S0-ATY-354

Essentials of Paralegalism

Second Edition

# Essentials of Paralegalism

Second Edition

William P. Statsky

West Publishing Company

ST. PAUL ▪ NEW YORK ▪ LOS ANGELES ▪ SAN FRANCISCO

Text Design: Roslyn Stendahl, Dapper Design
Copyediting: Connie Helgeson-Moen
Composition: Parkwood Composition
Illustrations: Randy Miyake
Cover Image: Detail of hand silkscreen printed cotton entitled "Up Your Alley," copyright © 1990 Dawn Zero Erickson. Photograph by Daniel A. Erickson.
Cover Design: Patricia Boman

Photo credits follow index.

WEST'S COMMITMENT TO THE ENVIRONMENT

In 1906, West Publishing Company began recycling materials left over from the production of books. This began a tradition of efficient and responsible use of resources. Today, up to 95 percent of our legal books and 70 percent of our college texts are printed on recycled, acid-free stock. West also recycles nearly 22 million pounds of scrap paper annually—the equivalent of 181,717 trees. Since the 1960s, West has devised ways to capture and recycle waste inks, solvents, oils, and vapors created in the printing process. We also recycle plastics of all kinds, wood, glass, corrugated cardboard, and batteries, and have eliminated the use of styrofoam book packaging. We at West are proud of the longevity and the scope of our commitment to our environment.

Production, Prepress, Printing and Binding by West Publishing Company.

COPYRIGHT © 1988,   By WEST PUBLISHING COMPANY
COPYRIGHT © 1993   By WEST PUBLISHING COMPANY
                    610 Opperman Drive
                    P.O. Box 64526
                    St. Paul, MN 55164-0526

Printed in the United States of America

00 99 98 97 96 95 94 93   8 7 6 5 4 3 2 1 0

Library of Congress Cataloging-in-Publication Data

Statsky, William P.
    Essentials of paralegalism / William P. Statsky. — 2nd ed.
        p.   cm.
    Includes bibliographical references and index.
    ISBN 0-314-01083-1 (soft)
      1. Legal assistants—United States.   I. Title.
KF320.L4S72   1993
340'.023'73—dc20   92-17280
                                                              CIP

■ Also by William P. Statsky

Case Analysis and Fundamentals of Legal Writing, 3d ed. St. Paul: West Publishing Company, 1989 (with J. Wernet)

Family Law, 3d ed. St. Paul: West Publishing Company, 1991
Inmate Involvement in Prison Legal Services: Roles and Training Options for the Inmate as Paralegal. American Bar Association, Commission on Correctional Facilities and Services, 1974

Introduction to Paralegalism: Perspectives, Problems, and Skills, 4th ed. St. Paul: West Publishing Company, 1992

Legal Desk Reference. St. Paul: West Publishing Co., 1991 (with B. Hussey, M. Diamond & R. Nakamura)

The Legal Paraprofessional as Advocate and Assistant: Roles, Training Concepts and Materials. Center on Social Welfare Policy and Law, 1971 (with P. Lang)

Legal Research and Writing: Some Starting Points, 4th ed. St. Paul: West Publishing Company, 1993

Legal Thesaurus/Dictionary: A Resource for the Writer and Computer Researcher. St. Paul: West Publishing Company, 1985
Legislative Analysis and Drafting, 2d ed. St. Paul: West Publishing Company, 1984

Paralegal Employment: Facts and Strategies for the 1990s, 2d ed. St. Paul: West Publishing Company, 1993

Paralegal Ethics and Regulation, 2d ed. St. Paul: West Publishing Company, 1993

Torts: Personal Injury Litigation, 2d ed. St. Paul: West Publishing Company, 1990

Rights of the Imprisoned: Cases, Materials and Directions. Indianapolis: Bobbs-Merrill Company, 1974 (with R. Singer)

What Have Paralegals Done? A Dictionary of Functions. National Paralegal Institute, 1973

■ For Patricia Farrell Statsky: A person whose ability and love
have sustained more than she knows

■ Preface

This book provides an introduction to a still-developing career whose members may one day outnumber attorneys in the traditional and untraditional law office. The day has long passed when so many had to ask, "What's a paralegal?" Today the most likely question is, "What's the most effective way to use a paralegal?" Even the United States Supreme Court has taken note of the role of paralegals in encouraging the "cost-effective delivery of legal services." A great deal has happened since the publication of the first edition of this book in 1980. Yet the dominant themes of the field continue to be challenge, promise, and the opportunity to rethink the major assumptions that have characterized the practice of law.

Changes in the Second Edition

In addition to updating the material in the book on employment, salaries, roles, ethics, certification, licensing, and other regulation issues, there are a number of large changes in the second edition:

- The ethics material has been extensively expanded, taken out of Chapter 3, and placed in a new Chapter 4 (Attorney Ethics and Paralegal Ethics).
- Chapter 5 (Introduction to the Legal System) has been rewritten. Yet, the major focus of the chapter continues to be an overview of the judicial, executive, and legislative process.
- Chapter 6 (Introduction to Legal Analysis) has been expanded; it now includes new components of introductory legal analysis.
- There is a greater emphasis throughout the chapters on the recent experiences of paralegals on the job, e.g., more quotations from successful paralegals on the ingredients of their success, more quotations on what life is like working in particular areas of the law.
- A glossary has been added.
- Each chapter includes a chapter outline, chapter summary, and key terms.
- The How to Study Law chapter (the old chapter 4) has been moved to the front of the book.

Teaching Aids and Supplements

The following teaching aids and supplements are available for use in conjunction with the fourth edition:

- *Study Guide and Workbook* (for student purchase) containing review questions and answers for all the chapters, short writing exercises, and other related material.

- *Instructor's Manual* covering each chapter of the book.
- *Transparency Masters* containing figures from the text that are easily used for overhead projection.
- *Test Bank*, prepared by Dorothy Moore (Fort Lauderdale College).
- *Westest Computerized Testing,* which offers the complete Test Bank on disk.
- *The Making of a Case* videotape, narrated by Richard Dysart of "L.A. Law." The subject matter covered gives students a better idea of what case law is, why it is important, and how cases are published.

Acknowledgments

It is difficult to name all the individuals who have provided guidance in the preparation of this book. Valuable suggestions for improvements in all or portions of the second edition were made by the reviewers: Therese Cannon, University of West Los Angeles; Jean Hellman, Loyola University; Jane Kaplan, New York City Technical College; Edie Koonce, Tulane University; Kathleen Mercer-Reed, University of Toledo; Dorothy Moore, Fort Lauderdale College; Virginia Noonan, Northern Essex Community College.

In addition, adopters of the first edition took part in a survey to help shape this revision. Many thanks to the following participants for their thoughtful comments: Philip Bruce Baker, Central Virginia Community College; Annetta Buster, Brown Mackie College; Robert L. Everett, Pitt Community College; Joanne Gurley, Lake Erie College; Ellen Hall, Utah Valley Community College; Alan Katz, Cape Fear Community College; Gail M. Krebs, Commonwealth College; D. Robert Lewis, Florida Career Institute; Dorothy B. Moore, Fort Lauderdale College; Larry Nordick, Moorhead State University; Judge Sam Soulé, Western Wyoming Community College; Deborah A. Waterman, Shawnee State University; Linda Wilke-Long, Central Community College; Warren W. Wilson, Lincoln School of Commerce.

Since I began my association with West Publishing Company in the early 1970s, I have worked with some very talented people. Ken Ziegler's leadership has kept West's Paralegal Series in the forefront of paralegal education. Among his inspired decisions has been to install Elizabeth Hannan in the important position of acquisitions editor.

For the second edition, Laura Mickelson of WESTLAW provided invaluable help in the chapter on computers in the law. I also want to acknowledge Carrie Kish, the promotion manager, and Sandra Gangelhoff, the production editor for this edition.

Looking back over the years, there are a number of people who have played important roles in my initiation and growth as a student of paralegal education. I owe a great debt to: Jean and Edgar Cahn, founders of the Antioch School of Law and its Legal Technician Program; Susan Tubb, a forceful advocate of quality in paralegal education; Bill Fry, Director of the National Paralegal Institute and a valued colleague since our days together at Columbia Law School when it launched one of the first paralegal training programs in the country, the Program for Legal Service Assistants; Michael Manna, Holly Fox, Ed Schwartz, and Julie Clark-Molloy, more recent collaborators in the field; and finally, MaBel Juanita Hill, Willie Nolden, and Linda Saunders, some of my early students who taught me so much.

■ Contents

■ *The "expanded use of well-trained assistants, sometimes called 'paralegals,' has been an important development. Today there are . . . double the number of . . . schools for training paralegals [than the number of schools for training attorneys]. . . . The advent of the paralegal enables law offices to perform high quality legal services at a lower cost. Possibly we have only scratched the surface of this development."*

Warren E. Burger, Chief Justice
of the United States Supreme Court, February 3, 1980

■ *"Paralegals are an absolutely essential component of quality legal services in the future."*

James Fellers, President,
American Bar Association, April 4, 1975

■ *"Employment is expected to continue to grow much faster than the average for all occupations through the year 2000."*

U.S. Department of Labor,
Occupational Outlook Handbook, 1988–89

How to Study Law in the Classroom and on the Job

■ Outline

Section A. Classroom Learning

Education does not come naturally to most of us. It is a struggle. This is all the more true for someone entering a totally new realm of training such as legal education. Much of the material will seem foreign and difficult. There is a danger of becoming overwhelmed by the vast quantity of laws and legal material that confronts you. How do you study law? How do you learn law? What is the proper perspective that a student of law should have about the educational process? These are our concerns in this introduction to the process of studying. In short, our theme is training to be trained—the art of effective learning.

The first step is to begin with a proper frame of mind. Too many students have false expectations of what legal education can accomplish. This substantially interferes with effective studying.

1. Your legal education has two phases. Phase I begins now and ends when you complete this training program. Phase II begins when this training program ends and is not completed until the last day of your employment as a paralegal.

You have entered a career that will require you to be a perpetual student. The learning never ends. This is true not only because the boundary lines of law are vast, but also because the law is changing every day. No one knows all of the law. Phase I of your legal education is designed to provide you with the foundation that will enable you to become a good student in Phase II.

2. *Your legal education has two dimensions: the content of the law (the rules) and the practical techniques of using that content in a law office (the skills).*

Rules.   There are two basic kinds of law:

Substantive Law: those nonprocedural rules that govern rights and duties; for example, the requirements for the sale of land;

Procedural Law: those rules that govern the mechanics of resolving a dispute in court or in an administrative agency; for example, the number of days within which a party must respond to a claim stated in a complaint.

The law library contains millions of substantive and procedural rules written by courts (in volumes called reporters), by legislatures (in volumes called statutory codes), and by administrative agencies (in volumes called administrative codes).

A substantial portion of your time in school will involve a study of the substantive and procedural law of your state, and often of the federal government as well.

Skills.   By far the most important dimension of your legal education will be the skills of using rules. Without the skills, the content of the law is close to worthless. Examples of legal skills include:

- How to interview a client.
- How to investigate the facts of a case.
- How to draft a complaint, the document that initiates a lawsuit.
- How to digest or summarize documents in a case file.
- How to do legal research in a law library.

The overriding skill that, to one degree or another, is the basis for all others is the skill of legal analysis (see Chapter 6). There are some who make the mistake of concluding that legal analysis is within the exclusive domain of the attorney. Without an understanding of legal analysis, however, paralegals cannot understand the legal system and cannot intelligently carry out many of the more demanding tasks they are assigned.

3. *You must force yourself to suspend what you already know about the law in order to be able to absorb (a) that which is new and (b) that which conflicts with your prior knowledge and experience.*

Place yourself in the position of training students to drive a car. Your students undoubtedly already know something about driving. They have watched others drive and maybe have even had a lesson or two from friends. It would be ideal, however, if you could begin your instruction from point zero. There is a very real danger that the students have picked up bad habits from others. This will interfere with their capacity to *listen* to what you are saying. The danger is that they will block out those things you are saying that do not conform to previously learned habits and knowledge. If the habits or knowledge are defective, your job as a trainer is immensely more difficult.

The same is true in studying law. Everyone knows something about the law from government or civics courses as a teenager and from the various treatments of the law in the media. It may be that some of you have been involved in the law as a party or as a witness in court. Others may have worked, or currently work, in law offices. Will this prior knowledge and experience be a help or a hindrance to you in your future legal education? For some it will be a help. For most of us, however, there is a danger of interference.

This is particularly so with respect to the portrayal of the law on TV and in the movies. Those who grew up with TV's *Perry Mason* probably came to the conclusion that most legal problems are solved by dramatically tricking a hostile witness on the stand into finally telling the truth. Not so. The practice of law is not an endless series of confessions and concessions that are pried loose from opponents. Nor is the more modern TV program *L.A. Law* much more helpful. Every attorney does not spend all day engaged in the kind of case that makes front page news. Recently, a paralegal left her job as a paralegal with a solo practitioner in order to take another paralegal position with a firm that she thought was going to be like *L.A. Law*. Three months later, she begged her old boss to take her back. She had discovered that there was a great gap between reality and *L.A. Law*. While excitement and drama can be part of the practice of law, they are not everyday occurrences. What is dominant is painstaking and meticulous hard work. This reality is almost never portrayed in the media.

It is strongly recommended that you place yourself in the position of a stranger to the material you will be covering in your courses, regardless of your background and exposure to the field. Cautiously treat everything as a new experience. Temporarily suspend what you already know. Resist the urge to pat yourself on the back by saying, "I already knew that" or "I already know how to do that." For many students, such statements cause a relaxation. They do not work as hard once they have convinced themselves that there is nothing new to learn. No problem exists, of course, if these students are right. The danger, however, is that they are wrong or that they are only partially right. Students are not always the best judge of what they know and of what they can do. Do not become too comfortable. Adopt the following healthy attitude: "I've dealt with that before, but maybe I can learn something new about it." Every new teacher, every new supervisor, every new setting is an opportunity to add a dimension to your prior knowledge and experience. Be open to these opportunities. No two people practice law exactly the same way. Your own growth as a student and as a paralegal will depend in large part on your capacity to listen for, explore, and absorb this diversity.

4. Be sure that you know the goals and context of every assignment.

Throughout your education, you will be given a variety of assignments: class exercises, text readings, drafting tasks, field projects, research assignments, examinations, etc. You should ask yourself the following questions about each one:

■ What are the goals of this assignment? What am I supposed to learn from it?

- How does this assignment fit into what I have already learned? What is the context of the assignment?

Successfully undertaking the assignment depends in part on your understanding of its goals and how these goals relate to the overall context of the course. How do you identify goals and context?

- Carefully listen to and take notes on what your teachers tell the class about the assignment.

- Ask teachers questions about their expectations for assignments. Demonstrate a polite but probing interest.

- If the teacher has given a particular assignment before to other classes, ask former students. If they have had any papers returned to them by the teacher, try to read some of them to determine what comments/criticisms the teacher has made on them. These observations will be additional clues to what the teacher is after.

- Take note of what the authors of your texts have expressly or implicitly told you about the importance or purpose of certain tasks.

- Ask fellow classmates about their understanding of purpose and context.

In short, be preoccupied by these concerns. *Do not undertake assignments in isolation or in a vacuum.*

As we will see in greater detail later, this advice applies on the job as well as in school. A strong indication of one's commitment—an essential ingredient for progress and advancement—is a sincere interest in the broader picture. Avoid gaining a reputation as someone who simply wants to "get the job done and get out as quickly as possible." While speed is sometimes critical, speed is never a substitute for efficiency and professionalism. The latter are directly dependent on the extent of your involvement, interest, and enthusiasm in carrying out a task. Boredom and incompetence often feed on each other.

This is not to say that you must be wildly enthusiastic about everything you do. Sustaining such enthusiasm is unrealistic. At a minimum, you want to avoid undertaking tasks routinely—even routine tasks! One way to accomplish this goal is to have a constant eye on the broader picture. Why are you being asked to do something in a certain way? Has it always been done this way? Are there more efficient ways? After the pressure of the immediate need has passed, can you think about and eventually propose a more effective *system* of handling the task?

Of course, there is a danger of going to the opposite extreme. You cannot be so preoccupied with purpose, context, and systems that you fail to complete the immediate job before you. Timing is important. Often the office will have no tolerance for suggestions for improvement until immediate deadlines have passed. This simply means that you must always be operating at two levels. First, the *now* level. Mobilize all of your resources to complete the task as efficiently as possible under the present work environment. Second, the *systems* level. Keep your mind open, and challenge your creativity to identify steps and procedures that might be taken in the future to achieve greater efficiency in accomplishing the task.

5. *Design a study plan.*

Make constant and current *lists* of everything that you must do. Divide the list into long-term projects (what is due next week or at the end of the semester) and short-term projects (what is due tomorrow). Have a plan for each day. Establish the following norm for yourself: every day you will focus in some way on *all* of your assignments. Every day you will review your long-term and short-term list. Priority, of course, will be given to the short-term tasks. Yet some time, however small, will also be devoted to the long-term tasks. At a minimum, this time can be used simply to remind yourself that these tasks are hanging over you and that you must make concrete commitments to devote substantial blocks of time to them in the immediate future. Make and renew these commitments every day. If possible, go beyond this. On a day that you will be mainly working on the short-term projects, try to set aside 5% of your time to the long-term projects, for instance, by doing some background reading or by preparing a very rough first draft of an outline. It is critical that you establish *momentum* toward the accomplishment of *all* your tasks. This is done by never letting anything sit on the back burner. Set yourself the goal of making at least *some* progress on everything every day. Without this goal, the momentum may be very difficult to sustain.

Once you have decided what tasks you will cover on a given study day, the next question is: In what *order* will you cover them? There are a number of ways in which you can classify the things that you must do—for example: (a) easy tasks that will require a relatively short time to complete, (b) complex tasks requiring more time, (c) tasks with time demands that will be unknown until you start them. At the beginning of your study time, spend a few seconds preparing an outline of the order in which you will cover the tasks that day and the approximate amount of time that you will set aside for each task. You may want to start with some of the easier tasks so that you can feel a sense of accomplishment relatively soon. Alternatively, you may want to devote early study time to the third kind of task listed above ("c") so that you can obtain a clearer idea of the scope and difficulty of such assignments. The important point is that you establish a *schedule*. It does not have to be written in stone. Quite the contrary. It is healthy that you have enough flexibility to revise your day's schedule in order to respond to unfolding realities as you study. Adaptation is not a sign of disorganization, but the total absence of an initial plan is.

6. *Add 50% to the time you initially think you will need to study a subject.*

You are kidding yourself if you have not set aside a *substantial* amount of time to study law outside the classroom. The conscientious study of law takes time—lots of it. It is true that some students must work and take care of family responsibilities. You cannot devote time that you do not have. Yet the reality is that limited study time leads to limited education.

Generally, people will find time for what they want to do. You may *wish* to do many things for which there will never be enough time. You will find the time, however, to do what you really *want* to do. Once you have decided that you want something badly enough, you will find the time to do it.

Most people waste tremendous amounts of time by worrying about all the things that they have to do and in taking rest periods from this worrying through socializing or other casual pursuits. How much *productive* time do you gain out of a single work hour? For most of us the answer is about twenty minutes. The rest of the hour is spent worrying, relaxing, repeating ourselves, socializing, etc. One answer to the problem of limited time availability is to increase the amount of *productive* time that you derive out of each work hour.

You may not be able to add any new hours to the clock, but you can add to your net productive time. How about moving up to thirty minutes an hour? Forty? You will be amazed at the time that you can "find" simply by making a conscious effort to remove some of the waste. When asked how a masterpiece was created, a great sculptor once responded: "You start with a block of stone and you cut away everything that is not art." In your study habits, start with a small block of time and work to cut away everything that is not productive.

There are no absolute rules on how much time you will need. It depends on the complexity of the subject matter you must master. It is probably accurate to say that most of us need to study more than we do—as a rule of thumb, about 50% more. You should be constantly on the alert for ways to increase the time you have available, or more accurately, to increase the productive time that you can make available.

Resolving time-management problems as a student will be good practice for you when you are confronted with similar (and more severe) time-management problems as a working paralegal. Many law offices operate at a hectic pace. One of the hallmarks of a professional is a pronounced reverence for deadlines and the clock in general. Time is money. An ability to find and handle time effectively can also be one of the preconditions for achieving justice in a particular case.

Soon you will be gaining a reputation among your fellow students, teachers, supervisors, and employers. One of the reputations that you should make a concerted effort to acquire is a reputation for hard work, punctuality, and conscientiousness about the time you devote to your work. In large measure, success follows from such a reputation. It is as important, if not more important, than raw ability or intelligence.

7. Create your own study area free from distractions.

It is essential that you find study areas that are quiet and free from distractions. Otherwise, concentration is obviously impossible. It may be that the worst places to study are at home or at the library, unless you can find a corner that is cut off from noise and people who want to talk. Do not make yourself too available. If you study in the corridor, at the first table at the entrance to the library, or at the kitchen table, you are inviting distraction. You need to be able to close yourself off for two to three hours at a time. It is important for you to interact with other people—but not while you are studying material that requires considerable concentration. You will be tempted to digress and to socialize. You are in the best position to know where these temptations are. You are also the most qualified person to know how to avoid the temptations.

8. Conduct a self-assessment of your prior study habits and establish a program to reform the weaknesses.

If you were to describe the way in which you study, would you be proud of the description? Here is a partial list of some of the main weaknesses of attitude or practice that students have in studying:

- The student has done well in the past with only minimal study effort. Why change now?
- No one else in the class appears to be studying very much. Why be different?
- The student learns best by listening in class. Hence instead of studying on one's own, why not wait until someone explains it in person?

- The student simply does not like to study; there are more important things to do in life.
- The student can't concentrate.
- The student studies with the radio on or with other distractions.
- The student gets bored easily. "I can't stay motivated for long."
- The student does not understand what he or she is supposed to study.
- The student skim reads.
- The student does not stop to look up strange words or phrases.
- The student studies only at exam time—crams for exams.
- The student does not study at a consistent pace. It's an hour here and there—no organized, regular study times.
- The student does not like to memorize.
- The student does not take notes on what he or she is reading.

What other interferences with effective studying can you think of? Or more important, which of the above items apply to you? How do you plead? In law, it is frequently said that you cannot solve a problem until you obtain the facts. What are the facts in the case of your study habits? Make your personal list of attitude problems, study patterns, or environmental interferences. Place these items in some order. Next, establish a plan for yourself. Which item on the list are you going to try to correct tonight? What will the plan be for this week? For next week? For the coming month? What specific steps will you take to try to change some bad habits? Do not, however, be too hard on yourself. Be determined but realistic. The more serious problems are obviously going to take more time to correct. Improvement will come if you are serious about improvement and regularly think about it. If one corrective method does not work, try another. If the fifth does not work, try a sixth. Discuss techniques of improvement with your fellow students and teachers. Prove to yourself that change is possible.

9. Conduct a self-assessment on grammar, spelling, and composition, and design a program to reform weaknesses.

The legal profession lives by the written word. Talking is important for some activities, but writing is crucial in almost every area of the practice of law. You cannot function in this environment without a grasp of the basics of spelling, grammar, and composition. A major complaint made by employers today is that paralegals are consistently violating these basics. The problem is very serious.

Step One. You must take responsibility for your training in grammar, spelling, and composition. Do not wait for someone to teach you these basics. Do not wait until someone points out your weaknesses. You must make a personal commitment to train yourself. If there are English courses available to you, great. It is essential, however, that you understand that a weekly class will not be enough.

Step Two. Raise your consciousness about the writing around you. Your training in writing cannot be compartmentalized. You must be constantly thinking about and worrying about writing. The concern should be a preoccupation. When you are reading a newspaper, for example, you should be conscious of the use of semicolons and paragraph structure in what you are reading. At least occasionally you should ask yourself why a certain punctuation mark was used by a writer. You are surrounded by writing. You read this writing for content. You must begin a conscious effort to focus on the structure of this writing as well.

Step Three.   Purchase several grammar books. Do not rely on only one grammar book. There are hundreds of texts on the market, and they each explain things differently, so you should consult more than one grammar book on difficult points. It must be admitted that some grammar books are poorly written! They are not always easy to use. They may give examples of grammar rules without clearly defining the rules. Or they may define the rules without giving clear examples of the application of the rules. A grammar book may be excellent for some areas of writing but weak for others. Hence, have more than one grammar book in your personal library.

You may have saved grammar books you used earlier in your education. In addition, go to second-hand bookstores. They often have a section on textbooks. Some of the best grammar books are old elementary texts that provide excellent overviews of the basics. Another way to cut down on the expense of purchase is to consider paperback texts. The characteristics to look for in making a purchase are:

- A comprehensive index.
- Clearly defined rules covering the basics.
- Numerous examples of the application of the rules.
- Exercises on the rules *with answers* so that you can check your own progress.

Step Four.   Use the grammar books almost as frequently as you would a dictionary. Have the books at your side every time you write. Force yourself to use these books regularly. The more often you use them now, the less you will need them later as you continue to improve. You will never be able to discard them entirely, however. You will need to consult them when doing any serious writing in the law. How often will you have to consult them? It depends on the extent of the weaknesses that you have and the frequency with which you begin consulting them now.

Step Five.   Improve your spelling. Use a dictionary often. Begin making a list of the words that you are spelling incorrectly. Work on these words. When you have the slightest doubt about the spelling of a word, check the dictionary. Again, the more often you take this approach now, the less often you will need to use the dictionary later.

Step Six.   Enroll in English and writing courses. Check offerings at local schools like adult education programs in the public schools or at colleges.

Step Seven.   Find out which law courses in your curriculum require the most writing from students. If possible, take these courses—no matter how painful you find writing to be. In fact, the more painful it is, the more you need to place yourself in an environment where writing is demanded of you on a regular basis.

Step Eight.   Simplify your writing. Cut down the length of your sentences. Minimize the use of semicolons that extend the length of sentences. Many people have the mistaken idea that legal writing must be "heavy," august, and flowery. This usually leads to verbosity. The best legal writing, no matter how technical, is evenly paced, clear, and concise.

Step Nine. Prepare a self-assessment of your weaknesses. Make a list of what you must correct. Then set a schedule for improvement. Set aside a small amount of time each day, say, ten minutes, during which you work on your writing weaknesses. Be consistent about this time. Do not wait for the weekend or for next semester when you will have more time. The reality is that you will probably never have substantially more time than you have now. The problem is not so much the absence of time as it is an unwillingness to dig into the task. Progress will be slow and you will be on your own. Hence, there is a danger that you will be constantly finding excuses to put it off.

10. *Consider forming a student study group, but be cautious.*

Students sometimes find it useful to form study groups. A healthy exchange with your colleagues can be very productive. One difficulty is finding students with whom you are compatible. Trial and error may be the only way to identify such students. A more serious concern is trying to define the purpose of the study group. It should not be used as a substitute for your own individual study. It would be inappropriate to divide a course into parts, with members of the group having responsibility for preparing notes on and teaching the assigned parts to the remainder of the group.

The group can be very valuable for mutual editing on writing assignments. Suppose, for example, that you are drafting complaints in a course. Photocopy a complaint that one member of the group drafts. The group then collectively comments upon and edits the complaint according to the standards discussed in class and in the materials of the course. Similarly, you could try to obtain copies of old exams in the course and collectively examine answers prepared by group members. Ask your teacher for fact situations that could be the basis of legal analysis memos (see Chapter 6) or other drafting assignments. Make up fact situations of your own. The student whose work is being scrutinized must be able to take constructive criticism. The criticism should be intense if it is to be worthwhile. Students should be asked to rewrite the draft after incorporating suggestions made. The rewrite should later be subjected to another round of mutual editing. Occasionally, you might want to consider asking your teacher to meet with your group in order to obtain further help in legal writing.

Do not hesitate to subject your writing to the scrutiny of your fellow students. You can learn a great deal from each other.

11. *Use your legal research skills to help you understand components of a course that are giving you difficulty.*

The law library is more than the place to go to find law that governs the facts of a client's case. A great deal of the material in the law library consists of explanations/summaries/overviews of the same law that you will be covering in your courses. Learn how to gain access to this material as soon as possible. Your legal research course should help you acquire this skill. You need to know how to use texts such as legal dictionaries, legal encyclopedias, treatises, annotations, etc. They will prove invaluable as outside reading to help resolve conceptual and practical difficulties you are having in class.

12. *Organize your learning through definitions or definitional questions.*

The most sophisticated question an attorney or paralegal can ask is: What does that word or phrase mean? What's the definition? To a very large extent, the practice of law is a probing for definitions of key words or phrases in the context of facts that have arisen. Can a five year old be liable for negligence? (What is *negligence?*) Can the government tax a church-run bingo game? (What is the *free exercise of religion?*) Can attorneys in a law firm strike and obtain the protection of the National Labor Relations Act? (What is a *covered* employee under the labor statute?) Can a person rape his or her spouse? (What is the definition of *rape?*) Can a citizen slander the president of the United States? (What is a *defamatory statement* and what are the definitions of the defenses to a slander action?) Etc.

For every course that you take, you will come across numerous technical words and phrases in class and in your readings. Begin compiling a list of these words and phrases for each class. Try to limit yourself to what you think are the major ones. When in doubt about whether to include something on your list, resolve the doubt by including it.

Then pursue definitions. Ask your teacher for definitions. Find definitions in your text and in the law library, for instance, in legal dictionaries, legal encyclopedias, treatises, annotations, legal periodical literature, statutory codes, etc.

For some words, you may have difficulty obtaining definitions. Do not give up your pursuit. Keep searching. Keep probing. Keep questioning. For some words, there may be more than one definition. Others may require definitions of the definitions.

Of course, you cannot master a course simply by knowing the definitions of all the key words and phrases involved. Yet these words and phrases are the *vocabulary* of the course and are the foundation and point of reference for learning the other aspects of the course. Begin with vocabulary.

Consider a system of three-by-five or two-by-three cards to help you learn the definitions. On one side of the card, place a single word or phrase. On the other side, write the definition with a brief page reference or citation to the source of the definition. Using the cards, test yourself periodically. If you are in a study group, ask other members to test you. Ask a relative to test you. Establish a plan of ongoing review.

13. *Translate important rules into checklists—developing your own practice manual.*

It is important that you learn how to write checklists that could be part of a manual. Every rule that you are told about or that you read about can be translated into a checklist. Checklist formulation should eventually become second nature to you. The sooner you start thinking in terms of dos, don'ts, models, etc., the better.

Suppose that you have before you the following statute of your state:

§1742. No marriage shall be solemnized without a license issued by the county clerk of any county of this state not more than thirty days prior to the date of the solemnization of the marriage.

One way to handle this statute is to create a checklist of questions that you would ask a client in order to determine whether the statute applies. (Breaking a statute down into its *elements* will assist you in identifying such questions, as you will see in Chapter 6.) Some of the questions would be:

1. Did you have a marriage license?
2. Where did you get the license? Did you obtain it from a county clerk in this state?
3. On what date did you obtain the license?
4. On what date did you go through the marriage ceremony (solemnization)? Were there more than thirty days between the date you obtained the license and the date of the ceremony?

These are the questions that must be asked as part of a large number of questions concerning the validity of a marriage. If you were creating a manual, the above questions in your checklist for section 1742 could go under the manual topic of "Marriage Formation" or "Marriage License." Whenever you have a class on this topic or whenever you analyze any law on this topic, you translate the lecture into checklists such as the brief one presented above.

To be sure, there are checklists written by others already in existence. They are found, for example, in manuals and practice books. Why create your own? First of all, your checklists are *not* intended as a substitute for those in manuals or practice books. You will undoubtedly make extensive use of the latter. You are encouraged to do so. Your checklists will supplement the others. More significantly, two of the best ways for you to learn how to use manuals are (a) to write checklists of your own and (b) to see the connection between the law (for example, a statute) and the guidelines and techniques within a checklist.

14. *Develop the skill of note taking.*

Note taking is essential in the law. You will regularly be told to "write it down" or "put it in a memo." Effective note taking is often a precondition to being able to do *any* kind of writing in the law.

First, take notes on what you are reading for class preparation and for research assignments. Do not rely exclusively on your memory. After reading hundreds of pages (or more), you will not be able to remember what you have read at the end of the semester, or even at the end of the day. Copy what you think are the essential portions of the materials you are reading. Be sure to include definitions of important words and phrases as indicated in guideline 12 above.

To be sure, note taking will add time to your studying. Yet you will discover that it was time well spent, particularly when you begin reviewing for an exam or writing your memorandum.

Second, take notes in class. You must develop the art of taking notes while simultaneously listening to what is being said. On the job, you may have to do this frequently. For example, when:

- Interviewing a client
- Interviewing a witness during field investigation
- Receiving instructions from a supervisor
- Talking with someone on the phone
- Taking notes during a deposition
- Taking notes from a witness giving testimony at trial

A good place to begin learning how to write and listen at the same time is during your classes.

Most students take poor class notes. This is due to a number of reasons:

- A student may write slowly.
- A student may not like to take notes; it's hard work.
- A student may not know if what is being said is important enough to be noted until after it is said—when it is too late because the lecture has gone on to something else.
- A student does not think it necessary to take notes on a discussion that the teacher is having with another student.
- A student takes notes only when he or she sees other students taking notes.
- Some teachers ramble.

A student who uses these excuses for not taking comprehensive notes in class will eventually be using similar excuses on the job when note taking is required for a case. This is unfortunate. You must overcome whatever resistances you have acquired to the admittedly difficult task of note taking. Otherwise you will pay the price in your schoolwork and on the job.

Common Abbreviations Used by Students in Litigation Classes

π	plaintiff	lee	lessee	jdr	joinder
Δ	defendant	CN	contributory negligence	b/p	burden of proof
θ	third party			s/l	statute of limitations
c.l.	common law	CpN	comparative negligence		
c/a	cause of action			s/f	statute of frauds
JV/π	jury verdict for plaintiff	rsb	reasonable	K	contract
		A/R	assumption of risk	T	tort
R&R	reversed & remanded	cz	cause	IT	intentional tort
		px cz	proximate cause	N	negligence
Dem	demurrer	ab dg	abnormally dangerous	SL	strict liability
$	suppose			A&B	assault & battery
Q	question	inj	injunction	4cb	foreseeable
O	owner	b.f.p.	bona fide purchaser	dfm	defamation
stat	statute			Dct	deceit
L	liable, liability	br/wrt	breach of warranty	lbl	libel
nj	injury			sld	slander
dmg	damages	dft	defect	impl	implied
dfs	defense	dsn	design	impt	imputed
Tp	trespass	WD	wrongful death	jfc	justification
pvg	privilege	Svv	survival	std	standard
Tfz	tortfeasor	m-	mal-, mis-	vln	violation
lz	license	m-pr	malpractice	pun	punitive
lzc	licensee	m-rep	misrepresentation	stfn	satisfaction
tpr	trespasser	n-	non-	rls	release
ktb	contribution	[	not, un-	rem	remedy
lr	lessor	[4cf	unforeseeable	p.f.	prima facie

Source: Prosser, Wade & Schwartz, *Cases and Materials on Torts*, p. 1263 (Foundation Press, 1976).

Of course, you do not want to write down everything, even if this were physically possible. You ought to make the assumption, however, that if it is important enough for someone to tell you something, it is important enough for you to make note of it.

If you do not know how to take shorthand, develop your own system of abbreviations. (See above figure.) Sometimes you will have to begin taking notes at the moment the person starts talking rather than wait until the end of what he or she is saying. Try different approaches to increasing the completeness of your notes.

If you are participating in class by talking with the teacher, it will obviously be difficult for you to take notes at the same time. After class, take a few moments to jot down some notes on what occurred during the discussion.

15. Studying rules—the role of memory.

Memory plays a significant role in the law. Applicants for the bar, for example, are not allowed to take notes into the exam room. An advocate in court or at an administrative hearing may be able to refer to notes, but the notes are of little value if the advocate does not have a solid grasp of the case. Most of the courses you will be taking have a memory component. This is true even for open-book exams, since you will not have time to go through all the material while responding to the questions.

Two mistakes are often made by students with respect to the role of memory:

- They think that memorizing things is beneath their dignity.
- They think that because they understand something, they know it sufficiently to be able to give it back in an examination.

Of course, you should not be memorizing what you do not understand. Rote memorization is close to worthless. Not so for important material that you comprehend. Yet you have not necessarily committed something to memory for later use, simply because you understand it.

Many systems for memorizing material can be effective:

- Reading it over and over
- Copying it
- Writing questions to yourself about it and trying to answer the questions
- Having other students ask you questions about it
- Making summaries or outlines of it
- Etc.

If you do not have a photographic mind, you must resort to such techniques. Try different systems. Ask fellow students for tips on how they make effective use of their memory.

You will have to find out from your teacher what material you will be expected to know for the course. You can also check with other students who have had this teacher in the past. It may not always be easy to find out how much a teacher expects you to know from memory. Teachers have been known to surprise students on examinations! Some teachers do not like to admit that they are asking their students to memorize a lot of material for their courses, yet they still give examinations that require a lot of memory preparation.

16. Studying skills—the necessity of feedback.

Memory obviously plays a less significant role in learning the skills of interviewing, investigation, legal analysis, drafting, coordinating, digesting, advocacy, and legal research. These skills have their own vocabulary that you must know, but it is your judgmental rather than your memory faculties that must be developed in order to become competent and excel in these skills.

They are developed primarily by *doing*—practice drills or exercises are essential. The learning comes from the feedback that you obtain while engaged in the skill exercises. What are the ways that a student obtains feedback?

- Evaluations on assignments and exams
- Role-playing exercises that are critiqued in class
- Comparisons between your work (particularly writing projects) with models provided by the teacher or that you find on your own in the library
- Critiques that you receive from fellow students in study groups

You must constantly be looking for feedback. Do not wait to be called on. Do not wait to see what feedback is planned for you at the end of the course. Take the initiative immediately. Seek conferences with your teachers. Find out who is available to read your writing or to observe your performance in any of the other skills. Set up your own role-playing sessions with your fellow students. Seek critiques of your rewrites even if rewriting was not required. Look for opportunities to critique other students on the various skills. Ask fellow students for permission to read their graded examinations so that you can compare their papers with your own. Create your own hypotheticals for analysis in study groups. (A *hypothetical* is simply a set of facts invented for the purpose of discussion and analysis.) Do additional reading on the skills. Become actively involved in your own skills development.

17. Studying ambiguity—coping with unanswered questions.

The study of law can be frustrating because there is so much uncertainty in the law. Legions of unanswered questions exist. Definitive answers to legal questions are not always easy to find, no matter how good your legal research techniques are. Every new fact situation presents the potential for a new law. Every law seems to have an exception. Furthermore, advocates frequently argue for exceptions to the exceptions. When terms are defined, the definitions often need definitions. A law office is not always an easy environment in which to work because of this reality.

The study of law is in large measure an examination of ambiguity that is identified, dissected, and manipulated.

The most effective way to handle frustration with this state of affairs is to be realistic about what the law is and isn't. Do not expect definitive answers to all legal questions. Search for as much clarity as you can, but do not be surprised if the conclusion of your search is further questions. A time-honored answer to many legal questions is: "It depends"! Become familiar with the following equation since you will see it used often:

If "X" is present, then the conclusion is "A," but if "Y" is so, then the conclusion is "B," but if "Z" is . . .

The practice of law may sometimes appear to be an endless puzzle. Studying law, therefore, must engage you in similar thinking processes. Again, look for precision and clarity, but do not expect the puzzle to disappear.

18. The value of speed-reading courses in the study of law.

In the study of law, a great deal of reading is required. Should you, therefore, take a speed-reading course? No, unless the course helps you *slow down* the speed of your reading! This advice may be quite distasteful to advocates (and salespersons) of speed-reading courses. The reality, however, is that statutes, regulations, and court opinions cannot be speed-read. They must be carefully picked apart and read word for word, almost as if you were translating from one language into another. If you are troubled by how long it takes you to read, do not despair. Do not worry about having to read material over and over again. Keep reading. Keep rereading. The pace of your reading will pick up as you gain experience. Never strive, however, to be able to fly through the material. Strive for comprehensiveness. Strive for understanding. For most of us, this will come through the slow process of note taking and rereading. It is sometimes argued that comprehension is increased through speed. Be careful of this argument. Reading law calls for careful thinking about what you read—and taking notes on these thoughts. There may be no harm in rapidly reading legal material for *the first time*. At your second, third, and fourth reading, however, speed is of little significance.

Section B. On-the-Job Learning: The Art of Being Supervised

A great deal of learning will occur when you are on the job. Some of it may come through formal in-house office training and by the study of office procedure manuals. Most of the learning, however, will come in day-to-day interaction with your supervisors as you are given assignments. The learning comes through *being* supervised. Being supervised is not always easy. It will take some effort on your part to maximize the learning potential of the experience. The following guidelines are designed to assist you in increasing this potential:

Don't play "king's clothes" with the instructions that you receive.

Recall the story of the king's clothes. The king was naked, but everybody kept saying what a beautiful wardrobe he had on. As new people arrived, they saw that he had no clothes, but they heard everyone talking as if he were fully dressed. The new people did not want to appear stupid, so they too began admiring the king's wardrobe. When paralegals are receiving instructions on an assignment, they play king's clothes when the pretend that they understand all the instructions but in fact do not. They do not want to appear to be uninformed or unintelligent. They do not want to give the impression that they are unsure of themselves. For obvious reasons, this is a serious mistake.

Whenever you are given an assignment in a new area—that is, an assignment on something that you have not done before—there should be a great deal that you do not understand. This is particularly true during your first few months on the job, when everything is new! Do not pretend to be something you are not. Constantly ask questions about new things. Do not be reluctant to ask for explanations. Learn how to ask for help. *It will not be a sign of weakness.* Quite the contrary. People who take steps to make sure that they fully understand all their instructions will soon gain a reputation for responsibility and conscientiousness.

Repeat the instructions to your supervisor before you leave the room.

Once your supervisor has told you what he or she wants you to do, do not leave the room in silence or with the general observation, "I'll get on that right away." Repeat the instructions back to the supervisor *as you understand them.* Make sure that you and your supervisor are on the same wavelength by explaining back what you think you were told to do. This will be an excellent opportunity for the supervisor to determine what you did or did not understand, and to provide you with clarifications where needed.

Supervisors will not always be sure of what they want you to do. By trying to obtain clarity on the instructions, you are providing them with the opportunity to think through what they want done. In the middle of the session with you, the supervisor may change his or her mind on what is to be done.

Write your instructions down.

Never go to your supervisor without pen and paper. Preferably, keep an instructions notebook, diary, or journal in which you record the following information:

- Notes on what you are asked to do
- The date you got the assignment
- The date by which the supervisor expects you to complete all or part of the assignment
- The date you actually complete the assignment
- Comments made by supervisors or others on what you submit

The notes will serve as your memory bank. Whenever any questions arise about what you were supposed to do, you have something concrete to refer to.

Insist on a due date and on a statement of priorities.

You need to know when an assignment is due. Ask for a due date *even if the supervisor tells you to "get to it when you can."* This phrase may mean "relatively soon" or "before the end of the month" to your supervisor, but not to you. If the supervisor says he or she does not know when it should be done, ask for an approximate due date. Tell the supervisor you want to place the assignment on your calendar so that it will not slip through the cracks because of all the other assignments.

Also ask what priority the assignment has. Where does it fit in with your other assignments? If you have more than enough to fill the day, you need to know what takes priority. If you do not ask for a priority listing, the supervisor will assume you are under no time pressures.

If the instructions appear to be complicated, ask your supervisor to separate and prioritize the tasks.

As you receive instructions, you may sometimes feel overwhelmed by all that is being asked of you. Many supervisors do not give instructions in clear, logical patterns. They may talk in a rambling, stream-of-consciousness fashion. When confronted with this situation, simply say:

> OK, but can you break that down for me a little more in terms of what you want me to do first? I think I will be able to do the entire assignment, but it would help if I approach it one step at a time. Where do you want me to start?

As often as possible, write your instructions and what you do in the form of checklists.

A methodical mind is one that views a project in "do-able" steps and that tackles one step at a time. You need to have a methodical mind in order to function in a busy law office. One of the best ways to develop such a mind is to think in terms of checklists. A checklist is simply a chronological sequencing of tasks that must be done in order to complete a project. Convert the instructions from your supervisor into checklists in the same manner as translating rules into checklists discussed earlier. In the process of actually carrying out instructions, you go through many steps—all of which could become part of a detailed checklist. The steps you went through to complete the task become a checklist of things to do in order to complete such a task in the future. To be sure, it can be time-consuming to draft checklists. Keep in mind, however, that:

- The checklists can be invaluable for other employees who are given similar assignments in the future.
- The checklists will be a benefit to you in organizing your own time and in assuring completeness.

You will not be able to draft checklists for everything that you do. Perhaps you will not be able to write more than one checklist a week. Perhaps you will have to use some of your own time to write checklists. Whatever time you can devote will be profitably spent so long as you are serious about writing and using the checklists. They may have to be rewritten or modified later. This should not deter you from the task, since most things that are worth doing require testing and reassessment.

Once you have a number of checklists, you have the makings of a how-to-do-it manual that you have written yourself.

Find out what manuals and checklists already exist in your office.

It does not make sense to reinvent the wheel. If manuals and checklists already exist in your office on the topic of your assignment, you should find and use them. The problem is that the how-to-do-it information is usually buried in the heads of the attorneys, paralegals, and secretaries of the office. No one has taken the time to write it all down. If this is *not* the case, you should find out where it is written down and try to adapt what you find to the assignment on which you are working.

Ask for a model.

One of the best ways to make sure you know what a supervisor wants is to ask whether he or she knows of any models that you could use as a guide for what you are being asked to do. Such models may be found in closed case files, manuals, formbooks, practice texts, etc. Care must be applied in using such material. Every new legal problem is potentially unique. What will work in one case may not work in another. A model is a guide, a starting point—and nothing more.

Do some independent legal research on your own on the instructions you are given.

Often you will be told what to do without being given more than a cursory explanation of why it needs to be done that way. But all the instructions you are given have some basis in the law. A complaint, for example, is served on an opposing party in a designated way because the law has imposed rules on how such service is to be made. You may be asked to serve a complaint in a certain way without being told what section of the state code (or of your court rules) *requires* it to be served in that way. It would be highly impractical to read all the law that is the foundation for an assigned task. It is not necessary to do so and you would not have time to do so.

What you can do, however, is to select certain instructions on certain assignments and do some background legal research to gain a greater appreciation for why the instructions were necessary. You will probably have to do such legal research on your own time unless the assignment you are given includes doing some legal research. Research can be time-consuming, but you will find it enormously educational. It can place a totally new perspective on the assignment and, indeed, on your entire job.

Ask secretaries and other paralegals for help.

Secretaries and paralegals who have worked in the office for a long period of time can be very helpful to you if you approach them properly. Everybody wants to feel important. Everybody wants to be respected. When someone asks for something in a way that gives the impression he or she is *entitled* to what is being sought, difficulties usually result. Think of how you would like to be approached if you were in the position of the secretary or paralegal. What would turn you off? What would make you want to go out of your way to cooperate with and assist a new employee who needs your help? Your answers (and sensitivity) to questions such as these will go a long way toward enabling you to draw on the experience of others in the office.

Obtain feedback on an assignment before the date it is due.

Unless the assignment you are given is a very simple one, do not wait until the date that it is due to communicate with your supervisor. If you are having trouble with the assignment, you will want to check with your supervisor as soon as possible and as often as necessary. It would be a mistake, however, to contact the supervisor only when trouble arises. Of course, you want to avoid wasting anyone's time, including your own. You should limit your contacts with a busy supervisor to essential matters. You could take the following approach with your supervisor:

> Everything seems to be going fine on the project you gave me. I expect to have it in to you on time. I'm wondering, however, if you could give me a few moments of your time. I want to bring you up to date on where I am so that you can let me know if I am on the right track.

Perhaps this contact could take place on the phone or during a brief office visit. Suppose that you have gone astray on the assignment without knowing it? It is obviously better to discover this before the date the assignment is due. The more communication you have with your supervisor, the more likely it is that you will catch such errors before a great deal of time is wasted.

Ask to participate in office and community training programs.

Sometimes there are training sessions for attorneys conducted in the law firm. You should ask that you be included. Bar associations and paralegal associations often conduct all-day seminars on legal topics relevant to your work. Seek permission to attend them if they are held during work hours.

Ask to be evaluated regularly.

For a number of reasons, evaluations are not given or are unhelpful when they are given:

- Evaluations can be time-consuming.
- Evaluators are reluctant to say anything negative, especially in writing.
- Most people do not like to be evaluated: it's too threatening to the ego.

Go out of your way to let your supervisor know that you want to be evaluated and that you can handle criticism. If you are defensive when you are criticized, you will find that the evaluations of your performance will go on behind your back! Such a work environment is obviously very unhealthy. Consider this approach that a paralegal might take with a supervisor:

> I want to know what you think of my work. I want to know where you think I need improvement. That's the only way I'm going to learn. I also want to know when I'm doing things correctly, but I'm mainly interested in your suggestions on what I can do to increase my skills.

If you take this approach *and mean it*, the chances are good that you will receive some very constructive criticism.

One step at a time.

Perhaps the most important advice you can receive in studying law is to concentrate on what is immediately before you. One step at a time. What are your responsibilities in the next fifteen minutes? Block everything else out. Make *the now* as productive as you can. Your biggest enemy is worry about the future: worry about the exams ahead of you, worry about your family, worry about the state of the world, worry about finding employment, etc. Leave tomorrow alone! Worrying about it will only interfere with your ability to make the most of what you must do now. Your development in the law will come slowly, in stages. Map out these stages in very small time blocks—beginning with the time that is immediately ahead of you. If you must worry, limit your concern to how to make the next fifteen minutes a more valuable learning experience.

☐ Summary

Legal education is a lifelong endeavor; a competent paralegal never stops learning about the law and the skills of applying it. A number of important guidelines will help you become a good student in the classroom and on the job. Do not let the media blur your understanding of what the practice of law is actually like. To avoid studying in a vacuum, be sure that you know the goals of an assignment, and how it fits into the other assignments. Organize your day around a study plan. Since the time demands on you will probably be greater than you anticipated, it is important that you design a system of studying. Step one is to assess your own study habits, such as how you

(Continued on next page)

☐ Summary *(Continued)*

handle distractions or how you commit things to memory. Then promise yourself that you will do something about your weaknesses

How many of the rules about the comma can you identify? Do you know when to use *that* rather than *which* in your sentences? How many of your paragraphs have topic sentences? On every page of your writing, are there zero spelling errors? You have entered a field where the written word is paramount. You must take personal responsibility—now—for the improvement of your grammar, spelling, and composition skills.

Use the law library to help you understand difficult areas of the law. But don't expect absolute clarity all the time. Seek out evaluations of your work. Become a skillful note taker. Get into the habit of looking for definitions and of translating rules into checklists.

These suggestions also apply once you are on the job. Don't pretend you understand what you don't. Repeat instructions back to your supervisor before you begin an assignment. Ask for due dates and priorities if you are given several things to do. Write down your instructions in your own notebook or journal. Find out if an assignment has been done by others in the past. If so, seek their help. Try to find a model and adapt it as needed. Ask for feedback before an assignment is due.

I

The Paralegal
in the Legal System

Contents

1

The Emergence and Development of a New Career in Law

■ Chapter Outline

Section A. Questions, Frustration, and Challenge

Welcome to the field! You probably fall into one or more of the following categories:

- You have never worked in a law office and have many questions about the career of a paralegal.

- You are employed or were once employed in a law office and now want to upgrade your skills.

- You have not made up your mind about whether to become an attorney and see the paralegal career as a way to learn more about the legal profession.

As Chief Justice Burger points out in the quote at the beginning of this book, the paralegal career is still in a state of development. By definition, therefore, a number of important questions still exist. The task of the first part of this book is to address these questions:

- What is a paralegal?
- Where do paralegals work?

■
"Paralegals: a novelty in the sixties, an asset in the seventies, a necessity in the eighties."
Hon. Richard A. Powers III, Magistrate, United States District Court for the Eastern District of Pennsylvania, 1986.
■

■
"Our profession is still growing and evolving. Be part of this evolution!"
Bobbi J. McFadden, President, Cincinnati Paralegal Association, 1991.
■

■ What are the functions of a paralegal?
■ How do I obtain a job?
■ What is the difference between an attorney and a paralegal?
■ What is the difference between a paralegal and the clerical staff of a law office?
■ How is the paralegal field regulated? Who does the regulating and for what purposes?
■ What are the ethical guidelines that govern paralegal conduct?
■ What is the future of the paralegal field?

Unfortunately *and* fortunately, definitive answers to these questions do not yet exist. As we shall see, considerable controversy surrounds many of them. It would be foolhardy for anyone to enter the field without having a comprehensive understanding of what the controversies are. According to Deanna Shimko-Herman, a paralegal in Milwaukee, "It is incumbent upon paralegals to be fully informed of the issues, and to operate from that informed base."[1] At times, however, the controversy seems to breed more confusion than constructive dialogue. This confusion can be frustrating to someone new to the field. From another point of view, however, this state of affairs presents you with the ultimate challenge of shaping your own answers to these questions. If Chief Justice Burger is correct that "we have only scratched the surface," the creative opportunities that exist for you are boundless. You will not simply be performing a job—you will be *helping to create a new profession*. This challenge would not exist if all the answers to the fundamental questions were already written in stone.

 ## Section B. Major Players: The Big Five

During our examination of this challenge, we will meet many organizations. Five in particular have had a dramatic influence on the development of paralegalism. These five (not necessarily listed in order of influence) are as follows:

■ National Federation of Paralegal Associations *(NFPA)*
■ National Association of Legal Assistants *(NALA)*
■ American Bar Association *(ABA)*
■ Your state's bar association
■ Your local paralegal association

While these organizations will be covered in some detail throughout the remaining chapters of the book, a brief word about each will be helpful at this point.

National Federation of Paralegal Associations (NFPA)

NFPA is an association of local associations. There are local paralegal associations throughout the country. Over sixty of them have affiliated with

---

[1]Shimko-Herman, *Should Paralegals Be Regulated with Limited Licensing?,* 17 On Point 10 (National Capital Area Paralegal Ass'n, February 1991).

NFPA. (See Appendix A). From its national headquarters in Kansas City, Missouri, NFPA promotes paralegalism through education and political action.

National Association of Legal Assistants (NALA)

NALA is primarily an association of individuals, although there are also a number of local paralegal associations that are affiliated with NALA. (See Appendix A.) From its national headquarters in Tulsa, Oklahoma, NALA is equally active in the educational and political arenas. One of the major differences between NALA and NFPA concerns the issue of certification. NALA has instituted a voluntary program of certifying paralegals through a series of examinations. For reasons we will explore in Chapter 3, NFPA strongly opposes this certification program.

American Bar Association (ABA)

The ABA is a voluntary association of attorneys; no attorney must be a member. Yet it is a powerful entity because of its resources, prestige, and the large number of attorneys who have joined. The ABA has a Standing Committee on Legal Assistants that has had a significant impact on the growth of the field. Recently, paralegals have been allowed to become Associate Members of the ABA, a development not everyone initially welcomed.

State Bar Association of Your State

Every state has at least one bar association that plays a major role in regulating attorneys under the supervision of the state's highest court. Most of the state bar associations have taken formal positions (in guidelines or ethical opinions) on the use of paralegals by attorneys. A few have followed the lead of the ABA and have allowed paralegals to become associate members. Whenever a paralegal issue arises, you will inevitably hear people ask, "What has the bar said about the issue?"

Your Local Paralegal Association

There are three main kinds of local paralegal associations: statewide, county or regionwide, and citywide.[2] In Appendix A, you will find a list of every local association in the country with an indication of whether it is affiliated with NFPA, affiliated with NALA, or unaffiliated. For a great many paralegals in the country, major career support and inspiration have come through active participation in their local paralegal association.

. . . .

While these five organizations will dominate our discussion of paralegalism, we will also be referring to other important groups, such as *LAMA*, the Legal Assistant Management Association (an association of people who supervise other paralegals in large law offices); and *ALA*, the Association of Legal Administrators (an association of people who manage law offices).

---

[2]In addition, there are associations of paralegals connected with particular schools.

■ **ASSIGNMENT 1.1**

It is not too early in your education to make contact with paralegal associations. In the back of this book, after the index, you will find several forms: "Paralegal Associations: Local" and "Paralegal Associations: National." By filling out and mailing the forms now, you can begin this contact.

 Section C. Job Titles

For convenience, this book uses the job title *paralegal*. An equally common and synonymous term is *legal assistant*. Not everyone uses one of these titles. In fact, there is considerable diversity in the job titles that are used. There is also controversy (for example, a recent lawsuit was brought to prevent certain people from calling themselves paralegals or legal assistants); and confusion (for example, there are some licensed attorneys who work under the title of legal assistant, particularly in the government).

To begin sorting through the maze, we examine three categories of people: employees of attorneys (the dominant category), self-employed individuals who work for attorneys (a growing but much smaller category), and self-employed individuals who provide their services directly to the public without attorney supervision (the smallest but most controversial category). In none of these categories is there universal agreement on what job title should be used. Some titles (paralegal, legal technician) are used in more than one category, but not always on a consistent basis.

1. Employees of Attorneys

The vast majority (over 95%) are employees of attorneys. They may be called:

paralegal	legal service assistant
legal assistant	paralegal specialist
certified legal assistant	junior legal assistant
senior legal assistant	legal technician
lawyer's assistant	legal paraprofessional
attorney assistant	case clerk
project assistant	legal assistant clerk
lay assistant	document clerk
lawyer's aide	depo summarizer

The most commonly used titles are paralegal and legal assistant. As indicated, these titles are synonymous.[3] They are as interchangeable as the words lawyer and attorney.

---

[3]Someone once proposed that the word *paralegal* be used primarily as an adjective and the phrase *legal assistant* primarily as a noun. Under this proposal, a legal assistant would perform paralegal tasks. The proposal has never been considered seriously.

All of the titles listed thus far are generic in the sense that they do not tell you what area of law the person works in. Other employee job titles are more specific:

litigation assistant	conflict-of-interest coordinator
corporate paralegal	family law paralegal
probate specialist	welfare paralegal
personal injury paralegal	international trade paralegal
real estate paralegal	worker's compensation paralegal
bankruptcy paralegal	claims negotiator
water law paralegal	

Occasionally, when the office wants its paralegal to perform more than one job, *hybrid titles* are used. For example, an office might call an employee a *paralegal/investigator,* a *paralegal/librarian,* or a *paralegal/legal secretary.*

When a paralegal becomes part of management in an office with a large number of paralegals, titles reflecting this new status are often used—such as paralegal supervisor, legal assistant manager, or case manager.

2. Self-Employed Individuals Working for Attorneys

All of the above titles cover people who are employees of attorneys in one law office. A much smaller number are *independent contractors* who have formed their own businesses that provide services to attorneys from more than one office. (Independent contractors are self-employed persons who control the methods of performing tasks; the objectives or end products of the tasks are controlled by those who buy their services.) They move from office to office for relatively short-term projects and periods, or they work in their own office on projects mailed to them (or transmitted by fax machine or by modem) from different attorneys around town. Such self-employed individuals have different titles such as:

freelance paralegal

independent paralegal

contract paralegal

3. Self-Employed Individuals Serving the Public

Finally, there is a controversial category of people who do not work for (and who are not supervised by) attorneys. They sell their services directly to the public. Among the titles used by such practitioners are:

legal technician	legal typist
limited practice officer	independent paralegal
certified closing officer	freelance paralegal
public paralegal	scrivener
forms practitioner	

Bar associations have often tried to prosecute these individuals for unauthorized practice of law. Yet there is a movement, in the form of limited licensing, toward legitimizing some of their activities. We will examine this in Chapter 3.

. . . .

Established paralegals are not always happy with the diversity of titles. For example, a number of paralegal associations object to anyone in the third category (self-employed individuals serving the public) using the word *paralegal* in his or her title. To avoid confusion in the mind of the public, such associations want to limit these words to those who work under the supervision of an attorney. They prefer the title *legal technician*, for example, to *independent paralegal*. One paralegal association refers to everyone in the third category as "non-paralegals"! For similar reasons, the National Association of Legal Assistants recently asked a court to prevent inmates from using the title of paralegal or legal assistant. They had completed a course in legal research to allow them to work on their own legal problems and those of fellow inmates.[4] Since they would not always be working under the supervision of attorneys, NALA wanted them to use a title other than paralegal or legal assistant.

There may come a time when a legislature or court will establish definitive titles for certain categories of individuals in this area. As the present time, however, official titles do not exist. There is no requirement, for example, that individuals be licensed by the state in order to work in any of the three categories listed above. Hence there are no rules on who can use titles such as paralegal or legal assistant. If a form of licensing is instituted, this may change. Again we will discuss this possibility in Chapter 3.

Section D. Job Definitions

What comes to mind when people think of a paralegal? Perhaps the most common definition is: a nonattorney who helps an attorney. While essentially correct, there are problems with this definition—as we will see. In this book, the following definition is used:

> A paralegal is a person with legal skills who works under the supervision of an attorney or who is otherwise authorized to use those skills; this person performs tasks that do not require all the skills of an attorney and that most secretaries are not trained to perform.

Definitions have been formulated by the American Bar Association, the National Association of Legal Assistants, and the National Federation of Paralegal Associations. American Bar Association:

> A legal assistant is a person, qualified through education, training, or work experience, who is employed or retained by a lawyer, law office, governmental agency, or other entity in a capacity or function which involves the performance, under the ultimate direction and supervision of an attorney, of specifically delegated substantive legal work, which work, for the most part, requires a sufficient knowledge of legal concepts that, absent such assistant, the attorney would perform the task.

National Association of Legal Assistants:

> Legal Assistants [also known as paralegals] are a distinguishable group of persons who assist attorneys in the delivery of legal services. Through formal education, training, and experience, legal assistants have knowledge and expertise

---

[4]*Alan Gluth et al vs. Arizona Department of Corrections* (CB-84-1626 PHX CAM) (United States Court of Appeals for the Ninth Circuit). See 17 Facts & Findings 6 (NALA, Fall 1990).

regarding the legal system and substantive and procedural law which qualify them to do work of a legal nature under the supervision of an attorney.

National Federation of Paralegal Associations:

A paralegal/legal assistant is a person qualified through education, training, or work experience to perform substantive legal work that requires knowledge of legal concepts and is customarily, but not exclusively, performed by a lawyer. This person may be retained or employed by a lawyer, law office, governmental agency, or other entity, or may be authorized by administrative, statutory or court authority to perform this work.

■ ASSIGNMENT 1.2

Assume that John Jones is authorized by law to represent clients in social security hearings for a fee. He works alone in his own office. Is John a legal assistant or paralegal under the ABA definition? Under the NALA definition? Under the NFPA definition?

Unless a law office employs a relatively large number of paralegals, career ladders usually do not exist. Yet career ladders are becoming increasingly common if there are three or more paralegals in the office. This requires more than one definition of a paralegal to reflect the different steps on the ladder—from the entry-level paralegal to the paralegal manager. In Figure 1.1 you will find an example of the definitions proposed by the Legal Assistant Management Association (LAMA), an organization of over 500 legal assistant managers. Of course, not all large offices use these titles or definitions, but their use is increasing.[5]

A number of points need to be made about the definition of a paralegal— or the absence of a definition about which everyone can agree:

1. To date, there is no official terminology imposed by law.

There are three ways that a person becomes a paralegal—by experience, by training, and by fiat.[6] See Figure 1.2. Twenty years ago, the first route was the most common way to become a paralegal. Today, the second route is the most common. While the third route still exists, those who enter the field this way are sometimes resented by paralegals who entered the field by experience or training.

Why do these three methods of becoming a paralegal exist? Primarily because there are no licensing or other laws on who can be a paralegal, at least at the present time. Consequently, there is nothing to prevent a law office from calling its messenger a paralegal! Bar associations, paralegal associations, and educators have attempted to formulate definitions, as we have seen, but nothing has emerged as universally acceptable. To some, this state of affairs is healthy since the absence of official terminology encourages diversity. To others, it is frustrating:

---

[5]For example, the legal assistant manager might be called a paralegal supervisor in some offices. For a more complete list, see Figure 2.2 in Chapter 2.

[6]Malone, *Let Your Staff Shine as "Paralegals,"* The Compleat Lawyer 4 (Winter 1990).

Unfortunately, some law firms seem to be using the phrases "legal assistant" and "paralegal" with alarming regularity without regard to the tasks being performed. And firms are hiring these people at a lower pay scale, thus lowering the salary of the average paralegal.[7]

2. Definitions are often phrased in the negative.

Some definitions do a better job of telling us what a paralegal is *not* than what one *is*. A paralegal is *not* an attorney, *not* a secretary, *not* a *law clerk* (someone studying to be an attorney), etc. This can be frustrating, as evidenced by the following statement of Karen Dodge, an Oregon paralegal: "I am, along with thousands of other legal assistants, more than a non-lawyer!"[8]

3. Many definitions have four main components.

- The paralegal is not an attorney.
- The paralegal has legal knowledge and skills.

FIGURE 1.1

Sample Job Descriptions of Paralegals in a Large Law Office Where a Career Ladder Exists

---

Legal Assistant Clerk

A person who, under the supervision of a legal assistant, performs clerical tasks such as document numbering, alphabetizing documents, labeling folders, filing, and any other project that does not require substantive knowledge of the transaction or litigation.

Legal Assistant [also called a Paralegal]

A person who assists an attorney in the practice of law. His or her duties can include factual research, document analysis, cite checking and shepardizing, drafting certificates and corporate transactional documentation, drafting pleadings, coordinating document productions, administering trusts and estates, assisting with pension plan administration, assisting with real estate transactions, and handling substantive functions in practice areas that do not require a law degree.

Senior Legal Assistant

An experienced legal assistant with the ability to supervise or train other legal assistants. He or she may have developed a specialty in a certain practice area.

Supervising Legal Assistant

Someone who spends about 50% of his or her time supervising other legal assistants, and about 50% on client cases as a legal assistant.

Case Manager

An experienced legal assistant who can coordinate or direct legal assistant activities on a major case or transaction.

Legal Assistant Manager [also called Paralegal Administrator, Paralegal Coordinator, Director of Legal Assistant Services, and Supervisor]

A person responsible for recruiting, interviewing, and hiring legal assistants. May also be responsible for training legal assistants, monitoring work assignments, and handling personnel and administrative matters that relate to legal assistants. May have budget responsibility for the legal assistant program, and play a role in salary and billing rate administration. The Legal Assistant Manager works few or no billable hours.

Source: Ernst & Young, *Legal Assistant Managers and Legal Assistants,* 388 (3rd ed. 1989), Legal Assistants Management Association.

---

[7] *Ka L'eo O* (Hawaii Ass'n of Legal Assistants, February 1983).
[8] Karen Dodge, Paragram (Oregon Legal Assistants Ass'n, September 1984).

By experience:	A secretary, office clerk, or other member of the clerical staff starts to perform paralegal responsibilities. Eventually, he or she is given the title of paralegal.
By training:	A graduate of a paralegal training program who has never worked in a law office is hired as a paralegal.
By fiat:	An office hires an individual with the title of paralegal even though he or she has never had any law office experience or paralegal training.

FIGURE 1.2

Three Ways to Become a Paralegal

- The paralegal works under the supervision of an attorney.
- The paralegal does not practice law.

4. *There are problems with each of these four components.*

First, there *are* some attorneys who are classified as paralegals. There are attorneys working in America, for example, who are licensed in a foreign country. Some states consider such attorneys to be paralegals. The same may be true of attorneys working in one state but licensed to practice in another state. Occasionally a suspended or disbarred attorney will try to continue work in the law as a paralegal. Under certain circumstances, as we will see in Chapter 4, such work is ethical and legal. Finally, there is nothing to prevent an attorney from applying for and receiving a paralegal job. This is not uncommon in a tight market where there are many unemployed attorneys looking for work.

Second, we learn very little when we are told that a paralegal has legal knowledge and skills. So do attorneys, law clerks, legal secretaries, investigators, many real estate brokers, bankers, etc.

Third, not all paralegals work under the supervision of an attorney. As we will see later, many paralegals working for the government are not supervised by attorneys. There are also special laws that permit nonattorneys to engage in legal work independent of attorneys. To be sure, most paralegals work in private law offices under the supervision of an attorney. Yet there are some who are otherwise situated.

Fourth, it is inaccurate to say that paralegals cannot practice law. The more correct statement of the principle is that paralegals cannot engage in the *unauthorized* practice of law. The existence of rules on the *un*authorized practice of law governing paralegals presupposes the existence of an *authorized practice of law* by paralegals. It is true that the spectrum of authorized practice for paralegals is quite narrow—but it does exist. In our society, the practice of law is not the exclusive domain of the attorney. This will be explored in greater detail in Chapters 3 and 4.

5. *The definitions that we have require further definitions.*

In law, the presence of a definition usually prompts a search for a definition of the definition! Paralegal definitions sometimes contain words and phrases such as *supervision, substantive legal work, practice of law, assistance,* etc. We must be concerned about what these words and phrases mean—they must be defined. These definitions will then probably require clarifications that are, in effect, further definitions. This phenomenon is not peculiar to paralegalism. The process of legal analysis itself calls for an extended series of definitions and subdefinitions, as we will demonstrate in Part II of this book.

Other disciplines face the same difficulty. In the medical profession, for example, a close counterpart to the paralegal is the *physician assistant*. The following is a proposed definition of this career:

> Physician assistant means an individual who is qualified by academic and clinical training to provide patient care services under the supervision and responsibility of a doctor of medicine or osteopathy.[9]

Among the major phrases in this definition that require further defining are: "qualified," "patient care services," and "supervision."

6. A title and definition should serve three main functions.

In the quest for an acceptable title and definition, there is a danger of losing sight of the reasons that should govern the search. A title and definition should:

- Convey enough information about the field to a prospective student.
- Convey enough information about the field to a prospective employer.
- Convey enough information about the field to the public, as prospective clients.

7. Unanimity may be unnecessary, undesirable, and impossible to achieve.

The above three purposes can arguably be served without ever achieving total agreement on terminology. We bang our heads against a stone wall when we insist on terminology that:

- Precisely and definitively distinguishes this career from that of other law office personnel.
- Includes everyone who should be included.
- Excludes everyone who should be excluded.

This is simply too much to ask because of the great diversity in the field. We do not yet know all the boundary lines. The wiser course at this stage of development is *not* to insist on trying to achieve unanimity.

8. Terminology and credentialization.

It does not seem to disturb anyone that we do not have a definitive definition of an attorney. An attorney is someone with a license to practice law. Attorneys are defined primarily by the *credential* that they hold. Any attempt to provide a descriptive definition poses substantial difficulties. There has been endless litigation, for example, on trying to define the *practice of law*. The same is true of terms such as *legal advice* and *professional judgment*. We will explore some of this controversy in Chapters 3 and 4. The point, however, is that a precise definition of an attorney (in terms of what an attorney does) is no more easy to identify than a precise definition of a paralegal. We should not ask of paralegalism that it achieve a level of definitional precision that the legal profession has never been able to achieve.

When a career is having difficulty defining itself, it sometimes tries to use credentialization as a way out of the difficulty. The paralegal career may also

[9]44 Federal Register 36,177 (No. 121, 6/21/79).

move in this direction. A paralegal may someday be defined primarily as some-one with a license or a certificate to be a paralegal. If this happens, the debate on role will not end. Shifting the question from "What is a paralegal?" to "What credentials should a paralegal have?" will not stop the controversy.

9. Functional Definition

While many organizations and individuals are engaged in a theoretical de-bate over the definition of a paralegal, the marketplace may be forcing a prac-tical definition on us. As we will see in a moment, there are several kinds of cases in which the winning party can force the losing party to pay the attorney fees *and the paralegal fees* of the winning party. (When this occurs, the parale-gal fees, of course, go to the supervising attorney of the paralegal; they do not go directly to the paralegal.) But everything a paralegal does on a case does *not* qualify for an award of paralegal fees. Consequently, if attorneys want to in-crease the chance of obtaining an award of paralegal fees, they must make sure that the tasks of the paralegal fit within the criteria for such an award. The main criterion is that the paralegal is performing tasks that are not purely secretarial or clerical. This reality may lead to a practical or functional definition of a para-legal: a person who performs tasks that qualify for an award of paralegal fees.

■ ASSIGNMENT 1.3

In this assignment, we explore what the world thinks a paralegal or legal as-sistant is. So much will depend on what the public has heard about this field. It is not as well known as other new occupations such as *paramedic*. In many parts of the country, the word *paramedic* is printed in large bold print on ambulances racing throughout the city. This visibility has increased the public's understanding of what a paramedic is. Media attention is also important. Many paralegals were disap-pointed, for example, when a prime-time attorney soap opera, *L.A. Law,* failed to include a paralegal for a role in the law firm that was the center of this very popular television program. Some wrote to the program producer to protest this glaring omission, but to no avail. This does not mean, however, that any kind of media attention would be welcomed. Shelly Widoff, a paralegal consultant in Boston, has her fingers crossed: "I just hope we all don't cringe when the media get hold of us on a TV sitcom." [10] Recently, many paralegals not only cringed but also vigorously protested when *Quincy,* a medical television program, portrayed a paralegal as an arch villain. Thankfully this occurred in only one of its episodes!

Douglas Parker, a litigation paralegal, believes that the public has "as many different perceptions of our occupational status as there are craters on the moon." [11] To gauge whether this is true in your community, contact the following individuals in your area. Ask each of them the question: "What is a paralegal or legal assistant?"

(a) A neighbor or friend who does not work in a law office and who has probably never been in a law office.
(b) A neighbor or friend who does not work in a law office but who has hired an attorney at least once in his or her life.
(c) A legal secretary.
(d) An attorney who has never hired a paralegal.
(e) An attorney who has hired a paralegal.
(f) A working paralegal who is not now in school.

---

[10]S. Widoff, *On the Docket,* 4 Legal Assistant Today 10 (January/February 1987).
[11]Parker, *Legal Assistants: A Case of Uncertain Identity,* 7 Legal Professional 10 (September/October 1989).

(g) A high school student.
(h) A student in a law school studying to be an attorney.
(i) A police officer.
(j) A person who runs a small business.
(k) A local judge.
(l) A clerk in a local court.

Take careful notes on their answers to the question. Compare the answers.

- What common ideas or themes did you find in the definitions?

- What two definitions were the most different? List the differences.

- Do you think that your survey raises any problems about the perception of paralegals in your area? If so, what are these problems, and how can they be solved?

■ Section E. Salaries

How much do paralegals make? While some data is available to answer this question, there is no definitive answer because of the great variety of employment settings. According to a 1991 study of over 2,600 paralegals by the National Association of Legal Assistants, the national average annual salary of paralegals was $27,082, with an average annual bonus of $1,793.[12] A 1991 study of 587 paralegals reported that the national average annual salary was $27,772.[13] It is important to note that none of these are entry-level salaries; most of the paralegals surveyed had been on the job for one or more years.[14] The Legal Assistant Management Association conducted one of the most comprehensive surveys of paralegal salaries in 1989. Over 6,000 paralegal salaries were examined. The results are reported in Figures 1.3 and 1.4. Note that a paralegal's salary will tend to increase in direct proportion to his or her experience (Figure 1.3) and level of responsibility (Figure 1.4). A number of other generalizations can be made about salaries across the country:

- Paralegals who work in the law departments of corporations (banks, insurance companies, other businesses) tend to make more than those who work in private law firms. In a 1989 survey of just under a thousand corporate law departments, the average salary for a paralegal was $29,973. About 150 of them reported receiving an average bonus of $2,243 (Altman & Weil).

- Paralegals who work in large private law firms tend to make more than those who work in smaller private law firms.

- Paralegals who work in large metropolitan areas (over a million in population) tend to make more than those who work in rural areas.

- Paralegals who work for the government in civil service positions tend to make less than those who work for large private law firms or corporations.

- Paralegals who work in legal aid or legal service offices that are funded by government grants and charitable contributions tend to make less than all other paralegals.

---

[12]NALA, *The Legal Assistant Profession: National Utilization and Compensation Survey Report,* 35 (1991).

[13]Milano, *Salary Survey Results,* 8 Legal Assistant Today 27 (May/June 1991).

[14]One study of a relatively small number of law offices in Colorado showed that the average salary for entry-level paralegals was $17,900. Acree, *The CBA Economic Survey,* 20 The Colorado Lawyer 451 (March 1991).

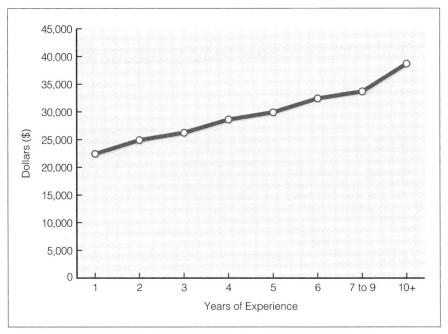

FIGURE 1.3
1989 Total Compensation (Median) by Years of Experience

Source: Ernst & Young, *Legal Assistant Managers and Legal Assistants,* ix (3rd ed. 1989).

FIGURE 1.4
1989 Average Compensation by Level of Responsibility

Position	NON-BONUS RECEIVERS	BONUS RECEIVERS		
	Total Compensation*	Base Salary*	Bonus	Total Compensation**
Legal Assistant Manager	$37,180	$43,112	$4,131	$47,243
Supervising Legal Assistant	$37,847	$39,819	$3,050	$42,868
Senior Legal Assistant	$34,925	$35,063	$3,091	$38,154
Case Manager	$29,636	$32,170	$4,787	$36,957
Legal Assistant	$25,636	$26,697	$1,781	$28,477
Legal Assistant Clerk	$17,888	$18,958	$850	$19,808

*1989 base salary
**1989 base salary plus 1988 bonus (does not include overtime where paid)

Source: Ernst & Young, *Legal Assistant Managers and Legal Assistants,* p. 16 (3rd ed. 1989).

- Paralegals working for attorneys who understand the value of paralegals tend to make more than those working for attorneys who have a poor or weak understanding of what paralegals can do.
- Paralegals who work in an office where there is a career ladder for paralegals, plus periodic evaluations and salary reviews, tend to make more than those who work in offices without these options.
- Paralegals who are career-oriented tend to make more than those less interested in a long-term commitment to paralegal work.

Paralegal salaries are related to the skills a paralegal has developed and the extent to which such skills are used by the office.

There are a few paralegals in the country—*very few*—who command salaries of over $100,000. Lee Henderson, for example, is such a paralegal; she works for a large Dallas law firm. "Lee Henderson, a paralegal with 25 years' experience in the mortgage banking business, supervises a staff of 38. Her department manages closings for residential mortgage loans. She has also helped develop computer programs to assist other departments."[15] Again, such salaries, while possible, are rare.

In addition to the payment of bonuses, other fringe benefits must also be considered, e.g., vacation time, health insurance, parking facilities. A comprehensive list of such benefits will be presented in Chapter 2. (See Figure 2.12.)

One final point to keep in mind about salaries. Once a person has gained training *and experience* as a paralegal, there are possibilities of using this background to go into other positions that are law-related. For example, a corporate paralegal in a law firm might leave the firm to take a higher-paying position for a corporation as a securities analyst, or an estates paralegal at a law firm might leave for a more lucrative position as a trust administrator at a bank. A more extensive list of these law-related jobs will be given at the end of Chapter 2.

Section F. Historical Perspective

In the late 1960s, most attorneys would draw a blank if you mentioned the words *paralegal* or *legal assistant*. According to Webster's *Ninth New Collegiate Dictionary,* the earliest recorded use of the word *paralegal* in English occurred in 1971. Today, the situation has changed radically. There are few offices that do not employ paralegals or that are not seriously thinking about

---

[15]Marcotte, *$100,000 a Year for Paralegals?*, 73 American Bar Association Journal 19 (October 1987).

hiring them. A recent survey reports that there is one paralegal for every four attorneys in law firms and one paralegal for every two attorneys in the law departments of corporations.[16] It has been estimated that the number of paralegals may eventually exceed the number of attorneys in the practice of law. The United States Bureau of Labor Statistics has projected that paralegals will constitute one of the fastest growing fields in the country, with a growth of over 75% between the years 1988 and 2000 (see Figure 1.5).

What has caused this dramatic change? The following factors have been instrumental in bringing paralegalism to its present state of prominence:

■ The pressure of economics.

■ The call for efficiency and delegation.

■ The promotion by bar associations.

■ The organization of paralegals.

■ The restructuring of professions and occupations generally.

1. The Pressure of Economics

Perhaps the greatest incentive to the development of paralegals has been arithmetic. Law firms simply add up what they earn without paralegals, add up

OCCUPATION	EMPLOYMENT		CHANGE IN EMPLOYMENT
	1988	Projected, 2000	1988–2000
Paralegals	83,000	145,000	+75.3%
Medical assistants	149,000	253,000	+70.0%
Home health aides	236,000	397,000	+67.9%
Radiologic technologies and technicians	132,000	218,000	+66.0%
Data processing equipment repairers	71,000	115,000	+61.2%
Medical record technicians	47,000	75,000	+59.9%
Medical secretaries	207,000	327,000	+58.0%
Physical therapists	68,000	107,000	+57.0%
Surgical technologies	35,000	55,000	+56.4%
Operations research analysts	55,000	85,000	+55.4%
Securities and financial services sales workers	200,000	309,000	+54.8%
Travel agents	142,000	219,000	+54.1%
Computer systems analysts	403,000	617,000	+53.3%
Physical and corrective therapy assistants	39,000	60,000	+52.5%
Social welfare service aides	91,000	138,000	+51.5%
Occupational therapists	33,000	48,000	+48.8%
Computer programmers	519,000	769,000	+48.1%
Human services workers	118,000	171,000	+44.9%
Respiratory therapists	56,000	79,000	+41.3%
Correction officers and jailers	186,000	262,000	+40.8%

Source: U.S. Department of Labor, Bureau of Labor Statistics, *Occupational Outlook Quarterly*, 6 (Spring 1990).

FIGURE 1.5

The Fastest Growing Occupations, 1988–2000

---

[16]Ernst & Young, *Legal Assistant Managers and Legal Assistants*, xi (3rd ed. 1989).

what they could earn with paralegals, compare the two figures, and conclude that the employment of paralegals is profitable. There "can be little doubt that the principal motivation prompting law firms to hire legal assistants is the economic benefit enjoyed by the firm." [17] The key to increased profits is *leveraging.* Leverage, often expressed as a ratio, is the ability to make a profit from the income-gathering work of others. The higher the ratio of paralegals to partners in the firm, the more profit to the partners (assuming everyone is generating income from billable time). [18]

In the best of all worlds, some of this increased profit will result in lower fees to the client. For example, Chief Justice Warren Burger feels that some attorneys charge "excessive fees for closing real-estate transactions for the purchase of a home. A greater part of that work can be handled by trained paralegals, and, in fact, many responsible law firms are doing just that to reduce costs for their clients." [19]

Figure 1.6 provides an example of the economic impact of using a paralegal. In the example, a client comes to a lawyer to form a corporation. [20] We will compare (a) the economics of an attorney and secretary working on the case, assuming a fee of $2,000, and (b) the economics of an attorney, secretary, *and* paralegal working on the same case, assuming a fee of $1,600. As you can see, with a paralegal added to the team, the firm's profit is increased almost 25% in spite of the lower fee, and the attorney has more billable time to spend elsewhere. Some studies have claimed an even higher profit increase because of the use of paralegals.

The example assumes that the attorney's fee is $200 per hour and that the attorney billed the client $40 per hour for the paralegal's time. According to a 1988 study of relatively large law firms, the billing rate that firms charged clients for paralegal work ranged from $41 to $60 an hour, and the average number of chargeable billable hours each paralegal reported in these firms was 1,350 per year. [21] A more recent study showed that the average paralegal fee allowed by the courts was $48.10 per hour. [22] (See also Figure 10.4 in Chapter 10.)

When a law firm bills clients for paralegal time, the paralegal becomes a *profit center* in the firm. In such cases, paralegals are not simply part of the cost of doing business reflected in the firm's *overhead;* [23] they generate revenue (and therefore, profit) for the firm. To calculate the amount of profit, the *rule of three* is often used as a general guideline. To be profitable, a paralegal must bill three times his or her salary. Of the total revenue brought in through paralegal bill-

---

[17]*The Expanding Role of Legal Assistants in New York State,* 7 (N.Y. State Bar Association, Subcommittee on Legal Assistants).

[18]The same, of course, is true of associates in the firm. The higher the ratio of associates to partners, the greater the profit to the partners.

[19]U.S. News & World Rep., Feb. 22, 1982 at p. 32.

[20]Adapted from Jespersen, *Paralegals: Help or Hindrance?* The Houston Lawyer 111, 114–16 (March/April 1977).

[21]Ernst & Young, *Legal Assistant Managers and Legal Assistants,* xii (3rd ed. 1989).

[22]Carla Teague, *Case Law Trends Affecting the Paralegal Profession,* 16 National Paralegal Reporter 18 (NFPA, Fall 1991). A 1991 survey of all members of NALA concluded that the average billing rate for NALA members was $55.00 per hour. NALA, *The Legal Assistant Profession,* see footnote 12 at p. 29.

[23]Overhead includes the cost of office space, furniture, equipment, and insurance, plus the cost of secretarial or other clerical staff whose time is usually not billed separately to clients.

TASK: TO FORM A CORPORATION		

a. Attorney and Secretary

	Time	
Function	**Attorney**	**Secretary**
1. Interviewing	1.0	0.0
2. Advising	1.0	0.0
3. Gathering information	1.0	0.0
4. Preparing papers	2.0	4.0
5. Executing and filing papers	1.0	1.0
	6.0	5.0

Assume that the attorney's hourly rate is $200 per hour. Assume that the overhead cost of maintaining a secretary is $20 per hour.

Attorney (6 × $200)	$1,200
Secretary (5 × $20)	100
Total cost	$1,300
Fee	$2,000
Less cost	1,300
Gross profit	$ 700

b. Attorney, Secretary, *and* Paralegal

	Time		
Function	**Attorney**	**Paralegal**	**Secretary**
1. Interviewing	0.5	0.5	0.0
2. Advising	1.0	0.0	0.0
3. Gathering information	0.0	1.0	0.0
4. Preparing papers	0.5	1.5	4.0
5. Executing and filing papers	0.5	0.5	1.0
	2.5	3.5	5.0

In addition, assume a paralegal hourly rate of $40 per hour.

Attorney (2.5 × $200)	$500
Paralegal (3.5 × $40)	140
Secretary (5 × $20)	100
Total cost	$740
Fee	$1,600
Less cost	740
Gross profit	$ 860

COMPARISON	

Fee: a. Attorney and Secretary	$2,000
b. Attorney, Secretary, and Paralegal	$1,600
Saving to client	$400
Increased profitability to lawyer ($860 vs. $700)	$160

By using a paralegal on the case, the attorney's profit increases almost 25% over the profit realized without the paralegal. Furthermore, the attorney has 3.5 hours that are suddenly available to work on other cases, bringing in additional revenue of $700 (3.5 × the attorney's hourly rate of $200).

FIGURE 1.6

The Profitability of Using Paralegals

ing, one-third is allocated to salary, one-third to overhead, and one-third to profit. Phrased another way, when the gross revenue generated through paralegal billing equals three times the paralegal's salary, the firm has achieved its minimum profit expectations.

For example:

Paralegal's salary:	$30,000
Paralegal rate:	$35 per hour

Billings the firm hopes this paralegal will generate: $90,000

Rule-of-three allocation:
—paralegal salary: $30,000
—overhead for this paralegal: $30,000
profit to the law firm: $30,000[24]

■ ASSIGNMENT 1.4

(a) In the example just given, how many billable hours per year would this paralegal have to produce in order to generate $30,000 per year in profits for the firm? Is this number realistic? If not, what must be done?

(b) Assume that a paralegal seeks a salary of $25,000 a year and that the law firm would like to be able to pay this salary. Using the "rule of three," if this person is able to generate 1,400 billable hours per year, how much must this paralegal's time be billed at in order for the attorney and the paralegal to be happy?

Paralegals can be even more profitable to the firm in cases where clients pay a fixed fee or a contingency fee. A *fixed fee* (e.g., $20,000) is paid regardless of the number of hours it takes the firm to complete the case—and regardless of the outcome of the case. A *contingency fee* is usually a percentage (e.g., 33%) that is paid only if the client wins, regardless of the number of hours it takes the firm to complete the case. In most cases where a client pays a fixed fee or a contingency fee, there is no hourly billing. Greater use of paralegals on such cases can lead to greater profits. The "more the attorney uses legal assistant services as opposed to attorney services," the less cost is incurred, "thereby maintaining more of the fee as a profit."[25]

Not every law firm agrees, however, that hiring paralegals inevitably leads to greater profits for the firm. A number of factors complicate the attempt to determine the economic effect of hiring paralegals. For example:

■ At some firms, there is a relatively high turnover of paralegals. This means increased in-house training costs for newly hired paralegals and, therefore, higher overhead.

■ Many attorneys are looking for work, particularly recent law school graduates. Some are working part-time for law firms,[26] or are accepting comparatively low-paying *staff attorney*[27] positions at the firms. These attorneys have no hope of ever becoming partners in the firm—unlike the traditional associates at the firm. In fee-generating cases, some firms may be more likely to delegate work to a part-time attorney or to a staff attorney than to paralegals, since the firm can bill an attorney's time at a higher rate. This tendency is even greater if the salary of this attorney is not significantly different from the salary of the paralegals in the firm. When low-salaried attorneys are available, some firms are not as convinced that it's economical to hire paralegals.

---

[24]Adapted from State Bar of Texas, *Attorneys' Guide to Practicing with Legal Assistants*, VI(3) (1986).

[25]L. Hangley, "The Role of the Legal Assistant" in *The Team Approach to Practice Development*, 5 (Professional Education Systems, 1989).

[26]Part-time attorneys are sometimes called "contract attorneys" or "project attorneys."

[27]Also referred to as second-tier attorneys.

- An experienced legal secretary can sometimes earn more than a new parale-gal. Where this is so, a firm might be tempted to assign some secretarial tasks to the paralegal. When this occurs, the profitability of paralegals may dimin-ish, since a firm cannot bill paralegal rates for secretarial tasks.

Yet such factors have not diminished the movement toward hiring increased numbers of paralegals. Furthermore, the cost-effectiveness of a paralegal should not be judged solely by the amount of revenue directly generated by his or her efforts. Paralegals often perform valuable but *nonbillable* tasks, such as recruit-ing new employees, managing other paralegals, updating and organizing plead-ings files, and doing most of the work on cases that the attorney would normally do for free (e.g., probating the estate of the attorney's brother-in-law). This, of course, enables attorneys to direct more of their efforts to fee-generating mat-ters. Furthermore, if a paralegal is not as profitable as an employer had hoped, the problem may be the lack of an effective strategy to incorporate paralegals into the office and to manage them effectively. "In fact, if the hiring, allocation and utilization of paralegals is not actively planned and managed by the law firm, productivity and profitability will not be improved." [28]

■ ASSIGNMENT 1.5

The following historical overview provides two theories to explain the develop-ment of paralegals. Why do you think the author feels that the "second has held the profession back"?

"Historically, the legal assistant's role evolved from efficient use of legal secretaries. There are two theories as to how this happened. One theory suggests that the attorney, seeing the benefit to his clients in providing increased services through the use of his legal secretary, provided his secretary with further education and training and she then per-formed substantive legal services. The other theory is that the attorney, looking for areas where he might bill his client for the secretary's service, determined that if he called his secretary a legal assistant, he could more easily charge for the secretarial services. Both of these approaches contributed to the evolution. While the first concept has elevated the paralegal profession, the second has held the profession back." [29]

Thus far the focus of our discussion has been law firm profit when the rev-enue generated by the law firm comes from the firm's own clients—through hourly fees, a fixed fee, or a contingent fee. Earlier we briefly mentioned another kind of case where the paralegal can play a significant role in the firm's profit picture. There are a number of special cases (for example, employment discrim-ination and antitrust violations), where *the losing side pays the attorney fees of the winning side.* Most courts agree that in addition to recovering attorney fees, the winning side can recover for its paralegal time spent in litigation. But in what amount? Two possibilities exist:

(a) Prevailing Market Rate for Paralegals.   This is the amount a law firm charges its clients for paralegal time, e.g., $50 an hour.

---

[28]A. Olson, *Law Firms, Paralegals and Profitability* 4 Journal of Paralegal Education and Practice 31, 32 (October 1987).
[29]L. Hangley, "The Role of the Legal Assistant" in *The Team Approach to Practice Development,* 3 (Professional Education Systems, 1989).

(b) Actual Cost to the Law Firm. This is the amount that the law firm pays to keep its paralegal, e.g., $20 an hour, to cover the paralegal's salary, fringe benefits, and other overhead items related to the paralegal.

There can be a dramatic difference between market rate and actual cost, since the former includes the profit that the firm makes through the paralegal. When a losing party must pay for the paralegal time of the winning party, how much is paid? Market rate or actual cost? Different states answer this question in different ways when the litigation involves a state matter.

For certain kinds of *federal* cases, however, the United States Supreme Court settled the question in the very important 1989 opinion of *Missouri v. Jenkins* when it ruled that the prevailing market rate was to be the standard of recovery. The relevant portions of this opinion are reprinted below.

The case involved a Kansas City suit in which a claim was made under § 1988 of the Civil Rights Act. The lower court awarded the winning party $40 an hour for paralegal time, which was the prevailing rate in Kansas City at the time. On appeal, the losing party argued that it should pay no more than $15 an hour, which represented the actual cost to the law firm of employing the paralegal. The United States Supreme Court did not accept this position.

Many consider this opinion to be a great victory for the paralegal movement. "Waves from the ripple effect" of the opinion "will wash the doorsteps

Missouri v. Jenkins
United States Supreme Court
491 U.S. 274,
109 S.Ct. 2463, 105 L.Ed.2d 229 (1989)

Justice BRENNAN delivered the opinion of the Court. . . . [T]o bill paralegal work at market rates makes economic sense. By encouraging the use of lower-cost paralegals rather than attorneys wherever possible, permitting market-rate billing of paralegal hours "encourages cost-effective delivery of legal services and, by reducing the spiraling cost of civil rights litigation, furthers the policies underlying civil rights statutes." *Cameo Convalescent Center, Inc. v. Senn,* 738 F.2d 836, 846 (CA7 1984), cert. denied, 469 U.S. 1106, 105 S.Ct. 780, 83 L.Ed.2d 775 (1985).*

Such separate billing appears to be the practice in most communities today.** In the present case, Missouri concedes that "the local market typically bills separately for paralegal services," Transcript of Oral Argument 14, and the District Court found that the requested hourly rates of $35 for law clerks, $40 for paralegals, and $50 for recent law graduates were the prevailing rates for such services in the Kansas City area. . . . Under these circumstances, the court's decision to award separate compensation at these rates was fully in accord with § 1988. . . .

* It has frequently been recognized in the lower courts that paralegals are capable of carrying out many tasks, under the supervision of an attorney, that might otherwise be performed by a lawyer and billed at a higher rate. Such work might include, for example, factual investigation, including locating and interviewing witnesses; assistance with depositions, interrogatories, and document production; compilation of statistical and financial data; checking legal citations; and drafting correspondence. Much such work lies in a gray area of tasks that might appropriately be performed either by an attorney or a paralegal. To the extent that fee applicants under § 1988 are not permitted to bill for the work of paralegals at market rates, it would not be surprising to see a greater amount of such work performed by attorneys themselves, thus increasing the overall cost of litigation.

Of course, purely clerical or secretarial tasks should not be billed at a paralegal rate, regardless of who performs them. What the court in *Johnson v. Georgia Highway Express, Inc.,* 488 F.2d 714, 717 (CA5 1974), said in regard to the work of attorneys is applicable by analogy to paralegals: "It is appropriate to distinguish between legal work, in the strict sense, and investigation, clerical work, compilation of facts and statistics and other work which can often be accomplished by non-lawyers but which a lawyer may do because he has no other help available. Such non-legal work may command a lesser rate. Its dollar value is not enhanced just because a lawyer does it."

** *Amicus* National Association of Legal Assistants reports that 77 percent of 1,800 legal assistants responding to a survey of the association's membership stated that their law firms charged clients for paralegal work on an hourly billing basis. Brief for National Association of Legal Assistants as *Amicus Curiae* 11.

of virtually every law office which employs or which is contemplating utilizing legal assistants in its delivery of legal services."[30] The highest Court in the land not only acknowledged the value of paralegals, but also provided a clear demonstration of how profitable paralegals can be in these kinds of cases. Equally important is the admonition of the Court's footnote that "purely clerical or secretarial tasks [performed by a paralegal] should not be billed at a paralegal rate." If a law firm wants to recover paralegal fees at market rates from the opposing side, the firm must be able to show that it gave the paralegal substantial, nonsecretarial tasks to perform in the case. In some law offices, a major complaint of paralegals is that they are not delegated enough challenging tasks. *Missouri v. Jenkins* should help combat this problem. Attorneys will be more inclined to use paralegals properly when they see that their economic livelihood is enhanced by doing so.[31]

It must be noted, however, that some courts do *not* adopt the approach of the United States Supreme Court in *Missouri v. Jenkins*. This opinion involved the interpretation of the Civil Rights Act. If another court is interpreting a different statute, it might reach a different conclusion on how to handle paralegal time. There are a few courts that refuse to allow any separate compensation for paralegal time. In such courts, paralegal fees are simply not recoverable. Yet the trend is definitely in the direction of following the approach of *Missouri v. Jenkins*.

■ ASSIGNMENT 1.6

(a) Earlier in this chapter, you were given sample job descriptions of paralegals in a large law office: legal assistant clerk, legal assistant, senior legal assistant, supervising legal assistant, case manager, and legal assistant manager. (See Figure 1.1). Assume that the law firm of Smith & Smith is large enough to have employees under all of these categories and that employees within each of them work on a major case for which an award of paralegal fees can be made. How would a court make a determination of paralegal fees in this case?

(b) What has been the impact of *Missouri v. Jenkins* in your state?

---

2. The Call for Efficiency and Delegation

Attorneys are overtrained for a substantial portion of the tasks that they perform in a law office. This is one of the major reasons that traditional law offices are charged with inefficiency. Paralegals have been seen as a major step toward reform. The results have been quite satisfactory as evidenced by the following comments from attorneys who have hired paralegals:[32]

> A competent legal assistant for several years has been effectively doing 25% to 35% of the actual work that I had been doing for many years prior to that time.

---

[30]*The Paralegal Factor*, 9 The California Lawyer 47 (June 1989).

[31]There is another dimension to these fee-award cases that should be considered. Suppose that an attorney seeks an award of *attorney* fees to cover time spent on tasks that the attorney should have delegated to a paralegal. In such a case, a court might refuse to award the attorney his or her normal hourly fee. One court phrased the problem this way: "Routine tasks, if performed by senior partners in large firms, should not be billed at their usual rates. A Michelangelo should not charge Sistine Chapel rates for painting a farmer's barn." *Ursic v. Bethlehem Mines*, 719 F.2d 670, 677 (3rd Cir. 1983).

[32]Oregon State Bar, Legal Assistants Committee, *Legal Assistant Survey* (1977).

> The results of our three attorney—three paralegal system have been excellent. Our office's efficiency has been improved and our clients are receiving better service.
>
> It has been our experience that clients now ask for the legal assistant. Client calls to the attorneys have been reduced an estimated 75%.

It has taken a *very* long time for attorneys to realize that something was wrong with the way they practiced law. The following historical perspective presents an overview of how attorneys came to this realization.[33]

During the American Colonial period, the general populace distrusted attorneys because many of them sided with King George III against the emerging independent nation. Some colonies tolerated the existence of attorneys, but established roadblocks to their practice. In 1641, for example, the Massachusetts Bay Colony prohibited freemen for hiring attorneys for a fee:

> "Every man that findeth himself unfit to plead his own cause in any court shall have libertie to employ any man against whom the court doth not except, to help him, Provided he gave him noe fee or reward for his pains."[34]

Furthermore, almost anyone could become an attorney without having to meet rigorous admission requirements.

Up until the nineteenth century, the attorney did not have assistants other than an occasional apprentice studying to be an attorney himself. The attorney basically worked alone. He carried "his office in his hat."[35] A very personal attachment and devotion to detail were considered to be part of the process of becoming an attorney and of operating a practice. In the early nineteenth century, George Wythe commented that:

> It is only by drudgery that the exactness, accuracy and closeness of thought so necessary for a good lawyer are engendered.[36]

The same theme came from Abraham Lincoln in his famous "Notes for a Law Lecture":

> If anyone . . . shall claim an exemption from the drudgery of the law, his case is a failure in advance.[37]

Attorneys would be somewhat reluctant to delegate such "drudgery" to someone working for them, according to this theory of legal education.

During this period, attorneys often placed a high premium on the personal relationship between attorney and client. As late as 1875, for example, Seward and his partners "would have none of the newfangled typewriters" because clients would "resent the lack of personal attention implied in typed letters."[38] The coming of the Industrial Revolution, however, brought the practice of law closer to industry and finance. Some law offices began to specialize. As attor-

---

[33]The research for part of the section on the historical background of paralegals was conducted by the author and subsequently used with his permission in the following article: Brickman, *Expansion of the Lawyering Process through a New Delivery System: The Emergence and State of Legal Paraprofessionalism* 71 Columbia Law Review 1153, 1169ff (1971).

[34]"Body of Liberties," cited in R. Warner, *Independent Paralegal's Handbook,* 8 (Nolo Press, 1986).

[35]Lee, *Large Law Offices,* 57 American Law Review 788 (1923).

[36]Lewis, ed., "George Wythe," in Great American Lawyers: A History of the Legal Profession in America, vol 1, 55 (1907).

[37]Nicolay & Hay, eds., "Notes for a Law Lecture," in Complete Works of Abraham Lincoln, 142 (1894). See also Frank, Lincoln as a Lawyer, 3 in (1961).

[38]Swaine, *The Cravath Firm and Its Predecessors: 1819–1947,* vol 1, 365, 449.

neys assumed new responsibilities, the concern for organization and efficiency grew. To be sure, large numbers of attorneys continued to carry their law offices "in their hats" and to provide an essentially one-to-one service. Many law offices in the 1850s, however, took a different direction.

Machines created new jobs. The typewriter introduced the typist. Librarians, investigators, bookkeepers, office managers, accountants, tax and fiduciary specialists, and research assistants soon found their way into the large law office. Although nonattorneys were primarily hired to undertake clerical or administrative responsibilities, they soon were delegated more challenging roles. As one study of a law firm noted with respect to several female employees who had been with the firm a number of years:

> In addition, these women were given considerable responsibility in connection with their positions as secretary or head bookkeeper. The head bookkeeper acted as assistant secretary to the partner-secretary of certain charitable corporations the firm represented. In this capacity, she recorded minutes of director's meetings, issued proxy statements, supervised the filing of tax returns for the organization and attended to other significant administrative matters.[39]

In this fashion, attorneys began delegating more and more nonclerical duties to their clerical staff. This was not always done in a planned manner. An employee might suddenly be performing dramatically new duties as emergencies arose on current cases and as new clients arrived in an already busy office. In such an environment, an attorney may not know what the employee is capable of doing until the employee does it. Despite its haphazard nature, the needs of the moment and *OJT* (on-the-job training) worked wonders for staff development.

By the 1960s, attorneys started to ask whether a new category of employee should be created. Instead of expanding the duties of a secretary, why not give the new duties to a new category of employee—the paralegal? A number of studies were conducted to determine how receptive attorneys would be to this idea on a broad scale. The results were very encouraging. The conclusion soon became inevitable that attorneys can delegate many tasks to paralegals without sacrificing quality of service. Today this theme has become a dominant principle of law office management. Most attorneys no longer ask, "Can I delegate?" Rather they ask, "Why *can't* this be delegated?" Or, "How can the delegation be effectively managed?" It is a given that substantial delegation is a necessity.

This is not to say, however, that all attorneys immediately endorse the paralegal concept with enthusiasm. Many are initially hesitant, as demonstrated by the following report on the hiring of legal assistants within the California Department of Health, Education, and Welfare (HEW):

> When the legal assistant program began in early 1977 in HEW, it was met with some skepticism, especially in offices in cities other than Sacramento. There was concern that the quality of the work might be diminished by legal assistants. However, team leaders and deputies are not only no longer skeptical, they are now enthusiastic supporters of the legal assistant program. The attorneys feel that the work product is at least as good, and more thorough, than that provided by attorneys, mainly because the legal assistants have developed an expertise in a narrow area of the law and the work is more stimulating to the legal assistants than it was to the attorneys.
>
> The legal assistants processed 152 cases in fiscal year 1977/78 and 175 cases in 1978/79. It was estimated that legal assistants are as efficient as attorneys in processing the preliminary phase of these cases. As a result, a legal

---

[39]Dodge, *Evolution of a City Law Office,* 1955 Wisconsin Law Review 180, 187.

assistant in this instance produces as many pleadings as a deputy attorney general would have produced in the same amount of time. For this reason the section has been able to provide a faster turnaround time for the client agencies.[40]

Proponents of greater use of paralegals in government argue that, in addition to efficiency, considerable savings can result from such use. For example, in order to save money and increase efficiency, a bill was introduced into the California Assembly:

> "to require each state agency and department that employs attorneys to begin to utilize a combination of hiring practices and attrition which will result in a ratio of one paralegal . . . to every five attorneys employed by the state by January 1, 1990."[41]

Unfortunately, this bill was not enacted into law—largely because of opposition from government attorneys.

Another call for more cost-effective methods of practicing law by the government came from the Council for Citizens Against Government Waste (the "Grace Commission") which recommended that the United States Department of Justice increase the ratio of paralegals to attorneys in order to achieve a savings of $13.4 million over three years. Soon thereafter, legislation was proposed in Congress to establish an Office of Paralegal Coordination and Activities in the Department of Justice to work toward the increased use of paralegals in the department.[42] While this proposal was not passed by Congress, the effort is typical of the momentum toward paralegal use throughout the practice of law.

3. The Promotion by Bar Associations

The bar associations assumed a large role in the development of paralegals. This has given great visibility to the field. In 1968, the House of Delegates of the American Bar Association established a Special Committee on Lay Assistants for Lawyers (subsequently renamed the Standing Committee on Legal Assistants), and resolved:

> (1) That the legal profession recognize that there are many tasks in serving client's needs which can be performed by a trained, non-lawyer assistant working under the direction and supervision of a lawyer;
>
>   (2) That the profession encourage the training and employment of such assistants. . . .[43]

Most of the state bar associations now have committees that cover the area of paralegal utilization. As we will see in Chapter 4, some of these committees have established guidelines for the use of paralegals in a law office. The real impact on the growth of paralegalism, however, has come from those bar association committees that deal with legal economics and law office management. Such committees have sponsored numerous conferences for practicing attorneys. These conferences, plus articles in bar association journals, have extensively promoted paralegals.

---

[40]*Study of Paralegal Utilization in the California Attorney General's Office,* 23, Management Analysis Section. California Department of Justice, (December 1980).

[41]Assembly Bill No. 2729 (January 21, 1986).

[42]H.R. 5107, 99th Cong., 2d Sess.

[43]Proceedings of the House of Delegates of the American Bar Association, 54 American Bar Association Journal 1017, 1021 (1968).

4. The Organization of Paralegals

Paralegals have been organizing. There are approximately 200 paralegal organizations throughout the country. (See list in Appendix A.) This has greatly helped raise everyone's consciousness about the potential of paralegalism. As indicated earlier, there are two major national associations, the National Federation of Paralegal Associations (NFPA) and the National Association of Legal Assistants (NALA). We will examine the work and the impact of these associations in the chapter on regulation. It is no longer true that attorneys are the sole organized voice speaking for paralegals and shaping the development of the field.

5. The Restructuring of Professions and Occupations Generally

The creation of new careers within an established profession or occupation is not unique to the law.

Doctors

There are approximately eleven paramedical personnel for every doctor in the United States. The hospital patient confronts a substantial number of non-doctor personnel: registered nurse, practical nurse, inhalation therapist, laboratory technician, occupational therapist, physical therapist, medical record librarian, medical technologist, cytotechnologist, radiologic technologist, radiation therapy technologist, nuclear medical technician, dietician, etc. It has been estimated that in the field of nursing alone, there are hundreds of different programs. The most recent stratification has been the licensing of the *physician assistant,* whose ranks were initially filled by many veterans who were medics or medical corpsmen while members of the armed services.

Dentists

There are approximately 250 dental assistant training programs, 175 dental hygiene training programs, and 30 dental laboratory technician training programs. The demand for "dental auxiliary personnel" has been steadily increasing.

A more radical development is denturism. A *denturist* is a nondentist who produces and dispenses removable dentures directly to the public. As might be expected, denturists are vigorously opposed by organizations such as the American Dental Association.

Teachers

Studies have shown that teachers spend from 20% to 70% of their time on nonteaching responsibilities. Teacher aides were initially created to relieve teachers of some of their clerical tasks so that they could spend more time on education. A growing number of aides, however, have been participating directly in the instructional process. It has been estimated that we may reach a ratio of one aide for every two teachers in the various departments of a large school.

Architects

The American Institute of Architecture reports that the 30,000 American architects need 127,000 supportive personnel in areas such as drafting, estimation, information and data processing, and graphic arts. More than 250 architecture technician programs are currently offered at colleges and institutes.

Law Enforcement

Auxiliary police, probation aides, and parole aides are becoming a standard part of law enforcement and correctional administration. In police science, for example, numerous programs have been developed to free the police officer from community relations responsibilities through the hiring of police aides so that the police officer can devote more energies to criminal work. The employment of ex-felons as probation and parole aides has been heralded as one of the most significant innovations in the field of corrections.

. . . .

The development of a new occupation is due to several different but related factors. One of these factors is *technological,* as we have seen. Just as there would be no such thing as an airline pilot without the development of the manned flight, there probably would never be the secretary in the modern sense without the development of the typewriter, telephone, etc.

Another basic factor is *economic.* As occupations become more and more complex (or more and more lucrative), the people who perform them begin to delegate their so-called routine tasks to other people who work for them. Nurses "paraprofessionalized" the field of medicine in this way. New specialists and subspecialists then emerged. Occupations not only "routinized down," but "specialized out." One example of the latter is the bank trust manager who is doing work that attorneys previously did. The ability of trust managers to specialize in one small area of the law allowed them to take away a share of the trust and estate market from attorneys. This was substantially due to economic forces; the generalist attorney simply could not compete with the services offered by this particular kind of banker. The public demand for the services of the latter is too acute for the legal profession to regain its full monopoly. The attorney, of course, saves face by agreeing to refrain from labeling the banker's activities "the practice of law." Underlying such a concession, however, are some elemental forces of economics.

The third major factor influencing the development of occupations is *social.* Society's insistence on universal education, for example, has led to the growth of a large civil-service teacher occupation. Urbanization has launched a variety of occupations, for example, social workers, criminologists, environmentalists, highway patrol officers, etc.

As occupations proliferate, competition among the occupations develops. This competition has led to some artificial results, the most prominent of which is a tendency to draw rigid jurisdictional lines among workers. Social workers are not psychologists; teachers are not social workers; attorneys are not accountants. We know, however, that such categorizations are misleading. Any one job often requires the individual to function within a variety of disciplines. Public school teachers, for example, would be quite surprised if told that they need have no skills in psychology, social work, or "police work" to perform in the urban classroom.

There is, however, security in the outward appearance of definitive boundary lines. Thirty years ago, researchers asked the following question at random: "Who are you?" Most often, they received a geographical answer ("I am a New Yorker"), then an ethnic answer ("I am a Canadian"), and finally an occupational answer ("I am a dentist"). The same question asked today produces an entirely different frequency of responses. An overwhelming majority of the respondents will base their answer on their occupation. We are what we *do*. Hence the increased tendency to insist on sharp career boundaries.

Within particular occupational categories, however, there is considerable turmoil over who should do what. As indicated, delegation within an occupation has created innumerable suboccupations or co-occupations. The best example of this is, again, the nurse. Doctors defined a series of functions that they were overtrained to perform. They then created the role of the nurse to undertake them. Nurses, in turn, defined a similar set of functions within their own sphere and delegated them to a new entity, the licensed practical nurse.

The legal profession is undergoing a comparable phenomenon. Typical of the progression in the law is the experience of the Paraprofessional Law Clinic at a state prison in Graterford, Pennsylvania. A group of inmates were authorized to set up a paralegal "law firm" to serve the needs of fellow inmates who need help processing their legal papers to challenge the validity of their incarceration. No attorneys are involved in the program, except for occasional outside attorneys who lend assistance to the paralegals on particular problems encountered in the firm's caseload. The most frustrating aspect of the program to the paralegals is its success. They have been able to win a large number of cases involving a miscalculation of sentence-time by prison administrators who have the responsibility of counting the day-to-day time owed by the inmates. Apparently the bureaucratic process of identifying the exact release date after deducting time served before trial, time earned for good behavior, etc., is complex. The prison staff often makes mistakes. During the first six months of the firm's existence, the paralegals claim to have had 15,924 days credited to the sentences of 103 inmates. Given the scope of the problem, the paralegals have been deluged with sentence computation cases; they have little time for anything else. While their success rate is a source of satisfaction to them, they are not happy with their caseload because they would prefer to work on cases that involve constitutional law, the so-called test cases. Their plan is to systematize computation cases and train other inmates to undertake them so that they can devote their energies to the more difficult cases. *In effect, these paralegals want to create a class of para-paralegals, or assistant paralegals, through delegation.* And so the process continues, leading potentially to an occupational structure of considerable stratification.

Delivery of Legal Services in Other Countries

England

The English legal profession has two main branches consisting of solicitors and barristers. The *solicitor* handles the day-to-day legal problems of the public with only limited rights to represent clients in certain lower courts. The bulk of litigation in the higher courts is provided by the *barrister*. When representation in such courts is needed, the solicitor arranges for the barrister to enter the case. Solicitors often employ one or more *Legal Executives,* who are the equivalent of the American paralegal. Legal Executives are delegated many responsibilities under the supervision of the solicitor. They undergo extensive training programs and take rigorous examinations at the Institute of Legal Executives. Once qualified, the Legal Executive obtains Fellowship in the Institute and is entitled to use the letters "F.Inst.L.Ex." after his or her name.

Canada

The Institute of Law Clerks of Ontario defines a *law clerk* as "a trained professional doing independent legal work, which may include managerial duties, under the direction and guidance of a lawyer and whose function is to relieve a lawyer of routine legal and administrative matters and assist him in the more complex ones." The title of legal assistant is more common outside Ontario. The number of legal assistants throughout Canada is estimated to be 4,000. One of the important organizations of legal assistants is the Canadian Association of Legal Assistants.

Japan

Attorneys are not the only providers of legal services in Japan. A separate category of workers called judicial scriveners has special authority to assist the public in preparation of legal documents such as contracts and deeds. The granting of this authority is conditioned on the successful completion of an examination.

Cuba

In Cuba, legal assistants work with attorneys in law offices or collectives called *bufetes*. The assistants draft legal documents, interview clients, conduct legal research, file papers in court, negotiate for trial dates, etc.

Russia

Attorneys-at-law in Russia are organized in lawyers' colleges. Membership in the colleges is granted to three kinds of individuals: first, graduates from university law schools; second, individuals with legal training of six months or more, with experience in judicial work, or at least one year as a judge, governmental attorney, investigator, or legal counsel; and third, persons without legal training but with at least three years' experience. Also, there are nonlawyer notaries who prepare contracts and wills for the public.

Finland

In Finland, only members of the Finnish Bar Association can use the title of advocate. Advocates, however, do not enjoy an exclusive right of audience in the courts. Litigants can plead their own case or retain a representative who does not have to be an advocate.

Germany

In Germany, as in many European countries, the *notary* has a major role in legal matters. As a skilled impartial advisor, the notary (who is not necessarily an attorney) oversees the contents of documents to insure that legal transactions will withstand court challenges. Notaries often advise parties on the legal implications of commercial affairs.

Section G. Stages in the Development of Paralegalism

Paralegalism became a self-conscious movement in the late 1960s. The following stages, or eras, of development summarize the progress of the field since

I.	1967–1971	The era of **discovery**
II.	1972–1976	The era of **education**
III.	1977–1981	The era of **politics**
IV.	1982–1986	The era of **management**
V.	1987—	The era of **credentialization**

FIGURE 1.7

Paralegal Development

then. A single theme characterizes each era, but there is overlap. The five themes have been discussed throughout the history of paralegalism. Yet, one theme dominates in each era.

The Era of Discovery

During this time, we were finding out what paralegals are and can do. It was a time of discovery. Attorneys experimented with new roles for nonattorneys in the delivery of legal services. Surveys and studies were undertaken. The results were reported at national conferences and within the literature. Since the results were impressive, the news spread quickly. Attorneys were told that there was a new way to practice law. The discovery of paralegals generated considerable enthusiasm, debate, and controversy. There is little doubt that paralegals are now a fixture in the vast majority of settings where law is practiced. The one possible exception is in some rural areas of the country where it is taking a little longer for attorneys to integrate paralegals into the practice of law. To this extent, the discovery of paralegals is still going on.

This is not to say that most attorneys hire paralegals or use them effectively. The expansion and development of paralegalism has by no means reached its peak. The point, however, is that the day has long passed when it was common within the legal profession to ask, "What's a paralegal?"

The Era of Education

In the early 1970s, there was an explosion in the creation of paralegal training programs. The American Bar Association introduced a controversial plan to approve paralegal schools, as we will see in Chapter 3. Texts for paralegals began to emerge from the law publishers. At times, it appeared that few schools were *not* considering the creation of a paralegal program. Today the growth in programs has leveled off; new programs are not as common as they were in the early 1970s.

A more recent development in the field has been the creation of programs for *continuing* education for employed paralegals. Almost every newsletter of paralegal associations throughout the country announces an upcoming seminar on substantive law topics (such as securities fraud or condominium conversions), or on paralegalism issues (such as overtime compensation or networking). These seminars may last several days or part of an afternoon in conjunction with the association's regularly scheduled monthly or annual meeting.

The Era of Politics

Politics, of course, has always been part of paralegal history. For example, during the era of education, paralegals began to organize into local and national associations to protect their own interests as well as to pursue their professional development. Between 1977 and 1981, however, a period of intense political debate began both among paralegals and between paralegals and attorneys. While the debate continues today, it is no longer the dominant theme, as it was in those years. For example,

- The lines were sharply drawn between the National Federation of Paralegal Associations and the National Association of Legal Assistants on the issue of whether the certification of paralegals was premature.

- There were intensive lobbying drives by paralegal associations to slow down regulatory efforts of some bar associations, and to insure that paralegals would be close participants with attorneys in this regulation. Strategies were planned within most paralegal associations on how to combat problems common to paralegals.

- New local paralegal associations were formed with the active encouragement of the older associations. Considerable debate existed within some of these new associations over whether to affiliate with the National Federation of Paralegal Associations, with the National Association of Legal Assistants, or to remain unaffiliated.

The Era of Management

Earlier in this chapter, factors such as economics and efficiency were listed as major reasons for the rapid expansion of paralegal use. While this enthusiasm has not died down, it became clear that the field needed a period of consolidation. Many law offices hired proportionately large numbers of paralegals within a short time. They were encouraged to expand by the promotional literature of the bar associations and by the increased income that the employment of the first paralegal generated. Some studies, however, have shown that a law office's increase in income tends to level off when larger numbers of paralegals are hired.[44]

Furthermore, not all offices are equipped to deal with the administrative problems that are found in an office with diverse personnel. Attorneys, for example, "who endorse the paralegal concept and hire recent graduates are often those whose workload is already too heavy. They have little time to provide individualized on-the-job training. The result is that paralegals feel frustrated with their lack of adequate preparation, and employers are disillusioned with their new employees."[45]

Attorneys are not trained as managers, yet management skills are fundamental to the effective use of paralegals. Hiring law office managers has helped, as has development of the relatively new career of legal administrator, but they have not eliminated the need for attorneys to educate themselves in the principles of management and systemization.

The mentality of the attorney is to work alone. Attorneys are trained to view each case as unique—every case can eventually be fought to the Supreme Court. This mentality and approach do not always encourage the attorney to delegate responsibility effectively. It certainly does not necessarily prepare the attorney to run an office in a businesslike and efficient manner. The skills required to have a law declared unconstitutional are radically different from the skills required to manage people. Unfortunately, paralegals can be victims of

---

[44]Bower, *Can Paralegals Be Profitable?* Michigan Bar Journal 173 (March 1980).
[45]American Bar Association, *NFPA/NALA Focus: Two Perspectives,* 3 Legal Assistant Update 90 (1983).

this defect in attorney training. It is not enough that paralegals are competent; they must also be *used* competently. Paralegals must be challenged and be secure in their relationship with attorneys and with other law office personnel.

There are, however, visible signs of change. Greater attention is given by many law schools to the problems of law office administration. The bar associations are also intensifying their efforts in this direction. Slowly, attorneys have come to the realization that the incorporation of paralegals into an office requires careful planning and an understanding of human nature. Management assistance is becoming available. There is now a vast body of experience on which to draw.

An important sign that change is on the way is the relatively recent creation of a new position in the larger law office—the legal assistant manager or paralegal administrator. Many firms with four or more paralegals have added a paralegal administrator to oversee the recruitment, training, assignment, and management of the office paralegals. The paralegal administrator (see Figure 2.2 in Chapter 2 for the different titles used for this position) often reports to an individual with broader management responsibility in the office, such as a legal administrator, office manager, managing partner, or chairperson of the management committee. Almost always, the paralegal administrator is someone with several years of experience as a paralegal who is intrigued by the invitation to move into management. Depending on the size of the office, some still perform paralegal duties on client cases in addition to their management duties. The number of paralegal administrators is growing every day. As indicated earlier, they recently formed a national organization—the Legal Assistant Management Association (LAMA).

Attorneys now realize that they need this kind of specialized help to incorporate paralegals into the practice of law. In the old days, many attorneys had the mistaken notion that they could immediately make a lot of money simply by hiring paralegals. Thankfully, we are moving out of this era.

The Era of Credentialization

The dust has not yet settled from all the controversies surrounding paralegalism. By the early 1980s none of the credentialing issues had been settled. Most people agreed that it was premature to launch extensive programs of licensing or certification. While some efforts in this direction were taken, as we will see in Chapter 3, the consensus was that more time was needed to sort out all the factors involved in a program of credentialization.

It is anticipated, however, that this will change. Momentum is building toward developing some form of official credentialization, such as limited licensing. According to Kay Field, former president of the National Association of Legal Assistants:

> Those of us who have worked hard to become qualified legal assistants resent the law firm who hires a high school girl to do the filing, [and] calls her a legal assistant. . . . We all agree that there needs to be some specific standards, but unfortunately we cannot all agree first of all who is to prepare them, secondly how stringent they will be, and lastly, who will enforce them. I say to you, however, that these matters must be addressed by us before they are done for us.[46]

---

[46]K. Field, *Legal Assistants: Where Do We Go from Here?* 10 Facts and Findings 17, 18 (National Association of Legal Assistants, May/June 1984).

President Field and her organization do not advocate licensing, but they do advocate action before it is too late. Intense debate rages among paralegals over the issue of credentialization, which we will examine in Chapter 3. There is a very real danger that while paralegals continue to fight among themselves over the issue, attorneys and legislatures might suddenly step in to impose a scheme of regulation and control that will satisfy no one. Unless paralegals resolve the issue, it will be resolved for them. How could this happen? One possible scenario is as follows: The legislature imposes a license requirement after widespread publicity is given to an incident of negligence committed by an untrained and unqualified paralegal. To prevent such precipitate action by the legislature, it is critical that paralegals collectively decide what they want and how it should be achieved. The next three chapters are designed to provide you with the data you need to participate in this still-emerging aspect of paralegalism.

☐ Chapter Summary

A *paralegal* is a person with legal skills who works under the supervision of an attorney or who is otherwise authorized to use those skills; this person performs tasks that do not require all the skills of an attorney and that most secretaries are not trained to perform. It is an exciting time to become a paralegal, even though many questions about the field remain to be resolved. There are three main categories of paralegals: those who are employed by attorneys (the largest), self-employed people working for attorneys, and self-employed people providing their services directly to the public. Within these categories, there is great diversity over the titles that are used. Nor is there universal agreement over the definition of a paralegal, or of the different kinds of paralegals. This diversity and lack of agreement are primarily caused by the fact that at present there are no licensing requirements to be a paralegal. People continue to enter the field by one of three routes: experience, training, or fiat. They do not enter through the vehicle of a unifying licensing system.

Paralegal salaries are influenced by a number of factors: experience, level of responsibility, kind of employer, geographic area, the employer's understanding of the paralegal's role, and the extent to which the paralegal is committed to the field as a career.

Bar associations and paralegal associations have promoted the value of paralegals extensively. The economic impact they have had on the practice of law is the major reason paralegals have flourished and grown so rapidly. In a properly leveraged firm, paralegals can be a "profit center" without any sacrifice in the quality of the service delivered by the firm. In most states, attorneys can charge their clients paralegal fees in addition to traditional attorney fees. Furthermore, under *Missouri v. Jenkins,* there are some cases in which a firm can obtain an award of paralegal fees at market rates from losing parties in litigation. Also, a paralegal can help attorneys redirect some of their energies from nonbillable to billable tasks. A firm operates more efficiently and profitably when it consistently and systematically delegates tasks to competent people with lower billing rates, so that other people with higher billing rates will be available to perform tasks at higher rates. This is not to say, however, that paralegals are always profitable to a firm. Proper use and supervision of paralegals are key components of profitability.

Since the late 1960s, paralegalism has gone through a number of stages. During the era of discovery, people were finding out what paralegals were capable of. This knowledge encouraged hundreds of institutions throughout the country to open paralegal schools during the era of education. The era of politics gave us a proliferation of paralegal associations at the national and local levels to address the emerging issues of this new field. In the era of management, greater attention was given to the ingredients of a successful paralegal-attorney relationship. Recognizing that attorneys have never been famous for their management skills, specialists emerged—for example, legal assistant managers—to help attorneys better integrate paralegals into an office. Today we are in the era of credentialization, during which we are likely to see limited licensing or other forms of official regulation.

Key Terms

NFPA
NALA
ABA
bar association
LAMA
ALA
paralegal
legal assistant
hybrid titles
independent contractor
freelance paralegal
independent paralegal
contract paralegal
nonparalegal
legal assistant clerk
senior legal assistant
supervising legal assistant

case manager
legal assistant manager
law clerk (America)
authorized practice of law
physician assistant
credentialization
paralegal fees
leveraging
delegation
apprentice
OJT
Standing Committee on Legal
    Assistants
denturist
solicitor
barrister
legal executive

law clerk (Ontario)
notary
profit center
overhead
rule of three
fixed fee
contingency fee
staff attorney
contract attorney
project attorney
associate
nonbillable tasks
fee generating
market rate
Missouri v. Jenkins

CHAPTER

2

Paralegal Employment

■ Chapter Outline

 ## Section A. The Job Market

For many paralegals seeking their first job, these are difficult times. Even many attorneys are having a hard time obtaining their first job. Most employers are inundated with job applications. According to one expert, for every $10,000 in salary you hope to earn as a paralegal, you will need to set aside one month of search time. "So if you want $25,000 per year, your search should take about two and one-half months. But do not be disappointed if it takes longer." [1]

Competition for paralegal jobs is likely to come from several sources:

■ Other recent graduates from paralegal training programs

■ Secretaries and clerks now working in law offices who want to be promoted into paralegal positions

■ Paralegals with a year or more of experience who are seeking a job change

■ People with no legal training or experience who walk into an office "cold" seeking a job

■ People with no legal training or experience but who have connections (a friend of an important client, a relative of a partner)

■ Frustrated attorneys applying for paralegal jobs!

---

[1]Wagner, *Tips & Traps for the New Paralegal,* 8 Legal Assistant Today 78 (March/April 1991).

FIGURE 2.1

Where Do
Paralegals Work
and in What
Percentages?

> I. Traditional private law firms
>   A. Small firm—1–10 lawyers (26%)
>   B. Medium firm—11–50 lawyers (15%)
>   C. Large firm—over 50 lawyers (30%)
> II. Untraditional private law firms (3%)
> III. Government
>   A. Federal government (4%)
>   B. State government (2%)
>   C. Local government (1%)
> IV. Legal Service/Legal Aid Offices (Civil Law) (3%)
> V. Law departments of corporations, banks, insurance companies, and other
>   businesses (8%)
> VI. Special interest groups or associations (1%)
> VII. Criminal law offices
>   A. Prosecution (1%)
>   B. Defense (1%)
> VIII. Freelance or independent paralegals (1%)
> IX. Service companies/consulting firms (1%)
> X. Related fields (3%)
>   A. Law librarian
>   B. Paralegal teacher
>   C. Paralegal supervisor/office administrator
>   D. Miscellaneous

Fortunately, the last category is relatively small, but such attorneys exist.[2] Recently, for example, a paralegal job announcement drew more than 100 responses from paralegals, plus "four from attorneys."[3]

In this environment, the two keys to success are *information* about the employment scene and *techniques* to market yourself. With these objectives in mind, we turn now to the following themes:

- Places where paralegals work
- Paralegal specialties
- Effective job-finding strategies
- Alternative career options

Section B. Where Paralegals Work

There are ten major locations where paralegals work. They are summarized in Figure 2.1, along with the approximate percentage of paralegals working in each location.

---

[2]There are even some unemployed attorneys who are angry at bar associations for promoting the hiring of paralegals. "In the current market, a young attorney might well work for the same salary as a paralegal." After all, "bar associations represent lawyers, not paralegals. It must be pointed out that paralegals steal jobs from lawyers recently admitted to the bar." Anonymous, *Buddy, Can You Spare a Job,* 46 The Shingle 25 (Philadelphia Bar Ass'n, Fall 1983).
[3]Zavalney, *The Price of Success,* 6 Texas Lawyer 10 (January 21, 1991).

1. Traditional Private Law Firms

Most paralegals today work for *private law firms*. While the need for paralegals may be just as great in the other categories, it is the traditional private law firms that have been doing most of the hiring. A "private" law firm is simply one that generates its income primarily from the fees of individual clients.

There are a number of characteristics of paralegals working for traditional private law firms, particularly the larger ones:

■ They are among the highest paid paralegals.

■ They tend to experience more law office management and personnel problems than other paralegals.

■ They tend to specialize more and hence have less variety in their work assignments.

■ They have been the most politically active paralegals in forming associations and in dealing with the bar associations.

■ They are predominantly women.

Figure 2.2 presents a survey of the employment of paralegals in many of the largest law firms in the country.

2. Untraditional Private Law Firms

Since the mid-1970s a new kind of private law firm (sometimes called a *legal clinic*) has come into existence. It also receives its income from fees, but it differs from the traditional law firm in a number of respects:

■ It tends to charge lower fees.

■ It tends to serve the middle class.

■ It has branch offices that are storefront in character (as opposed to a single downtown office in a plush suite on the 11th floor).

■ It tends to have a higher proportion of paralegals (there are more paralegals per attorney than in the traditional private law firm).

■ It is more likely to advertise and to use such devices as credit-card payment.

Such law firms have been controversial in the past. The traditional bar generally does not like these firms. The charge is that they are not dignified enough for the professional image that the bar wishes to project. In fact, during the early days, the bar went to court to try to force such firms out of existence. The bar lost, particularly over the issue of whether attorneys were allowed to advertise, as we will see in Chapter 4.

The number of untraditional law firms is relatively small, but they are growing. The fear of losing business has caused many small traditional firms to begin imitating some of the characteristics of the more aggressive new breed.

3. Government

The civil service departments of federal, state, and local governments have established standards and classifications for many different kinds of government paralegals. These paralegals work in four main areas of government:

■ In the office of the chief government attorney, e.g., attorney general, corporation counsel

FIGURE 2.2   Employment in Selected Large Law Firms*

Generally, a law firm is more likely to hire paralegals if it has hired them in the past, if it has a paralegal manager, and if it has many attorneys in the firm. This table tries to provide as much of this information as possible for selected—not all—large law firms in the country. Many law firms have branch offices. When you find two numbers separated by a slash, for example, 94/70, the first number is the total number in all offices of the firm (including headquarters), and the second number is the number in the city listed.

Law Firm (Number of Attorneys)	Title of Paralegal Manager	Number of Paralegals
Alabama		
Birmingham		
Balch & Bingham (66)		19
Bradley, Arant, Rose (97)		23
Burr & Forman (67)		12
Sirote & Permutt (94/70)		32
Alaska		
Anchorage		
Guess & Rudd (28)		6
Perkins Coie (336/19)		85/5
Arizona		
Phoenix		
Beus, Gilbert & Morrill (38)		15
Brown & Bain (125/79)	Paralegal Coordinator	48/24
Bryan, Cave, McPheeters (367/20)		76/8
Fennemore Craig (131/100)		15
Jennings, Strouss & Salmon (106)		17
Lewis & Roca (135/124)	Associate & Paralegal Coordinator	38
Mariscal, Weeks & McIntyre (33)		8
Meyer, Hendricks, Victor (56)		18
O'Connor, Cavanagh, Anderson (129/123)	Legal Administrator	24
Snell & Wilmer (238/171)	Paralegal Administrator	50/39
Squire, Sanders & Dempsey (430/29)		80/7
Streich, Lang, Weeks (140/125)		50/37
California		
Century City		
Irell & Manella (204/140)	Director of Legal Assistants	41
O'Melveny & Myers (560/64)		105/7
Costa Mesa		
Latham & Watkins (54)	Administrative Paralegal	13
Paul, Hastings, Janofsky (43)		9
Rutan & Tucker (106)		11

Continued

FIGURE 2.2   Employment in Selected Large Law Firms*—*Continued*

Law Firm (Number of Attorneys)	Title of Paralegal Manager	Number of Paralegals
California		
Los Angeles		
Adams, Duque & Hazeltine (89)		20
Alschuler, Grossman & Pines (41)	Paralegal Coordinator	7
Baker & Hostetler (503/85)		78/24
Baker & McKenzie (1580/70)	Paralegal Coordinator	11
Bottum & Feliton	Paralegal Manager	
Bryan, Cave, McPheeters (367/38)	Administrator	76/19
Buchalter, Nemer, Fields (179/124)	Paralegal Coordinator; General Litigation Paralegal Supervisor	55
Cox, Castle & Nicholson (95)		11
Dewey, Ballantine (394/39)	Senior Paralegal	81/8
Fadem, Berger & Norton	Paralegal Supervisor	
Finnegan, Henderson, Farabow	Director, Legal Assistant Services	
Frandzel & Share	Litigation Manager	
Gendel, Raskoff, Shapiro (49)	Paralegal Director	9
Gibson, Dunn & Crutcher (725/202)		145/60
Graham & James (385/104)		83/19
Hufstedler, Miller, Kaus	Paralegal Coordinator	10
Iwasaki, Thomas & Sheffield	Paralegal Coordinator	
Jones, Day, Reavis (1259/123)	Litigation Group/Administrative Assistant	21
Kindel & Anderson		11
Latham & Watkins (570/257)	Senior Legal Assistant	115/45
Lewis, D'Amato, Brisbois (197/104)		33/25
Loeb & Loeb (189/89)	Paralegal Administrator	26
Lyon & Lyon (50)	Paralegal & Data Processing Manager	14
Manatt, Phelps, Rothenberg (105)		15
McCutchen, Black, Verleger (95)		15
McKenna, Conner & Cuneo (197/43)	Paralegal Coordinator	12
Milbank, Tweed, Hadley (504/81)		12
Mitchell, Silberberg & Knupp (155/153)		22
Morgan, Lewis & Bockius (672/125)		113/21
Morrison & Foerster (588/118)		210/15
Munger, Tolles & Olson (83)		35
Musick, Peeler & Garrett (117)		20
O'Melveny & Myers (560/270)	Supervisor of Litigation Paralegal Services	136/80
Paul, Hastings, Janofsky (388/150)	Legal Assistant Administrator	55/31
Pillsbury, Madison, Sutro (625/46)		162/50
Pretty, Schroeder, Brueggemann	Paralegal Supervisor	

Continued

FIGURE 2.2   Employment in Selected Large Law Firms*—*Continued*

Law Firm (Number of Attorneys)	Title of Paralegal Manager	Number of Paralegals
California		
Los Angeles		
Rosen & Winston	Paralegal Coordinator	
Sheppard, Mullin, Richter (249/146)		21/18
Sidley & Austin (707/93)	Legal Assistant Coordinator	25
Skadden, Arps, Slate (1133/132)	Administrative Supervisor	77
Tuttle & Taylor (61)		16
Wyman, Bautzer, Kuchel (131/118)	Legal Assistant Manager	22
Newport Beach		
Gibson, Dunn & Crutcher (725/93)		165/15
O'Melveny & Myers (533/52)		136/10
Oakland		
Crosby, Heafey, Roach (192/225)		37
Donahue, Gallagher, Thomas	Paralegal Administrator	
King, Shapiro, Mittleman	Legal Assistant Coordinator	
Lempres & Wulfsberg	Legal Assistant Coordinator	
Palo Alto		
Brown & Bain (125/33)		48/20
Cooley, Godward, Castro (174/64)	Legal Assistant Manager	20
Brobeck, Phleger & Harrison (414/53)		136/12
Fenwick & West		30
Ware & Freidenrich (89)		14
Wilson, Sonsini, Goodrich (214)	Legal Assistant Coordinator	63
Riverside		
Best, Best & Krieger (114/74)		27
Sacramento		
Kronick, Moskovitz, Tiedemann (60)		12
Downey, Brand, Seymour (63)		10
San Diego		
Baker & McKensie (1580/27)	Paralegal Manager	16
Gray, Cary, Ames (183/170)	Paralegal Coordinator	28
Jennings, Engstrand & Henrickson (57)		13
Latham & Watkins (570/64)		174/16
Luce, Forward, Hamilton (146/134)		22
Schall, Boudreau & Gore	Legal Assistant Supervisor	
Seltzer, Caplan, Wilkins (53)	Paralegal Administrator	24
Solomon, Ward, Seidenwurm	Paralegal Coordinator	
Stutz, Gallagher & Artiano	Paralegal Coordinator	

Continued

FIGURE 2.2   Employment in Selected Large Law Firms*—*Continued*

Law Firm (Number of Attorneys)	Title of Paralegal Manager	Number of Paralegals
California		
San Francisco		
Brobeck, Phleger & Harrison (414/224)	Legal Assistant Manager	136/62
Bronson, Bronson & McKinnon (169/115)	Legal Assistant Administrator	64/25
Cooley, Godward, Castro (174/93)	Legal Assistant Administrator	36
Farella, Braun & Martel (75)	Director, Human Resources & Legal Support; Litigation Coordinator	39
Graham & James (385/133)		83/36
Handcock, Rothert & Bunshof (53)		43
Heller, Ehrman, White (355/193)	Legal Assistant Coordinator	143/55
Howard, Rice, Nemerovski (100)	Legal Assistant Administrator(s)	41
Jackson, Tufts, Cole (52)		24
Jeffer, Mangels, Butler (90/74)	Legal Assistant Coordinator	15
Landels, Ripley & Diamond (82)	Legal Assistant Manager	21
Long & Levit	Legal Assistant Manager	26
McCutchen, Doyle, Brown (274/198)	Paralegal Manager	59/52
Morrison & Foerster (588/245)	Legal Assistant Coordinator	175/125
Orrick, Herrington (258/167)	Legal Assistant Manager	62/34
Pettit & Martin (249/148)	Legal Assistant Manager	37/20
Pillsbury, Madison, Sutro (625/321)	Director, Legal Assistant & Computer Litigation Support Departments	116/58
Sedgwick, Detert, Moran (167/92)		39
Shartsis, Friese & Ginsburg (32)	Legal Assistant Supervisor	15
Thelen, Marrin, Johnson (361/168)	Legal Assistant Manager	86/62
San Jose		
Gibson, Dunn & Crutcher (738/19)		165/15
Hopkins & Carley (44)		11
Pillsbury, Madison, Sutro (625/44)	Information Resources Coordinator	162/14
Santa Monica		
Haight, Brown & Bonesteel (150/140)	Paralegal Training & Development Coordinator	44/41
Colorado		
Denver		
Coghill & Goodspeed	Paralegal Manager	
Davis, Graham & Stubbs (189/155)	Paralegal Coordinator	35/30
Gorsuch, Kirgis, Campbell (63)	Legal Assistant Coordinator	19
Hall & Evans (101)		43
Holland & Hart (229/144)	Legal Assistant Coordinator	37/22

Continued

FIGURE 2.2   Employment in Selected Large Law Firms*—*Continued*

Law Firm (Number of Attorneys)	Title of Paralegal Manager	Number of Paralegals
Colorado		
Denver		
Holme, Roberts & Owen (199/139)		54/40
Hopper, Kanouff, Smith	Legal Assistant/Manager	
Kirkland & Ellis (425/45)	Legal Assistant Supervisor	13
Rothgerber, Appel, Powers		15
Sherman & Howard (171/124)	Litigation Paralegal Supervisor	30/23
Tilly & Graves	Senior Legal Assistant	
Connecticut		
Hartford		
Cummings & Lockwood (159/28)		13
Day, Berry & Howard (220/151)	Legal Assistant Supervisor	50/39
Murtha, Cullina, Richter (92)		16
Robinson & Cole (141/120)		29
Schatz & Schatz (75)		11
Shipman & Goodwin (80)		23
Tyler, Cooper & Alcorn (84)		14
Updike, Kelly & Spellacy	Manager, Litigation Paralegals	12
Stamford		
Cummings & Lockwood (159/100)		25/13
Kelly, Drye & Warren (409/30)		47/10
Waterbury		
Carmody & Torrance (37)		12
Gager & Henry (34)		12
Delaware		
Wilmington		
Bayard, Handelman & Murdoc (28)		12
Elzufor, Austin & Drexler	Paralegal Supervisor	
Morris, James, Hitchens (38)		16
Morris, Nichols, Arscht (47)		14
Potter, Anderson & Corroon (51)		9
Prickett, Jones, Elliott (44)		11
Richards, Layton & Finger (76)	Paralegal Administrator	14
Young, Conaway, Stargatt (42)	Paralegal Supervisor	14
District of Columbia		
Akin, Gump, Strauss (485/233)	Legal Assistant Staff Manager	68
Anderson, Kill, Orlick (28)		16
Arent, Fox, Kintner (251/218)	Legal Assistant Administrator	40
Arnold & Porter (341/294)	Coordinator, Legal Assistant Programs	96

Continued

FIGURE 2.2 Employment in Selected Large Law Firms*—*Continued*

Law Firm (Number of Attorneys)	Title of Paralegal Manager	Number of Paralegals
District of Columbia		
Baker & Hostetler (503/96)	Paralegal Coordinator	78/15
Beverage & Diamond (59)		16
Brownstein, Zeidman & Schomer (69)		26
Bryan, Cave, McPheeters (367/49)		76/13
Cadwalader, Wickersham & Taft (295/62)	Coordinator of Legal Assistants	11
Covington & Burling (282/273)		76
Crowell & Moring (182)	Coordinator, Legal Assistants	45
Davis, Polk & Wardwell (433/36)	Legal Assistant Coordinator	123/20
Dewey, Ballantine (394/66)		81/24
Dickstein, Shapiro & Morin (160/135)		58/32
Dow, Lohnes & Albertson (224/166)	Transaction Coordinator; Manager of Information Services	47/31
Dunnells, Duvall, Bennett (65)	Paralegal Coordinator	12
Finnegan, Henderson, Farabow (103)	Director, Legal Assistant Services	30
Fried, Frank, Harris (397/126)		143/34
Fulbright & Jaworski (685/72)		160/14
Gibson, Dunn & Crutcher (725/101)		165/20
Heron, Burchette, Ruckert		28
Hogan & Hartson (334/289)	Legal Assistant Administrator	43/35
Howrey & Simon (174)	Legal Assistant Administrator	61
Hunton & Williams (471/63)		146/16
Jones, Day, Reavis (1259/123)	Litigation Group/Administrative Assistant	221/46
Kaplan, Russin & Vecchi (138)		19
Keller & Heckman (43)		14
Kirkland & Ellis (425/81)	Legal Assistant Supervisor	110/26
Kirkpatrick & Lockhart (315/84)		72/17
Melrod, Redman & Gartlan (66)	Paralegal Coordinator	13
McDermott, Will & Emery (520/71)	Paralegal Coordinator	
McKenna, Conner & Cuneo (197/122)	Paralegal Coordinator	36/28
Morgan, Lewis & Bockius (672/169)	Personnel Administrator	130/25
Newman & Holtzinger (69)	Senior Paralegal	22
Patton, Boggs & Blow (173/143)		23/13
Piper & Marbury (269/71)	Legal Assistant Administrator	10
Powell, Goldstein, Frazer (241/44)	Legal Assistant Coordinator	
Reed, Smith, Shaw (387/105)		85/18
Shaw, Pittman, Potts (248/231)	Director of Legal Assistants	52/46
Sidley & Austin (707/124)	Legal Assistant Administrator	27
Skadden, Arps, Slate (1133/164)	Paralegal Supervisor	
Squire, Sanders & Dempsey (430/82)		80/14
Steptoe & Johnson (232/220)	Director of Practice Support	42
Sutherland, Asbill & Brennan (244/134)	Chairman, Legal Assistant Committee	51/32

Continued

FIGURE 2.2   Employment in Selected Large Law Firms*—*Continued*

Law Firm (Number of Attorneys)	Title of Paralegal Manager	Number of Paralegals
District of Columbia		
Swidler & Berlin (86)	Paralegal Coordinator	45
Venable, Baetjer & Howard (295/67)		42/15
Weil, Gotshal & Manges (552/46)	Paralegal Coordinator	13
Wiley, Rein & Fielding (105)	Legal Assistant Administrator	21
Williams & Connolly (126)		20
Willkie, Farr & Gallagher (350/46)	Legal Assistant Supervisor	17
Wilmer, Cutler & Pickering (200)	Practice Area Manager	99
Florida		
Fort Lauderdale		
Fleming, O'Bryan & Fleming (34)		10
Holland & Knight (284/27)		39/9
Ruden, Barnett, McClosky (103)		33
Miami		
Anderson, Moss, Parks	Legal Assistant Coordinator	
Floyd, Pearson, Richman (31)		8
Fowler, White, Burnett (54)		14
Greenberg, Traurig, Hoffman (134)	Paralegal Manager	38
Mershon, Sawyer, Johnson (93)		12
McDermott, Will & Emery (520/30)		90/8
Mershon, Sayer, Johnston (77)		11
Shutts & Bowen (83)	Paralegal Supervisor	25
Steel, Hector & Davis (143/111)		18/12
Valdes-Fauli, Cobb, Petrey	Paralegal Supervisor	
Orlando		
Akerman, Senterfitt & Eidson (42)		9
Baker & Hostetler (503/35)		78/15
Gray, Harris & Robinson (32)		10
Lowndes, Drosdick, Doster (48)		9
McGuire, Voorhis & Wells (59)		22
Rumberger, Kirk, Caldwell	Legal Assistant Coordinator	
Tampa		
Carlton, Fields, Ward (150/107)		35/22
Fowler, White, Gillen (77)	Director of Personnel and Recruiting	21
Holland & Knight (284/74)	Legal Assistant Coordinator	39/16
Rudnick & Wolfe (246/17)	Personnel Manager	37/8
Shackleford, Farrior, Stallings (58)		10
Trenam, Simmons, Kemker (75)		16

Continued

FIGURE 2.2   Employment in Selected Large Law Firms*—*Continued*

Law Firm (Number of Attorneys)	Title of Paralegal Manager	Number of Paralegals
Georgia		
Atlanta		
Alston & Bird (221/179)	Legal Assistant Coordinator	36
Arnall, Golden & Gregory (62)	Senior Litigation Paralegal	21
Hurt, Richardson, Garner (89)	Paralegal Coordinator	16
Hyatt & Rhoads (49)		17
Jones, Day, Reavis (1259/102)		221/17
Kilpatrick & Cody (172/124)		35
King & Spalding (270/230)	Paralegal Coordinator	73
Long, Aldridge & Norman (90)	Human Resources Manager	22
Neely & Player (42)		14
Parker, Johnson, Cook	Coodinator, Paralegal Program	
Powell, Goldstein, Frazer (241/197)	Paralegal Manager	53
Schwall, Ruff & Goodman	Director of Administration	
Smith, Gambrell & Russell (90)	Paralegal Coordinator	10
Stokes, Shapiro, Fussell	Senior Legal Assistant	
Sutherland, Asbill & Brennan (244/110)	Paralegal Specialist	51/29
Troutman, Sanders, Lockerman (165)		28
Hawaii		
Cades, Schutte, Fleming (74)		16
Goodsill, Anderson, Quinn (81)		20
Illinois		
Chicago		
Altheimer & Gray (179)	Director, Corporate Support Group	27
Baker & McKenzie (1580/174)	Paralegal Coordinator	20
Bell, Boyd & Lloyd (206/165)		27/23
Cassiday, Schade & Gloor	Paralegal Director	
Chapman & Cutler (257/241)		18/16
Clausen, Miller, Gorman (121)		18
Coffield, Ungaretti, Harris (90)		17
Gardner, Carton & Douglas (204/163)		28/23
Hinshaw, Culbertson, Moelmann (279/155)	Paralegal Coordinator	32/16
Hopkins & Sutter (287/182)	Paralegal Coordinator	31/19
Jenner & Block (289/248)	Paralegal Manager	101/91
Jones, Day, Reavis (1259/83)		221/13
Katten, Muchin & Zavis (341/283)		42
Keck, Mahin & Cate (351/212)	Legal Assistant Coordinator	39/29
Kirkland & Ellis (425/259)	Manager of Legal Assistants; Legal Assistant Coordinator	110/77
Latham & Watkins (570/67)		174/12

Continued

FIGURE 2.2   Employment in Selected Large Law Firms*—*Continued*

Law Firm (Number of Attorneys)	Title of Paralegal Manager	Number of Paralegals
Illinois		
	Chicago	
Levin & Funkhouser (18)		14
Lord, Bissel & Brook (275/227)		41/33
Mayer, Brown & Platt (566/381)	Paralegal Coordinator	113/91
McDermott, Will & Emery (520/309)		90/57
Peterson, Ross, Schloerb (163/147)		35
Phelan, Pope & John (74)		18
Pretzel & Stouffer	Supervisor of Litigation Paralegals	
Ross & Hardies (166/128)		15
Rudnick & Wolfe (246/219)	Personnel Manager	37/31
Sachnoff & Weaver (103)		23
Schiff, Hardin & Waite (213/198)		31
Seyfarth, Shaw, Fairweather (318/176)		29/14
Sidley & Austin (707/414)	Paralegal Recruiting Coordinator	174/89
Skadden, Arps, Slate (1133/106)	Legal Assistant Supervisor	
Sonnenschein, Nath (300/207)	Paralegal Administrator	24
Vedder, Price, Kaufman (155/138)		17
Wildman, Harrold, Allen (194/191)	Paralegal Coordinator	24
Winston & Strawn (404/298)	Paralegal Manager; Legal Assistant Supervisor	33
Indiana		
	Indianapolis	
Baker & Daniels (182/139)		33
Barnes & Thornburg (202/118)		27/18
Bingham, Summers, Welsh (54)	Legal Assistant Supervisor	12
Bose, McKinney & Evans (48)		13
Ice, Miller, Donadio (165)	Chief Operating Officer	19
Kentucky		
	Lexington	
Greenebaum, Doll & McDonald	Paralegal Coordinator	
Stoll, Keenon & Park (63)		14
Wyatt, Tarrant & Combs (162/35)		
	Louisville	
Brown, Todd & Heyburn (131/100)	Paralegal Coordinator	22
Greenebaum, Doll & McDonald (67)	Administrative Paralegal Coordinator	11
Stites & Harbison (100)	Paralegal Administrator	
Wyatt, Tarrant & Combs (162/89)	Professional Personnel Administrator	28

Continued

FIGURE 2.2   Employment in Selected Large Law Firms*—*Continued*

Law Firm (Number of Attorneys)	Title of Paralegal Manager	Number of Paralegals
Louisiana		
New Orleans		
Adams & Reese (86)		50
Chaffe, McCall, Phillips	Paralegal Coordinator	
Carmouche, Gray, Hoffman (55)		13
Deutsch, Kerrigan & Stiles	Senior Paralegal	
Jones, Walker, Waechter (161/153)	Paralegal Manager, General Litigation Section	41
McGlinchey, Stafford, Cellini (137/123)		58
Milling, Benson, Woodward (71)		22
Phelps, Dunbar, Marks (161/95)		36/25
Stone, Pigman, Walther (62)		13
Maine		
Bangor		
Eaton, Peabody, Bradford (30)		14
Portland		
Bernstein, Shur, Sawyer (50)		17
Drummond, Woodsum, Plimpton (41)		8
Poerce, Atwood, Scribner (83)		18
Verrill & Dana (70)		16
Maryland		
Baltimore		
Frank, Bernstein, Conaway (200/133)	Assistant Director of Recruitment	35/25
Gordon Feinblatt, Rothman (72)		16
Melnicove, Kaufman, Weiner (78)		8
Miles & Stockbridge (192/107)		39/25
Montedonico & Mason (52)		10
Ober, Kalor, Grimes (107)		21
Piper & Marbury (269/195)	Recruiting Administrator	44/36
Semmes, Bowen & Semmes (165/144)		44
Smith, Somerville & Case (89)		18
Tydings & Rosenberg (32)	Paralegal Supervisor	12
Venable, Baetjer & Howard (295/167)		53
Weinberg & Green (146/134)		18
Whiteford, Taylor & Preston (138)		41
Massachusetts		
Boston		
Bingham, Dana & Gould (236/225)		41
Brown, Rudnick, Freed (114)	Corporate Paralegal Coordinator; Litigation Paralegal Supervisor	23

Continued

FIGURE 2.2   Employment in Selected Large Law Firms*—*Continued*

Law Firm (Number of Attorneys)	Title of Paralegal Manager	Number of Paralegals
Massachusetts		
Boston		
Burns & Levinson (103)		34
Campbell & Associates (31)		12
Choate, Hall & Stewart (165)		23
Fish & Richardson (38)		21
Foley, Hoag & Eliot (149/138)		28/25
Gaston & Snow (272/174)	Paralegal Coordinator	55/30
Goodwin, Proctor & Hoar (288)	Director of Administration & Human Resources	39
Goulston & Storrs (91)		16
Hale & Dorr (324/293)	Manager of Paralegal Services	63
Hill & Barlow (93)		22
Hutchins & Wheeler (83)		13
Mintz, Levin, Cohn (188/167)		36
Nutter, McClennen & Fish (168/160)	Paralegal Coordinator	20
Palmer & Dodge (144)	Legal Assistant Coordinator	22
Rackemann, Sawyer & Brewster (60)	Paralegal Administrator	17
Ropes & Gray (312/289)	Director of Paralegal Services; Senior Legal Assistant Coordinator	47/44
Sullivan & Worcester (133/114)	Paralegal Manager	28/23
Testa, Hurwitz & Thiobeault (82)	Paralegal Manager	13
Warner & Stackpole (49)	Executive Director	10
Widett, Slater & Goldman (83)	Director of Personnel	15
Worcester		
Bowditch & Dewey (59)	Paralegal Administrator	16
Fletcher, Tilton & Whipple	Paralegal Manager	
Michigan		
Detroit		
Butzel, Long, Gust (85)	Legal Assistant Coordinator	16
Clark, Klein & Beaumont (86)		10
Dickinson, Wright, Moon (213/138)		37
Dykema Gossett (312/162)		37
Honigman, Miller, Schwartz (236/182)	Manager of Legal Assistants	55/40
Kitch, Saurbier, Drutchas (90)		23
Miller, Canfield, Paddock (239/123)		43
Plunkett & Cooney (150/105)		25
Vandeveer, Garzia, Tonkin (48)		28
Grand Rapids		
Miller, Johnson, Snell (77)		13
Varnum, Riddering, Schmidt (119)		18
Warner, Norcross & Judd (96)	Director of Administration	16

Continued

FIGURE 2.2   Employment in Selected Large Law Firms*—*Continued*

Law Firm (Number of Attorneys)	Title of Paralegal Manager	Number of Paralegals
Minnesota		
Minneapolis		
Bowman & Brooke (23)		19
Dorsey & Whitney (352/269)	Senior Legal Assistant Supervisor	70/45
Faegre & Benson (233/184)		47/39
Fredrikson & Byron (100)		22
Gray, Plant, Mooty (86)		19
Larkin, Hoffman, Daly (84)		22
Leonard, Street & Deinar (89)		17
Lindquist, Vennum (94)	Human Resources Manager	15
Mackall, Crounse & Moore (49)		11
Maslon, Edelman, Borman (43)		20
Oppenheimer, Wolff & Donnelly (251/178)	Legal Assistant Manager	36/27
Popham, Haik, Schnobrich (175/129)	Legal Assistant Manager	39/33
Robins, Kaplan, Miller (190/117)	Legal Assistant Manager	60/52
St. Paul		
Briggs & Morgan (143/76)	Paralegal Coordinator	24
Doherty, Rumble & Butler (77)		13
Mississippi		
Jackson		
McDavid, Noblin & West (8)		8
Thomas, Price, Alston (27)		15
Watkins, Ludlam & Stennis (50)	Legal Assistant Coordinator	18
Missouri		
Kansas City		
Blackwell, Sanders, Matheny (72)		12
Polsinelli, White, Vardeman	Legal Assistant Coordinator	
Shook, Hardy & Bacon (151/127)	Paralegal Supervisor	44
Shughart, Thomson & Kilroy	Paralegal Coordinator	
Stinson, Mag & Fizzell (146/133)	Litigation Paralegal Coordinator	23
St. Louis		
Armstrong, Teasdale, Schlafly (162/118)		22
Bryan, Cave, McPheeters (367/181)		76/37
Coburn, Croft & Putzell (70)		14
Greensfelder, Hemker & Gale (81)		11
Husch, Eppenberger, Donohue (74)		10
Lewis, Rice & Fingersh (141/90)		18
Peper, Martin, Jensen (80)		14
Sandberg, Phoenix & von Gontard (37)		10
Stolar Partnership (44)		12
Thompson & Mitchell (176/124)		20/16

Continued

FIGURE 2.2   Employment in Selected Large Law Firms*—*Continued*

Law Firm (Number of Attorneys)	Title of Paralegal Manager	Number of Paralegals
Nebraska		
Omaha		
Fraser, Stryker, Vaughn (31)		7
Kutak, Rock & Campbell (205/90)	Manager of Litigation Support Services	44/14
Nevada		
Las Vegas		
Lionel, Sawyer & Collins (52)		12
Reno		
Hill, Cassas, deLipkau (135)		23
New Hampshire		
Concord		
Sullivan, Hollis & Soden (40)		26
Manchester		
Devine, Millimet, Stahl (48)		16
McLane, Graf, Raulerson (50)		16
Sheehan, Phinney, Bass (52)		19
New Jersey		
Morriotown		
Pitney, Hardin, Kipp (155)	Administrator of Litigation Paralegals	15
Porzio, Bromberg & Newman (30)	Paralegal Coordinator	40
Riker, Danzig, Scherer (116)	Paralegal Manager	20
Stanely & Fisher (116)	Paralegal Manager, Litigation	32
Newark		
Carpenter, Bennett & Morrissey (78)		13
Crummy, Del Deo, Dolan (105)	Paralegal Administrator	25
McCarter & English (182/159)	Paralegal Coordinator	48/34
Sills, Cummis, Zuckerman (138/128)	Paralegal Coordinator	40
Roseland		
Hannoch Weisman (150/128)	Director of Paralegal Service	33
Lowenstein, Sandler, Kohl (132/115)	Corporate Supervisor; Litigation Paralegal Supervisor	27
Woodbridge		
Greenbaum, Rowe, Smith (81)	Legal Assistant Coordinator	21
Wilentz, Goldman & Spitzer (138/122)	Paralegal Manager	34/28

Continued

FIGURE 2.2 Employment in Selected Large Law Firms*—*Continued*

Law Firm (Number of Attorneys)	Title of Paralegal Manager	Number of Paralegals
New Mexico		
Albuquerque		
Eaves, Darling & Porter	Supervising Paralegal	
Modrall, Sperling, Roehl (68)	Legal Assistant Coordinator	21
Poor Law Firm (37)		10
New York		
Buffalo		
Damon & Morey (55)		17
Hodgson, Russ, Andrews (135/108)		34
Jaeckle, Fleischmann & Mugel (81)		17
Moot & Sprague (61)		15
Phillips, Lytle, Hitchcock (136/98)		52/34
Saperston & Day (80)		17
New York City		
Anderson, Kill, Olick (182/150)		100
Battle, Fowler (127)		21
Bower & Gardner (218/212)		54
Breed, Abbott & Morgan (117)	Legal Personnel Coordinator	20
Brown & Wood (242/195)	Legal Assistant Supervisor	49
Cadwalader, Wickersham & Taft (295/208)	Director of Legal Assistants	40/36
Cahill, Gordon & Reindel (287/273)	Legal Assistant Coordinator	76/68
Carter, Ledyard & Milburn (76)	Paralegal Supervisor	27
Chadbourne & Parke (276/220)	Legal Assistant Manager	55
Cleary, Gottlieb, Steen (429/270)	Coordinator of Paralegal Services	66
Coudert Brothers (360/172)	Legal Personnel Manager	61/33
Cravath, Swaine & Moore (309/301)	Manager of Legal Assistants	117
Davis, Polk & Wardwell (433/378)	Manager, Corporate Assistants; Manager, Litigation Assistants	123/114
Debevoise & Plimpton (349/288)	Manager, Legal Assistant Department	81
Dewey, Ballantine (394/287)	Legal Assistant Administrator	81/53
Dilworth, Paxson, Kalish (145)	Paralegal Supervisor	20
Dreyer & Traub (95)		37
Fish & Neave (102)		35
Fitzpatrick, Cella, Harper (49)		27
Fried, Frank, Harris (397/250)	Legal Assistant Manager	143/75
Hughes, Hubbard & Reed (244/179)		35/27
Kaye, Scholer, Fierman (399/305)	Manager of Legal Assistants	88/65
Kramer, Levin, Nessen (140)	Paralegal Coordinator	33
LeBoeuf, Lamb, Leiby (405/218)	Paralegal Supervisor	110/80
Lord, Day, Lord (205/193)		45

Continued

FIGURE 2.2 Employment in Selected Large Law Firms*—*Continued*

Law Firm (Number of Attorneys)	Title of Paralegal Manager	Number of Paralegals
New York		
New York City		
Milbank, Tweed, Hadley (504/350)		116/91
Milgram, Thomajan & Lee (85)		21
Morgan & Finnegan (76)	Paralegal Coordinator	34
Mudge, Rose, Guthrie (304/237)		72/52
Patterson, Belknap, Webb (144/138)	Paralegal Manager	40/35
Parker, Chapin, Flattau (130)		21
Paul, Weiss, Rifkind (411/382)	Paralegal Supervisor	116
Proskauer, Rose, Goetz (425/350)	Corporate Paralegal Supervisor	90/84
Reid & Priest (203/159)		28/20
Rogers & Wells (337/255)	Litigation Legal Assistant Supervisor; Corporate Legal Assistant Coordinator; Real Estate Legal Assistant Coordinator	40
Rosenman & Colin (229/223)	Paralegal Coordinator	40
Rubin, Baum, Levin (54)		24
Schulte, Roth & Zabel (162/161)	Litigation Legal Assistant/ Supervisor	34
Shey & Gould (292/252)	Legal Assistant Manager; Corporate Paralegal Supervisor	82/69
Shearman & Sterling (624/478)	Legal Assistant Manager	112/105
Sidley & Austin (707/66)	Paralegal Manager	174/20
Simpson, Thacher & Bartlett (442/431)	Paralegal Coordinator	128
Skadden, Arps, Slate (1133/583)	Director of Legal Assistant Services	433
Stroock, Stroock & Lavan (339/250)	Litigation Paralegal Supervisor	74/29
Sullivan & Cromwell (366/303)	Director of Paralegal Services	73/60
Weil, Gotshall & Manges (552/392)	Legal Assistant Manager	137/108
White & Case (462/311)	Manager of Legal Assistants; Coordinator of Evening Legal Assistants	64
Whitman & Ransom (255/149)		34/24
Willkie, Farr & Gallagher (350/281)	Corporate Supervisor; Director of Litigation Services	74/58
Wilson, Elser, Moskowitz (379/222)	Legal Assistant Supervisor	30
Winthrop, Stimson, Putnam (289/222)	Legal Assistant Manager	42/29
Winston & Strawn (404/91)	Legal Assistant Manager	62
Rochester		
Chamberlain, D'Amanda, Oppenheimer (31)		13
Harter, Secrest & Emery (93)		30
Harris, Beach, Wilcox (96)		15
Nixon, Hargrave, Devans (259/142)	Manager of Paralegal Services	46
Phillips, Lytle, Hitchcock (136/24)		52/10
Woods, Oviatt, Gilman (40)		11

Continued

FIGURE 2.2   Employment in Selected Large Law Firms*—*Continued*

Law Firm (Number of Attorneys)	Title of Paralegal Manager	Number of Paralegals
New York		
Syracuse		
Bond, Schoeneck & King (143/98)		29/19
Hiscock & Barclay (95)		26/11
North Carolina		
Charlotte		
Kennedy, Covington, Lobdell (74/68)		17/13
Moore & Van Allen (62)	Legal Assistant Coordinator	18
Robinson, Bradshaw & Hinson (66)		14
Smith, Helms, Mulliss (147/64)		60/19
Greensboro		
Smith, Helms, Mulliss (147/69)		60/41
Raleigh		
Hunton & Williams (471/33)		142/10
Maupin, Taylor, Ellis (59)		12
Moore & Van Allen	Legal Assistant Coordinator	
Poyner & Spruill (106/70)		28/17
Winston-Salem		
Petree, Stockton & Robinson (70)		10
Womble, Carlyle, Sandridge (182/125)		48
Ohio		
Cincinnati		
Dinsmore & Shohl (133/122)	Paralegal Administrator	38
Frost & Jacobs (167/141)		49
Graydon, Heed & Ritchey (63)		12
Keating, Muething & Klekamp (61)		15
Taft, Stettinius & Hollister (154/133)	Administrator	26
Thompson, Hine & Flory (348/65)		61/20
Cleveland		
Arter & Hadden (337/126)	Paralegal Coordinator	77/20
Baker & Hostetler (503/173)	Paralegal Manager	78/29
Benesch, Friedlander, Coplan (174/127)		28/19
Calfee, Halater & Griswold (150/147)		24
Hahn, Laeser & Parks (73)		16
Jones, Day & Reavis (1259/228)	Administrative Assistant	221/41
McDonald, Hopkins, Burke (62)		18
Squire, Sanders & Dempsey (430/185)	Chairman, Legal Assistant Personnel Committee	80/33
Thompson, Hine & Flory (348/166)	Legal Assistant Manager	61/29

Continued

FIGURE 2.2   Employment in Selected Large Law Firms*—*Continued*

Law Firm (Number of Attorneys)	Title of Paralegal Manager	Number of Paralegals
Ohio		
Columbus		
Arter & Hadden (337/61)		77/10
Baker & Hostetler (503/84)		78/10
Bricker & Eckler (82)		22
Carlile, Patchen, Murphy (33)		9
Emens, Hurd, Kegler (63)		11
Porter, Wright, Morris (214/134)	Paralegal Administrator	40
Schottenstein, Zox & Dunn (79)		10
Schwartz, Kelm, Warren (39)	Director, Paralegal Services	12
Squire, Sanders & Dempsey (430/87)		80/18
Thompson, Hine & Flory (348/36)		61/13
Vorys, Sater, Seymour (255/203)	Paralegal Administrator	56
Toledo		
Fuller & Henry (53)		10
Nathan & Roberts	Paralegal Administrator	
Schumaker, Loap & Kendrick (69)		7
Oklahoma		
Oklahoma City		
Crowe & Dunlevy (91)		22
Tulsa		
Conner & Winters (45)		9
Gable & Gotwals (46)		7
Hall, Estill, Hardwick (79)		32
Oregon		
Portland		
Bullivant, Houser (61)	Paralegal Manager	14
Davis, Wright, Tremaine (238/60)		22/9
Miller, Nash, Wiener (104)	Coordinator, Litigation Legal Assistants	15
Schwabe, Williamson & Wyatt (151/125)		21
Sears, Lubersky, Bledsoe (86)		15
Stoel, Rives, Boley (220/153)	Legal Assistant Manager	40/11
Pennsylvania		
Philadelphia		
Ballard, Spahr, Andrews (218/158)	Senior Legal Assistant	51/32
Blank, Rome, Comisky (227/204)		35
Clark, Ladner, Fortenbaugh (51)		17
Cohen, Shapiro, Polisher (83)		14
Cozen & O'Connor (136/106)		46

Continued

FIGURE 2.2 Employment in Selected Large Law Firms*—*Continued*

Law Firm (Number of Attorneys)	Title of Paralegal Manager	Number of Paralegals
Pennsylvania		
Philadelphia		
Dechert, Price & Rhoades (384/254)	Paralegal Coordinator	82/58
Dilworth, Paxson, Kalish (155/116)	Paralegal Supervisor, Litigation Department	27/20
Drinker, Biddle & Reath (217/178)	Senior Legal Assistant	56/36
Duane, Morris, Heckscher (223/167)		56/42
Fox, Rothchild, O'Brien (118)		25
Hoyle, Morris & Kerr (60)	Legal Assistant Administrator	36
Mesirov, Gelman, Jaffe (102)		33
Montgomery, McCracken, Walker (160/146)	Paralegal Coordinator	35/32
Morgan, Lewis & Bockius (672/173)		113/50
Pechner, Dorfman, Wolffe (62)		11
Pepper, Hamilton & Scheetz (355/177)	Legal Assistant Administrator	73/39
Rawle & Henderson (72)		19
Reed, Smith, Shaw (387/61)	Paralegal Coordinator	24
Saul, Ewing, Remick (183/152)	Litigation Support Manager	42
Schnader, Harrison, Segal (245/199)	Supervisor of Legal Assistants	45
Stradley, Ronon, Stevens (80)		19
White & Williams (101)		42
Wolf, Block, Schorr (244/221)		40/38
Pittsburgh		
Buchanan Ingersoll (190/174)	Legal Assistant Coordinator	33
Eckert, Seamans, Cherin (201/155)	Paralegal Coordinator	27/24
Kirkpatrick & Lockhart (315/190)	Legal Assistant Coordinator	83
Klett, Lieber, Rooney (63)	Director of Paralegal Services	13
Reed, Smith, Shaw (387/201)	Paralegal Manager	85/37
Wilkes-Barre		
Rosenn, Jenkins & Greenwald (46)		18
Rhode Island		
Providence		
Edwards & Angell (170/93)		34
Hinckley, Allen, Snuder (78)		22
Gamma Law Associates	Paralegal Manager	
Roberts, Carroll, Feldstein	Paralegal Manager	
Tillinghast, Collins & Graham (51)		14
South Carolina		
Charleston		
Sinkler & Boyd (50/19)	Legal Assistant Coordinator	15/9
Young, Clement, Rivers	Paralegal Coordinator	

Continued

FIGURE 2.2   Employment in Selected Large Law Firms*—*Continued*

Law Firm (Number of Attorneys)	Title of Paralegal Manager	Number of Paralegals
South Carolina		
Columbia		
Nelson, Mullins, Riley (86)	Legal Assistant Coordinator	35
Greenville		
Leatherwood, Walker, Todd (40)		13
Wyche, Burgess, Freeman (22)		8
Tennessee		
Nashville		
Baker, Worthington, Crossley (94/34)		16
Bass, Berry & Sims (80/77)		25
Boult, Cummings, Conners (33)	Administrator/Paralegal Coordinator	13
Farris, Warfield, Kanaday (46)		13
Hartwell, Martin & Stegall (24)		10
Manier, Herod, Hollabaugh (41)		11
Texas		
Austin		
Brown, Maroney, Oaks (81)	Legal Assistant Coordinator	32
Clark, Thomas, Winters (74)		17
Graves, Dougherty, Hearon (71)		13
Fulbright & Jaworski (685/33)		160/12
Johnson & Gibbs (312/32)		40/13
Small, Craig, Werkenthin (63)		25
Vinson & Elkins (503/33)		174/21
Dallas		
Akin, Gump, Strauss (485/167)	Legal Assistant Staff Manager	109/32
Arter & Hadden (337/61)	Paralegal Coordinator	24
Baker & Botts (407/76)	Legal Assistant Coordinator	13
Baker, Mills, Glast (88)		22
Carrington, Coleman, Sloman (81)	Legal Assistant Administrator	18
Cowles & Thompson (69)		25
Fulbright & Jaworski (685/66)		160/16
Gardere & Wynne (200)		46
Gibson, Dunn & Crutcher (738/33)		165/11
Goodwin, Carlton & Maxwell (100)		20
Haynes & Boone (246/161)	Legal Assistant Coordinator; Litigation Support Coordinator	47
Hughes & Luce (156/133)		30/26
Jackson & Walker (216/144)	Legal Assistant Manager	35/25
Jenkins & Gilchrist (199/148)		32/24
Johnson & Gibbs (312/230)		40

Continued

FIGURE 2.2   Employment in Selected Large Law Firms*—*Continued*

Law Firm (Number of Attorneys)	Title of Paralegal Manager	Number of Paralegals
Texas		
Dallas		
Jones, Day, Reavis (1259/162)	Administrative Assistant	221/40
Locke, Purnell, Rain (190/183)		33
Page & Addison (28/24)		16/14
Riddle & Brown (50)		20
Shank, Irwin, Conant	Paralegal Coordinator	
Strasburger & Price (183/169)	Legal Assistant Coordinator	51
Thompson & Knight (213/198)	Legal Assistant Coordinator	46
Vial, Hamilton, Koch (85)		29
Wendel Turley (21)		24
Winstead, McGuire, Sechrest (180/128)	Paralegal Coordinator	41/37
El Paso		
Grambling & Mounce (37)		11
Kemp, Smith, Duncan (82)		18
Scott, Hulse, Marshall (40)		15
Fort Worth		
Cantey & Hanger (75)		16
Kelly, Hart & Hallman (76)		14
Houston		
Andrews & Kurth (287/202)	Legal Assistant Coordinator for Litigation	93/27
Arnold, White & Durkee (67)	Paralegal Coordinator	27
Baker & Botts (407/259)	Legal Assistant Manager	95/62
Baker, Brown, Sharman (60)	Legal Assistant Coordinator	15
Beirne, Maynard & Parsons (21)		12
Bracewell & Patterson (207/155)		40/36
Butler & Binion (171/140)	Legal Assistant Coordinator	45/28
Davis & McFall (33)	Paralegal Coordinator	20
Fulbright & Jaworski (685/337)	Coordinator, Legal Assistants	160/68
Hutcheson & Grundy (66)	Legal Assistant Coordinator	14
Jackson & Walker (216/54)		35/13
Liddell, Sapp, Zivley (178/130)		35/27
Lorance & Thompson (33)		11
Mayer, Day, Caldwell (70)		16
Porter & Clements (47)		11
Sewell & Riggs (53)		11
Sheinfeld, Maley & Key (71)		17
Vinson & Elkins (495/387)	Legal Assistant Manager; Legal Assistant Recruiter	174/146
Weil, Gotshal & Manges (552/60)	Legal Assistant Coordinator	22

Continued

FIGURE 2.2 Employment in Selected Large Law Firms*—*Continued*

Law Firm (Number of Attorneys)	Title of Paralegal Manager	Number of Paralegals
Texas		
San Antonio		
Cox & Smith (82)		19
Fulbright & Jaworski (685/48)		100/10
Groce, Locke & Hebdon (82)	Personnel Administrator	27
Matthews & Branscomb (82)	Legal Assistant Supervisor	19
Utah		
Salt Lake City		
Ray, Quinney & Nebeker (73)		11
Van Cott, Bagley, Cornwall (78)		11
Virginia		
Fairfax		
Hazel & Thomas (166/61)		32
Wilkes, Artis, Hedrick (40)		13
McLean		
McGuire, Woods, Battle (336/67)		94/19
Watt, Tieder, Killian (46)		13
Richmond		
Browder & Russell (44)	Paralegal Manager	17
Hunton & Williams (471/241)	Legal Services Manager; Human Resources Administrator	146/77
Mays & Valentine (131/111)		29
McGuire, Woods, Battle (336/180)	Legal Assistant Administrator	111/58
Sands, Anderson, Marks (42)		12
Williams, Mullen, Christian (58)	Personnel Manager	18
Washington		
Seattle		
Betts, Patterson & Mines (51)	Paralegal Coordinator	15
Bogle & Gates (235/159)		78/53
Davis, Wright, Tremaine (238/125)	Legal Assistant Coordinator	20
Foster, Pepper & Shefelman (138/105)		21
Gibson, Dunn & Crutcher		18
Helsell, Fetterman, Martin (49)		13
Lane, Powell, Spears (241/133)	Paralegal Manager	43/37
Oles, Morrison & Rinker (32)		10
Perkins Coie (336/178)	Legal Assistant Coordinator	85/47
Preston, Thorgrimson, Shidler (207/125)	Coordinator/Litigation Legal Assistants and Clerks	41/25
Reed, McClure, Moceri (46)		18
Riddall, Williams, Bullitt (73)	Personnel Manager	14

Continued

FIGURE 2.2   Employment in Selected Large Law Firms*—*Continued*

Law Firm (Number of Attorneys)	Title of Paralegal Manager	Number of Paralegals
Washington		
Seattle		
Stoel, Rives, Boley (220/60)		40/11
Williams, Kastner & Gibbs (80)	Paralegal Coordinator	18
Wilson, Smith, Cochran		18
West Virginia		
Charleston		
Bowles, Rice, McDavid (66/47)		17/12
Huntington		
Jenkins, Fenstermaker, Krieger (16)		5
Wisconsin		
Milwaukee		
Foley & Lardner (410/210)		56/25
Geofrey & Kahn (88)		23
Quarles & Brady (207/162)		27/22
Whythe & Hirschboeck (60)		10

*Sources: West's Legal Directory; National Association of Legal Placement Directory; National Law Journal (September 26, 1988; September 18, 1989; September 24, 1990); PIC's National Law Network; California Lawyer (November 1990); Legal Assistants Management Association Directory (1990); and independent checking.

- In the general counsel's office of individual agencies
- In other departments of individual agencies, e.g., enforcement department, civil rights division
- In the office of individual legislators, legislative committees, legislative counsel, or the legislative drafting office of the legislature

Federal Government

Thousands of paralegals work for the federal government in the capital (Washington, D.C.) and the main regional cities of the federal government (Boston, New York, Philadelphia, Atlanta, Chicago, Kansas City, Dallas, Denver, Seattle, and San Francisco). The most important job classification for this position is the *Paralegal Specialist* (GS-950).[4] This position is described in the following excerpt from the *Office of Personnel Management Handbook*, X-118. Note the extensive responsibility that these individuals have. The ending of this description is quite remarkable: paralegals perform "duties requiring discretion and independent judgment" which "may or may not be performed under the direction of a lawyer." There is no doubt that government paralegals have a range of responsibility that is broader than paralegals working anywhere else in the country.

---

[4]GS stands for *General Schedule,* which is the main pay-scale system used by the federal government. The number 950 is the occupational code for the Paralegal Specialist.

Description of Work

Paralegal specialist positions involve such activities as (a) legal research, analyzing legal decisions, opinions, rulings, memoranda, and other legal material, selecting principles of law, and preparing digests of the points of law involved; (b) selecting, assembling, summarizing and compiling substantive information on statutes, treaties, contracts, other legal instruments, and specific legal subjects; (c) case preparation for civil litigation, criminal law proceedings or agency hearings, including the collection, analysis and evaluation of evidence, e.g., as to fraud and fraudulent and other irregular activities or violations of laws; (d) analyzing facts and legal questions presented by personnel administering specific Federal laws, answering the questions where they have been settled by interpretations of applicable legal provisions, regulations, precedents, and agency policy, and in some instances preparing informative and instructional material for general use; (e) adjudicating applications or cases on the basis of pertinent laws, regulations, policies and precedent decisions; or (f) performing other paralegal duties requiring discretion and independent judgment in the application of specialized knowledge of particular laws, regulations, precedents, or agency practices based thereon. These duties may or may not be performed under the direction of a lawyer.

The largest numbers of Paralegal Specialists are employed in the following units of the federal government:[5]

U.S. Department of Health & Human Services
U.S. Department of Justice
U.S. Court System
U.S. Department of Treasury
U.S. Department of Transportation
U.S. Department of the Army
U.S. Department of the Interior
U.S. Equal Employment Opportunity Commission
U.S. General Services Administration
U.S. Department of Energy
U.S. Department of State
U.S. Department of Labor

Paralegal Specialists are not the only individuals using special legal skills in the federal government. The following law-related occupations, filled mainly by nonattorneys, should be considered:

Legal Clerk	Contract Specialist
Legal Technician	Contract Representative
Immigration Specialist	Labor Relations Specialist
Foreign Affairs Analyst/Officer	Employee Relations Specialist
Civil Rights Analyst	Wage & Hour Compliance Specialist
Social Services Representative	Mediation Specialist
Equal Employment Opportunity Specialist	Investigator
	Regulatory Analyst
Hearings and Appeals Officer	Legislative Analyst
Legal Instruments Examiner	Land Law Examiner
Public Utilities Specialist	Copyright Examiner
Tax Law Specialist	Copyright Technician
Patent Advisor	Railroad Retirement Claims
Patent Examiner	Examiner

---

[5]J. Harris, *The Paralegal's Guide to U.S. Government Jobs*, 3 (Federal Reports, 1986).

Patent Technician
Intelligence Analyst
Internal Revenue Officer
Import Specialist
Environmental Protection Specialist
Security Specialist
Freedom of Information Act
  Specialist

Estate Tax Examiner
Workers Compensation Claims
  Examiner
Unemployment Compensation
  Claims Examiner

When there is an opening for a Paralegal Specialist or for one of the positions listed above, the individual agency with this opening may do its own recruiting or may recruit through the Office of Personnel Management[6] (formerly called the Civil Service Commission), which oversees hiring procedures throughout the federal government. For a list of job information centers in your area where you can inquire about paralegal and other law-related positions in the federal government, see Appendix C.

State Government

When looking for work as a paralegal in the *state* government, find out if your state has established civil service classification standards for paralegal positions. See Figure 2.3 for some of this data. In addition, locate a directory of agencies, commissions, boards, or departments for your state, county, and city governments. You want to find a list of all (or most of the major) government offices. Many local public libraries will have a government directory. Alternatively, check the offices of state and local politicians, such as governor, mayor, commissioner, alderman, representative, or senator. They will probably have such a directory. Finally, check your local phone book for the sections on government offices. Contact as many of them as you can to find out whether they employ paralegals. If you have difficulty obtaining an answer to this question, find out where their attorneys are located. Sections or departments that employ attorneys will probably be able to tell you about paralegal employment opportunities. In your search, include a list of all the courts in the state. Judges and court clerks may have legal positions open for nonattorneys.

In addition to the statewide personnel departments listed in Figure 2.3, many government offices have their own personnel department that will list employment openings. Also, whenever possible, talk with attorneys and paralegals who already work in these offices. They may know of opportunities that you can pursue.

Do not limit your search to paralegal or legal assistant positions. Legal jobs for nonattorneys may be listed under other headings, such as research assistant, legal analyst, administrative aide, administrative officer, executive assistant, examiner, clerk, and investigator. As we have seen, this is also true for employment in the federal government.

4. Legal Service/Legal Aid Offices (Civil)

Community or neighborhood legal service offices and legal aid offices exist throughout the country. (See *Directory of Legal Aid & Defender Offices,* published by the National Legal Aid & Defender Association.) They obtain most of their funds from the government, often in the form of yearly grants to provide

---

[6] 1900 E. St. NW, Wash. D.C. 20415 (202-606-1800).

FIGURE 2.3   Summary Chart—Survey of State Government Job Classifications for Paralegals

GOVERNMENT	POSITION	RESPONSIBILITIES	QUALIFICATIONS	SALARY

Alabama
Personnel Dept.
64 N. Union St., rm.
  402
Montgomery, AL 36130-
  2301
205-261-3389
	Legal Assistant
	10/22/82
	(11502?)
		▪ Perform legal research
		▪ Draft pleadings
		▪ Interview witnesses in preparation for trial
		▪ Conduct routine investigations
		▪ Prepare and interpret legal documents in noncomplex cases
		▪ Prepare summaries of documents
		▪ Perform office administrative duties
			Graduation from an accredited legal assistant program
			OR
			possession of a legal assistant certificate
				$15,366–$23,369 per year

Other positions to check in Alabama: Docket Clerk (11501); Legal Opinions Clerk (11505); Contract Clerk (119.267-018); Legal Investigator (119.267-022); Title Examiner (119.287-010); Appeals Referee (119.267-014).				
Alaska Dept. of Administration Division of Personnel Pouch C Juneau, AK 99811 907-465-4430	Paralegal Assistant I 4/1/84 (7105-13)	▪ Interview clients ▪ Obtain statements and affidavits ▪ Conduct investigations ▪ Perform legal research ▪ Coordinate witness scheduling ▪ Represent clients at hearings	Certificate from a state paralegal training program OR Associate of Arts program with a major in paralegal, criminal justice, or law studies OR 3 years of experience as legal secretary, court clerk, etc.	$26,460–$36,048 per year
Other positions to check in Alaska: Legal Assistant II (7106); Investigator II (7707); Latent Fingerprint Examiner (7756).				

American Samoa
Dept. of Human
  Resources
American Samoa
  Government
Pago Pago, AS 96799
684-633-4489
	Legal Assistant I
	(E2-09-7524)
		▪ Conduct routine investigations
		▪ Perform legal research
		▪ Review citations for traffic court cases
		▪ Interview witnesses
		▪ Present traffic cases in court
		▪ Prepare orders to show cause
			A bachelor's degree with a major in police science, corrections, or a related field	$9,317–$15,167 per year

Other positions to check in American Samoa: Legal Assistant II (E2-10-7525); Legal Assistant III (E2-11-7526); Paralegal (12-13-7552).				
Arizona Dept. of Administration Personnel Division 1831 West Jefferson St. Phoenix, AZ 85007 602-542-5482	Legal Assistant 1/11/77 (74510)	▪ Perform legal research ▪ Help prepare briefs and pleadings ▪ Take statements and depositions ▪ Interview complainants ▪ Index laws	2 years of college study in relevant courses (experience involving legal terminology and legal research procedures can substitute for the education requirement)	$16,618–$23,937 per year

Continued

FIGURE 2.3   Summary Chart—Survey of State Government Job Classifications for Paralegals—*Continued*

GOVERNMENT	POSITION	RESPONSIBILITIES	QUALIFICATIONS	SALARY
Arizona		■ Serve papers ■ Help answer court calendars		
Other positions to check in Arizona: Legal Assistant I, Legal Assistant II (Child Support Enforcement Administration)				
Arkansas Office of Personnel Management P.O. Box 3278, 1509 West 7th St. Little Rock, AR 72203 501-682-1507	Legal Assistant 7/1/77 7/1/79-R (R177)	■ Receive legal questions from agency attorneys ■ Collect and evaluate information on the questions ■ Provide reports (orally or in memo form) to attorneys ■ File pleadings and briefs ■ Maintain law library	The education equivalent of completion of 1 year of law school, including a course in legal bibliography	$14,118 per year

California
State Personnel Board
801 Capitol Mall
P.O. Box 944201
Sacramento, CA 94244-
  2010
916-445-5291
ALSO:
Dept. of Personnel
  Administration
1115 11th St., 1st Fl.
Sacramento, CA 95814-
  3860
916-322-5193
	Legal Assistant
	3/13/75
	9/20/78
	(CW55, 1820)
		■ Assist in reviewing legal documents to determine if they comply with the law
		■ Analyze proposed legislation
		■ Digest and index opinions, testimony, depositions, and other trial documents
		■ Perform research of legislative history
		■ Assist in drafting complaints and other pleadings
		■ Perform routine legal research
			2 years of legal clerical experience in California government
			OR
			3 years in a law office
				$2,009–
				$2,418 per month

	Legal Analyst 7/2/81 (LE18, 5237)	■ Investigate and analyze facts ■ Coordinate witnesses ■ Draft interrogatories ■ Draft pleadings ■ Summarize discovery documents ■ Supervise other staff	1 year as a state Legal Assistant OR 2 years in another paralegal job and 15 semester hours or 22 quarter units in a paralegal curriculum or equivalent to graduation from college	$2,278– $2,700 per month
Colorado Dept. of Personnel State Centennial Bldg. 1313 Sherman St. Denver, CO 80203 303-866-2321	Legal Assistant 6/23/82 ("A" 77500) ("B" 77501)	■ Provide discovery and investigation assistance ■ Digest and index legal documents ■ Check legal citations ■ Take notes during deposition	Bachelor's degree and approved paralegal studies program (experience can substitute for general education)	Legal Assistant A $2,025– $2,713 per month

Continued

FIGURE 2.3   Summary Chart—Survey of State Government Job Classifications for Paralegals—*Continued*

GOVERNMENT	POSITION	RESPONSIBILITIES	QUALIFICATIONS	SALARY
Colorado		■ Prepare simple pleadings and briefs ■ Maintain case files ■ Prepare statistical reports ■ Perform legal research		Legal Assistant B $2,344–$3,141 per month

Connecticut
Personnel Div.
Dept. of Administration
  Services
165 Capital Ave.
Hartford, CT 06106-
  1630
203-566-3081
	Paralegal Specialist I 10/1/87 (6140)(NL16)	■ Act as liaison between legal and clerical staff
		■ Perform legal research
		■ Assist in drafting legal documents
		■ Maintain tickler systems
		■ Present written and oral argument at administrative hearings
		■ Maintain records
			2 years of experience working for a lawyer
			OR
			A designated number of college courses in law or paralegal studies
			
			(Note: substitutions are allowed)
				$970–$1,168 biweekly

Other positions to check in Connecticut: Paralegal Specialist II (6141, NL 20); Legal Office Administrator (5373, 9389c, MP 18).				
Delaware State Personnel Office Townsend Bldg. P.O. Box 1401 Dover, DE 19901 302-736-4195	Legal Assistant 8/75 (12846)	■ Review documents to assess consistency with law ■ Summarize cases ■ Draft pleadings, deeds, and other documents ■ Interview clients and witnesses ■ Assist in investigations ■ File documents in court	Enough education and/or experience to demonstrate competence in research, drafting filing, interviewing, record keeping, and communication (oral and written)	$17,400 per year
Other positions to check in Delaware: License Investigator (Dept. of Administrative Services); Clerk of Court I (Family Court) (12311); Law Library Assistant.				
District of Columbia D.C. Personnel Office 613 G St. NW, Rm 306 Wash. D.C. 20001-3798 202-727-6400	Paralegal Specialist	Similar to Paralegal Specialist positions in the federal government. (See page 81)		
Florida Dept. of Administration Division of Personnel Management Services 330 Carlton Bldg. Tallahassee, FL 32399 904-488-5823	Paralegal Specialist 1/1/84 (7703) (0807)	■ Take affidavits from victims and witnesses ■ Perform legal research under supervision ■ Maintain case files and tickler system	Completion of legal assistant training course OR Bachelor's degree with major in allied legal services OR	$1,220–$1,975 per month

Continued

FIGURE 2.3   Summary Chart—Survey of State Government Job Classifications for Paralegals—*Continued*

GOVERNMENT	POSITION	RESPONSIBILITIES	QUALIFICATIONS	SALARY
Florida		■ Perform notary functions ■ Prepare case summaries ■ Draft pleadings	4 years of experience as a paralegal or legal secretary	
Other positions to check in Florida: Appeals Coordinator/Clerk (Public Employees Relations Commission) (7704); Legal Trainee (7706)				
Georgia State Merit System of Personnel Administration 200 Piedmont Ave. Atlanta, GA 30334-5100 404-656-2705	Legal Assistant 1/1/81 (44330)	■ Perform legal research ■ Review litigation documents ■ Summarize law ■ Develop forms and procedures	2 years of legal experience involving legal research, interpreting laws, or relevant administrative responsibilities	$20,310–$32,052 per year
Other positions to check in Georgia: Law Clerk (44340)—requires a law degree OR two years of legal assistant experience; Para-Legal (nonmerit position in State Law Department); Research Assistant (nonmerit position in State Law Department).				
Guam Civil Service Commission Kumision I Setbision Sibit P.O. Box 3156 Agana, GU 96910 011-671-649-NORM Dept. of Administration Division of Personnel P.O. Box 3156 Agana, GU 96910 011-671-472-8194	Paralegal I 12/83 (2.810)	■ Perform legal research ■ Index public laws ■ Prepare updates to administrative laws ■ Draft bills and simple pleadings ■ Compile laws by subject matter ■ Interview clients and witnesses	3 years of experience working with laws and procedures OR A bachelor's degree OR Completion of a course leading to certification as a paralegal OR Equivalent experience and training	$13,930–$18,610 per year
Other position to check in Guam: Legal Clerk I (2.805).				
Hawaii Dept. of Personnel Services 830 Punchbowl St. Honolulu, HI 96813 808-548-7405	Legal Assistant II 4/15/83 (2.141)	■ Act as conduit between attorneys and client, e.g., provide legal information ■ Perform legal research ■ Summarize laws ■ Collect and evaluate evidence for trial ■ Perform cite checks ■ Index depositions	4 years of legal experience OR Graduation from an accredited legal assistant training program	$1,690–$2,326 per month
Idaho Personnel Commission 700 West State Boise, ID 83720 208-334-2263	Idaho currently does not have any job classifications for paralegal work. The Legal Assistant position (05916) was phased out. The Office of the Attorney General does, however, employ a paralegal in its Consumer Protection Unit and in its Natural Resource Division.			

Continued

FIGURE 2.3   Summary Chart—Survey of State Government Job Classifications for Paralegals—*Continued*

GOVERNMENT	POSITION	RESPONSIBILITIES	QUALIFICATIONS	SALARY

Illinois
Dept. of Central
  Management Services
Bureau of Personnel
505 Stratton Office
  Bldg.
Springfield, IL 62706
217-782-2141
312-917-2141 (Chicago)
	Paralegal Assistant
	11/17/83
	(1887, 30860)
	(RC-062-12)
		■ Write legal memo-
		  randa and other doc-
		  uments for attorneys
		■ Analyze hearing
		  transcripts
		■ Excerpt data from
		  transcripts
		■ Prepare statistical
		  reports
		■ Edit, index, and
		  proofread decisions
		■ Perform legal
		  research
			Knowledge and skill
			equivalent to four years
			of college and knowl-
			edge and skills relevant
			to job responsibilities
				$1,643—
				$2,102 per
				month

Other position to check in Illinois: Legal Research Assistant (1888) (23350) (MC-02) (RC-028-13).				
Indiana State Personnel Dept. Rm. 513, State Office Bldg. 100 North Senate Ave. Indianapolis, IN 46204 317-232-3056	The state has no special classifications for paralegals working in the state government. In the Offices of Attorney General, however, the Consumer Protection Division now has Complaint Analyst positions that have been filled with paralegals. Complaint Analysts act as a mediator between the consumer and the business against which the consumer has a complaint. Each Complaint Analyst handles at least 200 cases.			

Iowa
Dept. of Personnel
Grimes State Office
  Bldg.
E. 14th St. & Grand
  Ave.
Des Moines, IA 50319
515-281-3351
	Paralegal
	(Office of Attorney
	General)
	(45004)
		■ Represent the state at
		  revocation hearings
		■ Write administrative
		  appeal briefs
		■ Resolve appeals not
		  needing a hearing
		■ Initiate suggestions to
		  improve hearing
		  procedures
			2-year paralegal degree	$787–
				$1,024
				biweekly

Other position to check in Iowa: Administrative Assistant I (00708).				

Kansas
Dept. of Administration
Div. of Personnel
  Services
Landon State Office
  Bldg.
900 SW Jackson St.
Topeka, KS 66612-1251
913-296-4278
	Legal Assistant
	6/83
	(D3 1961)
		■ Perform legal
		  research
		■ Draft pleadings
		■ Compile administra-
		  tive transcript
		■ Conduct
		  investigations
			Completion of a Legal
			Assistant training pro-
			gram of at least 60 se-
			mester hours.
				$1,630–
				$2,294 per
				month

Kentucky
Dept. of Personnel
Capitol Annex, Rm. 373
Frankfort, KY 40601
502-564-4460
	Paralegal
	12/1/85
	(9856)
		■ Conduct analytical
		  research
		■ Investigate cases
		■ Interview complain-
		  ants and witnesses
		■ Draft documents
			Bachelor's degree in
			paralegal science
			  .OR
			Post-baccalaureate cer-
			tificate in paralegal
			studies
				$1,139–
				$1,826 per
				month

Continued

FIGURE 2.3 Summary Chart—Survey of State Government Job Classifications for Paralegals—*Continued*

GOVERNMENT	POSITION	RESPONSIBILITIES	QUALIFICATIONS	SALARY
Kentucky		▪ Provide general assistance to attorneys in litigation	OR Completion of a 2-year program in paralegal studies (Note: paralegal experience can be substituted)	
Other positions to check in Kentucky: Paralegal Senior (9857); Law Clerk (9801).				
Louisiana Dept. of Civil Service P.O. Box 94111 Capitol Station Baton Rouge, LA 70804-9111 504-342-8083	Paralegal Assistant 6/3/86 (113470) (C1 PA)	▪ Perform legal research ▪ Draft pleadings ▪ Interview potential trial witnesses ▪ Compose briefs and memoranda ▪ Collect delinquent payments ▪ Index legal opinions ▪ Maintain law library	1 year of law school OR Paralegal certification OR A baccalaureate degree and 30 semester hours of paralegal courses OR 2 years of paralegal school with 30 semester hours of paralegal courses	$1,180– $1,770 per month
Other position to check in Louisiana: Legal Research Assistant (70490).				
Maine Bureau of Human Resources State Office Bldg. State House Station 4 Augusta, ME 04333 207-289-3761	Paralegal Assistant (0016/U336)	▪ Assist attorney in title search ▪ Perform legal research ▪ Assist attorney at hearings ▪ Conduct investigations	4 years of college and 1 year of paralegal experience OR Graduation from an approved paralegal course	$21,507– $28,787 per year
Other positions to check in Maine: Legal Researcher (0018, 02045, 0979, 20E); Law Clerk (secretarial position with paralegal duties)(0061, 41255, 202.362-014, 0380, 0880, 18R); Workers Compensation Assistant (036900).				
Maryland Dept. of Personnel State Office Bldg. #1 301 W. Preston St. Baltimore, MD 21201 301-225-4715 800-492-7845	Legal Assistant I (10/31/47) (9/3/68) 0589	▪ Perform legal research ▪ Conduct investigations ▪ File pleadings ▪ Prepare affidavits ▪ Maintain docket file ▪ Coordinate employee activities	High school diploma or certificate and 4 years of experience as a clerk or secretary in a law office (Note: One year of paralegal education can substitute for two years of experience)	$17,261– $22,609 per year
Other positions to check in Maryland: Legal Assistant (209, 13); Legal Assistant II (1292); Para-l egal I (e.g., Howard County Office of State's Attorney).				

Continued

FIGURE 2.3   Summary Chart—Survey of State Government Job Classifications for Paralegals—*Continued*

GOVERNMENT	POSITION	RESPONSIBILITIES	QUALIFICATIONS	SALARY
Massachusetts Dept. of Personnel Administration One Ashburton Pl. Boston, MA 02108 617-727-3555	Paralegal Specialist 5/11/88 (10-R39) (Group 31)	■ Perform legal research ■ Analyze statutes ■ Digest the law ■ Prepare briefs and answers to interrogatories ■ Interview parties ■ Evaluate evidence ■ Develop case tracking systems ■ Schedule appointments	2 years of experience in legal research or legal assistant work (Note: An associate's degree or a higher degree with a major in paralegal studies can be substituted for the required experience)	$24,490– $32,691 per year
Michigan Dept. of Civil Service Capitol Commons Center 400 South Pine St. P.O. Box 30002 Lansing, MI 48909 517-373-3020	Paralegal III 5/81 (8020403, BA, 7)	■ Perform legal research ■ Conduct investigations ■ Draft legal documents ■ Prepare interrogatories ■ Digest and index laws ■ Serve and file legal papers	Associate degree in a paralegal program OR Equivalent combination of experience and education to perform the job	$10.43– $12.78 per hour
Other positions to check in Michigan: Paralegal IV (8020404, BA, 7); Paralegal VB (8020405, BA, 7); Paralegal VI (8031106, BA, 7). Note: The Legal Assistant I position requires a law degree.				
Minnesota Dept. of Employee Relations 520 LaFayette Rd. St. Paul, MN 55101 612-296-8366	Legal Technician 2/75 3/76 (17526C)	■ Perform legal research ■ Prepare legal documents ■ Collect documents for attorney	Completion of paralegal training program OR 2 years of varied paralegal experience OR 1 year of law school	$20,609– $25,829 per year
Other positions to check in Minnesota: Legal Technician-Farm Real Estate (Dept. of Agriculture); Legal Text Edit Specialist (001936, 206).				
Mississippi State Personnel Board 301 N. Lamar St. Jackson, MS 39201 601-359-1406	Paralegal Specialist 7/83 (1848-PR 188- 269, D)	■ Interpret and explain laws to staff ■ Assist in preparing legal documents ■ Review reports ■ Assist in referring cases for prosecution ■ Train and supervise staff in research ■ Perform research	Bachelor's degree in paralegal studies or a related field and 1 year of experience	$17,323 per year
Other position to check in Mississippi: Legal Clerk I (1962-PR 081-162, B) (clerical position with paralegal duties).				
Missouri Office of Administration Division of Personnel P.O. Box 388 Jefferson City, MO 65102 314-751-4162	Paralegal or legal assistant positions are not found under the Missouri Merit System. Individual agencies not covered by the Merit System, however, may have such positions.			

Continued

FIGURE 2.3 Summary Chart—Survey of State Government Job Classifications for Paralegals—*Continued*

GOVERNMENT	POSITION	RESPONSIBILITIES	QUALIFICATIONS	SALARY
Montana Dept. of Administration Personnel Division Mitchell Bldg., Rm. 130 205 Roberts St. Helena, MT 59620 406-444-3871	Paralegal Assistant I 1/80 (119004)	■ Perform legal research ■ Compile citations and references; check cites ■ Assemble exhibits ■ Explain laws ■ Arrange interviews and depositions ■ File pleadings ■ Supervise clerical staff	Completion of paralegal training program OR Education and experience equivalent to a bachelor's degree with courses in business, economics, law, etc.	Grade 11 $16,092–$22,236 per year
Other positions to check in Montana: Paralegal Assistant II (119005); Agency Legal Services Investigator (168155).				
Nebraska Dept. of Personnel Box 94905 Lincoln, NE 68509-4905 402-471-2075	Legal Aide I 5/1/78 C318131	■ Perform legal research ■ Proofread legal material ■ Help draft regulations ■ Help maintain hearing room tapes and films	Any combination of training and/or experience that will enable the applicant to possess the required knowledge, ability, and skills	$13,054 per year
Other position to check in Nebraska: Legal Aide II (C318132).				
Nevada Dept. of Personnel 209 E. Musser St. Capitol Complex Carson City, NV 89710 702-885-4050 800-992-0900	Legal Assistant 7/1/89 (2.155)	■ Digest information in files ■ Explain status of case to clients or to the public ■ Offer advice on procedures ■ Interview clients and witnesses ■ Schedule depositions ■ Organize and prepare exhibits	Completion of 1-year or 2-year paralegal course AND Legal secretarial experience or training OR Any combination of education and experience to demonstrate entry level knowledge, skills, and abilities	$18,803–$25,136 per year
Other positions to check in Nevada: Legal Assistant II (2.159); Legal Research Assistant (7.750).				
New Hampshire Division of Personnel State House Annex 25 Capitol St., Rm. 1 Concord, NH 03301 603-271-3261	Paralegal I 2/4/76 1/27/87 (6793-15)	■ Evaluate complaints of violations of state law ■ Interview business owners and consumers ■ Perform legal research ■ Examine contracts, agreements, and related legal documents to insure they comply with the law	4 years of college with 9 semester credits in law topics related to paralegal studies and 6 months of experience in research or investigation	$19,110–$22,542 per year
Other positions to check in New Hampshire: Paralegal II (6792-18); Legal Coordinator and Contracts Monitor (5668-22); Legal Research Assistant (5676-23); Legal Research Aide I (5670-16); Legal Research Aide II (5671-18); Legal Aide (5660-14).				

Continued

FIGURE 2.3   Summary Chart—Survey of State Government Job Classifications for Paralegals—*Continued*

GOVERNMENT	POSITION	RESPONSIBILITIES	QUALIFICATIONS	SALARY
New Jersey Dept. of Personnel Front & Montgomery Sts. CN 317 Trenton, NJ 08625 609-292-4144	Paralegal Technician Assistant 2/4/87 (A13-30459)	■ Perform legal research under close supervision ■ Help draft noncomplex memoranda ■ Help prepare correspondence ■ Help prepare pleadings ■ Perform cite checks ■ Proofread legal documents	Completion of an approved course of paralegal training	$25,535–$35,266 per year
Other positions to check in New Jersey: Legal Services Assistant I (A18-72743); Paralegal Technician, Law and Public Safety (A17-30461); Paralegal Technician, Casino Control Commission (X17-98648); Research Analyst (A18-03171); Research Analyst—Civil Service (A18-03171); Supervising Research Analyst—Div. of Youth and Fam. Services (A28-03184B).				
New Mexico State Personnel Office 810 W. San Mateo Rd. Santa Fe, NM 87503 505-827-8190	Legal Assistant I 8/29/79 (1330)	■ Provide help in legal research ■ Prepare affidavits and exhibits ■ Serve legal papers ■ Prepare and maintain records ■ Handle routine legal correspondence	Education and legal experience equaling 4 years. The experience can be gained as a paralegal. An Associate's Degree in paralegal studies can substitute for 3 years of experience.	$14,891–$24,760 per year
Other position to check in New Mexico: Legal Assistant II (1331).				
New York Dept. of Civil Service One Harriman State Office Bldg. Albany, NY 12239 518-457-3701	Legal Assistant I 2/10/84 (26-880)	■ Compile and organize documents ■ Help prepare legal documents and forms ■ Respond to inquiries and complaints ■ Maintain files ■ Monitor legislation ■ Perform legal research	Associate's degree in paralegal studies OR Completion of general practice legal specialty training AND Passing a test on law and procedure	$25,786 per year
Other positions to check in New York: Legal Assistant Trainee I (00-107); Legal Assistant II (26-881).				
North Carolina Office of State Personnel 116 West Jones St. Raleigh, NC 27603-8004 919-733-7108	Paralegal I 6/82 (NC 1422) (INCAC 8G.0402)	■ Draft legal instruments ■ Prepare routine opinions ■ Handle complaints and inquiries from the public ■ Administer the law office ■ Perform legal research	Graduation from a certified paralegal school and 1 year of paralegal experience	$19,783–$31,428 per year
North Dakota Central Personnel Division	Legal Assistant I 4/87 (0701)	■ Perform legal research ■ Maintain case files	The equivalent of 2 years of college in a curriculum appropriate	$1,219–$1,882 per month

Continued

FIGURE 2.3 Summary Chart—Survey of State Government Job Classifications for Paralegals—*Continued*

GOVERNMENT	POSITION	RESPONSIBILITIES	QUALIFICATIONS	SALARY

North Dakota
Office of Management &
  Budget
State Capitol, 14th Fl.
Bismarck, ND 58505
701-224-3290
		■ Maintain law library
		■ Assist attorneys in
		  litigation
		■ Perform general sec-
		  retarial duties
			to prelaw and 2 years of
			related experience.	

Other position to check in North Dakota: Legal Assistant II (0702).				

Ohio
Dept. of Administrative
  Services
Div. of Personnel
30 E. Broad Street
Columbus, OH 43266
614-466-3455
	Legal Aide
	8/84
	(63810)
		■ Perform legal
		  research
		■ Conduct
		  investigations
		■ Draft legal documents
		■ Draft responses to le-
		  gal questions
		■ Assist attorneys at
		  hearings
		■ File legal papers
		■ Maintain legal
		  records
			Completion of certifica-
			tion program for
			paralegals
			OR
			Completion of desig-
			nated courses, e.g., le-
			gal research, case anal-
			ysis, legal analysis, civil
			procedure
				$9.01–
				$10.58 per
				hour

Other positions to check in Ohio: Hearing Assistant (63821); Hearing Officer (63831).				

Oklahoma
Office of Personnel
  Management
2101 N. Lincoln Blvd.
Oklahoma City, OK
  73105
405-521-2171
800-522-8122
	Legal Research
	Assistant
	7/1/81
	(K101 FC: K10)
		■ Perform legal
		  research
		■ Conduct
		  investigations
		■ Assist attorneys in
		  litigation
		■ File pleadings
		■ Maintain law library
			Completion of approved
			legal research assistant
			program
			OR
			Completion of 18 se-
			mester hours of law
			school
				$1,691–
				$2,256 per
				month

Other positions to check in Oklahoma: Legal Assistant I; Legal Assistant II (Office of the Municipal Counselor, Oklahoma City).				

Oregon
Executive Dept.
Personnel & Labor Rela-
  tions Div.
155 Cottage St. N.E.
Salem, OR 97310-0310
503-378-3020
	Paralegal Specialist
	(1526)
		■ Organize complex
		  facts
		■ Communicate with
		  experts
		■ Analyze cases
		■ Assist attorneys in
		  litigation
		■ Arrange for case
		  settlements
		■ Answer
		  interrogatories
			Experience and training
			that demonstrate the
			knowledge and skills re-
			quired for the position
				$2,140–
				$2,845 per
				month

Other positions to check in Oregon: Paralegal I (1523); Paralegal II (1524); Paralegal III (1525); Investigator (C1031); Special Investigator (X 1032); Legal Assistant (C0680).				

Pennsylvania
Office of Administration
Bureau of Personnel
517 Finance Bldg.
Harrisburg, PA 17105
717-787-5545
	Legal Assistant I
	6/89
	(0701)
		■ Review work of field
		  personnel for possi-
		  ble legal implications
		■ Summarize cases
		■ Prepare reports
			1 year of experience as
			legal assistant trainee
			OR
			4 years of experience in
			clerical work, investiga-
			tion, or enforcement
				$16,919–
				$26,171 per
				year

Continued

FIGURE 2.3 Summary Chart—Survey of State Government Job Classifications for Paralegals—*Continued*

GOVERNMENT	POSITION	RESPONSIBILITIES	QUALIFICATIONS	SALARY
Other positions to check in Pennsylvania: Legal Assistant II (07020), Legal Assistant Supervisor (07030), Legal Assistant Manager (07040).				

Rhode Island
Office of Personnel
  Administration
289 Promenade St.
Providence, RI 02908
401-277-2160
	Paralegal Aide
	11/24/85
	(02461300)
		■ Perform legal
		  research
		■ Conduct
		  investigations
		■ Answer questions by
		  interpreting laws
		■ Assist in litigation
		■ Maintain files
			Completion of an ap-
			proved paralegal train-
			ing program
			OR
			Paraprofessional experi-
			ence in an extensive le-
			gal service program
				$18,380–
				$19,965 per
				year

South Carolina
Budget and Control
  Board
Division of Human Re-
  source Management
1201 Main St.
P.O. Box 12547
Columbia, SC 29211
803-737-0900
	Paralegal Assistant I
	4/84
	(2066)
		■ Obtain and assemble
		  witness statements,
		  reports, and exhibits
		■ Draft and proofread
		  pleadings
		■ Maintain tickler
		  system
		■ Assist in document
		  control
			Certification from an ap-
			proved paralegal
			program
			OR
			High school diploma
			and 1 year of experi-
			ence with a South Caro-
			lina attorney
				$17,821–
				$26,731 per
				year

Other positions to check in South Carolina: Paralegal Assistant II (2067); Legal Aide (2065).				
South Dakota Bureau of Personnel 500 E. Capitol Pierre, SD 57501-5070 605-773-3148	South Dakota does not have positions within state government specifically titled paralegal, legal assistant, legal technician, or legal aide. Individuals performing these functions are usually classified as administrative assistants, secretaries, or exempt professionals.			

Tennessee
Dept. of Personnel
505 Deaderick St.
Nashville, TN 37243-
  0635
615-741-2958
	Legal Assistant
	7/1/84
	(02350)
		■ Perform legal re-
		  search e.g., cite
		  checking
		■ Draft regulations
		■ Maintain law library
		■ Answer routine inquir-
		  ies on laws and
		  regulations
			Completion of an ap-
			proved curriculum in
			paralegal studies
				$1,128–
				$1,677 per
				month

Texas
State Auditor's Office
P.O. Box 12067
419 Reagan State Office
  Bldg.
Austin, TX 78711-2067
512-463-5788
	Legal Assistant I
	9/1/89
	(3570)
		■ Perform legal
		  research
		■ Compile citations and
		  references
		■ Research land titles
		■ Assemble exhibits
		■ Help prepare legal
		  documents
		■ File pleadings in
		  court
			Completion of a parale-
			gal training program
			OR
			The equivalent in
			experience
				$20,772–
				$26,160 per
				year

Other positions to check in Texas: Legal Assistant II (3572); Legal Assistant III (3574); Administrative Technician II (Office of Attorney General).				

Utah
Department of Human
  Resource
  Management
2229 State Office Bldg.
Salt Lake City, UT
  84114
801-538-3025
	Paralegal
	9/30/89
	(18750)
		■ Digest pretrial data
		■ Maintain calendar/
		  docket systems
		■ Draft subpoenas, mo-
		  tions, etc.
		■ Assist at depositions
		  and hearings
		■ Interview witnesses
			Certificate of paralegal
			studies, plus 2 years
			work experience, prefer-
			ably in a legal field
				$18,325–
				$27,165 per
				year

Continued

FIGURE 2.3   Summary Chart—Survey of State Government Job Classifications for Paralegals—*Continued*

GOVERNMENT	POSITION	RESPONSIBILITIES	QUALIFICATIONS	SALARY
Utah Other position to check in Utah: Paralegal (18751).				

Vermont
Agency of
   Administration
Dept. of Personnel
110 State St.
Montpelier, VT 05602
802-828-3497
	Paralegal
	Technician
	8/11/89
	(081800)
	(P.G. 18)
		■ Assist attorneys in
		   litigation
		■ Conduct
		   investigations
		■ Interview parties
		■ Perform legal
		   research
		■ Audit records
		■ Interpret laws
		■ Draft briefs and legal
		   documents
			1 year of experience in
			investigatory, analytical,
			research or paralegal
			duties; plus 3 years of
			additional experience at
			or above a senior cleri-
			cal or technical level
			
			(Note: 30 college cred-
			its in legal or paralegal
			studies can substitute
			for the 3 years of addi-
			tional experience.)
				$20,072–
				$30,305 per
				year

Other position to check in Vermont: State Investigator—Civil Rights.				

Virginia
Office of Compensation
   Management
Dept. of Personnel and
   Training
101 N. 14th St.
Richmond, VA 23219-
   3657
804-225-2131
	Legal Assistant
	11/1/83
	(21521)
		■ Help supervise cleri-
		   cal staff
		■ Monitor compliance
		   requirements
		■ Draft briefs and fact
		   narratives
		■ Perform legal
		   research
		■ Prepare witnesses
		   and exhibits
		■ Manage law library
			Paralegal course work
			or training preferred,
			plus experience in judi-
			cial and quasi-judicial
			systems and in the ap-
			plication of legal
			principles
				$18,723–
				$25,572 per
				year

Washington D.C. (See District of Columbia)				

Washington State
Dept. of Personnel
600 S. Franklin
P.O. Box 1789
Olympia, WA 98504
206-586-0194
	Legal Examiner I
	9/14/89
	(4661)
		■ Assist in litigation
		■ Assist in
		   investigations
		■ Perform legal
		   research
		■ Collect and organize
		   economic data
		■ Help organize large
		   volume of documents
			2 years of experience
			as a legal assistant
			OR
			Completion of approved
			2 year paralegal or le-
			gal assistant course
			OR
			4-year college degree
			and either completion of
			a 10-month legal assis-
			tant program or 1-year
			of experience as parale-
			gal or legal assistant
				$1,647–
				$2,081 per
				month

Other positions to check in Washington: Legal Examiner II (4662); Legal Examiner III (4663).				

West Virginia
Civil Service System
1900 Washington St.
   East, Rm. B-456
Charleston, WV 25305
304-348-3950
	Para-Legal Assistant
	10/7/74
	10/21/80
	(0550)
		■ Perform legal
		   research
		■ Write abstracts of
		   evidence
		■ Supervise clerical
		   staff
		■ Maintain case
		   records
		■ Summarize legal
		   literature
			Completion of approved
			Para-Legal Assistant
			program
			OR
			2 years of relevant legal
			experience under the
			supervision of an
			attorney
				$1,064–
				$1,920 per
				month

Continued

FIGURE 2.3   Summary Chart—Survey of State Government Job Classifications for Paralegals—*Continued*

GOVERNMENT	POSITION	RESPONSIBILITIES	QUALIFICATIONS	SALARY
West Virginia		■ Maintain statistical records ■ Monitor pending legislation ■ Prepare legal documents		
Other position to check in West Virginia: Child Advocate Para-Legal (8098).				
Wisconsin Dept. of Employment Relations 149 East Wilson St. P.O. Box 7855 Madison, WI 53707 608-266-9820	Legal Assistant I 4/79 (PR2-08)	■ Abridge transcripts of testimony ■ Prepare appendices for appellate briefs ■ Paginate appeal records ■ Collect and organize facts for trial preparation ■ Draft routine pleadings ■ Conduct elementary research	There must be reasonable assurance that the applicant has the skills and knowledge to perform the tasks. "Under current civil service statutes, the state of Wisconsin does not require specific credentials unless it can be established that the position needs professional licensing."	$10.03–$14.02 per hour
Other positions to check in Wisconsin: Legal Assistant II (PR2-09); Legal Assistant I—Confidential (PR1-08) (Dept. of Justice, Attorney General); Administrative Assistant IV (PR1-13).				
Wyoming Personnel Division Department of Administration and Fiscal Control 2001 Capitol Ave. Cheyenne, WY 82002 307-777-6713	There are no paralegal or legal assistant classifications in Wyoming state government. The closest may be the positions of Executive Secretary and Legal Investigator (LE52).			

legal services to the poor. The clients do not pay fees. These offices make extensive use of paralegals with titles such as:

Administrative Benefits
  Representative
Administrative Hearing
  Representative
AFDC Specialist (Aid to Families
  with Dependent Children)
Bankruptcy Law Specialist
Case Advocate
Case Specialist
Community Law Specialist
Disability Law Specialist
Domestic Relations Specialist

Employment Law Specialist
Food Stamp Specialist
Generalist Paralegal
Health Law Specialist
Housing/Tenant Law Specialist
Immigration Paralegal
Information and Referral Specialist
Legal Assistant
Legal Research Specialist
Legislative Advocate
Paralegal

Paralegal Coordinator	Social Security Specialist
Paralegal Supervisor	Tribal Court Representative
Public Entitlement Specialist	Veterans Law Specialist
Senior Citizen Specialist	Wills Procedures Specialist

As we will see in Chapter 3, many administrative agencies permit nonattorneys to represent citizens at hearings before those agencies. Legal service and legal aid offices take advantage of this authorization. Their paralegals undertake extensive agency representation. (See Figure 2.4 for a sample job announcement that lists paralegal duties, including work at hearings, on behalf of clients.) The distinction between attorneys and paralegals in such offices is less pronounced than in any other setting. Unfortunately, however, such paralegals are among the lowest paid because of the limited resources of the offices where they work.

Another way in which legal services are provided to poor people (sometimes referred to as *indigents*) is through *judicare.* This is a system of paying private attorneys for legal services to the poor on a case-by-case basis. Instead of receiving a government grant to open up an office that will serve only the poor, the Judicare attorney maintains a private office and bills the government whenever legal services are delivered to the poor. These attorneys often employ paralegals.

Further variations on methods by which paralegals are used to deliver legal services to the poor include:

- Paralegals who work in special institutions such as mental health hospitals or prisons
- Paralegals who are senior citizens providing legal services to senior citizens at nursing homes, neighborhood centers, and similar locations

5. Law Departments of Corporations, Banks, Insurance Companies, and Other Businesses

Not every corporation or business in the country uses a law firm to handle all of its legal problems. Many have their own in-house law department under the direction of an attorney who is often called the *general counsel* or *corporate counsel.*[6] The attorneys in this department have only one client—the corporation or business itself. Examples include manufacturers, retailers, transportation companies, publishers, general insurance companies, real estate and title insurance companies, estate and trust departments of large banks, hospitals, universities, etc. In increasing numbers, paralegals are being hired in these settings. The average corporate law department employs seventeen attorneys, two paralegals, two nonattorney professionals, and fourteen legal support personnel.[7] Paralegal salaries are relatively high because the employer (like the large traditional private law office) can afford to pay good wages.

---

[6]Even if a corporation has its own law department, however, it may still occasionally hire an outside law firm in special situations such as complex litigation.

[7]Stanton, *Stepping Up to the Bar,* 35 Occupational Outlook Quarterly 3, 7 (Spring 1991).

FIGURE 2.4

Sample Job Description for Paralegal in Legal Service Office

Gulf Coast Legal Foundation

Positions Open for Paralegals Experienced in Welfare

The Gulf Coast Legal Foundation, formerly the Houston Legal Foundation, has three positions open for paralegals with experience in welfare law. However, if experienced persons do not apply, we will seriously consider applicants with no more educational qualifications than a GED. We are discouraging law students and law graduates from applying. Our program has five neighborhood offices in Houston and Galveston and will expand to Fort Bend and Brazoria Counties. Our paralegals are assigned to specialty units. These positions are for the welfare unit where the goal is to increase the number of AFDC (Aid to Families with Dependent Children) families by 12,000 in the county and the number of SSI (Supplemental Social Security Income) recipients by 1,500 in the county, and to increase the level of benefits. The welfare unit represents the local welfare rights organization, which has ten years of history, parent councils of Title XX day care centers, and in cooperation with another unit, groups of handicapped people. The paralegal would maintain a direct service caseload of state welfare appeals and SSI hearings as well as some unemployment, health claims and other administrative matters. Each paralegal will be expected to handle six pending hearings and perform one research task each month after a training period of half a year. And do their own typing. The paralegal would also maintain a library of state manuals and social security materials. The paralegal would also be expected to participate in saturation leafleting, to attend some group meetings, and to perform minor educational services. The supervising attorney of the welfare unit would supervise the paralegal. The unit will have a total of five lawyers and six paralegals.

Because of inadequate public transportation, the paralegal would be responsible for transporting clients to welfare centers and maintaining a personal automobile.

Applicants should furnish their scores on the SAT or GRE exam, a writing sample, and detailed information concerning any prior legal services experience. We will weigh mathematical skills over writing skills. Our program will give preference to experienced paralegals who intend to continue a career as a paralegal. Our program also has an affirmative action policy for the hiring of women and members of minority groups. Our program serves a substantial Mexican-American population and must give an additional preference to applicants who speak Spanish fluently.

The salary range can go up to the equivalent of a moderately experienced attorney.

---

6. Special Interest Groups or Associations

Many special interest groups exist in our society: unions, business associations, environmental protection groups, taxpayer associations, consumer protection groups, trade associations, citizen action groups, etc. The larger groups have their own offices, libraries, and legal staff, including paralegals. The legal work often involves monitoring legislation, lobbying, preparing studies, etc. Direct legal services to individual members of the groups are usually not provided. The legal work relates to the needs (or a cause) of the organization as a whole. Occasionally, however, the legal staff will litigate test cases of individual members that have broad impact on the organization's membership.

A different concept in the use of attorneys and paralegals by such groups is *group legal services*. Members of unions or groups of college students, for example, pay a monthly fee to the organization for which they are entitled to designated legal services, such as preparation of a will or divorce representation. The members pay *before* the legal problems arise. Group legal service systems are a form of legal insurance. The group legal service office will usually employ paralegals.

7. Criminal Law Offices

Criminal cases are brought by government attorneys who are called prosecutors, district attorneys, or attorneys general. Defendants are represented by private attorneys if they can afford the fees. If they are indigent, they are assigned private counsel whose fees are paid by the government, or they are represented by public defenders who work in a special office set up by government funds to represent the poor. The use of paralegals in the practice of criminal law is increasing, particularly due to the encouragement of organizations such as the National District Attorneys Association and the National Legal Aid & Defender Association.

8. Freelance Paralegals

As we learned in Chapter 1, most *freelance paralegals* are self-employed individuals who sell their services to attorneys. They are also called independent paralegals and contract paralegals. They perform their services in their own office or in the offices of the attorneys who hire them for special projects. Often they advertise in publications read by attorneys, such as legal newspapers and bar association journals. Such an ad might look something like this:

> **Improve the quality and**
> ******cost-effectiveness******
> **of your practice with the help of:**
> **Lawyer's Assistant, Inc.**

In addition, these paralegals will usually have a flyer or brochure that describes their services. Here is an excerpt from such a flyer:

> Our staff consists of individuals with formal paralegal training and an average of five years of experience in such areas as estates and trusts, litigation, real estate, tax, and corporate law. Whether you require a real estate paralegal for one day or four litigation paralegals for one month, we can provide you with reliable qualified paralegals to meet your specific needs.

The attorneys in a law firm may be convinced of the value of paralegals but not have enough business to justify hiring a full-time paralegal employee. A freelance paralegal may be an alternative.

For an overview on how to start a freelance business, see Appendix D.

As we saw in Chapter 1, there are also self-employed paralegals who sell their services directly to the public. They, too, are sometimes called freelance paralegals, although the terms legal technician and independent paralegal are more common. Relatively few paralegals are engaged in this kind of business. This may change, however, as a number of states seriously consider a form of limited licensing to authorize what they do. We will examine this possibility in Chapter 3.

9. Service Companies/Consulting Firms

Service companies and consulting firms also sell services to attorneys, but usually on a broader and more sophisticated scale than the freelance paralegal does. Examples include:

- Selecting a computer system for a law office
- Designing and managing a computer-assisted document control system for a large case
- Digesting discovery documents

- Helping a law firm establish a branch office
- Designing a filing or financial system for the office
- Incorporating a new company in all fifty states
- Conducting a trademark search
- Undertaking a UCC (Uniform Commercial Code) search and filing in all fifty states

In order to accomplish such tasks, these service companies and consulting firms recruit highly specialized staffs of management experts, accountants, economists, former administrators, etc. More and more paralegals are joining these staffs, particularly paralegals with prior law office experience.

10. Related Fields

Experienced paralegals have also been using their training and experience in a number of nonpractice legal fields. Many are becoming law librarians at firms. Paralegal schools often hire paralegals to teach courses and to work in administration, in such areas as admissions, internship coordination, placement, etc. Law offices with large numbers of paralegals have hired paralegal administrators or supervisors to help recruit, train, and manage the paralegals. Some paralegals have become legal administrators or office managers with administrative responsibilities throughout the firm. It is clear that we have not seen the end of the development of new roles for paralegals within the law firm or in related areas of the law. At the end of the chapter, a more extensive list of such roles will be provided. (See Figure 2.15.)

Section C. Paralegal Specialties: A Dictionary of Functions

"The question so often asked of us is, 'What exactly do you do?' "
Douglas Parker, Paralegal, Pasadena, California, 1989.

We now examine forty-five areas of specialty work throughout the ten categories of paralegal employment just discussed. Paralegals often work in more than one of these specialties, and there is considerable overlap in the functions performed. The trend, however, is for paralegals to specialize. This follows the pattern of most attorneys.

Paralegal Specialties

1. Administrative law
2. Admiralty law
3. Advertising law
4. Antitrust law
5. Banking law
6. Bankruptcy law
7. Civil rights law
8. Collections law
9. Communications law
10. Construction law
11. Contract law
12. Corporate law
13. Criminal law
14. Employee benefits law
15. Entertainment law
16. Environmental law
17. Estates, trusts, and probate law
18. Ethics and professional responsibility
19. Family law
20. Government contract law
21. Immigration law
22. Insurance law
23. Intellectual property law
24. International law
25. Judicial administration

26. Labor and employment law
27. Landlord and tenant law
28. Law librarianship
29. Law office administration
30. Legislation
31. Litigation
32. Military law
33. Municipal finance law
34. Oil and gas law
35. Parajudge
36. Pro bono work

37. Public sector
38. Real estate law
39. Social security law
40. Tax law
41. Tort law
42. Tribal law
43. Water law
44. Welfare law
45. Worker's compensation law
Note: Paralegal in the White House

1. Administrative Law

I. Government Employment

Many paralegals work for specific administrative agencies. (See also Figure 2.3 for a list of paralegal functions in state agencies.) They might:

A. Handle questions and complaints from citizens.
B. Draft proposed regulations for the agency.
C. Perform legal research.
D. Provide litigation assistance in the agency and in court.
E. Represent the government at administrative hearings where authorized.
F. Manage the law office.
G. Train and supervise other nonattorney personnel.

II. Representation of Citizens

Some administrative agencies authorize nonattorneys to represent citizens at hearings and other agency proceedings. (See also *immigration law, pro bono work, public sector, social security law,* and *welfare law.*)

A. Interview client.
B. Conduct investigation.
C. Perform legal research.
D. Engage in informal advocacy at the agency.
E. Represent the client at agency hearing.
F. Draft documents for submission at hearing.
G. Monitor activities of the agency—for example, attend rule-making hearings to take notes on matters relevant to particular clients.
H. Prepare witnesses, reports, and exhibits designed to influence the drafting of regulations at the agency.

■ *Comment on Paralegal Work in this Area:*

We "have a great deal of autonomy and an opportunity to develop expertise in particular areas." We have our "own caseloads, interview clients and then represent those clients at administrative hearings." Georgia Ass'n of Legal Assistants, *Sallye Jenkins Sapp, Atlanta Legal Aid; Sharon Mahaffey Hill, Georgia Legal Services,* 10 ParaGraph 5 (1987).

When I got my first case at a hearing before the State Department of Mental Health, I was "scared to death!" But the attorneys in the office were very supportive. "They advised me to make a good record, noting objections for the transcript, in case of future appeal. Making the right objections was scary." Milano, *New Responsibilities Being Given to Paralegals,* 8 Legal Assistant Today 27, 28 (November/December 1990).

2. Admiralty Law

This area of the law, also referred to as maritime law, covers accidents, injuries, and death connected with vessels on navigable waters. Special legislation exists in this area, such as the Jones Act. (See also *international law, litigation,* and *tort law.*)

I. Investigation

A. Obtain the facts of the event involved.
B. Arrange to board the vessel to photograph the scene of the accident.
C. Collect facts relevant to the seaworthiness of the vessel.
D. Take statements from witnesses.

II. Legal Research

A. Research liability under the applicable statutes.
B. Research special procedures to obtain compensation.

III. Subrogation

A. Handle small cargo subrogation files.
B. Prepare status reports for clients.

IV. Litigation

A. Draft complaints and other pleadings.
B. Respond to discovery requests.

C. Monitor maritime files to keep track of discovery deadlines.

D. Coordinate projects by expert witnesses.

E. Provide general trial assistance.

■ *Comment on Paralegal Work in this Area:*

Jimmie Muvern, CLA (Certified Legal Assistant), works for a sole practitioner in Baton Rouge, Louisiana who specializes in maritime litigation: "If there is a doubt regarding the plaintiff's status as a Jones Act seaman, this issue is generally raised by a motion for summary judgment filed well in advance of trial, and it is good practice for the legal assistant who may be gathering facts regarding the client's accident to also gather facts from the client and from other sources which might assist the attorney in opposing summary judgment on the issue of the client's status as a Jones Act seaman." J. deGravelles & J. Murvin, *Who Is a Jones Act Seaman?* 12 Facts & Findings 34 (NALA, April 1986).

3. Advertising Law

(See also *administrative law* and *intellectual property law*.)

I. Compliance Work

A. *Advertising:* Review advertising of company products in order to identify possible claims made in the advertising about the product. Collect data needed to support the accuracy of claims made in advertising pursuant to regulations of the Federal Trade Commission and company guidelines.

B. *Labels:* Review labels of company products to insure compliance with the regulations on deception of the Federal Trade Commission. Insure compliance with the Food & Drug Administration and company policy on:
1. Product identity,
2. New weight statement,
3. Ingredient list,
4. Name and address of manufacturer/distributor,
5. Nutrition information.

C. *Product promotions:* Review promotions for company products (coupons, sweepstakes, bonus packs, etc.) to insure compliance with Federal Trade Commission guidelines, state laws, and company policy.

II. Inquiries and Complaints

A. Keep up-to-date on government regulations on advertising.

B. Help company attorney respond to inquiries and complaints from the public, a competitor, the Federal Trade Commission, the Food & Drug Administration, the state's attorney general, etc.

■ *Comment on Paralegal Work in this Area:*

"On the surface, my job certainly does not fit the 'traditional' paralegal role. If a fortune teller had ever read my coffee grounds, I might have learned that my paralegal career would include being part of the production of commercials and labels for household products I had grown up with. . . . My employer, the Proctor & Gamble Company, is one of the largest consumer product companies in the United States." Its "Legal Division consists of forty attorneys and nine paralegals. Advertising law is challenging. It requires ingenuity, fast thinking and mastery of tight deadlines." Kothman, *Advertising Paralegal Finds Own Label,* National Paralegal Reporter 12 (NFPA, Spring 1990).

4. Antitrust Law

(See also *administrative law, corporate law, criminal law,* and *litigation.*)

I. Investigation/Analysis

A. Accumulate statistical and other technical data on a company or industry involved in litigation. Check Securities & Exchange Commission (SEC) filings, annual reports, advertising brochures, etc.

B. Prepare reports on economic data.

C. Obtain data from government bodies.

D. Find and interview potential witnesses.

II. Administrative Agency

A. Monitor the regulations and decisions of the Federal Trade Commission.

B. Prepare drafts of answers to requests for information from the Federal Trade Commission.

III. Litigation

A. Assist in drafting pleadings.

B. Request company witness files in preparation for deposition.

C. Schedule depositions.

D. Draft form interrogatories.

E. Prepare special exhibits.

F. Organize, index, and digest voluminous records and lengthy documents.

G. Prepare trial notebook.

H. Attend trial and take notes on testimony of witnesses.

I. Cite check briefs of attorneys.

J. Provide general trial assistance.

■ *Comment on Paralegal Work in this Area:*

When Mitchell became a permanent employee at the firm, "he was given three days' worth of files to read in order to familiarize himself with the [antitrust] case. At this point in the case, the firm had already gone through discovery of 27,000 documents. Mitchell analyzed and summarized documents with the other ten paralegals hired to work on the case. With a major case such as this one, paralegals did not have a regular nine to five work day. Mitchell frequently worked seventy hours a week (for which he was paid overtime). In January, Mitchell and his team were sent across the country to take depositions for the case. His air transportation, accommodations, and meals were all 'first class,' but this was not a vacation; he worked around the clock." R. Berkey, *New Career Opportunities in the Legal Profession*, 47 (Arco, 1983).

5. Banking Law

Paralegals employed by banks often work in the bank trust department. They also work in bank legal departments, where they become involved with litigation, real estate, bankruptcy, consumer affairs, and securities law. In addition to banks, paralegals work for savings and loan institutions and other commercial lenders. Finally, some paralegals are employed in law firms that specialize in banking law. The following overview of duties is limited to the paralegal working for the legal department of a bank. (See also *administrative law, corporate law, estates law,* and *municipal finance law.*)

I. Claims

Assist legal staff in assessing bank liability for various claims, such as negligence and collection abuse.

II. Compliance Analysis

Determine whether the bank is complying with the regulations and statutes that regulate the banking industry.

III. Monitoring

Keep track of the activities of the various banking regulatory agencies and of the legislative committees with jurisdiction over banks.

IV. Litigation

Assist attorneys litigating claims.

V. Miscellaneous

A. Draft and/or review loan applications and accompanying credit documents.
B. Perform document analysis on
   1. Financial statements,
   2. Mortgages,
   3. Assignments,
   4. Security agreements.
C. Conduct UCC (Uniform Commercial Code) searches.
D. Assemble closing documents.
E. Arrange for and attend loan closings.
F. Prepare notarization of documents.
G. Monitor recordation.
H. Act as liaison among supervising attorney at the bank, the loan officer, and the customer.
I. Perform routine legal research and analysis for the Compliance Department.

■ *Comment on Paralegal Work in this Area:*

Ruth Sendecki is "the first legal assistant" at Merchants National Bank, one of the Midwest's largest bank holding companies. Most paralegals employed at banks today work in the trust department; Ruth, however, works with "general banking" at Merchants. Before this job, she worked at a bank, but not in a legal capacity. "You don't have to limit yourself to a law firm. You can combine being a legal assistant with other interests." Her "primary responsibility is in the commercial loan department. . . . She also serves the mortgage loan, correspondent banking and the international banking departments." According to her supervisor at the bank, "She is readily accessible for the benefit of the attorney, the loan officer and the customer to facilitate completion of the arrangements for both sides." Furthermore, she "is expanding her knowledge base, and other departments are drawing on her knowledge." Kane, *A Banker with the $oul of a Legal Assistant,* 5 Legal Assistant Today 65 (July/August 1988).

6. Bankruptcy Law

Paralegals in this area of law may be employed by a law firm that represents the debtor (e.g., an individual, a business); a creditor (e.g., a bank-mortgagee); or the trustee in bankruptcy. (A trustee in bankruptcy does not have to be a lawyer. Some paralegals with bankruptcy experience have in fact become trustees.) A few paralegals work directly for a bankruptcy judge as a clerk or deputy in Bankruptcy Court. The following overview assumes the paralegal works for a firm that represents the debtor. (See also *banking law, collections law, contract law,* and *litigation.*)

A. Help client fill out an extensive questionnaire on assets and liabilities. May visit client's place of business to determine the kinds of records kept there.

B. Help client assemble documents:
1. Loan agreements,
2. Deeds of trust,
3. Security agreements,
4. Creditor lists,
5. Payables lists,
6. Employment contracts,
7. Financial statements,
8. Leases, etc.

II. Investigation

A. Confirm amounts of indebtedness.

B. Identify secured and unsecured claims of creditors.

C. Check UCC (Uniform Commercial Code) filings at the secretary of state's office and at county clerk's office.

D. Check real property records in the clerk's office of the county where the property is located.

E. Verify taxes owed; identify tax liens.

F. Identify exempt property.

III. Asset Control

A. Open bankruptcy file.

B. Prepare inventories of assets and liabilities.

C. Arrange for valuation of assets.

IV. Creditor Contact

A. Answer inquiries of creditors on the status of the case.

B. Request documentation from creditors on claims.

V. Drafting

A. Original bankruptcy petition.

B. Schedule of liabilities.

C. Statement of affairs.

D. Status reports.

E. Final account.

VI. Coordination

A. Serve as liaison with trustee in bankruptcy.

B. Coordinate meeting of creditors.

C. Prepare calendar of filing and other deadlines.

■ *Comment on Paralegal Work in this Area:*

"As a legal assistant, you can play a major role in the representation of a Chapter 11 debtor. From prefiling activities through confirmation of the plan of reorganization, there are numerous duties which you can perform to assist in the successful reorganization of the debtor." Morzak, *Organizing Reorganization*, 5 Legal Assistant Today 33 (January/February).

"Bankruptcy work is unusual in a number of ways—extremely short statutes of limitation, for example. . . . The field is one in which there's lots of opportunity for paralegals. The paralegal does everything except sign the papers. . . . Most attorneys do not like bankruptcy, but if you do all the legwork for them, you can make a lot of money for them." Johnson, *The Role of the Paralegal/Legal Assistant in Bankruptcy and Foreclosure*, AALA News 7 (Alaska Ass'n of Legal Assistants, March 1987).

7. Civil Rights Law

(See also *labor and employment law, pro bono work,* and *public sector.*)

I. Government Paralegal

A. Help identify and resolve discrimination complaints (based on sex, race, age, etc.) made by government employees against the government.

B. Help government attorneys litigate discrimination complaints (based on sex, race, age, etc.) brought by citizens against the government, against other citizens, or against companies.

II. Representation of Citizens

Assist law firms representing citizens in their discrimination complaints against the government, other citizens, or companies:

A. In court.

B. In special agencies created to hear discrimination cases, such as the Equal Employment Opportunity Commission or the Human Rights Commission.

■ *Comment on Paralegal Work in this Area:*

"One aspect that Matthews likes is that each case is a different story, a different set of facts. 'There is a lot of interaction with people in the courts and with the public. We do a great deal of civil rights litigation, everything from excessive police force to wrongful termination. Sometimes there are as many as 60 witnesses. The lawyers depend on me to separate the witnesses out and advise them which ones would do best in the courtroom. A lot of times the lawyer does not know the witness and has not seen the witness until the person is in the courtroom testifying.' For one case, Matthews reviewed more than 1,000 slides taken in a nightclub, looking for examples of unusual or rowdy behavior. The slides included everything from male strippers to people flashing. Autopsy and horrible injury photographs are also part of the job." *Broadening into the Paralegal Field*, 39 The Docket 7 (NALS, January/February 1991).

8. Collections Law[8]

(See also *banking law, bankruptcy law, contract law,* and *litigation.*)

I. Acceptance of Claims

A. Open file.

B. Prepare index of parties.

C. Prepare inventory of debts of debtor.

II. Investigation

A. Conduct asset check.

B. Verify address.

C. Verify filings at secretary of state's office and county clerk's office (e.g., UCC filings).

D. Contact credit bureau.

E. Verify information in probate court, registry of deeds, etc.

III. Litigation Assistant (Civil Court, Small Claims Court)

A. Draft pleadings.

B. Arrange for witnesses.

C. File documents in court.

D. Assist in settlement/negotiation of claim.

E. Assist in enforcement work, such as:

1. Wage attachment (prejudgment attachment),

2. Supplementary process,

3. Execution,

4. Seizure of personal property.

■ *Comment on Paralegal Work in this Area:*

"O.K.—So, it [collections work] is not the nicest job in the world, but somebody has to do it, right? If the attorney you work for does not want to do it, there are plenty more in town who will. For a paralegal working in this area, there is always something new to learn. . . . It is sometimes difficult to see the results of your labor right away in this kind of work, as very few files are paid in full and closed in a short period of time. It is disheartening to go through many steps and possibly spend a great deal of time just trying to get someone served or to locate someone, and then end up with nothing. I will admit that collections can be very frustrating, but boring they are not!" Wexel, *Collections: Persistence Pay$ Off,* The Paraview (Metrolina Paralegal Ass'n, April 1987).

"I currently have responsibility for some 400 collection cases. My days are spent on the phone talking to debtors, drafting the necessary pleadings, executing forms, and hopefully depositing the money collected.

The exciting part of collection is executing on a judgment. We were successful in garnishing an insurance company's account for some $80,000 when they refused to pay a judgment that had been taken against them. We have also gone with the Sheriff to a beer distributorship two days before St. Patrick's Day to change the locks on the building housing gallons and gallons of green beer. The debtor suddenly found a large sum of money to pay us so that we would release the beer in time for St. Patrick's day." R. Swoagerm, *Collections Paralegal,* The Citator 9 (Legal Assistants of Central Ohio, August 1990).

9. Communications Law

(See also *administrative law* and *entertainment law.*)

I. Government Paralegal

Assist attorneys at the Federal Communications Commission (FCC) in regulating the communications industry—for example, help with rule-making, license applications, hearings.

II. Representation of Citizens or Companies

A. Draft application for licenses.

B. Prepare compliance reports.

C. Prepare exemption applications.

D. Prepare statistical analyses.

E. Monitor activities of the FCC.

F. Assist in litigation.

1. Within the FCC,

2. In court.

■ *Comment on Paralegal Work in this Area:*

The current specialty of Carol Woods is the regulation of television and radio. "I am able to do work that is important and substantive, and am able to work independently. I have an awful lot of contact with clients, with paralegals at the client's office, and with government agencies. One of the liabilities of private practice for both attorneys and paralegals is that there is so much repetition and you can get bored. A lot of times as a paralegal you can't call the shots or know everything that goes into the planning of a project. However, when you can participate in all facets of a project, it's great!" A. Fins, *Opportunities in Paralegal Careers,* 84 (Nat'l Textbook Co., 1979).

10. Construction Law

(See also *contract law, litigation,* and *tort law.*)

I. Claims Assistance

A. Work with engineering consultants in the preparation of claims.

---

[8]See Commercial Law League of America, Seminar, *A Paralegal Approach to the Practice of Commercial Law* (11/14/75).

II. Data Collection

A. Daily manpower hours,

B. Amount of concrete poured,

C. Change of orders.

III. Document Preparation

A. Prepare graphs.

B. Prepare special studies—for example, compare planned with actual progress on construction project.

C. Prepare documents for negotiation/settlement.

D. Help draft arbitration claim forms.

IV. Assist in litigation.

■ *Comment on Paralegal Work in this Area:*

"Because of the complex factual issues that arise with construction disputes, legal assistants are critical in identifying, organizing, preparing, and analyzing the extensive relevant factual information. In many cases, whether a party wins or loses depends on how effectively facts are developed from documents, depositions, interviews, and site inspections. Thus, a successful construction litigation team will generally include a legal assistant skilled in organization and management of complex and voluminous facts. . . . Construction litigation also provides legal assistants with a very distinctive area for expertise and specialization." M. Gowen, *A Guide for Legal Assistants* 229 (Practicing Law Institute, 1986).

11. Contract Law

The law of contracts is involved in a number of different paralegal specialties. (See also *advertising law, antitrust law, banking law, bankruptcy law, collections law, construction law, corporate law, employee benefits law, entertainment law, family law, government contract law, insurance law, intellectual property law, international law, labor and employment law, landlord-tenant law, municipal finance law, oil and gas law, real estate law,* and *tax law.*)

I. Contract Review

A. Review contracts to determine compliance with terms.

B. Investigate facts involving alleged breach of contract.

C. Do legal research on the law of contracts in a particular specialty.

II. Litigation Assistance

III. Preparation of Contract Forms

A. Separation agreements,

B. Employment contracts,

C. Contracts for sale, etc.

■ *Comment on Paralegal Work in this Area:*

"The . . . paralegal also assists two attorneys in drafting reviewing, researching, revising and finalizing a variety of contracts, including Entertainment, Participant and Operational Agreements. Much of the . . . paralegal's time is spent studying existing contracts looking for provisions that may answer any inquiries or disputes. With hundreds of agreements presently active, researching, reviewing, amending, terminating, revising and executing contracts is an everyday activity for [the] . . . Legal Department." Miquel, *Walt Disney World Company's Legal Assistants: Their Role in the Show,* 16 Facts and Findings 29, 30 (NALA, January 1990).

"Initially, my primary job was to review contracts, and act as Plan Administrator for the 401(k). I was also involved in the negotiation and development of a distributor agreement to market SPSS software to the Soviet Union. Most contract amendments were to software license agreements. The pace picked up when I was promoted to Manager of Human Services, while retaining all of my previous responsibilities." Illinois Paralegal Ass'n, *Spotlight on . . . Laurel Bauer,* 20 Outlook 21 (Winter 1991).

12. Corporate Law

Paralegals involved in corporate law mainly work in one of two settings: law firms that represent corporations, and legal departments of corporations. Corporate legal departments often are run by an attorney called the general counsel. (See also *banking law, employee benefits law, insurance law, labor and employment law, real estate law,* and *tax law.*)

I. Incorporation and General Corporate Work

A. Preincorporation.

   1. Check availability of proposed corporate name and, if available, reserve it.

   2. Draft preincorporation subscriptions and consent forms for initial board of directors where required by statute.

   3. Record articles of incorporation.

   4. Order corporate supplies.

B. Incorporation.

   1. Draft and file articles of incorporation with appropriate state agency.

      a. Subchapter S corporation,

      b. Close corporation,

      c. Nonprofit corporation.

   2. Draft minutes of initial meetings of incorporators and directors.

3. Draft corporate bylaws.

4. Obtain corporate seal, minute book, and stock certificate book.

5. Prepare necessary documents to open a corporate bank account.

C. Directors meetings.

1. Prepare and send out waivers and notices of meetings.

2. Draft minutes of directors meetings.

3. Draft resolutions to be considered by directors:

   a. Sale of stock,

   b. Increase in capitalization,

   c. Stock splits,

   d. Stock option,

   e. Pension plan,

   f. Dividend distribution,

   g. Election of officers.

D. Shareholders meetings (annual and special).

1. Draft sections of annual report relating to business activity, officers, and directors of company.

2. Draft notice of meeting, proxy materials, and ballots.

3. Prepare agenda and script of meeting.

4. Draft oath and report of judge of elections when required.

5. Maintain all of the corporate minute books and resolutions.

E. Draft and prepare general documents:

1. Shareholder agreement,

2. Employment contract,

3. Employee benefit plan,

4. Stock option plan,

5. Trust agreement,

6. Tax return,

7. Closing papers on corporate acquisition.

8. See also drafting tasks listed above in reference to directors and shareholders meetings.

II. Public Sale of Securities

A. Compile information concerning officers and directors for use in Registration Statement.

B. Assist in research of blue sky requirements.

C. Closing:

1. Prepare agenda,

2. Obtain certificates from state agencies with respect to good standing of company and certified corporate documents,

3. Prepare index and organize closing binders.

III. Research

A. Legislative reporting: keep track of pending legislation that may affect office clients.

B. Extract designated information from corporate records and documents.

C. Assemble financial data from records on file at SEC and state securities regulatory agencies.

D. Undertake short- and long-term statistical and financial research on companies.

E. Perform legal research.

IV. General Assistance

A. Maintain tickler system (specifying, for example, next corporate meeting, upcoming trial, appellate court dates, etc.).

B. Monitor the daily law journal or newspaper in order to identify certain cases on calendars of courts, current court decisions, articles, etc. and forward such data in the journal or newspaper to appropriate office attorneys.

C. Act as file managers for certain clients (index, digest, and monitor documents in the file; prepare case profiles; etc.).

D. Maintain corporate forms file.

V. Miscellaneous

A. Prepare documents for qualification to do business in foreign jurisdictions.

B. Prepare filings with regulatory agencies.

C. Assist in processing patent, copyright, and trademark applications.

D. Coordinate escrow transactions.

E. Work on certificates of occupancy.

F. Prepare documents needed to amend bylaws or articles of incorporation.

G. Prepare interrogatories.

H. Digest deposition testimony.

I. Perform cite checks.

■ *Comment on Paralegal Work in this Area:*

"When the majority of people describe a legal assistant or a paralegal, they often think of courtroom battles, million dollar lawsuits and mountains of depositions. For those of us in the corporate area, these sights are replaced with board room battles, million dollar mergers and mountains of prospectus. Some of us have NEVER seen the inside of a courtroom or have never touched a pleading. I guess it can be said that 'we don't do windows, we don't type, and we don't do litigation.' A corporate paralegal is never without a multitude of projects that offer excitement or anxiety. This isn't to say, however, that the corporate field is without its fair share of boredom. . . . The future is only limited by your imagination. Not every paralegal wants the drama of a landmark case. Some of us are quite content seeing a client's company written up in the *Wall Street Journal* for the first time!" D. Zupanovich, *The Forming of a Corporate Paralegal*, 2 California Paralegal 4 (July/September 1990).

"The company I work for is a major worldwide producer of chemicals. . . . I recently had to obtain some technical information about the computer system at a hotel in a foreign country in order to set up documents on a diskette that would be compatible with the computer system in that country before one of the attorneys went there for contract negotiations. . . . One of the most thrilling experiences I have had since working for the company was that of working on the closing of a leveraged buyout of a portion of our business in Delaware. To experience first-hand the intensity of the negotiating table, the numerous last-minute changes to documents, the multitudinous shuffle of papers, and the late, grueling hours was both exhausting and exhilarating." Grove, *Scenes from a Corporate Law Department,* The Paraview 2 (Metrolina Paralegal Ass'n, February 1990).

"Even 'dream jobs' have their moments of chaos. After only two months on the job [at Nestle Foods Corporation] Cheryl had to prepare for a Federal Trade Commission Second Request for Production of Documents relating to an acquisition. She suddenly was thrown into the job of obtaining and organizing over 6,000 documents from around the world, creating a document database and managing up to 10 temporary paralegals at a time. Of course, this preparation included weekends and evenings for a six-week period. Cheryl calls December the 'lost month.' " Scior, *Paralegal Profile: Corporate Paralegal,* Post Script 14 (Manhattan Paralegal Ass'n, April/May 1990).

- ■ *Quotes from Want Ads:*

Law firm seeks paralegal for corporate work: "Ideal candidate is a self-starter with good communications skills and is willing to work overtime." "Ability to work independently is a must." Paralegal needed to assist corporate secretary: "Analytical, professional attitude essential. Knowledge of state and/or federal regulatory agencies required." "Ability to work under pressure." "All candidates must possess excellent writing and drafting skills." "Ideal candidate is a self-starter with good communication/research skills and is willing to work overtime." "Candidate having less than three years experience in general corporate legal assistance need not apply." Position requires "word processing experience and ability to manage multiple projects." Position requires "intelligent, highly motivated individual who can work with little supervision." "Great opportunity to learn all aspects of corporate business transactions." Position requires "career-minded paralegal with excellent organizational and communications skills, keen analytical ability and meticulous attention to detail." Position

requires "an experienced paralegal with a strong blue-sky background particularly in public and private real estate syndication." Applicant must have "excellent academic credentials, be analytical, objective, and dedicated to performing thorough quality work and to displaying a professional attitude to do whatever it takes to get the job done and meet deadlines."

13. Criminal Law[9]

(See also *litigation* and *military law.*)

I. Paralegal Working for Criminal/Civil Division Prosecutor

A. Log incoming cases.

B. Help office screen out cases that are inappropriate for arrest, cases that are eligible for diversion, etc.

C. Act as liaison with police department and other law enforcement agencies.

D. Prepare periodic, statistical, caseload reports.

E. Interview citizens seeking the prosecution of alleged wrongdoers; prepare case files.

F. Help the Consumer Fraud Department resolve minor consumer complaints—for instance, contact the business involved to determine whether a settlement of the case is possible without prosecution.

G. Conduct field investigations as assigned.

H. Prepare documents for URESA cases (Uniform Reciprocal Enforcement of Support Act).

I. Monitor status of URESA cases.

J. Help office maintain its case calendar.

K. Act as liaison among the prosecutor, the victim, and witnesses while the case is being prepared for trial and during the trial.

L. Act as general litigation assistant during the trial and the appeal.

II. Paralegal Working for Defense Attorney

A. Interview defendants to determine eligibility for free legal defense (if the paralegal works for a public defender).

B. Conduct comprehensive interview of defendant on matters relevant to the criminal charge(s).

C. Help the defendant gather information relevant to the determination of bail.

---

[9]See J. Stein & B. Hoff, *Paralegals and Administrative Assistants for Prosecutors* (Nat'l District Attorneys Ass'n, 1974); and J. Stein, *Paralegals: A Resource for Defenders and Correctional Services* (1976).

D. Help the defendant gather information relevant to eligibility for diversion programs.

E. Conduct field investigations as assigned; interview witnesses.

F. Help obtain discovery, particularly through police reports and search warrants.

G. Act as general litigation assistant during the trial and the appeal.

■ *Comment on Paralegal Work in this Area:*

"Ivy speaks with an obvious love for her current job in the State Attorney's office. In fact, she said she would not want to do anything else! She also said there is no such thing as a typical day in her office, which is one of the many aspects of her job she enjoys. She not only helps interview witnesses and prepare them for trial, but she often must locate a witness, requiring some detective work! Ivy assisted in a case involving an elderly woman who was victimized after the death of her husband. The woman was especially vulnerable because of her illiteracy. Through the help of the State Attorney's office, the woman was able to recover her money and get assistance with housing and learning to read. Ivy continues to keep in touch with the woman and feels the experience to be very rewarding." Frazier, *Spotlight on Ivy Hart-Daniel,* JLA News 2 (Jacksonville Legal Assistants, Inc., January 1989).

"Kitty Polito says she and other lawyers at McClure, McClure & Kammen use the firm's sole paralegal not only to do investigations but 'to pick cases apart piece by piece.' Polito credits legal assistant Juliann Klapp with 'cracking the case' of a client who was accused by a co-defendant of hitting the victim on the back of the head. At trial, the pathologist testified that the victim had been hit from left to right. Klapp passed a note to the attorneys pointing out that such a motion would have been a back-handed swing for their right-handed client. Thus it was more likely that the co-defendant, who is left-handed, was the one who hit the victim. The defendant won." Brandt, *Paralegals' Acceptance and Utilization Increasing in Indy's Legal Community,* 1 The Indiana Lawyer 1 (June 20, 1990).

14. Employee Benefits Law[10]

Employee benefits paralegals work in a number of different settings: in law firms, banks, large corporations, insurance companies, or accounting firms. The following overview of tasks covers a paralegal working for a law firm. (See also *contract law, corporate law, labor and employment law, social security law,* and *worker's compensation law.*)

---

[10]Rocky Mountain Legal Assistants Association, *The Use of the Legal Assistant* (1975).

I. Drafting of Employee Plans

A. Work closely with the attorney, the plan sponsor, the plan administrator, and the trustee in preparing and drafting qualified employee plans, such as:
   1. Stock bonus plans,
   2. Profit sharing plans,
   3. Money purchase pensions,
   4. Other pension plans,
   5. Trust agreements,
   6. Individual Retirement Account (IRA) plans,
   7. Annuity plans,
   8. HR-10 or Keogh plans,
   9. Employee stock ownership plans,
   10. Life and health insurance plans,
   11. Worker's compensation plans,
   12. Social security plans.

II. Document Preparation and Program Monitoring

A. Gather information.
B. Determine eligibility for participation and benefits.
C. Notify employees of participation.
D. Complete input forms for document assembly.
E. Assemble elections to participate.
F. Determine beneficiary designations.
G. Record elections to contribute.
H. Allocate annual contributions to individual participant accounts.
I. Prepare annual account statements for participants.
J. Identify any potential discrimination problems in the program.

III. Government Compliance Work Pertaining To:

A. Tax requirements for qualifications, amendment, and termination of plan.
B. Department of Labor reporting and disclosure requirements.
C. Insurance requirements.
D. Welfare and Pension Plans Disclosure Act requirements.
E. ERISA requirements (Employee Retirement Income Security Act).
F. Pension Benefit Guaranty Corporation requirements.

IV. Miscellaneous

A. Help draft summary plan descriptions for distribution to employees.
B. Help prepare and review annual reports of plans.

C. Continue education in current law of the field—for instance, become a Certified Employee Benefit Specialist (CEBS).

■ *Comment on Paralegal Work in this Area:*

"Michael Montchyk was looking to use his undergraduate degree in statistics. . . . He now works for attorneys specializing in employee benefits, where understanding numbers and familiarity with the law are key skills." Lehren, *Paralegal Work Enhancing Careers of Many,* Philadelphia Business Journal 9B (August 6, 1990).

"This area is not for everybody. To succeed, you need considerable detail orientation, solid writing skills, self-motivation, the ability to keep up with a legal landscape that is never the same, and a knack for handling crisis situations which arise when least expected." Germani, *Opportunities in Employee Benefits,* SJPA Reporter 7 (South Jersey Paralegal Ass'n, January 1989).

15. Entertainment Law

(See also *contract law, corporate law,* and *intellectual property law.*)

I. Types of Client Problem Areas

A. *Copyright and trademark law:* Applying for government protection for intellectual property, such as plays, films, video, music, and novels.

B. *Contract law:* Help negotiate and draft contracts, and ensure their enforcement.

C. *Labor law:* Assist in compliance with the contracts of unions or guilds.

D. *Corporate law:*
   1. Assist in formation of business organizations.
   2. Work on mergers.
   3. Maintain compliance with federal and state reporting laws and regulations.

E. *Tax law:* planning and compliance.
   1. Report passive royalty income, talent advances, residuals, etc.
   2. Allocate expenditures to specific projects.

F. *Family law:* Assist with prenuptial agreements, divorces, child custody, etc.

II. Tasks

A. Register copyrights.

B. Help a client affiliate with his or her guild.

C. Monitor remake and sequel rights to films.

D. Prepare documents to grant a license to use client's music.

E. Check title registrations with the Motion Picture Association of America.

F. Read scripts to determine whether clearances are needed for certain kinds of material and references.

G. Apply for permits and licenses.

H. Calculate costs of property rights.

■ *Comment on Paralegal Work in this Area:*

"I am a paralegal in the field of entertainment law, one of the fastest growing, and, to me, most exciting areas of the paralegal profession, and one whose duties are as varied as the practices of the lawyers for whom we work. . . . I started in a very large Century City firm whose entertainment practice covers everything from songwriters to financing of major motion pictures, and from major recording stars and producers to popular novelists. . . . My specialty (yes, a specialty within a specialty) is music. . . . My husband is also an entertainment paralegal who works for 20th Century Fox. . . . Never, ever a dull moment!" Birkner, *Entertainment Law: A Growing Industry for the Paralegal,* 2 California Paralegal Magazine 7 (April/June 1990).

16. Environmental Law[11]

(See also *legislation, litigation, oil and gas law, real estate law,* and *water law.*)

I. Research

A. Research questions pertaining to the environment, land use, water pollution, and the National Environmental Policy Act.
   1. Locate and study pertinent state and federal statutes, case law, regulations, and law review articles.
   2. Obtain secondary materials (maps, articles, books) useful for broadening the information base.
   3. Contact, when appropriate, government officials or other informants for data or answers.
   4. Obtain and develop personality profiles of members of Congress, members of relevant bureaucracies, and other political figures.
   5. Help prepare memoranda of findings, including citations and supporting documents.

B. Develop research notebooks for future reference. When new topics arise in environmental law, prepare notebooks to facilitate future research on similar topics.

C. Prepare bibliographies on environmental topics.

II. Drafting

A. Draft memoranda regarding new federal and state laws, regulations, or findings of research.

---

[11]Colorado Bar Association Legal Assistant Committee. These tasks have been approved by the Committee, not by the Board of Governors of the Colorado Bar.

B. Draft memoranda discussing pertinent issues, problems, and possible solutions regarding public policy developments.

C. Draft narrative histories of legislation regarding political impulses, the impact of administrative and court rulings, and substantive and technical differences between drafts of legislation or results of amendments.

D. Draft and edit articles on coastal management programs and problems, conservation, water pollution, and the National Environmental Policy Act.

E. Edit environmental impact statements.

F. Assist in the preparation of briefs.

   1. Check citations for pertinence and accuracy.

   2. Develop table of contents, list of authorities, and certificate of service.

III. Hearing Participation

A. Locate and schedule witnesses.

B. Gather pertinent research materials (including necessary local documents, maps, and specific subject matter).

IV. Litigation: Provide General Trial Assistance

■ *Comment on Paralegal Work in this Area:*

Mary Peterson's firm has made a specialty of environmental and land use law. In a recent major hazardous waste case, "we will try to prove that the paint companies, dry cleaning stores and even the federal government, which used the property to build aircraft during the war" are responsible. "Some of the toxic waste dumped there were cited by federal agencies even back to 1935." Her job is to investigate the types of hazardous wastes and, with the help of the Freedom of Information Act, gather all available evidence. Then she studies it, duplicates, indexes, and writes summaries, which she distributes to the partners and associates. It's a case that has taken eight months so far and may go on for several years "because you don't know what you will uncover tomorrow. The toxins and pollutants could be different. There is no standard, just a constantly changing picture." Edwards, *The General Practice Paralegal* 8 Legal Assistant Today 49, 55 (March/April 1991).

17. Estates, Trusts, and Probate Law

(See also *banking law, collections law, employee benefits law, family law,* and *social security law.*)

I. Estate Planning

A. Collect data (birth dates, fair market value of assets, current assets and liabilities, etc.).

B. Prepare preliminary drafts of wills or trusts from sample forms.

C. Perform investment analysis in order to provide attorney who is fiduciary of estate with information relevant to investment options.

II. Office Management

A. Maintain tickler system.

B. Maintain attorney's calendar.

C. Open, index, monitor, and keep current all components of the client's trust and estate office file.

D. Operate computer in connection with accounting aspects of trusts and estates administered by the office.

E. Act as office law librarian (keeping loose-leaf texts up-to-date, etc.).

F. Train secretaries and other paralegals in the system used by the office to handle trusts, estates, and probate cases.

G. Selectively discard certain mail and underline significant parts of other mail.

III. Estate of Decedent

A. Assets phase.

   1. Collect assets (such as bank accounts, custody accounts, insurance proceeds, social security death benefits, safety deposit box contents, and apartment contents).

   2. Assist in the valuation of assets.

   3. Maintain records (for example, record and file wills and trusts, vault inventories, powers of attorney, property settlements, fee cards, bill-payment letters).

   4. Notify beneficiaries.

   5. Prepare profiles of wills and trusts for attorney review.

B. Accounting phase.

   1. Prepare preliminary drafts of federal and state death tax returns.

   2. Apply the income-principal rules to the estate.

   3. Organize data relevant to the tax implications of estates.

   4. Prepare accountings: final and accounts current (this involves setting up a petition for a first and final accounting).

C. Termination-distribution phase.

   1. Apply for the transfer of securities into the names of the people entitled.

   2. Draw checks for the signature of executors.

   3. Monitor legacies to charitable clients.

   4. File and prepare tax waivers.

5. Assist with the closing documents.
6. Calculate distributable net income.
7. Follow up on collection and delivery.

IV. Litigation

1. Perform legal research.
2. Conduct factual research (investigation)—for instance, track down the names and addresses of all possible claimants and contact them.
3. Prepare sample pleadings.
4. Digest depositions (review, condense, point out inconsistencies, etc.).
5. Prepare drafts of interrogatories.
6. Prepare drafts of answers to interrogatories.
7. Notarize documents.
8. Act as court witness as to decedent's signature and other matters.
9. Assist with litigation.

■ *Comment on Paralegal Work in this Area:*

"What I like best about estate planning is that you work with people on a very individual basis. I don't think that in many other areas of law you get that one-on-one contact with the client. . . . You're working with people while they are thinking about the most important things in their lives—their families, their wealth and how to distribute it, and what they want to happen after they pass on. A lot of the clients contact me directly with their questions for the attorneys. Some of the widows especially are more comfortable calling me with their questions. They seem to think their questions might be 'stupid' and they're embarrassed to ask the attorneys directly. I can take their questions and see that the attorneys respond to them promptly." Bassett, *Top Gun Patricia Adams: Legal Assistant of the Year,* 6 Legal Assistant Today 70, 74 (July/August 1990).

"The position can be very stressful. But it is seldom boring. My typical day involves responding to many telephone inquiries from clients, dictating memos or letters requesting additional information concerning life insurance policies, valuation of assets, or simply sending notice of an upcoming hearing "to all persons entitled," etc. I draft virtually all documents needed in the administration of an estate, beginning with the initial petition for probate. . . . The decedent may have had an interest in a closely-held business, or leave minor or handicapped children, or leave a spouse with no knowledge of the family assets; these all require additional attention. Every case is different. Probate paralegals to some extent must be 'snoopy,' because you do learn a great deal about people, both deceased and living. In most cases your client is facing a difficult time with trepidation and it is your role to provide confidence. The end results are very rewarding." Rose, *Still a Probate Paralegal,* 12 The Journal 5 (Sacramento Ass'n of Legal Assistants, August 1990).

■ *Quotes from Want Ads:*

Law firm seeks someone with "good communication and organizational skills, [who] is self-motivated, relates well with attorneys, clients, and staff, is detail oriented, has a teamwork attitude, a pleasant personality, and is a non-smoker." Bank has opening for "trust tax administrator, with emphasis on personal and trust planning." Paralegal must have "technical understanding of wills and estate plans and terminology. Must be self-starter." "This is a full-time position with extensive responsibility for both court-supervised and noncourt-supervised estates and trusts." Position requires a person who "enjoys writing and proofreading, and who has excellent grammatical skills." Job is "for individual who enjoys the complexity and detail of accounting and bookkeeping in a legal environment." "Applicants must be prepared to handle tax work."

18. Ethics and Professional Responsibility

Paralegals in this area work in two main settings: (1) in large law firms as a conflicts specialist, helping the firm determine whether conflicts of interest exist and (2) in state disciplinary agencies that investigate complaints against attorneys for unethical behavior.

I. Law Firm (*Conflicts Specialist* or *Conflicts Manager*)

A. Research
   1. Identify all persons or companies related to the prospective client.
   2. Determine whether the firm has ever represented the prospective client and/or any of its related parties.
   3. Determine whether the firm has ever represented an opponent of the prospective client and/or any of its related parties.

B. *Reports:* Notify attorney in charge of professional-responsibility matters of data indicating possible conflicts.

C. *Database work:* update information in client-list database on current and past clients.

II. Disciplinary Agency

A. Screen incoming data on new ethical complaints against attorneys.

B. Help investigate complaints.

C. Provide general litigation assistance to disciplinary attorneys during the proceedings at the agency and in court.

■ *Comment on Paralegal Work in this Area:*

Jane Palmer "does all the research on every prospective client, identifying all the related parties." Her computerized database tells her if the firm has ever represented a party on either side, or been adverse to them. "The most valuable thing has been my experience with the firm, developing somewhat of a corporate memory. The job takes extreme attention to detail. You may not always have all the information you need, so you have to be a detective. Quick response is important; so is making sure to keep things confidential." Sacramento Ass'n of Legal Assistants, *New Responsibilities Given to Paralegals*, The Journal 5 (February 1991).

19. Family Law[12]

(See also *contract law, employee benefits law, estates law, litigation, pro bono work,* and *public sector.*)

I. Telephone Screening of Clients

II. Commencement of Action

A. Interview client to obtain initial information for pleadings.

B. Prepare initial pleadings, including petition, summons and waiver of service, affidavit as to children, and response.

C. Draft correspondence to clients, courts, and other attorneys.

D. Arrange for service of process.

III. Temporary Orders

A. Prepare motions for temporary orders or temporary injunctions.

B. Draft notice and set hearings.

C. Assist in settlement negotiations.

D. Draft stipulations for temporary orders after negotiations.

IV. Financial Affidavits

A. Work with clients to gather and compile financial information.

B. Analyze income and expense information provided by client.

C. Work with accountants, financial advisors, brokers, and other financial experts retained by client.

D. Retain appraisers for real estate, business, and personal property.

E. Prepare financial affidavits.

V. Discovery

A. Prepare discovery requests.

B. Assist clients—gather documents and data to respond to discovery requests.

C. Help prepare responses to discovery requests.

D. Organize, index, and summarize discovered materials.

VI. Settlement Negotiations

A. Assist attorney in analysis of proposed settlements.

B. Research legal questions and assist in drafting briefs and memoranda.

C. Assist in drafting separation agreements.

VII. Hearings

A. Help prepare for final orders hearings.

B. Research legal questions and assist in drafting briefs and memoranda.

C. Assist in the preparation of trial exhibits and trial notebooks.

D. Arrange for expert witnesses and assist in preparing witnesses and clients for trial.

E. Attend hearings.

F. Prepare decree.

VIII. Post-Decree

A. Prepare documents for transfers of assets.

B. Arrange for the filing and recording of all transfer documents.

C. Review bills for tax-deductible fees and help prepare opinion letters to client.

D. Draft pleadings for withdrawal from case.

IX. Special Projects

A. Develop forms for gathering information from client.

B. Maintain files on the following: separation-agreement provisions, current case law, resource materials for clients, and experts in various fields (e.g., custody, evaluation, and business appraisals).

■ *Comment on Paralegal Work in this Area:*

Karen Dunn, a family law paralegal, "draws considerable satisfaction from a divorce case where the client was a woman in her sixties whose husband had left her, a situation which created predictable distress, notably during discussion of financial aspects. She was able to tell me things she couldn't tell the attorney. I found out she had a thyroid condition, so she was able to get more money in the end. I worked with her on the financial affidavit and drafted temporary orders to provide child support and spousal maintenance until the decree was entered." Edwards, *The General Practice Paralegal* 8 Legal Assistant Today 49, 54 (March/April 1991).

"As the only paralegal in a one-attorney family law practice, my job responsibilities are numerous. I work for an attorney who believes her paralegal should handle nearly all the legal functions she does, with the exception

---

[12]See footnote 11.

of appearing in court on behalf of clients, taking depositions and giving legal advice. My skills are used to the maximum, as I gather and organize all case information, allowing the attorney to prepare for court and be more cost-effective. I am the liaison person between clients and the attorney. I am able to deal with the human, emotional aspects of our clients, and not just the technical aspects of the law. As each person is different, so is every case, which makes this job a continuing challenge." Lenihan, *Role of the Family Law Paralegal*, 10 Paragraph 6 (Oregon Legal Assistants Ass'n, August 1987).

■ *Quotes from Want Ads:*

Position is "excellent for a highly motivated person with excellent organizational skills and the ability to interface with clients." "Two swamped attorneys need reliable paralegal to work in fully computerized office. Must have excellent research and writing skills." Applicant must be "self-motivated, well-organized person who has initiative and can assume responsibility." Position requires "ability, experience, and attention to detail." "Looking for very professional applicants."

20. Government Contract Law[13]

(See also *administrative law, construction law, contract law, litigation,* and *water law.*)

I. Calendar

A. Maintain calendar for court and appeals board appearances.
B. Record dates briefs are due, etc.

II. Claims

A. Gather, review, summarize, and index client files.
B. Assist in drafting contract claims.
C. Conduct preliminary research on selected legal issues.

III. Appeals

A. Draft and answer interrogatories and requests for production of documents.
B. Summarize and index answers to discovery.
C. Assist in drafting appeal.
D. Prepare questions for witnesses and summarize prior testimony.
E. Maintain documents during hearing.

IV. Post-Hearing Briefs

A. Summarize and index transcripts.
B. Assist with analysis of government's brief.

C. Conduct preliminary research on selected issues.
D. Assist in drafting the post-hearing brief.

21. Immigration Law

(See also *administrative law, family law, international law, labor and employment law,* and *public sector.*)

I. Problem Identification

A. Help individual who has difficulty in obtaining:
  1. Visa,
  2. Permanent residency based on occupation,
  3. Nonimmigrant status,
  4. Citizenship status.
B. Help individuals who are faced with deportation proceedings.

II. Providing Information on

A. Visa process,
B. Permanent residency process,
C. Nonimmigrant status process,
D. Registration process,
E. Citizenship process,
F. Deportation process.

III. Investigation

Assist the individual in obtaining data and documentation on birth, travel, residency, etc.

IV. Referral

Refer individuals to foreign consulates, nationality organizations, government officials, etc., for assistance concerning their immigration status.

V. Applications/Forms

Assist the individual in filling out visa applications, permanent residency applications, etc.

VI. Monitor Consular Processing Procedure

■ *Comment on Paralegal Work in this Area:*

"This is not a specialty for the faint-hearted or the misanthrope. The immigration paralegal may deal with much more than the timely filing of paperwork. One distinguishing feature of immigration work is our knowledge of intensely personal aspects of the client's life. We know his criminal record, the success and failure of his personal life, how much money he makes, and his dreams and aspirations. . . . Some clients have a very laissez-faire attitude towards perjury, and may invite the paralegal to participate without a blush. In America, [said one client] you lie *to* your attorney. In my country, you cook up the lie *with* your attorney." Myers & Raman, *Sweet-Talking Clients and Intransigent Bureaucrats,* 15 National Paralegal Reporter 4 (NFPA, Winter 1991).

[13]Berg, C. *Annual Survey* (San Francisco Association of Legal Assistants, Dec. 19, 1973).

22. Insurance Law

Paralegals in this area work for law firms that represent insurance companies who are defendants in litigation, often personal injury litigation. They also work for insurance companies themselves. The following overview covers the latter. (See also *corporate law, employee benefits law, litigation, social security law,* and *worker's compensation law.*)

I. Compliance

A. Analyze government regulations on the insurance industry.

B. Prepare applications for new insurance products to obtain approval from Department of Insurance.

II. Claims

A. Assist in processing disputed claims.

B. Provide trial assistance by coordinating activities of company attorneys with outside counsel representing the company.

III. Monitoring and Research

A. Monitor regulations of agencies and statutes of the legislatures that affect the insurance industry, including the committees of the legislature with jurisdiction over the industry.

B. Provide factual and legal research on inquiries that come into the office from agents and brokers.

■ *Comment on Paralegal Work in this Area:*

"Compliance is an insurance industry term which refers to keeping the company and its products in compliance with state and federal law, and procuring licenses for the company in unlicensed states. Compliance is a good field for paralegals because there is opportunity to work autonomously and also to advance within most companies." [I am a] Senior Compliance Analyst [at a life insurance company]. I have met many paralegals who are compliance analysts, compliance specialists, and compliance managers." Maston, *Insurance,* The Citator 8 (Legal Assistants of Central Ohio, August 1990).

23. Intellectual Property Law

(See also *contract law* and *entertainment law.*)

I. Copyrights

A. Application

1. Help client apply for registration of copyright for a novel, play, or other work with the Copyright Office.

2. Collect data, such as nature of the work, date completed, name of creator/author, name of owner of the work, etc., for application.

3. Help identify the classification for the copyright.

4. Examine the certificate of copyright registration for accuracy.

5. File the application.

B. Marketing

1. Identify potential users/licensees of the copyright.

2. Help prepare contracts.

C. Infringement

1. Conduct investigations to determine whether an infringement exists—for example, compare the copyrighted work with the alleged infringing work.

2. Provide general litigation assistance.

II. Patent

A. Application

1. Help the inventor apply for a patent with the U.S. Patent and Trademark Office.

2. Help the inventor describe the invention—for example, assemble designs, diagrams, and notebooks.

3. Conduct a patent search. Check technical libraries to determine the current state of the art.

4. Determine filing fees.

5. Help the client apply for protection in foreign countries.

6. Monitor the responses from government offices.

7. Examine certificate of patent for accuracy.

B. Marketing the invention

1. Help identify licensees. Solicit bids, conduct financial checks, study the market, etc.

2. Help prepare contracts.

C. Infringement

1. Conduct investigation on products that may have violated the patent.

2. Provide general litigation assistance.

III. Trademarks

A. Registration

1. Research trademark files or order search of trademark or trade name preliminary to an application before the U.S. Patent and Trademark Office.

2. Examine indexes and directories.

3. Conduct investigations to determine when the mark was first used, where, on what products, etc.

4. Prepare foreign trademark applications.

5. Respond to official actions taken by government offices.

6. Examine the certificate of trademark for accuracy.

7. Maintain files for renewals.

B. Infringement

1. Conduct investigations into who else used the mark when, where, in what market, etc.

2. Provide general litigation assistance.

■ *Comment on Paralegal Work in this Area:*

"With the right training, trademark paralegals can find richly rewarding experiences waiting for them, whether they remain in paralegal work or go on to build careers in some other facet of trademark law. Trademark work is very dynamic." Wilkinson, *The Case for a Career in Trademark Law,* 7 Legal Professional 29 (November/December 1989).

"Paula Rein was a trademark paralegal before such a job title was even invented. Her career has spanned over 19 years, leading her to some of the biggest corporations and law firms in New York City. Her extensive knowledge of trademark administration has made her one of the most resourceful trademark paralegals in her occupation. In her current 'diversified position,' at a law firm that specializes in intellectual property, she works on the cases of clients in the food and service industries and professional associations. Paula thrives in her current position." Scior, *Paralegal Profile,* Postscript 13 (Manhattan Paralegal Ass'n, December 1989).

24. International Law

Example: a paralegal working on a "dumping" case in international trade.

I. Investigation

A. Examine the normal behavior in the industry/market affected.

B. Do statistical research (cost and price data).

C. Prepare profiles of domestic competitors.

II. Preparation of Documents

A. Help prepare for presentation before the Commerce Department.

B. Help prepare for presentation before the Court of International Trade.

III. Accounting Research

IV. Coordination of Data From:

A. Members of Congress,

B. Foreign embassies,

C. State Department,

D. U.S. Special Trade Representative.

■ *Comment on Paralegal Work in this Area:*

Steven Stark works "40–50 hours a week, specializing in international legal assisting, a hot area, while the Japanese are busy buying up American properties. [Steve became the liaison for the firm's Tokyo branch office. He originally expected to stay at the firm only three years, but found that] the longer you're here, the more they value you. New things still come up. You work with the constant tension of everyone being expected to perform at a very high level, at all times. This is a high-stakes game, with million and billion dollar deals. It's a peaked, emotional atmosphere, with long hours." Milano, *Career Profiles,* 8 Legal Assistant Today 35, 38 (September/October 1990).

25. Judicial Administration

Most courts have clerks to help with the administrative aspects of deciding cases. In addition, a few courts have paralegals that work for the court. They perform some of the functions of the administrative clerks, such as determining whether the parties have been properly notified of trial dates, checking filings and proposed orders from attorneys to determine whether anything appears inappropriate or premature, or obtaining additional information for a judge.

■ *Comment on Paralegal Work in this Area:*

"The Shreveport City Court has employed me as its paralegal in the civil department for the past six years. The Baton Rouge City Court employs several paralegals." We handle many matters such as determining if the legal delays for pleading have expired "before initialing the pleading and passing it on to the clerk or judge for signature. The most important task is the handling of default judgments. I must certify that proper service has been made. Perhaps I could be called a 'nitpicker' about these cases, but the judge acts on my certificate that everything is in order. It is always challenging to stay informed on our constantly changing procedural laws; I must keep a set of the Civil Procedure at my desk." Waterman, *The Court's Paralegal,* 3 NWLPA News 5 (Northwest Louisiana Paralegal Ass'n, November 1990).

26. Labor and Employment Law

(See also *civil rights law, contract law, employee benefits law,* and *worker's compensation law.*)

I. Investigation

Look into:

A. Sexual harassment.

B. Wrongful discharge.

C. Violation of occupational safety and health laws.

D. Violation of labor laws involving collective bargaining, union organization, grievance and arbitration procedures.

E. Violation of Civil Rights Act protecting against discrimination on the basis of race, national origin, sex, or physical handicap.

F. Violation of Age Discrimination in Employment Act.

G. Violation of Americans with Disabilities Act.

II. Compliance

Assist companies in the design and implementation of policies on:

A. Drug and alcohol testing.

B. AIDS in the workplace.

C. Race, sex, and age discrimination.

III. Litigation Assistance

A. Help handle labor disputes before the National Labor Relations Board, State Labor Relations Board, Civil Service Commission, Human Rights Board, and the courts.

B. Perform a variety of tasks:

1. Maintain the files.
2. Digest and index data in files.
3. Arrange for depositions.
4. Help draft petition and other pleadings.
5. Maintain tickler system of due dates.
6. Prepare exhibits.
7. Prepare statistical data.
8. Help prepare appeal.

■ *Comment on Paralegal Work in this Area:*

"My experience in the labor and employment area has proven to be both diverse and unique. It is diverse because of the various labor-related issues accessible to me as a paralegal. It is unique because it is an area of specialty which involves very few paralegals in my part of the state." Batke, *Labor and Employment Paralegal,* The Citator 3 (Legal Assistants of Central Ohio, August 1990).

"In the labor law area, I was responsible for doing background research, preparing witnesses and drafting arbitration briefs. I also assisted with the drafting of revised language during contract negotiations with unions." Diebold, *A Paralegal of Another Kind,* 16 Facts and Findings 38 (NALA, March 1990).

27. Landlord and Tenant Law

Paralegals in real estate law firms occasionally become involved in commercial lease cases, such as a dispute over the interpretation of the lease of a supermarket at a large shopping mall. Such landlord-tenant cases, however, are not as common as the cases that arise between landlords and tenants who live in the apartments they rent. For example, a landlord of a small apartment seeks to evict a tenant for nonpayment of rent. Many of these cases are handled by publicly funded legal service or legal aid offices which do not charge fees. (See *public sector, oil and gas law,* and *real estate law.*)

■ *Comment on Paralegal Work in this Area:*

"The Legal Action Center is the largest nongovernmental social service agency in the state. As a paralegal, Virginia Farley handles all eviction calls to the landlord-tenant unit. Three afternoons a week are designated intake times. She screens all eviction cases, determines whether the applicant is eligible for free assistance according to the Center's guidelines, recommends a plan once a case is accepted and assists in carrying out the plan under an attorney's supervision. [After arriving in the city], Virginia made a commitment to work directly with the poor and started serving as a volunteer in five organizations until a job opened up for her at the Legal Action Center." Roche, *Paralegal Profile,* 4 Findings and Conclusions 5 (Washington Ass'n of Legal Assistants, November 1987).

28. Law Librarianship

There is a separate degree that a law librarian can obtain. This degree, however, is not a requirement to be a law librarian. There are a number of small or medium-sized law offices that are hiring paralegals to perform library chores exclusively or in combination with paralegal duties on cases. (See also *law office administration* and *litigation.*)

I. Administration

A. Order books for law library.

B. File loose-leaf material and pocket parts in appropriate volumes.

C. Pay bills of library vendors.

D. Test and recommend computer equipment, software, and services for the law library.

E. Prepare budget for library.

II. Cite Checking

A. Check the citations in briefs, speeches, articles, opinion letters, and other legal documents to determine the accuracy of quoted material.

B. Check the citations to determine the accuracy of citation format according to the Uniform System of Citation (the Bluebook), local court rules, or other system required by the office.

III. Research

A. Undertake factual research projects as information resource.

B. Perform legal research.

IV. Training

A. Train office staff in traditional legal research techniques.

B. Train office staff in computer research, for example, WESTLAW.

C. Train office staff in cite checking.

■ *Comment on Paralegal Work in this Area:*

"I suppose my entry into the law librarianship profession might be considered unorthodox because I had no formal educational courses in librarianship. My experience was that of working first as a legal secretary and later evolving into a legal assistant. My job in a small general practice firm included taking care of the office library such as filing supplements and pocket parts (because no one else would do it!!); doing the bookkeeping and paying the bills. [I did some legal research] as an extension of legal drafting. . . . In all my working years (and they are many) I had the greatest satisfaction from my work as a law librarian because each day I learned new things." Lewek, *The Legal Assistant as Law Librarian,* 17 Facts & Findings 28 (NALA, March 1991).

29. Law Office Administration

At the beginning of Chapter 10, you will find a detailed job description of the legal administrator and of the legal assistant manager. (See Figures 10.2 and 10.3.) Some experienced paralegals move into management positions at a law office. This might involve helping to administer the *entire* office, or *one component* of it, such as the administration of all the legal assistants in the office, the administration of the legal assistants and other support personnel working on a large case, or the administration of the computer operation in the office. There are some smaller law offices that seek paralegals to perform office management duties along with paralegal duties. (See also *law librarianship* and *litigation*.)

■ *Comment on Paralegal Work in this Area:*

In 1984, the partners at the firm decided to upgrade their legal assistant program and needed a nonlawyer to run it. They offered Linda Katz the new position. "The firm is segmented into practice areas, with legal assistants dispersed throughout the areas. They report to supervising attorneys for work assignments each day. I serve as administrative supervisor, assuring consistency in how legal assistants are treated and utilized, and what opportunities they have for benefits and advancement." Milano, *Career Profiles,* 8 Legal Assistant Today 35 (September/October 1990).

"A good paralegal litigation manager [in a large document case] has both strong paralegal skills and strong management skills. Such a manager must be able to analyze the case's organizational needs, develop methods to cope with them effectively, and often must act as paralegal, office manager and computer expert—all in a day's work." Kaufman, *The Litigation Manager,* 6 Legal Professional 55 (July/August 1989).

30. Legislation

I. Monitoring

Keep track of all events, persons, and organizations involved in the passing of legislation relevant to the clients of the firm.

II. Legislative History

Compile the legislative history of a statute.

III. Drafting of Proposed Legislation

IV. Lobbying

A. Prepare reports and studies on the subject of proposed legislation.

B. Arrange for and help prepare witnesses who will testify at legislative hearings.

■ *Comment on Paralegal Work in this Area:*

Margo Horner "is a legislative analyst for the Nat'l Federation of Independent Business (NFIB). With paralegal training and a masters degree in history, her job is research, creating legislative strategy, working with [legislators] and their staffs to produce legislation favorable to [NFIB]. Margo likes the frenetic tempo of her life." Smith, *Margo,* 1 Legal Assistant Today 14 (Summer 1984).

31. Litigation

I. File Monitoring

A. Index all files.

B. Write case profile based on information in the files.

C. Read attorney briefs to check accuracy of the information in the litigation file.

D. Organize and index documents obtained through discovery.

E. Code documents into the computer.

II. Investigation

A. Gather documents:

1. Medical records,
2. Police records,
3. Birth and death records,
4. Marriage records,
5. Adoption and custody records,
6. Incorporation records.

B. Research records. For instance:

1. Prepare a profit history report of a company.

2. Identify corporate structure of a parent company and its subsidiaries.

3. Trace UCC (Uniform Commercial Code) filings.

4. Find out from court dockets if a particular merchant is being sued, has sued before, etc. Does any pattern exist?

5. Identify the "real owner" of an apartment building.

6. Check housing code agency to find out if a landlord has other building code violations against it on record.

C. Gather facts (other than documents). In a wide range of cases (such as real estate, corporate, criminal, divorce, and custody), the investigator substantiates facts, follows leads for possible evidence in connection with litigation, etc.

III. Discovery

A. Draft interrogatories.

B. Draft answers to interrogatories.

C. Draft deposition questions.

D. Prepare witnesses for deposition.

E. Prepare witness books for deposition.

F. Arrange time and place of deposition.

G. Draft requests for admissions.

H. Draft requests for production of documents.

I. Index and digest discovery data.

J. Work with computer programmer in the design of a system to manage discovery documents.

IV. Filings/Serving

In court, at agencies, on parties, on attorneys, etc.

V. General Assistance

A. Arrange for clients and others to be interviewed.

B. Arrange for expert witnesses to appear in court or at depositions.

C. Reconstruct (from a large collection of disparate records and other evidence) what happened at a particular time and place.

D. Assist clients in completing information questionnaire, especially in class-action cases.

E. Help organize the trial notebook containing items the attorney will need during the trial, such as charts and tables to be used as exhibits at trial.

F. Sit at counsel's table at trial to take notes and suggest questions for attorney to ask witnesses.

G. Attend (and report on) hearings in related cases.

H. Supervise document encodation on a computer project related to a case in litigation.

I. Prepare and evaluate prospective jurors from jury book and during voir dire.

J. Help prepare appeal documents—for example, the notice of appeal.

VI. Legal Research

A. Shepardize; perform cite check.

B. Write preliminary memos and briefs.

C. Prepare bibliographies of source materials related to litigation.

VII. Pleadings

Write preliminary draft of pleadings using standard forms and/or adapting other pleadings written by attorneys on similar cases.

VIII. Expert Analysis

Assist in obtaining expert opinions for attorneys on:

A. Taxation.

B. Accounting.

C. Statistics.

D. Economics (for example, calculation of damages).

IX. Court Witness

A. Act as witness as to service of process.

B. Act as witness as to data uncovered or photographed (such as the condition of an apartment building).

■ *Comment on Paralegal Work in this Area:*

"There are boxes and boxes with an infinite number of documents to be indexed. There are depositions to be summarized. There are cases whose cites need checking. There are trips to the courthouse downtown. There is red-lining of documents to determine changes between two documents. There is Bates-stamping of documents. And there are the exciting trips to visit clients." Lasky, *Impressions of a New Paralegal,* 17 Reporter 5 (Los Angeles Paralegal Ass'n, February 1988).

"I organized. I tabbed and tagged, listed and labelled, hoisted and hole-punched, folded and filed, boxed and Bates-stamped, indexed and itemized, sorted and summarized." Klinkseick, *Aim High,* 16 On Point 4 (Nat'l Capital Area Paralegal Ass'n, July/August 1990).

"Initially, it was overwhelming with the number of files and the names to learn and things to remember, but with help, I learned skills and techniques and polished them day after day as each new case brought with it new quirks and new challenges. I've attended depositions, PTO shaft inspections, and pig farm operations. I've calculated medical expenses, reviewed medical records, and been baffled at how salesmen keep time records! But the ultimate of all experiences, I have to admit, are the trials. You prepare and prepare and hope that you haven't missed any of the details. Then before you know it, the jury has been selected and you're off! The trials keep your adrenaline flowing. They frazzle your patience. They show you your limitations. They elevate you when you win. They shake your confidence when you lose." Riske, *In the Limelight,* 7 Red River Review 4 (Red River Valley Legal Assistants, North Dakota, August 1990).

"For almost six years now . . . , I've experienced the variety (and the drudgery) of preparing civil cases for trial. I've spent countless hours photocopying documents never read by any judge or jury, or worst of all, by anyone else. I've tracked down witnesses and encouraged them to talk only to find out that they know nothing about the case. In this business of endless paper where no two cases are alike, I've come to understand . . . that flexibility is essential and a sense of humor is invaluable in dealing with people, be they stressed-out attorneys or reluctant witnesses." Vore, *A Litigation Recipe* 16 On Point 4 (Nat'l Capital Area Paralegal Ass'n, November 1990).

Rebecca McLaughlin tells of a particularly memorable event during her experience as a paralegal. "It was a few minutes after 12:00 noon on Friday, and presiding Judge Barbour always recesses court at precisely 12:30 on Fridays. The Government's star witness was on the stand and denied he had ever seen a certain letter. One of the trial attorneys motioned me to counsel table and asked if we had any proof that the witness had, in fact, seen this letter." Since there were well over 900 defense exhibits, almost 300 Government exhibits, and well over 40 file cabinets filled with supporting documents, Rebecca felt little hope for success in finding out quickly. "She hurried across the street to the office, found the witness' original copy of the letter with his handwritten notes in the margin, and returned to the courtroom with a BIG SMILE. The witness was impeached with his own document minutes before recess. . . . Later, Rebecca received a well-deserved standing ovation from the attorneys, and all the trial team members. It was the highlight of her career." Johnson, *MALA Spotlight: Rebecca McLaughlin,* 8 The Assistant 17 (Mississippi Ass'n of Legal Assistants, July 1989).

■ *Quotes from Want Ads:*

"Excellent writing skills and attention to detail are absolute requirements." "Plaintiff's medical malpractice firm seeks non-smoker with word processing abilities." Position requires "extensive writing, document summarizing, and medical records research." Must have an ability "to work independently in handling cases from inception through trial preparation; familiarity with drafting law motions pleadings essential." High-energy candidate "needs to be assertive and should have an excellent academic background." "Wanted: a sharp, take-charge litigation paralegal." "Knowledge of computerized litigation support is a plus; good communications

and organizational skills are a must." "Applicant must possess a thorough working knowledge of all phases of trial work." "Successful candidate will be professional, prompt, pleasant and personable. No egomaniacs or job hoppers, please." "Overtime flexibility required." "Defense litigation paralegal needed. Must be a self-starter with the ability to accept unstructured responsibility." "Applicant must have a thorough knowledge of state and federal court procedures." Position requires an ability "to organize and manage documents in large multiparty litigation." "Applicants must possess strong supervisory, analytic, writing, and investigative skills, and an ability to perform under pressure." "Position requires good analytical and writing skills, and the ability to organize and control several projects simultaneously." "Deposition summarizer needed; work in your own home on your own computer." "Part-time proofreader for deposition summaries needed."

32. Military Law

In the Navy, a nonattorney who assists attorneys in the practice of law is called a *legalman.* Depending upon the assignment, the legalman can work in a large variety of areas of the law—for example, admiralty law, contracts, and military justice. The following job functions, however, are not limited to any particular branch of the armed services.

I. Military Proceedings

A. Assist in processing the following proceedings:
   1. Special court-martial.
   2. General court-martial.
   3. Courts of inquiry.
   4. Line of duty investigations.
   5. Reclassification board proceedings.

B. Prepare all special orders designating membership of special and general court-martial and courts of inquiry.

C. Assure that charges are properly prepared and that specifications are complete and accurate.

D. Make initial determination on jurisdiction of court, status of accused, and subject matter of offenses.

E. Examine completed records of investigations and other records requiring legal review to ensure that they are administratively correct.

F. Prepare all special court-martial orders promulgating sentence.

G. Assure that records of court-martial are correct and complete before disposing of case.

H. Transmit bad-conduct discharge court-martial cases to appropriate officials.

II. Claims Against the Government

A. Conduct examinations.

B. Process claims against the United States—for instance, federal tort claims.

C. Manage claim funds.

D. Undertake research on FLITE (Federal Legal Information Through Electronics).

E. Write briefs.

III. Administrative Duties

A. Maintain control records of all court-martial and claims cases within command.

B. Maintain law library.

C. Examine and distribute incoming correspondence, directives, publications, and other communications.

D. Supervise cataloging and filing of publications, books, periodicals, journals, etc.

E. Maintain records of discipline within command.

F. Administer office budget.

G. Orient new personnel and monitor their training.

IV. Court Reporting

A. Use the steno-mask for recording legal proceedings.

B. Prepare charges to the jury.

C. Mark exhibits as they are entered into evidence.

D. Transcribe and assemble records of the proceeding.

■ *Comment on Paralegal Work in this Area:*

"I have been working for the Office of the Staff Judge Advocate (SJA) at Fort Ord, California. The SJA is the Army's lawyer. We serve a military community of just over 90,000 people. Staff within the SJA consists of a combination of military and civilian attorneys, paralegals, legal clerks and court reporters. I am responsible for claims filed against the federal government under the Federal Tort Claims Act. I am responsible for discovery and investigative efforts, determining legal issues, writing memorandums of law and recommending settlement or denial. Job satisfaction for paralegal professionals is high in the U.S. government. I know that, should I desire to re-enter the civilian work sector, my experience and knowledge of the government legal systems will uniquely qualify me to work for any firm which deals with the government." Richards, *Marching to a Different Drummer: Paralegal Work in the Military,* 2 California Paralegal Magazine 8 (October/December 1990).

33. Municipal Finance Law[14]

(See also *banking law* and *corporate law*.)

---

[14]See footnote 11.

I. Document Preparation

A. Basic documents:

1. Prepare first drafts of basic documents, including bonds, indentures of trust, financing agreements, and all other related documents.

2. Attend drafting sessions and note changes required to initial drafts.

3. Prepare second and subsequent drafts by incorporation of revisions and red-line changes.

B. Closing documents:

1. Prepare first drafts of all closing documents.

2. Prepare second and subsequent drafts by incorporation of revisions and red-line changes.

C. Draft official statement/private offering memorandum:

1. Prepare first drafts.

2. Attend drafting sessions.

3. Perform due diligence to verify the information and data contained in the offering document.

4. Prepare second and subsequent drafts by incorporation of revisions and red-line changes.

II. Coordination

A. Establish timetable and list of participants.

B. Distribute documents to participants.

C. Coordinate printing of bonds and offering documents.

D. File all documents as required.

E. Coordinate publication of notices of meetings and elections, ordinances, public hearing notices, etc.

III. Closing

A. Prepare checklist.

B. Arrange and assist in preclosing and closing.

C. File any documents necessary to be filed prior to closing.

D. Secure requisite documents to be prepared or furnished by other participants.

E. Perform all post-closing procedures:

1. File all documents or security agreements.

2. Supervise preparation of closing binders.

IV. Formation of Special Districts

A. Prepare documents necessary to organize the district.

B. File documents with municipality or county and district court.

C. Prepare documents for organizational meeting of district.

V. Elections (Formation of District or for Bond Election)

Draft election documents and obtain all necessary election materials.

VI. Develop and Maintain Research Files

A. IDB procedures for municipalities.

B. Home rule charters.

C. Demographic and economic statistics.

D. Memoranda noting statutory changes.

E. Interoffice research memoranda.

F. Checklists for each type of financing.

34. Oil and Gas Law

Some paralegals who work in the area of oil and gas law are referred to as *land technicians* or *landmen*. (See also *real estate law*.)

I. Collect and analyze data pertaining to land ownership and activities that may affect the procurement of rights to explore, drill for, and produce oil or gas.

II. Help acquire leases and other operating rights from property owners for exploration, drilling, and producing oil, gas, and related substances.

III. Monitor the execution of the leases and other operating agreements by ensuring that contract obligations are fulfilled (e.g., payment of rent).

IV. Help negotiate agreements with individuals, companies, and government agencies pertaining to the exploration, drilling, and production of oil or gas.

V. Assist in acquiring oil- and gas-producing properties, royalties, and mineral interests.

VI. Process and monitor the termination of leases and other agreements.

VII. Examine land titles.

■ *Comment on Paralegal Work in this Area:*

"As an oil and gas paralegal, my practice encompasses many different areas of law including real estate, litigation, bankruptcy, and securities, as well as contact with various county, state, and federal government agencies. I frequently spend time searching real estate records in counties . . . for information on leases to determine such things as who has been assigned an interest in the lease. I have worked in mechanic's lien foreclosures, partition actions, and bankruptcy cases. While researching such things as regulatory information and oil prices, I have obtained information from the Federal Energy Regulatory Commission offices in Washington. The variety of work requires a working knowledge of several areas of law, and is always challenging and interesting." Hunt,

Oil and Gas, The Citator (Legal Assistants of Central Ohio, August 1990).

35. Parajudge

In many states, the judge presiding in certain lower courts does not have to be an attorney. Such courts include justice of the peace courts and local magistrates courts.

Administrative agencies often hold hearings conducted by hearing officers, referees, or administrative law judges (ALJ). Frequently, these individuals are not attorneys, particularly at state and local agencies.

36. Pro Bono Work

Pro bono work refers to services provided to another person at no charge. Law firms often give their attorneys time off in order to take pro bono cases—for example, to defend a poor person charged with a crime. Paralegals are also encouraged to do pro bono work. This is done on their own time or on law firm time with the permission of their supervisor. The following are examples of pro bono work performed by paralegals:

I. Abused Women

A. Draft request for protective order.

B. Draft divorce pleadings.

II. AIDS Patients

A. Interview patients and prepare a memorandum of the interview for the pro bono attorney supervising the paralegals.

B. Assist patients with guardianship problems.

C. Draft powers of attorney.

III. Homeless

A. Handle Supplemental Security Income (SSI) claims.

B. Make referrals to shelters and drug programs.

■ *Comment on Paralegal Work in this Area:*

"Asked to share her favorite pro bono experience, Therese Ortega, a litigation paralegal, answered that to choose was too difficult; any time her efforts result in a benefit to the client, 'I get a warm glow.' One occasion she obviously cherishes was the fight on behalf of some low-income kidney dialysis patients whose eligibility for transportation to and from treatment was threatened. 'Perseverance and appeals paid off,' she says. Rides were re-established through the hearing process, then by information conferences. Finally, the cessation notices stopped." *Spotlight on Therese Ortega,* 13 The Journal 3 (Sacramento Ass'n of Legal Assistants, March 1991).

37. Public Sector

A paralegal in the *private sector* works in an office whose funds come from client fees or from the budget of the corporate treasury. Every other setting is generally considered the *public sector*. More specifically, the latter refers to those law offices that provide civil or criminal legal services to the poor for free. Often, the services consist of helping clients obtain government benefits such as public housing, welfare, medical care, etc. Such services are referred to as *public benefits,* and providing such assistance is called practice of public benefits law. Some of the paralegals who are employed by these offices are called Public Benefits Paralegals. The offices operate with government grants, charitable contributions, and the efforts of volunteers. They are called Legal Aid Society, Legal Aid Foundation, Legal Services Office, Office of the Public Defender, etc. (See also *administrative law, bankruptcy law, civil rights law, criminal law, family law, landlord and tenant law, litigation, pro bono work, social security law, welfare law,* and *worker's compensation law.*)

■ *Comment on Paralegal Work in this Area:*

"If someone asked me what I disliked most about my job, I would have to answer: the size of my paycheck. That is the only drawback of working for a nonprofit law firm—[the Community Legal Aid Society which represents elderly and handicapped persons]. Everything else about my job is positive." For example, to "be an integral part of a case where a landlord is forced by the Courts to bring a house up to code and prevent a tenant from being wrongfully evicted is a great feeling." The positive aspects of the job "more than compensate for the size of the paycheck." Hartman, *Job Profile,* Delaware Paralegal Reporter 5 (Delaware Paralegal Ass'n, November 1988).

"Mr. Watnick stressed that the organization doesn't have the luxury of using paralegals as "xeroxers" or errand runners. Staff paralegals have their own caseloads and represent clients before Administrative Law Judges—with a dramatically high rate of success." Shays, *Paralegals in Human Service,* Postscript 16 (Manhattan Paralegal Ass'n, March/April 1990).

38. Real Estate Law

(See also *banking law, contract law,* and *landlord and tenant law.*)

I. General

Assist law firms, corporations, and development companies in transactions involving land, houses, condominiums, shopping malls, office buildings, redevelopment projects, civic centers, etc.

A. Research zoning regulations.

B. Prepare draft of the contract of sale.

C. Title work:
1. If done outside, order title work from the title company; arrange title insurance.
2. If done in-house:
    a. Examine title abstracts for completeness,
    b. Prepare a map based on a master title plat or the current government survey map,
    c. Help construct a chain of title noting defects, encumbrances, liens, easements, breaks in the chain, etc.,
    d. Obtain releases of liens, payoff statements for existing loans, etc.
    e. Help draft a preliminary title opinion.

D. Mortgages:
1. Assist in obtaining financing,
2. Review mortgage application,
3. Assist in recording mortgage.

E. Closing:
1. Arrange for a closing time with buyer, seller, brokers, and lender. Obtain letter confirming date of closing.
2. Collect the data necessary for closing. Prepare checklist of expenses:
    a. Title company fee,
    b. Lender's fee,
    c. Attorney's fee,
    d. Taxes and water bills to be prorated,
    e. Tax escrow, discharge of liens.
3. Prepare and organize the documents for closing:
    a. Deed,
    b. Settlement statement,
    c. Note and deed of trust,
    d. Corporate resolutions,
    e. Performance bond,
    f. Waivers.
4. Check compliance with the disclosure requirements of the Real Estate Settlement Act.
5. Arrange for a rehearsal of the closing.
6. Attend and assist at the closing—for example, take minutes, notarize documents.

F. Foreclosure:
1. Order foreclosure certificate.
2. Prepare notice of election and demand for sale,
3. Compile a list of parties to be notified,
4. Monitor publication of the notice.
5. Assist with sale documents—for example, prepare bid letter.

G. Eminent Domain:
1. Photograph or videotape the property taken or to be taken by the state,
2. Prepare inventory of the property taken,
3. Help client prepare business records pertaining to the value of the property,
4. Arrange for appraisals of the property,
5. Order and review engineering reports regarding soil,
6. Review tax appeals records on values claimed by the property owner,
7. Mail out notice of condemnation.

H. Office management:
1. Maintain office tickler system,
2. Maintain individual attorney's calendar,
3. Be in charge of the entire client's file (opening it, keeping it up-to-date, knowing where parts of it are at all times),
4. Train other staff in the office system of handling real estate cases.

II. Tax-exempt Industrial Development Financing

A. Undertake a preliminary investigation to establish facts relevant to:
1. Project eligibility,
2. The local issuer,
3. Cost estimates of the financing.

B. Prepare a formal application to the issuer.

C. Prepare a timetable of approvals, meetings, and all other requirements necessary for closing.

D. Prepare a preliminary draft of portions of the proposal memorandum (relating to the legal structure of the financing) that is submitted to prospective bond purchasers.

E. Obtain confirmation from the Treasury Department that the company is in compliance with the financing covenants of current external debt instruments.

F. Obtain insurance certificates.

G. Write the first draft of the resolutions of the board of directors.

H. Write the preface and recital of documents for the legal opinion of the company.

I. Contact the bank to confirm the account numbers, amount of money to be transferred, and investment instructions.

J. Prepare a closing memorandum covering the following documents:
1. Secretary's certificate including resolutions of the board of directors, the certified charter and bylaws of the company, and the incumbency certificate,
2. UCC-1 financing statements,
3. Requisition forms,
4. Certificate of authorized company representative,
5. Deed,
6. Legal opinion of the company,
7. Transfer instruction letter,
8. Officer's certificate.

K. Confirm that the money has been transferred to the company's account on the day of closing.

L. Order an updated good-standing telegram.

M. Send a copy of the IRS election statement.

N. Assemble, monitor, and distribute documents to appropriate departments.

■ *Comment on Paralegal Work in this Area:*

"Although it may look boring to the untrained eye, and sound boring to the untrained ear, for those of us whose livelihoods depend upon it, real estate law is *interesting* and *exciting*. There is always something new to learn or a little flaw to resolve. What can be better than having clients come to you and thank you for your assistance in what would have been a complete disaster without your knowledge and expertise to get them through? I call that total job satisfaction. I am now capable of doing everything in a real estate settlement from opening the file to walking into the settlement room and disbursing the funds. It is not uncommon for me to receive calls from attorneys in the area asking me how certain problems can be solved. That boosts my ego more than any divorce case every could!" Jaeger, *Real Estate Law Is a Legal Profession Too!,* 14 On Point 9 (Nat'l Capital Area Paralegal Ass'n, June 1988).

At a paralegal conference, Virginia Henderson made a seminar presentation on her duties as a paralegal. Her "candor and energetic enthusiasm concerning her profession were encouraging and motivating. She was very explicit about her duties as a commercial real estate paralegal, explaining that attorney supervision is lessened once the paralegal assumes more responsibility and exhibits initiative as far as his/her duties are concerned. It was refreshing to listen to a veteran of the paralegal profession speak so optimistically about the profession's limitless potential. Here's to having more paralegals as seminar speakers!" Troiano, *Real Estate,* Newsletter 12 (Western New York Paralegal Ass'n, November/December 1987).

"As a foreclosure legal assistant, one of my worst fears is to have a client call and say, 'Remember the Jones property you foreclosed for us last year? Well, we're trying to close on this and it seems there's a problem with the title. . . .' Oh no, what *didn't* I do! Mortgage foreclosure litigation is fraught with all kinds of pitfalls for the inexperienced and the unwary. An improper or faulty foreclosure could not only be disastrous for the client, it can also be a malpractice nightmare for the law firm." Hubbell, *Mortgage Foreclosure Litigation: Avoiding the Pitfalls,* 16 Facts and Findings 10 (NALA, November 1989).

■ *Quotes from Want Ads:*

"Ideal candidate must possess exceptional organization, communication, writing and research skills and be willing to work overtime." "We need a team player with high energy." Position requires an ability to work independently on a wide variety of matters and to meet deadlines." "Experience in retail real estate or real estate financing a must." "Should be assertive and have excellent analytical skills." Position requires a "self-motivated person. We seek a TIGER who can accomplish much with a minimum of supervision." "Knowledge of state and federal securities law a plus." "Must be flexible and possess high integrity." Position requires a "self-starter able to deal effectively with executive management, outside counsel, escrow and title companies, brokers, leasing agents, and clients."

39. Social Security Law

(See also *administrative law, public sector,* and *welfare law.*)

I. Problem Identification

Identify whether:
A. Person is denied benefits.
B. Recipient is terminated from disability payments.
C. Recipient is charged with receiving overpayment.
D. Medicare waivers/appeals are involved.

II. Case Preparation

A. Investigate relevant facts.
B. Perform legal research.
C. Engage in informal advocacy with Social Security employees.

III. Representation

A. Represent clients at administrative hearings regarding SSI (Supplemental Security Income).
B. Represent clients at administrative hearings regarding SSD (Social Security Disability)

IV. Appeal

A. Help attorney prepare a court appeal of the agency's decision.

■ *Comment on Paralegal Work in this Area:*

"Paralegal representation of a claimant in a Social Security Disability hearing is the closest to a judicial setting that a paralegal may expect to become involved in. For the paralegal, this can be a very complex and challenging field. It can also be extremely rewarding, bringing with it the satisfaction of successfully representing a claimant in a quasi-judicial setting." Obermann, *The Paralegal and Federal Disability Practice in Maine,* MAP Newsletter (Maine Ass'n of Paralegals, January 1988).

40. Tax Law

(See also *corporate law, employee benefits law, estates law,* and *real estate law.*)

I. Compile all necessary data for the preparation of tax returns:

A. Corporate income tax,
B. Employer quarterly tax,
C. Franchise tax,
D. Partnership tax,
E. Sales tax,
F. Personal property tax,
G. Individual income tax,
H. Estate tax,
I. Gift tax.

II. Communicate with client to obtain missing information.

III. Compile supporting documents for the returns.

IV. Draft extensions-of-time requests.

V. Make corrections in the returns based upon new or clarified data.

VI. Compute the tax liability or transfer client information to computer input sheets for submission to a computer service that will calculate the tax liability.

VII. Organize and maintain client binder.

VIII. Compute cash flow analysis for proposed real estate syndication.

IX. Compile documentation on the valuation of assets.

X. Maintain the tax law library.

XI. Read loose-leaf tax services and other periodic tax data to keep current on tax developments. Bring such developments to the attention of others in the office.

XII. Supervise and train other nonattorney staff within the tax department of the office.

■ *Comment on Paralegal Work in this Area:*

"A legal assistant with the firm for the past 13 years, Pat [Coleman] spends a lot of time in her office. She is surrounded by her work, and one gets the idea that Pat knows exactly what is in every file and could put her hand on any information that is needed. Notes are taped next to the light switch; the firm's monthly calendar highlighting important meetings is readily available, and helps her track her many deadlines. Pat is an Enrolled Agent (which permits her to practice before the Treasury Department) and has a lot of tax background, and is competent in that area as well as bookkeeping. One of her least favorite tax forms is the 990 required of not-for-profit organizations. The 990 tax form is second only to private foundation returns when it comes to being pesky and tricky." Howard, *Patricia Coleman of Chicago Creates Her Niche in Taxes, Trusts and ERISA,* 3 Legal Assistant Today 40 (Winter 1986).

41. Tort Law

A tort is a civil wrong that has injured someone. Paralegals who work on PI (personal injury) cases are mainly litigation assistants. The major torts are negligence, defamation, strict liability, and wrongful death. Paralegals in this area are also often involved in worker's compensation cases for injuries that occur on the job. (See *admiralty law, litigation,* and *worker's compensation.*)

■ *Comment on Paralegal Work in this Area:*

"Personal injury/products liability cases can be fascinating, challenging, and educational. They also can be stressful, aggravating and very sad. I have been involved in a great many cases in my career, on both sides of the plaintiff/defendant fence. Some of the cases seemed frivolous and somewhat 'ambulance chasing' in nature. Others were significant cases in which the plaintiff had wrongfully suffered injury. There are many talents a good personal injury/products liability paralegal must have. He or she must be creative, tenacious, observant and able to communicate well with people." Lee, *Personal Injury/Products Liability Cases,* 11 Newsletter 7 (Dallas Ass'n of Legal Assistants, November 1987).

"Recently, Mary Mann, a paralegal who works on product liability litigation, was asked by her attorney to track down a specific medical article [on a subject relevant to a current case]. The attorney only had a vague description of the article, a possible title, and the name of the organization that might have published it. In her search Mary spoke by phone to people in New York, Atlanta, Washington, and finally to a doctor in Geneva, Switzerland, who spoke very little English. In her effort to make herself understood by the doctor, Mary continued to speak louder and louder in very simplistic and basic English phrases, as people tend to do when con-

fronted by a language barrier. She is sure her efforts to maintain a professional demeanor were humorous to those passing by her office. However, she did succeed in getting the article and in the process gained a friend in Switzerland!" Fisher, *Spotlight: Mary Mann,* 7 The Assistant 14 (Mississippi Ass'n of Legal Assistants, April/June 1988).

"Asbestos litigation . . . opened up in the late 1970's with the law suits initiated against the Johns-Mansville Corporation. In 1982 Mansville filed a Chapter 11 bankruptcy to protect its assets from the thousands of claims being filed against it." Huge numbers of paralegals were employed in this litigation. For those paralegals working *for* Johns-Mansville on the defense team, "the question of morality arose. I get asked about the morality of my job constantly. For me, personal moral judgment does not enter into it. Our legal system is based on the availability of equal representation for both sides. I think I play a small part in making that system work." Welsh, *The Paralegal in Asbestos Litigation,* 10 Ka Leo O' H.A.L.A. 6 (Hawaii Ass'n of Legal Assistants, February/March 1987) (reprint from newsletter of the East Bay Ass'n of Legal Assistants).

■ *Quotes from Want Ads:*

"Medical malpractice law firm seeks paralegal who is a self-starter, has good communication skills, is organized and detail-oriented." Position in PI [personal injury] firm requires "a take-charge person to handle case details from beginning to end." "Prefer person with experience in claims adjustment, medical records, or nursing." Position requires "dynamic, highly-motivated individual who will enjoy the challenge of working independently and handling a wide variety of responsibilities." "Excellent writing skills a must." "Should be able to perform under pressure." Manufacturer of consumer products "seeks paralegal with engineering background." Must be mature enough to handle "heavy client contact." Position requires "ability to read and summarize medical records."

42. Tribal Law

Tribal courts exist on Indian reservations that have jurisdiction over many civil and criminal cases in which both parties are Native Americans. Parties are often represented by tribal court advocates who are nonattorney Native Americans. In addition, the judges are often nonattorneys. (See *litigation.*).

43. Water Law[15]

(See also *administrative law* and *real estate law.*)

---

[15]See footnote 11.

I. Water Rights

Investigate and analyze specific water rights and water rights associated with property:

A. Do research at Department of Water Resources regarding decrees, tabulations, well permits, reservoirs, diversion records, maps, and statements.

B. Communicate in writing and orally with Department of Water Resources personnel regarding status of water rights and wells.

C. Communicate in writing and orally (including interviews) with District Water Commissioners regarding status of water rights and wells, historic use, and use on land.

D. Communicate in writing and orally (including interviews) with property owners and managers, ranch managers, ditch company personnel, etc. regarding status of water rights and wells, historic use, and use on land.

E. Do research at other agencies and offices (such as the Bureau of Land Management, state archives, historical societies, public libraries).

F. Prepare historic use affidavits.

G. Prepare reports regarding investigation and analysis of the status of water rights and wells, historic use, and use on land.

H. Prepare maps, charts, diagrams, etc. regarding status of water rights and wells, historic use, and use on land.

II. Real Estate Transactions

A. Draft documents for the purchase and sale, encumbrance, or lease of water rights and wells.

B. Perform standup title searches in county clerk and recorder's offices.

C. Perform due diligence investigations.

D. Prepare for and assist at closings.

III. Well Permit Applications

A. Prepare well permit documents for filing— applications, land ownership affidavits, statements of beneficial use, amendments to record, extensions of time.

B. Coordinate and monitor the well permitting and drilling process.

C. In writing and orally, communicate with Department of Water Resources personnel, well drillers, and client.

IV. Water Court Proceedings—

Certain district courts have special jurisdiction over water right proceedings. Proceedings are governed by the Rules of Civil Procedure for District Courts and by local water court and district court rules.

A. Prepare water court documents for filing applications, statements of opposition, draft rulings and orders, stipulations, withdrawals of opposition, and affidavits.

B. Maintain diligence filing tickler system. Work with client to record and maintain evidence of diligence.

C. Review, route, and maintain a file of water court resumes.

D. Review, route, and maintain a file of term day notices and orders. Prepare attorneys for term day and/or attend term day.

V. Monitor Publications

Read *Reporter,* water court resumes, and register for new water law cases and Department of Water Resources regulations.

44. Welfare Law

(See also *administrative law, pro bono work, public benefits,* and *social security law.*)

I. Problem Identification

A. Perform preliminary interview:

　1. Identify nonlegal problems for referral to other agencies,

　2. Open a case file or update it,

　3. Using a basic fact sheet (or form), record the information collected during the interview,

　4. Determine next appointment,

　5. Instruct client on what to do next, such as obtain medical and birth records, etc.,

　6. Arrange for client to see office attorney.

B. Categorize welfare problems:

　1. Help client learn what benefits exist in programs such as:

　　a. Welfare

　　b. Social Security

　　c. Medicare

　2. Help client fill out application forms.

　3. Deal with client who objects to home visits by caseworkers or attempt by welfare department to force him or her to take a job or enter a training program.

　4. Help client when welfare department wants to reduce the amount of client's welfare check or terminate public assistance altogether.

II. Problem Resolution

A. Consult with attorney immediately:

　1. Summarize facts for the attorney,

　2. Submit the case record to the attorney,

3. Obtain further instructions from attorney.

B. Refer nonlegal problems to other agencies:
   1. Give name and address of agency to client,
   2. Search for an appropriate agency,
   3. Contact agency for the client.

C. Investigate:
   1. Verify information (call caseworker, visit welfare office, etc.)
   2. Search for additional information.
   3. Record relevant facts.
   4. Consult with attorney on difficulties encountered.

D. Analyze laws:
   1. Check office welfare law manual,
   2. Consult with office attorneys,
   3. Contact legal service attorneys outside office,
   4. Do research in law library.

E. Be an informal advocate (to determine if the problem can be resolved without a hearing or court action).
   1. Make sure everyone (welfare department, client, etc.) understands the issue,
   2. Provide missing information,
   3. Pressure the welfare department (with calls, letters, visits, etc.),
   4. Maintain records such as current and closed files.

F. Be a formal advocate:
   1. Prior hearing (administrative review)
      a. Determine if such hearing can be asked for and when request must be made,
      b. Draft letter requesting such hearing,
      c. Prepare for hearing (see "Fair Hearing" below),
      d. Conduct hearing (see "Fair Hearing" below),
      e. Follow-up (see "Fair Hearing" below).
   2. Fair Hearing
      a. Determine if the hearing can be asked for and when request must be made,
      b. Draft letter requesting the hearing,
      c. Prepare for the hearing:
         i. In advance of hearing, request that the welfare department send the paralegal the documents it will rely on at the hearing.
         ii. In advance of hearing, make sure that everyone (department representatives, client, etc.) is going to the hearing on the same issues.
         iii. Organize other relevant documents such as cancelled check stubs.
         iv. Find witnesses (other than client).
         v. Prepare all witnesses (for example, explain what hearing will be about; conduct a brief role-playing experience to acquaint them with the format and what the paralegal will be seeking from them as witnesses).
         vi. Map out a preliminary strategy to use in conducting the hearing.
         vii. Make a final attempt to resolve the issues without a hearing.
         viii. Make sure client and other witnesses will appear (e.g., give address of the hearing, take them to the hearing on the date of the hearing).
      d. Conduct the hearing:
         i. Make sure the name, address, and title of everyone present is identified for the record.
         ii. Make opening statement summarizing client's case.
         iii. Ask for a postponement if the client has not appeared or if an emergency has arisen requiring more time to prepare.
         iv. Clearly state what relief the client is seeking from the hearing.
         v. If confusion exists on the issues, fight for a statement of the issues most favorable to the client.
         vi. Take notes on the opening statement of the welfare department representative.
         vii. Complain if welfare department failed to provide sufficient information in advance of the hearing.
         viii. Present the client's case.
            a. submit documents.
            b. conduct direct examination of own witnesses.
            c. conduct re-direct examination of own witnesses (if allowed).
            d. cite the law.
         ix. Rebut case of welfare department.
            a. object to their documents.
            b. object to their use of jargon.
            c. object to their interpretation of the law.
            d. cross-examine their witnesses.
            e. re-cross-examine their witnesses (if allowed).

        x. Make closing statement summarizing the case of the client and repeating the result the client is seeking.

   e. Follow up:

        i. Pressure the hearing officer to reach a result without undue delay.

        ii. Request a copy of the transcript of the hearing.

        iii. When a result is reached, pressure the welfare department to abide by it.

        iv. Consult with attorney to determine whether the hearing result should be appealed in court.

3. Court

   a. Prepare preliminary draft of the legal argument to be made on appeal,

   b. Assist the attorney in gathering the documents for appeal; interview the witnesses for appeal, etc.,

   c. Be a general assistant for the attorney at court proceedings,

   d. File papers in court,

   e. Serve the papers on opponents.

G. Miscellaneous

1. Train other paralegals.

2. Write pamphlets on welfare law for distribution in the community.

3. Organize the community around welfare issues.

45. Worker's Compensation Law

(See also *administrative law, labor and employment law,* and *litigation.*)

I. Interviewing

A. Collect and record details of the claim (date of injury, nature and dates of prior illness, etc.).

B. Collect or arrange for the collection of documents, such as medical records, employment contract, etc.

C. Schedule physical examination.

II. Drafting

A. Draft claim for compensation.

B. Draft request for hearing.

C. Draft medical authorization.

D. Draft demand for medical information in the possession of respondent or insurance carrier.

E. Draft proposed summary of issues involved.

III. Advocacy

A. Informal: Contact (call, visit, write a letter to) the employer and/or the insurance carrier to determine whether the matter can be resolved without a formal hearing or court action.

B. Formal: Represent claimant at the administrative hearing.

IV. Follow-up

A. Determine whether the payment is in compliance with the award.

B. If not, draft and file a statutory demand for proper payment.

C. If such a statutory demand is filed, prepare a tickler system to monitor the claim.

■ *Comment on Paralegal Work in this Area:*

"I have been working as a paralegal in this area for more than seven years. This is one of the areas of the law [in this state] in which a paralegal can perform almost all of the functions to properly process a Workers' Compensation claim. A Workers' Compensation practice must be a very high volume in order to be [profitable]. Thus paralegal assistance in handling a large case load is an absolute necessity. An extensive volume of paperwork is processed on a daily basis. Client contact is a major portion of a paralegal's responsibilities. With a large case load, it is physically impossible for an attorney to communicate with each and every client on a regular basis. It is not unusual for a paralegal in this field to work on several hundred files each week." Lindberg, *Virtually Limitless Responsibilities of a Workers' Compensation Paralegal,* Update 6 (Cleveland Ass'n of Paralegals, July 1989).

"The Company's two worker's compensation paralegals are responsible for reviewing each claimant's file, preparing a summary of medical reports, outlining the issues, and reviewing with the adjusters any questions or circumstances of the case before the claimant's disposition. In addition, they draft any necessary subpoenas, witness lists and settlement stipulations for their respective attorneys, and collect information and draft letters to the Special Disability Trust Fund outlining the Company's theory of reimbursement for second injury cases." Miquel, *Walt Disney World Company's Legal Assistants: Their Role in the Show,* 16 Facts and Findings 29, 30 (NALA, January 1990).

> **Note**
>
> **A PARALEGAL IN THE WHITE HOUSE**
> **MEG SHIELDS DUKE**
> **NEW ROLES IN THE LAW CONFERENCE REPORT, 93 (1982)**
>
> [After working as a paralegal on the Reagan-Bush Campaign Committee], I'm a paralegal in the White House Counsel's office. I believe I'm the first paralegal in this office, in the White House. They've had law clerks in the past, but never have they hired a paralegal. There's one paralegal to nine attorneys at the moment. I think that's ridiculous and I hope we'll change that in the next several months to a year. But my responsibilities here are varied. Everybody is still trying to determine what their turf is. But for the first couple of months I've worked on a lot of transition matters, which might be expected. I was the coordinator for our transition audit, congressional transition audit, from the Hill, which just ended a few weeks ago. I have engaged in drafting correspondence concerning the use of the president's name; the use of his image; our policy on gifts acceptance by public employees; drafting standards of conduct for public employees in the White House; job freeze litigation; those few controversial things. The last few weeks of my time have been devoted to the Lefever nomination. It's all been fascinating. Anyway, there are a number of areas that we also get involved in, the ethics of government act, for example. It's the first time it has been applied across the board to a new administration. It has been very, very time consuming for all our staff. I've been assisting in that, reviewing each individual file for high level government employees. As I said, I'm in the counsel's office now and intend to stay for a couple of years. But I would like to start my own paralegal firm. I have a close friend who started her own paralegal firm in Florida and we've talked often in the past of expanding it to Washington and a few other cities West where we'd like to spend some time. We're investigating the possibilities of reopening another firm here in Washington at some point, maybe in the next year and a half. But I think there is a place for more paralegals in the public sector, at least in the White House area, and I understand the Department of Justice of course has many, but I'd like to see it expanded and I'd also like to see more people branching out and trying this independent approach because I think it's fun. It's risky, but it's worth it.

"In my experience, most entry-level candidates are unprepared to effectively market themselves to law firms and corporations in this increasingly competitive marketplace. It is no longer enough simply to have a paralegal certificate. An individual must be able to sell him or herself effectively through the use of a well-written resume and cover letter, and be prepared to develop strong interviewing skills."
Tami M. Coyne, May 1990.

"Getting the job you want requires planning, determination, hard work, and follow-through. Don't give up!"
Lindi Massey, January 1991.

Section D.   Finding a Job: Employment Strategies

The following strategies are primarily for individuals who have never worked with attorneys or held a paralegal job. Many of the strategies, however, are also relevant to people who have worked in law offices as secretaries or who are paralegals and wish to find other employment opportunities in the field.

General Strategies for Finding Employment

1. Begin now
2. Start compiling a Job Hunting Notebook
3. Organize an employment workshop
4. Locate working paralegals
5. Go on informational interviews
6. Locate potential employers
7. Prepare a resume, cover letter, and writing sample
8. Prepare for the job interview

Strategy 1: Begin Now

You should begin preparing for the job hunt on the first day of your first paralegal class. Do *not* wait until the program is almost over. Whether or not there is a placement office at your school, you should assume that obtaining a job will be your responsibility. For most students, the job you get will be the job *you* find.

While in school, your primary focus should be on compiling an excellent academic record. *In addition,* you must start the job search now. It is not too early, for example, to begin compiling the lists called for in the Job Hunting Notebook that we will examine later. When school is over, be prepared to spend a substantial amount of additional time looking for employment. Since most students in the country will not have employment lined up before they graduate, time must be set aside for the search. How much time? There is, of course, no absolute answer to this question. It is clear, however, that a half-hearted, part-time effort will probably not be successful. Simply sitting back and sending out a stack of resumes is rarely effective! Since this is a "buyer's market" where there are many more applicants than available jobs, a conscientious search could involve four to six hours a day for several months. This may surprise—and disappoint—many graduates of paralegal programs. Yet this time frame is a reality throughout the legal profession. It applies to the majority of attorneys and legal administrators looking for work as well as to paralegals. *Being* a paralegal requires determination, assertiveness, initiative, and creativity. *Finding* paralegal work will require these same skills. This is not a field for the faint of heart who are easily discouraged.

It may be that there is still a lot of uncertainty in your mind about the kinds of employment options that exist. How can you begin looking for a job if you don't yet know what kind of job you would like to have? First of all, many of the suggested steps in this chapter will be helpful regardless of the kind of job you are pursuing. More important, however, the very process of going through these steps will help you clarify your employment objectives. As you begin seeking information and leads, the insights will come to you.

At this point, keep an open mind, be conscientious, and begin now.

Strategy 2: Begin Compiling a Job Hunting Notebook

Later in this chapter, you will find an outline for a Job Hunting Notebook that you should start preparing now. Following the outline, there are sample pages for the various sections in the Notebook. (See page 160.)

Strategy 3: Organize an Employment Workshop

In Figure 2.1 at the beginning of this chapter, you were given a list of the major categories (and subcategories) of paralegal employment. Begin organizing an employment conference or workshop consisting of a panel of paralegals from as many of the categories and subcategories of paralegals as you can locate in your area. Try to find at least one paralegal to represent each category and subcategory. The guest paralegals could be asked to come to an evening or Saturday session to discuss topics such as:

- How I obtained my job
- My recommendations for finding work
- Dos and don'ts in the employment interview
- What I do (what a typical day consists of)
- What were the most valuable parts of my legal education

While you might want to ask a teacher or the director of the program at your school to help you organize the workshop, it is recommended that you make it a student-run workshop. It will be good practice for you in taking the kind of initiative that is essential in finding employment. You might want to consider asking the nearest paralegal association to co-sponsor the workshop with your class. (See question 5 in the letter found at the end of the index of this book.)

Have a meeting of your class in which a chairperson is selected to help coordinate the event. Then divide up the tasks of contacting participants, arranging for a room, preparing an agenda for the workshop, etc. You may want to invite former graduates of your school to attend as panel speakers or as members of the audience. The ideal time for such a workshop is a month or two after you begin your coursework. This means that you need to begin organizing immediately.

Strategy 4: Locate Working Paralegals

Perhaps the most significant step in finding employment is to begin talking with paralegals who are already employed. They are the obvious experts on how to find a job! They are probably also very knowledgeable about employment opportunities in their office and in similar offices in the area. (See Job Hunting Notebook, p. 168.)

Attend paralegal association meetings. See Appendix A for a list of paralegal associations. Contact the one nearest you and ask about joining. There may be a special dues or fee structure for students.

Ask if the association has a *job bank* service. Here is what a paralegal who recently used this service had to say:

> I gained access to an opening to a wonderful job at a law firm exclusively listed in the Minnesota Association of Legal Assistants (MALA) Job Bank. . . . I would never have heard about the position if I hadn't been a member of MALA. *Merrill Advantage* (Spring 1990).

Not all associations, however, have job bank services, and those that do have them may not make them available to students.

Try to obtain copies of current and past issues of the monthly or bimonthly newsletters of all the local paralegal associations in your area. Some of these newsletters give listings of job openings that mention specific employers. If so, try to contact the employers to determine if the position is still open. If it is no longer open, ask if you could send your resume to be kept on file in the event a position becomes available in the future. Also, try to speak to the paralegal who filled the position in order to ask for leads to openings elsewhere.

Ask the local paralegal association if it has a job-finding manual for paralegals in your area. Find out about attending various association meetings. Try to participate in committees. The more active you are as a student member, the more contacts you will make. If there is no paralegal association near you, organize one—beginning with your own student body and past graduates of your school.

Paralegal newsletters often announce continuing education conferences and seminars for paralegals. Similar announcements are found in the newsletters of the two major national paralegal associations: the National Federation of Paralegal Associations *(National Paralegal Reporter)*, and the National Association of Legal Assistants *(Facts and Findings)*. Employed paralegals attend these events in large numbers. Hence they are excellent ways in which to meet experienced paralegals.

Paralegals sometimes attend continuing education conferences conducted by the local bar association, particularly those bar associations where paralegals are allowed to become associate members. You should also find out if there is an association of legal secretaries and of legal administrators in your area. If so, they might conduct workshops or meetings that you can attend. At such meetings and elsewhere, try to talk with individual legal secretaries and legal administrators about employment opportunities for paralegals where they work.

Strategy 5: Go on Informational Interviews

An *informational interview* is an opportunity for you to sit down with someone, preferably where he or she works, to learn about a particular kind of employment. Unlike a job interview, where you are the one interviewed, *you* do the interviewing in an informational interview. You ask questions that will help you learn what life is like working at that kind of office. Your goal is to find out if a particular kind of paralegal practice interests you.

> If, for example, you are a real "people" person who finds antitrust theory fascinating, you should listen to antitrust paralegals discussing their day-to-day work. You may hear that most of them spend years in document warehouses with one lawyer, two other paralegals and a pizza delivery man as their most significant personal contacts. That information may influence your decision about antitrust as a career path.[16]

Do *not* try to turn an informational interview into a job interview. While on an informational interview, it is inappropriate to ask a person for a job. Toward the end of the interview, you can delicately ask for leads to employment and you can ask how the person obtained his or her job, but these inquiries should be secondary to your primary purpose of obtaining information about the realities of work at that kind of office. Do not use an informational interview as a subterfuge for a job interview that you are having difficulty obtaining.

The best people to interview are employed paralegals whom you have met through the steps outlined in Strategy 4. While attorneys and legal administrators may also be willing to grant you informational interviews, the best people to talk to are those who were once in your shoes. Simply say to a paralegal you have met, "Would it be possible for me to come down to the office where you work for a brief informational interview?" If he or she is not familiar with this kind of interview, explain its limited objective. Some may be too busy to grant such interviews, but you have nothing to lose by asking, even if you are turned down. As an added inducement, consider offering to take the paralegal to lunch. In addition to meeting this paralegal, you also want to try to have at least a brief tour of the office where he or she works. Observing how different kinds of employees interact with each other and with available technology in the office will be invaluable.

Here are some of the questions you should ask on an informational interview.

- What is a typical day for you in this office?
- What kinds of assignments do you receive?
- How much overtime is usually expected? Do you take work home with you?

---

[16]Gainen, *Information Interviews: A Strategy,* Paradigm (Baltimore Ass'n of Legal Assistants, November/December 1989).

- How do the attorneys interact with paralegals in this kind of practice? Who does what? How many different attorneys does a paralegal work with? How are assignment priorities set?
- How do the paralegals interact with secretaries and other support staff in the office?
- What is the hierarchy of the office?
- What kind of education best prepares a paralegal to work in this kind of office? What courses are most effective?
- What is the most challenging aspect of the job? The most frustrating?
- How are paralegals perceived in this office?
- Are you glad you became this kind of paralegal in this kind of office? Would you do it over again?
- What advice would you give to someone who wants to become a paralegal like yourself?

Several of these questions are also appropriate in a job interview, as we will see later.

One final word of caution. Any information you learn at the office about clients or legal matters must be kept confidential, even if the person you are interviewing is casual about revealing such information to you. This person may not be aware that he or she is disclosing confidential information. Carelessness in this regard is not uncommon.

Strategy 6: Locate Potential Employers

There are a number of ways to locate attorneys:

a. Placement office
b. Personal contacts
c. Ads
d. Through other paralegals
e. Employment agencies
f. Directories and other lists
g. Courts and bar association meetings

(See Job Hunting Notebook, p. 168).

For every attorney that you contact, you want to know the following:

- Has the attorney hired paralegals in the past?
- If so, is the attorney interested in hiring more paralegals?
- If the attorney has never hired paralegals before, might he or she consider hiring one?
- Does the attorney know of other attorneys who might be interested in hiring paralegals?

The last point is particularly important. Attorneys from different firms often talk with each other about their practice, including their experiences with paralegals or their plans for hiring paralegals. Hence always ask about other firms. If you obtain a lead, begin your contact with the other firm by mentioning the name of the attorney who gave you the lead. You might say, "Mary Smith told me that you have hired paralegals in the past and might be interested in hiring another paralegal," or "John Jones suggested that I contact you concerning possible employment at your firm as a paralegal."

a. Placement Office.   Start with the placement office of your paralegal school. Talk with staff members and/or check the bulletin board regularly. If your school is part of a university that has a law school, you might want to check the placement office of the law school as well. While paralegal jobs are usually not listed there, you may find descriptions of law firms with the number of attorneys and paralegals employed. (See Figure 2.2.) It would be useful for you to identify the major resources for obtaining attorney jobs, such as special directories, lists or ads in bar publications, legal newspapers, etc. In particular, try to find the following resource used by unemployed attorneys and law students: *Directory of Legal Employers,* which is published by the National Association of Law Placement. (The Directory can also be used on WESTLAW, page 420, if you have access to this computer legal research system.) Such resources might provide leads on contacting offices about paralegal employment.

b. Personal Contacts.   Make a list of attorneys who fall into the following categories:

- Personal friends
- Friends of friends
- Attorneys you have hired
- Attorneys your relatives have hired
- Attorneys your former employers have hired
- Attorneys your friends have hired
- Teachers
- Politicians
- Neighbors
- Etc.

You should consider contacting these attorneys about their own paralegal hiring plans as well as for references to other attorneys. Don't be reluctant to take advantage of any direct or indirect association that you might have with an attorney. Such contacts are the essence of networking. (See Job Hunting Notebook, page 168).

c. Ads.   You should regularly check the classified pages of your daily newspaper as well as the legal newspaper for your area. If you are seeking employment in another city, the main branch of your public library and the main library of large universities in your area may have out-of-town newspapers. If you have friends in these other cities, they might be willing to send you clippings from the classified ads of their newspapers. There are several *national* legal newspapers that sometimes have paralegal employment ads. These include the *National Law Journal* and the *American Lawyer.* Law libraries often subscribe to such newspapers.

Look for ads under the headings "Paralegal" or "Legal Assistant." For example:

PARALEGAL
  TRUST ACCOUNTANTS
For details see our ad in
this section headed
  ACCOUNTANT

PARALEGALS Fee Pd.
Salary Open. Corporate &
Real Estate positions. Superior writing ability is a
necessity. Must be able to
work under pressure. Superior opportunities. Contact . . .

**PARALEGAL
(CORPORATE)**
Large downtown Boston law firm seeks expd Corporate Paralegal. Oppty for responsibility & growth, Must have strong academic background. Computer literacy a plus. Salary commensurate with exp. Send resume in confidence to: X2935 TIMES

LEGAL ASSISTANT
Large West Palm Beach, Florida, firm wishes to employ legal assistant with immigration/naturalization experience, in addition to civil litigation, research & pleading abilities. Knowledge of Germanic languages helpful. Full fringe benefits/profit sharing. Salary negotiable. Contact . . .

For detailed quotes from want ads for a variety of different kinds of paralegal jobs, see pages 108–126.

Some ads are placed by private employment agencies that specialize in legal placements. The ad may not give the name and address of the employer seeking the paralegal. Instead, it will direct interested parties to an intermediary, such as a newspaper, which forwards all responses to the employer. Such ads are called "blind ads."

You will find that most want ads seek paralegals with experience in a particular area of practice. Hence if you are a recent graduate of a paralegal school who is looking for a beginning or entry-level position, you may not meet the qualifications sought in the ads.[17] Should you apply for such positions nevertheless? Suppose, for example, that an add seeks "a corporate paralegal with two years of experience." You might consider answering such an ad as follows:

> I am responding to your ad for a corporate paralegal. I do not have the experience indicated in the ad, but I did take an intensive course on corporate law at my paralegal school, and I'm wondering whether I could send you my resume so that you could consider what I have to offer.

If the answer is no, you can certainly ask for leads to anyone else who might be hiring individuals like yourself.

When reading want ads, do not limit yourself to the entries for "Paralegal" and "Legal Assistant." Also look for headings for positions that may be law related, such as "Research Assistant," "Legislative Aide," "Law Library Assistant." For example:

RESEARCH ASSISTANT

IMMEDIATE POSITION
Social Science Research Institute in downtown looking for coder/editor of survey instruments. Post Box L3040.

PROOFREADER
Leading newspaper for lawyers has an immediate opening for a proofreader of manuscripts and galleys. Attention to detail, some night work. Past experience preferred. Low teens. Call Nance, 964-9700, Ext. 603.

LEGISLATIVE ASSISTANT/SECRETARY
Good skills essential, dwntwn location, send resume/sal. requirements to Post Box M 8341.

---

[17]At the end of this chapter, we will examine the catch-22 problem of "no job/no experience" and "no experience/no job" when we discuss "your second job."

| RECRUITMENT COORDINATOR | LEGISLATIVE ASST/ADMIN | ADMINISTRATOR—LAW |

RECRUITMENT COORDINATOR

Local office of national law firm seeks individual to coordinate attorney recruiting and paralegal program. B.A. required and 1–3 year's personnel, recruitment, or paralegal experience preferred. Salary commensurate with experience. E.O.E. Please send resume and salary requirements to LT Box 9-24-2101.

LEGISLATIVE ASST/ADMIN—If you are looking for that foot in the door, apply up on CAPITOL HILL, here's the job for you. Newsmaking Congressman seeks dedicated indiv to handle challenging & rewarding duties. Track legislation, handle corresp & mailing. Get involved in the fast-paced world of Capitol Hill. Good typg. Call Tues–Fri 8:30–4.

LIBRARY/CLERICAL—permanent, full-time pos. at lge law firm library. Duties incl. looseleaf filing, processing new books & periodicals, shelving books, and some typing. Exper. w/looseleaf filing pref. Good benefits and excel. leave policy. Respond to Post Box No. M8272.

ADMINISTRATOR—LAW

Medium-size established law firm seeks manager with administrative, financial, and personnel experience and EDP familiarity to supervise all non-legal office activities. Salary commensurate with experience. Equal opportunity employer. Applicants should send resumes with salary requirements to LT Box 9-17-2085.

Of course, some of the above jobs may not be what you are looking for. They may not be directly related to your legal training and experience. Nevertheless, you should read such ads carefully. Some might be worth pursuing.

On most classified pages, you will find many ads for legal secretaries or word processors. You might want to respond to such ads as follows:

I saw your ad for a legal secretary. I am a trained paralegal and am wondering whether you have any openings for paralegals. If not, I would greatly appreciate your referring me to any attorneys you know who may be looking for paralegals.

What about applying for a clerical position in a law office? Many paralegals take the view that this would be a mistake. In a tight employment market, however, some paralegals believe that a secretarial or typing job would be a way to "get a foot in the door," and hope that they will eventually be able to graduate into a position in the office that is commensurate with their paralegal training. Such a course of action is obviously a very personal decision that you must make on your own. It is not uncommon for clerical staff to be promoted to paralegal positions in a firm. It is also not uncommon, however, to get stuck in a clerical position.

Should you ever respond to want ads *for attorneys?* Such ads are common in legal newspapers and magazines. Of course, a paralegal cannot claim to be an attorney. But any office that is looking for attorneys obviously has a need for legal help. Hence, consider these possible reasons for responding to such ads, particularly when they give the name and address of the office seeking the attorney:

■ Perhaps the office is *also* looking for paralegal help but is simply not advertising for it (or you have not seen the want ad for paralegals).

- Perhaps the office is having difficulty finding the attorney it is seeking and would consider hiring a paralegal for a temporary period of time to perform paralegal tasks *while* continuing the search for the attorney.
- Perhaps the office has never considered hiring a paralegal *instead of* an attorney, but would be interested in exploring the idea.

Many of these employers may be totally uninterested in a response by a paralegal to an ad for an attorney. Yet none of the possibilities just described is irrational. The effort might be productive. Even if you are given a flat rejection, you can always use the opportunity to ask the person you contact if he or she knows of any other offices that are hiring paralegals.

Finally, a word about want ads placed *by a paralegal* seeking employment. Should you ever place an ad in a publication read by attorneys, such as the journal of the bar association, or the legal newspaper for your area? Such ads can be expensive and are seldom productive. Nevertheless, if you have a particular skill—for example, if you are a former nurse trained as a paralegal and are seeking a position in a medical malpractice firm, an ad might strike a responsive chord.

d. Through Other Paralegals.   In Strategy 4 above, we discussed methods to contact working paralegals. Once you talk with a paralegal, you can, of course, obtain information about contacting the employing attorney of that paralegal.

e. Employment Agencies.   There have always been employment agencies for the placement of attorneys. Many of these agencies also handle paralegal placement. Recently, a number of agencies have been opened to deal primarily with paralegal placement. Here is an example of an ad from such an agency:

Help Wanted

Paralegal Agency   Fee Paid

**Paralegal Placement Experts Recognized by
Over 200 Law Firms and Corporations**

PENSIONS

Outstanding law firm seeks 1+yrs pension paralegal exper. Major responsibilities, quality clients & liberal benefits. Salary commensurate w/exper.

LITIGATION

SEVERAL positions open at LAW FIRMS for litigation paralegals. Major benefits incl bonus.

MANAGING CLERK

Midtown law firm seeks 1+ yrs exper as a managing clerk. Work directly w/top management. Liberal benefits.

These are just a few of the many paralegal positions we have available. Call us for professional career guidance.

Look for such ads in the classified pages of general circulation and legal newspapers. Check your yellow pages under "Employment Agencies." If you are not sure which of the listed agencies cover legal placements, call several at random and ask which agencies in the city handle paralegal placement or legal placement in general. Caution is needed, however, in using such agencies. Some of them know very little about paralegals, in spite of their ads claiming to place paralegals. You may find that the agency views a paralegal as a secretary with a little extra training.

All employment agencies charge a placement fee. You must check whether the fee is paid by the employer or by the employee hired through the agency. Read the agency's service contract carefully before signing. Question the agency about the jobs they have available—for instance, whether evening work is expected or what typing requirements there are, if any.

Finally, you should find out if a paralegal *staffing agency* exists in your area. This is an employment agency that provides part-time employment at law offices. Most of the people placed are paralegals with experience in a particular area of practice. The paralegals are often paid by the agency, which in turn is paid by the offices. Law firms and corporate law departments may prefer part-time paralegals because of the low overhead costs involved, the availability of experienced people on short notice for indefinite periods, and the ability to end the relationship without having to go through the sometimes wrenching experience of terminating permanent employees.

f. Directories and Other Lists of Attorneys.   Find out whether there is a directory or list of attorneys in your area. Ask a librarian at any law library in your area. Your yellow pages will also list attorneys generally or by specialty.

Also check with a librarian about national directories of attorneys. One of the major directories is the *Martindale-Hubbell Law Directory* which gives descriptions of law firms by state and city or county (see Figure 2.5). For each firm, you are given brief biographies of the attorneys (listing bar memberships, colleges attended, etc.) as well as the areas of practice for the firm. (In 1992, Martindale-Hubbell started to include information on paralegals and other legal support personnel in law firms.) Also inquire about the availability of specialty lists of attorneys. Examples include criminal law attorneys, corporate counsel, bankruptcy attorneys, black attorneys, women attorneys, etc. Read whatever biographical data is provided on the attorneys. If there is something you have in common with a particular attorney (for example, you were both born in the same small town or you both went to the same school), you might want to mention this fact in a cover letter or phone conversation.

If you have access to either of the two major computer research systems—WESTLAW or LEXIS—you can locate attorneys online. LEXIS gives you the entire *Martindale-Hubbell Law Directory*. WESTLAW has created its own directory: *West's Legal Directory*. See Figure 2.6.

Finally, you may want to examine the *Directory of Legal Employers*, published by the National Association of Law Placement. As mentioned earlier, it lists the names and addresses of law firms and corporations that hire attorneys. But it will also indicate the number of paralegals employed by the offices listed in the directory. There are two places where you can find this directory: in the placement offices of most law schools and on WESTLAW.

g. Courts and Bar Association Meetings.   You can also meet attorneys at the courts of your area—for example, during a recess or at the end of the day. Bar association committee meetings are sometimes open to nonattorneys. When the other strategies for contacting attorneys do not seem productive, consider going to places where attorneys congregate. Simply introduce yourself and ask if they know of paralegal employment opportunities at their firms or at other firms. If you meet an attorney who practices in a particular specialty, it would be helpful if you could describe your course work or general interest in that kind of law. If you are doing some research in that area of the law, you might begin by asking for some research leads before you ask about employment.

FIGURE 2.5
Excerpt from a Page in Martindale-Hubbell Law Directory

POYATT, ROYCROFT & MACDONALD
Established In 1968

731 SHADY LANE
DALLAS, TEXAS 75202
Telephone: 214-555-6720

Fax: 214-555-6730

Fort Worth, Texas Office: 34 Main Street, Suite 10, 77001
Telephone: 817-555-9224.   Fax: 817-555-9220

Poyatt, Roycroft & MacDonald was founded in 1968 by Kathleen Poyatt, Greg Roycroft and Julie MacDonald, former classmates and graduates of the University of Texas Law School. Starting with a local general practice, the firm now serves the entire state and maintains two fully-staffed offices offering a wide range of legal services. The firm encourages continuing professional development, and all partners and associates participate in continuing legal education seminars, professional association activities and civic affairs.

MEMBERS OF FIRM

KATHLEEN POYATT, born Plano, Texas, May 13, 1940; admitted to bar, 1967, Texas and U.S. Court of Appeals, Fifth Circuit. *Education:* Tulane University (B.A., with honors, 1962); University of Texas (J.D., cum laude, 1967). Phi Beta Kappa; Phi Delta Phi; Order of the Coif. Associate Editor, Texas Law Review, 1966–1967. Certified Public Accountant, Texas, 1971. Member, Advisory Board, Dallas Family Planning Council, 1982–1984. Legal Counsel, Dallas Board of Realtors, 1986–1987. *Member:* Dallas and American Bar Associations; State Bar of Texas (Chair, Committee on Trust Administration, Estate Planning and Probate Section, 1989–); American Judicature Society. (Board Certified, Estate Planning and Probate Law, Texas Board of Legal Specialization). LANGUAGES: Spanish and French. SPECIAL AGENCIES: Texas Council on Charitable Trusts. REPORTED CASES: Mastalia v. Fairty, 145 S.E. 2d 1405. TRANS-ACTIONS: Bankruptcy of Braniff Airlines, 1982; The Keepwell Foundation, 1990. AREAS OF CONCENTRATION: Trust Administration, Banking and Creditors' Rights, Trial, Litigation and Real Estate.

JULIE MACDONALD, born Nashville, Tennessee, August 29, 1940; admitted to bar, 1967, Texas and U.S. District Court, Northern District of Texas. *Education:* University of Tennessee at Memphis (B.A., with honors, 1962); University of Texas (J.D., with honors, 1967). Alpha Lambda Delta; Phi Kappa Phi; Phi Beta Kappa. Member, Tennessee State Board of Professional Responsibility, 1983–1984; Dallas Association of Young Lawyers; The Association of Trial Lawyers of America. *Member:* Dallas (*Member:* Real Estate and Commercial Real Estate Morning Section; Continuing Education Committee) and American (*Member:* Real Property Section; Continuing Education Committee). Bar Associations; State Bar of Texas; Dallas Association of Young Lawyers; The Association of Trial Lawyers of America, LANGUAGES: Spanish and Italian. SPECIAL AGENCIES: Texas Council on Taxation Trusts. REPORTED CASES: Cunoo v. Banks, 466 S.E. 2d 6609; Kyle v. Smily, 432 S.E. 2d 4599. TRANSACTIONS: The Hines foundation, 1989. AREAS OF CONCENTRATION: Trials and Appeals, Estate Planning, Real Estates, Banking and Taxation.

LEGAL SUPPORT PERSONNEL
PARALEGAL

LINDA DAVIS, born Maurice, Louisiana, August 16, 1962. *Education:* Interstate Paralegal Institute. Certified Legal Assistant, Texas, 1985. President, Dallas Paralegal Association, 1987. Secretary, Texas State Paralegal Association, 1988. *Member:* National, State and Local Paralegal Association. Legal Research, Drafting Legal Pleadings, Client Correspondence, Deposition Summaries and File Investigations.

---

b. Miscellaneous.   Go to a recent reporter volume or advance sheet of a reporter volume containing court opinions of your state. At the beginning of each opinion, there is a list of the attorneys who represented the parties in that case. You can obtain their addresses from standard directories such as those mentioned above. If the opinion is on an area of law in which you have an interest, call the attorneys after you have read the opinion. Ask a question or two about the case and that area of the law. Then ask about employment opportunities for paralegals in that area.

Look for ads in legal newspapers in which an attorney is seeking information about a particular product involved in a suit that is contemplated or underway. Or read feature stories in this newspaper on major litigation that is about to begin. If the area of the law interests you, contact the law firms in-

FIGURE 2.6

Sample Screen from West's Legal Directory

Name:	Jones, James E
City:	Boston
State:	Massachusetts
Position:	Partner
Firm:	Smith, Jones & White
Address:	1000 State Street, Exchange Plaza, Boston, MA 90001
Phone:	(617)722-7777
Electronic Mail:	Fax Area Code (617) Phone 722-7776
Born:	May 20, 1947, Dallas, TX. U.S.A.
Education:	Baylor University, Waco, Texas (J.D., 1973), Cum Laude
	University of Texas, Austin, Texas (B.A., 1969)
Admitted:	Massachusetts 1975
	Texas 1973
	Federal Court 1979
Fraternities:	Phi Alpha Delta
Directorships:	Massachusetts Commerce Association, 1980–Present
Affiliations:	American Bar Association
	State Bar of Massachusetts
Representative Clients:	Semi-Conductor, Inc.
	BCA National Bank
Representative Cases:	Thayer v. Smith, 560 S.W.2d 137 (1989)
Practice:	50% Patent, Trademark, Copyright
	25% Corporations Law
	25% Litigation
Foreign Languages:	Russian
Certified Specialty:	Patent, Trademark, Copyright--U.S. Patent & Trademark Office
Published Works:	*Corporations and Business Law*, 1981, CAB Publishing Company

volved to ask about employment opportunities for paralegals. Many firms hire additional paralegals, particularly for large cases.

Find the bar journal of your local or state bar associations in the law library. The articles in the journal are often written by attorneys from the state. If the subject of an article interests you, read it and call the author. Ask a question or two about the topic of the article and the area of the law involved. Then ask about employment opportunities for paralegals in that area.

Strategy 7: Prepare Your Resume, Cover Letter, and Writing Sample

The cardinal principle of resume writing is that the resume must fit the job you are seeking. Hence, you must have more than one resume or you must rewrite your resume for each kind of paralegal job you are seeking. A resume is an *advocacy* document. You are trying to convince someone (a) to give you an interview and ultimately (b) to offer you a job. You are not simply communicating information about yourself. A resume is *not* a summary of your life or a one-page autobiography. It is a very brief *commercial* in which you are trying to sell yourself as a person who can make a contribution to a particular prospective employer. Hence the resume must stress what would appeal to this employer. You are advocating (or selling) yourself effectively when the form and content of the resume has this appeal. Advocacy is required for several reasons. First, there are probably many more applicants than jobs available. Second, most prospective employers ignore resumes that are not geared to their particular needs.

Before examining sample resumes, we need to explore some general guidelines that apply to *any* resume.

Guidelines on Drafting an Effective Resume

1. Be concise and to the point. Generally, the resume should fit on one page. A longer resume is justified only if you have a unique education or experience that is directly related to law or to the particular law firm or company in which you are interested.

2. Be accurate. Studies show that about 30% of all resumes contain inaccuracies. Recently, a legal administrator felt the need to make the following comment (to other legal administrators) about job applicants: "I'm sure we have all had experiences where an applicant has lied on an application about experience, previous salary scales, length of time with previous employers, training, skills, and anything else they can think of that will make them appear more attractive."[18] While you want to present yourself in the best possible light, it is critical that you not jeopardize your integrity. All of the data in the resume should be verifiable. Prospective employers who check the accuracy of resumes usually do so themselves, although some use outside organizations such as the National Credential Verification Service.

3. Include personal data—that is, name, address, zip code, and phone (with area code) where you can be reached. (If someone is not always available to take messages while you are away, invest in an answering machine.) Do not include a personal photograph or data on your health, height, religion, or political party. You do not have to include information that might give a prospective employer a basis to discriminate against you illegally, such as your marital status or the names and ages of your children. Later we will discuss how to handle such matters in a job interview.

4. Provide a concise statement of your career objective at the top of the resume. (It should be pointed out, however, that some people recommend that this statement be included in the cover letter rather than in the resume.) The career objective should be a quick way for the reader to know whether your goal fits the needs of the prospective employer. Hence, *the career objective should be targeted to a particular employer.* An overly general career objective gives the unfortunate effect of a "mass-mailing resume." Suppose, for example, you are applying for a position as a litigation paralegal at a forty-attorney law firm that is looking for someone to help with scheduling and document handling on several cases going on simultaneously.

Don't say: **Career Objective**—A position as a paralegal at an office where there is an opportunity for growth.

Do say: **Career Objective**—A position as a litigation paralegal at a medium-sized law firm where I will be able to use and build on the organization skills I developed in my prior employment and the case management skills that I have learned to date.

---

[18]Jacobi, *Back to Basics in Hiring Techniques,* The Mandate, 1 (Ass'n of Legal Administrators, San Diego Chapter, October 1987).

The first statement is too flat and uninformative. Its generalities could fit just about *any* paralegal job. Even worse, its focus is on the needs of the applicant. The second statement is much more direct. While also referring to the needs of the applicant, the second statement goes to the heart of what the employer is looking for—someone to help create order out of the complexity of events and papers involved in litigation.

5. Next, state your prior education and training.[19] (See Job Hunting Notebook, page 164, page 165.) List each school or training institution and the dates attended. Use a reverse chronological order—that is, start the list with the most current and work backwards. Do not include your high school unless you attended a prestigious high school, you have not attended college, or you are a very recent high school graduate. When you give your legal education:

a. List the major courses.

b. State specific skills and tasks covered in your courses that are relevant to the job you are applying for. Also state major topic areas covered in the courses that demonstrate a knowledge of (or at least exposure to) material that is relevant to the job. For example, if you are applying for a corporate paralegal job, relevant courses could be stated as follows:

> **Corporate Law:** This course examined the formation of a corporation, director and shareholder meetings, corporate mergers, and the dissolution of corporations; we also studied sample shareholder minutes and prepared proxy statements. Grade received: B+.

> **Legal Bibliography:** This course covered the basic law books relevant to researching corporate law, including the state code. We also covered the skills of using practice books, finding cases on corporate law through the digests, etc. Grade received: A−.

c. List any special programs in the school, such as unique class assignments, term papers, extensive research, moot court, internship, or semester projects. Give a brief description if any of these programs are relevant to the job you are applying for.

d. State any unusually high grades: give overall grade point average (GPA) if it is distinctive.

List any degrees, certificates, or other recognition that you earned at each school or training institution. Include high aptitude or standard test scores. If the school or institution has any special distinction or recognition, mention this as well.

6. State your work experience. (See Job Hunting Notebook, pages 161–163.) List the jobs you held, your job title, the dates of employment, and the major duties that you performed. (Do not state the reason you left each job, although you should be prepared to discuss this if you are granted an interview.) Again, work backwards. Start with the most current (or your present) employment. The statement of duties is particularly important. If you have legal experience, emphasize specific duties and tasks that are directly relevant to the position you are seeking—for example, include that you drafted corporate minutes or prepared incorporation papers. Give prominence to such skills and tasks on the resume. Nonlegal experience, however, can also be relevant. Every

---

[19]If you already have experience as a paralegal and are seeking to change jobs, the next section of the resume should be work experience, followed by education and training.

prior job says something about you as an individual. Phrase your duties in such jobs in a manner that will highlight important personality traits. (See p. 163.) In general, most employers are looking for people with the following characteristics:

- Emotional maturity
- Intelligence
- Willingness to learn
- Ability to get along with others
- Ability to work independently (someone with initiative and self-reliance who is not afraid of assuming responsibility)
- Problem-solving skills
- Ability to handle time pressures and frustration
- Loyalty
- Stability, reliability
- Energy

As you list duties in prior and current employment settings, do *not* use any of the language just listed. But try to state duties that tend to show that these characteristics apply to you. For example, if you had a job as a camp counselor, state that you supervised 18 children, designed schedules according to predetermined objectives, prepared budgets, took over in the absence of the director of the camp, etc. A listing of such duties will say a lot about you as a person. You are someone who can be trusted, you know how to work with people, you are flexible, etc. These are the kind of conclusions that you want the reader of your resume to reach. Finally, try to present the facts to show a growth in your accomplishments, development, and maturity. Note that *action verbs* were used in examples just given: supervised, designed, prepared, took over. Concentrate on such verbs. Avoid weak verbs such as "involved in" or "was related to."

7. State other experience and skills that do not fall within the categories of education and employment mentioned above. (See Job Hunting Notebook, p. 163.) Perhaps you have been a homemaker for 20 years, you raised five children, you worked your way through college, you were the church treasurer, a cub scout volunteer,. etc In a separate category on the resume called "Other Experience," list such activities and state your duties in the same manner mentioned above to demonstrate relevant personality traits. Hobbies can be included (without using the word "hobby") when they are distinctive and illustrate special talents or achievement.

8. State any special abilities (for example, that you can design a database or speak a foreign language), awards, credentials, scholarships, membership associations, leadership positions, community service, publications, etc., that have not been mentioned elsewhere on the resume.

9. No one has a perfect resume. There are facts about all of us that we would prefer to downplay or avoid, e.g., sudden change in jobs, school transfer because of personal or family difficulties, low aptitude test scores. There is no need to point out these facts, but in a job interview you must be prepared to discuss any obvious gaps or problems that might be evident from your resume. Thus far we have been outlining the format of a *chronological resume* in which your education, training, and experience are presented in a chronological se-

quence from the present backwards. (See Figure 2.8.) Later we will examine how a *functional resume* might be more effective than a chronological resume in handling difficulties such as sudden changes or gaps in employment. (See Figure 2.9.)

10. At the end of the resume, say, "References available on request." On a separate sheet of paper, type the names and addresses of people who know your abilities and who could be contacted by a prospective employer. If the latter is seriously considering you for a position, you will probably be asked for the list. This will most likely occur during a job interview. Generally, you should seek the permission of people you intend to use as references. Call them up and ask if you can list them as references in your job search.

11. Do not include salary requirements or your salary history on the resume. Leave this topic for the interview.

12. The resume should be neatly typed, grammatically correct, and readable. Be sure that there are no spelling errors or smudge spots from erasures or fingerprints. In this regard, if you can't make your resume *perfect,* don't bother submitting it. Avoid abbreviations except for items such as street, state, degrees earned, etc. Do not make any handwritten corrections. Proofread carefully. Ask someone else to proofread the resume for you to see if you missed anything.

You do not have to use complete sentences in the resume. Sentence fragments are adequate as long as you rigorously follow the grammatical rule on parallelism. For example, say, "research*ed* securities issues, draf*ted* complaints, serv*ed* papers on opposing parties." Do not say, "researched securities, drafting complaints, and I served papers on opposing parties." When you present a series or a list, be consistent in using words ending in "ed" or ending in "ing," etc. Do not suddenly change from an "ed" word to an "ing" word or add personal pronouns on only some of the items in the series or list.

Leave generous margins. Cluster similar information together and use consistent indentation patterns so that readers can easily scan the resume and quickly find those categories of information in which they are most interested.

The resume should have a professional appearance. Consider having your resume typeset on quality paper (with matching envelopes) by a commercial printing company or word processing service. Obtain multiple copies of your resume. Avoid submitting a resume that was obviously reproduced on a poor-quality Xerox machine at a corner drugstore. The resume is often the first contact that a prospective employer will have with you. You want to convey the impression that you know how to write and organize data. Furthermore, it is a sign of respect to the reader when you show that you took the time and energy to make your resume professionally presentable. Law offices are *conservative* environments. Attorneys like to project an image of propriety, stability, accuracy, and order. Be sure that your resume also projects this image.

13. Again, the resume concentrates on those facts about you that show you are particularly qualified *for the specific job you are seeking.* The single most important theme you want to convey in the resume is that you are a person who can make a contribution to *this* organization. As much as possible, the reader of the resume should have the impression that you prepared the resume for the particular position that is open. In style and content, the resume should emphasize what will be pleasing to the reader and demonstrate what you can contribute to a particular office. (See Figure 2.7.)

The last guideline is very important. You cannot comply with it unless you have done some *background research* on the law office where you are applying

FIGURE 2.7

The Resume as an Advocacy Document

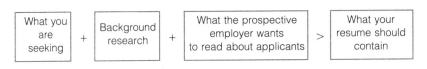

and, if possible, on the person who will be receiving the resume. How do you do this background research? First and foremost, you want to try to contact employees, particularly paralegals, who work there now or who once worked there. That's why Strategy 4, outlined above, on ways to locate working paralegals is so important.

In addition, consult one of the directories of attorneys, such as the *Martindale-Hubble Law Directory* or *West's Legal Directory,* discussed earlier. Ask a librarian for a current directory of attorneys used in your state. Many large firms have brochures on their firms which are part of marketing strategies to find new clients. They may also have newsletters that they send to their current clients. Such brochures and newsletters may not be available to the general public unless someone within the firm gives you access to them.

If you are applying for a position in the law department of a large corporation, call the public relations office of the corporation and ask for promotional literature and a copy of its annual report. Many law libraries have directories of corporate counsel which you should check. In addition, most general libraries have directories, such as *Standard & Poor's Register of Corporations, Directors and Executives* and *Moody's Bank and Finance Manual,* that provide information on such companies. Ask the librarian what other sources provide profiles of businesses.

Here is a partial checklist of information you want to obtain through background research on a prospective employer or job (see also page 156):

- Why has the office decided to hire a paralegal now? What needs or problems prompted this decision?
- What kind of law is practiced at the office? What are its specialties?
- How is the office structured and governed? By management committee?
- How old is the office? Has it expanded recently? If so, in what areas?
- What kinds of clients does the office have? A variety of small clients? Several large clients that provide most of the fees?
- If the office is the law department of a corporation, what are the company's main products or services?
- How many attorneys are in the office?
- How many paralegals? What kind of work do they do? Does the office understand the role of paralegals? What kinds of complaints have the paralegals had about the office? What are the advantages and disadvantages of working in the office?
- Has the office had personnel problems? High turnover?
- Does the office operate through systems? If not, how does it feel about developing such systems?

If you do your homework on a prospective employer, you will have begun collecting answers to such questions so that you can tailor your resume to these answers. You will select those aspects of your prior employment or education, for example, that suggest or demonstrate you are able to handle the demands of the job.

Of course, for many jobs, you will *not* be able to obtain answers to these questions, no matter how much background research you do. You will simply have to do the best you can to predict what the "correct" answers are and structure your resume, cover letter, and writing samples accordingly.

The main point, however, is that a lot of preparation is needed before you approach a prospective employer. Much time and energy must be expended. A conscientious and organized job search will be good preparation for the career ahead of you. *The same kind of motivation, creativity, and aggressiveness that is needed to find a good job is also needed to perform effectively as a paralegal and to advance in this field.* The cornerstone of achievement and success is a heavy dosage of old-fashioned hard work.

Figure 2.8 is an example of a *chronological resume,* the most common and traditional format used by many applicants today. As indicated earlier, this re-

<table>
<tr><td colspan="2" align="center">**JOHN J. SMITH**
43 BENNING ROAD SE
SALEM, MARYLAND 21455
(301) 456-0427</td></tr>
<tr><td>**Career Objective**</td><td>Position as a paralegal at a small law firm in the area of probate, trusts, and estates in a firm where my accounting and legal skills will be used and where there are opportunities for growth.</td></tr>
<tr><td>**Education**</td><td>Jan. 1989–Jan. 1990 Maynard Paralegal Institute.
Courses:
Trusts and Estates: The course presented an overview of probate procedure in Maryland. We covered how to conduct a client conference to collect the basic facts and how to prepare the 105 short form.
Tax I: An introduction to the taxation of estates and general income tax; fundamentals of accounting; valuation of personal and real assets.
Introduction to Law   Civil Procedure
Family Law   Legal Research
Litigation
Internship: Part of the curriculum at Maynard involved a six-week internship placement at a law firm; I was placed at Donaldson and Tannance, a general practice firm in Salem. Tasks undertaken at the internship: drafted answers to interrogatories in a divorce case on the ground of mental cruelty; maintained the office's tickler system; completed cite checking and shepardizing for an appellate brief.
Sept. 1987–June 1988 Jefferson Junior College Courses:
Business Law   Sociology
English I, II   Chemistry
Introduction to Psychology   Creative Writing
French I</td></tr>
<tr><td>**Employment**</td><td>1985–1988 Teller, Salem National Bank
Responsibilities: received deposit and withdrawal requests; trained new tellers, supervised note department in the absence of the assistant manager.
1980–1984 Driver, ABC Biscuit Company</td></tr>
<tr><td>**Honors**</td><td>1985 Junior Achievement Award for Outstanding Marketing</td></tr>
<tr><td>**Associations**</td><td>Financial Secretary, Salem Paralegal Association
Regional Representative, National Federation of Paralegal Associations
Member, National Association of Legal Assistants</td></tr>
<tr><td>**References**</td><td>Available on request.</td></tr>
</table>

FIGURE 2.8
Sample Chronological Resume

FIGURE 2.9

Sample Functional
Resume[20]

Jane Doe
18 East 7th Avenue
Denver, Colorado 80200
303-555-1198

JOB OBJECTIVE

A position in a legal office requiring skills in communications, research, and organization, leading toward training for and work as a paralegal.

BRIEF SUMMARY OF BACKGROUND

Bachelor of Arts and Bachelor of Science (Education) with major in English and minor
in Library Science. Taught creative writing and communications to high school jun-
iors and seniors; worked several years as research and index assistant in records
and research department of large, international organization; worked part-time on a
volunteer basis in schools and libraries as librarian and reading tutor.

PROFESSIONAL SKILLS RELATED TO CAREER OBJECTIVE

Communications Skills

Taught communications to high school seniors; read extensively in international publications during nonworking years; conducted workshops on library skills and sto-
rytelling to children and young adults; participated in workshops with educators on
reading skills; served as Circulation Representative for *The Christian Science Monitor,* which included promoting and selling subscriptions by telephone and in person.
Gained considerable writing experience while working toward college degree in
English.

Clerical Skills

Facility with [a] vocabulary and spelling; [b] rules of diction and usage; [c] typing
(80 wpm); [d] filing (helped revise and maintain many files including administrative,
subjective, alpha-chrono combinations); [e] systems (maintained and circulated library collections and maintained catalog card files).

Research Skills

As librarian: helped students and teachers research and retrieve information and
materials on various subjects; ordered, received, processed, and shelved library
materials.

As research assistant: indexed correspondence; researched files for information using subject index; collated information on various subjects.

Analytical and Organizational Skills

Handled all phases of management of school library; planned for materials needed;
ordered to meet those needs; supervised assistants; set up revised filing systems;
helped engineer departmental move to new quarters.

EMPLOYMENT HISTORY

9/84–Present	Lincoln Elementary School 100 Oak Street, Denver, Colorado 80000 *Title:* Teacher's Aide (Part-time)
6/76–6/84	International Church Center Executive Department, Records and Research Section 465 E. 8th St., Boston, Massachusetts 02127 *Title:* Research and Index Assistant (1 year full-time; 7 years part-time)
4/84–6/84	Latin Preparatory School 16 Adams Court, Dorchester, Massachusetts 02139 *Title:* School Librarian (substitute)
2/83–6/84	James P. O'Reilly Elementary School 74 Statler Road, Boston, Massachusetts 02140 *Title:* School Librarian (volunteer)
9/74–6/75	Roosevelt High School 16 Main St., Minneapolis, Minnesota 55162 *Title:* English Teacher

Continued

EDUCATION

1983–1984	University of Massachusetts, Boston Campus Special courses included: Library and Urban Children; Design Management
1979–1980	Harvard Extension, Problems in Urban Education
1909–1973	University of Minnesota, Minneapolis, B.S. and B.A., *Major:* English *Minor:* Library Science

SCHOOL ACTIVITIES

National Honor Society; Dramatic Club; Creative Writing Club; YWCA; Member, Minnesota Dance Company, 1969–1973.

REFERENCES

Available on request.

FIGURE 2.9

Sample Functional Resume[20]
—Continued

sume presents your education, training, and work history in reverse chronological sequence, beginning with the most recent events and working backwards.

A *functional resume,* on the other hand, clusters certain skills or talents together regardless of the period in which they were developed. See Figure 2.9. This style of resume can be particularly useful when you want to downplay large gaps in education, when you are making a radical change of careers, or when your skills were not gained in paralegal education, training, or employment. The functional resume should not, however, ignore the chronological sequence of the major training and work events of your life, since a prospective employer will want to know what this sequence is. Note that the functional resume in Figure 2.9 has a skill cluster early in the resume, after which there is the historical overview in reverse chronological order. Because of this format, the emphasis of the resume is on the skills or abilities highlighted at the beginning.

Cover Letter

The *cover letter* should state how you learned of the office. It should also highlight and amplify those portions of the resume that are relevant to the position you are seeking. Without being unduly repetitive of the resume, explain how you are qualified for the job. Like the resume itself, the cover letter should give the impression that you are a professional. It is also important that you communicate a sense of enthusiasm about the position.

Note that the cover letter in Figure 2.10 is addressed to a specific person. It would be inappropriate to send a "To Whom It May Concern" letter. Find out the exact name of the person to whom the resume should be sent. If you are not sure, call the office and ask.

One final, critically important point about the cover letter: it must be grammatically correct and contain no spelling errors. Your standard must be perfection. While this is also true of the resume, it is particularly true of the cover letter. When the envelope is opened, the first thing that is read is the cover letter. Most of us are *unaware of how poor our grammar is.* We have been lulled into a sense of security because readers of what we write—including teachers—

---

[20]Rocky Mountain Legal Assistants Association, *Employment Handbook for Legal Assistants,* 26–8 (1979).

FIGURE 2.10
Cover Letter

> 43 Benning Road SE
> Salem, Maryland 21455
> 301/456-0427
> March 13, 1990
>
> Linda Stenner, Esq.
> Stenner, Skidmore & Smith
> 438 Bankers Trust Bldg.
> Suite 1200
> Salem, Maryland 21458
>
> Dear Ms. Stenner:
>
> Michael Diamond, Esq. told me that your firm may have an opening for a trusts and estates paralegal. I am enclosing my resume for your consideration. I am very interested in working in the field of probate, trusts, and estates. The course work that I did at Maynard Institute and my prior work at the Salem National Bank provided me with an appreciation of the complexity of this area of the law. I find the field fascinating.
>
> I am fully aware of the kind of attention to detail that a paralegal in this field must have. If you decide to check any of my references, I am confident that you will be told of the high level of discipline and responsibility that I bring to the tasks I undertake.
>
> I have two writing samples that may be of interest to you: a draft of a will that I prepared in my course on trusts and estates, and a memorandum of law on the valuation of stocks. These writing samples are available on request.
>
> I would appreciate the opportunity to be interviewed for the paralegal position at your firm. I feel confident that my training and experience have prepared me for the kind of challenge that this position would provide.
>
> Sincerely,
>
> John J. Smith

seldom complain unless we make an egregious error. People read primarily for content; they do not focus on grammar and spelling. Hence you must provide this focus on your own. In the section on studying at the beginning of this book, there are suggestions for improving your writing skills. In the meantime, proofread, proofread, proofread; and then find others to proofread everything that you intend to submit in writing to a prospective employer.

Writing Samples

You should be constantly thinking about writing samples based upon the course work you do and any legal employment or internship experiences you have had. If your writing sample comes from a prior job or internship, be sure that the confidentiality of actual parties is protected by "whiting out" or changing their names.[21] In addition, consider preparing other writing samples *on your own.* For example:

■ a brief memorandum of law on the application of a statute to a set of facts that you make up

---

[21] "It is always inappropriate to hand a prospective employer anything that has current, active case information anywhere in it: case names and numbers, court and internal file numbers, names, addresses, telephone numbers of deponents, names of plaintiffs, defendants, and third parties in the body of the document." Fitzgerald, *Ethics and the Job Hunting Paralegal,* 18 Reporter (Los Angeles Paralegal Ass'n, November 1989).

- a pleading such as a complaint
- a set of interrogatories
- articles of incorporation and bylaws for a fictitious corporation
- an analysis of a recent court opinion
- an in-take memorandum of law based on an interview that you role-play with another student
- an annotated bibliography on a particular topic
- a brief article that you write for a paralegal newsletter on an aspect of your legal education or work experience as a paralegal

Prepare a file of all your writing samples. (See Job Hunting Notebook, page 167.) If possible, try to have a teacher, practicing attorney, or paralegal review each sample. Rewrite it based on their comments. You must take the initiative in preparing writing samples and in soliciting feedback from knowledgeable contacts that you make. You need to have a large pool of diverse writing samples from which to choose once you begin the actual job hunt. Start preparing these samples now.

Strategy 8: The Job Interview

Once you have overcome the hurdles of finding a prospective employer who will read your cover letter and resume, the next problem is to arrange for a job interview. In your cover letter, you may want to add the following sentence at the end: "Within the next two weeks, I will give you a call to determine whether an interview would be possible." This strategy does not leave the matter entirely up to the prospective employer as to whether there will be further contact with you. You must be careful, however, not to appear too forward. Some may resent this approach. On the other hand, you have little to lose by trying it several times to see what response you obtain.

Always try to have a paralegal, attorney, administrator, or secretary in the office arrange the interview for you with the person who will be doing the hiring and/or interviewing. Hopefully, your background research into the office will enable you to identify such an in-house person who will put in a word for you.

Job Interview Guidelines

(See Job Hunting Notebook, page 169.)

"Attired in your best interviewing suit, you nervously navigate your way to the reception area of what you hope will be your future employer's office. You are a comfortable ten minutes early. Upon arrival you are directed to the office of the interviewer, whom you greet with a smile and pleasant handshake. She offers you a cup of coffee, which you wisely refuse, since you may spill it. She then looks you in the eye and poses her first question. 'Why are you interested in working for this company?' [Suddenly you go blank!] All thoughts leave your mind as you pray for the ability to speak." Cunningham, *A Planned Approach to Interviewing*, 5 The LAMA Manager 1 (Legal Assistants Management Association, Fall 1989).

1. Be sure you have the exact address, room number, and time of the interview. Give yourself sufficient time to find the office. If the area is new to you, be sure that you have precise directions. It would be unfortunate to start your contact with the office by having to provide excuses for being late. Arrive at least

ten minutes early. You will probably be nervous and will need to compose yourself before the interview. It is important that you are as relaxed as possible.

2. Try to find out in advance who will be interviewing you. Don't be surprised, however, if the person who greets you is a substitute for the person originally scheduled to conduct the interview. There are a number of different kinds of people who might conduct the interview: the law office manager, the managing attorney, the supervising attorney for the position, the paralegal supervisor, a staff paralegal, or a combination of the above if you are interviewed by different people on the same day or on different days. The style of the interview may be quite different depending on who conducts it. Someone with management responsibility might stress the interpersonal dimensions of the position, whereas a trial attorney might give you the feeling that you are being cross-examined. Try to determine whether you are being interviewed by the person who has the final authority to hire you. In many offices, you will be interviewed by someone whose sole task is to screen out unacceptable applicants. If you make it through this person, the next step will usually be an interview with the ultimate decision-maker. Whenever you know or suspect that you will be interviewed by an attorney, try to obtain his or her professional biography through *Martindale-Hubbell* or other directories. You might be lucky enough to get to talk with someone who has been interviewed by this person before (such as a paralegal now working at the office, a fellow job seeker, or someone at the local paralegal association) so that you can obtain a sense of what to expect.

3. Although relatively uncommon, you may have to face a *group interview*. There could be several interviewers questioning you at once. Alternatively, one or more interviewers could interview you along with, and at the same time as, other candidates for the job.

4. Make sure that you are prepared for the interview. Review the guidelines discussed above on writing your resume. In the resume and in the interview, you are trying to sell yourself. Many of the principles of resume writing apply to the interview. Know the kinds of questions you will probably be asked. Rehearse your responses. Write down a series of questions (tough ones) and ask a friend to role-play an interview with you. Have your friend ask you the questions and critique your responses. Also take the role of the interviewer of your friend so that you can gauge both perspectives. Be prepared to handle a large variety of questions. See Figure 2.11. Keep in mind, however, that no matter how much preparation you do, you may still be surprised by the course the interview takes. Be flexible enough to expect the unexpected. If you are relaxed, confident, *and prepared,* you will do fine.

5. You are not required to answer potentially illegal questions—for instance, "Are you married?" Some employers use the answers to such irrelevant questions to practice illegal sex discrimination. You need to decide in advance how you will handle them if they are asked. You may want to ask why the question is relevant. Or you may simply decide to steer the interview back to the qualifications that you have and the commitment that you have made to a professional career. A good response might be, "If you're concerned that my marital status may affect my job performance, I can assure you that it will not." Follow this up with comments about dedication and job commitment. It may be the perfect time to offer references.[22] Whatever approach you take, be sure to remain courteous.

---

[22]Reitz, *Be Steps Ahead of Other Candidates: Understand the Interview Game,* 5 Legal Assistant Today 24, 84 (March/April 1988).

- **Open-Ended Questions** (which are calculated to get you to talk, giving the listener an idea of how you organize your thoughts)
    (1) Tell me about yourself.
    (2) What kind of position are you seeking?
    (3) What interests you about this job?

- **Closed-Ended Questions** (which can be answered by one or two words)
    (4) When did you receive your paralegal certificate?
    (5) Did you take a course in corporate law?

- **Soft-Ball Questions** (which should be fairly easy to answer if you are prepared)
    (6) What are your interests outside of school and work?
    (7) What courses did you enjoy the most? Why? Which were least rewarding? Why?
    (8) Do your grades reflect your full potential? Why or why not?
    (9) Why did you leave your last job?
    (10) How have you grown or developed in your prior jobs? Explain.
    (11) How were you evaluated in your prior jobs?
    (12) What are your strengths as a worker?
    (13) Describe an ideal work environment. What would your "dream job" be?
    (14) What factors make a job frustrating? How would you handle these factors?
    (15) What do you hope to be doing in ten years? What are your long-term goals?
    (16) If you are hired, how long are you prepared to stay?
    (17) Are you interested in a job or a career? What's the difference?
    (18) Why did you become a paralegal?
    (19) What problems do you think a paralegal might face in a busy law office? How would you handle these problems?
    (20) Can you work under pressure? When have you done so in the past?
    (21) How flexible are you in adapting to changing circumstances? Give examples of your flexibility in the last year.
    (22) How do you feel about doing routine work?
    (23) Do you prefer a large or a small law office? Why?
    (24) What accomplishment in your life are you most proud of? Why?
    (25) What salary expectations do you have? What was your salary at your last position?
    (26) What other questions do you think I should ask in order to learn more about you?
    (27) What questions would you like to ask me about this office?

- **Tension Questions** (which are calculated to put you on the spot in order to see how you handle yourself)
    (28) No one is perfect. What are your weaknesses as a worker?
    (29) Have you ever been fired from a position? Explain the circumstances.
    (30) Why have you held so many jobs?
    (31) Name some things that would be unethical for an attorney to do. What would you do if you found out that the attorney supervising you was doing these things?
    (32) Are you a competitive person? If not, why not? If you are, give some examples over the last six months that demonstrate this characteristic.
    (33) Is there something in this job that you hope to accomplish that you were not able to accomplish in your last job?

FIGURE 2.11

The Six Categories of Job Interview Questions

Continued

FIGURE 2.11

The Six Categories
of Job Interview
Questions—
Continued

(34) Do you type? If not, are you willing to learn?

(35) Do you smoke? If so, how would you handle a work environment that is totally smoke-free, including the washrooms?

(36) Where else have you interviewed for a job? Have you been turned down?

(37) Why wouldn't you want to become an attorney now?

(38) Everyone makes mistakes. What is the biggest mistake that you made in any of your prior jobs and how did you handle it?*

(39) No job is perfect. What is the least appealing aspect of the job you are seeking?

(40) There are over 50 applicants for this one position. Why do you think you are the most qualified?

(41) If you are offered this position, what are the major concerns that you would have about taking it?

(42) What would make you want to quit a job?

(43) Give some examples of when you have shown initiative over the last six months in school or at your last job.

- **Hypothetical Questions** (in which you are asked how you would handle a stated fact situation)

(44) If you were told, "This isn't any good, do it again, and get it right this time," what would you do?

(45) If you find out on Friday afternoon that you're expected to come in on Saturday, what would you do?**

(46) Assume that you are given the position here and that you work very closely on a day-to-day basis with an attorney. After a six-month period, what positive and negative comments do you think this attorney would make about you as a worker?

(47) Suppose that your first assignment was to read through and summarize 4,000 documents over an eight-month period. Could you do it? Would you want to do it?

(48) Assume that two airplanes crash into each other and that your firm represents one of the passengers who was killed. What kind of discovery would you recommend?

- **Potentially Illegal Questions** (because the questions are not relevant to the candidate's fitness and ability to do most jobs)

(49) Are you married? Do you plan to marry?

(50) Do you have any children? If so, how old are they? Who takes care of your children?

(51) If you do not have any children now, do you plan to have any in the future?

(52) How old are you?

(53) What is your religion?

(54) What is your political affiliation?

---

*Moralez, *Sample Interview Questions*, 11 Paragram (Oregon Legal Assistant Ass'n, May 1988).

**Wendel, *You the Recruiter*, 5 Legal Assistant Today 31 (September/October 1987).

6. Avoid being critical of anyone. Do not, for example, "dump on" your prior employer or school. Criticizing or blaming other organizations, even if justified, is likely to give the interviewer the impression that you will probably end up blaming *this* organization if you get the job and difficulties arise.

7. What about being critical of yourself? You will be invited to criticize yourself when you are asked the seemingly inevitable question, "What are your weaknesses?" You may want to pick a *positive* trait and express it as a negative.

For example: "I tend to get frustrated when I'm not given enough to do. My goal is not just to collect a paycheck. I want to make a contribution." Or: "I think I sometimes have expectations that are too high. There is so much to learn, and I want it all now. I have to pace myself, and realize that the important goal is to complete the immediate task, even if I can't learn every conceivable aspect of that task at the present time." Or: "I get irritated by carelessness. When I see someone turn in sloppy work, or work that is not up to the highest standards, it bothers me."

If you use any of these approaches, be sure that you are able to back them up when you are asked to explain what you mean. You will probably be asked to give concrete examples of such "weaknesses."

8. If you have done the kind of background research on the office mentioned earlier, you will have a fairly good idea what the structure and mission of the office is. Interviewers are usually impressed by applicants who demonstrate this kind of knowledge during the interview. It will be clear to them which applicants have done their homework. A major goal of the interview is to relate your education and experience to the needs of the office. To the extent possible, you want to know what these needs are before the interview so that you can quickly and forcefully demonstrate that you are the person the office is looking for. Most offices decide to hire someone because they have a problem—for example, they need someone with a particular skill, they need someone to help them expand, or they need someone who can get along with a particularly demanding supervising attorney. If you are not sure, ask the interviewer directly why the office has decided to add a paralegal. The success of the interview is directly related to your ability to identify the problem of the office and to demonstrate how you can solve it for them.

9. If the paralegal job is in a certain specialty, such as probate or corporate law, you must be prepared to discuss that area of the law. You may be asked questions designed to assess your familiarity with the area. Prior to the interview, spend some time reviewing your class notes. Skim through a standard practice book for that area of the law in the state. Be sure that you can back up anything you said in your resume about prior involvement with the area in your school or work experience. Such discussions are always an excellent opportunity for you to present writing samples in that field of the law. (Be sure to bring extra copies of such writing samples and of your resume).

10. Dress conservatively. "It is recommended that a man be clean shaven, wear a dark suit (gray or navy blue), a white shirt, and a muted-tone tie. Shoes should be polished. A woman should wear a skirt-suit or a blazer and skirt, plain blouse, neutral-colored stockings, and a simple hairdo. A minimal amount of jewelry and no perfume are the rule. . . . To complete these 'uniforms,' a briefcase is a necessity. It symbolizes that you are a professional. Women may want to keep their purses in their briefcases."[23]

11. Be sure that you project yourself positively. Take the initiative in greeting the interviewer. A firm handshake is recommended. Maintain good posture and eye contact. Remember that everything you do will be evaluated. The interviewer will be making mental notes on your body language. Avoid appearing ill at ease or fidgety. Many feel that the practice of law is a battlefield. The interviewer will be forming an opinion of whether you "fit in."

12. Try to avoid the topic of salary until the end of the interview when you have completed the discussion of the job itself. Preferably, let the interviewer

---

[23]Berkey, *Successful Interviewing,* 5 Legal Assistant Today 66 (September/October 1987).

raise the issue. Think through how you will handle the topic, but try to avoid discussing it until the appropriate time arises. If asked what salary you are seeking, give a salary range rather than a single rigid figure. Always relate salary to the specific skills and strengths that you would be able to bring to the office, rather than to the "going rate." You need to know what the going rate is—check recent salary surveys of local and national paralegal associations—so that the salary range you seek is realistic. But avoid using the going rate as the first and sole reason for your position on salary.

13. Be an active participant in the interview even though you let the interviewer conduct the interview. Help keep the discussion going.

14. Be enthusiastic, but not overly so. You want to let the office know that you really want the job, not because you are desperate but because you see it as a challenge offering professional development. You are qualified for the job and you feel that the office is the kind of place that recognizes valuable contributions from its workers.

15. Be yourself. Do not try to overwhelm the interviewer with your cleverness and charm.

16. Be prepared to leave the following documents with the interviewer: extra copies of your resume, a list of references, and writing samples.

17. Ask the interviewer if you can be given the opportunity to talk with one or more paralegals currently working at the office. It will be another sign of your seriousness.

18. Ask your own questions of the interviewer. In effect, you are interviewing the office as much as the other way around. Come with a written list and don't be afraid to let the interviewer see that you have a checklist of questions that you want to ask. It is a sign of an organized person. There is a great deal of information about the job that you could inquire about. From your background research about the job, you should already have some of this information, but you can now verify what you know. You want to ask pertinent and intelligent questions that will communicate to the interviewer that you are serious about the paralegal field, that you are prepared, and that you grasp what the interviewer has been telling you about the job and the office.

Below are some of the topics that you could cover in your own questions. See also Figure 2.12 and Figure 2.13 for ideas on questions.

- What type of person is the office seeking to hire?
- What prompted the office to seek this type of person?
- What are some examples of paralegal responsibilities? Will the paralegal specialize in certain tasks or areas of the law? (Ask for a description of a typical workday of a paralegal at the firm.)
- What skills will the paralegal need for the job? Digesting? Investigation? Research? Drafting? Interviewing?
- How many attorneys are in the firm? Is the number growing, declining, remaining constant?
- How is the firm managed or governed? Managing partner? Management committees? Legal administrator? Is there a policy manual for the firm?
- How many paralegals are in the firm? Is the number growing, declining, remaining constant? Are all the paralegals at the firm full-time? Does the firm use part-time or freelance paralegals? Has the firm considered hiring a paralegal coordinator?
- Is there a career ladder for paralegals in the firm?

- How long has the firm used paralegals? What is the average length of time a paralegal stays with the firm? What are the feelings of firm members on the value of paralegals to the firm? Why is this so? How would firm members describe an ideal paralegal employee? Do all members of the firm feel the same about paralegals? What reservations, if any, do some members of the firm have about paralegals?

- What other personnel does the firm have (secretaries, computer staff, library staff, clerks, messengers, part-time law students, etc.)? How many of each are there? What relationship does the paralegal have with each?

- What kind of supervision does a paralegal receive? Close supervision? From one attorney? Several?

- Will the paralegal work for one attorney? Several? Will the paralegal have his or her own case load? Is there a paralegal pool available to many attorneys?

- What kind of client contact will the paralegal have? Phone? Meetings? Interviews? Document inspection at client's office?

- What kind of correspondence will the paralegal be preparing? Letters that the paralegal will sign? Letters for attorney to sign? Memos?

- What opportunities does a paralegal have for further learning? Office training programs? (Do paralegals attend new-attorney training sessions?) Does the firm encourage outside training for paralegals, e.g., from paralegal associations, bar associations, area schools?

- Will the paralegals be attending staff meetings? Strategy sessions with attorneys?

- How are paralegals evaluated in the office? Written evaluations? Oral? How often?

- Are paralegals required to produce a set number of billable hours? Per day? Per week? Per month? Annually? What is the hourly rate at which a paralegal's time is billed to a client? Do different paralegals in the office bill at different rates? If so, what determines the difference?

- How often are paralegals required to record their time? Daily, hourly, in ten-minute segments, etc.?

- What secretarial assistance is available to the paralegal? None? A personal secretary? Secretary shared with an attorney? Use of a secretarial pool? Will the paralegal do any typing? Light typing? His or her own typing? Typing for others?

- Does the job require travel?

- What equipment will the paralegal be using? Word processor, typewriter, copier, dictaphone, research computer?

- Office space for the paralegal? Private office? Shared office? Partitioned office?

- Compensation and benefits—See Figure 2.12, Checklist of Possible Paralegal Fringe Benefits.

19. After you have thoroughly explored the position during the interview, if you still want the job, ask for it. Be sure that you make a specific request. Some interviewers go out of their way to stress the difficult aspects of the job in order to gauge your reaction. Don't leave the interviewer with the impression

FIGURE 2.12

Checklist of
Possible Paralegal
Fringe Benefits

Compensation:

_____ Salary Increase Policy (amount? criteria for determining? frequency of review? who reviews?)

_____ Overtime (frequency? method of compensation?)

_____ Bonus (method for determining? frequency?)

_____ Cost-of-Living Adjustment (frequency? method for determining?)

_____ Other Incentive Programs, like Profit Sharing Plan

_____ Pension/Retirement Plan (defined benefit? defined contribution? other?)

_____ Tax Deferred Savings Plan

_____ Other Investment Plan

Insurance:

_____ Basic Medical (full coverage? partial?)

_____ Major Medical (full coverage? partial?)

_____ Dependent Medical Insurance (fully paid? partially paid?)

_____ Supplemental Medical (fully paid? partially paid?)

_____ Dental (full coverage? partial?)

_____ Maternity Leave (full coverage? partial?)

_____ Eye Care/Glasses (full coverage? partial?)

_____ Life Insurance (full coverage? partial?)

_____ Physical Disability (short term? long term? full coverage? partial?)

_____ Sick Days (number? carry-over of unused sick leave allowed?)

Professional Activities:

_____ Time Off for Association Events

_____ Association Dues Paid

_____ Association Dinner Events Paid

_____ Tuition Reimbursement for Paralegal Classes

_____ Tuition Reimbursement for Law School

Other:

_____ Vacation (number of days? carry over of unused vacation allowed?)

_____ Personal Leave Days (number allowed?)

_____ Child Care Assistance

_____ Paid Holidays (number?)

_____ Parking (fully paid? partially paid?)

_____ Leased Car

_____ Mileage Allowance

_____ Club Membership

_____ Fitness Center

_____ Refreshments on the Job

_____ Sports Tickets

_____ Entertainment Allowance

_____ Free Legal Advice and Representation by the Firm on Personal Matters

Comparability:

_____ Paralegal Fringe Benefits Similar to Those of New Attorneys?

_____ Paralegal Fringe Benefits Similar to Those of Secretaries?

_____ Policy Manual on Paralegal Use in Office (available?)

_____ Evaluation (method? frequency?)

_____ Career Ladder for Paralegals in Office (criteria for advancement?)

_____ Supervision of Paralegal (by attorney? by paralegal manager? by legal administrator?)

_____ Supervision by Paralegal (secretary? assistant to paralegal?)

_____ Work Assignments (who delegates? one attorney? several? paralegal manager?)

_____ Availability of Secretarial Assistance

_____ Paralegal Turnover in Office (low? high?)

_____ Client Contact (frequent? rare?)

_____ Attendance at Trials (frequent? rare?)

_____ Sit at Counsel's Table (frequent? rare?)

_____ Billable Hours: hourly rate?

_____ Billable Hours: quota? (monthly quota? annual quota?)

_____ Time Spent on Non-Billable Matters (frequent? rare? type?)

_____ Office Space (private? shared?)

_____ Use of Computers (frequent? rare?)

_____ Availability of Word Processing Department to Paralegal (frequent? rare?)

_____ Typing (own work? attorney's work?)

_____ How Management Perceives Paralegals (professionals? administrative? support staff? combination?)

_____ Flexible Work Schedule

_____ Travel Required (frequent? rare? type?)

_____ Attendance at Attorney Strategy Meetings (frequent? rare?)

_____ Attendance at Management Meetings (frequent? rare?)

_____ Office Training for Paralegals (kind? frequency?)

_____ In-House Attorney Training Available to Paralegals (frequent? rare?)

_____ CLE (Continuing Legal Education) for Attorneys Available to Paralegals (frequent? rare?)

_____ Business Cards Provided

_____ Name on Door

_____ Name on Letterhead Stationery of Law Office

_____ Has Own Letterhead Stationery

_____ Office Correspondence (does paralegal ever sign under own name?)

_____ Attendance at Attorney Retreats (frequent? rare?)

_____ Attendance at Attorney Social Functions (frequent? rare?)

FIGURE 2.13

Checklist of Factors that Help Determine the Quality of the Work Environment of a Paralegal

that you may be having second thoughts if in fact you still want the job after you have had all your questions answered.

Follow-Up Letter

After the interview, always send a letter to the person who interviewed you. In a surprising number of cases, the follow-up letter is a significant factor in obtaining the job. In the letter:

■ Thank the person for the interview.

- Tell the person that you enjoyed the interview and the opportunity to learn about the office.
- State that you are still very interested in the position.
- Briefly restate why you are qualified for the position.
- Clarify any matters that arose during the interview.
- Submit references or writing samples that may have been asked for during the interview.

Keep a copy of all such letters. In a notebook, maintain accurate records on the dates you sent out resumes, the kinds of resumes you sent, the dates of interviews, the names of people you met, your impressions, the dates when you made follow-up calls, etc. (See page 171.)

If you are turned down for a job, find out why. Call the office to try to obtain more information than is provided in standard rejection statements. Politely ask what could have improved your chances. Finally, use the occasion to ask for any leads to other prospective employers.

■ ASSIGNMENT 2.1

Role-play an interview in class. The instructor will decide what kind of job the interview will be for, and will select students to play the role of interviewer and interviewee. The interviewer should ask a variety of questions such as those presented above in the guidelines for handling a job interview. The rest of the class will evaluate the performance of the interviewee. What mistakes did he or she make? How should he or she have dealt with certain questions? Was he or she confident? Overconfident? Did he or she ask the right questions of the interviewer? Were these questions properly timed? What impressions did the interviewee convey of himself or herself? Make a list of dos and don'ts for such interviews.

 ## Section E. The Job Hunting Notebook

Purchase a large three-ring, loose-leaf notebook for your Job Hunting Notebook. Include in it the outline of sections listed below. Following the outline, create at least one page for each section.

There are a number of purposes for the Notebook:

- To help you identify your strengths based on past legal or nonlegal employment, training, and other life experience.
- To help you organize this data for your resumes.
- To provide you with checklists of contacts that you should start making immediately.
- To help you prepare for job interviews.
- To provide a place to store copies of resumes, cover letters, writing samples, follow-up letters, notes on job leads and strategies, personal impressions, etc.
- To keep a calendar on all aspects of the job search.

The Notebook is your own personal document. No one else will see it unless you choose to share its contents with others.

Outline of Job Hunting Notebook

Part I. Resume & Writing Sample Preparation

1. Prior and Current Nonlegal Employment—Analysis Sheet
2. Prior and Current Legal Employment—Analysis Sheet
3. Prior and Current Volunteer Activity—Analysis Sheet
4. Other Life Experiences—Analysis Sheet
5. Nonlegal Education & Training—Analysis Sheet
6. Legal Education & Training—Analysis Sheet
7. Notes on Resume Writing
8. Draft of General Resume
9. Drafts of Specialized Resumes
10. Writing Samples

Part II. Contacts for Employment

11. Contacts—Attorneys You Already Know or with Whom You Have Indirect Association
12. Contacts—Employed Paralegals
13. Contacts and Tasks—General

Part III. Legwork in the Field

14. Job Interview Checklist
15. Job Interview—Analysis Sheet
16. Record Keeping

. . . .

1. Prior and Current Nonlegal Employment—Analysis Sheet

2. Prior and Current Legal Employment—Analysis Sheet

3. Prior and Current Volunteer Activity—Analysis Sheet

We begin by analyzing your experience in nonlegal jobs (e.g., cashier, truck driver); then in legal jobs (e.g., legal secretary, investigator); and finally in volunteer activity (e.g., church sale coordinator, political campaign assistant). Make a list of these jobs and volunteer activities. Start a separate sheet of paper for each entry on your list, and then do the following:

- State the name, address, and phone number of the place of employment or location of the volunteer work.
- State the exact dates you were there.
- State the names of your supervisors there. (Circle the name of supervisors who had a favorable impression of you. Place a double circle around the name of each supervisor who would probably write a favorable recommendation for you, if asked.)
- Make a list of every major task you performed there. Number each task, starting with number 1. (As you write this list, leave a three-inch *left-hand margin* on the paper. In front of the number for each task, place as many of the following letters that apply to that task. When an explanation or description is called for, provide it on attached sheets of paper.)

B   The task required you to conform to a *budget*. (Briefly describe the budget, including its size and who prepared it.)

C   There was some *competition* in the office about who is the person most qualified to perform it. (Briefly describe why you were the most qualified.)

E   *You were evaluated* on how well you performed the task. (Briefly describe the evaluation of you.)

EI   To perform the task, you occasionally or always had to *exercise initiative;* you did not just wait for detailed instructions. (Briefly describe the initiative you took.)

ET   You occasionally or frequently had to devote *extra time* to perform the task. (Briefly describe the circumstances.)

J/C   It was not a mechanical task; you had to exercise some *judgment* and/or *creativity* to perform it. (Briefly describe the kind of judgment or creativity you exhibited.)

M   *Math* skills were involved in performing the task. (Briefly describe what kind of math you had to do).

OD   *Others depended* on your performing the task well. (Briefly describe who had to rely on your performance and why.)

OT   You always or regularly performed the task *on time.*

OW   To perform the task, you had to coordinate your work with *other workers;* you did not work alone. (Briefly describe the nature of your interaction with others.)

P   You had some role in *planning* how the task would be performed; you were not simply following someone else's plan. (Briefly describe your planning role.)

PI   You did not start out performing the task; you were formally or informally *promoted into* it. (Briefly describe what you did before being asked to perform this task and the circumstances of the promotion.)

PP   You are *personally proud* of the way you performed the task. (Briefly describe why.)

R   You made *recommendations* on how the task could be more efficiently performed or better integrated into the office. (Briefly describe the recommendations you made and what effect they had.)

RR   You *received recognition* because of how well you performed the task. (Briefly describe what recognition you received and from whom.)

SE   To perform the task, you had to operate *some equipment* such as computers or motor vehicles. (Briefly describe the equipment and the skills needed to operate it.)

SO   To perform the task, you had to *supervise others* or help supervise others. (Briefly describe whom you supervised and what the supervision entailed.)

T   You *trained* others to perform the task. (Briefly describe this training.)

TP   You had to work under *time pressures* when you performed the task; you didn't have forever to perform it. (Briefly describe these pressures.)

W   There was some *writing* involved in performing the task. (Briefly describe what kind of writing you did.)

Include other characteristics of the task that are not covered in this list.

4. Other Life Experiences—Analysis Sheet

Circle *each* of the following experiences that you have had. Do not include experiences that required schooling, since these experiences will be covered elsewhere in the Notebook. Do not include experiences that involved volunteer work unless you have not already included them elsewhere in the Notebook. Attach additional sheets as indicated and where more space is needed.

- Raised a family alone
- Helped raise a family
- Traveled extensively
- Read extensively in a particular field on your own
- Learned to operate a computer on your own
- Learned a language on your own
- Learned a craft on your own, such as weaving or fixing cars
- Learned an art on your own, such as painting or sculpture
- Developed a distinctive hobby requiring considerable skill
- Other life experiences (list each)

Attach a separate sheet of paper for *each* of the life experiences or activities that you listed above. Write the activity at the top of the sheet. Answer the following questions for each activity:

a. How long did you engage in this activity?

b. Have you ever tried to teach this activity to someone else? If so, describe your efforts.

c. Do you think you could teach this activity to others? Explain your answer.

d. Which of the following characteristics do you think are necessary or helpful in being able to perform the activity competently? Do not focus at this point on whether you possess these characteristics. Simply compile a list of what would be helpful or necessary.

Intelligence	Compassion	Patience
Creativity	Responsibility	Dependability
Perseverance	Punctuality	Determination
Drive	Self-confidence	Stamina
Independence	Poise	Self-control
Talent	Efficiency	Grace
Understanding	Skill	Dexterity
Cleverness	Competitiveness	Sophistication
Spirit	Congeniality	Stick-to-itiveness
Conviction	Judgment	Will power
Fortitude	Strength	Zeal
Ambition	Know-how	Experience
Ability to work with others	Imagination	Others? (list)

e. Ask *someone else* (whom you trust and who is familiar with you) to look at the list. Ask this person if he or she would add anything to the list. Then ask him or her to identify which of these characteristics apply to *you* for this activity.

f. Now it's your turn. Which of these characteristics do *you* think apply to you for this activity?

g. If there are any major differences in the answers to (e) and (f) above, how do you explain the discrepancy? Are you too hard on yourself? Do you tend to put yourself down and minimize your strengths?

5. *Nonlegal Education and Training—Analysis Sheet*

On a separate sheet of paper, list every school or training program *not* involving law that you have attended or are now attending (whether or not you completed it), starting with the most recent. Include four-year colleges, two-year colleges, vocational training schools, weekend seminars, work-related training programs, internships, church training programs, hobby training programs, self-improvement training, etc. Include everything since high school.

Devote a separate sheet of paper to each school or training program, writing its name at the top of the sheet and answering the following questions for it. If more than one course was taught, answer these questions for two or three of the most demanding courses.

a. What were the exact or approximate dates of attendance?

b. Did you complete it? What evidence do you have that you completed it? A grade? A certificate? A degree?

c. Were you required to attend? If so, by whom? If not, why did you attend?

d. How did you finance your attendance?

e. What requirements did you meet in order to attend? Was there competition to attend? If so, describe in detail.

f. Describe the subjects taught. What was the curriculum?

g. How were you evaluated?

h. What evidence of these evaluations do you have? Could you obtain copies of them?

i. Describe in detail any writing that you had to do, such as exams or reports. Do you have copies of any of these written items? If not, could you obtain copies? Could any of these items be rewritten now for use as a writing sample?

j. What skills other than writing did you cover, such as organization, research, speaking, reading, manual dexterity, machine operation, interpersonal relations?

k. What evidence do you have or could you obtain that shows you covered these skills and how well you did in them?

l. Did you receive any special award or distinction? If so, describe it and state what evidence you have or could obtain that you received it.

m. Make a list of every favorable comment you can remember that was made about your work. What evidence of these comments do you have or could you obtain?

n. Was the experience meaningful in your life? If so, explain why. How has it affected you today?

o. What, if anything, did you do that called for extra effort or work on your part beyond what everyone else had to do?

p. Have you ever tried to teach someone else what you learned? If so, describe your efforts. If not, could you? Describe what you could teach.

q. List each teacher who knew you individually. Circle the name of each teacher who would probably write you a letter of recommendation if asked.

r. Would any other teacher or administrator be able to write you a letter of recommendation based on the records of the school or program? If so, who?

s. Does the school or program have a reputation for excellence? If so, describe its reputation.

6. *Legal Education and Training—Analysis Sheet*

On a separate sheet of paper, list every *legal* course or training program that you have ever taken—formal or informal. Include individual classes, seminars, internships, etc., at formal schools, on the job, or through associations. Devote a separate sheet of paper to each course or program, writing its name at the top of the sheet and answering the following questions for it.

a. What were the exact dates of attendance?

b. Did you complete it? What evidence do you have that you completed it? A grade? A certificate?

c. What requirements did you meet in order to attend? Was there competition to attend? If so, describe in detail.

d. What text(s) did you use? Photocopy the table of contents in the text(s) and circle those items that you covered.

e. Attach a copy of the syllabus and circle those items in the syllabus that you covered.

f. Make two lists: a list of the major themes or subject areas that you were required to *know* or understand (content) and a list of the things that you were asked to *do* (skills).

g. Make a detailed list of everything that you were asked to write for the course or program, such as exams, memos, research papers, other reports. For every written work product other than exams, give the specific topic of what you wrote. Describe this topic in at least one sentence.

h. Which of these written work products could you now *rewrite* as a writing sample? Whom could you ask to evaluate what you rewrite to insure that it meets high standards?

i. Describe in detail everything else you were asked to do other than mere reading assignments. Examples: role-play a hearing, visit a court, verbally analyze a problem, interview a client, evaluate a title abstract, search a title, operate a computer, find something in the library, investigate a fact.

j. How were you evaluated? What evidence do you have or could you obtain of these evaluations?

k. Did you receive any special award or distinction? If so, describe it and state what evidence you have or could obtain that you received it.

l. Make a list of every favorable comment you can remember that was made about your work. What evidence of these comments do you have or could you obtain?

m. What, if anything, did you do that called for extra work or effort on your part beyond what everyone else had to do?

n. Describe the most valuable aspect of what you learned.

o. Have you ever tried to teach anyone else what you learned? If so, describe your efforts. If not, could you? Describe what you could teach.

p. Describe every individual who evaluated you. Could you obtain a letter of recommendation from these individuals?

7. *Notes on Resume Writing*

It is important that you have an open mind about resumes. There is no correct format. Different people have different views. In the best of all worlds, you will be able to do some background research on the law office where you are applying for work and you will learn what kind of resume (in form and content) that office prefers. When this type of research is not possible, you must do the best you can to predict what kind of a resume will be effective .

On this page in the Notebook, you should collect ideas about resumes from a wide variety of people such as:

Teachers	Program administrators
Working paralegals	Unemployed paralegals
Paralegal supervisors	Legal administrators
Fellow students	Attorneys whom you know
Personnel officers	Authors of books and articles on finding employment
Placement officers	
Legal secretaries	Others

You want to collect divergent viewpoints on questions such as the following:

- What is an ideal resume?
- What are the major mistakes that a resume writer can make?
- What is the best way to phrase a career objective?
- How long should the resume be?
- In what order should the data in the resume be presented?
- How detailed should the resume be?
- What kind of personal data should be included and omitted?
- How do you phrase educational experiences to make them relevant to the job you are seeking?
- How do you phrase employment experiences to make them relevant to the job you are seeking?
- How do you show that nonlegal experiences (school or work) can be relevant to a legal job?
- How do you handle potentially embarrassing facts, e.g., frequent job changes, low course grades?
- What should the cover letter for the resume say?

8. *Draft of General Resume*

Prepare a general resume and include it here. We are calling it general because it is not directed at any specific job. It should be comprehensive with no page limitation. Use the guidelines, questions, and checklists in this Notebook to help you identify your strengths. The resumes you write for actual job searches will be shorter, specialized, and tailored to the job you are seeking.

Before you write specialized resumes, however, you should write a general one that will be your main point of reference in preparing these other resumes. The general resume will probably never be submitted anywhere. Take at least one full day to compile and carefully think about the data needed for the general resume.

9. Drafts of Specialized Resumes

Every time you write a resume that is tailored to a specific job, include a copy here. Also include several practice copies of specialized resumes. While taking a course in corporate law, for example, write a resume in which you pursue an opening at a law office for a corporate paralegal. For each resume that you write (practice or real), solicit the comments of teachers, administrators, fellow students, working paralegals, attorneys, etc. Include these comments in this section of the Notebook.

10. Writing Samples

The importance of collecting a large pool of writing samples cannot be overemphasized. Even if you eventually use only a few of them, the value of preparing them is enormous. The following characteristics should apply to *each* writing sample:

- It is your own work.
- It is clearly and specifically identified. The heading at the top tells the reader what the writing is.
- It is typed (handwritten work should be typed).
- There are no spelling or grammatical errors in it.
- Its appearance is professional.
- Someone whom you respect has evaluated it before you put it in final form.
- You feel that it is a high-quality product.
- It does not violate anyone's right to privacy or confidentiality. (If the sample pertains to real people or events, you have disguised all names or other identifying features.)

There are two main kinds of writing samples: those that are assigned in school or at work and those you generate on your own.

Examples of Required Work That You Could Turn into a Writing Sample

- A memorandum of law
- A legal research report or memo
- An answer to a problem in a textbook
- An exam answer
- An intake memorandum of law
- A complaint
- An answer to a complaint
- A motion
- A set of interrogatories
- Answers to a set of interrogatories
- An index to discovery documents
- A digest of one or more discovery documents
- Other memos, studies, or reports
- Articles of incorporation and bylaws

Any of the above writing samples could be generated on your own if they are not required in your coursework. Ask your teachers or supervisors to help you identify written pieces that you could create. Also consider writing an article for one of the many newsletters of paralegal associations (see Appendix A). The article could cover an aspect of your education or work experience. Or consider writing a review of a recent paralegal book. Even if what you write is not published in a newsletter, it might still become a writing sample if it meets the criteria listed above.

11. Contacts—Attorneys You Already Know or with Whom You Have Indirect Association

Make a list of attorneys as described in Strategy 6 in this chapter, page 135. Not only do you want to know whether any of these attorneys are interested in hiring paralegals, but equally important, you want to know if they can give you any leads to other employers who might be interested in hiring.

12. Contacts—Employed Paralegals

You want to talk with as many employed paralegals as you can in order to obtain leads to possible positions, as well as general guidelines for the job search. Make a list of all the paralegals that you contact and what they tell you. If they have nothing useful to say at the present time, ask them if you could check back with them in several months and if you could leave your name and number with them in the event that they come across anything in the future. See page 132 for ideas on how to locate employed paralegals.

13. Contacts and Tasks—General

Below you will find a general checklist of contacts and tasks that you should consider in your job search. Take notes on the results of these contacts and tasks and include these notes here if they are not included elsewhere in the Notebook. Your notes should include what you did, when, whom you contacted, what was said, what follow-up is still needed, etc.

- Attorneys with whom you already have a direct or indirect association
- Employed paralegals
- Other paralegals searching for work; they may be willing to share leads that were unproductive for them, especially if you do likewise
- Contacts provided by your placement office
- Want ads in general circulation newspapers
- Want ads in legal newspapers
- Want ads and job bank openings listed in paralegal newsletters
- General directories of attorneys, such as *Martindale-Hubbell*
- Special directories of attorneys, such as the *Directory of Corporate Counsel*
- Information from placement offices of local law schools
- Employment agencies specializing primarily in attorney placement
- Employment agencies specializing in paralegal placement
- Staffing agencies specializing in support staff and paralegal placement
- Bar association meetings open to the public

- Legal secretaries who may have leads
- Legal administrators who may have leads
- Local attorneys of record printed in reporter volumes
- Local attorneys who have written articles in bar journals
- Stories in legal newspapers on recent large cases that are in litigation or are about to go into litigation (page 140)
- Local and national politicians who represent your area
- Service companies and consulting firms (page 99)

14. *Job Interview Checklist*

1. _____ Exact location of interview
2. _____ Time of arrival
3. _____ Professional appearance in dress
4. _____ Extra copies of resume
5. _____ Extra copies of writing samples
6. _____ Name of person(s) who will conduct interview
7. _____ Background research on the firm or company so that you know the kind of law it practices, why it is considering hiring paralegals, etc.
8. _____ Role-playing of job interview in advance with a friend
9. _____ Preparation for difficult questions that might be asked, such as why you left your last job so soon after starting it
10. Preparation of questions that you will ask regarding:
  _____ Responsibilities of position
  _____ Skills needed for the position
  _____ Methods of supervision
  _____ Office's prior experience with paralegals
  _____ Career ladder for paralegals
  _____ Relationship between paralegals, secretaries, and other clerical staff
  _____ Client contact
  _____ Opportunities for growth
  _____ Methods of evaluating paralegals
  _____ Continuing education
  _____ Billable hours expected of paralegals
  _____ Availability of systems
  _____ Working conditions (typing, photocopying, office, etc.)
  _____ Travel
  _____ Overtime
  _____ Equipment use
  _____ Compensation and fringe benefits (see Figure 2.12)
11. _____ Follow-up letter

15. *Job Interview—Analysis Sheet*

Write out the following information *after* each job interview that you have.

1. Date of interview
2. Name, address, and phone number of firm or company where you interviewed
3. Name(s) and phone number(s) of interviewer(s)
4. Kind of position that was open
5. Date you sent the follow-up letter
6. What you need to do next (send list of references, send writing samples, provide missing information that you did not have with you during the interview, etc.)
7. Your impressions of the interview (how you think you did, what surprised you, what you would do differently the next time you have an interview)
8. Notes on why you did not get the job

16. *Record Keeping*

You need a system to keep track of the steps taken to date. See Figure 2.14, Record Keeping & the Job Search. In addition, keep a calendar in which you record important future dates, such as when you must make follow-up calls, when the local paralegal association meets, etc.

■ Section F. Your Second Job

If you examine want ads for paralegals (p. 136), you will find that most prospective employers want paralegals with experience. The market for such individuals is excellent. But if you are *new* to the field, you are caught in the dilemma of not being able to find a job without experience and not being able to get experience without a job. How do you handle this classic Catch-22 predicament?

■ You work even harder to compile an impressive resume. You make sure that you have collected a substantial writing-sample file. Such writing samples are often the closest equivalent to prior job experience available to you.

■ When you talk to other paralegals, you seek specific advice on how to present yourself as an applicant for the first job.

■ You consider doing some volunteer work as a way to acquire experience for your resume. Legal service offices (page 83) and public interest law firms (page 98) often encourage volunteer work. A recent law school graduate struggling to start a practice may be another option.

■ You may have to reassess what you will accept for your first job. Perhaps you can eventually turn the first job into a more acceptable position. You may simply use it to gain the experience necessary for landing a better second job.

■ Pray for luck.

FIGURE 2.14 Record Keeping & the Job Search

CALLS MADE TO:	DATE	RESUME SENT TO:	DATE	FOLLOW-UP	DATE	WRITING SAMPLES PROVIDED TO:	DATE	INTERVIEW	DATE	FOLLOW-UP	DATE

FIGURE 2.15

Positions for
Experienced
Paralegals

- Paralegal supervisor
- Law office administrator (Legal administrator)
- Law firm marketing administrator
- Paralegal consultant
- Freelance/independent paralegal
- Law librarian/assistant
- Paralegal teacher
- Paralegal school administrator
- Placement officer
- Bar association attorney referral coordinator
- Court administrator
- Court clerk
- Sales representative for legal publisher/vendor
- Investigator
- Customs inspector
- Compliance and enforcement inspector
- Occupational safety and health inspector
- Lobbyist
- Legislative assistant
- Real estate management consultant
- Real estate specialist
- Real estate portfolio manager
- Land acquisitions supervisor
- Title examiner
- Independent title abstractor
- Abstractor
- Systems analyst
- Computer analyst
- Computer sales representative
- Bank research associate
- Trust officer (Trust administrator)
- Trust associate
- Assistant loan administrator
- Fiduciary accountant
- Financial analyst/planner
- Investment analyst
- Assistant estate administrator
- Enrolled agent
- Equal employment opportunity specialist
- Employee benefit specialist/consultant
- Pension specialist
- Pension administrator
- Compensation planner
- Corporate trademark specialist

Continued

■ Corporate manager

■ Securities analyst

■ Securities compliance officer

■ Insurance adjustor

■ Actuarial associate

■ Claims examiner

■ Claims coordinator

■ Director of risk management

■ Environmental specialist

■ Editor for a legal or business publisher

■ Recruiter, legal employment agency

■ Personnel director

■ Administrative law judge

■ Arbitrator

■ Mediator

■ Internal security inspector

■ Evidence technician

■ Demonstrative evidence specialist

■ Fingerprint technician

■ Polygraph examiner

■ Probation officer

■ Parole officer

■ Corrections officer

■ Politician

■ Etc.

FIGURE 2.15

Positions for
Experienced
Paralegals—
Continued

Once you have had several years of experience and have demonstrated your competence, you will find many more employment options available to you. You will find it substantially easier to negotiate salary and articulate your skills in a job interview. You can also consider other kinds of employment where your legal training, skills, expertise, and experience are valuable. It is not uncommon for a paralegal to be recruited by former or active clients of a first employer. Numerous business contacts are made in the course of a job; these contacts could turn into new careers. In Figure 2.15 you will find a list of some of the types of positions that paralegals have taken after they demonstrated their ability and acquired legal experience.

In short, you face a different market once you have acquired a record of experience and accomplishment. You are in greater demand in law firms and businesses. Furthermore, your legal skills are readily transferable to numerous law-related positions.

Chapter Summary

Someone once said that finding a job is a job in itself. This is especially true in the current market. It will take determination to find what you want. The first step is to become informed about where paralegals work and what they do at those locations. The first part of this chapter was designed to provide you with this information. The major employers of paralegals are private law firms, the government, legal service offices, corporations, and other businesses. While other settings also exist, these are the largest. After examining these settings, we looked at approximately 45 specialties such as bankruptcy and criminal law. Our focus was the identification of paralegal functions in the specialties and a paralegal perspective of what life is like in each. For the specialties where most paralegals work—litigation, corporate law, estates, and real estate—quotations from job ads identified traits and skills employers want.

In the second half of the chapter, we turned to strategies for finding employment. The strategies addressed the following questions: When should you begin the search? How do you compile a Job Hunting Notebook? How do you organize an employment workshop? How do you locate working paralegals in order to obtain leads to employment? How do you arrange an informational interview? How can you use local paralegal associations as a resource? How do you locate potential employers? How do you do background research on potential employers? What should your resume contain? What is an effective cover letter? What kinds of writing samples should you prepare, and when should you start preparing them? How should you prepare for a job interview? What kinds of questions should you anticipate? What kinds of questions should you ask? How can you organize all of the contacts, events, and pieces of paper that are involved in a comprehensive job search?

Finally, we examined alternative career opportunities for paralegals, particularly for those who have gained paralegal experience on the job.

Key Terms

private law firm
legal clinic
paralegal manager
paralegal specialist
general schedule (GS)
Office of Personnel
    Management
neighborhood legal service
    office
judicare
indigents
corporate counsel
special interest groups
group legal services
assigned counsel
legal insurance

public defender
freelance paralegal
service company
consulting firm
paralegal specialties
conflicts specialist
legalman
landmen
private sector
public sector
public benefits
PI cases
tort
job bank
National Paralegal Reporter
Facts & Findings

informational interview
networking
blind ad
staffing agency
Martindale-Hubbell
chronological resume
functional resume
cover letter
group interview
open-ended question
closed-ended question
hypothetical question
CLE

3

The Regulation of Paralegals

■ Chapter Outline

■ Section A. Kinds of Regulation

The activities of paralegals could be regulated in seven important ways:

- Laws on the unauthorized practice of law and on the *authorized* practice of law by nonattorneys
- State licensing
- Regulation of education
- Self-regulation
- Fair Labor Standards Act
- Tort Law (e.g., the negligence of paralegals and of attorneys who employ them)
- Ethical rules

The first six of these methods of regulation are covered in this chapter. Ethics will be examined in the next chapter. As we explore these methods, you should keep in mind the terminology of regulation outlined in Figure 3.1.

FIGURE 3.1

The Terminology of Regulation

Accreditation is the process by which an organization evaluates and recognizes a program of study (or an institution) as meeting specified qualifications or standards.

Approval means the recognition that comes from accreditation, certification, licensure, or registration. As we will see, the American Bar Association uses the word "approval" as a substitute for "accreditation" of paralegal education programs.

Certification is the process by which a nongovernmental organization grants recognition to an individual who has met qualifications specified by that organization. Three of the most common qualifications are:

- Graduating from a school or training program, or

- Passing a standard examination, or

- Completing a designated period of work experience.

Once certification has been bestowed by one or a combination of these methods, the individual is said to have been *certified*. If the certification comes from a school or training program, some prefer to say that the person has been *certificated*. (Occasionally a government agency will have what it calls a certification program. This program may be similar to those described above, or it may in fact be a license program.)

Code is any set of rules that regulates conduct.

Ethics are rules that embody standards of behavior to which members of an organization are expected to conform.

Guideline is suggested conduct that will help an applicant obtain accreditation, certification, licensure, registration, or approval.

Licensure is the process by which an agency of government grants permission to persons meeting specified qualifications to engage in an occupation and/or to use a particular title.

Limited Licensure (also called *specialty licensure*) is the process by which an agency of government grants permission to persons meeting specified qualifications to engage in designated activities that are customarily (but not always exclusively) performed by another license holder. (If, in the future, paralegals are granted a limited license in a particular state, they will be authorized to sell designated services—now part of the attorney monopoly— directly to the public in that state.)

Registration or *enrollment* is the process by which individuals or institutions list their names on a roster kept by an agency of government or by a nongovernmental organization. There may or may not be qualifications that must be met before one can go on the list.

Regulation is any governmental or nongovernmental method of controlling conduct.

◼ Section B. Unauthorized and Authorized Practice of Law

(a) Defining the Practice of Law

Every state has laws on who can be an attorney and on the *unauthorized practice of law*. In many states it is a *crime* to practice law illegally. It is not a crime to represent yourself, but you risk going to jail if you practice law on behalf of someone else. Why such a harsh penalty? Legal problems often involve complicated, serious issues. A great deal can be lost if citizens do not receive competent legal assistance. To protect the public, the state has established a system of licensing attorneys to provide this assistance and to punish anyone who tries to provide it without the license.

The *practice of law* involves three major kinds of activities:

- Representing someone in court or in an agency proceeding

- Preparing and drafting legal documents for someone

- Providing legal advice on someone's rights and obligations

The essence of legal advice is to relate the law to an individual's specific legal problem.

Suppose that you write a self-help book on how to sue your landlord. The book lists all the laws, provides all the forms, and gives precise guidelines on how to use the laws and the forms. Are you practicing law? No, since you are not addressing the *specific* legal problem of a *specific* person. It is not the practice of law to sell legal books or similar materials to the general public even if a member of the public uses them for his or her specific legal problem. Now suppose that you open an office in which you sell the book and even type the forms for customers. Practice of law? No, *unless you provide individual help in filling out the forms.* You can type the forms so long as the customer does all the thinking about what goes in the forms! So too:

- It is proper for a nonattorney to charge citizens a fee to type legal forms in order to obtain a divorce. But it is the unauthorized practice of law to provide personal assistance on how to fill out the forms.

- It is proper for a nonattorney to charge citizens a fee to type their will or trust. But it is the unauthorized practice of law to provide personal assistance on what should go in the will or trust.

For years, attorneys have complained that large numbers of individuals were crossing the line by providing this kind of personal assistance. Bar associations often asked the state to prosecute many of them. Yet some charged that the attorneys were less interested in protecting the public than in preserving their own monopoly over the practice of law. Perhaps the most famous recent case involving this controversy was that of Rosemary Furman and the Florida Bar.

Rosemary Furman: Folk Hero?

Rosemary Furman, a former legal secretary, believes that you should be able to solve simple legal problems without hiring an attorney. Hence she established the Northside Secretarial Service in Jacksonville, Florida. She compiled and sold packets of legal forms (for $50) on divorce, name changes, and adoptions. The price *included her personal assistance in filling out and filing the forms.* The Florida Bar Association and the Florida courts moved against her with a vengeance for practicing law illegally. She was convicted and sentenced to 30 days in jail.

Widespread support for Ms. Furman developed. Her case soon became a cause célèbre for those seeking increased access to the legal system for the poor and the middle class.[1] Many were outraged at the legal profession and the judiciary for their treatment of Ms. Furman.

The CBS program *60 Minutes* did a story that was favorable to her cause. Other national media, including *Newsweek,* covered the case. Warner Brothers considered doing a docudrama on the story. Rosemary Furman struck a responsive chord when she claimed that for every $50 she earned, an attorney lost $500. An editorial in the *Gainesville Sun* said, "Throw Rosemary Furman in jail? Surely not after the woman forced the Florida bar and the judiciary to confront its responsibility to the poor. Anything less than a 'thank you' note would indeed show genuine vindictiveness on the part of the legal profession" (Nov. 4, 1984). There were, however, other views. An editorial in *USA Today* said, "If she can give legal advice, so can charlatans, frauds, and rip-off artists" February 2, 1984).

The events in the Rosemary Furman story are as follows:

- 1978 & 1979: The Florida Bar Association takes Rosemary Furman to court, alleging that she is practicing law without a license.

- 1979: The Florida Supreme Court rules against her. She is enjoined from engaging in the unauthorized practice of law.

---

[1] Peoples & Wertz, *Update: Unauthorized Practice of Law,* 9 Nat'l Paralegal Reporter 1 (Nat'l Federation of Paralegal Associations, February 1985).

■ 1982: The Florida Bar Association again brings a complaint against her business, alleging that she was continuing the unauthorized practice of law.

■ 1983: Duval County Circuit Judge A. C. Soud, Jr. finds her in contempt of court for violating the 1979 order. The judge makes this decision in a nonjury hearing. She is then ordered to serve 30 days in jail.

■ 1984: The United States Supreme Court refuses to hear the case. This has the effect of allowing the state jail sentence to stand. The Court is not persuaded by her argument that she should have been granted a jury trial of her peers rather than have been judged solely by members of a profession (attorneys and judges) that was biased against her.

■ Her attorneys ask the Florida Supreme Court to vacate the jail sentence if she agrees to close her business.

■ The Florida Bar Association tells the Florida Supreme Court that the jail term is a fitting punishment and should be served.

■ November 13, 1984: The Florida Supreme Court orders her to serve the jail sentence for practicing law without a license. (451 So.2d 808)

■ November 27, 1984: Rosemary Furman is granted clemency from the 30-day jail term by Florida Governor Bob Graham and his Clemency Board. She does not have to go to jail.

■ Furman and her attorneys announce that they will work on a constitutional amendment defining the practice of law to make it easier for citizens to avoid dependency on attorneys in civil cases. Says Ms. Furman, "I have only begun to fight."

This case has had an impact in Florida and elsewhere in the country. Recently, for example, Florida has been considering a dramatic change in the definition of unauthorized practice of law. Under this proposal, it "shall not constitute the unauthorized practice of law for nonlawyers to engage in limited oral communications to assist a person in a completion of a legal form approved by the Supreme Court of Florida. Oral communications by nonlawyers are restricted to those communications reasonably necessary to elicit factual information to complete the form and inform the person how to file the form."[2] Later in this chapter, we will discuss the even more dramatic concept of *limited licensing* for paralegals, which is being considered in a number of states. Some have referred to these developments as "the long shadow of Rosemary Furman."

---

[2] Florida Bar News 12 (August 1, 1989).

■ ASSIGNMENT 3.1

(a) Define the practice of law in your state. Quote from your state code, court rules, or other official authority that is available.

(b) Would Rosemary Furman have been prosecuted for the unauthorized practice of law in your state today?

Legal Assistant regulation is on the horizon in one form or another, [and possibly in many forms]. It is imperative that we approach the regulation "can of worms" from an informed and knowledgeable vantage point, and that we participate in the formative process.
Gail White Nicholson, Vice-President, Greenville Association of Legal Assistants, 1991

The Furman case involved direct competition with attorneys. More indirect competition comes from people engaged in law-related activities, such as accountants, claims adjusters, real estate agents, life insurance agents, and officers of trust departments of banks. For years, bar associations complained about such activities. In many instances, they challenged the activities in court as the unauthorized practice of law. The problem was so pervasive that some bar associations negotiated a "statement of principles" (sometimes called a treaty) with these occupations in an attempt to identify boundary lines and methods of resolving difficulties. Most of these treaties, however, have been ineffective in defining the kinds of law-related activities that can and cannot be performed by nonattorneys. A tremendous amount of effort and money is needed to negotiate, monitor, and enforce the treaties. The resources are simply not available. Furthermore, there is a concern that such efforts by attorneys to restrain competition might violate the antitrust laws, as we will see later in the chapter.

Some practitioners of law-related occupations have gone directly to the legislature to seek enactment of statutes that authorize what would otherwise be the unauthorized practice of law. In many instances, they have been successful. For example:

Ga.Code Ann. § 9-401 (Supp. 1970). § 9-401. . . . Provided that, a title insurance company may prepare such papers as it thinks proper, or necessary, in connection with a title which it proposes to insure, in order, in its opinion, for it to be willing to insure such title, where no charge is made by it for such papers.

Utah Code Ann. 1968, 61-2-20. § 61-2-20. Rights and privileges of real estate salesmen—brokers.—It is expressly provided that a real estate salesman shall have the right to fill out and complete forms of legal documents necessary to any real estate transaction to which the said broker is a party as principal or agent, and which forms have been approved by the commission and the attorney general of the state of Utah. Such forms shall include a closing real estate contract, a short-form lease, and a bill of sale of personal property.

Tenn. Code Ann. § 62-1325 (1955). § 62-1325. Licensed Real Estate Brokers may draw contracts to option, buy, sell, or lease real property.

The effect of such statutes is to allow members of designated occupations to perform certain legal tasks that are intimately related to their work without having to hire attorneys or without forcing their clients to hire them.

(b) Authorized Practice of Law

Examine the following phrase closely: unauthorized practice of law by nonattorneys. If there is such a thing as the *un*authorized practice of law, then, by implication, there must be an *authorized* practice of law. And indeed there is. The treaties and statutes discussed above are examples of this. There are also other areas where nonattorneys are given a special authorization to practice law. Occasionally attempts are made to call what they do something other than the *practice of law*, but as we will see, these attempts conflict with reality since the nonattorneys are doing what attorneys do within the sphere of the special authorization. These special authorizations have been vigorously opposed by attorneys on the ground that the authorizations conflict with the privileged domain of attorneys. The latter are not always this blunt in stating their opposition. The objection is usually couched in terms of "protection of the public," but in large measure, the opposition has its roots in turf protection. Attorneys are not above engaging in battles for economic self-preservation.

Some members of the public view attorneys as fighters, people who will pursue an issue to the bitter end. While this trait may place attorneys in a favorable light in the eyes of clients for whom they are doing battle, many feel that the aggressive inclination of the attorney can be counterproductive. Administrative agencies, for example, are often suspicious of the involvement of attorneys. They are viewed as combatants who want to turn every agency decision into an adversarial proceeding. Agencies often see courtroom gymnastics and gimmicks as the attorney's primary mode of operation. The attorney is argumentative to a fault.

This image of the attorney as someone who complicates matters is best summed up by an old accountant's joke that taxation becomes more and more complex in direct proportion to attempts by attorneys to *simplify* the tax law. Whether or not this view of the attorney is correct, it has accounted for some erosion of the legal profession's monopoly over the practice of law.

The unavailability of attorneys has also helped produce this result. A vast segment of our population has legal complaints that are never touched by attorneys. This is due, in part, to the fact that most of these complaints do not involve enough money to attract attorneys.

We now turn to a fuller exploration of these themes under the following headings:

1. Court "representation" by nonattorneys
2. Attempted restrictions on the activities of the "jailhouse lawyer" and the broader policy considerations raised by such restrictions
3. Agency representation by nonattorneys

(1) Court Representation

In the vast majority of courts in this country, only attorneys can represent someone in a judicial proceeding. There are, however, some limited—but dramatic—exceptions.

In Maryland, a nonattorney employee of a nonprofit legal service office can represent tenants in a summary ejectment proceeding in the District Court of Maryland! A special Lay Advocacy Program oversees this form of court advocacy by nonattorneys.[3] Another extraordinary example exists in North Dakota where lay advocates assist women who are petitioners seeking protective orders in domestic violence cases. Some judges "encourage and allow" the lay advocate "to conduct direct and cross-examination of witnesses and make statements to the court." A proposal has been made to formalize this activity by creating a new position called a Certified Domestic Violence Advocate. Under this proposal, the following activities of this nonattorney would *not* be considered the unauthorized practice of law: helping a petitioner fill out printed forms, sitting with the petitioner during court proceedings, and making written or oral statements to the court.[4]

There are some lower courts in the country, particularly in the West, where parties can have nonattorneys represent them. Examples include Justice of the Peace Courts, Magistrates Courts, and Small Claims Courts. It is relatively rare, however, for parties to have any representation in such courts.

[3]*Lay Advocacy Program Defends Indigent Tenants*, 6 Bar Bulletin 3 (Maryland Bar Ass'n, January 1991). Annotated Code of Maryland § 10–101 (1991 Supp).
[4]*Role of Lay Advocates in Domestic Violence Proceedings*, 15 Note Pad 1 (State Bar Ass'n of North Dakota, April 5, 1991).

As we learned in Chapter 2, Tribal Courts on Indian reservations have jurisdiction over designated civil and criminal matters involving Native Americans. In many of these courts, both parties are represented by nonattorney advocates.

Government employees occasionally act in a representative or semi-representative capacity in court proceedings, even though they are not attorneys. In North Carolina cases involving the termination of parental rights, for example, the United States Supreme Court has noted the role of nonattorneys:

> In fact, . . . the North Carolina Departments of Social Services are themselves sometimes represented at termination hearings by social workers instead of by lawyers.[5]

It is well known that attorneys waste a good deal of pretrial time traveling to court and waiting around simply to give documents to the judge and to set dates for the various stages of pretrial and trial proceedings. Another problem is that an attorney may have to be in two different courtrooms at the same time. For example, the time spent at an early morning hearing may be unexpectedly extended so that the attorney cannot appear at a previously scheduled mid-morning proceeding in another courtroom on a different case. In such situations, wouldn't it be helpful if the attorney's paralegal could "appear" in court for the limited purpose of delivering papers to the judge, asking for a new date, or presenting some other message? *In most states, such activity is strictly prohibited.*

On August 16, 1982, a Kentucky paralegal learned about this prohibition in a dramatic way. Her attorney was involved in a trial at the Jefferson Circuit Court. He asked the paralegal to go to another courtroom during "Motion Hour," where attorneys make motions or schedule future proceedings on a case. He told her to ask for a hearing date on another case that he had pending. She did so. When the case was called during "Motion Hour," she rose, identified herself as the attorney's paralegal, and gave the message to the judge, asking for the hearing date. Opposing counsel was outraged. He verbally assaulted the paralegal in the courtroom and filed a motion to hold the paralegal and her attorney in contempt of court for the unauthorized practice of law. When a hearing was later held on this motion, members of a local paralegal association packed the courtroom. Tensions were high. When the judge eventually *denied* the motion, after a hearing on the matter, the audience broke out into loud applause. "Apparently the judge concluded that [the paralegal] had rendered no service involving legal knowledge or advice, but had merely transmitted to the court [the attorney's] message regarding disposition of the motion, that is, she had been performing a function that was administrative, not legal in nature."[6]

About twenty years earlier, a celebrated Illinois opinion, *People v. Alexander,*[7] took a position similar to this Kentucky court. In this opinion, the defendant was an unlicensed law clerk who appeared before the court to state that his employing attorney could not be present in court at the moment because he was trying a case elsewhere. On behalf of his employer, the law clerk requested a continuance. The defendant's actions were challenged. It was argued that any

---

[5]*Lassiter v. Dept. of Social Services,* 452 U.S. 18, 29, 101 S.Ct. 2153, 2161, 68 L.Ed.2d 640, 651 (1981).

[6]Winter, *No Contempt in Kentucky,* 7 Nat'l Paralegal Reporter 8 (Nat'l Federation of Paralegal Associations, Winter 1982).

[7]53 Ill. App. 2d 299, 202 N.E.2d 841 (1964).

People v. Alexander

Appellate Court of Illinois, First District

53 Ill. App. 2d 299, 202 N.E.2d 841 (1964)

In the case of People ex rel. Illinois State Bar Ass'n v. People's Stock Yards State Bank, 344 Ill. 462, at page 476, 176 N.E. 901, at page 907, wherein a bank was prosecuted for the unauthorized practice of law, the following quotation is relied upon:

> "According to the generally understood definition of the practice of law in this country, it embraces the preparation of pleadings, and other papers incident to actions and special proceedings, and the management of such actions and proceedings on behalf of clients before judges and courts * * *."

Since this statement relates to the appearance and management of proceedings in court on behalf of a client, we do not believe it can be applied to a situation where a clerk hired by a law firm presents information to the court on behalf of his employer.

We agree with the trial judge that clerks should not be permitted to make motions or participate in other proceedings which can be considered as "managing" the litigation. However, if apprising the court of an employer's engagement or inability to be present constitutes the making of a motion, we must hold that clerks may make such motions for continuances without being guilty of the unauthorized practice of law. Certainly with the large volume of cases appearing on the trial calls these days, it is imperative that this practice be followed.

In Tull v. Samuel Phillipson & Co., 250 Ill.App. 247 (1928) the court said at page 250:

> "It is well known in this county where numerous trial courts are sitting at the same time the exigencies of such a situation require that trial attorneys be represented by their clerical force to respond to some of the calls, and that the court acts upon their response the same as if the attorneys of record themselves appeared in person."

After that opinion was handed down, the number of judges was substantially increased in the former Circuit and Superior Courts and the problem of answering court calls has at least doubled. We cannot add to the heavy burden of lawyers who in addition to responding to trial calls must answer pre-trial calls and motion calls—all held in the morning—by insisting that a lawyer must personally appear to present to a court a motion for a continuance on grounds of engagement or inability to appear because of illness or other unexpected circumstances. To reduce the backlog, trial lawyers should be kept busy actually trying lawsuits and not answering court calls.

appearance by nonattorneys before a court in which they give information as to the availability of counsel or the status of litigation constitutes the unauthorized practice of law. The Illinois court took the unique position that this was not the practice of law. The reasoning of the court is presented in the excerpt from the opinion printed above.

It must be emphasized that most states would *not* agree with Kentucky and Illinois. Most states would prohibit nonattorneys from doing what was authorized in these two states. Fortunately, however, there are at least a few additional states that have begun to move in the direction of the minority view.

The Allen County Bar Association of Indiana has taken the bold move of permitting paralegals to perform what hitherto had been considered attorney functions in court. A paralegal is authorized:

■ To "take" default judgments

■ To "set" pretrial conferences, uncontested divorces, and all other hearing dates

■ To "file" stipulations or motions for dismissal

■ Etc.

The paralegal, however, must perform these tasks with court personnel other than judges; nonattorneys cannot communicate directly with judges.

The vast majority of attorneys in the country would be amazed to learn what is going on in Allen County. Once the shock subsides, however, these attorneys will probably see the wisdom and common sense of what Allen County has done and begin to think of ways to try it themselves.

The rules of the Allen County program are as follows:

Paralegal Rules of Practice
Allen County Bar Association (Indiana)

1. Generally, a legal assistant employee shall be limited to the performance of tasks which do not require the exercising of legal discretion or judgment that affects the legal right of any person.

2. All persons employed as legal assistants shall be registered [see Figure 3.2] by their employer law firm with the Allen County Circuit and Superior Court Administrator and the Clerk of the Allen Superior and Circuit Courts. Said law firm shall, by affidavit, state that it shall be bound and liable for the actions of its legal assistant employee, and that any and all actions or statements made by such personnel shall be strictly and completely supervised by his employer member of the Bar. All documents the legal assistant presents or files must contain the attorney's signature, either as an attorney for the petitioning party, or a statement affixed indicating that the documents were prepared by said attorney. Each law firm shall certify in writing that the legal assistant employee is qualified in each field in which they will act with the Courts (probate, dissolution of marriage, collection, etc.). A copy of such statement and certification shall be given to such legal assistant and shall be carried by such person whenever activity with the Court is pursued by such person. There shall be one legal assistant certified by each law office desiring same, but [an] alternate shall be allowed in case of illness, vacation or unavailability. However, in those instances where a single law firm has more than one full time legal assistant, each of whom operate in separate specialized areas, a certification can be had by more than one person, showing that such person's specialization on a full time basis is limited to one specific area. Otherwise, there should be a limit of one person certified as a legal assistant per law firm.

3. Such employee shall be limited to the following acts:

(a) Such employee may take default judgments upon the filing of an affidavit in each case stating the amount of damages and that proper service was obtained sworn to by affidavit.

(b) Such employee shall have authority to set Pre-Trial Conferences, Uncontested Divorces, and all other hearing dates.

(c) Such employee shall have authority to obtain trust account deposits at the Allen County Clerk's Office but only in the name of his employer firm.

(d) Such employee shall have authority to file stipulations or motions for dismissal.

(e) Such an employee shall have the authority to do all filing of documents and papers with the Clerk of the Allen Superior Courts and Circuit Court where such documents and papers are not to be given to anyone authorized to affix a judge's signature or issue Court orders.

(f) Notwithstanding the limitations of subparagraph (e) above, such employee shall have the authority to obtain from the law clerk the signature stamp of the judge on non-discretionary standard orders and notices, such as notice of hearing, and orders to appear and to answer interrogatories on the filing of a Verified Motion for Proceedings Supplemental. Note: Standard orders which depart from the usual format, restraining orders, suit and support orders, bench warrants, and body attachments must be secured by an attorney.

(g) Such employee is not to negotiate with opposing litigants within the Courthouse nor confer with a judge on legal matters. Matters requiring communications with a judge, require an attorney.

(h) Where circumstances permit, attorneys shall take precedence over such employees in dealings with courts and clerks.

Note again that the above program does not allow the paralegal to talk directly with a judge in performing the authorized tasks. ("Matters requiring communications with a judge, require an attorney.") Why such a restriction? Wouldn't it make sense to allow paralegal-judge communication on some procedural matters that are of a routine nature? *No,* would be the response of most bar associations.

Yes, however, is the refreshing response of several county bar associations in the state of Washington. Under the sponsorship of the Seattle-King County

FIGURE 3.2

Allen County
Circuit and
Superior Court
Certification of
Legal Assistants

STATEMENT OF CERTIFICATION

This is to certify that _____
is employed by the law firm of _____.
Said law firm binds itself and takes full responsibility and liability for the actions of its legal
assistant employee above-named and that any and all actions or statements made by such
personnel shall be strictly and completely supervised by a member of the Bar of the State
of Indiana. This is to certify that the above-mentioned legal assistant is qualified to assist
an attorney in the _____ area of law.

LAW FIRM OF:_____

BY:_____

STATE OF INDIANA, COUNTY OF ALLEN, SS:

Subscribed and sworn to before me, a Notary Public in and for said County and State, this
_____ day _____ , 19_____ .

_____

Notary Public

Bar Association and the Tacoma-Pierce County Bar Association, paralegals are allowed to "present" certain orders to judges. The orders must be those that the parties have already agreed on, or must be ex parte (which means involving one party only). In presenting such orders to a judge, the paralegal must obviously deal directly with—and perhaps even communicate with—an almighty judge! The prohibition in Allen County, Indiana on communicating with a judge does not exist in these two counties of Washington state.

(2) The Jailhouse Lawyer

A *jailhouse lawyer* is a nonattorney who helps fellow prisoners with their legal problems. Some prisons attempted to prevent the jailhouse lawyer from providing this legal assistance even though no meaningful alternatives for such assistance were provided by the prisons. This prohibition was struck down, however, by the United States Supreme Court in *Johnson v. Avery* in 1969. The basis of the opinion was that without the jailhouse lawyer, prisoners may not have access to the courts. The concurring opinion of Justice Douglas has become one of the most widely quoted and influential statements in the field of paralegalism.

Johnson v. Avery

Supreme Court of the United States, 1969.
393 U.S. 483, 89 S.Ct. 747, 21 L.Ed.2d 718

Mr. Justice DOUGLAS, concurring.

While I join the opinion of the Court [in striking down the prohibition on the activities of jailhouse lawyers] I add a few words in emphasis of the important thesis of the case.

The increasing complexities of our governmental apparatus at both the local and the federal levels have made it difficult for a person to process a claim or even to make a complaint. Social security is a virtual maze; the hierarchy that governs urban housing is often so intricate that it takes an expert to know what agency has jurisdiction over a particular complaint; the office to call or official to see for noise abatement, for a broken sewer line, or a fallen tree is a mystery to many in our metropolitan areas.

A person who has a claim assertable in faraway Washington, D.C., is even more helpless, as evidenced by the increasing tendency of constituents to rely on their congressional delegation to identify, press, and process their claims.

We think of claims as grist for the mill of the lawyers. But it is becoming abundantly clear that more and more of the effort in ferreting out the basis of claims and the agencies responsible for them and in preparing the almost endless paperwork for their prosecution is work for laymen. There are not enough lawyers to manage or supervise all of these affairs; and much of the basic work done requires no special legal talent. *Yet there is a closed-shop philosophy in the legal profession that cuts down drastically active roles for laymen. . . . That traditional, closed-shop attitude is utterly out of place in the modern world where claims pile high and much of the work of tracing and pursuing them requires the patience and wisdom of a layman rather than the legal skills of a member of the bar.* [Emphasis added.]

"If poverty lawyers are overwhelmed, some of the work can be delegated to sub-professionals. New York law permits senior law students to practice law under certain supervised conditions. Approval must first be granted by the appellate division. A rung or two lower on the legal profession's ladder are laymen legal technicians, comparable to nurses and lab assistants in the medical profession. Large law firms employ them, and there seems to be no reason why they cannot be used in legal services programs to relieve attorneys for more professional tasks." Samore, Legal Services for the Poor, 32 Albany L.Rev. 509, 515–516 (1968).

The plight of a man in prison may in these respects be even more acute than the plight of a person on the outside. He may need collateral proceedings to test the legality of his detention or relief against management of the parole system or against defective detainers lodged against him which create burdens in the nature of his incarcerated status. He may have grievances of a civil nature against those outside the prison. His imprisonment may give his wife grounds for divorce and be a factor in determining the custody of his children; and he may have pressing social security, workmen's compensation, or veterans' claims.

While the demand for legal counsel in prison is heavy, the supply is light. For private matters of a civil nature, legal counsel for the indigent in prison is almost nonexistent. Even for criminal proceedings, it is sparse. While a few states have post-conviction statutes providing such counsel, most states do not. Some states like California do appoint counsel to represent the indigent prisoner in his collateral hearings, once he succeeds in making out a prima facie case. But as a result, counsel is not on hand for preparation of the papers or for the initial decision that the prisoner's claim has substance.

Notes

1. "Jailhouse lawyers, or *writ writers,* as they are sometimes called, have always been part of prison society. But in recent years their numbers as well as the amount of litigation they generate, his increased substantially. In 1985, prisoners filed 33,400 petitions in federal and state courts. . . ." One

Jailhouse lawyer,
Fernando Jackson,
Soledad Prison, California

jailhouse lawyer at Soledad prison "devotes sixteen hours a day to his legal work, subscribes to dozens of legal publications (at a cost of $1,800 a year), and files a steady stream of lawsuits." Suing "has become almost a national pastime. Prisoners act no differently from other citizens in a litigious society." Kroll, *Counsel Behind Bars: Jailhouse Lawyers . . .*, 7 California Lawyer 34 (June 1987).

2. The *Johnson* opinion stressed that the prison provided *no* alternative to the jailhouse lawyer. If alternatives had been available, the inmate would not be allowed to practice law. In *Williams v. U.S. Dep't of Justice*, 433 F.2d 958 (5th Cir. 1970), the court held that the presence of law students in the prison could be an alternative, but only if it is demonstrated that the students are meeting the need for inmate legal services. If the inmates had to wait a considerable period of time, for example, before they could be interviewed by the law students, then no alternative existed and the jailhouse lawyer could not be prevented from helping other inmates.

3. In *Gilmore v. Lynch*, 319 F. Supp. 105 (N.D. Cal. 1970), affirmed by the United States Supreme Court in *Younger v. Gilmore*, 404 U.S. 15 (1971), the court held that California either had to satisfy the legal needs of its prisoners or expand the prison law library to include a more comprehensive collection of law books. See also *Bounds v. Smith*, p. 187.

4. Finally, the right of an inmate to assist a fellow inmate in legal matters does *not* extend to representing the inmate in court. *Guajardo v. Luna*, 432 F.2d 1324 (5th Cir. 1970). Nor can a nonattorney represent an inmate in court even if this nonattorney is not an inmate himself or herself. This latter point was decided by the United States Supreme Court in *Hackin v. Arizona*, 389 U.S. 143 (1967).

5. How far can the rationale of *Johnson* be extended? Suppose, for example, it is demonstrated that many claimants before state administrative agencies are not receiving legal services because attorneys cannot be afforded. Would the *Johnson* opinion permit paralegal representation before such agencies even if the latter prohibited it? What is the difference between an inmate's right to have access to the courts and *anyone's* right to complain to an agency? How do you think Justice Douglas would handle the case if it came before him?

"Although the *Johnson* case is admittedly narrow in scope, it does nevertheless, give aid and comfort to the view that whenever lawyers are unavailable for whatever reason, society will sanction alternative systems for the delivery of legal services. The paramount consideration will not be ethics nor the exclusivity of the right to practice law, but rather it will be the facilitation of access routes to the grievance machinery set up for the resolution of claims. If lawyers are not available to assist the citizenry with these claims, then the question arises as to whether skilled nonlawyers represent a viable alternative. The inevitability of this question becomes clear when we listen to the statistics on the demand for the services of a lawyer. Estimates have been made to the effect that if every lawyer devoted full time to the legal needs of the poor, there would still be a significant shortage of lawyers for the poor. If the legal needs of the middle class are added, the legal service manpower shortage becomes overwhelming." Statsky, W. and Lang, P., *The Legal Paraprofessional as Advocate and Assistant: Roles, Training Concepts and Materials*, 49–50 (1971).

See also Statsky, W., *Inmate Involvement in Prison Legal Services: Roles and Training Options for the Inmate as Paralegal* (American Bar

Procunier v. Martinez

Supreme Court of the United States, 1974.
416 U.S. 396, 94 S.Ct. 1800, 40 L.Ed.2d 244

The District Court also enjoined continued enforcement of Administrative Rule MV-IV-02, which provides in pertinent part:

"Investigators for an attorney-of-record will be confined to not more than two. Such investigators must be licensed by the State or must be members of the State Bar. Designation must be made in writing by the Attorney."

By restricting access to prisoners to members of the bar and licensed private investigators, this regulation imposed an absolute ban on the use by attorneys of law students and legal paraprofessionals to interview inmate clients. In fact attorneys could not even delegate to such persons the task of obtaining prisoners' signatures on legal documents. The District Court reasoned that this rule constituted an unjustifiable restriction on the right of access to the courts. We agree.

The constitutional guarantee of due process of law has as a corollary the requirement that prisoners be afforded access to the courts in order to challenge unlawful convictions and to seek redress for violations of their constitutional rights. This means that inmates must have a reasonable opportunity to seek and receive the assistance of attorneys. Regulations and practices that unjustifiably obstruct the availability of professional representation or other aspects of the right of access to the courts are invalid. Ex parte Hull, 312 U.S. 546, 61 S.Ct. 640, 85 L.Ed. 1034 (1941).

The District Court found that the rule restricting attorney-client interviews to members of the bar and licensed private investigators inhibited adequate professional representation of indigent inmates. The remoteness of many California penal institutions makes a personal visit [by attorneys] to an inmate client a time-consuming undertaking. The court reasoned that the ban against the use of law students or other paraprofessionals for attorney-client interviews would deter some lawyers from representing prisoners who could not afford to pay for their traveling time or that of licensed private investigators. And those lawyers who agreed to do so would waste time that might be employed more efficaciously in working on the inmates' legal problems. Allowing law students and paraprofessionals to interview inmates might well reduce the cost of legal representation for prisoners. The District Court therefore concluded that the regulation imposed a substantial burden on the right of access to the courts.

Bounds v. Smith

Supreme Court of the United States, 1977
430 U.S. 817, 97 S.Ct. 1491, 52 L.Ed.2d 72

[In this opinion the Supreme Court is again concerned with the need of prisoners to have access to the courts and the use of nonlawyers in helping to obtain that access. The Court held that prisons must assist inmates in the preparation and filing of meaningful legal papers by providing the inmates with adequate law libraries or adequate assistance from persons trained in the law. The Court rejected the claim that nonlawyer inmates were ill-equipped to use the "tools of the trade of the legal profession." In the Court's experience, nonlawyer petitioners are capable of using law books to file cases raising claims that are "serious and legitimate" whether or not such petitioners win the cases. In outlining the options available to a prison, the Court specifically referred to paralegals:]

It should be noted that while adequate law libraries are one constitutionally acceptable method to assure meaningful access to the courts, our decision here . . . does not foreclose alternative means to achieve that goal. Nearly half the States and the District of Columbia provide some degree of professional or quasi-professional legal assistance to prisoners. . . . Such programs take many imaginative forms and may have a number of advantages over libraries alone. Among the alternatives are the training of inmates as paralegal assistants to work under lawyers' supervision, the use of paraprofessionals and law students, either as volunteers or in formal clinical programs, the organization of volunteer attorneys through bar associations or other groups, the hiring of lawyers on a part-time consultant basis, and the use of full-time staff attorneys, working either in new prison legal assistance organizations or as part of public defender or legal services offices.

Association, Commission on Correctional Facilities and Services, Resource Center on Correctional Law and Legal Services, 1974).

. . . .

Two other important Supreme Court cases involving nonattorneys in prison need to be considered: *Procunier v. Martinez* and *Bounds v. Smith*. See page 187.

■ ASSIGNMENT 3.2

Jim Mookely is an attorney who represents fifty inmates on a consolidated case in the state court. The inmates are in fourteen different institutions throughout the state. Jim asks the director of the state prison system to allow his paralegal, Mary Smith, to interview all fifty inmates at a central location. The director responds as follows:

- He refuses to transport the inmates to one location. The inmates would have to be interviewed at the institutions where they are currently living.

- He refuses to let anyone in any institution unless the individual has either a law degree *or* has been through the prison's two-week orientation program totaling twenty hours in the evening at the state capital.

Mary Smith has not taken the orientation program, and it would be very inconvenient for her to do so since she lives 150 miles from the capital. How would *Johnson, Procunier,* or *Bounds* apply to this problem?

---

(3) Agency Representation

A considerable number of administrative agencies will permit a paralegal or other nonattorney to represent clients at the agency. These individuals are usually called agents, practitioners, or representatives. They engage in informal advocacy for their clients at the agency or formal advocacy, including representation at an adversarial administrative hearing. (A proceeding is adversarial if another side appears in the controversy, whether or not the other side is represented. If there is no other side present in the matter before the agency, the proceeding is considered nonadversarial.) Often the issues before the agency are economic, statistical, or scientific, but legal issues are also involved. It is clear that in conducting an adversarial hearing before an agency, the nonattorney can be practicing law in a manner that is remarkably similar to an attorney's representation of a client in court. Our study of this phenomenon will begin with federal administrative agencies, and then we will cover state agencies.

Nonattorney Practice before Federal Administrative Agencies. For federal agencies, Congress has passed a statute, the Administrative Procedure Act, that gives each federal agency the power to decide for itself whether only attorneys can represent clients before it:

Administrative Procedure Act 5 U.S.C.A. § 555 (1967). (b) A person compelled to appear in person before an agency is entitled to be accompanied, represented, and advised by counsel or, if permitted by the agency, by other qualified representative. . . .

When a federal agency decides to use this power to permit nonattorney representation, it can simply allow anyone to act as the agent or representative of another before the agency, or it can establish elaborate qualifications or standards of admission to practice before it. If the agency takes the latter course, its qualifications or standards could include a specialized test to demonstrate competency in the subject matter regulated by the agency, minimum educational or experience requirements, registration or enrollment on the agency's approved roster of representatives, and an agreement to abide by designated ethical rules of practice—a violation of which could result in suspension and "disbarment."

The United States Patent Office has established criteria for individuals to practice (as *registered agents*) before this agency by drafting and filing applications for patents, searching legal opinions on patentability, etc.[8] In 1982, there were approximately 12,000 registered agents who had met this criteria at the agency. Of this number, about 1,900 (or 15.8%) were nonattorneys. At the Interstate Commerce Commission, close to 10,000 nonattorney "practitioners" have been authorized to represent clients at ICC proceedings that often involve issues such as rate increases and service extensions for railroads and other transportation carriers.[9] Perhaps the largest use of nonattorneys in federal agencies is at the Internal Revenue Service within the Treasury Department.[10] Any certified public accountant is authorized to practice before the IRS. There are over 190,000 members of the American Institute of Certified Public Accountants, most of whom are not attorneys.[11] In addition, the IRS has enrolled, i.e., registered, thousands of nonattorneys to represent taxpayers at all administrative proceedings within the IRS. These individuals, called *enrolled agents,* charge clients fees for their services. (Once a dispute goes to court, however, an attorney must take over.) To become an enrolled agent, an individual must either pass a written IRS examination or prove that he or she once worked at the IRS for five years interpreting and applying tax laws. In most states there are organizations of enrolled agents; the major national organization is the National Association of Enrolled Agents.

While many federal agencies allow nonattorney representation, it is not true that extensive numbers of nonattorneys actually use the authority they have. A recent study by the American Bar Association of thirty-three federal administrative agencies reached the following conclusion: "We found that the overwhelming majority of agencies studied permit nonlawyer representation in both adversarial and nonadversarial proceedings. However, most of them seem to encounter lay practice very infrequently (in less than 5% of adjudications), while only a few encounter lay practice as often as lawyer practice. Thus, although universally permitted, lay practice before federal agencies rarely occurs."[12]

One agency where nonattorney representation is fairly high (about 15%) is the Social Security Administration. Paralegals are frequently appointed by clients (see Figure 3.3) to represent them before the agency. In 1983, a study compared the success of clients at hearings based upon the kind of representation they received. The results were as follows:

■ 59% of clients were successful when represented by attorneys.

■ 54.5% of clients were successful when represented by nonattorneys.

■ 43.7% of clients were successful when they represented themselves.[13]

---

[8]37 C.F.R. 1.341–1.348 (1983).

[9]49 C.F.R. 1103.1–1103.5 (1983).

[10]31 C.F.R. 10.3–10.75 (1983); 20 U.S.C. 1242 (1975).

[11]Rose, *Representation by Non-Lawyers in Federal Administrative Agency Proceedings* (Administrative Conference of the United States, 1984); Vom Baur, *The Practice of Non-Lawyers before Administrative Agencies,* 15 Federal Bar Journal 99 (1955).

[12]ABA Standing Committee on Lawyers' Responsibility for Client Protection, *Report of 1984 Survey of Nonlawyer Practice before Federal Administrative Agencies* (October 19, 1984).

[13]DSS/OHA *Participant Involvement in Request for Hearing Cases for Fiscal 1983,* Table 6, (May, 1984).

FIGURE 3.3
Appointment of
Representative

DEPARTMENT OF
HEALTH AND HUMAN SERVICES
SOCIAL SECURITY ADMINISTRATION

NAME (Claimant) (Print or Type)   SOCIAL SECURITY NUMBER

WAGE EARNER (if different)   SOCIAL SECURITY NUMBER

Section I   APPOINTMENT OF REPRESENTATIVE

I appoint this individual _____
                                              (Name and Address)

to act as my representative in connection with my claim or asserted right under:

☐ Title II   ☐ Title XVI   ☐ Title IV FMSHA   ☐ Title XVIII
  (RSDI)   (SSI)   (Black Lung)   (Medicare Coverage)

I authorize this individual to make or give any request or notice; to present or elicit evidence; to obtain information; and to receive any notice in connection with my pending claim or asserted right wholly in my stead.

SIGNATURE (Claimant)   ADDRESS

TELEPHONE NUMBER   DATE

(Area Code)

Section II   ACCEPTANCE OF APPOINTMENT

I, _____, hereby accept the above appointment. I certify that I have not been suspended or prohibited from practice before the Social Security Administration; that I am not, as a current or former officer or employee of the United States, disqualified from acting as the claimant's representative; and that I will not charge or receive any fee for the representation unless it has been authorized in accordance with the laws and regulations referred to on the reverse side hereof. In the event that I decide not to charge or collect a fee for the representation, I will notify the Social Security Administration. (Completion of Section III satisfies this requirement.)

I am a / an _____
                    (Attorney, union representative, relative, law student, etc.)

SIGNATURE (Representative)   ADDRESS

TELEPHONE NUMBER   DATE

(Area code)

Section III (Optional)   WAIVER OF FEE

I waive my right to charge and collect a fee under Section 206 of the Social Security Act, and I release my client (the claimant) from any obligations, contractual or otherwise, which may be owed to me for services I have performed in connection with my client's claim or asserted right.

SIGNATURE (Representative)   DATE

WAIVER OF DIRECT PAYMENT

I ONLY waive my right to direct certification of a fee from the withheld past-due benefits of my client (the claimant). I do NOT, however, waive my right to petition for and be authorized to charge and collect a fee directly from my client.

SIGNATURE (Representative)   DATE

Form **SSA-1696-U4** (3-88)   (See Important Information on Reverse)
Detroy prior editions
                                                        FILE COPY

Fees can be charged by attorneys or paralegals for these services, but the agency must specifically approve the fee. This is not to say, however, that attorneys and paralegals are treated alike. If an attorney successfully represents a claimant, the agency will deduct up to 25% of the claimant's award, which will be paid directly to the attorney to cover fees. On the other hand, if a paralegal successfully represents a claimant, the paralegal must collect the fee directly from the client, since the Social Security Administration will not deduct anything from the award in such cases.[14]

Nonattorney Practice before State Administrative Agencies.   At the *state* level, there is often a similar system for authorizing nonattorneys to provide represen-

---
[14]42 U.S.C. 406 (1975).

tation at many, but by no means all, state administrative agencies. Many states have their own version of the federal Administrative Procedure Act quoted above.

Of course, the organized bar has never been happy with this special authorization given to nonattorneys within federal or state administrative agencies. Since there are state statutes on who can practice law (and often criminal penalties for nonattorneys who practice law in violation of these statutes), how can an administrative agency allow a nonattorney to engage in activity that is clearly the practice of law? The answer to this question is somewhat different for federal and state agencies.

If the agency permitting nonattorney representation is a *federal* agency (for example, the United States Patent Office, the Interstate Commerce Commission, the Internal Revenue Service, and the Social Security Administration), its authorization takes precedence over any *state* laws on the practice of law that would prohibit it. This principle was established in the United States Supreme Court case of *Sperry v. State of Florida ex rel the Florida Bar.*[15] The case involved a nonattorney who was authorized to represent clients before the United States Patent Office. The Florida Bar claimed that the nonattorney was violating the state practice-of-law statute. The Supreme Court ruled that the *Supremacy Clause* of the United States Constitution gave federal laws supremacy over conflicting state laws. The Court also said:

> Examination of the development of practice before the Patent Office and its governmental regulation reveals that: (1) nonlawyers have practiced before the Office from its inception, with the express approval of the Patent Office and to the knowledge of Congress; (2) during prolonged congressional study of unethical practices before the Patent Office, the right of nonlawyer agents to practice before the Office went unquestioned, and there was no suggestion that abuses might be curbed by state regulation; (3) despite protests of the bar, Congress in enacting the Administrative Procedure Act refused to limit the right to practice before the administrative agencies to lawyers; and (4) the Patent Office has defended the value of nonlawyer practitioners while taking steps to protect the interests which a State has in prohibiting unauthorized practice of law. We find implicit in this history congressional (and administrative) recognition that registration in the Patent Office confers a right to practice before the Office without regard to whether the State within which the practice is conducted would otherwise prohibit such conduct.
>
> Moreover, the extent to which specialized lay practitioners should be allowed to practice before some 40-odd federal administrative agencies, including the Patent Office, received continuing attention both in and out of Congress during the period prior to 1952. The Attorney General's Committee on Administrative Procedure which, in 1941, studied the need for procedural reform in the administrative agencies, reported that "[e]specially among lawyers' organizations there has been manifest a sentiment in recent years that only members of the bar should be admitted to practice before administrative agencies. The Committee doubts that a sweeping interdiction of nonlawyer practitioners would be wise. . . ."

Suppose, however, that a *state* agency permits nonattorney representation. Can this be challenged by the bar? The issue may depend on who has the *power* to regulate the practice of law in a particular state. If the state legislature has this power, then the agency authorization of nonattorney representation is valid, since the agency is under the jurisdiction and control of the legislature. So

[15]373 U.S. 379, 83 S.Ct. 1322, 10 L.Ed.2d 428 (1963).

long as the nonattorney representation is based on a statute of the legislature, it is valid. If, however, the state judiciary has the power to control the practice of law in a state, then the courts may be able to invalidate any nonattorney representation that is authorized by the agency.

Nonattorneys who have the authority to provide representation at an administrative agency may do so as independent paralegals, or as full-time employees of attorneys. The following ethical opinion from California involves the latter—a paralegal employee of a law firm. The opinion discusses some of the issues that are involved when the law firm wants its paralegal to use the special authorization for nonattorney representation at a particular administrative agency—the Worker's Compensation Appeals Board. Later in Chapter 4 we will examine some of the ethical issues involved in this opinion in greater depth.

Formal Opinion 1988–103
State Bar Committee on
Professional Responsibility and Conduct
California

Issue

May a law firm, having advised its clients of its intention to do so, delegate authority to a paralegal employee to make appearances at Workers' Compensation Appeals Board hearings and to file petitions, motions, or other material?

Digest

A law firm may delegate such authority, provided that the paralegal employee is adequately supervised.

Authorities Interpreted

Rules 3-101, 3-103 and 6-101 of the Rules of Professional Conduct of the State Bar of California.

* * *

Issue

A client has contracted for the services of a law firm for representation in a matter pending before the Workers' Compensation Appeals Board (hereinafter "WCAB"). The law firm employs and intends to utilize the services of the paralegal in connection with the proceedings pending before the WCAB to make appearances, file petitions and present motions.

The client has consented to the law firm utilizing the services of the paralegal, after being informed as to the potential consequences of representation by a person of presumably lesser qualification and skill than may be reasonably expected of an attorney. In addition, the status of the employee as a paralegal rather than an attorney will be fully disclosed at all proceedings at which the paralegal appears and on all documents which the paralegal prepares.

Discussion

It is unlawful for any person to practice law in this state without active membership in the State Bar of California. (Bus. & Prof. Code, ¶6125) The practice of law includes the performing of services in any matter pending in a court or administrative proceeding throughout its various stages, as well as the rendering of legal advice and counsel in the preparation of legal instruments and contracts by which legal rights are secured. (cf. *Smallberg v. State bar* (1931) 212 Cal. 113.)

It has been held that the representation of claimants before the Industrial Accident Commission (predecessor to the WCAB) constitutes the performance of legal services. (*Bland v. Reed* (1968) 261 Cal.App.2d 445, 448.) However, the representation by a nonattorney of an applicant before the WCAB is expressly authorized by Labor Code 5501 and 5700 as follows:

> The application may be filed with the appeals board by any party in interest, his attorney, or other representative authorized in writing . . . . Either party may be present at any hearing, in person, by attorney, or by any other agent, and may present testimony pertinent under the pleading.

Thus, the principal issue is whether an attorney may hire a nonattorney to engage in conduct on behalf of the attorney's client which the employee is authorized to perform independently, but which, if performed by the attorney, would constitute the practice of law.

It is the opinion of the Committee that because the client has been informed about and has consented to the involvement of the paralegal, no violation occurs with respect to dishonesty or deceit. (See Bus. & Prof. Code, ¶6106, 6128, subd.(a).) In addition, if the status of the employee as a paralegal rather than attorney is fully disclosed at all proceedings at which the paralegal appears and on all documents which the paralegal prepares, no violation of the prohibition on an attorney lending his or her name to be used as an attorney by a person not licensed to practice law will occur. (See Bus. & Prof. Code, ¶6105.)

In addition, because Labor Code sections 5501 and 5570 expressly authorize nonattorneys to represent applicants before the WCAB, the proposed arrangements would not constitute a violation of Rule of Professional Conduct 3-101(A), which provides as follows:

> A member of the State Bar shall not aid any person, association, or corporation in the *unauthorized* practice of law. (Emphasis added.)

Further, there is no indication that the facts presented that the relationship between the paralegal and the law firm would constitute a partnership in violation of Rule of Professional Conduct 3-103, which provides as follows:

> A member of the State Bar shall not form a partnership with a person not licensed to practice law if any of the activities of the partnership consist of the practice of law.

The pivotal consideration is that the client contracted for the services of the law firm, rather than a paralegal, for representation. However, since the safeguards mentioned above have been taken to avoid misleading or deceiving the client or any one else regarding the status of the paralegal, the Committee finds no ethical insufficiency inherent in the participation of paralegals.

A lawyer or law firm contemplating entering into such an arrangement should remember that an attorney stands in a fiduciary relationship with the client. (*Krusesky v. Baugh* (1982) 138 Cal.App.3d 562, 567.) When acting as a fiduciary, the law imposes upon a member the strictest duty of prudent conduct as well as an obligation to perform his or her duties to the best of the attorney's ability. (*Clark v. State Bar* (1952) 39 Cal.2d 161, 167; and cf. Bus. & Prof. Code, ¶6067; Rule of Professional Conduct 6-101(A).) However, an attorney does not have to bear the entire burden of attending to every detail of the practice, but may be justified in relying to some extent on nonattorney employees. (*Moore v. State Bar* (1964) 62 Cal.2d 74, 80; *Vaughn v. State Bar* (1972) 6 Cal.3d 847, 857.)

The attorney who delegates responsibilities to his or her employees must keep in mind that he or she, as the attorney, has the duty to adequately supervise the employee. In fact, the attorney will be subject to discipline if the lawyer fails to adequately supervise the employee. (*Chefsky v. State Bar* (1984) 36 Cal.3d 116, 123; *Palomo v. State bar* (1984) 36 Cal.3d 785; *Gassman v. State Bar* (1976) 18 Cal.3d 125.)

What constitutes adequate supervision will, of course, depend on a number of factors, including, but not limited to, the complexity of the client matter, the level of experience of the paralegal and the facts of the particular case.

It is the opinion of the Committee that, even though the paralegal will be providing substantive legal services to the client, adequate supervision under these unique facts does not require the attorney to ensure that the paralegal performs the services in accordance with the level of competence that would be expected of the attorney under rule 6-101.

So long as the paralegal is adequately supervised and the law firm does not mislead the client that the services will be performed in accordance with the attorney level of competence or that an attorney will be handling the matter, the Committee does not believe the attorney would be in violation of the Rules of Professional Conduct.

This opinion is issued by the Standing Committee on Professional Responsibility and Conduct of the State Bar of California. It is advisory only. It is not binding upon the courts, the State Bar of California, its Board of Governors, or any persons or tribunals charged with regulatory responsibility or any member of the State Bar.

■ ASSIGNMENT 3.3

Make a list of every state and local administrative agency in your state. Have a class discussion in which students identify as many state and local agencies as they can. Then divide the total number of agencies by the number of students in the class so that each student will be assigned the same number of agencies. For your agencies, find out whether nonattorneys can represent citizens. What are the requirements, if any, to provide this representation informally (e.g., calling or writing the agency on behalf of someone else) or formally (e.g., representing someone else at an agency hearing)? Check your state statutes. Check the regulations of the agency. If possible, call the agency to ask what its policy is and whether it can refer you to any statutes or regulations on the policy.

■ **ASSIGNMENT 3.4**

Paul is a nonattorney who works at the Quaker Draft Counseling Center. One of the clients of the center is Dan Diamond. Paul says the following to Mr. Diamond:

> You don't have anything to worry about. The law says that you cannot be drafted until you have had an administrative hearing on your case. I will represent you at that hearing. If you are drafted before that hearing, I will immediately draft a habeas corpus petition that can be filed at the United States District Court.

Any problems with Paul's conduct?

 Section C. Licensing of Paralegals

Many occupations (electricians, brokers, nurses, etc.) are licensed by the government. To date, *no* federal, state, or local government has imposed a licensing requirement on traditional paralegals. Proposals for licensing have been made in some legislatures, but none has been enacted into law. For paralegals who work under the supervision of attorneys, licensing is arguably unnecessary, since the public is protected by this supervision. But what about the relatively small number of independent paralegals who work directly with the public without attorney supervision? Many have argued that there *is* a need to license them in order to protect the public. The phrase *limited licensing* refers to a government authorization to perform a designated number of activities that are now part of the attorney monopoly. While no limited licensing proposal has yet been enacted into law, the likelihood of passage is very real in spite of substantial attorney opposition. Before covering limited licensing, let's examine efforts to enact broad-based licensing schemes covering all activities of all paralegals.

Broad-Based Licensing

A number of states have proposed legislation to license all paralegals. Many of these proposals confuse the word *certification* with *licensure*. Certification is usually a statement by a *non*governmental organization that a person has met certain qualifications. Licensure, on the other hand, is a permission or authorization *by a government* to engage in a certain activity.

In 1977, for example, the Michigan legislature gave serious consideration to passing the Legal Assistant Act to "regulate the practice of legal assistants." Under this proposal, a nine-member commission would be created to establish the requirements for the "certification" of legal assistants. Even though the proposal uses the word *certification*, it was a licensure program, since it would establish the qualifications to engage in a particular occupation. If this legislation had been enacted, a person could not be a legal assistant in Michigan without passing a statewide examination and having the educational credentials identified by the commission.

This plan was *not* adopted in Michigan. Such licensing schemes are usually vigorously opposed by paralegal associations as being premature, unnecessary, and unduly restrictive. A commonly voiced fear is that the license might limit what paralegals are now authorized to do without a license, and that some competent paralegals who now work in law offices might not fit within rigid eligibility criteria that might be established for the license. The organized bar is also opposed to broad-based licensing. The following excerpts from bar association reports give some of the reasons why:

North Carolina Bar, *Report of Special Committee on Paralegals* 3 (1980)

Several states have considered the possibility of adopting a licensing statute for paralegals, but none has done so. Licensing itself is subject to great public and legislative concern at present. So long as the work accomplished by non-lawyers for lawyers is properly supervised and reviewed by a licensed and responsible attorney, there would seem to be no need for a further echelon of licensing for the public's protection. Furthermore, licensing might be more dangerous than helpful to the public. The apparent stamp of approval of a license possibly could give the impression to the public that a person having such a license is qualified to deal directly with and give legal advice to the public. Although the Committee would not attempt to close the door on licensing of paralegals in the future if circumstances change and if, for example, the use of independent, non-lawyer employee paralegals were to become widespread, present conditions, at least, do not call for any program of licensing for paralegals.

Illinois State Bar Association, *Report on the Joint Study Committee on Attorney Assistants* 6 (6/21/77)

Our Joint Committee arose because there was a suggestion that attorney assistants be licensed. After due consideration we recommend no program of licensure or certification of attorney assistants or other lay personnel.

We are opposed to licensure because the standards on which licensure are to be based are difficult or impossible to formulate. Furthermore, we have started with a premise that precedes this conclusion; to wit: no delegation of any task to an attorney assistant shall diminish the responsibility of the attorney for the services rendered. We believe that any program which purports to say who is "licensed" and who is "not licensed" creates a standard which will diminish the attorney's responsibility. It furthermore may exclude from useful and desirable employment people who, under the supervision and control of an attorney, may perform useful tasks but who may not meet the standards of licensure involved.

We are further opposed to licensure because of the danger that it poses to the public. If a group of persons appears to be authorized to perform tasks directly for the public, without the intervening control of an attorney, it would be humanly inevitable that many of the licensed persons would try to deal directly with the public. We think these risks would be substantially increased by licensure.

■ **ASSIGNMENT 3.5**

How would you characterize the opposition to licensure expressed in the above excerpts from the bar reports? Do you think there is a conflict of interest in attorneys making these judgments about paralegal control? Explain.

Limited Licensing

As we saw earlier, some independent, or freelance, paralegals have their own businesses, through which they sell their services to attorneys. A smaller number work directly for the public without attorney supervision. For example, a paralegal might sell divorce forms and type them for clients. This is not the illegal practice of law, so long as no legal advice is given in the process. One of the reasons Rosemary Furman got into trouble was that she gave such advice along with the forms she typed, and hence was charged with the unauthorized practice of law by the Florida bar.

Some have argued that the law that led to the prosecution of people like Rosemary Furman should be changed. Why not grant them a limited license (sometimes called a specialty license) to practice law? Remarkably, a suggestion to this effect was actually made by a Commission of the American Bar Association! The ABA does not favor broad-based licensing of all paralegals. In a 1986 report, however, an ABA Commission on Professionalism cautiously suggested—on page 52 of the report—that there be "limited licensing of paralegals" and "paraprofessionals" to perform certain functions such as handling some real estate closings, drafting simple wills, and performing certain tax work. The report argued that such a proposal could help reduce the cost of legal services:

> No doubt, many wills and real estate closings require the services of a lawyer. However, it can no longer be claimed that lawyers have the exclusive possession of the esoteric knowledge required and are therefore the only ones able to advise clients on any matter concerning the law.[16]

This remarkable proposal caused quite a stir. Many refer to the controversy it created as the "page 52 debate." For years, many attorneys were suspicious of paralegalism because of a fear that paralegals might eventually be licensed and compete with attorneys. Then along comes a report of an ABA Commission that recommends licensing! Yet it must be remembered that neither the report nor the Commission speaks for the entire ABA. In fact, the proposal in the report "drew the ire" of other ABA members *and is unlikely to be given serious consideration by the ABA as a whole any time soon.* This will not, however, prevent continued suggestions in favor of some form of licensing—even from within segments of the ABA itself.

Before paralegals had time to recover from the drama of the "page 52 debate," another shock wave arrived. In 1989, the State Bar of California stated that there was "an overwhelming unmet need" for better access to legal services, and created a *Commission on Legal Technicians* to study whether independent paralegals can help meet this need. Its answer was *yes!* The Commission recommended that the California Supreme Court adopt a Rule of Court authorizing nonattorneys to engage in the practice of law in the following three areas: bankruptcy law, family law, and landlord-tenant law. (Other areas might be added later.) As "licensed independent paralegals," they would not be required to have attorney supervision. They could open an office and sell their services directly to the public. In effect, the state's rules on the unauthorized practice of law would be abolished for those services. Court representation, however, would not be included. If a client needed to go to court, an attorney would have to be hired. This "limited license" program would be administered by the California State Department of Consumer Affairs with help from an Advisory Committee consisting of two independent paralegals, one attorney, and four members of the public who are not independent paralegals or attorneys.

Here are some of the other features of the proposal:

■ Applicants for the license must be at least 18 years of age.

■ Applicants must submit fingerprints.

---

[16]*In the Spirit of Public Service: A Blueprint for Rekindling of Lawyer Professionalism* , 52 (ABA, Comm'n on Professionalism, 1986).

- Applicants must take and pass a two-part written examination: (1) a general knowledge examination, including an ethics section, and (2) a specialty exam in an area of practice. In order to be licensed, an applicant must take and pass both the general and specialty examinations within a two-year period.

- Applicants must meet minimum levels of education and/or experience, as recommended by the Advisory Committee. However, as of the date of implementation of the enabling legislation, persons who have practiced in the field for two years should have the right to take the examination without additional entry requirements. (The last sentence constitutes the grandfathering provision of the proposal.)

- For license renewal, licensees must fulfill annual continuing education requirements.

- Complaints and investigations would be handled by the Department of Consumer Affairs' centralized services.

- A client security fund would be established to provide compensation to victims of independent paralegal thefts. The initial annual fee would be $25.00 per licensee and the Advisory Committee would develop recommended guidelines for disbursement, including an appropriate cap to be placed on each claim paid by the fund.

- Standards for denial of licensure and for discipline would be established.

- The Supreme Court would approve a code of professional conduct for licensed independent paralegals.

The reaction among paralegals to this proposal has been surprisingly mixed. The two national paralegal associations—the National Association of Legal Assistants (NALA) and the National Federation of Paralegal Associations (NFPA)—have taken very different positions. As we will see later, this is not the first time that these two giants have clashed over the issue of regulating paralegals.

The National Association of Legal Assistants is *against* the California proposal for a number of reasons. First, the proposal does not provide guidelines to determine the kinds of bankruptcy, family law, or landlord-tenant cases an independent paralegal is competent to handle. Many of these cases are complex at the outset or become complex as they unfold. Such cases require the attention of an attorney. Independent paralegals are not in the best position to determine when a case is beyond their skills. Second, the licensing of independent paralegals could eventually lead to a climate in which traditional paralegals and legal assistants who work for attorneys would have to become licensed. Third, the licensing of independent paralegals will lead to open warfare with attorneys and to public disillusionment with the legal system. "For all practical purposes, . . ." the independent paralegals covered by the California proposal ". . . will become direct and fierce competitors of . . . lawyers who will not look kindly upon these untrained 'mini-lawyers.' It is only a matter of time . . . [until] the inevitable will occur; the public will have a bad experience working with one of these untrained, inadequately educated non-lawyers and it will become further disillusioned with the legal system. Thus the results will further blacken the public's image of lawyers and the law profession." [17] Finally, NALA objects to the use

---

[17]National Ass'n of Legal Assistants, *Statement to . . . State Bar of California* (1991).

Demonstration in front of the California State Bar Association on the issue of limited licensing.

of the word *paralegal* for anyone who does not work under the supervision of an attorney.

The National Federation of Paralegal Associations, on the other hand, has taken a different approach. While not directly endorsing or opposing the California proposal, the NFPA has laid out the conditions under which it will support "regulation of paralegals who deliver legal services directly to the public." The conditions are as follows:

- the regulation expands the utilization of paralegals to deliver cost-efficient legal services,
- there is a demonstrated public need,
- the regulation includes minimum criteria for performing independent paralegal services such as experience under the supervision of an attorney or of a licensed paralegal,
- the paralegals pass a performance-based proficiency examination.

Applying these conditions to the California proposal, the NFPA would probably favor the proposal, although, as indicated, no formal position has been taken on it.

As revolutionary as this proposal is, there is another proposal in California from *HALT (Help Abolish Legal Tyranny)* that is even more radical. HALT is a national legal consumer group. It has proposed that nonattorneys be allowed to practice law in fourteen specialty areas.[18] A Board of Legal Technicians in the Department of Consumer Affairs would decide which of these specialty areas require registration (involving little more than providing information about yourself), and which require licensing (involving passing an examination).

---

[18]The areas are: immigration law, family law, housing law, public benefits law, litigation support law, conservatorship and guardianship law, real estate law, liability law, estate administration law, consumer law, corporate/business law, intellectual property law, estate planning law, bankruptcy law. (Under the HALT proposal, other specialty areas might be added later.)

Other states are also considering proposals for limited licensing. In Illinois, for example, an Independent Paralegal Licensing Act was introduced in the legislature. The origin of this plan is quite interesting. A paralegal student designed a regulation plan as part of a class assignment. When this student went to work for an Illinois state legislator, the plan eventually became the basis of the licensing plan that was actually introduced in the legislature!

As you might expect, many attorneys have been intensely opposed to any form of limited licensing. A former president of the State Bar of California said, "It's like letting nurses do brain surgery." Here are some other comments from attorneys: "This is the worst thing since the plague!" They think "just about everybody should be able to practice law. I guess they think everybody should be able to slice open a belly and remove an appendix." "I cannot think of anything that would be more injurious to the public." This is an idea "whose time has not yet come." And "this is potentially the most fractious and controversial issue ever confronted" by the bar association. So far, such opposition has been successful since none of the limited license proposals have been enacted into law.

A much more modest form of limited licensing, however, has in fact been enacted into law in the state of Washington. A totally new category of worker has been created in the real estate industry, the *Limited Practice Officer* (LPO), also referred to as a Closing Certified Officer. This individual is a nonattorney with the authority "to select, prepare and complete legal documents incident to the closing of real estate and personal property transactions." [19] The State Supreme Court has created a Limited Practice Board to which applicants apply for "admission" to become an LPO. (See Figure 3.4.) The Board approves the form of the documents that the LPO can "select, prepare, and complete" in a closing, e.g., deeds, promissory notes, guaranties, deeds of trust, reconveyances, mortgages, satisfactions, security agreements, releases, Uniform Commercial Code documents, assignments, contracts, real estate excise tax affidavits, and bills of sale. Like the system for regulating attorneys, an LPO applicant must demonstrate "good moral character" and pass a combined essay and multiple-choice examination on the law. Once certified, LPOs can be disciplined for violating their authority. At present, there are no educational requirements to become an LPO, although such requirements are anticipated. LPOs must provide proof of financial responsibility by such means as purchasing a liability insurance policy ("errors and omissions insurance coverage") or showing that coverage exists under a bond taken out by their employer.

■ ASSIGNMENT 3.6

(a) Compare the LPO program in Washington with the two proposals for limited licensing in California.

(b) Do you agree with NALA's position on limited licensing, or that of NFPA? Why?

What are the chances of a licensing requirement becoming law? Even though proposals for broad-based licensing continue to appear, passage is unlikely in view of widespread opposition from attorneys and paralegals. Limited licensing, on the other hand, may eventually become a reality, in spite of the

---

[19]Washington Supreme Court Rule 12(a).

FIGURE 3.4

Application for
Admission to
Limited Practice as
a Limited Practice
Officer in the State
of Washington
under the
Admission to
Practice Rule 12

To the Washington State Limited Practice Board:

I hereby apply for a limited license to practice law in the State of Washington as a limited practice officer under the Admission to Practice Rule 12.

Applicant's Name in Full _____

Last   First   Middle

Applicant's Date of Birth _____

Month   Day   Year

Applicant's Business Address _____

Address

_____

City   State   Zip Code

Applicant's Business Phone (   ) _____

Area Code   Number

Applicant's Home Address _____

Address

_____

City   State   Zip Code

Applicant's Home Phone (   ) _____

Area Code   Number

Applicant's Social Security Number _____

Please list:

Employers/Supervisors	**From**	**To**	**Telephone Number**
(Past five years) Attach separate sheet if needed.			

position of NALA. The LPO program in Washington represents a small crack in the door. Will current proposals, such as those under serious consideration in California and Illinois, eventually kick the door through?

It is becoming increasingly difficult for attorneys to oppose limited licensing on the basis of the need to protect the public. A system now exists for identifying and punishing unscrupulous and incompetent attorneys; a similar system could be designed to regulate independent paralegals. And, of course, no one is proposing the equivalent of allowing nondoctors to perform brain surgery. The proposals for limited licensing simply try to identify services that do not require all of the skills of an attorney.

Perhaps the most compelling argument for limited licensing is the fact that attorneys have priced themselves out of the market. Recent studies continue to document a vast unmet need for legal services in our society. Attorneys, however, point to the reforms that have made legal services more accessible at a lower cost. See Figure 3.5. Yet, in spite of these reforms and in spite of the dramatic increase in the number of attorneys coming out of our law schools, the unmet need for legal services among the poor and middle class continues to grow. Here, for example, are some of the conclusions of legal-needs studies covering two large states:

> Each year in Illinois, by conservative estimates, 300,000 low-income families face approximately 1,000,000 civil legal problems for which they do not receive legal help.[20]

---

[20]Illinois State Bar Association and Chicago Bar Association, *Illinois Legal Needs Study* 5 (1989).

FIGURE 3.5
Reforms in the
Practice of Law

- *Pro bono work.* Many law firms and corporations give their attorneys time off to provide free legal services to the poor.
- *Simplified forms.* Bar associations have helped create legal forms that are relatively easy for the public to use without the assistance of an attorney.
- *Prepaid legal services.* Some companies and unions have developed programs of legal insurance under which participants pay a set amount each month for designated legal services that might be needed while the participant is in the program.
- *Attorney advertising.* Advertising has arguably made the public more aware of legal services and more inclined to use such services.
- *Publicly funded legal services.* The bar associations have consistently supported increased funding by the government for organizations that provide free legal services to the poor.
- *Traditional paralegals.* The increased use of paralegals by attorneys can lead to lower client costs since the billing rate for paralegal time is considerably lower than the billing rate for most attorneys.

The poor in New York face nearly 3,000,000 civil legal problems per year without legal help. Not more than 14% of their overall need for legal assistance is being met.[21]

The statistics are even more alarming if the legal needs of the middle class are included. In the light of these numbers, critics are calling for drastic reform.

In areas such as divorce and bankruptcy, an increasingly large underground network of nonattorneys are providing low-cost legal services to citizens. Why not bring these nonattorneys out into the open? Subject them to testing and other license requirements to help ensure competence and honesty. While many attorneys see this cure as worse than the disease, others are more receptive to the idea.

Each state must make its own determination of whether limited licensing should be adopted. It is quite possible that one or two states will take the plunge in the near future and enact limited licensing. Will your state do so? Keep in mind that even if it does, it will probably affect very *few* paralegals in your state. The likelihood is that the requirement will apply only to those paralegals who do not work for attorneys. This means that the vast majority of paralegals in the state who work for attorneys would continue as they are—with no license requirement. It is true that some paralegals favor limited licensing for traditional paralegals who work under the supervision of attorneys in order to expand what they are allowed to do for attorneys. But any movement toward such expansion is considerably weaker than the current momentum toward licensing independents.

. . . .

When a licensing proposal—or a proposal for any kind of paralegal regulation—comes before the legislature, here are some of the steps that should be taken immediately:

*What to Do When the Legislature Proposes Legislation
to Regulate Paralegals*

1. Obtain a copy of the proposed legislation or bill as soon as possible. If you know the name of the legislator sponsoring the bill, write or call him or her

---

[21]New York State Bar Association, *New York Legal Needs Study: Draft Final Report*, 196 (1989).

directly. Otherwise contact the office of the Speaker of the House, Speaker of the Assembly, President of the Senate, etc. Ask how you can locate the proposed bill.

2. Find out the exact technical status of the bill. Has it been formally introduced? Has it been assigned to a committee? What is the next scheduled formal event on the bill?

3. Immediately inform the sponsoring legislator(s) and the relevant committee(s) that you want an opportunity to comment on the bill. Find out if hearings are going to be scheduled on the bill. Make known your interest in participating in such hearings. Your goal is to slow the process down so that the bill is not rushed into enactment. Be particularly alert to the possibility that the paralegal bill may be buried in proposed legislation on a large number of related or unrelated topics. Again, there is a real danger that the bill will get through relatively unnoticed.

4. Determine why the paralegal bill is being proposed. What is the *public* reason given for the proposal of the bill? More important, what is the underlying *real* reason for the proposal? Perhaps some special interest or small group (real estate agents, for instance) is seeking a special privilege in a law-related field. Yet the language of the bill they are proposing may be so broad that paralegals will be adversely affected.

5. Alert your local paralegal association. It needs to be mobilized in order to express an organized position on the bill. Contact the major national paralegal associations: NFPA and NALA (see Appendix A). Do they know about the proposed legislation? Have they taken a position? They need to be activated.

6. If your local bar association has a paralegal committee, seek its support.

7. Launch a letter-writing campaign. Make sure that large numbers of paralegals in the area know about the bill and know how to express their opinion to the legislature.

8. Ask local paralegal schools to take a position.

. . . .

Keep in mind that we are talking about mandatory *licensing* by the state, not voluntary *certification* by entities such as paralegal associations. The certification debate will be covered later in the chapter.

■ ASSIGNMENT 3.7

(a) Do you favor broad-based licensing for every paralegal? Limited licensing? Will licensing advance or restrict the development of paralegalism?

(b) If all attorneys in the country drastically cut their fees, would there be a need for paralegal licensing?

(c) There are some tasks that even paralegals who work for attorneys cannot perform, such as taking the deposition of a witness. Should there be limited licensing to authorize such tasks?

■ ASSIGNMENT 3.8

Evaluate the following observation: "The emerging professions and the more established professions have frequently sought greater regulation of their occupational group. They are often motivated, despite the obligatory language on protection of the public interest, to do so in efforts to establish their 'territorial imperative' or to establish barriers to entry into the profession and thereby enhance their economic self-interest." Sapadin, *A Comparison of the Growth and Development of the Physician Assistant and the Legal Assistant,* in Journal of the American Association for Paralegal Education: Retrospective 1983, 142 (1983).

Section D. Bar Association Control of Paralegal Education

Since the early 1970s, the American Bar Association has been "approving" paralegal training programs after a recommendation is made by its standing Committee on Legal Assistants, all of whose members are attorneys. There is no requirement that a school be ABA-approved in order to train paralegals. In fact, most training programs are not so approved. The approval process is voluntary, and the majority of programs have decided *not* to apply for approval. A program must meet state government accreditation standards, but it does not have to seek the approval of the ABA or of any other bar association.

The ABA approval process has been controversial from its inception. Those who oppose total attorney control of paralegalism feel that the bar associations are inappropriate mechanisms to regulate training institutions. Since a major objective of attorneys is to increase their profits by employing paralegals, critics argue that it is a conflict of interest for attorneys to control the field totally. When regulatory decisions must be made on matters such as the approval of schools, whose interest would the attorneys be protecting in making these decisions? The interest of the paralegals? The interest of the public? Or the profit interest of the attorney-regulators?

The ABA has been somewhat sensitive to this criticism, and, as we will see, at one time considered withdrawing from the approval process. In recent years, challenges have been made to the monopoly that bar associations exercise over the practice of law. In 1975, the United States Supreme Court sent shock waves throughout the legal profession when the Court ruled that attorneys were no longer exempt from the *antitrust* laws, and that some minimum fee schedules are a violation of these laws.[22] In 1979, an antitrust charge was brought against the ABA on the ground that its paralegal-school approval process was designed to eliminate competition from, and restrict entry into, the market for recruitment, training, and placement of paralegals. The ABA won this case.[23] Despite the victory, the ABA remains vulnerable to future challenge.

Note that the ABA uses the word *approval* rather than accreditation in describing its process of exercising control over educational institutions. Yet the process meets the accepted definition of accreditation presented in Figure 3.1 at the beginning of this chapter. The use of the more euphemistic word *approval* may be an indication that the ABA is itself not sure whether it should be in the business of regulating paralegal education. Indeed, in 1981, the House of Delegates of the ABA instructed its Committee on Legal Assistants to terminate ABA involvement in the approval process. However, some schools that had al-

---

[22]Goldfarb v. Virginia State Bar, 421 U.S. 773 (1975).
[23]*Paralegal Institute, Inc. v. American Bar Association,* 475 F. Supp. 1123 (E.D.N.Y. 1979).

ready received approval objected. As a result, the Committee proposed and the House of Delegates accepted an alternative system of approving schools.

The alternative was the creation of an ABA Approval Commission to implement the approval process. The final decision on approval of individual schools is still left in the hands of the ABA. The Commission makes its recommendations on approval to the Committee on Legal Assistants, which in turn makes it recommendations to the House of Delegates of the ABA. The major difference between the Committee and the Commission is that the latter must contain nonattorney members. There are eleven members of the Commission, all of whom are appointed by the president of the ABA on advice from the Committee:

- Three attorneys (one of whom has taught in a paralegal program)
- One attorney who represents the ABA Committee on Legal Assistants
- One paralegal nominated by the National Federation of Paralegal Associations (NFPA)
- One paralegal nominated by the National Association of Legal Assistants (NALA)
- Two representatives nominated by the American Association for Paralegal Education (AAfPE)
- One representative nominated by the Association of Legal Administrators (ALA)
- One nonlegal educator
- One representative of the general public

The ABA does not view the Commission as a permanent institution. The plan is to phase it out over a period of years and to replace it with an *independent accrediting* body that is equally broad based. It is unclear, however, whether this replacement is feasible. It depends on the willingness of paralegal schools to submit themselves to this still-voluntary approval process. Furthermore, an independent body would be very expensive to run. Its revenues would come from fees paid by the schools that apply for approval and for renewals of approval. If large numbers of schools continue to bypass a national accrediting or approval entity, the process will lose both the political and financial support it needs. Since there is no realistic hope that an independent accrediting body will be formed, the ABA will probably continue its approval program indefinitely.

■ **ASSIGNMENT 3.9**

Who should control accreditation? Are there too many attorneys on the ABA Approval Commission? Too few paralegals? Could there be too many paralegals on such a body? Do you favor an independent accrediting entity? Who should run it? Should it be voluntary?

Only one thing is sure: change is on the horizon. The legal profession can no longer feel secure in its privileged position, as the following speech demonstrates.

The Legal Profession:
A Bow to the Past—a Glimpse of the Future

by J. Sims

[Mr. Sims was the Deputy Assistant Attorney General in the Antitrust Division of the United States Department of Justice. The following are excerpts from a speech he delivered on February 11, 1977, before a conference of the Federation of Insurance Counsel in Arizona.]

Today, in Los Angeles, legal services are being advertised on television. That fact alone gives us some idea of how much change has come to the legal profession in the last few years.

That change has not always come easy, but the fact that it has come so far, so fast, tells us quite a bit about what will happen in the future. We lawyers as a group have grumbled and argued, fought and yelled, struggled and been confused—but there are now lawyers advertising on television. Even a casual observer cannot fail to appreciate the significance of this change.

Competition, slowly but surely, is coming to the legal profession. This opening of traditional doors,the breaking of traditional barriers is the result of many forces—the number of new lawyers, the awakening of consumerism, the growing realization that the complexity of our society requires legal assistance in more and more areas. But one contributing factor has been antitrust litigation and the Department of Justice. . . .

[T]he Supreme Court fired the shot heard 'round the bar [o]n June 16, 1975. [I]n a unanimous decision [Goldfarb v. Virginia State Bar, 421 U.S. 773 (1975)], the Court held that the minimum fee schedule challenged by the Goldfarbs violated Section 1 of the Sherman Act. This decision broke the dam and released the flood of change that we see engulfing the profession today. For better or worse, the Goldfarbs had set in motion a series of events that were to change the character of the legal profession forever.

The Court decided several things in *Goldfarb*, but the most important was that the legal profession was subject to the antitrust laws—there was no "professional exemption." The response to *Goldfarb* was fascinating. A large number of private suits were filed challenging various aspects of bar regulation. . . .

[An] area sure to be controversial in the future is unauthorized practice. There is already at least one antitrust challenge, against the Virginia State Bar, seeking to prohibit the bar from promulgating unauthorized practice opinions. This case, which involves title insurance, is a direct challenge to the extraordinary power that the legal profession now has—in most states—to define the limits of its own monopoly. It would be strange indeed for a state to hand over to, say its steel industry, not only the power to regulate entry into the industry and the conduct of those within it, but also the power to define what the industry was. In many states, that is exactly the power the organized bar now has, and that power is being challenged as inconsistent with the antitrust laws.

The heart of this challenge is that lawyers shouldn't be deciding what is the practice of law—defining the scope of the legal monopoly. The papers filed in that case . . . indicate that the objection is not to such a decision being made; the objection is to the State's delegation of that power to the profession.

In fact, of course, the principle behind this lawsuit could be expanded not only to other subject matter areas, but also to arrangements between the organized bar and other professions which have as their basic result the division of commercial responsibilities.

For example, the American Bar Association has entered into "statements of principles" with respect to the practice of law with a variety of other professions and occupations ranging from accountants to claim adjusters, publishers, social workers, and even professional engineers [page 178]. These documents generally set forth the joint views of the professions as to which activities fall within the practice of law and which activities are proper for members of the other profession. They nearly all provide that each profession will advise its clients to seek out members of the other profession in appropriate circumstances.

As a general rule, two competitors may not agree with each other to allocate markets, or bids, or even functions; if they do, they violate the antitrust laws. At the least, this traditional antitrust principle raises some questions about the legal effect of such "statements of principles."

[T]he efforts of the bar to limit the scope of paralegal responsibilities and, in some jurisdictions, to seek a certification requirement for paralegals are seen by many as simply another effort to preserve and protect the legal services monopoly. Many believe that non-lawyers could perform many tasks reserved today for people with law degrees.

■ **ASSIGNMENT 3.10**

What are the implications of Mr. Sims' remarks on the role of bar associations in regulating paralegal education?

Section E. Should Paralegals Become Part of Bar Associations?

At present, no paralegals are full members of any bar associations. In 1981, however, the State Bar of Texas created a Legal Assistant Division of the bar. Its unique aspect is that all of its regular members *must* be paralegals. Hence, while paralegals cannot become members of the bar association, they can become members of a Division of the bar association. The Division is not a mere advisory committee of the bar; it is part of the bar association itself, which means that it is under the ultimate control of the Board of Directors of the State Bar of Texas.

The qualifications for membership in the Division are as follows:

■ The applicant must *not* be a Texas attorney.

■ The applicant must perform "substantial paralegal services in rendering direct assistance to an attorney." (Someone who does occasional paralegal work would not qualify.)

■ The applicant's supervising attorney must certify that the applicant performs substantial paralegal services for that attorney.

Members pay annual dues of $25.

The bylaws of the Division state its purpose as follows: "to enhance legal assistants' participation in the administration of justice, professional responsibility and public service in cooperation with the State Bar of Texas." All the officers of the Division are paralegals elected by the membership. The budget of the Division, however, must be approved by the State Bar of Texas.

The Division has been very popular among paralegals in Texas; by the middle of 1990, almost 2,000 paralegals had joined. The State Bar of Michigan recently adopted a similar program by creating a Legal Assistant Section of the bar consisting of legal assistants who are *affiliate members* of the bar. Other bar associations have also created special membership categories. There are, for example, *associate members* of the Columbus Bar Association (Ohio), associate members of the Bar Association of San Francisco, paralegal affiliate members of the Association of Trial Lawyers of America, and associate members of the American Immigration Lawyers Association.[24] Not all bar associations, however, have moved in this direction. The Louisiana State Bar Association, for example, voted in 1989 *not* to offer associate membership to paralegals because "the occupation of paralegals has not been sufficiently defined so as to provide guidance as to who is a trained and qualified paralegal, and who is not."[25]

---

[24]As of 1991, associate membership status existed or was under serious consideration in the following states either in the bar itself or in one of its committees or sections: Alaska, Arizona, Colorado, Connecticut (pending), District of Columbia, Florida, Illinois, Massachusetts, Michigan, Missouri (St. Louis County Bar only), New Jersey, New Mexico, North Dakota, Ohio (pending), Pennsylvania (pending), Texas, Wisconsin (pending), and West Virginia. Maze, *Bar Associate Membership Status for Legal Assistants,* 17 Facts & Findings 6 (NALA, March 1991).

[25]Landers, *Louisiana State Bar Association Decides Against Associate Membership for Paralegals,* 4 The Advocate (Louisiana State Paralegal Ass'n, August 1989).

■ ASSIGNMENT 3.11

Does the state, city, or county bar association where you live have a membership category for paralegals? If so, what are the eligibility requirements for membership and what are the benefits of membership?

What about the major national bar association—the American Bar Association (ABA)? For a long time, many argued that paralegals should become affiliated with the ABA in some way. In 1982 the ABA Committee on Legal Assistants proposed that the ABA create a new category of membership for paralegals. The National Association of Legal Assistants (NALA) warmly endorsed the proposal, while the National Federation of Paralegal Associations (NFPA) opposed it. Initially the House of Delegates of the ABA rejected the proposal of the Committee on the ground that the addition of this nonattorney membership category would further "dilute" the primary attorney category. Eventually, however, this objection was overcome. The House of Delegates agreed to accept a *legal assistant associate* category of membership. (For an application form, see Figure 3.6.) An ABA member who supervises the legal assistant must sign the latter's application for associate membership. As of 1991, there were 1,200 Legal Assistant Associates in the ABA.

As indicated, not all paralegals endorsed the concept of associate or affiliate membership in bar associations when the idea was first proposed. Here are some typical comments in opposition:

I haven't been able to understand why paralegals would want to become second class members of an organization that represents the interests of another profession. [Some paralegals view associate membership] as a positive development, while the very idea is enough to raise the blood pressure of other paralegals.[26]

[It is] in the public interest that the allied legal professions remain autonomous. [It is] necessary and advisable that paralegals retain primary control in the development of the paralegal profession.[27]

It is a recognized and uncontested fact that the purpose of any bar association is to promote and protect attorneys and their practice of law, rather than legal assistants. Further, associate members do not participate in the administrative and substantial legal decisions which are made by the Bar Association, e.g., no vote on dues, by-laws, budget or substantive issues of membership requirements. [A separate identity may] eliminate possible conflicts of interest on issues where attorneys and legal assistants hold differing perspectives and opinions regarding the future of legal practice.[28]

Those who viewed paralegals as an autonomous, self-directed profession tended to disagree with the effort to join bar associations in any form. Yet this point of view is *not* shared by the majority of paralegals today. The momentum is toward more and more bar associations creating membership categories for paralegals. The reasons are best summed up by the following comment made

---

[26]Whelen, *An Opinion: Bar Association's Paralegal Non-Voting Membership*, 15 At Issue 9 (San Francisco Ass'n of Legal Assistants, May 1987).
[27]*NFPA Findings*, 8 The Journal 3 (Sacramento Ass'n of Legal Assistants, January 1986).
[28]Heller, *Legal Assistant Associate Membership in the ABA*, 14 On Point 1, 14 (Nat'l Capital Area Paralegal Ass'n, August 1988).

FIGURE 3.6

ABA Associate Membership Application

ABA ASSOCIATE APPLICATION
(Valid Through August 31, 1991)

Membership Department • American Bar Association • 750 North Lake Shore Drive, Chicago, Illinois 60611, (312) 988-5522 FAX: (312) 988-6281

ADDRESS

Please print the way you wish your name and address to appear in the ABA records and on your Associate card and certificate. All materials will be sent to this address.

Name ______________________

Firm/Agency/Organization ______________________

Address ______________________

____

City ____________ State ______ Zip Code ________

Country ______________________

This address is my ☐ Home ☐ Business ☐ Both

Home Phone ( )________ Business Phone ( )________

Birth Date ____/____/____ Gender ☐ Male ☐ Female

EMPLOYMENT

Employer ______________________

Your Title ______________________

Number of Years in this position ______________________

For Judicial Associate applicants only, please indicate:
☐ Judge ☐ Court administrator ☐ Federal court executive

Employment Setting (Check one):
[1] Law Firm [2] Corporate Law Dept. [3] Gov't. [4] Judiciary
[5] Law School [6] Legal Service/Public Defense Agency [7] Military
[9] Other ______________________

Number of attorneys at this office:
[A] Solo [B] 2-5 [C] 6-9 [D] 10-19 [E] 20-99 [F] 100+

EDUCATION

Institution ______________________

Type of Degree or Certificate ______________________

REQUIRED CERTIFICATION

I certify that I meet the criteria for the category of Associate affiliation I have selected (as defined on page 2).

If elected an Associate of the American Bar Association, I will abide by its Constitution and Bylaws, and the authority of the Board of Governors with respect to Associates.

Signature (required) ______________________

ANNUAL ASSOCIATE DUES ARE $75

The ABA year runs from Sept. 1 to Aug. 31. Associates who join after October 1st receive a pro-rated credit toward next year's dues. Section dues are not pro-rated. *Some Associate categories REQUIRE you to join an ABA section. They are indicated by an *.* These required section dues are reflected in the total annual dues.

Check your selection(s):	**Total Annual Dues**
☐ Administrative Law Associate Administrative Law and Regulatory Practice Section* ($25.00)	$100.00
☐ Bar Executive Associate	$ 75.00
☐ Criminal Justice Associate Criminal Justice Section* ($25.00)	$100.00
☐ Educational Associate Legal Education and Admissions to the Bar Section* ($25.00)	$100.00
☐ Governmental Business Associate	$ 75.00
☐ Industrial Organization Economist Associate	$ 75.00
☐ International Associate	$ 75.00
Jurisdiction(s) in which admitted to practice ________ ________ Admission year(s): ________ Bar associations or legal organizations of which applicant is a member, and any offices held in them ________	
☐ Judicial Associate Judicial Administrative Division* ($25.00)	$100.00
☐ Law Librarian Associate	$ 75.00
☐ Law Office Administrative Associate Law Practice Management Section* ($27.50)	$102.50
☐ Legal Assistant Associate	$ 75.00
Supervising Attorney Verification: I, ________, ABA Membership I.D. Number: ________, a member of the Bar of the State of ________ verify that the above applicant for Legal Assistant Associate does or has performed for me in a capacity which meets the requirements described on page 2. Attorney Signature (required) ________	

Subtotal (from above) $ ________

Subtotal for additional sections (from page 4) $ ________

Total $ ________

FULL PAYMENT (Must be enclosed)

☐ Check enclosed (payable to ABA)
☐ VISA ☐ MasterCard

Card Number ________ Exp. Date ________

Signature ________

International Associates:
Please make payment in U.S. funds drawn on a U.S. bank, or a wire transfer through the First National Bank of Chicago, Account Number 50-03997 (include your name, address and "New Applicant" on the transfer for reference). **Your application CANNOT otherwise be processed.**

Associate Dues for the American Bar Association and ABA sections, divisions and forum committees are not deductible as charitable contributions for federal income tax purposes. However, such dues may be deductible as business expense.

Associate dues include a basic subscription to the *ABA Journal,* and Section dues include basic subscriptions to the section publications as shown on page 4.

Legal Assistant Associate: Persons who, although not members of the legal profession, are qualified through education, training, or work experience, are employed or retained by a lawyer, law office, governmental agency, or other entity in a capacity or function which involves the performance, under the direction and supervision of an attorney, of specifically-delegated substantive legal work, which work, for the most part, requires a sufficient knowledge of legal concepts such that, absent that legal assistant, the attorney would perform the task.

AMERICAN BAR ASSOCIATION ASSOCIATE AFFILIATION

Article Three of the ABA Constitution and Bylaws provides for the establishment of classes of Associates, composed of non-members with whom affiliation is considered to be in the interest of the Association. Associates are not members of the Association and do not, as a group, constitute a membership classification. Associates of the American Bar Association, except for International Associates, are non-lawyers who are not eligible for membership within the Association, but serve within the legal profession. Pursuant to Article 21.12 of the Association Bylaws, persons who are ineligible to be members of the Association may qualify for election by the Board of Governors as Associates if they are in one of the classifications listed above, and satisfy such further eligibility requirements as may be approved by the Board.

PRIVILEGES OF ASSOCIATES

1. To attend meetings of the Association, including sessions of the House of Delegates and the Assembly, and to enjoy any floor privileges extended to non-members.
2. To receive Association publications that are regularly provided to all members of the Association.
3. To be appointed to any Committee or Commission of the Association for which non-members are eligible for appointment.
4. To participate in the economic benefit programs available to ABA members, with the exception of the insurance programs of the American Bar Endowment.
5. To affiliate with one or more of the sections of their choice, upon application and payment of the annual section dues then in effect. All Associates under the age of 36 shall automatically become Associates of the Young Lawyers Division (see page 4).

-2-

before the ABA created the associate membership category:

> It is time our profession stopped being paranoid about ABA Associate Membership and open our eyes to opportunities presented to us. [We should not be spending time] dreaming up reasons to reject a chance for growth and improved relations within the established legal community. No guarantees have been given to assure us that associate membership would be beneficial, but why close *any* doors opened to us? If just a few paralegals would like to take advantage of this opportunity, why slam the door in their faces? The spirit of cooperation and teamwork within the legal community are the key reasons to encourage associate membership.[29]

■ **ASSIGNMENT 3.12**

(a) Should paralegals become a formal part of bar associations? What effect do you think associate membership would have on existing paralegal associations? Strengthen them? Destroy them? Is it healthy or unhealthy for paralegals to organize themselves as independent entities? Is it healthy or unhealthy for them to be able to challenge the organized bar? What is the conflict-of-interest argument against associate membership? Do you agree with this argument?

(b) Should a paralegal association allow *attorneys* to become associate members of the *paralegal* association? Why or why not?

(c) Under the ABA associate membership category, what kinds of paralegals are excluded from membership? Is such exclusion a good idea?

(d) To become an associate or affiliate member of a bar association, the applicant usually must obtain the signed statement of an attorney-employer asserting or attesting certain facts about the applicant—for instance, that he or she is a paralegal who works for the attorney. The statement is called an attorney attestation. For example, to obtain affiliate membership in the State Bar of Michigan, the attorney must "hereby attest" that the applicant "is employed by me and is recognized as a legal assistant (paralegal) and that he/she, under the supervision and direction of a lawyer, performs the services" specified elsewhere on the application. Some *paralegal* associations require the same kind of attorney attestation as a condition of allowing paralegals to join the paralegal association. Do you think attorney attestation is a good idea for associate/affiliate membership in a bar association? For full membership in a paralegal association?

(e) As indicated elsewhere in this book, there are a fairly large number of paralegals who have moved on to management positions as paralegal coordinators or legal assistant managers. Should these individuals become members of traditional paralegal associations?

■ Section F. Self-Regulation by Paralegals: The Certification Debate

As we have seen, there are two major national associations of paralegals:

■ National Federation of Paralegal Associations (NFPA): An association of associations; its membership consists of state and local paralegal associations

■ National Association of Legal Assistants (NALA): an association of individuals, plus a number of state and local paralegal associations, and several student paralegal associations

---

[29]Anderson, *ABA Associate Membership: A Different Perspective,* 3 Findings and Conclusions 7 (Washington Ass'n of Legal Assistants, August 1987).

In Appendix A, there is a list of state and local paralegal associations, with a notation of whether they are part of NFPA, part of NALA, or unaffiliated.

NALA is *not* a member of NFPA, and vice versa. In fact, the two groups take very different positions on a number of issues, two of the most important of which are limited licensing of independent paralegals and certification of all paralegals. Earlier in this chapter we examined the clash of views on limited licensing. We turn now to the older and perhaps more bitter debate over certification. NALA has created two major certification programs for paralegals—the Certified Legal Assistant (CLA) program and the Certified Legal Assistant Specialist (CLAS) program. The major opponent of the very existence of these programs has been NFPA. The following two excerpts present a detailed description of the position of both associations on certification. At the end of the descriptions, you will be asked which side is correct.

The Case for Certification[30]
by Jane H. Terhune

[Jane H. Terhune is a past president of the National Association of Legal Assistants. She is employed as a legal assistant for the firm of Hall, Estill, Hardwick, Gable, Collingsworth & Nelson, Tulsa, Oklahoma.]

Professional competence of an *individual* can be assessed by two recognized mechanisms: licensing or certification. Accreditation or approval, on the other hand, examines educational *programs* to determine whether they meet established standards of quality. Although the ABA has an institutional approval process, this paper is concerned only with the assessment of *individual* competence and therefore will not deal with the issue of institutional accreditation or approval.

Since the early 1970s legal assistants have obtained employment by means of formal training, in-house training, or other law office experience. While each method of training has certain advantages, no one method has proven superior to the others. Thus the dilemma: how can prospective employers or clients assess or legal assistants demonstrate paralegal skills and knowledge when there is no standard for performance?

Is licensing the appropriate mechanism to assure professional competence of legal assistants at this time? Several states have recently considered it, but none has yet adopted it. It is generally agreed that requirements for licensing would either severely limit the growth and development of the still new paralegal field or be so weak as to be meaningless. Licensing,

by definition, is a mandatory requirement and is usually administered and controlled by government entities or well-established and strong professional associations. It is doubtful that state legislatures can define the legal assistant profession well enough to regulate it effectively at this time. Therefore, licensing appears to be impractical as well as premature.

Certification, on the other hand, is a voluntary professional commitment that appears to be a practical alternative, and the National Association of Legal Assistants believes that one national certification program is preferable to a multitude of possible state programs. Certification is not new or unique. Many professions and paraprofessions have developed and supported certification as an alternative to licensing or other forms of regulation. Certification recognizes expertise and proven ability without limiting entrance into or employment in the field, and the same standards are applied regardless of the individual's background or training. Furthermore, a certification program can help guide educational institutions in developing and evaluating their legal assistant curricula. It is argued that certification would limit the development of the paralegal field, but the PLS (Professional Legal Secretary) certification of legal secretaries has in no way interfered with their employment. To the contrary, secretaries with the Certified PLS title are regarded as professionals in their respective fields.

In 1974, as part of an effort to set high professional standards for legal assistants while the field was in its early development, the NALA Certifying Board for Legal Assistants was created. It was composed of nine members—five legal assistants (working in different areas of the law), two paralegal educators, and two attorneys. The composition of the Board has remained the same to date, and in number is similar to many certification boards or committees in other fields. During the first year of its existence the Certifying Board

---

[30] American Bar Association, Standing Committee on Legal Assistants, *Legal Assistant Update '80* 5–16 (1980). This article has been updated to reflect current positions of NALA and NFPA.

acted mainly as a feasibility study group. All known national professional associations with certification programs were contacted for advice and guidance. Paralegal educators were contacted for information about their programs as well as entrance and graduation requirements. Legal assistant duties and responsibilities in various areas of the law were surveyed, and correspondence with the Institute of Legal Executives in England began. Our English counterparts were anxious to share their ten years of experience with NALA. After several months of gathering information, replies were tabulated and summarized and the NALA Certifying Board for Legal Assistants was ready to embark on its task. Its first task was to create an examination. Passing this examination would enable a legal assistant to become a CLA—Certified Legal Assistant.

Although many legal assistants work in special areas of law rather than as generalists, there are general skills and knowledge which apply to all legal fields and, for this reason, general subjects or topics were selected for inclusion in the examination.

The CLA Examination—Outline

The two-day CLA examination contains objective questions, such as multiple choice, true/false, and matching. There are also essay questions and short answer questions. The examination covers the follow areas:

Communications. This section of the CLA examination contains questions on:

word usage	capitalization	grammar
number usage	vocabulary	correspondence
punctuation	word division	nonverbal communication
sentence structure	concise writing	

Ethics. This section deals with ethics in the legal assistant's contacts with employers, clients, co-workers, and the general public. Unauthorized practice, ethical rules, practice rules, and confidentiality are among the topics tested by this section. Knowledge of the American Bar Association Rules of Professional Conduct and the National Association of Legal Assistants, Inc., Code of Ethics and Professional Responsibility is required for this examination.

Human Relations and Interviewing Techniques. The Human Relations portion encompasses professional and social contacts with the employer, clients, and other office visitors, co-workers, including subordinates, and the public outside of the law office. For this reason, the legal assistant should be familiar with authorized practice, ethical rules, practice rules, delegation of authority, consequences of delegation, and confidentiality.

Interviewing techniques cover basic principles, as agreed upon by most authors on the subject, definitions of terms of basic principles, and handling of specialized interviews. Subject areas included in this section of the examination are:

General considerations for the interviewing situation: courtesy, empathy, and physical setting	Manner of questions
	Use of checklists for specific matters
Initial Roadblocks—lapse of time, prejudice, etc.	Special-handling situations: the elderly, the very young

The test covers initial and subsequent interviews as well as both client and witness interviews.

Judgment and Analytical Ability.   The sections of this part deal with (1) analyzing and categorizing facts and evidence; (2) the legal assistant's relationship with the lawyer, the legal secretary, the client, the courts, and other law firms; (3) the legal assistant's reactions to specific situations; (4) handling telephone situations; and (5) reading comprehension and data interpretation.

Legal Research.   It is extremely important for the legal assistant to be able to use the most important tool of the legal profession—the law library. The purpose of the legal research section of the CLA Examination is to test your knowledge of the use of state and federal codes, the statutes, the digests, case reports, various legal encyclopedias, court reports, shepardizing, and research procedure.

Legal Terminology.   The sections of this part deal with (1) Latin phrases; (2) legal phrases or terms in general; and (3) utilization and understanding of common legal terms. The questions involve legal terminology and procedures used in general practice.

Substantive Law.   The substantive law section of the CLA examination is divided into nine parts: (1) general (which includes American Legal System); (2) bankruptcy; (3) corporate; (4) estate planning and probate; (5) contract; (6) litigation; (7) real estate; (8) criminal; and (9) administrative law. Each examinee will be required to take the first part and must select four out of the remaining eight parts.

After passing the examination, a legal assistant may use the *CLA (Certified Legal Assistant)* designation, which signifies certification by the National Association of Legal Assistants, Inc. CLA is a service mark duly registered with the U.S. Patent and Trademark Office (No. 1131999). Any unauthorized use is strictly forbidden.

Based on the premise that education, a commitment of all professionals, is a never ending process, Certified Legal Assistants are required periodically to submit evidence of continuing education in order to maintain certified status. The CLA designation is for a period of five years, and if the CLA submits proof of continuing education in accordance with the stated requirements, the certificate is renewed for another five years. Lifetime certification is not permitted.

Continuing education units are awarded for attending seminars, workshops or conferences in areas of substantive law or a closely related area. The seminars, etc., do not have to be sponsored by NALA, although all NALA seminars and workshops qualify.

The development of the specific test items was a time-consuming and difficult project. Rather than employ professional testing companies unfamiliar with the legal assistant field, it was decided that the Certifying Board, composed of legal assistants, attorneys, and educators from the legal assistant field, was best qualified to prepare the exams. Then followed a series

of meetings to review, refine, and evaluate the proposed exams. The exams were pilot-tested, testing times were noted, results were systematically analyzed, and problems were identified. Every question in each section was carefully scrutinized for "national scope," and questions which did not apply to all states were removed from the exam.

Eligibility Requirements for CLA Examination

Applicants for the Certified Legal Assistant examination must meet one of the following three requirements at the time of filing the application.

1. Graduation from a legal assistant program that is:
   a) Approved by the American Bar Association; or
   b) An associate degree program; or
   c) A post-baccalaureate certificate program in legal assistant studies; or
   d) A bachelor's degree program in legal assistant studies; or
   e) A legal assistant program which consists of a minimum of sixty semester hours (or equivalent quarter hours) of which at least fifteen semester hours (or equivalent quarter hours) are substantive legal courses.

2. A bachelor's degree in any field plus one (1) year's experience as a legal assistant.

3. A high school diploma or equivalent plus seven (7) years' experience as a legal assistant under the supervision of a member of the Bar plus evidence of a minimum of twenty (20) hours of continuing legal education credit to have been completed within a two (2) year period prior to the application date.

Applicants meeting any one of these criteria may take the exam. They need not be members of the National Association of Legal Assistants to apply for or receive the CLA (Certified Legal Assistant) certification.

The CLA examination was first offered in November, 1976, at regional testing centers. Approximately 50% of the first group of applicants passed the entire exam, and the board was particularly pleased that the passing percentage was uniform throughout the country, a fact which seemed to indicate that the test was free of state or regional bias. Although the passing rate has fluctuated slightly in subsequent testing, the uniformity has been maintained. In the March 1990 exam, there was a 51.5% pass rate, as 504 of 977 legal assistants passed the test. As of April 1991, there were 4,265 CLAs in the country. The following states have the most CLAs:

Florida:	1120	Colorado:	122
Texas:	967	Kansas:	106
Arizona:	316	Iowa:	77
Oklahoma:	202	Louisiana	73
California:	157	New Mexico:	63

Certification is an ambitious and expensive project for a young professional association. Over $20,000 and thousands of hours were initially invested in the CLA program, but the National Association of Legal Assistants believes it has been a wise investment. Traditionally, where new professions do not set their own standards, related professions or governments have done so for them. NALA felt a responsibility to develop a quality national certification program for legal assistants desiring professional recognition. The CLA exam has been in use for a number of years, but work on the project continues. The question bank is continually expanded so that an indefinite number of exam versions can be created, and questions are being reviewed and updated constantly.

Specialty Certification

Recently NALA launched a major new component of its CLA program. It is now possible for someone who has already achieved CLA status to take additional examinations in order to receive *Specialty Certification* in one or more of the following areas:

- **Civil Litigation** covers Federal Rules of Civil Procedure, Federal Rules of Evidence, and Federal Rules of Appellate Procedure; document control; drafting pleadings; abstracting information; and general litigation procedures.

- **Probate and Estate Planning** covers general probate and trust law, federal estate tax, fiduciary income tax, drafting wills and trusts, and estate planning concepts.

- **Corporate and Business Law** covers the knowledge and applications of those principles of contract, tort, property, agency, employment, administrative, corporate, and partnership law which commonly constitute the subject matter known as business law. Examinees must be thoroughly familiar with the Uniform Commercial Code, Uniform Partnership Act, Uniform Limited Partnership Act, Model Business Corporate Act, as well as with the regulatory authority of those federal agencies which affect the business relationship such as the SEC, FTC, OSHA, and EPA.

- **Criminal Law and Procedure** covers an applicant's knowledge in the area of criminal procedure and law from arrest through trial. The examination covers components of substantive criminal law, procedural matters, and constitutional rights guaranteed to defendants. Applicants must be thoroughly familiar with the Federal Rules of Criminal Procedure, Federal Rules of Evidence, the Model Penal Code, and major United States Supreme Court cases.

- **Real Estate** covers the applicant's knowledge in the area of real estate purchases, sales, terminology, actions affecting title, landlord-tenant relations, oil and gas, easements, abstracts, title insurance, liens, cluster developments, types of conveyances, methods of passing title included in conveyances, legal remedies associated with real estate, and legal descriptions of real estate.

Each of these specialty examinations takes four hours to complete. Upon passing one of them, the legal assistant becomes a *CLAS—a Certified Legal Assistant Specialist.* The CLA examination tests broad *general* skills required of *all* legal assistants. Specialty certification, on the other hand, recognizes significant competence in a *particular* field. Yet both the CLA exam and the CLAS exam are similar in that they do not test the law of any particular state. They are national in scope, since NALA believes that standard national examinations will ensure uniformity of professional standards as well as permit legal assistants to move from one state to another without loss of certified status.

From the inception of the CLAS program in 1982 up to 1990, 298 legal assistants have achieved CLAS status in the country.

The Case Against Certification
by Judith Current

[Judith Current is a past president of the National Federation of Paralegal Associations. She is employed as a legal assistant in the firm of Holme, Roberts & Owen, Denver, Colorado.]

The National Federation of Paralegal Associations (NFPA) is a professional organization composed of fifty-two state and local paralegal associations representing over 17,000 paralegals across the country. NFPA was founded in 1974 and adopted the following purposes in 1975:

- to constitute a unified national voice of the paralegal profession
- to advance, foster, and promote the paralegal concept
- to monitor and participate in developments in the paralegal profession
- to maintain a nationwide communications network among paralegal associations and other members of the legal community

NFPA has continued to foster these goals through its established policies and activities. In 1977 NFPA adopted its Affirmation of Responsibility (p. 279).

NFPA recognizes that certification of paralegals is of national concern, but it feels that there has been insufficient study as to the impact of certification and the means by which certification should be administered. NFPA will only support a certification program which is coordinated by a national, broadly based, autonomous body in which paralegals have at least equal participation with attorneys and other members.

The topic of certification of legal assistants has been of concern to NFPA since its inception. It has found every certificate proposal advanced to date to be seriously lacking in the understanding of the true nature of the profession, particularly its diversity, and the proposals have offered a structure that provides little or no representation to the persons most affected, the legal assistants themselves.

Specifically, its reservations fall within the following areas:

Need/Prematurity

Since there is tremendous diversity in the functions and classifications of paralegals, it is extremely difficult to create generalized standards that can be fairly applied. This problem may eventually find an acceptable solution; but it will require much study and considerable input from all affected sectors.

No studies have been conducted that have demonstrated a need for certification. A study conducted by the American Bar Association in 1975 concluded that certification was premature. The California State Bar in 1978 rejected a proposal for certification and accreditation after nearly two years of study. Other states have similarly rejected certification. Until a need for certification is clearly demonstrated, certification will be premature.

Premature regulation runs a risk of foreclosing yet unseen avenues of development, as well as creating yet another layer of costly bureaucracy when, in fact, none may be needed. NFPA sees nothing to prevent, and everything to encourage, an extremely cautious approach to the enactment of any program of certification. Meanwhile, the normal mechanisms of the marketplace, the existing unauthorized practice laws and ethical guidelines, the increasing numbers of legal assistants with demonstrable experience, and the ever-growing reputations of various training programs can serve as guidelines for those who seek the sorts of yardsticks that certification might provide.

Impact of Certification

No studies have been conducted that satisfactorily assess the potential impact of certification on the delivery of legal services. Some of the possible negative effects include:

1. *The growth, development, and diversity of the paralegal profession could be diminished by certification.* The paralegal profession has been developing steadily without a demonstrated need for such regulation. Regulating the profession could curtail development into new areas, stifling the potential growth of the field and unnecessarily limiting the role of the paralegals in the delivery of legal services.

2. *Certification could result in a decrease of the availability of legal services to the poor.* Legal aid offices [page 83] are economically dependent upon paralegals who represent clients at various administrative hearings. Most of these paralegals are in-house trained specialists who are paid lower salaries than private sector paralegals. If certification is implemented, it is conceivable that administrative agencies may initiate a system in which only certified paralegals, or attorneys, would be allowed to represent clients at the hearings. Many paralegals successfully working in this area might not meet the educational or testing requirements imposed by certification, and the legal aid offices would not be able to meet the salary demands that would be made by certified paralegals.

3. *Innovation in paralegal education programs could diminish as a result of certification.* Schools would be forced by necessity to gear their courses to a certification examination rather than to the needs of the legal community and the marketplace. While some standardization of training programs might be desirable in the future, it would be premature at this time because the training programs have not been in existence long enough to determine which types of programs are most effective and because the paralegal profession is still in a dynamic stage of development. Experimentation and variety are currently essential to the field of paralegal education.

4. *Entry into the profession could be curtailed by certification.* At the present time, a paralegal can enter the profession in a variety of ways, including formal education, in-house training, promotion from legal secretary, or a combination thereof. Certification could limit these entry paths by establishing prescribed educational requirements.

No Acceptable Model for Certification

In the opinion of NFPA, no acceptable model or program of certification has yet been devised. Oregon is the only state to have adopted a certification program, but it was discontinued shortly after it began because of a lack of interest from paralegals and attorneys in the state. NFPA questions the propriety of the Oregon State Bar controlling the certification of paralegals, and deplores the fact that the paralegals were denied equal representation on the certifying board. The Oregon program failed adequately to recognize specialization and failed to make any distinctions between the tasks which may be performed by a certified paralegal and those which may be performed by an uncertified paralegal. Thus, certification did not enhance the position of paralegals in Oregon.

NFPA feels that the certification program conducted by the National Association of Legal Assistants (NALA) is unacceptable. The criteria for eligibility to take the certification examination is not based on objective data. The examination, in the Federation's opinion, contains questions irrelevant to a practicing paralegal and is not an effective measure of a person's ability to work successfully as a paralegal. The NALA certification program is not officially recognized by a governmental body, and a person certified under this program is not allowed to perform any tasks other than those which may also be performed by uncertified paralegals.

Control and Representation

No certification program will be acceptable to NFPA unless it is developed, implemented, and controlled by an autonomous group which is composed of an equal number of attorneys, paralegals, paralegal educators, and members of the public. Self-regulation is unacceptable to NFPA since self-regulation can become self-interest, and self-interest can conflict with the public interest. NFPA strongly believes that bar control of paralegals is inappropriate in that such regulation may meet the interests of the organized bar and lawyers but not necessarily the interests of the public or the paralegal profession. NFPA also questions the propriety of the organized bar attempting to regulate another profession.

National Coordination

NFPA believes that any program of certification will be most efficient and equitable if it is developed as a national program rather than on a state-by-state basis. A national program would eliminate duplication of effort on the part of each individual state. It would allow for mobility and would avoid a conflict of standards between states.

NFPA recommends that the need for and possible methods of certification be studied in much greater depth, and that this study be conducted by an autonomous group which provides equal representation to paralegals, attorneys, paralegal educators, and members of the public. NFPA also recommends that bar associations work with paralegals and educators to educate lawyers in the proper and effective utilization of paralegals and that paralegals work to promote the growth and the development of the profession through support of and participation in the local and national paralegal associations.

■ ASSIGNMENT 3.13

(a) Which side is correct? Conduct a debate in your class on the advantages and disadvantages of certification.

(b) Do you agree with NFPA that self-regulation is unacceptable?

Certification in Florida

Florida Legal Assistants (FLA) is a statewide paralegal association that is affiliated with the National Association of Legal Assistants. Florida is a big NALA state; over 25% of all CLAs in the country live in Florida. Several years ago, FLA began its own exam on Florida law for those legal assistants who had passed the CLA exam of NALA. In 1984, FLA launched the Certified Florida Legal Assistant Examination. A person who is a CLA and passes this exam on Florida law can become a *CFLA—a Certified Florida Legal Assistant*. Like the CLA exam, the CFLA exam is voluntary; no one is required to take it. The program is not endorsed by any of the bar associations in Florida. It is run exclusively by FLA. "Some legal assistants view the CFLA designation as a step up from NALA's CLA designation."[31]

Certification in Texas?

The Florida certification program was inaugurated with relative calm. The exact opposite occurred when certification proposals emerged in Texas. As we saw earlier, there is a *Legal Assistant Division* within the State Bar of Texas. A survey of the members of the Division revealed very high interest in adopting a voluntary certification program specifically for Texas. Over 76% of the members indicated that they would take a certification exam if it were offered. Consequently, the Division drafted two certification proposals and conducted a series of hearings on them in 1986. The proposals were as follows:

Proposal 1. The Division would develop and administer its own two-day exam on generic topics (such as legal analysis and communications) and on Texas law. Only legal assistants with at least two years working experience as a legal assistant would be eligible to take the exam.

Proposal 2. The Division would join forces with NALA and give two exams. NALA would administer its two-day Certified Legal Assistant (CLA) exam. Then the Division would administer its half-day exam designed with a focus on Texas law. Anyone who had previously passed the CLA exam would be required to have worked as a legal assistant in Texas for one year before taking the Division's Texas exam.

---

[31]Morris, *State Certifying Test for Legal Assistants in Florida: Is Arizona Next?*, The Digest, p. 1 (Arizona Paralegal Ass'n, October 1989).

These two proposals stirred great controversy in Texas and throughout the country. The National Federation of Paralegal Associations (NFPA) vigorously opposed both proposals, raising many of the same arguments against certification discussed earlier. But the Dallas Association of Legal Assistants (which is a member of NFPA) criticized NFPA for its opposition. The National Association of Legal Assistants (NALA) endorsed the Texas move toward certification. Of course, this is not surprising in view of NALA's history of supporting certification. And NALA would play a major role if the second proposal were adopted.

The debate was not limited to NFPA and NALA. Eight public hearings were held throughout Texas, and 187 persons submitted written comments. *But no clear consensus emerged from the hearings on the two proposals.* There was considerable confusion about the nature, purpose, and scope of the two proposals, and indeed, about the value of certification itself.

In spite of these difficulties, there is continued interest in developing a state-specific certification program in Texas within the structure of the state bar association. The most recent proposal under consideration is the establishment of a series of voluntary specialty examinations on Texas law to recognize "advanced professional competency" within a particular specialty. The likelihood of enacting such a proposal is very high. The bar's Legal Assistants Committee has appointed a Certification Committee to study it.

Position of the American Bar Association on Certification

The ABA has taken the following positions on paralegal certification:

1. Certification of *minimal,* or *entry-level,* paralegal competence is *not* appropriate.
2. Voluntary certification of *advanced* paralegal competence or proficiency in specialty areas of the law *might* be appropriate *if* it were administered by the appropriate body.
3. The ABA is *not* the appropriate body to undertake a program of certifying paralegals in advanced competence or proficiency in specialty areas of the law.
4. A voluntary program of certifying advanced paralegal competence or proficiency in specialty areas of the law, if undertaken at all, should be undertaken on a national basis by a board that includes attorneys, paralegals, educators, and members of the general public.
5. Since such a board does not presently exist, there should not be any certification at this time.

According to the ABA, certification of minimal competence does not have the benefits that would justify the time, expense, and effort to implement it. Furthermore, any of the benefits would be outweighed by potential detriment from it. A major danger the ABA sees is that such certification could evolve into licensure, which the ABA opposes.

But the ABA does see benefit in certifying paralegals in areas of specialization *after* they have been on the job. This kind of advanced certification would be a way of recognizing professional advancement. "Such certification would be a measure of quality of work and experience. Its function would be to demonstrate to employers or prospective employers a high degree of legal assistant competence in a particular area of practice that has already been obtained, rather than just the potential for such competence."[32]

The ABA feels, however, that advanced certification must be administered by the appropriate body. This body should be broad based, including attorneys, paralegals, educators, and members of the public. The ABA recognizes that it is *not* such a body. Neither is the National Association of Legal Assistants nor the National Federation of Paralegal Associations. In fact, such a body simply does not exist. It would take a great deal of money, energy, and political skill to create one. Beyond a lot of rhetoric, no one is even trying.

Hence, as a practical consequence, it can be said that the ABA is opposed to *any* certification at this time.

■ ASSIGNMENT 3.14

When a new local paralegal association is formed, it is often lobbied by NALA and by NFPA to become a part of one of these national organizations. The local association will usually make one of three decisions: affiliate with NALA, affiliate with NFPA, or remain unaffiliated. If you were a member of a local association faced with the decision of whether to join NALA, NFPA, or stay unaffiliated, what would your vote be? Why?

■ ASSIGNMENT 3.15

Is it a good idea to have two national associations? Why or why not?

Throughout this book the importance of paralegal associations has been stressed. They have had a major impact on the development of paralegalism. Many state and local bar associations as well as the ABA have felt the effect of organized paralegal advocacy through the associations.

As soon as possible, you should join a paralegal association. Find out if the association allows students to become members. (See the form at the end of this book after the index.) If an association does not exist in your area, you should form one and decide whether you want to become part of the National Federation of Paralegal Associations or the National Association of Legal Assistants. The paralegal association is your main voice in the continued development of the field. Join one now and become an active member. In addition to the educational benefits of membership and the job placement services that many associations provide, you will experience the satisfaction of helping shape your career in the years to come. Attorneys and the bar associations should not be the sole mechanism for controlling paralegals.

G. Fair Labor Standards Act

Yes, I am paid overtime. I am paid at time and a half rate. I agree with being paid overtime. If the attorney asks me to work additional long hours and weekends, then yes I do believe I should be compensated for yielding my free time

---

[32]ABA Standing Committee on Legal Assistants, *Position Paper on the Question of Legal Assistant Licensure or Certification,* 5 Legal Assistant Today 167 (1986).

for work. This does not make me any less of a professional. My professionalism will show through my work product.[33]

My firm doesn't pay paralegals overtime, and I don't want to be classified as a person eligible for overtime. For one thing, people paid overtime are non-professionals, and I don't think of myself as a non-professional. I feel that my salary, salary increases, and bonuses reflect a degree of compensation for the extra hours I work.[34]

One of the hot topics in the field is GOD: the Great Overtime Debate. "The mere mention of the subject of overtime in any group of working legal assistants is guaranteed to spark a prolonged session of horror-story telling." [35] The topic is so controversial that one paralegal association recently established a hotline to answer questions confidentially. Some paralegals have filed—and won—lawsuits against their employers for failure to pay *overtime compensation* for hours worked beyond forty hours in a week.

There is a definite body of law that determines whether overtime compensation must be paid; the issue is not dependent on the preferences of individual paralegals. The governing law is the federal *Fair Labor Standards Act*,[36] which is enforced by the Wage and Hour Division of the U.S. Department of Labor. Under the Act, overtime compensation must be paid to employees unless they fall within one of the three "white collar" exemptions. Exempt employees are those who work in a professional, administrative, or executive capacity.[37] The vast majority of traditional paralegals do *not* fit within any of these exemptions. Since they are nonexempt, they *are* entitled to the protection of the Act. Phrased another way, they are not considered professionals, administrators, or executives under the Act and must therefore be paid overtime compensation. If, however, the paralegal is a supervisor with extensive management responsibilities over other employees, an exemption may apply. But this would cover only a small segment of the paralegal population. The following opinion letter explains the position of the government on this issue. As you will see, the criteria

---

[33]*The Member Connection,* 14 Facts & Findings 7 (NALA, June 1988).

[34]*The Membership Responds,* 9 The ParaGraph (Georgia Ass'n of Legal Assistants, September/October 1987).

[35]Acosta, *Let's Talk About Overtime!,* 10 Ka Leo O' H.A.L.A. 6 (Hawaii Ass'n of Legal Assistants, August/September 1987).

[36]29 U.S.C.A. §§ 201 *et seq.* (1976).

[37]The Professional Employee Exemption:

- Primary duty consists of work requiring knowledge of an advanced type in a field customarily acquired by a prolonged course of specialized intellectual instruction and study. (Such course of study means at least a baccalaureate degree or equivalent.)

- Work requires the consistent exercise of judgment and discretion.

- Work is predominantly intellectual and varied in character, as opposed to routine, mental or physical work.

The Administrative Employee Exemption:

- The employee's primary duty consists of work related to management policies or general business operations.

- The employee regularly exercises discretion and independent judgment.

The Executive Employee Exemption:

- The employee's primary duty consists of the management of the enterprise.

- The employee regularly supervises two or more other employees. 29 C.F.R. part 541 (1983).

used to distinguish exempt from nonexempt employees are the actual job responsibilities of the employee, not the job title or compensation policy of the office.

■ ASSIGNMENT 3.16

(a) If you had a choice, would you want to receive overtime compensation as an entry-level paralegal?

(b) Surveys have shown that between 20–40% of nonexempt paralegals today do *not* receive overtime compensation. Can you explain this startling fact?

Wage and Hour Division
United States Department of Labor
September 27, 1979

This is in further reply to your letter of July 12, 1979, . . . concerning the exempt status under section 13(a)(1) of the Fair Labor Standards Act of paralegal employees employed by your organization. . . .

The specific duties of the paralegal employees (all of which occur under an attorney's supervision) are interviewing clients; identifying and refining problems; opening, maintaining, and closing case files; acting as the liaison person between client and attorney; drafting pleadings and petitions, and answering petition, and interrogatories; filling pleadings and petitions; acting as general litigation assistant during court proceedings; digesting depositions, and preparing file profiles; conducting formal and informal hearings and negotiations; preparing and editing newsletters and leaflets for community development and public relations purposes; performing outreach services; coordinating general activities with relevant local, State, and Federal agencies; assisting in establishing and implementing community legal education programs; and working as a team with other employees to deliver quality legal services. You state that the job requires at least two years of college and/or equivalent experience.

[The Fair Labor Standards] Act provides a complete minimum wage and overtime pay exemption for any employee employed in a bona fide executive, administrative, or professional capacity . . . . An employee will qualify for exemption if all the pertinent tests relating to duties, responsibilities, and salary . . . are met. In response to your first question, the paralegal employees you have in mind would not qualify for exemption as bona fide professional employees as discussed in section 541.3 of the regulations, since it is clear that their primary duty does not consist of work requiring knowledge of an advanced type in a field of science or learning customarily acquired by a prolonged course of specialized intellectual instruction and study, as distinguished from a general academic education and from an apprenticeship and from training in the performance of routine mental, manual, or physical processes.

With regard to the status of the paralegal employees as bona fide administrative employees, it is our opinion that their duties do not involve the exercise of discretion and independent judgment of the type required by section 541.2(b) of the regulations. The outline of their duties which you submit actually describes the use of skills rather than discretion and independent judgment. Under section 541.207 of the regulations, this requirement is interpreted as involving the comparison and evaluation of possible courses of conduct and acting or making a decision after the various possibilities have been considered. Furthermore, the term is interpreted to mean that the person has the authority or power to make an independent choice, free from immediate direction or supervision with respect to matters of significance.

The general facts presented about the employees here tend to indicate that they do not meet these criteria. Rather, as indicated above, they would appear to fit more appropriately into that category of employees who apply particular skills and knowledge in preparing assignments. Employees who merely apply knowledge in following prescribed procedures or determining whether specified standards have been met are not deemed to be exercising independent judgment, even if they have some leeway in reaching a conclusion. In addition, it should be noted that most jurisdictions have strict prohibitions against the unauthorized practice of law by lay persons. Under the American Bar Association's Code of Professional Responsibility, a delegation of legal tasks to a lay person is proper only if the lawyer maintains a direct relationship with the client, supervises the delegated work, and has complete professional responsibility for the work produced. The implication of such strictures is that the paralegal employees you describe would probably not have the amount of authority to exercise independent judgment with regard to legal matters necessary to bring them within the administrative exemption. . . .

With regard to your [other] questions, all non-exempt employees, regardless of the amount of their wages, must be paid overtime premium pay of not less than one and one-half times their regular rates of pay for all hours worked in excess of forty in a work-week. The fact that an employee did not obtain advanced approval to work the overtime does not relieve the employer from complying with the overtime provisions of the Act.

We hope this satisfactorily responds to your inquiry. However, if you have any further questions concerning the application of the Fair Labor Standards Act to the situation you have in mind, please do not hesitate to let us know.

Sincerely,

C. Lamar Johnson
Deputy Administrator

Section H. Tort Liability of Paralegals

Thus far we have discussed a number of ways that paralegal activities are or could be regulated:

- Criminal liability for violating the statutes on the unauthorized practice of law
- Special authorization rules on practice before administrative agencies and other tribunals
- Licensing
- Bar rules on paralegal education
- Self-regulation
- Labor laws

Finally, we come to *tort liability,* which is another method by which society defines what is and is not permissible. A tort is a private wrong or injury other than a breach of contract or the commission of a crime, although some breaches of contract and crimes can also constitute torts.

Two questions need to be kept in mind. First, when are paralegal employees *personally liable* for their torts? Second, when are employers *vicariously liable* for the torts of their paralegal employees? (As we will see, vicarious liability simply means being liable because of what someone else has done or failed to do.) The short answer to the first question is: *always.* The short answer to the second question is: *when the wrongdoing by the paralegal was within the scope of employment.* After covering both questions, we will then examine the separate question of when malpractice insurance will pay for such liability.

Several different kinds of wrongdoing are possible. The paralegal might commit:

- The tort of negligence
- An intentional tort, such as battery.
- An act which is both a crime (such as embezzlement) *and* an intentional tort (such as conversion).

A client who is injured by any of these torts can sue the paralegal in the same manner that a patient in a hospital can sue a nurse. Paralegals are not relieved of liability simply because they work for, and function under the supervision of, an attorney. Every citizen is *personally* liable for the torts he or she commits. The same is true of criminal liability.

Next we turn to the employers of paralegals. Are they *also* liable for wrongdoing committed by their paralegals? Assume that the supervising attorneys did nothing wrong themselves. For example, the attorney did not commit the tort or crime as an active participant with the paralegal, or the attorney was not careless in selecting and training the paralegal. Our question is: Can an attorney be liable to a client solely because of the wrongdoing of a paralegal? When such liability applies, it is called *vicarious liability,* which exists when one person is liable solely because of what someone else has done or failed to do. The answer to our question is found in the doctrine of *respondeat superior,* which makes employers responsible for the torts of their employees or agents when the wrongdoing occurs within the scope of employment.[38]

Hence, if a tort is committed by a paralegal within the scope of employment, the client can sue the paralegal or the attorney, or both. This does not mean that the client recovers twice; there can be only one recovery for a tort. The client is simply given a choice in bringing the suit. In most cases, the primary target of the client will be the employer, who is the so-called *deep pocket,* meaning the one who has resources from which a judgment can be satisfied.

Finally we need to examine what is meant by *scope of employment.* Not every wrongdoing of a paralegal is within the scope of employment simply because it is employment related. The test is as follows: Paralegals act within the scope of employment when they are furthering the business of their employer, which for our purposes is the practice of law. Slandering a client for failure to pay a law firm bill certainly furthers the business of the law firm. But the opposite is probably true when a paralegal has an argument with a client over a football game and punches the client during their accidental evening meeting at a bar. In the latter example, the client could not sue the paralegal's employer for the intentional tort of battery under the doctrine of *respondeat superior,* because the battery was not committed while furthering the business of the employer. Only the paralegal would be liable for the tort under such circumstances.

The most common tort committed by attorneys is negligence. This tort occurs when a client is injured because of a failure to use the ordinary skill, knowledge, and diligence normally possessed and used, under similar circumstances, by a member of the profession in good standing. In short, the tort is committed by failure to exercise the reasonable care expected of an attorney. An attorney is not, however, an insurer. Every mistake will not lead to negligence liability even if it causes harm to the client. The harm must be due to an unreasonable mistake, such as forgetting to file an action in court before the statute of limitations runs out.

When a paralegal commits negligence for which the attorney becomes liable under *respondeat superior,* the same standard applies. Since the work product of the paralegal blends into the work product of the supervising attorney, the attorney becomes as fully responsible for what the paralegal did as if the attorney had committed the negligence. Unreasonableness is measured by what a

[38]We are talking here of vicarious *civil* liability, or more specifically, the tort liability of employers because of the torts committed by their employees. Employers are not subject to vicarious *criminal* liability. If a paralegal commits a crime on the job, only the paralegal goes to jail (unless the employer actually participated in the crime).

reasonable attorney would have done, not what a reasonable paralegal would have done.

There have not been many tort cases in which paralegals have been sued for wrongdoing in a law office. Yet as paralegals become more prominent in the practice of law, more are expected to be named as defendants. The most common kinds of cases involving paralegals have occurred when the paralegal was a notary and improperly notarized signatures under pressure from the supervising attorney.

■ **ASSIGNMENT 3.17**

Mary Smith is a paralegal at the XYZ law firm. One of her tasks is to file a document in court. She negligently forgets to do so. As a result, the client has a default judgment entered against her. What options are available to the client?

■ **ASSIGNMENT 3.18**

Go to the *American Digest System*. Give citations to and brief summaries of court cases on the topics listed in (a) and (b) below. Start with the Descriptive Word Index volumes of the most recent Decennial. After you check the appropriate key numbers in that Decennial, check those key numbers in all the General Digest volumes that follow the most recent Decennial. Then check for case law in at least three other recent Decennials. Once you obtain citations to case law in the digest paragraphs, you do not have to go to the reporters to read the full text of the opinions. Simply give the citations you find and brief summaries of the cases as they are printed in the digest paragraphs.

(a) Cases, if any, dealing with the negligence of attorneys in the hiring and supervision of legal secretaries, law clerks, investigators, and paralegals. (If there are many, select any five cases.)

(b) Cases, if any, dealing with the negligence of doctors and/or hospitals in the hiring and supervision of nurses, paramedics, and other medical technicians. (If there are many, select any five cases.)

■ Section I. Malpractice Insurance

Legal *malpractice* generally refers to wrongful conduct by an attorney for which an injured party (the attorney's client) can receive damages. Just as doctors purchase malpractice insurance against suits by their patients, so too attorneys can buy such insurance to cover suits against them by their clients for alleged errors and omissions. We need to examine how paralegals fit into this picture.

Until the 1940s, not many attorneys bought malpractice insurance because suits by clients were relatively rare. Today, the picture has changed radically; cautious attorneys do not practice law without such insurance against their own malpractice. "Statistically, the new attorney will be subjected to three claims before finishing a legal career." [39] Hence, very few attorneys are willing to *go bare*, that is, practice without insurance. This change has been due to a number

---

[39] R. Mallen & J. Smith, *Legal Malpractice,* 3rd ed., 2 (1989).

FIGURE 3.7

Malpractice
Liability Claims
Against Attorneys

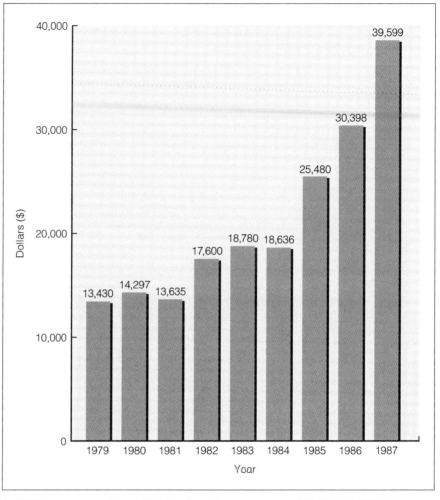

In 1979 the average claim paid, including all expenses, was $13,430. By 1987 this amount rose 295% to a new average of $39,599.

Source: St. Paul Fire & Marine Insurance Company

of factors. As the practice of law becomes more complex, the likelihood of error increases. Furthermore, the public is becoming more aware of its right to sue. In spite of disclaimers by attorneys that they are not guaranteeing any results, client expectations tend to be high, and hence clients are more likely to blame their attorney for an unfavorable result. And attorneys are increasingly willing to sue each other. In fact, some attorneys have developed a legal malpractice specialty in which they take clients who want to sue other attorneys. As malpractice awards against attorneys continue to rise (see Figure 3.7), the market for malpractice insurance has dramatically increased. And so has the cost. In some cities, the premium for insurance is over $6,000 per year per attorney.

There are two kinds of professional liability insurance policies covering attorney malpractice: occurrence policies and claims-made policies. An *occurrence policy* covers all occurrences (such as negligent error or omission) during the period the policy is in effect, even if the claim on such an occurrence is not actually filed until after the policy expires. Insurance companies are reluctant to write such policies because of the length of time it sometimes takes to uncover the existence of the negligent error or omission. Here's an example: An attorney makes a careless mistake in drafting a will that is not discovered until the person who hired the attorney dies many years later. Under an occurrence policy, the attorney is protected if the mistake occurred while the policy was in effect, even if the actual claim was not filed in court until after the policy terminated. The most common kind of policy sold by insurance companies today is the *claims-made policy* under which coverage is limited to claims actually filed (made) during the period in which the policy is in effect.[40]

Malpractice policies usually cover all the attorneys *and* the nonattorney employees of the law office. One policy, for example, defines the individuals covered—"the insured"—as follows:

> The insured includes the firm, all lawyers within the firm, and all non-lawyer employees, as well as former partners, officers, directors and employees solely while they acted on behalf of the insured firm.[41]

Such inclusion of employees is not always automatic, however. The policies of some insurance companies do not include paralegals or secretaries unless the law firm specifically requests coverage for them and pays an additional premium for their inclusion. Paralegals should therefore ask their employers if their malpractice policy explicitly covers paralegals.

What about freelance or independent paralegals who sell their services to attorneys? Although they may not be considered employees of the firm, they will usually be covered under the firm's policy in the same manner as full-time, in-house paralegal employees. So long as the employing attorney supervises and is responsible for the conduct of the paralegal, the malpractice policy usually provides coverage. In the language of one widely used policy, coverage is provided for "any other person for whose acts, errors or omissions the insured is legally responsible,"[42] which would include freelance paralegals.

Nevertheless, some freelance paralegals have explored the possibility of obtaining their own malpractice insurance policies. To date, most traditional insurance companies have not made such policies available, although there are exceptions. Complete Equity Markets, Inc., for example, offers "Paralegals Professional Indemnity Insurance" as a claims-made policy. For approximately $1,800 a year, a paralegal can purchase $250,000 worth of malpractice insurance. Since most paralegals work for an attorney and are already covered under the attorney's policy, few paralegals have purchased their own policy. Yet if paralegals are eventually granted a form of limited license that authorizes them to sell their services directly to the public, separate paralegal malpractice policies will become common and may even be mandated as a condition of receiving the license.[43]

---

[40]It is possible for a claims-made policy to cover a negligent error or omission that took place *before* the effective date of the policy, but most companies exclude coverage for prepolicy claims that the attorney knows about or could have reasonably foreseen at the time the policy is applied for.

[41]Home Insurance Companies, Professional Liability Insurance.

[42]American Home Assurance Company, Lawyers Professional Liability Policy.

[43]As we saw earlier, most Enrolled Agents are nonlawyers who are authorized to provide certain tax services to the public. The National Association of Enrolled Agents offers a "Professional Liability Insurance Plan" through the St. Paul Fire and Marine Insurance Company. The Association's brochure says, "You can now secure protection against an unexpected lawsuit or penalty for damages arising from services you provide as an Enrolled Agent." Attorneys are not eligible to purchase this insurance.

☐ Chapter Summary

Criminal prosecution may result from violating statutes on the unauthorized practice of law. In general, they prohibit nonattorneys from appearing for another in a representative capacity, drafting legal documents, and giving legal advice. Nonattorneys can sell forms and other legal materials but cannot give individual help in using them.

There are some major exceptions to the prohibitions on nonattorney conduct. In a limited number of circumstances, nonattorneys are authorized to do what would otherwise constitute the unauthorized practice of law. For example:

- In most states, a real estate broker can draft sales contracts.

- Several specialized courts allow nonattorneys to represent clients in court, although this is rare.

- A few states allow paralegals to "appear" in court to request a continuance or a new date for the next hearing in a case.

- An inmate can "practice law" in prison—for example, he or she can draft court documents for and give legal advice to another inmate if the prison does not offer adequate alternative methods of providing legal services.

- Many administrative agencies, particularly at the federal level, allow nonattorneys to represent clients before the agencies.

A number of states have considered broad-based licensing (which would cover all activities of all paralegals) and limited licensing (which would cover specified activities of those paralegals, often called legal technicians, who are not supervised by attorneys). To date, neither kind of licensing has been enacted. Relatively soon, however, a limited-license requirement will probably be enacted in one or two states. While this would be a dramatic event, it would affect very few paralegals, since limited licensing would not apply to paralegals who work for attorneys.

All paralegal schools in the country must be licensed by their state. There is no requirement that they be accredited by the bar association. The American Bar Association, however, has an "approval" process whereby a school can be approved by the ABA.

A number of bar associations allow paralegals to become associate or affiliate members. For example, the American Bar Association has a membership category called Legal Assistant Associate.

Certification has been a major point of disagreement between the National Association of Legal Assistants (NALA) and the National Federation of Paralegal Associations (NFPA). NALA has instituted a national test that leads to certification as a Certified Legal Assistant (CLA). Even though this is a voluntary program, NFPA opposes its very existence.

The Fair Labor Standards Act requires employers to pay overtime compensation to employees unless they function in an executive, administrative, or professional capacity. Paralegal managers with major responsibility for the supervision of other paralegals would fall within one of the exceptions, and hence would not be entitled to overtime compensation. All other paralegals, however, do not fall within an exception and therefore must be paid overtime compensation.

If a paralegal commits a tort, such as negligence, he or she is personally liable to the defendant. Under the theory of *respondeat superior,* the supervising attorney is also liable for the wrong committed by the paralegal if it occurred within the scope of employment. Most attorneys have a claims-made malpractice insurance policy that covers their employees.

Key Terms

accreditation	limited licensure	treaties
approval	specialty licensure	certified domestic violence
certification	registration	advocate
certified	regulation	ex parte order
certificated	practice of law	jailhouse lawyer
ethics	unauthorized practice of law	writ writer
guideline	authorized practice of law	*Johnson v. Avery*
licensure	statement of principles	Administrative Procedure Act

registered agent
agency practitioner
enrolled agent
supremacy clause
page 52 debate
legal technician
licensed independent
     paralegal
HALT
limited practice officer
pro bono
prepaid legal services
legal insurance
approval commission

antitrust
monopoly
associate members
affiliate members
attorney attestation
CLA
CLAS
CFLA
specialty certification
legal assistant division
entry-level certification
advanced certification
GOD
Fair Labor Standards Act

overtime compensation
Wage and Hour Division
exempt paralegal
nonexempt paralegal
tort liability
personal liability
vicarious liability
respondeat superior
deep pocket
malpractice
go bare
occurrence policy
claims-made policy

4

Attorney Ethics and Paralegal Ethics

■ Chapter Outline

Section A. The Ten Commandments of an Ethical Conservative

When it comes to ethics, *a paralegal must be conservative.* To an ethical conservative, the question is not, "What can I get away with?" but rather, "What is the right thing to do?" With this guideline in mind, we will examine many ethical principles in this chapter. Some of the most important are presented in Figure 4.1.

Section B. Enforcing Ethics

Ethics and Sanctions

Ethics are rules that embody standards of behavior to which members of an organization must conform. The organization is often an association of individuals in the same occupation—for example, attorneys, paralegals, stockbrokers, or accountants. The ethical rules of some organizations are enforced by *sanctions.* A sanction is any penalty or punishment imposed for unaccepta-

FIGURE 4.1

Paralegal Ethics:
The Ten
Commandments of
a Conservative

1. Know the ethical rules governing attorneys. If you understand when attorneys are vulnerable to charges of unprofessional conduct, you will be better able to help them avoid such charges.

2. Know the ethical rules governing paralegals. At the start of your paralegal career, promise yourself that you will adhere to rigorous standards of professional ethics, even if these standards are higher than those followed by people around you.

3. Never tell anyone who is not working on a case anything about that case. This includes your best friend, your spouse, and your relatives.

4. Assume that people outside your office do not have a clear understanding of what a paralegal or legal assistant is. Make sure that everyone with whom you come in contact (clients, attorneys, court officials, agency officials, the public) understand that you are not an attorney.

5. Know what legal advice is and refuse to be coaxed into giving it, no matter how innocent the question asked of you appears to be.

6. Never make contact with an opposing party in a legal dispute, or with anyone closely associated with that party, unless you have the permission of your supervising attorney and of the attorney for the opposing party, if the latter has one.

7. Don't sign your name to anything if you are not certain that what you are signing is 100% accurate and that the law allows a paralegal to sign it.

8. Never pad your time sheets. Insist that what you submit is 100% accurate.

9. Know the common rationalizations for misrepresentation and other unethical conduct:
   - it's always done
   - the other side does it
   - the cause of our client is just
   - if I don't do it, I will jeopardize my job

   Promise yourself that you will not allow any of these rationalizations to entice you to participate in misrepresentation or other unethical conduct.

10. If what you are asked to do doesn't feel right, don't proceed until it does.

ble conduct.[1] Other organizations, however, have ethical rules that are not tied to any system of enforcement.

All of the major national paralegal associations have adopted ethical rules, as we shall see later in the chapter, but none are enforced by sanctions. No paralegal, for example, has ever been thrown out of a paralegal association for unethical conduct. It could happen, but it is unlikely since it is very expensive to establish and operate an enforcement system. Paralegal associations simply do not have the resources that would be required.

Attorneys, on the other hand, *are* subject to enforceable ethical rules. These rules attempt to govern everything an attorney does in the practice of law. Of course, one of the things an attorney does is employ paralegals. Hence, as we will see, there are rules on how an attorney can use paralegals ethically. Unethical use of paralegals can subject the attorney to sanctions.

Paralegals and Attorney Ethics

Can a paralegal *also* be sanctioned for violating these ethical rules? No. The rules govern attorney conduct only.[2] Since paralegals cannot join a bar associ-

---

[1]Another meaning of the word *sanction* is to authorize or to give formal approval. Example: the court *sanctioned* the payment of attorney fees.

[2]Remarkably, there is one jurisdiction—the District of Columbia—that allows a nonattorney to become a full owner/partner of a law firm! This individual must agree to abide by the ethical code that governs attorneys. In D.C., therefore, the ethical rules governing attorneys *do* apply to nonattorneys. (The first nonattorney to become a partner of a law firm was an accountant.)

ation as full members, they cannot be sanctioned by a bar association or by any other agency set up to monitor attorney conduct. Serious wrongdoing by paralegals may result in their being fired and might subject them to negligence suits or to criminal prosecution (as we saw in Chapter 3,) but they cannot be punished for unethical conduct by the entity that regulates attorneys.

This does not mean, however, that paralegals can ignore the ethical rules governing attorneys. Quite the contrary. *One of the paralegal's primary responsibilities is to help an attorney avoid being charged with unethical conduct.* (A recent seminar conducted by the Los Angeles Paralegal Association was entitled "Law Firm Ethics: How to Keep Your Attorneys off '60 Minutes' "!) Hence, the paralegal must be intimately familiar with ethical rules. Our goal in this chapter is to provide you with that familiarity.

Courts, Legislatures, and Bar Associations

In most states, the regulation of attorneys is primarily under the control of the highest court in the state (often called the Supreme Court), which determines when an attorney can be granted a license to practice law and under what conditions the license will be taken away or suspended because of unethical conduct. Since the state legislature may also exert some regulatory authority over attorneys, a dispute occasionally arises over which branch of government can control a particular aspect of the practice of law. The judiciary often wins this dispute and becomes the final authority. In practice, however, the judicial branch and the legislative branch usually share regulatory jurisdiction over the practice of law, with the dominant branch being the judiciary. The day-to-day functions of regulation are delegated to an entity such as a state bar association and a disciplinary board or grievance commission.

There are three kinds of bar associations:

- National (for example, American Bar Association, Association of Trial Lawyers of America, Hispanic National Bar Association)
- State (for example, Illinois State Bar Association, State Bar of Montana)
- Local (for example, Boston Bar Association, San Diego County Bar Association)

All national and local bar associations are voluntary; no attorney is required to be a member. The majority of state bar associations in the country are *integrated,* which simply means that membership is required as a condition of practicing law in the state. (Integrated bar associations are also referred to as *mandatory* or *unified* bar associations. See Figure 4.2.) There is a state bar association in every state. Most, but not all, are mandatory.

Under the general supervision of the state's highest court, the state bar association has a large role in regulating most aspects of the practice of law. For example, dues charged by integrated bar associations are used to fund the state's system of enforcing ethical rules. States that do not have integrated bar associations often have a *registration* requirement. Each attorney in the state registers to practice law and pays a registration fee that is used to fund that state's system of enforcing the ethical rules. Even in these states, the state bar association has a great influence over the regulation of attorneys. Given this dominant role of bar associations, the method of regulating attorneys in America is essentially that of self-regulation: attorneys regulating attorneys.[3]

---

[3]This is so even in states that allow nonattorneys to serve on boards or commissions that regulate an aspect of the legal profession.

FIGURE 4.2

States with Unified
Bar Associations
(1991)

Alabama	Idaho	Montana	North Dakota	Utah
Alaska	Kentucky	Nebraska	Oklahoma	Virginia
Arizona	Louisiana	Nevada	Oregon	Washington
California	Michigan	New Hampshire	South Carolina	West Virginia
Florida	Mississippi	New Mexico	South Dakota	Wisconsin
Georgia	Missouri	North Carolina	Texas	Wyoming

There is no national set of ethical rules that applies to every state. Each state can adopt its own rules to regulate the attorneys licensed in that state. The rules are found in documents with various names, such as code of ethics, canons of ethics, code of professional responsibility, model rules. In fact, however, there is considerable similarity in the rules that the states have adopted. The reason for this similarity is the influence of the American Bar Association.

As indicated, the American Bar Association is a voluntary national bar association; no attorney must belong to it. Yet approximately 55% of the attorneys in America do belong to the ABA. It publishes ethical rules but does *not* discipline attorneys for unethical conduct. The role of the ABA in this area is to write ethical rules and to *propose* to the individual states that they be accepted. A state is free to adopt, modify, or reject them. The current recommendation of the ABA is found in a document called the *Model Rules of Professional Conduct.*[4] This document has been very influential throughout the country. Many states adopted it with relatively minor changes.

Accusation of Unethical Conduct

When an attorney is charged with unethical conduct, the case is investigated by a disciplinary body appointed by the state's highest court. The name

---

[4]The *Model Rules of Professional Conduct* is a 1983 revision of the ABA's *Model Code of Professional Responsibility*. The latter document consists of three main parts. First, there are nine *canons,* which are general statements of norms that express the standards of professional conduct expected of attorneys. Second, and more important, there are *disciplinary rules* (abbreviated DR), which are mandatory statements of the minimum conduct below which no attorney can fall without being subject to disciplinary action. Third, there are *ethical considerations* (abbreviated EC) which represent the objectives toward which each member of the profession should strive.

for this body differs from state to state, e.g., the Grievance Commission, the Attorney Registration and Disciplinary Commission, the Committee on Professional Conduct, the Board of Professional Responsibility.

A hearing is held to determine whether unethical conduct was committed by the accused attorney. The commission, committee, or board then makes its recommendation to the state's highest court which makes the final determination of whether to accept this recommendation. A number of sanctions can be imposed by the court. See Figure 4.3.

Section C. The Ethical Rules

We turn now to an overview of specific ethical rules that apply to attorneys. Where appropriate, a paralegal perspective on the rules will be presented. At the end of the overview, there will be a more concentrated focus on paralegals, particularly on ethical issues not covered earlier in the chapter. The overview is based on the ABA *Model Rules of Professional Conduct.* The rule numbers used in the discussion (such as Model Rule 1.5) refer to these *Model Rules,* which will either be quoted or summarized.

1. Competence

An attorney shall provide competent representation to a client. Model Rule 1.1

A *competent* attorney uses the *knowledge* and *skill* that are reasonably necessary to represent a particular client. What is reasonably necessary depends on the complexity of the case. A great deal of knowledge and skill, for example, may be needed when representing a corporate client accused of complicated antitrust violations.

How do attorneys obtain this knowledge and skill? They draw on the general principles of legal analysis and legal research learned in law school. But more importantly, they take the time needed to *prepare* themselves. They spend time in the law library. They talk with their colleagues. In some instances, they formally associate themselves with more experienced attorneys in the area. Attorneys who fail to take these steps are acting unethically if their failure means that they do not have the knowledge and skill reasonably necessary to represent a particular client.

Some attorneys have so many clients that they could not possibly give proper attention to each. Always looking for more lucrative work, they run the risk of neglecting the clients they already have. As a consequence, they might miss court dates or other filing deadlines, lose documents, fail to determine what law governs a client's case, etc. Such an attorney is practicing law "from the hip"—incompetently and unethically.

> Example: Mary Henderson, Esq. has a large criminal law practice. She agrees to probate the estate of a client's deceased son. She has never handled such a case before. Five years go by. No progress is made in determining who is entitled to receive the estate. If some minimal legal research had been done, Henderson would have been able to close the case within six months of taking it.

Henderson has probably acted unethically. The failure to do basic research on a case is a sign of incompetence. The need for such research is clear in view

FIGURE 4.3

Attorney Sanctions
for Unethical
Conduct

DISBARMENT:	The termination of the right to practice law. The disbarment can be permanent or temporary. If it's temporary, the attorney will be allowed to apply for readmission after a designated period.
SUSPENSION:	The removal of an attorney from the practice of law for a specified minimum period, after which the attorney can apply for reinstatement. An *interim suspension* is a temporary suspension pending the imposition of final discipline.
REPRIMAND:	A public declaration that the attorney's conduct was improper. This does not affect his or her right to practice. Reprimand is also called *censure* or *public censure*.
ADMONITION:	A nonpublic declaration that the attorney's conduct was improper. The mildest form of punishment that can be imposed, it does not affect his or her right to practice. An admonition is also known as a *private reprimand*.
PROBATION:	Allowing the attorney to continue to practice but under specified conditions, such as submitting to periodic audits of client funds controlled by the attorney or making restitution to a client whose funds were wrongly taken by the attorney.

of the fact that she has never handled a probate case before. Either she must take the time to find out how to probate the estate, or she must contact another attorney with probate experience and arrange to work with this attorney on the case. Not doing either is unethical.

The vast majority of graduates of law schools need a good deal of on-the-job study and guidance before they are ready to handle cases of any complexity. A law school education does little more than help ensure that the attorney is equipped to go out and *continue* learning through experience and legal research. A good attorney is always learning the law—long after law school is over. The first day on the job for new attorneys is often a very nerve-wracking event because they are acutely aware of how much they do *not* know.

In addition to sanctions for unethical conduct, an attorney's incompetence may have other consequences as well. The client might try to sue the attorney for negligence in a legal malpractice case. (Such suits were discussed in Chapter 3.) If the client is a criminal defendant who was convicted, he or she may try to appeal the conviction on the ground that the attorney's incompetence amounted to a denial of the effective "Assistance of Counsel" guaranteed by the 6th Amendment of the U.S. Constitution.

Paralegal Perspective:

- "An attorney who utilizes a legal assistant's services is responsible for determining that the legal assistant is competent to perform the tasks assigned, based on the legal assistant's education, training, and experience . . . ."[5] While the attorney has this supervisory responsibility, paralegals also have a responsibility to maintain their own competence.

- If you are given assignments that are beyond your knowledge and skill, let your supervisor know. Either you must be given training with close supervision, or you must be given other assignments. A "lawyer should explain to

---

[5]ABA Standing Committee on Legal Assistants, *Model Guidelines for the Utilization of Legal Assistant Services,* Draft, Comment to Guideline 1 (March 1991). (Hereinafter cited as ABA *Model Guidelines.*)

the legal assistant that the legal assistant has a duty to inform the lawyer of any assignment which the assistant regards as beyond his capability." [6]

■ After you complete an assignment, look for an opportunity to ask your supervisor how you could have improved your performance on the assignment. Do not wait for a year-end evaluation to learn what you can do to become a more competent paralegal.

■ Find out which attorneys, administrators, paralegals, and secretaries in the office have a reputation for explaining things well. Spend time with such individuals even if you do not work with them on a daily basis. Take them to lunch. Find time to sit with them on a coffee break. Ask lots of questions. Let them know you respect high-quality work and appreciate anything they can tell you to help you increase your competence.

■ Take the initiative in continuing your formal paralegal education after you are employed. Do not wait for someone to suggest further training. Find out what seminars and conferences are being conducted by paralegal associations and bar associations in your area. Attend those that are relevant to your job even if you must pay for them yourself.

2. Diligence/Unwarranted Delay

An attorney shall act with reasonable diligence and promptness in representing a client. Model Rule 1.3

An attorney must make reasonable efforts to expedite litigation. Model Rule 3.2

Angry clients often complain that attorneys take forever to complete a case, and keep clients in the dark about what is happening. "He never answers my calls." "It took months to file the case in court." "He keeps telling me that everything is fine, but nothing ever gets done." Such complaints do not necessarily indicate unethical behavior by the attorney. Events may be beyond the control of the attorney. For example, the court calendar is crowded, the other side is not responding. Yet this does not excuse a lack of regular communication with clients to keep them reasonably informed about the status of their case.

Other explanations for a lack of diligence and promptness, however, are more serious:

■ The attorney is disorganized. The law office has not developed adequate systems to process cases. The delays are due to careless mistakes and a lack of skill.

■ The attorney is taking many more cases than the office can handle. Additional personnel should be hired to do the needed work, or new cases should not be accepted.

Often, the failure to use reasonable diligence and promptness causes harm to the client. For example, the attorney neglects to file a suit before the statute of limitations has run against the client. Unreasonable procrastination, however, can be unethical even if such harm does not result.

Another problem is the attorney who intentionally seeks numerous delays in an effort to try to wear the other side down. It is unethical to engage in such

---

[6]Section 20–110, Committee Commentary, *New Mexico Rules Governing the Practice of Law* (Judicial Pamphlet 16).

dilatory practices. Attorneys must use reasonable efforts to expedite litigation, consistent with protecting the interests of their clients.

Paralegal Perspective:

■ An overloaded attorney probably works with an overloaded paralegal. Successful paralegals often take the initiative by asking for additional work. But reason must prevail. If you have more work than you can handle, you must let your supervisor know. Otherwise, you might be contributing to the problem of undue procrastination.

■ Learn everything you can about office systems. Find out how they are created. After you have gained some experience in the office, you should start designing systems on your own initiative.

■ When a busy attorney is in court or cannot be disturbed because of pressing work on another case, someone in the office should be available to communicate with clients who want to know the status of their case. In many offices, the paralegal is in a position to provide this information. The role is delicate, however, since in addition to asking about the status of their case, clients often asks questions that call for legal advice. Giving such advice may constitute the unauthorized practice of law. Later we will examine in greater depth the temptations and pressures on a paralegal to give legal advice.

3. Fees

An attorney's fee shall be reasonable. Model Rule 1.5(a)

There is no absolute standard to determine when a fee is excessive and therefore unreasonable. A number of factors must be considered: the amount of time and labor involved, the complexity of the case, the experience and reputation of the attorney, the customary fee in the locality for the same kind of case, etc.

> Examples: In 1979, a court ruled that $500 an hour was excessive in a simple battery case involving a guilty plea and no unusual issues. In 1984, a court ruled that a fee of $22,500 was excessive in an uncomplicated real estate case involving very little time. The case was settled through the efforts of someone other than the attorney.

The basis of the fee should be communicated to the client before or soon after the attorney starts to work on the case. This is often done in the contract of employment called a *retainer*.[7]

At one time, bar associations published a list of "recommended fees" that should be charged for designated kinds of services. These *minimum-fee schedules* have now been prohibited by the United States Supreme Court. They constitute illegal price fixing by the bar in violation of the antitrust laws.

Contingent fees can sometimes present ethical problems. A contingent fee is a fee that is dependent on the outcome of the case. (Other kinds of fees will be examined in Chapter 10.)

---

[7]Another meaning of the word *retainer* is the amount of money or other assets that will serve as an advance payment for services. Depending on the agreement reached, the retainer may or may not be refundable in the event that the attorney-client relationship ends before all the legal services are performed.

> Example: An attorney signs a retainer to represent a client in an automobile negligence case. If the jury awards the client damages, the attorney will receive 30% of the award. If the client loses the case, the attorney receives no fee.

This is a contingent fee since it is dependent on the outcome of the negligence case.

The benefit of a contingent fee is that it provides an incentive for an attorney to take the case of a client who does not have funds to pay an attorney while the case is pending. But contingent fees are not ethical in every case, even if the amount to be received by the successful attorney is otherwise reasonable. A contingent fee in a criminal case, and in most divorce cases, for example, is unethical.

> Example: Gabe Farrell is a client of Sam Grondon, Esq. in a criminal case where Gabe is charged with murder. Gabe agrees to pay Grondon $100,000 if he is found innocent. Grondon will receive nothing if Gabe is convicted of any crime.

This fee agreement is unethical. Contingent fees are not allowed in criminal cases. Note the pressures on Grondon. He arguably has no incentive to try to negotiate a guilty plea to a lesser charge, since such a plea would mean a conviction and, hence, no fee. In such a situation, the attorney's own personal interest (obtaining the $100,000) could conflict with the interest of the client (receiving a lesser penalty through a negotiated plea). Similar pressures can arise in family-law cases.

> Example: To obtain a divorce from his wife, a client hires an attorney. The fee is $25,000 if the divorce is granted.

As the case develops, suppose there is a glimmer of hope that the husband and wife might reconcile. Hence, the attorney's interest (obtaining the $25,000) could conflict with the interest of the client (reconciling). This might lead the attorney to discourage the reconciliation or to set up roadblocks to it. Reconciliation obviously removes the possibility of the contingency—obtaining the divorce—from occurring. In family law cases, therefore, contingent fees are unethical if the fee is dependent on securing a divorce, on the amount of alimony obtained, on the amount of support obtained, or on the amount of a property settlement in lieu of alimony or support. Model Rule 1.5(d). This is so even if the terms of the contingent fee are otherwise reasonable.

One final theme should be covered: *fee splitting*. The splitting or division of a fee refers to a single client bill covering the fee of two or more attorneys who are not in the same firm.

> Example: John Jones, Esq. is hired by a singer who is charging her record company with copyright infringement and breach of contract. Jones calls in Randy Smith, Esq., a specialist in copyright law from another firm. Both work on the case. The singer receives one bill for the work of both attorneys even though they work for different law firms.

The attorneys are splitting or dividing the fee between them.[8] This arrangement is proper under certain conditions. For example, the total fee must be reasonable, and the client must be told about the participation of all the attorneys and not object.

Suppose, however, that the attorney splits the fee with a nonattorney.

---

[8]The attorney who refers a case to another attorney receives what is called a *referral fee* or *forwarding fee* from the latter.

> Example: Frank Martin is a freelance investigator. He refers accident victims to a law firm. For every client he refers to the firm, he receives 25% of the fee collected by the firm.

> Example: Helen Gregson is a chiropractor. She refers medical malpractice cases to a law firm which compensates her for each referral.

These are improper divisions of fees with nonattorneys—even if the amount of the division is reasonable and the clients brought in by Martin or Gregson consent to their receiving a part of the fee. An attorney cannot share with a nonattorney a portion of a fee paid by particular clients. The rationale behind this prohibition is that the nonattorney might exercise some control over the attorney and thereby jeopardize the attorney's independent judgment.

For the same reason, an attorney cannot form a partnership with a nonattorney if any of the activities of the partnership consist of the practice of law. If the office practices law as a corporation, a nonattorney cannot own any interest in the company or be a director or officer.[9]

Paralegal Perspective:

■ An attorney or law firm may include paralegals and other nonattorney employees in a compensation or retirement plan, even though the plan is based in whole or in part on a profit-sharing arrangement. Model Rule 5.4(a)(3).

> Example: Frank is a paralegal at a law firm. The firm has a retirement plan under which the firm contributes a portion of its profits into the plan. Frank is a member of this retirement plan.

The firm is not acting unethically. In most states, paralegals can receive compensation and retirement benefits that are based on the fees received by the firm so long as they are not receiving all or part of *particular* legal fees. "The linchpin of the prohibition [against splitting fees with a legal assistant] seems to be the advance agreement of the lawyer to 'split' a fee based on a preexisting contingent arrangement. There is no general prohibition against a lawyer who enjoys a particularly profitable period recognizing the contribution of the legal assistant to that profitability with a discretionary bonus. Likewise, a lawyer engaged in a particularly profitable specialty of legal practice is not prohibited from compensating the legal assistant who aids materially in that practice more handsomely than the compensation generally awarded to legal assistants in that geographic area who work in law practices that are less lucrative. Indeed, any effort to fix a compensation level for legal assistants and prohibit greater compensation would appear to violate the federal antitrust laws." [10]

■ A related restriction in many states is that an attorney cannot give a paralegal any compensation for referring business to the attorney. "It appears clear that a legal assistant may not be compensated on a contingent basis for a particular case or paid for 'signing up' clients for a legal practice." [11]

---

[9]Wolfram, C., *Modern Legal Ethics,* § 9.2.4 (1986). In the District of Columbia, however, where nonattorneys are allowed to be owner-partners in law firms, nonattorneys can obviously share legal fees with attorneys. See footnote 2.

[10]ABA *Model Guidelines,* Comment to Guideline 9, see footnote 5.

[11]Ibid.

- Attorneys must not allow their paralegals to accept cases, to reject cases, or to "set fees." The responsibility "for establishing the amount of a fee to be charged for a legal service" may not be delegated to a paralegal.[12]

- "A lawyer may include a charge for the work performed by a legal assistant in setting a charge for legal services."[13] As we saw in Chapter 1, most attorneys bill clients for paralegal time. Paralegals record their time on time sheets that become the basis of bills sent to clients. The amount that an attorney bills for paralegal time must be reasonable. Reasonableness is determined by a number of factors, such as the experience of the paralegal, the nature of the tasks the paralegal undertakes, and the market rate for paralegals in the area.

- *Double billing* must be avoided. The paralegal's time should not have already been figured into the attorney's hourly rate. Some states ask the attorney to submit an affidavit to support the amount claimed for the paralegal's time. The affidavit must give a detailed statement of the time spent and services rendered by the paralegal, a summary of the paralegal's qualifications, etc. In New Mexico, the attorney must disclose to the client the amount to be charged for the services of the paralegals in the office.

- As a paralegal, your time records should be contemporaneous, that is, made at approximately the same time as the events you are recording. Try to avoid recording time long after you perform tasks that require time records.

- Time sheets must also be accurate; padding is clearly unethical. Padding occurs when someone records time that was not in fact spent. When a client is billed on the basis of time sheets that have been padded, fraud has been committed. Padding is a serious problem in the practice of law:

  > [It] occurs most typically when attorneys are under the gun to bill a large number of hours. Everyone knows of lawyers who begin work at 8:00, leave the office at 6:00 and yet bill 10 hours a day—a feat that utterly amazes me. Whether it be eating lunch, talking to a spouse, working with support staff, reading advance sheets or just taking a break, some portion of every day is spent on non-billable matters. [A young Midwestern associate at a medium-sized firm says] padding or fabrication of entries is encouraged, or at the very least tolerated, at his firm, and many others, to judge from his friends' experiences. The pressure to pad is intense.[14]

  Unfortunately, paralegals can find themselves under a similar pressure, which, of course, should be resisted.

  > One of the most common temptations that can corrupt a paralegal's ethics is to inflate billable hours, since there is often immense pressure in law firms to bill high hours for job security and upward mobility. Such "creative billing" is not humorous; it's both morally wrong and illegal. It's also fraudulent and a plain and simple case of theft.[15]

---

[12]ABA *Model Guidelines*, Guideline 3(b), see footnote 5.

[13]ABA *Model Guidelines*, Guideline 8, see footnote 5.

[14]Doe, *Billing: Is "Padding" Widespread?*, 76 American Bar Ass'n Journal 42 (December 1990).

[15]Smith, *AAfPE National Conference Highlights*, 8 Legal Assistant Today 103 (January/February 1991).

4. Crime or Fraud by an Attorney

An attorney must not engage in criminal or fraudulent conduct. Model Rule 8.4

Sadly, it is not uncommon for an attorney to be charged with criminal conduct, such as theft of client funds, *insider trading* and securities fraud, falsifying official documents, or tax fraud. Since such conduct obviously affects the attorney's fitness to practice law, sanctions for unethical conduct can be imposed in addition to prosecution in a criminal court. Once an attorney is convicted of a serious crime in court, a separate disciplinary proceeding is often instituted to suspend or disbar the attorney for unethical conduct growing out of the same incident.

Paralegal Perspective:

- Value your integrity above all else. A paralegal in Oklahoma offers the following advice: "Insist on the highest standards for yourself and for your employer. One small ethical breach can lead to a series of compromises with enormous" disciplinary and "legal malpractice consequences."[16]

- If your supervisor is charged with criminal conduct, the chances are good that you will be questioned by prosecutors, and you might become a suspect yourself.

- In the highly charged, competitive environment of a law office, there are attorneys who are willing to violate the law in the interest of winning. Be sensitive to the overt and subtle pressures on you to participate in such violations. Talk with other paralegals who have encountered this problem. Don't sit in silence. If there is no one in the office with whom you can frankly discuss the elimination of these pressures, you must consider quitting. (See Section F of this chapter.)

- Paralegals who are also notaries are sometimes asked by their supervisors to notarize documents that should *not* be notarized. In fact, paralegals "are most often named as defendants for false notarization of a signature."[17] Such acts may not be covered in malpractice liability insurance policies since they are intentional acts. Be extremely cautious of what you are asked to sign.

- At some law firms, employees have succumbed to the temptation of using a "hot tip" that crosses their path in a corporate takeover case.[18] Assume that Company X is planning to merge with Company Y. The news is not yet public. When it does become public, the value of the stock in Company X is expected to rise dramatically. You work at a law firm that represents Company X and you find out about the planned merger while at work. If you buy stock in Company X before the announcement of the merger, you would benefit from the increased value of the stock that would result after the announcement. This might be an illegal use of inside information. In a dramatic recent case, a paralegal who worked at a securities law firm in Boston was charged with insider trading by the Securities and Exchange Com-

---

[16]Tulsa Ass'n of Legal Assistants, *Hints for Helping Your Attorney Avoid Legal Malpractice,* TALA Times (August 1989).

[17]Race, *Malpractice Maladies,* Paradigm 12 (Baltimore Ass'n of Legal Assistants, July/August 1989).

[18]Milford, *Law Firms Expected to Take Steps to Avert Insider Trading Scandals,* The News Journal D3 (October 16, 1989).

mission (SEC). While working on a case involving a proposed merger, she learned certain information which she gave to outside investors who used it to make illegal profits in the stock market. The story made national news. One headline read, "SEC Says Boston Paralegal Gave Tip Worth $823,471." Soon after the incident, she was fired. All employees of law firms must be extremely careful. Innocently buying stock as a personal investment could turn into a nightmare. One attorney "recommends that any paralegal who would like to buy or sell securities should check first with a corporate attorney in the firm to see if the firm represents the issuer or a company negotiating with the issuer. If it does, an accusation of 'insider trading' might later be made." [19] The same caution applies when a member of the paralegal's immediate family buys or sells such securities.

- Another problem area is the use of so-called *pirated software*. Many businesses buy one copy of computer software and then copy it so that other employees in the office can use it on other terminals. This is illegal, and can subject violators to fines and other criminal penalties.

- In all aspects of your career as a paralegal, adopt the motto, "If it doesn't feel right, it probably isn't."

5. Crime or Fraud by a Client

An attorney shall not counsel a client to engage in conduct the attorney knows is criminal or fraudulent. Model Rule 1.2(d)

The client hires the attorney and controls the purpose of the attorney-client relationship. Furthermore, the client is entitled to know the legal consequences of any action he or she is contemplating. This does not mean, however, that the attorney must do whatever the client wants.

Example: The president of a corporation hires Leo Richards, Esq. to advise the company on how to dump toxic waste into a local river.

Note that the president has not asked Richards *if* the dumping is legal. It would be perfectly ethical for Richards to answer such a question. In the example, the president asks *how* to dump. If Richards feels that the dumping can legally take place, he can so advise the president. Suppose, however, that it is clear to Richards that the dumping would violate the federal or state criminal code. Under such circumstances, it would be unethical for Richards to advise the president on how to proceed with the dumping. The same would be true if the president wanted help in filing an environmental statement that misrepresented the intentions of the company. Such an application would be fraudulent, and an attorney must not help someone commit what the attorney knows is fraudulent conduct.

When attorneys are later charged with unethical conduct in such cases, their defense is often that they did not know the conduct proposed by the client was criminal or fraudulent. If the law applicable to the client's case is unclear, an attorney can make a good faith effort to find a legal way for the client to achieve his or her objective. The point at which the attorney crosses the ethical line is when he or she *knows* the client is trying to accomplish something criminal or fraudulent.

---

[19]Shays, *Ethics for the Paralegal*, Postscript 15 (Manhattan Paralegal Ass'n, August/September 1989).

Paralegal Perspective:

■ An attorney will rarely tell paralegals or other staff members that he or she knows the office is helping a client do something criminal or fraudulent. But you might learn that this is so, particularly if there is a close, trusting relationship between you and your supervising attorney. You must let this attorney or some other authority in the office know you do not feel comfortable working on such a case.

6. Frivolous Legal Positions

An attorney must not bring a frivolous claim or assert a frivolous defense. Model Rule 3.1

A client has a right to an attorney who is a vigorous advocate. But there are limits on what this can entail. It is unethical, for example, for an attorney to assert *frivolous positions* as claims or defenses. There are two major tests for determining when a legal position is frivolous: the good-faith test and the intentional-injury test. First, a position is frivolous if the attorney is unable to make a good-faith argument that existing law supports the position, or the attorney is unable to make a good-faith argument that existing law should be changed or reversed to support the position. A position is not necessarily frivolous simply because the attorney happens to think that the client will ultimately lose. The key is whether there is a good-faith argument to support the position. If the attorney can think of absolutely no rational support for the position, it is frivolous. Since the law is often unclear, it is difficult to establish that an attorney is acting unethically under the test of good faith. Second, a position is frivolous if the client's primary purpose in having the position asserted is to harass or maliciously injure someone.

Paralegal Perspective:

■ In the heat of controversy, tempers can run high. Attorneys do not always exhibit the detachment expected of professionals. They may so thoroughly identify with the interests of their clients that they lose perspective. Paralegals working for such attorneys may get caught up in the same fever, particularly if there is a close attorney-paralegal working relationship on a high-stakes case that has lasted a considerable time. The momentum is to do whatever it takes to win. While this atmosphere can be exhilarating, it can also create an environment where less and less attention is paid to the niceties of ethics.

7. Safekeeping Property

An attorney shall hold client property separate from the attorney's own property. Model Rule 1.15

A law office often receives client funds or funds of others connected with the client's case—for example, attorneys receive money as trustees of a will or trust, as escrow agents in closing a business deal, or as settlement of a case. Such funds should be held in separate accounts, with complete records kept on each. The attorney should not *commingle* (i.e., mix) law firm funds with client funds. It is unethical to place everything in one account. This is so even if the firm maintains accurate records on what amounts in the single account belong to which clients and what amounts belong to the firm. In a commingled account, the danger is too great that client funds will be used for nonclient purposes.

Paralegal Perspective:

■ Use great care whenever your responsibility involves client funds, such as receiving funds from clients, opening bank accounts, depositing funds in the proper account at a bank, and making entries in law firm records on such funds. It should be fairly obvious to you whether an attorney is violating the rule on commingling funds. It may be less clear whether the attorney is improperly using client funds for unauthorized purposes. Attorneys have been known to "borrow" money from client accounts and then return the money before anyone discovers what was done. They may even arrange to pay the account interest while using the money. Elaborate bookkeeping and accounting gimmicks might be used to disguise what is going on. Such conduct is unethical even if the attorney pays interest and eventually returns all the funds. In addition, the attorney may eventually be charged with theft or criminal fraud. Of course, anyone who knowingly assists the attorney could be subject to the same consequences.

8. False Statements and Failure to Disclose

An attorney shall not knowingly:
   (1) make a false statement of material fact or law to a tribunal,
   (2) fail to disclose a material fact to a tribunal when disclosure is necessary to avoid assisting a client to commit a criminal or fraudulent act,
   (3) fail to tell a tribunal about laws or other authority directly against the position of the attorney's client if this law or authority is not disclosed by opposing counsel, or
   (4) offer evidence that the attorney knows is false. Model Rule 3.3(a)

One of the reasons the general public holds the legal profession in low esteem is their perception that attorneys seldom comply with the above rules. Our legal system is *adversarial,* which means that legal disputes are resolved by neutral judges after listening to fiercely partisan opponents. In effect, the parties do battle through their attorneys. This environment does not always encourage the participants to cooperate in court proceedings. In fact, quite the opposite is often true. In extreme cases, attorneys have been known to lie to the court, to offer knowingly false evidence, etc. Under Model Rule 3.3(a), such conduct is unethical.

Subsection (3) of Model Rule 3.3(a) is particularly startling.

Example: Karen Singer and Bill Carew are attorneys who are opposing each other in a bitter case involving a large sum of money. Singer is smarter than Carew. Singer knows about a very damaging but obscure case that goes against her client. But because of sloppy research, Carew does not know about it. Singer never mentions the case and it never comes up during the litigation.

Singer must pay a price for her silence. She is subject to sanctions for a violation of her ethical obligation of disclosure under Model Rule 3.3(a)(3).

Another controversial part of Model Rule 3.3(a) is subsection (2) requiring disclosures that involve criminal or fraudulent acts. Since this raises issues of confidentiality, we will discuss such disclosures later when we cover confidentiality.

Paralegal Perspective:

■ Be aware that an attorney who justifies the use of deception in one case will probably repeat such deceptions in the future on other cases. To excuse the deception, the attorney will often refer to the necessity of protecting the client or to the alleged evilness of the other side. Deceptions are unethical despite such justifications.

■ Chances are also good that employees of such an attorney will be pressured into participating in deception—for example, give a false date to a court clerk, help a client lie (commit perjury) on the witness stand, help an attorney alter a document to be introduced into evidence, or improperly notarize a document.

■ Do not compromise your integrity no matter how much you believe in the cause of the client, no matter how much you detest the tactics of the opposing side, no matter how much you like the attorney for whom you work, and no matter how important this job is to you.

9. Withdrawal

An attorney must withdraw from a case: if continuing would result in a violation of ethical rules or other laws; if the client discharges the attorney, or if the attorney's physical or mental condition materially impairs his or her ability to represent the client. Model Rule 1.16(a)

Attorneys are not required to take every case. Furthermore, once they begin a case, they are not obligated to stay with the client until the case is over. If, however, the case has already begun in court after the attorney has filed a notice of appearance, *withdrawal* is usually improper without the permission of the court.

There are circumstances in which an attorney *must* withdraw from a case that has begun:

■ Representation of the client would violate ethical rules—for example, the attorney discovers that he or she has a conflict of interest with the client which cannot be cured (i.e., corrected or overcome) by the consent of the client.

■ Representation of the client would violate the law—for example, the client insists that the attorney provide advice on how to defraud the Internal Revenue Service.

■ The client fires the attorney. (An attorney is an agent of the client. Clients are always free to dismiss their agents.)

■ The attorney's physical or mental condition has deteriorated (through problems with alcohol, depression due to marital problems, etc.) to the point where the attorney's ability to represent the client has been materially impaired.

An attorney has the option of withdrawing if the client insists on an objective that the attorney considers repugnant (such as pursuing litigation solely to harass someone), or imprudent (such as refiling a motion the attorney feels is an obvious waste of time and likely to incur the anger of the court). Model Rule 1.16(b)(3).

Paralegal Perspective:

■ When you have a close working relationship with an attorney, you become aware of his or her professional strengths and personal weaknesses, particularly in a small law office. Bar associations around the country are becoming increasingly concerned about the *impaired attorney,* someone who's not functioning properly due to alcohol, drugs, or related problems. A paralegal with such an attorney for a supervisor is obviously in a predicament. Seemingly small problems have the potential of turning into a crisis. If it is not practical to discuss the situation directly with the attorney involved, you need to seek the advice of others in the firm.

10. Confidentiality of Information

An attorney must not reveal information relating to the representation of a client unless (a) the client consents to the disclosure or (b) the attorney reasonably believes the disclosure is necessary to prevent a client from committing a criminal act that is likely to result in imminent death or substantial bodily harm. Model Rule 1.6

Information is confidential if others do not have a right to receive it. When access to information is restricted in this way, the information is considered *privileged.* While our primary focus in this section is on the ethical dimensions of confidentiality, we also need to examine confidentiality in the related contexts of the attorney-client privilege and the attorney work-product rule.

Ethics and Confidentiality

The ethical obligation to maintain *confidentiality* applies to *all* information that relates to the representation of a client, whatever its source. Note that the obligation is broader than so-called secrets or matters explicitly communicated in confidence. Confidentiality has been breached in each of the following examples:

> At a party, an attorney tells an acquaintance from another town that the law firm is representing Jacob Anderson, whose employer is trying to force him to retire.

> At a bar association conference, an attorney tells an old law school classmate that a client named Brenda Steck is considering a suit against her brother over the ownership of property left by their deceased mother.

> A legal secretary carelessly leaves a client's file open on his desk where a stranger (e.g., another client) can and does read parts of it.

The rule on confidentiality is designed to encourage clients to discuss their case fully and frankly with their attorney, including embarrassing and legally damaging information. Arguably, a client would be reluctant to be open with an attorney if he or she had to worry about whether the attorney might reveal the information to others. The rule on confidentiality makes it unethical for attorneys to do so.

Of course, a client can always consent to an attorney's disclosure about the client—*if* the client is properly consulted about the proposed disclosure in advance. Furthermore, sometimes the client implicitly authorizes disclosures because of the nature of his or her case. In a dispute over alimony, for example, the attorney would obviously have to disclose certain financial information about the client to a court or to opposing counsel during the settlement negotiations.

Disclosure can also be ethically permissible in cases involving future criminal conduct.

Example: An attorney represents a husband in a bitter divorce action against his wife. During a meeting at the law firm, the husband shows the attorney a gun which he says he is going to use to kill his wife later the same day.

Can the attorney tell the police what the husband said? Yes. It is not unethical for an attorney to reveal information about a crime if the attorney reasonably believes that disclosure is necessary to prevent the client from committing a criminal act that could lead to someone's imminent death or substantial bodily harm.

Finally, some disclosures can be proper in suits between attorney and client. Suppose, for example, that the attorney later sues the client for nonpayment of a fee, or the client sues the attorney for malpractice. In such proceedings, an attorney can reveal information about the client if the attorney reasonably believes disclosure is necessary to present a claim against the client or to defend against the client's claim.

Attorney-Client Privilege

The *attorney-client privilege* serves a similar function as the ethical rule on confidentiality. The two doctrines overlap. The attorney-client privilege is an *evidentiary* rule that applies to judicial and other proceedings in which an attorney may be called as a witness or otherwise required to produce evidence concerning a client. Under the attorney-client privilege, the attorney can refuse to disclose communications with his or her client whose purpose was to facilitate the provision of legal services for the client. The privilege also applies to employees of an attorney with respect to the same kind of communication— those whose purpose was to facilitate legal services.

Who May Not Testify Without Consent

Colorado Revised Statutes (1984 Cum. Supp.)
13-90-107 (1)(b)

An attorney shall not be examined without the consent of his client as to any communication made by the client to him or his advice given thereon in the course of professional employment; nor shall an attorney's secretary, paralegal, legal assistant, stenographer, or clerk be examined without the consent of his employer concerning any fact, the knowledge of which he has acquired in such capacity.

The *ethical* rule on confidentiality tells us when sanctions can be imposed on attorneys for disclosing confidential client information to anyone outside the law office. The *attorney-client privilege* tells us when attorneys (and their employees) can refuse to answers questions pertaining to confidential client information.

Attorney Work-Product Rule

Suppose that, while working on a client's case, an attorney prepares a memorandum or other in-house document that does *not* contain any confidential communications. The memorandum or document, therefore, is *not* protected by the attorney-client privilege. Can the other side force the attorney to provide a copy of the memorandum or document? Are they *discoverable,* meaning that an opposing party can obtain information about it during discovery? This question leads us to the work-product rule.

Under this rule, the *work product* of an attorney is considered confidential. Work product consists of any notes, working papers, memoranda, or similar documents and tangible things prepared by the attorney in anticipation of litigation. An example is a memorandum the attorney writes to the file indicating his or her strategy in litigating a case. Attorneys do not have to disclose their work product to the other side. It is not discoverable.[20] To the extent that such documents are not discoverable, they are privileged. (The work-product rule is sometimes referred to as the work-product privilege.)

Inadvertent Disclosure of Confidential Material

The great fear of law office personnel is that the wrong person will obtain material that should be protected by ethics, by the attorney-client privilege, or by the work-product rule. This can have devastating consequences. For example, if a stranger overhears a confidential communication by a client to the attorney or to the attorney's paralegal, a court might rule that the attorney-client privilege has been waived. At a recent paralegal conference, a speaker told a stunned audience that a paralegal in her firm accidentally faxed a strategy memo on a current case to the opposing attorney! The paralegal punched in the wrong phone number on the fax machine!

Paralegal Perspective:

■ Attorneys must instruct their paralegals and other nonattorney assistants on the obligation not to disclose information relating to the representation of a client. "It is the responsibility of a lawyer to take reasonable measures to ensure that all client confidences are preserved by a legal assistant."[21]

■ As we shall see later, the two major national paralegal associations also stress the ethical obligation of confidentiality in their own ethical codes:

  ▪ "A legal assistant must protect the confidences of a client, and it shall be unethical for a legal assistant to violate any statute . . . controlling privileged communications." Canon 7. National Association of Legal Assistants, Code of Ethics and Professional Responsibility (page 280).

  ▪ "A paralegal shall preserve client confidences and privileged communications. Confidential information and privileged communications are a vital part of the attorney, paralegal, and client relationship. The importance of preserving confidential and privileged information is understood to be an uncompromising obligation of every paralegal." IV. National Federation of Paralegal Associations, Affirmation of Professional Responsibility (page 280).

■ There are *many* temptations on paralegals to violate confidentiality. For example, a paralegal inadvertently reveals confidential information:

  ▪ while networking with other paralegals at a paralegal-association meeting;

  ▪ during animated conversation with another paralegal at a restaurant or on an elevator;

---

[20]An exception exists if the "party seeking discovery has substantial need of the materials in the preparation of his case" and is unable to obtain them without undue hardship by other means. This test is rarely met. Federal Rule of Civil Procedure 26(b)(3).

[21]ABA *Model Guidelines*, Guideline 6, see footnote 5.

- after returning home from work during casual discussions with a relative, spouse, or roommate about interesting cases at the office.

Recall the scope of the rule: *all* information relating to the representation of a client must not be revealed. Some paralegals make the mistake of thinking that the rule applies only to damaging or embarrassing information or that the rule simply means you should not reveal things to the other side in the dispute. Not so. The rule is much broader. *All* information relating to the representation of a client must not be revealed to *anyone* who is not working on the case in the office.

- In Missouri, the obligation of silence is even broader. The paralegal must not disclose information—"confidential or otherwise"—relating to the representation of the client.[22] In Texas, confidential information includes both privileged information and unprivileged client information. An attorney must "instruct the legal assistant that all information concerning representation of a client (indeed even the fact of representation, if not a matter of public record) must be kept strictly confidential."[23] In Philadelphia, paralegals are warned that it is "not always easy to recognize what information about your firm's clients or office is confidential. Moreover, a client of your office might be offended to learn that a . . . firm employee has discussed the client's business in public, even if the information mentioned is public knowledge. The easiest rule is to consider *all* work of the office to be confidential: do not discuss the business of your office or your firm's clients with any outsider, no matter how close a friend, at any time, unless you are specifically authorized by a lawyer to do so."[24] Under guidelines such as these, there is very little that paralegals can tell someone about their work!

- During the war, sailors were told that "loose lips sink ships." The same applies to law firms. One law firm makes the following statement to all its paralegals, "Throughout your employment, you will have access to information that must at all times be held in strictest confidence. Even the seemingly insignificant fact that the firm is involved in a particular matter falls within the orbit of confidential information. Unless you have attorney permission, do not disclose documents or contents of documents to anyone, including firm employees who do not need this information to do their work."[25]

- If you attend a meeting on a case outside the law office, ask you supervisor whether you should take notes or prepare a follow-up memorandum on the meeting. Let the supervisor decide whether your notes or the memo might be discoverable.[26]

- Be *very* careful when you talk with clients in the presence of third persons. Overheard conservations might constitute a waiver of the attorney-client privilege.

- Use a stamp marked *privileged* on protected documents.

---

[22]*Guidelines for Practicing with Paralegals,* Missouri Bar Ass'n (1987).

[23]State Bar of Texas, *General Guidelines for the Utilization of the Services of Legal Assistants by Attorneys* (1981). Rule 1.01, Texas Disciplinary Rules of Professional Conduct (1990).

[24]*Professional Responsibility for Nonlawyers,* Professional Responsibility Committee of the Philadelphia Bar Ass'n (1989) (emphasis added).

[25]*Orientation Handbook for Paralegals* 2 (Lane, Powell, Moses & Miller, 1984).

[26]Daniels, *Privileged Information for Paralegals,* 17 At Issue 15 (San Francisco Ass'n of Legal Assistants, November 1990).

■ During a job interview, be very careful about submitting writing samples that contain confidential information, such as privileged communications or the identity of clients at law offices where you may have worked or volunteered in the past.[27] Your lack of professionalism in carelessly referring to confidential information during an interview will probably destroy your chances of getting the job.

11. Conflict of Interest

An attorney should avoid a conflict of interest with his or her client.

"Like obscenity, *conflicts of interest* are difficult to define, but easy to recognize." [28] A conflict of interest is divided loyalty that actually or potentially places one of the participants to whom undivided loyalty is owed at a disadvantage. Such conflicts can exist in many settings.

> Example: Bill Davenport is a salesman who does part-time work selling the same type of product manufactured by two competing companies.

Davenport has a conflict of interest. How can he serve two masters with the same loyalty? Normally, a company expects the undivided loyalty of people who work for it. How can Davenport apportion his customers between the two companies? There is an obvious danger that he will favor one over the other. The fact that he may try to be fair in his treatment of both companies does not eliminate the conflict of interest. A *potential* certainly exists that one of the companies will be disadvantaged. It may be that the two companies are aware of the problem and are not worried. This does not mean that there is no conflict of interest; it simply means that the affected parties have consented to take the risks involved in the conflict.

The same kind of conflict can exist in other settings.

> Example: Frank Jones is the head of the personnel department of a large company. Ten people apply for a job, one of whom is Frank's cousin.

Frank has a conflict of interest. He has loyalty to his company (pressuring him to hire the best person for the job) and a loyalty to his cousin (pressuring him to help a relative). There is a potential that the company will be disadvantaged, since Frank's cousin may not be the best qualified for the job.

The conflict exists even if the cousin *is* the best qualified, and even if Frank does *not* hire his cousin for the job, and even if the company *knows* about the relationship but still wants Frank to make the hiring decision. For conflict of interest to exist, all you need is the potential for disadvantage due to *divided loyalties;* you do not have to show that disadvantage actually resulted.

In a law office, a number of conflict-of-interest issues can arise:

(a) Business transactions with a client

(b) Loans to a client

(c) Gifts from a client

---

[27]As we will see later, you may have to disclose the names of cases and clients in order to help the office decide whether you are "tainted" with a conflict of interest and hence could cause the disqualification of the office if you are hired. But this disclosure should occur only when the employment discussions are getting serious *and* with the knowledge of your former employers.

[28]Holtzman, *Conflicts of Interest,* 14 Legal Economics 55 (October 1988).

(d) Multiple representation

(e) Former client/present adversary

(f) Law firm disqualification

(g) Switching jobs and "the Chinese wall"

As we examine each of these topics, our central concern is whether the independence of the attorneys' professional judgment is compromised in any way because of conflicting interests.

(a) Business Transactions with a Client

Attorneys sell professional legal advice and representation. When they go beyond such services and enter a business transaction with the client, a conflict of interest can arise.

> Example: Janet Bruno, Esq. is Len Oliver's attorney in a real estate case. Oliver owns an auto repair business for which Bruno has done legal work. Oliver sells Bruno a 30% interest in the repair business. Bruno continues as Oliver's attorney.

Serious conflict-of-interest problems may exist here. Assume that the business runs into difficulties and Oliver considers bankruptcy. He goes to Bruno for legal advice on bankruptcy law. Bruno has dual concerns: to give Oliver competent legal advice and to protect *her own* 30% interest in the business. Bankruptcy may be good for Oliver but disastrous for Bruno's investment. How can an attorney give a client independent professional advice when the advice may go against the attorney's own interest? Bruno's concern for her investment creates the potential that Oliver will be placed at a disadvantage. Divided loyalties exist.

This is not to say, however, that it is always unethical for an attorney to enter a business transaction with a client. If certain strict conditions are met, it can be proper.

> *An attorney shall not enter a business transaction with a client, unless*
> *(i) the terms of the business transaction are fair and reasonable to the client and are fully disclosed to the client in understandable language in writing, and*
> *(ii) the client is given reasonable opportunity to seek advice on the transaction from another attorney who is not involved with the transaction or the parties, and*
> *(iii) the client consents to the business transaction in writing.*
> Model Rule 1.8(a)

In our example, Oliver must be given the chance to consult with an attorney other than Bruno on letting Bruno buy a 30% interest in the business. Bruno would have to give Oliver a clear, written explanation of their business relationship. And the relationship must be fair and reasonable to Oliver.

(b) Loans to a Client

An attorney, like all service providers, wants to be paid. Often a client does not have the resources to pay until *after* the case is over.

> Example: Harry Maxell, Esq. is Bob Stock's attorney in a negligence action in which Stock is seeking damages for serious injuries caused by the defendant. Since the accident, Stock has been out of work and on welfare. While the case is pending, Maxell agrees to lend Stock living expenses and court-filing fees.

The loan covering *living expenses* creates a conflict-of-interest problem. Suppose that the defendant in the negligence case makes an offer to settle the case with Stock. Should he accept the offer? There is a danger that Maxell's advice on this will be colored by the fact that he has a financial interest in Stone—he wants to have his loan repaid. The amount of the offer to settle may not be enough to cover the loan. Should he advise Stock to accept the offer? It may be in Stock's interest to accept the offer but not in Maxell's own interest. Such divided loyalty is an unethical conflict of interest. Model Rule 1.8(e).

The loan covering *litigation expenses,* such as filing fees and other court costs, is treated differently. The amount of such a loan is usually relatively small, and hence unlikely to interfere with the independence of the attorney's judgment. In our example, Maxell's loan to cover the cost of the filing fees is proper.

(c) Gifts from a Client

Clients sometimes make gifts to their attorneys or to the spouse or relative of their attorneys. Such gifts rarely create ethical problems except when a document must be prepared to complete the gift.

> Example: William Stanton, Esq. has been the family attorney of the Tarkinton family for years. At Christmas, Mrs. Tarkinton gives Stanton a television set and tells him to change her will so that Stanton's ten-year-old daughter would receive funds for a free college education.

If a document is needed to carry out the gift, it is unethical for the attorney to prepare that document. Its preparation would create a conflict of interest. In our example, the gift of money for college involves a document—Mrs. Tarkinton's will. Note the conflict. It would be in Mrs. Tarkinton's interest to have the will written so that she, and the executor of her will, retained considerable flexibility when questions arise on how much to pay for the college education. (For example, is there to be a maximum amount? Is room and board included?) And they need flexibility on the effect of contingencies, such as a delay or an interruption in going to college. (What happens if the daughter does not go to college until after she marries and raises her own children?) Other questions could arise as well. Stanton, of course, would want the will drafted so that his daughter received the most money possible; he does not want any contingencies in the will that might threaten receipt of the funds. It is in his interest to prepare the will so that Mrs. Tarkinton and her executor have very little flexibility.

Because of this conflict, an attorney cannot prepare a document such as a will, trust, or contract that results in any substantial gift from a client to the attorney or to the attorney's children, spouse, parents, or siblings. If a client wants to make such a gift, *another* attorney must prepare the document.[29] There is, however, one exception. If the client is *related* to the person receiving the gift, the attorney can prepare the document. Model Rule 1.8(c).

There does not appear to be any ethical problem in taking the gift of the television set from Mrs. Tarkinton. No documents are involved.

(d) Multiple Representation

A client is entitled to the independent professional judgment and vigorous representation of an attorney. Rarely can this occur in a case of *multiple repre-*

---

[29]This other attorney should not be a member of the same law firm. See the related discussion (later) on imputed disqualification.

sentation (also referred to as *common representation*), where the same attorney represents both sides in a legal dispute.

> Example: Tom and Henry have an automobile accident. Tom wants to sue Henry for negligence. Both Tom and Henry ask Mary Franklin, Esq. to represent them in the dispute.

Franklin has a conflict of interest. How can she give her undivided loyalty to both sides? Tom needs to prove that Henry was negligent; Henry needs to prove that he was not negligent, and perhaps that Tom was negligent himself. How can Franklin vigorously argue that Henry was negligent and at the same time vigorously argue that Henry was not negligent? How can she act independently for two different people who are at odds with each other? Since Tom and Henry have *adverse interests,* she cannot give each her independent professional judgment. (Adverse interests are simply opposing purposes or claims.) The difficulty is not solved by Franklin's commitment to be fair and objective in giving her advice to the parties. Her role as attorney is to be a *partisan advocate* for the client. It is impossible for Franklin to play this role for two clients engaged in a dispute where they have adverse interests. An obvious conflict of interest would exist. In every state, it would be unethical for Franklin to represent Tom and Henry in this case.

Furthermore, this is a case in which consent is *not* a defense. Even if Tom and Henry agree to allow Franklin to represent both of them, it would be unethical for her to do so. The presence of adverse interests between the parties makes it unethical for an attorney to represent both sides.

Suppose, however, that the two sides do not have adverse interests. There are cases that must go before a court even though the parties are in agreement about everything.

> Example: Jim and Mary Smith are separated, and both want a divorce. They have been married only a few months. There are no children and no marital assets to divide. George Davidson, Esq. is an attorney that Jim and Mary know and trust. They decide to ask Davidson to represent both of them in the divorce.

Can Davidson ethically represent both sides here? There are some states that *will* allow him to do so, on the theory that there is not much of a conflict between the parties. Jim and Mary want the divorce, there is no custody battle, and there is no property to fight over. All they need is a court to decree that their marriage is legally over. Hence the potential for harm caused by multiple representation in such a case is almost nonexistent. Other states, however, disagree. They frown on multiple representation in so-called "friendly divorces" of this kind.

There is no absolute ban on all multiple representation in the Model Rules, although such representation is certainly discouraged.

> *An attorney shall not represent a client if the representation of that client will be directly adverse to another client, unless*
>   *(i) the attorney reasonably believes the representation will not adversely affect the relationship with the other client, and*
>   *(ii) both clients consent after consultation about the risks of the multiple representation.* Model Rule 1.7

In the Smith example, both conditions can probably be met. Such a divorce is little more than a paper procedure since there is no real dispute between the parties. Hence Davidson would be reasonable in believing that his representation of Jim would not adversely affect Mary, and vice versa. Davidson can represent both sides so long as Jim and Mary consent to the multiple representation after Davidson explains whatever risks might be involved.

Nevertheless, attorneys are urged *not* to engage in multiple representation even if it is ethically proper to do so under the standards listed above. The case may have been "friendly" at the outset, but years later when everything turns sour, one of the parties inevitably attacks the attorney for having had a conflict of interest. Cautious attorneys always avoid multiple representation.

(e) Former Client/Present Adversary

As indicated earlier, clients are encouraged to be very open with their attorney since the latter needs to know favorable and unfavorable information about the client in order to evaluate the legal implications of the case. The more trust that exists between them, the more frank the client will usually be. Assume that such a relationship exists and that the case is eventually resolved. Months later, another legal dispute arises between the same parties, but this time the attorney represents the other side!

> Example: Helen Kline, Esq. represented Paul Andrews in his breach-of-contract suit against Richard Morelli, a truck distributor. Andrews claimed that Morelli failed to deliver five trucks that Andrews ordered. A court ruled in favor of Morelli. Now, a year later, Andrews wants to sue Morelli for slander. After accidentally meeting at a conference, they started discussing the truck suit. Morelli allegedly called Andrews a liar and a thief. In the slander suit, Andrews hires Michael Manna, Esq. to represent him. Morelli hires Helen Kline, Esq.

A former client is now an adversary. Kline once represented Andrews; she is now representing a client (Morelli) who is an adversary of Andrews. Without the consent of the former client (Andrews), it is unethical for Kline to *switch sides* and represent Morelli against him. Model Rule 1.9(a). Consent is needed *when the second case is the same as the first one or when the two are substantially related.* The slander suit is substantially related to the breach-of-contract suit, since they both grew out of the original truck incident.

If the cases are the same or are substantially related, the likelihood is strong that the attorney will use information learned in the first case to the detriment of the former client in the second case. Kline undoubtedly found out a good deal about Andrews when she represented him in the breach-of-contract case. She would now be in a position to use that information *against* him while representing Morelli in the slander case.

Kline had a duty of loyalty when she represented Andrews. This duty does not end once the case is over and the attorney fees are paid. The duty continues if the same case arises again or if a substantially related case arises later—even if the attorney no longer represents the client. A conflict of interest exists when Kline subsequently acquires a new client who goes against Andrews in the same case or in a substantially related case. This, of course, is what happened in our example. Her duty of undivided loyalty to the second client would clash with her *continuing* duty of undivided loyalty to the former client in the original case.

Suppose, however, that an attorney *can* take the second case against a former client because the second case is totally unrelated to the first. There is still an ethical obligation to refrain from using any information relating to the representation in the first case to the disadvantage of the former client in the second case. There is no ethical ban on taking the case, but if there is any information in the office relating to the first case, that information cannot be used against the former client in the second case.[30]

(f) Law Firm Disqualification

If an attorney is disqualified from representing a client because of a conflict of interest, every attorney in the *same law firm* is also disqualified unless the client being protected by this rule consents to the representation.

> Example: Two years ago, John Farrell, Esq. of the law firm of Smith & Smith represented the stepfather in a custody dispute with the child's grandmother. The stepfather won the case, but the grandmother was awarded limited visitation rights. The grandmother now wants to sue the stepfather for failure to abide by the visitation order. John Farrell no longer represents the stepfather. The grandmother asks John Farrell to represent her. He declines because of a conflict of interest, but sends her to his law partner, Diane Williams, Esq., down the corridor at Smith & Smith.

The *stepfather* would have to consent to the representation of the grandmother by Williams. There would certainly be a conflict of interest if John Farrell tried to represent the grandmother against the stepfather. The custody dispute and the visitation dispute are substantially related. Once one attorney in a firm is disqualified because of a conflict of interest, every other attorney in that firm is also disqualified. (This is known as *imputed disqualification* or *vicarious disqualification*.) The entire firm is treated as one attorney. The disqualification of any one "tainted" attorney in the firm contaminates the entire firm. In our example, Farrell's partner (Williams) is disqualified because Farrell would be disqualified. Model Rule 1.10.

(g) Switching Jobs and "the Chinese Wall"

Finally we need to consider the conflict-of-interest problems that can arise from changing jobs. We just saw that there can be an imputed disqualification of an entire law firm because one of the attorneys in the firm has a conflict of interest with a client. If that attorney now goes to work for a *new* firm, can there be an imputed disqualification of the new firm because of the same conflict of interest?

> Example: Kevin Carlson, Esq. works at Darby & Darby. He represents Ajax, Inc. in its contract suit against World Systems, Inc. The latter is represented by Polk, Young & West. Carlson quits his job at Darby & Darby and takes a job at Polk, Young & West.

While Carlson was at Darby and Darby, he obviously acquired confidential information about Ajax. Clearly, he cannot now represent World Systems in the contract litigation against Ajax. Blatant side-switching of this kind is highly unethical. But what about other attorneys at Polk, Young & West? Is the *entire* firm contaminated and hence disqualified from continuing to represent World Systems because of the hiring of Carlson? If other attorneys at Polk, Young & West are allowed to continue representing World Systems against Ajax, there would be pressures on Carlson to tell these attorneys what he knows about Ajax. Must Polk, Young & West therefore withdraw from the case? The states do not all answer this question in the same way.

---

[30]While this duty might exist, it is not easy to enforce. Think of how difficult it might be to prove that the attorney in the second case used information obtained in the first case.

In many states, the answer is *yes,* because the tainted attorney[31]—Carlson—possesses confidential information about Ajax, and the case at the new firm involves the same or substantially the same matter as at the prior firm. The confidential information learned at the prior firm would be material to the matter being handled by the new firm. In these states, the only way to avoid disqualification is if Ajax waives its right to object. Ajax must be told that Carlson now works at Polk, Young & West, which represents World Systems, and must consent to allowing an attorney at Polk, Young & West (other than Carlson) to continue to represent World Systems in the case. It is unlikely, however, that Ajax will give this consent. Why would it want to take the chance that Carlson will reveal confidential communications to his new colleagues at Polk, Young & West?

To avoid the drastic penalty of imputed disqualification, law firms often promise to build a *Chinese wall* (sometimes called an *ethical wall* or *cone of silence*) around the attorney who created the conflict of interest—the *tainted* or *contaminated* attorney. The goal of the wall is to screen the tainted attorney from any contact with a case where earlier confidentiality could be compromised. In many states, however, this promise is *ineffective* to avoid the disqualification. Yet there are states that are more sympathetic to a firm that wants to avoid the disqualification, depending on how involved the tainted attorney was in the case while at the previous firm and on the quality of the wall at the new firm.

The screening of the Chinese Wall should take several forms. For example:

- The tainted attorney promises not to discuss what he or she knows with anyone in the new firm.

- Those working on the case in the new firm promise not to discuss it with the tainted attorney.

- The tainted attorney works in an area that is physically segregated from work on the case in the new firm.

- The files in the case are locked so that the tainted attorney will have no access to the files. In addition, colored labels or "restricted flags" are placed on each of these files to indicate that they are off limits to the tainted attorney.

- All employees in the new firm are formally told that if they learn anything about the case, they must not discuss it with the tainted attorney.[32]

A tainted employee around whom a Chinese Wall is built is called a *quarantined* employee.

As indicated, there are states where a Chinese Wall will *not* be successful in preventing the imputed disqualification of the new firm.[33] There is skepticism that the tainted attorney will be able to resist the pressure to disclose what he or she knows in spite of these screening mechanisms. "Whether the screen is breached will be virtually impossible to ascertain from outside the firm."[34]

Yet again, not all states take this position. There are states that will not order a disqualification if the court can be convinced that harm to the former

---

[31]Also called the *contaminated* attorney or *infected* attorney.

[32]Another dimension of the Chinese Wall is to forbid the tainted attorney from earning any profit or financial gain from the case in question.

[33]The Model Rules explicitly recognize a Chinese Wall to prevent imputed disqualification only where the attorney has moved from a government position to private employment. Model Rule 1.11.

[34]C. Wolfram, *Modern Legal Ethics* § 7.6.4 (1986).

FIGURE 4.4
Computer Software
Used for Conflicts
Checks

```
            LEGALMASTER Conflicts Found
Conflicts checked for case: SAMUE—(10 matches on 3 names)
Rubin (2 matches)
     CSP-          CLNT Rubin Phillip
     FFIC-5        JUDGE Rubin Laurie
Samuel* (6 matches)
     GREGS-1       OPATT Samuels Fritz
     SCOTT-1       EXPRT Samuels Phillip J.
     SMITH-PI      JUDGE Samuels Norman I.
     IBM-          OPATT Samuels Jacob
     CSP-          OPATT Samuels Jacob
     ISIS-2        EXPRT Samuelson Juan
Savag* (2 matches)
     IBM-          CLNT Savage Norm
     GRUPE-7       CLNT Savage Emily
             Press any key to exit.
```

Legalmaster's Conflicts Module. Computer Software for Professionals, Inc.

client can be avoided. This is most likely to happen if the Wall was in place at the new firm at the outset of the employment transfer, if the new firm built the Wall before the other side raised the conflict-of-interest issue, and, most important, if the tainted attorney's involvement in the case at the old firm was relatively minor. This, of course, was not true for Kevin Carlson, Esq. in our example, since he actually represented Ajax while at Darby & Darby.

Imputed disqualification is a drastic consequence of job switching. In the Carlson example, somebody at Polk, Young & West made a major blunder in hiring Carlson. Before hiring him, a *conflicts check* should have been performed in order to determine whether he might taint the new firm and, if so, whether a Chinese Wall could prevent disqualification. This is done by obtaining the names of the clients Carlson and his old law firm (Darby & Darby) worked for and by determining whether the new firm (Polk, Young & West) ever worked *against* any of them.[35] Unfortunately, law firms often perform such conflicts checks carelessly or not at all.

Some large firms assign paralegals to perform the check under the supervision of an attorney. This paralegal will enter data on parties into a "conflicts index system" and compare it with data already in the system to identify potential conflicts. Computer programs (such as the one shown in Figure 4.4.) have been developed to assist in the task.

Insurance companies that issue malpractice policies to attorneys are very concerned about conflicts of interests that can arise from a *lateral hire,* in which a law firm hires an attorney from another law firm. The same concerns exist when one law firm buys or merges with another law firm. In Figure 4.5, you will find a series of questions one insurance company asks of all law firms applying for malpractice insurance.

Paralegal Perspective:

■ "A lawyer should take reasonable measures to prevent conflicts of interest resulting from a legal assistant's other employment or interests insofar as

---

[35]For each client that is a corporation, the firm should also cross-check the names of the parent corporation, all subsidiary corporations, and the names of chief executive officers. If the client is a partnership, the same kind of check is needed for the names of all general partners.

FIGURE 4.5

Questions on Malpractice Insurance Application about Conflict-of-Interest Avoidance

ADMINISTRATIVE SYSTEMS AND PROCEDURES—CONFLICT OF INTEREST	YES	NO
22. Do you have a written internal control system for maintaining client lists and identifying actual or potential conflicts of interest?	☐	☐
23. How does the firm maintain its conflict of interest avoidance system? ☐ Oral/Memory ☐ SIngle Index Files ☐ Multiple Index Files ☐ Computer		
24. Have the firm members disclosed in writing, all actual conflicts of interest and conflicts they reasonably believe may exist as a result of their role as director, officer, partner, employee, or fiduciary of an entity or individual other than the applicant firm?	☐	☐
25. Do firm members disclose to their clients, in writing, all actual conflicts of interest and conflicts they reasonably believe may exist?	☐	☐
26. Upon disclosure of actual or potential conflicts, do firm members always obtain written consent to perform ongoing legal services?	☐	☐
27. Has the firm acquired, merged with, or terminated a formal business relationship with another firm within the last three years?	☐	☐
28. Does the firm's conflict of interest avoidance system include attorney-client relationships established by predecessor firms, merged firms, and acquired firms?	☐	☐
Source: The St. Paul Companies, Professional Liability Application for Lawyers.		

such other employment or interests would present a conflict of interest if it were that of the lawyer." [36] Many paralegals change jobs one or more times in the course of their careers. Such changes can create the same kind of conflicts problems that result when attorneys change jobs:

Example: Paul Benton is a paralegal who works for Sands, Leonard & Wiley. One of the cases Paul works on is Mary Richardson v. Jane Quigly. Sands, Leonard & Wiley represents Richardson. The law firm of Neeley & Neeley represents Quigly. Before the case is resolved, Paul quits in order to take a job as a paralegal with Neeley & Neeley.

Neeley & Neeley is now in a position to determine what Paul found out about Richardson while he worked for Sands, Leonard & Wiley. The latter firm will probably ask a court to force Neeley & Neeley to withdraw from the case because it hired a tainted paralegal—Paul. The courts in some states will do just that. In these courts, imputed disqualification can result from tainted paralegals as well as from tainted attorneys. Yet other states say that paralegals should not be treated the same as attorneys. Under this view, a court is more likely to accept a Chinese Wall built around a tainted paralegal (who becomes a quarantined paralegal) as an alternative to disqualifying the law firm this paralegal recently joined. This view is represented in the ethics opinion of the American Bar Association (Informal Opinion 88-1526) printed below. It must be emphasized, however, that not all states follow this opinion.

■ In a recent, dramatic case, a San Francisco law firm was disqualified from representing nine clients in asbestos litigation involving millions of dollars.

---

[36]ABA *Model Guidelines*, Guideline 7, see footnote 5.

The sole reason for the disqualification was that the firm hired a paralegal who had once worked for a law firm that represented the opponents in the asbestos litigation. Soon after the controversy arose, the disqualified firm laid off the tainted paralegal who brought this conflict to the firm. He was devastated when he found out that he was being let go. "I was flabbergasted, totally flabbergasted." He has not been able to find work since.[37] The case was widely reported throughout the legal community. A front-page story in the *Los Angeles Daily Journal* said that it "could force firms to conduct lengthy investigations of paralegals and other staffers before hiring them." [38]

■ One law firm makes the following statement to all its paralegals, "If you or a temporary legal assistant working under your supervision were formerly employed by opposing counsel, this could be the basis for a motion to disqualify [this law firm.] So also could personal relationships such as kinship with the opposing party or attorney or dating an attorney from another firm. Make your attorney aware of such connections." [39]

■ If you have worked (or volunteered) for an attorney in the past in *any* capacity (as a paralegal, as an investigator, as a secretary, etc.), you should make a list of all the clients and cases with which you were involved. When you apply for a new job, your list may be relevant to whether the law firm will be subject to disqualification if you are hired. You must be careful, however, with the list. Do not attach it to your resume and randomly send it around town! Until employment discussions have become serious, do not show it to the prospective employer. Furthermore, try to notify prior attorneys with whom you have worked that you are applying for a position at a law firm where its "conflicts check" on you must include knowing what cases you worked on with previous attorneys. Giving them this notice is not always practical, and may not be required. Yet it is a safe procedure to follow whenever possible.

■ Freelance paralegals who work for more than one attorney on a part-time basis are particularly vulnerable to conflict-of-interest charges. For example, in a large litigation involving many parties, two opposing attorneys might unknowingly use the same freelance paralegal to work on different aspects of the same case, or might use two different employees of this freelance paralegal. Another example is the freelance paralegal who worked on an earlier case for a client and now works on a different but similar case in which that client is the opponent. The California Association of Freelance Paralegals has attempted to address this problem in Article 11 of its proposed Code of Ethics: "A freelance paralegal shall avoid conflicts of interest relating to client matters. The freelance paralegal shall not accept any case adverse to the client of [an attorney who hires the paralegal] if the latter case bears a substantial connection to the earlier one or if there is a possibility that the two cases are substantially related, regardless of whether confidences were in fact imparted to the freelance paralegal by the attorney or the attorney's client in the earlier case." [40] There are practical problems with such rules. It is not always easy

[37]Motamedi, *Landmark Ethics Case Takes Toll on Paralegal's Career, Family,* 7 Legal Assistant Today 39 (May/June 1990). *In re Complex Asbestos Litigation,* 232 Cal.App.3d 572, 283 Cal.Rptr. 732 (Cal.Ct.App. 1991).

[38]M. Hall, *S.F. Decision on Paralegal Conflict May Plague Firms,* 102 Los Angeles Daily Journal 1, col. 2 (September 25, 1989).

[39]Orientation Handbook for Paralegals 3 (Lane, Powell, Moses & Miller, 1984).

[40]California Ass'n of Freelance Paralegals, "CAFP's Proposed Code of Ethics," Article 11, *Freelancer* 9 (July/August 1991).

to determine whether two cases are "adverse" or bear a "substantial connection" with each other. If there is doubt, it is in the economic self-interest of the freelance paralegal *not* to tell the attorney since he or she will most likely refuse to hire the paralegal rather than take the risk of later disqualification because of contamination injected into the case by this paralegal. Finally, conducting a conflicts check could be somewhat difficult for a busy, experienced freelance paralegal who has worked for scores of attorneys and hundreds of clients over the years.

Standing Committee on Ethics and Professional Responsibility of the American Bar Association
Informal Opinion 88-1526

A law firm that employs a nonlawyer who formerly was employed by another firm may continue representing clients whose interests conflict with the interests of clients of the former employer on whose matters the nonlawyer has worked, as long as the employing firm screens the nonlawyer from information about or participating in matters involving those clients and strictly adheres to the screening process described in this opinion and as long as no information relating to the representation of the clients of the former employer is revealed by the nonlawyer to any person in the employing firm. In addition, the nonlawyer's former employer must admonish the nonlawyer against revelation of information relating to the representation of clients of the former employer.

The Committee is asked whether, under the ABA Model Rules of Professional Conduct (1983, amended 1987), a law firm that hires a paralegal formerly employed by another lawyer must withdraw from representation of a client under the following circumstances. The paralegal has worked for more than a year with a sole practitioner on litigation matters. One of those matters is a lawsuit which the sole practitioner instituted against a client of the law firm that is about to hire the paralegal and wishes to continue to defend the client. The paralegal has gained substantial information relating to the representation of the sole practitioner's client, the plaintiff in the lawsuit. The employing firm will screen the paralegal from receiving information about or working on the lawsuit and will direct the paralegal not to reveal any information relating to the representation of the sole practitioner's client gained by the paralegal during the former employment. The Committee also is asked whether the paralegal's former employer must take any actions in order to comply with the Model Rules.

Responsibilities of Employing Firm

The Committee concludes that the law firm employing the paralegal should not be disqualified from continuing to defend its client in the lawsuit, as long as the law firm and the paralegal strictly adhere to the screening process described in this Opinion, and as long as no information relating to the representation of the sole practitioner's client is revealed by the paralegal to any person in the employing firm.

The Model Rules require that a lawyer make reasonable efforts to ensure that each of the lawyer's nonlawyer employees maintains conduct compatible with the professional obligations of the lawyer, including the nondisclosure of information relating to the representation of clients. This requires maintaining procedures designed to protect client information from disclosure by the lawyer's employees and agents. . . .

It is important that nonlawyer employees have as much mobility in employment opportunity as possible consistent with the protection of clients' interests. To so limit employment opportunities that some nonlawyers trained to work with law firms might be required to leave the careers for which they are trained would disserve clients as well as the legal profession. Accordingly, any restrictions on the nonlawyer's employment should be held to the minimum necessary to protect confidentiality of client information.

Model Rule 5.3 imposes general supervisory obligations on lawyers with respect to nonlawyer employees and agents. The obligations include the obligation to make reasonable efforts to ensure there are measures in effect to assure that the nonlawyer's conduct is compatible with the professional obligations of the lawyer. With respect to new employees who formerly worked for other lawyers, these measures should involve admonitions to be alert to all legal matters, including lawsuits, in which any client of the former employer has an interest. The nonlawyer should be cautioned: (1) not to disclose any information relating to the representation of a client of the former employer; and (2) that the employee should not work on any matter on which the employee worked for the prior employer or respecting which the employee has information relating to the representation of the client of the former employer. When the new firm becomes aware of such matters, the employing firm must also take reasonable steps to ensure that the employee takes no action and does no work in relation to matters on which the nonlawyer worked in the prior employment, absent client consent after consultation.

Circumstances sometimes require that a firm be disqualified or withdraw from representing a client when the firm employs a nonlawyer who formerly was employed by another firm. These circumstances are present either: (1) where information relating to the representation of an adverse party gained by the nonlawyer while employed in another firm has been revealed to lawyers or other personnel in the new firm . . .; or (2) where screening would be ineffective or the nonlawyer necessarily would be required to work on the other side of the same or a substantially related matter on which the nonlawyer worked or respecting which the nonlawyer has gained information relating to the representation of the opponent while in the former employment. If the employing firm employs the nonlawyer under those circumstances, the firm must withdraw from representing the client, unless the client of the former employer consents to the continued representation of the person with conflicting interests after being apprised of all the relevant factors.

Responsibilities of Former Employer

Under Model Rule 5.3, lawyers have a duty to make reasonable efforts to ensure that nonlawyers do not disclose information relating to the representation of the lawyers' clients while in the lawyer's employ and afterwards. On the facts presented to the Committee here, once the lawyer learns that the paralegal has joined the opposing law firm, the lawyer should consider advising the employing firm that the paralegal must be isolated from participating in the matter and from revealing any information relating to the representation of the lawyer's client. If not satisfied that the employing firm has taken adequate measures to prevent participation and disclosures, the lawyer should consider filing a motion in the lawsuit to disqualify the employing law firm from continuing to represent the opponent. . . .

Therefore, the lawyer who hires the paralegal, under the circumstances before the Committee, must screen the paralegal from participating in the lawsuit with the employing law firm. Both the employing firm and the sole practitioner should admonish the paralegal not to disclose information relating to the representation of the plaintiff in the lawsuit and also of any other client of the sole practitioner for whom the paralegal formerly worked while with the former employer.

The standards expressed in this Opinion apply to all matters where the interests of the clients are in conflict and not solely to matters in litigation. The Committee also notes that these standards apply equally to all nonlawyer personnel in a law firm who have access to material information relating to the representation of clients and extends also to agents who technically may be independent contractors, such as investigators.

12. Communication with the Other Side

In representing a client, an attorney shall not communicate with a party on the other side about the subject of the case if the attorney knows that the party is represented by another attorney. The latter attorney must consent to such a communication. Model Rule 4.2

If the other side is not represented, an attorney must not give him or her the impression that the attorney is uninvolved. The attorney should not give this person advice other than the advice to obtain his or her own attorney. Model Rule 4.3

The ethical concern here is that an attorney will take an unfair advantage of the other side.

Example: Dan and Theresa Kline have just separated and are thinking about a divorce. Each claims the marital home. Theresa hires Thomas Farlington, Esq. to represent her. Farlington calls Dan to ask him if he is interested in settling the case.

It is unethical for Farlington to contact Dan about the case if Farlington knows that Dan has his own attorney. Farlington must talk with Dan's attorney. Only the latter can give Farlington permission to communicate with Dan. If Dan does not have an attorney, Farlington can talk with Dan, but he must not allow Dan to be misled about Farlington's role. Farlington works for the other side; he is not disinterested. Dan must be made to understand this fact. The only advice Farlington can give Dan in such a situation is to seek his own attorney.

Paralegal Perspective:

■ The ethical restrictions on communicating with the other side apply to the employees of an attorney as well as to the attorney. "The lawyer's obligation is to ensure that the legal assistants do not communicate directly with parties known to be represented by an attorney, without that attorney's consent, on the subject of such representation."[41] You must avoid improper communication with the other side. If the other side is a business or some other large organization, do not talk with anyone there unless your supervisor tells you that it is ethical to do so. Never call the other side and pretend you are someone else in order to obtain information.

■ If your office allows you to interview someone who is not represented by an attorney, you cannot give this person any advice other than the advice to secure his or her own attorney.

13. Solicitation

In person, an attorney may not solicit employment from a prospective client with whom the attorney has no family or prior professional relationship when a significant motive for doing so is the attorney's monetary gain.[42] Model Rule 7.3

People in distress are sometimes so distraught that they are not in a position to evaluate their need for legal services. They should not be subjected to pressures from an attorney who shows up wanting to be hired, particularly if the attorney is not a relative or has never represented them in the past.[43] Such in-person solicitation is unethical.

Example: Rachael Winters, Esq. stands outside the police station and gives a business card to any individual being arrested. The card says that Winters is an attorney specializing in criminal cases.

Winters is obviously looking for prospective clients. Doing so in this manner is referred to as *ambulance chasing,* which is a pejorative term for aggressively tracking down anyone who probably has a legal problem in order to drum up business. There is no indication either that Winters is related to any of the people going into the police station or that she has any prior professional relationship with them (for example, they are *not* former clients). Winters appears to have one goal: finding a source of fees. Hence her conduct is unethical. Such direct, in-person, one-on-one solicitation of clients in this way is not allowed. The concern is that an attorney who approaches strangers in trouble

---

[41]Section 20-104, Committee Commentary, *New Mexico Rules Governing the Practice of Law* (Judicial Pamphlet 16).

[42]This prohibition also applies to *live* telephone conversations in which the attorney seeks to be hired.

[43]Furthermore, the improper solicitation of clients and promotion of litigation constitutes the crime of *barratry* in some states. For example, in 1990 three attorneys and an employee of a law firm were indicted in Texas on charges that they illegally sought clients at hospitals and funeral homes after twenty-one students were killed and sixty-nine were injured in a school bus accident. *4 Said to Have Used Bus Crash to Get Business for Law Firm,* New York Times 8, col. 5 (April 7, 1990).

may exert undue influence on them. This is less likely to occur if the solicitation comes in the mail, even if it is sent to individuals known to need legal services.

> Example: An attorney obtains the names of homeowners facing foreclosure and sends them the following letter: "It has come to my attention that your home is being foreclosed on. Federal law may allow you to stop your creditors and give you more time to pay. Call my office for legal help."

While critics claim that such solicitation constitutes "ambulance chasing by mail," the technique is ethical in most states so long as it is truthful and not misleading.[44] *In-person* solicitation, however, is treated differently because of the obvious pressure that it imposes. It is "easier to throw out unwanted mail than an uninvited guest."[45]

Paralegal Perspective:

■ An unscrupulous attorney may try to use a paralegal to solicit clients for the office.

> Example: Bill Hill is a senior citizen who lives at a home for senior citizens. Andrew Vickers, Esq. hires Bill as his "paralegal." His sole job is to contact other seniors with legal problems and to refer them to Vickers.

Andrew Vickers is engaging in unethical solicitation through Bill Hill. Attorneys cannot hire a paralegal to try to accomplish what they cannot do themselves. Nor can they use a *runner*[46]—an employee or independent contractor who contacts personal-injury victims or other potential clients in order to solicit business for an attorney.

■ See also the related discussion above on splitting fees with nonattorneys.

14. Advertising

An attorney may advertise services on radio, on TV, in the newspaper, or through other public media as long as the ad is neither false nor misleading and does not constitute improper in-person solicitation. Model Rule 7.2

There was a time when almost all forms of advertising by attorneys were prohibited. Traditional attorneys considered advertising to be highly offensive to the dignity of the profession. In 1977, however, the United States Supreme Court stunned the legal profession by holding that truthful advertising cannot be completely banned.[47] The First Amendment protects such advertising. Furthermore, advertising does not pose the same danger as in-person solicitation by an attorney. A recipient of advertising is generally under very little pressure to buy the advertised product—in this case, an attorney's services. Hence, attorneys can ethically use truthful, nonmisleading advertising to the general public in order to generate business.

Studies have shown that over one-third of all attorneys in the country engage in some form of advertising. Most of it consists of listings in the Yellow

---

[44]*Shapero v. Kentucky Bar Ass'n*, 486 U.S. 466, 108 S.Ct. 1916, 100 L.Ed.2d 475 (1988). Some states impose additional requirements on mail solicitations—for example, the phrase "Advertising Material" must be printed on the outside of the envelope, and the word "advertisement" must be printed at the top of each page of the letter.

[45]Metzner, *Strategies That Break the Rules*, National Law Journal, 16 (July 15, 1991).

[46]Also called a *capper* if the person uses fraud or deception in the solicitation.

[47]*Bates v. State Bar of Arizona*, 433 U.S. 350, 97 S.Ct. 2691, 53 L.Ed.2d 810 (1977).

Pages. The use of other marketing tools is also on the rise. Revenue for television advertising, for example, was more than $89 million in 1989.[48] Former Chief Justice Warren Burger commented that some attorney ads "would make a used-car dealer blush with shame." Proponents of attorney advertising, however, claim that it has made legal services more accessible to the public and has provided the public with a better basis for choosing among available attorneys.

15. Reporting Professional Misconduct

Attorneys with knowledge that another attorney has committed a serious violation of the ethical rules must report this attorney to the appropriate disciplinary body. Model Rule 8.3

Attorneys may pay a price for remaining silent when they become aware of unethical conduct. The failure of an attorney to report another attorney may mean that both attorneys can be disciplined for unethical behavior. Not every ethical violation, however, must be reported. The ethical violation must raise a substantial question of the attorney's honesty, trustworthiness, or fitness to practice law.

Paralegal Perspective:

■ If a paralegal is aware of unethical conduct of his or her own attorney supervisor, is it unethical for the paralegal to fail to report the attorney to the bar association? No. As indicated earlier, the ethical rules under consideration here apply only to attorneys. Yet the paralegal is still in a predicament. If there is no one to talk to at the firm, he or she must decide whether to remain at this job. Sooner or later, unethical attorneys will probably ask or pressure their paralegal to participate in unethical conduct.

16. Appearance of Impropriety

How would you feel if you were told that, even though you have not violated any rule, you are still going to be punished because what you did *appeared* to be improper? That would be the effect of an obligation to avoid even the appearance of impropriety. In some states, however, it *is* unethical for attorneys to engage in such appearances.[49] The ABA Model Rules, however, does not list appearance of impropriety as an independent basis of determining unethical conduct. To be disciplined in states that have adopted the Model Rules, an attorney must violate one of the specific ethical rules. Yet even in these states, there are conservative attorneys who are as worried about apparent impropriety as they are about specific, actual impropriety.

17. Unauthorized Practice of Law

An attorney shall not assist a nonattorney in the unauthorized practice of law. Rule 5.5(b)

In Chapter 3, we saw that it is a crime in many states for a nonattorney to engage in the *unauthorized practice of law.* Our main focus in Chapter 3 was

---

[48]Hornsby, *The Complex Evolution of Attorney Ad Regs,* Nat'l Law Journal S4 (August 6, 1990).
[49]See Canon 9 of the *ABA Code of Professional Responsibility* (1981). "A lawyer should avoid even the appearance of professional impropriety."

the nonattorney who works for an office other than a traditional law office. An example would be a do-it-yourself divorce office that sells kits and typing services. Now our focus is the nonattorney who works under the supervision of an attorney in a law office. We want to explore the ways in which attorneys might be charged with unethically assisting *their own paralegals* engage in the unauthorized practice of law. For example, an attorney might allow a paralegal to give legal advice, to conduct depositions, or to sign court documents. These areas will be discussed below along with an overview of other major ethical issues involving paralegals.

18. Paralegals

We turn now to a more direct treatment of when attorneys can be disciplined for the unethical use of paralegals. We will cover the following topics:

(a) Paralegals, the ABA Model Code, and the ABA Model Rules
(b) Misrepresentation of paralegal identity or status
(c) Doing what only attorneys can do
(d) Absentee, shoulder, and environmental supervision

(a) Paralegals, the ABA Model Code, and the ABA Model Rules

The first major statement by the American Bar Association on the ethical use of paralegals by attorneys came in its *Model Code of Professional Responsibility:*

> DR 3-101(A): A lawyer shall not aid a nonlawyer in the unauthorized practice of law.

> EC 3-6: A lawyer often delegates tasks to clerks, secretaries, and other lay persons. Such delegation is proper if the lawyer maintains a direct relationship with his client, supervises the delegated work, and has complete professional responsibility for the work product. This delegation enables a lawyer to render legal services more economically and efficiently.[50]

A 1967 opinion elaborated on these standards:

American Bar Association
Formal Opinion 316 (1967)

A lawyer can employ lay secretaries, lay investigators, lay detectives, lay researchers, accountants, lay scriveners, non-lawyer draftsmen or non-lawyer researchers. In fact, he may employ non-lawyers to do any task for him except counsel clients about law matters, engage directly in the practice of law, appear in court or appear in formal proceedings as part of the judicial process, so long as it is he who takes the work and vouches for it to the client and becomes responsible for it to the client. In other words, we do not limit the kind of assistance that a lawyer can acquire in any way to persons who are admitted to the Bar, so long as the non-lawyers do not do things that lawyers may not do or do the things that lawyers only may do.

From these documents we learn that an attorney can hire a paralegal and is responsible for what the paralegal does. There are two levels of this responsibility: civil liability for malpractice and ethical liability for violation of ethical rules.

[50]See footnote 4 on the meaning of DR and EC in the ABA Model Code.

Example: The law firm of Adams & Adams represents Harold Thompson in his negligence suit against Parker Co. At the firm, Elaine Stanton, Esq. works on the case with Peter Vons, a paralegal whom she supervises. Peter neglects to file an important pleading in court, and carelessly gives confidential information about Thompson to the attorney representing Parker. All of this causes Thompson great damage.

Stanton is fully responsible to the client, Thompson, who might decide to bring a malpractice suit in court against her. She cannot hide behind the fact that her paralegal was at fault. (See the discussion of malpractice liability and respondeat superior in Chapter 3.)

What about ethics? Can Stanton be reprimanded, suspended, or disbarred because of what her paralegal did? None of the materials quoted above answer this question. Responsibility to a client for malpractice often raises separate issues from responsibility to a bar association (or other disciplinary body) for unethical conduct. The two kinds of responsibility can be closely interrelated because the same alleged wrongdoing can be involved in the malpractice suit and in the disciplinary case. Yet the two proceedings are separate and should be examined separately.

In 1983, the ABA replaced the *Model Code of Professional Responsibility* with its *Model Rules of Professional Conduct.* The Model Rules, which have been our main focus in this chapter, are more helpful in telling us when attorneys are subject to ethical sanctions because of their paralegals. This is done in *Model Rule 5.3*, covering paralegals. All attorneys in the law firm are not treated the same in Rule 5.3. As you read this rule, note that different standards of ethical responsibility are imposed on the following three categories of attorneys:

- Any attorney in the firm
- A partner in the firm
- An attorney in the firm with direct supervisory authority over the paralegal

---

Model Rules of Professional Conduct
Rule 5.3. Responsibilities
Regarding Nonlawyer Assistants

With respect to a nonlawyer employed or retained by or associated with a lawyer:

(a) a partner in a law firm shall make reasonable efforts to ensure that the firm has in effect measures giving reasonable assurance that the person's conduct is compatible with the professional obligations of the lawyer;

(b) a lawyer having direct supervisory authority over the nonlawyer shall make reasonable efforts to ensure that the person's conduct is compatible with the professional obligations of the lawyer; and

(c) A lawyer shall be responsible for conduct of such a person that would be a violation of the Rules of Professional Conduct if engaged in by a lawyer if:

(1) the lawyer orders or ratifies the conduct involved; or

(2) the lawyer is a partner in the law firm in which the person is employed, or has direct supervisory authority over the person, and knows of the conduct at a time when its consequences can be avoided or mitigated but fails to take reasonable remedial action.

Comment:

Lawyers generally employ assistants in their practice, including secretaries, investigators, law student interns, and paraprofessionals. Such assistants, whether employees or independent contractors, act for the lawyer in rendition of the lawyer's professional services. A lawyer should give such assistants appropriate instruction and supervision concerning the ethical aspects of their employment, particularly regarding the obligation not to disclose information relating to representation of the client, and should be responsible for their work product. The measures employed in supervising nonlawyers should take account of the fact that they do not have legal training and are not subject to professional discipline.

Let us analyze Rule 5.3 by applying it to Elaine Stanton, Esq. in our example. First of all, under 5.3(c)(1), *any* attorney in the firm who "orders" the paralegal to commit the wrongdoing in question is ethically responsible for that conduct. The same is true if the attorney "ratifies" (that is, approves or endorses) the wrongdoing after the paralegal commits it. There is no indication in the example that Stanton or any other attorney in the firm told Peter not to file the pleading in court, or told him to give confidential information about Thompson to the other side. Nor is there any indication that an attorney approved of Peter's conduct after it occurred.[51] Therefore, Rule 5.3(c)(1) does not apply.

We need to know whether Stanton is a partner in the firm. If so, she has an ethical obligation under 5.3(a) to "make reasonable efforts to ensure that the firm has in effect measures giving reasonable assurance" that the paralegal's conduct "is compatible with the professional obligations of the lawyer." Hence a partner cannot completely ignore office paralegals in the hope that someone else in the firm is monitoring them. Reasonable steps must be taken by every partner to establish a system of safeguards. Here are some examples:

■ Make sure that all paralegals in the firm are made aware of the ethical rules governing attorneys in the state.

■ Make sure that all paralegals in the firm are made aware of the importance of deadlines in the practice of law and of the necessity of using date-reminder (tickler) techniques.

In the example, Peter Vons is supervised by Elaine Stanton, Esq. Hence she is an attorney with "direct supervisory authority" over Peter. Rule 5.3(b) governs the conduct of such attorneys. This section requires her to "make reasonable efforts to ensure" that the paralegal's conduct "is compatible with the professional obligations of the lawyer."

Assume that Stanton is charged with a violation of Rule 5.3(b) because her paralegal, Peter, failed to file an important pleading in court and disclosed confidential information about a client. At Stanton's disciplinary hearing, she would be asked a large number of questions about how she supervised Peter. For example:

■ How do you assign tasks to Peter?

■ How do you know if he is capable of handling an assignment?

■ How often do you meet with him after you give him an assignment?

■ How do you know if he is having difficulty completing an assignment?

■ Has he made mistakes in the past? If so, how have you handled them?

Peter might be called as a witness in her disciplinary hearing and be interrogated extensively. For example:

■ How were you trained as a paralegal?

■ What kinds of assignments have you handled in your paralegal career?

■ How long have you worked for Elaine Stanton?

■ How does she evaluate your work?

■ What do you do if you have a question on an assignment but she is not available in the office?

---

[51]By Peter's conduct, we mean both what he did (disclose confidential information) and what he failed to do (file the papers in court).

- Why didn't you file the court document on time?
- Describe the circumstances under which you revealed confidential information to the opponent in the Thompson case.

All of these questions of Stanton and of Peter would be designed to find out if Stanton made "reasonable efforts" to ensure that Peter did not violate ethical standards. Note that attorney supervisors do not have to guarantee that a paralegal will act ethically. They simply have to "make reasonable efforts" that this will occur. The above questions are relevant to whether Stanton exerted such efforts with respect to Peter.

Another basis of ethical liability under the Model Rules is Rule 5.3(c)(2). Both a partner and a supervisory attorney can be subject to discipline if they knew about the paralegal's misconduct yet failed to take reasonable corrective steps at a time when such steps would have avoided or minimized ("mitigated") the damage. At their disciplinary hearing, a partner and/or a supervising attorney would be asked questions such as:

- When did you first find out that Peter did not file the court document?
- What did you do at that time? Why didn't you act sooner?
- When did you first find out that Peter spoke to opposing counsel?
- What did you do at that time? Why didn't you act sooner?

So, too, Peter might be asked questions at the hearing relevant to when his supervising attorney (Stanton) or any partner in the firm found out about what he had done—and what they did when they found out.

(b) Misrepresentation of Paralegal Identity or Status

"It is the lawyer's responsibility to take reasonable measures to ensure that clients, courts, and other lawyers are aware that a legal assistant, whose services are utilized by the lawyer in performing legal services, is not licensed to practice law." [52] People who come into contact with paralegals must not think that they are attorneys. Paralegals should not misrepresent their status intentionally or accidentally. The following status issues need to be covered:

- Titles
- Disclosure of status
- Business cards
- Letterhead
- Signature on correspondence
- Advertisements, announcement cards, signs, lists, and directories
- Name on court documents

What Title Can Be Used?   There are no ethical problems with the titles *paralegal* or *legal assistant*. No one is likely to think that persons with such titles are attorneys. There are some bar associations that prefer titles that are even more explicit in communicating nonattorney status—for example, *lawyer's assistant* and *nonattorney assistant*. Yet, they are seldom used because of the widespread acceptance and clarity of the titles *paralegal* and *legal assistant*. Some years ago,

---

[52]ABA *Model Guidelines,* Guideline 4, see footnote 5.

the Philadelphia Bar Association said that the latter titles should be given only to employees that possessed "the requisite training and education." No state, however, is this explicit in stating who can use the titles.

It is unethical to call a paralegal an "associate" or to refer to a paralegal as being "associated" with a law firm. The title, "paralegal associate," for example, should not be used. The common understanding is that an associate is an attorney. In Iowa, similar problems exist with the title, "Certified Legal Assistant," as we shall see shortly. (See Figure 4.7).

Note on Disbarred or Suspended Attorney as Paralegal. When attorneys have been disbarred or suspended from the practice of law for ethical improprieties, they may try to continue to work in the law as a paralegal for an attorney willing to hire them. Some states will not allow this because it shows disrespect for the court that disciplined the attorney and because of the high likelihood that the individual will engage in the unauthorized practice of law by going beyond paralegal duties. Other states are more lenient but impose other restrictions, such as not allowing a disbarred or suspended attorney to have any client contact while working as a paralegal.

Should Paralegals Disclose Their Nonattorney Status to Clients, Attorneys, Government Officials, and the General Public? Yes, this disclosure is necessary. The more troublesome questions are: What kind of disclosure should you make and when must you make it? Compare the following communications by a paralegal:

- "I work with attorney Ward Brown at Brown & Tams."
- "I am a paralegal."
- "I am a legal assistant."
- "I am not an attorney."

The fourth statement is the clearest expression of nonattorney status. The first is totally unacceptable since you have said nothing about your status. For most contacts, the second and third statements will be ethically sufficient to overcome any misunderstanding about your nonattorney status. Yet there might be members of the public who are confused about what a paralegal or legal assistant is. Hence, the only foolproof communication in all circumstances is the fourth.

In some states, the disclosure of nonattorney status is necessary only if a client, an attorney, a government official, or a member of the public is unaware of this status. Other states say that the paralegal should always disclose his or her nonattorney status at the outset of the contact. According to one state, "common sense suggests a routine disclosure at the outset of the conversation." Furthermore, the failure to provide an oral clarification of status is *not* cured simply by handing over a business card that says you are a paralegal or a legal assistant.

Do not assume that a person with whom you come in contact knows you are not an attorney; the safest course is to assume the opposite!

May a Paralegal Have a Business Card? Every state allows paralegals to have their own business cards as long as their nonattorney status is clear. (See Figure 4.6.) At one time, some states wanted the word *nonlawyer* used along with the paralegal's office title. This is rarely required today. Since paralegals are not allowed to solicit business for their employer, the card may not be used for this

ABEL MUSSER SOKOLOSKY &CLARK

ATTORNEYS AT LAW

DEBRA J. HOBBS
LEGAL ASSISTANT

ONE LEADERSHIP SQUARE
211 N. ROBINSON, SUITE 600
(405) 239-7046   OKLAHOMA CITY, OK 73102

Ethically proper in every state.

FIGURE 4.6

Paralegal
Business Card

John Simpson, CLA

PARALEGAL

PHONE
(319) 456-9103

JONES, DAY, OVERTON & DAVIS, P.C.
8262 PRESTWICK DR.
WATERLOO, IA 50702

Ethically proper in every state *except* in Iowa.

FIGURE 4.7

Paralegal
Business Card

---

purpose. The primary focus of the card must be to identify the paralegal rather than the attorney for whom the paralegal works. Finally, there must be nothing false or misleading printed on the card. In most states, a paralegal who is a *Certified Legal Assistant (CLA)* can include this fact on their card. In Iowa, however, this is not permitted, as we will see when we discuss signatures on correspondence. (See Figure 4.7.)

May the Letterhead of Law Firm Stationery Print the Name of a Paralegal?   States differ in their answer to this question, although most now agree that nonattorneys' names can be printed on law-firm letterhead if their title is also printed so that their nonattorney status is clear. (See Figure 4.8.) Before 1977, almost all states did *not* allow attorney stationery to print the names of nonattorney employees. The concern was that the letterhead would be used as a form of advertising by packing it with names and titles in order to make the office look impressive. This concern, however, evaporated in 1977 when the Supreme Court held that all forms of attorney advertising could not be banned.[53] After this date, most states withdrew their objection to the printing

---

[53]See footnote 47 above.

FIGURE 4.8

Attorney
Letterhead that
Prints Paralegal
Names

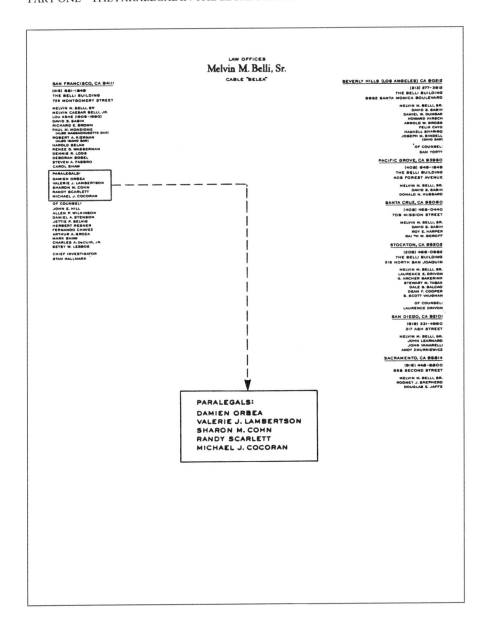

of paralegal names on attorney letterhead as long as no one would be misled into thinking that the paralegals were attorneys. In Michigan, it was recommended, but not required, that attorneys and nonattorneys be printed on different sides of the stationery to "enhance the clarification that the paraprofessional is not licensed to practice law." A few states adhere to the old view that only attorney names can be printed on law-firm letterhead. Yet, to the extent that it is still based on a prohibition of attorney advertising, this view is subject to challenge.

May a Paralegal Write and Sign Letters on Attorney Stationery?   There is never an ethical problem with a paralegal writing a letter that will be reviewed and signed by an attorney. Suppose, however, that the attorney wants the paralegal to sign his or her own name to the letter. Most states will permit this if certain conditions are met. For example, a title must be used that indicates the signer's nonattorney status, and the letter must not give legal advice.

The following formats are proper:

Sincerely,	Sincerely,	Sincerely,
Leonard Smith Paralegal	Pauline Jones Legal Assistant	Jill Strauss Legal Assistant for the Firm

The following formats, however, pose difficulties:

Sincerely,	Sincerely,	Sincerely,
William Davis	John Simpson, CLA	Mary Page Certified Legal Assistant

The first format is ethically improper. The lack of a title could mislead the reader into thinking that William Davis is an attorney. In most states, using the designations "CLA" or "Certified Legal Assistant" is also proper. (See Chapter 3 for a discussion of the CLA program.) In Iowa, however, they cannot be used. "A reader might think that CLA was a legal degree;" and if "Certified Legal Assistant" is used, "the public might be misled about his or her nonlawyer status." Hence, the second and third formats just shown cannot be used in Iowa. Presumably this also applies to a business card with the CLA designation. (See Figure 4.7.) This is an extreme view and is unlikely to be followed elsewhere.

In most states, there are no limitations on the persons to whom a paralegal can send letters. Yet there are a few states (such as New Jersey) where only an attorney can sign a letter to a client, to an opposing attorney, or to a court. A very minor exception to this rule would be "a purely routine request to a court clerk for a docket sheet." A paralegal can sign such a letter. This also is an extreme position. So long as the paralegal's nonattorney status is clear, and so long as an attorney is supervising the paralegal, restrictions on who can be the recipient of a paralegal-signed letter make little sense.

May an Attorney Print the Name of a Paralegal in an Advertisement, an Announcement Card, a Door Sign, an Outdoor Sign, a Law Directory or Law List, an Office Directory, or a Telephone Directory? Attorneys communicate to the public and to each other through advertisements, law directories or lists (that print the names of practicing attorneys), office directories, general telephone directories, door signs, outdoor signs, and announcement cards (that announce that the firm has moved, opened a new branch, merged with another firm, taken on a new partner, etc.). It is relatively rare that an attorney will want to print the name of his or her paralegal in one of these vehicles of communication. In a small city or town, however, a solo practitioner or small law firm might want to do so. While several states will not allow attorneys to do this, most states that have addressed the issue say it is ethically permissible if nothing false or misleading is said about the paralegal and the latter's nonattorney status is clear.

May an Attorney Print the Name of a Paralegal on a Court Document? Formal documents that are required in litigation, such as appellate briefs, memoranda supporting a motion, complaints, or other pleadings, must be signed by an attorney representing a party in the dispute. With rare exceptions, the document cannot be signed by a nonattorney, no matter how minor the formal document may be. In most states, a paralegal can sign a letter on a routine matter to a clerk or other nonjudge, but formal litigation documents require an attorney's signature.

Suppose, however, that the attorney wishes to print on a document the name of a paralegal who worked on the document *in addition to* the attorney's name and signature. The attorney may simply want to give a measure of recognition to the efforts of this paralegal. Most states permit this as long as there is no misunderstanding as to the paralegal's nonattorney status, and no attempt is made to substitute a nonattorney's signature for an attorney's signature.

Occasionally, a court opinion will recognize the contribution of a paralegal. Before the opinion begins, the court lists the names of the attorneys who represented the parties. The name of a paralegal might be included with these attorneys. Here, for example, is the list of attorneys that includes the name of a paralegal (Becky Strickland) in the case of *United States v. Cooke*, 625 F.2d 19 (4th Cir. 1980):

> Thomas J. Keith, Winston-Salem, N.C., for appellant.
> David B. Smith, Asst. U.S. Atty. (H. M. Michaux, Jr., U.S. Atty., Durham, N.C., Becky M. Strickland, Paralegal Specialist on brief), for appellee.
> Before HALL and PHILLIPS, Circuit Judges, and HOFFMAN, Senior District Judge.

(c) Doing What Only Attorneys Can Do

There are limitations on what attorneys can ask their paralegals to do. We just examined one such limitation: paralegals should never be asked to sign court documents. The failure to abide by these limits might subject the attorney to a charge of unethically assisting a nonattorney to engage in the unauthorized practice of law. The areas we need to examine are as follows:

- Legal advice
- Nonlegal advice
- Drafting documents
- Real estate closings
- Depositions
- Executions of wills
- Settlement negotiations
- Court appearances
- Counsel's table
- Administrative hearings

May a Paralegal Give Legal Advice? Unfortunately, it is not easy to define legal advice or the practice of law. According to the American Bar Association:

> It is neither necessary nor desirable to attempt the formulation of a single, specific definition of what constitutes the practice of law. Functionally, the practice of law relates to the rendition of services for others that call for the professional judgment of a lawyer. The essence of the professional judgment of the lawyer is his educated ability to relate the general body and philosophy of law to a specific legal problem of a client. . . . Where this professional judgment is not involved, non-lawyers, such as court clerks, police officers, abstracters, and

many governmental employees, may engage in occupations that require a special knowledge of law in certain areas. But the services of a lawyer are essential in the public interest whenever the exercise of *professional judgment* is required.[54]

The major way that an attorney communicates this professional judgment is through *legal advice.* According to the ABA, it occurs when "the general body and philosophy of law" is related or applied "to a specific legal problem." You are giving legal advice when you tell a particular person how the law might affect a particular legal problem or how to achieve a particular legal result that solves or avoids such a problem. Giving such advice is the unauthorized practice of law, whether or not you charge for the advice and whether or not your advice is correct.

Compare the following sets of statements:

General Information about the Law	Information about the Law as Applied to a Specific Person
"The Superior Court is located at 1223 Via Barranca."	"Your case must be heard in the Superior Court which is located at 1223 Via Barranca."
"There are several different kinds of bankruptcy."	"There are several different kinds of bankruptcy, but you should file under Chapter 13."
"The failure to pay child support will lead to prosecution."	"Your failure to pay child support will lead to prosecution."

Arguably, the statements in the second column constitute legal advice; general information about the law has been related or applied to a particular legal problem of a particular person. The legal questions or problems addressed are: What court can hear (has jurisdiction over) *your* case? What kind of bankruptcy should *you* file? Can *you* be prosecuted for not paying child support?

The statements in the first column do not appear to focus on any particular person's legal problem. Hence such statements do not constitute legal advice, at least not explicitly. But we need to examine some of these statements more closely. When you tell someone that there are "several different kinds of bankruptcy," are you, by implication, telling that person that he or she should consider, and may qualify for, at least one of the kinds of bankruptcy? When you tell someone that the "failure to pay child support will lead to prosecution," are you, by implication, telling that person that his or her failure to pay child support will lead to his or her prosecution? The moment there is a focus on a particular person's legal problem, you are in the realm of legal advice. This focus can be express or implied. Hence, whenever *any* statement about the law is made, you must ask yourself two questions:

- Am I trying to relate legal information to any particular person's legal problem? (If so, I am giving express legal advice.)

- Could a person reasonably interpret what I am saying as relating legal information to a particular person's legal problem even if this is not my intent? (If so, I am giving implied legal advice.)

Great care is sometimes needed to avoid giving legal advice.

---

[54]EC 3–5, *ABA Model Code of Professional Responsibility* (1981).

There are a number of circumstances that increase the likelihood that statements can reasonably be interpreted as giving implied legal advice. For example:

- The statement is made by someone who works in the law, such as an attorney, paralegal, or legal secretary.
- The statement is made by someone who has helped the person with his or her legal problems in the past.
- The statement is made by someone who knows that the person has a current legal problem.
- The person is distressed about his or her current legal problem.

Under such circumstances, the person is likely to interpret *any* statement about the law as being relevant to his or her particular legal problem.

A number of paralegals have pointed out how easy it is to fall into the trap of giving legal advice:

> Legal assistants should be alert to all casual questions [since your answers] might be interpreted as legal advice.[55]

> Most of us are aware of the obvious, but we need to keep in mind that sometimes the most innocent comment could be construed as legal advice.[56]

> A . . . typical scenario, particularly in a small law office where legal assistants have a great deal of direct client contact, is that the clients themselves will coax you to answer questions about the procedures involved in their cases, and lead you into areas where you would be giving them legal advice. Sometimes this is done innocently—because the attorney is unavailable and they are genuinely unaware of the difference between what you can do for them and what their legal counsel is authorized to do. . . . They will press you for projections, strategy, applicable precedents—in short, legal advice. Sometimes you are placed in situations where you are not adequately supervised and your own expertise may be such that you know more about the specialized area of law than the attorney does anyway. . . . We have all walked the thin line between assisting in the provision of legal services and actually practicing law.[57]

When a paralegal gives legal advice in these circumstances, he or she is engaged in the unauthorized practice of law. An attorney who permits this to occur, or who fails to take the preventive steps required by Model Rule 5.3, is aiding the paralegal in the unauthorized practice of law—and hence is acting unethically.

There are a number of situations, however, in which a paralegal *can* give legal advice. First, a paralegal can tell a client precisely what the attorney tells the paralegal to say, even if the message constitutes legal advice. The paralegal, however, cannot elaborate on or explain this kind of message from the attorney. Paralegals "may be authorized to communicate legal advice so long as they do not interpret or expand on that advice."[58] Second, the paralegal may be working in an area of the law where nonattorneys are authorized to represent clients, such as social security hearings. (See Chapter 3.) In such areas, the authorization includes the right to give legal advice.

---

[55]King, *Ethics and the Legal Assistant*, 10 ParaGram 2 (Oregon Legal Assistants Ass'n, August 1987).
[56]DALA Newsletter 2 (Dallas Ass'n of Legal Assistants, December 1990).
[57]Spiegel, *How to Avoid the Unauthorized Practice of Law*, 8 The Journal 8–10 (Sacramento Ass'n of Legal Assistants, February 1986).
[58]ABA *Model Guidelines*, Comment to Guideline 3, see footnote 5.

May a Paralegal Give a Client Nonlegal Advice?   Yes. An attorney may allow a paralegal to render specialized advice on scientific or technical topics. For example, a qualified paralegal can give accounting advice or financial advice. The danger is that the nonlegal advice might also contain legal advice or that the client might reasonably interpret the nonlegal advice as legal advice.

May a Paralegal Draft Legal Documents?   Yes. A paralegal can draft any legal document as long as an attorney supervises and reviews the work of the paralegal. Some ethical opinions say that the document must lose its separate identity as the work of a paralegal and must leave the office as the work product of an attorney. In West Virginia, for example, "anything delegated to a nonattorney must lose its separate identity and be merged in the service of the lawyer." The key point is that an attorney must stand behind and be responsible for the document.

May a Paralegal Attend a Real Estate Closing?   The sale of property is finalized at an event called a real estate closing. Many of the events at the closing are formalities, such as signing and exchanging papers. Occasionally, however, some of these events turn into more substantive matters where negotiation, legal interpretation, and legal advice are involved.

In most states, paralegals can attend closings in order to assist their attorney-supervisor. The tough question is whether they can attend alone and conduct the closing themselves. Chicago has one of the most liberal rules. There, paralegals can conduct the closing without the attorney-supervisor being present if no legal advice is given, if all the documents have been prepared in advance, if the attorney-supervisor is available by telephone to provide help, and if the other attorney consents. In some states, additional conditions must be met before allowing paralegals to act on their own. For example, the closing must take place in the attorney's law office with the attorney readily accessible to answer legal questions. It must be noted, however, that this is a minority position. Most states would say that it is unethical for an attorney to allow a paralegal to conduct a real estate closing alone.

May a Paralegal Conduct a Deposition?   No. Paralegals can schedule depositions, can assist in preparing a witness who will be deposed (called the deponent), can take notes at the deposition, and can summarize deposition transcripts, but they cannot conduct the deposition. Asking and objecting to questions arc attorney-only functions.

May a Paralegal Supervise the Execution of a Will?   In Connecticut, the execution of a will must be supervised by an attorney. A paralegal can act as a witness to the execution, but an attorney must direct the procedure. Most other states would probably agree, although few have addressed this question.

May a Paralegal Negotiate a Settlement?   Some states allow a paralegal to negotiate with a nonattorney employee of an insurance company, such as a claims adjuster, as long as the paralegal is supervised by an attorney. Most states, however, limit the paralegal's role to exchanging messages from the supervising attorney, and do not allow any actual give-and-take negotiating by the paralegal.

May a Paralegal Make a Court Appearance?   In the vast majority of courts, a paralegal cannot perform even minor functions in a courtroom, such as asking a judge for a hearing date. As we saw in Chapter 3, very few exceptions to this rule exist. Only attorneys can act in a representative capacity before a judge. There are, however, a small number of specialized courts, like the small claims court of some states, where you do not have to be an attorney to represent parties. This exception, however, is rare. Finally, as mentioned earlier, a paralegal should not sign a formal court document that is filed in litigation.

May a Paralegal Sit at Counsel's Table During a Trial?   In many courts, only attorneys can sit at counsel's table during a trial. Yet, in some courts a paralegal is allowed to sit with the attorneys if permission of the presiding judge is obtained. This is referred to as sitting *second chair* in the courtroom.

May a Paralegal Represent Clients at Administrative Hearings?   Yes, when this is authorized at the particular state or federal administrative agency. (See Chapter 3.)

(d) Absentee, Shoulder, and Environmental Supervision

It is difficult to overestimate the importance of attorney supervision in the arena of ethics. Almost every ethical opinion involving paralegals (and almost every attorney malpractice opinion involving paralegals) stresses the need for effective supervision. The justification for the very existence of perhaps 95% of paralegal activity is this supervision. Indeed, one of the main reasons many argue that paralegal licensing is not necessary is the protective cover of attorney supervision.

What is meant by supervision? The extremes are easy to identify. Figure 4.9 provides this spectrum of extremes. *Absentee supervision* refers to the attorney who is either never around or never available. Once tasks are assigned, paralegals are on their own. At the other extreme is *shoulder supervision,* practiced by attorneys who are afraid to delegate. When they do get up enough courage to delegate something, they constantly look over the shoulder of the paralegal, who is rarely left alone for more than two-minute intervals. Such attorneys suffer from *delegatitis,* the inordinate fear of letting anyone do anything for them.

Both kinds of supervision are misguided. If you work for an attorney who practices absentee supervision, disaster is just around the corner. You may feel flattered by the confidence placed in you; you may enjoy the challenge of independence; you may be highly compensated because of your success. But you are working in an office that is traveling 130 miles per hour in a 50 miles per hour zone. Any feeling of safety in such an office is illusory. Shoulder supervision, on the other hand, provides safety at the expense of practicality. Perpetual step-by-step surveillance will ultimately defeat the economy and efficiency motives that originally led the office to hire paralegals.

Perhaps the most effective kind of supervision is *environmental supervision,* or what might be called *holistic supervision.* It is far broader in its reach than the immediate task delegated to a paralegal. It addresses the essential question: What kind of environment will lead to a high-quality paralegal work product without sacrificing economy? The components of this kind of supervision

FIGURE 4.9

Levels of Supervision: The Spectrum of Extremes

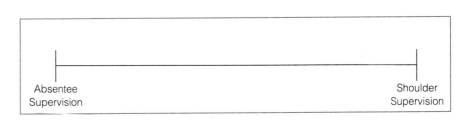

are outlined in Figure 4.10. Environmental supervision requires *hiring* the right people, *training* those people, *assigning* appropriate tasks, *providing* the needed resources, *monitoring* the progress, *reviewing* the end product, and *rewarding* competence.

FIGURE 4.10

"Environmental Supervision": The Ethical Ideal

1. Before paralegals are hired, the office undertakes a study of its practice in order to identify what tasks paralegals will perform and what levels of ability will be required to perform those tasks.

2. As part of the interview process, the office conducts background checks on applicants for paralegal jobs in order to ensure that competent people are hired who already have the needed skills or who are trainable so that they can acquire these skills on the job.

3. A program of orientation and training is created to introduce paralegals to the office and to prepare them for the tasks ahead.

4. Paralegals are given a copy of the ethical rules governing attorneys in the state. In addition to reading these rules, they are given training on the meaning of the rules.

5. Paralegals are told what to do if they feel that an ethical problem exists. Lines of authority are identified if the paralegal needs to discuss the matter with someone other than, or in addition to, his or her immediate supervisor.

6. The office does not assume that every attorney knows how to supervise paralegals. Paralegals are assigned to attorneys who have the required supervisory sensitivity and skill. Furthermore, the office is always looking for ways to increase this sensitivity and skill.

7. An attorney reviews all paralegal work. While paralegals may be given discretion and asked to exercise judgment in the tasks assigned, this discretion and judgment is always subjected to attorney review.

8. No task is assigned that is beyond the capacity of the paralegal. Specialized instruction always accompanies tasks the paralegal has not performed before.

9. Once a task is assigned, the paralegal is told where to receive assistance if the immediate supervisor is not available. This lack of availability, however, is relatively rare.

10. For tasks that the office performs on a recurring basis, manuals, office procedures, checklists, or other written material are available to the paralegal to explain how the tasks are performed and where samples or models can be found. If such *systems* material does not currently exist, the office has realistic plans to create such material.

11. To cut down on misunderstanding, every paralegal assignment includes the following information:
    - A *specific due date.* ("Get to this when you can" is unacceptable and unfair.)
    - A *priority assessment.* ("Should everything else be dropped while I do this assignment?")
    - A *context.* ("How does this assignment fit into the broader picture of the case?")
    - A *financial perspective.* ("Is this billable time?")

12. At reasonable times before the due date of selected assignments, the supervisor monitors the progress of the paralegal to ensure that the work is being done professionally and accurately.

13. A team atmosphere exists at the office among the attorneys, paralegals, secretaries, and other employees. Everyone knows each other's functions, pressures, and potential as resources. A paralegal never feels isolated.

14. Evaluations of paralegal performance are constructive. Both the supervisor and paralegal feel that there are opportunities for further learning.

15. The office sends the paralegal to training seminars conducted by paralegal associations and bar associations to maintain and to increase the paralegal's skills.

16. The office knows that an unhappy employee is prone to error. Hence the office ensures that the work setting of the paralegal encourages personal growth and productivity. This includes matters of compensation, benefits, work space, equipment, and advancement.

Unfortunately, most law offices do *not* practice environmental supervision as outlined in Figure 4.10. The chart represents the ideal. Yet you need to know what the ideal is so that you can advocate for the conditions that will help bring it about.

Thus far, our discussion on supervision has focused on the traditional paralegal who works full time in the office of an attorney. We also need to consider the freelance paralegal who works part-time for one or more attorneys. Very often this freelance or independent paralegal works in his or her own office. (See Chapters 1 and 3, and Appendix D.) How can attorneys fulfill their ethical obligation to supervise such paralegals?

> Example: Gail Patterson has her own freelance business. She offers paralegal services to attorneys who hire her for short-term projects which she performs in her own office.

Arguably, attorneys who hire Gail often do not provide the same kind of supervision that they can provide to a full-time paralegal who works in their office. We saw earlier that Model Rule 5.3(c)(2) says that an attorney has the responsibility to take steps to avoid the consequences of an ethical violation by a paralegal or to mitigate the consequences of such a violation. Suppose that Gail commits an ethical impropriety—for example, she reveals confidential communications. Since she works in her own office, the attorney who hired her may not learn about this impropriety in time to avoid or mitigate its consequences. Conflict of interest is another potential problem. Gail works for many different attorneys and hence many different clients of those attorneys. It is possible that she could accept work from two attorneys who are engaged in litigation against each other without either attorney knowing that the other has hired Gail on the same case. (See the earlier discussion of this problem on page 258.)

A few bar associations have declared that it is ethically improper for an attorney to hire a freelance paralegal because of the difficulties of providing meaningful supervision. It is not enough that the attorney vouches for, and takes responsibility for, the final product submitted by the freelance paralegal. Ongoing supervision is also needed under Model Rule 5.3. Not many states, however, have addressed this area of ethics. In the future, we will probably see the creation of new standards to govern this kind of paralegal.

◼ Section D. Doing Research on an Ethical Issue

1. At a law library, ask where the following two items are kept:
   - The code or rules of ethics governing the attorneys in your state
   - The ethical opinions that interpret the code or rules
2. Contact your state bar association. Ask what committee or other body has jurisdiction over ethics. Contact it to find out if it has published any opinions, guidelines, or other materials on paralegals. Also ask if there is a special committee on paralegals. If so, find out what it has said about paralegals.
3. Do the same for any other bar associations in your area, such as city or county bar associations.
4. At a law library, ask where the following two items are kept:
   - The ABA's Model Rules of Professional Conduct
   - The ethical opinions that interpret these Model Rules as well as the earlier Model Code of Professional Responsibility of the ABA

5. Examine the *ABA/BNA Lawyers' Manual on Professional Conduct.* This is a loose-leaf book containing current information on ABA ethics and the ethical rules of every state.

6. Other material to check in the library:
   - C. Wolfram, *Modern Legal Ethics* (1986) (treatise)
   - *The Georgetown Journal of Legal Ethics* (periodical)
   - *Lawyers' Liability Review* (newsletter)

7. Computer research in either WESTLAW or LEXIS will enable you to do legal research on the law of ethics in your state. (See Chapter 9.) Here, for example, is a query (i.e. question) you could use to ask WESTLAW to find cases in your state in which a paralegal was charged with the unauthorized practice of law:

     paralegal "legal assistant" /p "unauthorized practice"

   After you instructed WESTLAW to turn to the database containing the court opinions of your state, you would type this query at the keyboard in order to find out if any such cases exist.

8. Another way to find court opinions on ethics in your state is to go to the digest covering the courts in your state. Use its index to find cases on ethical issues.

Section E. Ethical Codes of the Paralegal Associations

As indicated at the beginning of this chapter, there are no binding ethical rules published by paralegal associations. Yet the two major national associations—the National Federation of Paralegal Associations (NFPA) and the National Association of Legal Assistants (NALA)—have written ethical codes. These important documents of NFPA and of NALA are presented below, followed by a broader document of NALA, its Model Standards and Guidelines.

Affirmation of Professional Responsibility
of the National Federation of Paralegal Associations

Preamble

The National Federation of Paralegal Associations recognizes and accepts its commitment to the realization of the most basic right of a free society, equal justice under the law.

In examining contemporary legal institutions and systems, the members of the paralegal profession recognize that a redefinition of the traditional delivery of legal services is essential in order to meet the needs of the general public. The paralegal profession is committed to increasing the availability and quality of legal services.

The National Federation of Paralegal Associations has adopted this *Affirmation of Professional Responsibility* to delineate the principles of purpose and conduct toward which paralegals should aspire. Through this Affirmation, the National Federation of Paralegal Associations places upon each paralegal the responsibility to adhere to these standards and encourages dedication to the development of the profession.

I. Professional Responsibility

A paralegal shall demonstrate initiative in performing and expanding the paralegal role in the delivery of legal services within the parameters of the unauthorized practice of law statutes.

Discussion: Recognizing the professional and legal responsibility to abide by the unauthorized practice of law statutes, the Federation supports and encourages new interpretations as to what constitutes the practice of law.

II. Professional Conduct

A paralegal shall maintain the highest standards of ethical conduct.

Discussion: It is the responsibility of a paralegal to avoid conduct which is unethical or appears to be unethical. Ethical principles are aspirational in character and embody the fundamental rules of conduct by which every paralegal should abide. Observance of these standards is essential to uphold respect for the legal system.

III. Competence and Integrity

A paralegal shall maintain a high level of competence and shall contribute to the integrity of the paralegal profession.

Discussion: The integrity of the paralegal profession is predicated upon individual competence. Professional competence is each paralegal's responsibility and is achieved through continuing education, awareness of developments in the field of law, and aspiring to the highest standards of personal performance.

IV. Client Confidences

A paralegal shall preserve client confidences and privileged communications.

Discussion: Confidential information and privileged communications are a vital part of the attorney, paralegal, and client relationship. The importance of preserving confidential and privileged information is understood to be an uncompromising obligation of every paralegal.

V. Support of Public Interests

A paralegal shall serve the public interests by contributing to the availability and delivery of quality legal services.

Discussion: It is the responsibility of each paralegal to promote the development and implementation of programs that address the legal needs of the public. A paralegal shall strive to maintain a sensitivity to public needs and to educate the public as to the services that paralegals may render.

VI. Professional Development

A paralegal shall promote the development of the paralegal profession.

Discussion: This Affirmation of Professional Responsibility promulgates a positive attitude through which a paralegal may recognize the importance, responsibility and potential of the paralegal contribution to the delivery of legal services. Participation in professional associations enhances the ability of the individual paralegal to contribute to the quality and growth of the paralegal profession.

Code of Ethics and Professional Responsibility
of the National Association of Legal Assistants

Preamble

It is the responsibility of every legal assistant to adhere strictly to the accepted standards of legal ethics and to live by general principles of proper conduct. The performance of the duties of the legal assistant shall be governed by specific canons as defined herein in order that justice will be served and the goals of the profession attained.

The canons of ethics set forth hereinafter are adopted by the National Association of Legal Assistants, Inc., as a general guide, and the enumeration of these rules does not mean there are not others of equal importance although not specifically mentioned.

Canon 1

A legal assistant shall not perform any of the duties that lawyers only may perform nor do things that lawyers themselves may not do.

Canon 2

A legal assistant may perform any task delegated and supervised by a lawyer so long as the lawyer is responsible to the client, maintains a direct relationship with the client, and assumes full professional responsibility for the work product.

Canon 3

A legal assistant shall not engage in the practice of law by accepting cases, setting fees, giving legal advice, or appearing in court (unless otherwise authorized by court or agency rules).

Canon 4

A legal assistant shall not act in matters involving professional legal judgment as the services of a lawyer are essential in the public interest whenever the exercise of such judgment is required.

Canon 5

A legal assistant must act prudently in determining the extent to which a client may be assisted without the presence of a lawyer.

Canon 6

A legal assistant shall not engage in the unauthorized practice of law and shall assist in preventing the unauthorized practice of law.

Canon 7

A legal assistant must protect the confidences of a client, and it shall be unethical for a legal assistant to violate any statute now in effect or hereafter to be enacted controlling privileged communications.

Canon 8

It is the obligation of the legal assistant to avoid conduct which would cause the lawyer to be unethical or even appear to be unethical, and loyalty to the employer is incumbent upon the legal assistant.

Canon 9

A legal assistant shall work continually to maintain integrity and a high degree of competency throughout the legal profession.

Canon 10

A legal assistant shall strive for perfection through education in order to better assist the legal profession in fulfilling its duty of making legal services available to clients and the public.

Canon 11

A legal assistant shall do all other things incidental, necessary, or expedient for the attainment of the ethics or responsibilities imposed by statute or rule of court.

Canon 12

A legal assistant is governed by the *American Bar Association Model Code of Professional Responsibility* and the *American Bar Association Model Rules of Professional Conduct.*

Model Standards and Guidelines for Utilization of Legal Assistants

of the National Association of Legal Assistants

Preamble

Proper utilization of the services of legal assistants affects the efficient delivery of legal services. Legal assistants and the legal profession should be assured that some measures exist for identifying legal assistants and their role in assisting attorneys in the delivery of legal services. Therefore, the National Association of Legal Assistants, Inc., hereby adopts these Model Standards and Guidelines as an educational document for the benefit of legal assistants and the legal profession.

Definition

Legal assistants* are a distinguishable group of persons who assist attorneys in the delivery of legal services. Through formal education, training, and experience, legal assistants have knowledge and expertise regarding the legal system and substantive and procedural law which qualify them to do work of a legal nature under the supervision of an attorney.

Standards

A legal assistant should meet certain minimum qualifications. The following standards may be used to determine an individual's qualifications as a legal assistant:

1. Successful completion of the Certified Legal Assistant (CLA) examination of the National Association of Legal Assistants, Inc.;

2. Graduation from an ABA approved program of study for legal assistants;

3. Graduation from a course of study for legal assistants which is institutionally accredited but not ABA approved, and which requires not less than the equivalent of 60 semester hours of classroom study;

4. Graduation from a course of study for legal assistants, other than those set forth in (2) and (3) above, plus not less than six months of in-house training as a legal assistant;

5. A baccalaureate degree in any field, plus not less than six months in-house training as a legal assistant;

6. A minimum of three years of law-related experience under the supervision of an attorney, including at least six months of in-house training as a legal assistant; or

7. Two years of in-house training as a legal assistant.

For purposes of these standards, "in-house training as a legal assistant" means attorney education of the employee concerning legal assistant duties and these Guidelines. In addition to review and analysis of assignments, the legal assistant should receive a reasonable amount of instruction directly related to the duties and obligations of the legal assistant.

Guidelines

These Guidelines relating to standards of performance and professional responsibility are intended to aid legal assistants and attorneys. The responsibility rests with an attorney who employs legal assistants to

---

*Within this occupational category some individuals are known as paralegals.

educate them with respect to the duties they are assigned and to supervise the manner in which such duties are accomplished.

Legal assistants should:

1. Disclose their status as legal assistants at the outset of any professional relationship with a client, other attorneys, a court or administrative agency or personnel thereof, or members of the general public.
2. Preserve the confidences and secrets of all clients; and
3. Understand the attorney's Code of Professional Responsibility and these Guidelines in order to avoid any action which would involve the attorney in a violation of that Code, or give the appearance of professional impropriety.

Legal assistants should not:

1. Establish attorney-client relationships, set legal fees, give legal opinions or advice, or represent a client before a court; nor
2. Engage in, encourage, or contribute to any act which could constitute the unauthorized practice of law.

Legal assistants may perform services for an attorney in the representation of a client, provided:

1. The services performed by the legal assistant do not require the exercise of independent professional legal judgment;
2. The attorney maintains a direct relationship with the client and maintains control of all client matters;
3. The attorney supervises the legal assistant;
4. The attorney remains professionally responsible for all work on behalf of the client, including any actions taken or not taken by the legal assistant in connection therewith; and
5. The services performed supplement, merge with, and become the attorney's work product.

In the supervision of a legal assistant, consideration should be given to:

1. Designating work assignments that correspond to the legal assistants' abilities, knowledge, training, and experience;

2. Educating and training the legal assistant with respect to professional responsibility, local rules and practices, and firm policies;
3. Monitoring the work and professional conduct of the legal assistant to ensure that the work is substantively correct and timely performed;
4. Providing continuing education for the legal assistant in substantive matters through courses, institutes, workshops, seminars, and in-house training; and
5. Encouraging and supporting membership and active participation in professional organizations.

Except as otherwise provided by statute, court rule or decision, administrative rule or regulation, or the attorney's Code of Professional Responsibility; and within the preceding parameters and proscriptions, a legal assistant may perform any function delegated by an attorney, including, but not limited to, the following:

1. Conduct client interviews and maintain general contact with the client after the establishment of the attorney-client relationship, so long as the client is aware of the status and function of the legal assistant, and the client contact is under the supervision of the attorney.
2. Locate and interview witnesses, so long as the witnesses are aware of the status and function of the legal assistant.
3. Conduct investigations and statistical and documentary research for review by the attorney.
4. Conduct legal research for review by the attorney.
5. Draft legal documents for review by the attorney.
6. Draft correspondence and pleadings for review by and signature of the attorney.
7. Summarize depositions, interrogatories, and testimony for review by the attorney.
8. Attend executions of wills, real estate closings, depositions, court or administrative hearings, and trials with the attorney.
9. Author and sign letters, provided the legal assistant's status is clearly indicated and the correspondence does not contain independent legal opinions or legal advice.

Section F. An Ethical Dilemma: Your Ethics or Your Job!

Throughout this chapter we have stressed the importance of maintaining your integrity through knowledge of and compliance with ethical rules. There may be times, however, when this is much easier said than done. Consider the following situations:

- You are not sure whether an ethical violation is being committed. Nor is anyone else in the office sure. Like so many areas of the law, ethical issues can be complex.
- You are sure that an ethical violation exists, and the violator is your supervisor!
- You are sure that an ethical violation exists, and the violators are everyone else in the office!

You face a potential dilemma (1) if no one seems to care about the ethical problem or, worse, (2) if your supervising attorney is the one committing the ethical impropriety or (3) if the entire office appears to be participating in the impropriety. People do not like to be told that they are unethical. Rather than acknowledge the fault and mend their ways, they may turn on the accuser, the one raising the fuss about ethics. Once the issue is raised, it may be very difficult to continue working in the office.

You need someone to talk to. In the best of all worlds, it will be someone in the same office. If this is not practical, consider contacting a teacher whom you trust. Paralegal associations are also an excellent source of information and support. A leader in one paralegal association offers the following advice:

> I would suggest that if the canons, discipline rules, affirmations, and codes of ethics do not supply you with a clear-cut answer to any ethical question you may have, you should draw upon the network that you have in being a member of this association. Getting the personal input of other paralegals who may have been faced with similar situations, or who have a greater knowledge through experience of our professional responsibilities, may greatly assist you in working your way through a difficult ethical situation.[59]

Of course, you must be careful not to violate client confidentiality during discussions with someone outside the office. Never mention actual client names or any specific information pertaining to a case. You can talk in hypothetical terms. For example, "an attorney working on a bankruptcy case asks a paralegal to. . . ." Once you present data in this sterilized fashion, you can then ask for guidance on the ethical implications of the data.

If handled delicately, most ethical problems that bother you can be resolved without compromising anyone's integrity or job. Yet the practice of law is not substantially different from other fields of endeavor. There will be times when the clash between principle and the dollar or the ego cannot be resolved to everyone's satisfaction. You may indeed have to make a choice between your ethics and your job.

■ ASSIGNMENT 4.1

(a) What is the name of the code of ethics that governs attorneys in your state?

(b) To what body or agency does a client initially make a charge of unethical conduct against his or her attorney in your state?

(c) List the steps required to discipline an attorney for unethical conduct in your state. Begin with the complaint stage and conclude with the court that makes the final decision. Draw a flow chart that lists these steps.

---

[59]Harper, *Ethical Considerations for Legal Assistants,* Compendium (Orange County Paralegal Ass'n, April 1987).

■ ASSIGNMENT 4.2

Paul Emerson is an attorney who works at the firm of Rayburn & Rayburn. One of the firm's clients is Designs Unlimited, Inc. (DU), a clothing manufacturer. Emerson provides corporate advice to DU. Recently Emerson made a mistake in interpreting a new securities law. As a consequence, DU had to postpone for six months the issuance of a stock option. Has Paul acted unethically?

■ ASSIGNMENT 4.3

(a) Three individuals in Connecticut hire a large New York law firm to represent them in a proxy fight in which they sought control of a Connecticut bank. They lose the proxy fight. The firm then sends these individuals a $358,827 bill for 895 hours of work over a one month period. Is this bill unethical? What further facts would you like to have to help you answer this question?

(b) Victor Adams and Len Patterson are full partners in the law firm of Adams, Patterson & Kelly. A client contacts Patterson to represent him on a negligence case. Patterson refers the case to Victor Adams who does most of the work. (Under an agreement between them, Patterson will receive 40% and Adams will receive 60% of any fee paid by this client.) Patterson does not tell the client about the involvement of Adams in the case. Any ethical problems?

(c) An attorney establishes a bonus plan for her paralegals. A bonus will be given to those paralegals who bill a specified number of hours in excess of a stated minimum. The amount of the bonus will depend on the amount billed and collected. Any ethical problems?

■ ASSIGNMENT 4.4

Mary works in a law firm that charges clients $125 an hour for attorney time and $55 an hour for paralegal time. She and another paralegal, Fred, are working with an attorney on a large case. She sees all of the time sheets that the three of them submit to the firm's accounting office. She suspects that the attorney is padding his time sheets by overstating the number of hours he works on the case. For example, he lists thirty hours for a four-day period when he was in court every day on another case. Furthermore, Fred's time is being billed at the full $55 an hour rate even though he spends about 80% of his time typing correspondence, filing, and other clerical duties. Mary also suspects that her attorney is billing out Mary's time at the attorney rate rather than the paralegal rate normally charged clients for her time. Any ethical problems? What should Mary do?

■ ASSIGNMENT 4.5

Smith is an attorney who works at the firm of Johnson & Johnson. He represents Ralph Grant, who is seeking a divorce from his wife, Amy Grant. In their first meeting, Smith learns that Ralph is an experienced carpenter but is out of work and has very little money. Smith's fee is $150 an hour. Since Ralph has no money and has been having trouble finding work, Smith tells Ralph that he won't have to pay the fee if the court does not grant him the divorce. One day while Smith is working on another case involving Helen Oberlin, he learns that Helen is looking for a carpenter. Smith recommends Ralph to Helen, and she hires him for a small job. Six months pass. The divorce case is dropped when the Grants reconcile. In the meantime, Helen Oberlin is very dissatisfied with Ralph's carpentry work for her; she claims he didn't do the work he contracted to do. She wants to know what she can do about it. She tries to call Smith at Johnson & Johnson but is told that Smith does not work there anymore. Another attorney, Georgia Quinton, Esq. helps Helen. Any ethical problems?

■ ASSIGNMENT 4.6

John Jones is a paralegal working at the XYZ law firm. The firm is handling a large class action involving potentially thousands of plaintiffs. John has been instructed to screen the potential plaintiffs in the class. John tells those he screens out (using criteria provided by the firm) in writing or verbally that "unfortunately, our firm will not be able to represent you." Any ethical problems?

■ ASSIGNMENT 4.7

A paralegal quits the firm of Smith & Smith. When she leaves, she takes client documents she prepared while at the firm. The documents contain confidential client information. The paralegal is showing these documents to potential employers as writing samples.

(a) What is the ethical liability of attorneys at Smith & Smith under Model Rule 5.3?

(b) What is the ethical liability of attorneys at law firms where she is seeking employment under 5.3?

(c) What is the paralegal's liability?

■ ASSIGNMENT 4.8

(a) Mary Smith is a paralegal at the ABC law firm. She has been working on the case of Jessica Randolph, a client of the office. Mary talks with Ms. Randolph often. Mary receives a subpoena from the attorney of the party that is suing Ms. Randolph. On the witness stand, Mary is asked by this attorney what Ms. Randolph told her at the ABC law office about a particular business transaction related to the suit. Randolph's attorney (Mary's boss) objects to the question. What result?

(b) Before Helen became a paralegal for the firm of Harris & Derkson, she was a chemist for a large corporation. Harris & Derkson is a patent law firm where Helen's technical expertise in chemistry is invaluable. Helen's next-door neighbor is an inventor. On a number of occasions he discussed the chemical makeup of his inventions with Helen. Regarding one of these inventions, the neighbor is being charged by the government with stealing official secrets to prepare the invention. Harris & Derkson represent the neighbor on this case. Helen also works directly on the case for the firm. In a prosecution of the neighbor, Helen is called as a witness and is asked to reveal the substance of all her conversations with the neighbor concerning the invention in question. Does Helen have to answer?

■ ASSIGNMENT 4.9

Bob and Patricia Fannan are separated, and they both want a divorce. They would like to have a joint-custody arrangement in which their son would spend time with each parent during the year. The only marital property is a house, which they agree should be sold, with each to get one half of the proceeds. Mary Franklin, Esq. is an attorney whom Jim and Mary know and trust. They decide to ask Franklin to represent both of them in the divorce. Any ethical problems?

■ ASSIGNMENT 4.10

Alice is a freelance paralegal with a specialty in probate law. One of the firms she has worked for is Davis, Ritter & Boggs. Her most recent assignment for this firm has been to identify the assets of Mary Steck, who died six months ago. One of Mary's assets is a 75% ownership share in the Domain Corporation. Alice learns a great deal about this company, including the fact that four months ago it had difficulty meeting its payroll and expects to have similar difficulties in the coming year.

Alice's freelance business has continued to grow because of her excellent reputation. She decides to hire an employee with a different specialty so that her office can begin to take different kinds of cases from attorneys. She hires Bob, a paralegal with four years of litigation experience. The firm of Jackson & Jackson hires Alice to digest a series of long deposition documents in the case of Glendale Bank v. Ajax Tire Co. Jackson & Jackson represents Glendale Bank. Peterson, Zuckerman & Morgan represents Ajax Tire Co. Alice assigns Bob to this case. Ajax Tire Co. is a wholly owned subsidiary of the Domain Corporation. Glendale Bank is suing Ajax Tire Co. for fraud in misrepresenting its financial worth when Ajax Tire Co. applied for and obtained a loan from Glendale Bank.

Any ethical problems?

■ ASSIGNMENT 4.11

Assume that you owned a successful freelance business in which you provided paralegal services to over 150 attorneys all over the state. How should your files be organized in order to avoid a conflict of interest?

■ ASSIGNMENT 4.12

Joan is a paralegal who works for the XYZ law firm, which is representing Goff in a suit against Barnard, who is represented by the ABC law firm. Joan calls Barnard and says, "Is this the first time that you have ever been sued?" Barnard answers, "Yes it is. Is there anything else that you would like to know?" Joan says *no* and the conversation ends. Any ethical problems?

■ ASSIGNMENT 4.13

Mary is a paralegal who is a senior citizen. She works at the XYZ legal service office. One day she goes to a senior citizens center and says the following:

> All of you should know about and take advantage of the XYZ legal service office where I work. Let me give you just one example why. Down at the office there is an attorney named Armanda Morris. She is an expert on insurance company cases. Some of you may have had trouble with insurance companies that say one thing and do another. Our office is available to serve you.

Any ethical problems?

■ ASSIGNMENT 4.14

(a) What restrictions exist on advertising by attorneys in your state? Give an example of an ad on TV or in the newspaper that would be unethical. On researching an ethical issue, see page 278.

(b) In *Bates v. State Bar of Arizona,* 433 U.S. 350 (1970), the United States Supreme Court held that a state could not prohibit all forms of lawyer advertising. Has *Bates* been cited by state courts in your state on the advertising issue? If so, what impact has the case had in your state? To find out, shepardize *Bates.*

■ **ASSIGNMENT 4.15**

Mary Jackson is a paralegal at Rollins & Rollins. She is supervised by Ian Gregory. Mary is stealing money from the funds of one of the firm's clients. The only attorney who knows about this is Dan Roberts, Esq., who is not a partner at the firm and who does not supervise Mary. Dan says and does nothing about Mary's actions. What ethical obligations does Dan have under Model Rule 5.3?

■ **ASSIGNMENT 4.16**

John Smith is a paralegal who works for the firm of Beard, Butler, and Clark. John's immediate supervisor is Viola Butler, Esq. With the full knowledge and blessing of Viola Butler, John Smith sends a letter to a client of the firm (Mary Anders). Has Viola Butler acted unethically in permitting John to send out this letter? The letter is as follows:

Law Offices of
Beard, Butler, and Clark
310 High St.
Maincity, Ohio 45238
512-663-9410

Attorneys at Law   *Paralegal*

Ronald Beard   **John Smith**
Viola Butler
Wilma Clark

May 14, 1991

Mary Anders
621 S. Randolph Ave.
Maincity, Ohio 45238

Dear Ms. Anders:

    Viola Butler, the attorney in charge of your case, has asked me to let you know that next month's hearing has been postponed. We will let you know the new date as soon as possible. If you have any questions don't hesitate to call me.

Sincerely,

John Smith
Legal Intern

JS:wps

■ ASSIGNMENT 4.17

Under what circumstances, if any, would it be appropriate for you to refer to a client of the office where you work as "my client"?

■ ASSIGNMENT 4.18

John Jones is a paralegal who works for an attorney named Linda Sunders. Linda is away from the office one day and telephones John, who is at the office. She dictates a one-line letter to a client of the office. The letter reads, "I advise you to sue." Linda asks John to sign the letter for her. The bottom of the letter reads as follows:

Linda Sunders
by John Jones

Any ethical problems?

■ ASSIGNMENT 4.19

Mary is a paralegal who works at the XYZ law firm. She specializes in real estate matters at the firm. Mary attends a real estate closing in which her role consists of exchanging documents and acknowledging the receipt of documents. Analyze this problem on the basis of the following variations:

(a) The closing takes place at the XYZ law firm.

(b) The closing takes place at a bank.

(c) Mary's supervising attorney is not present at the closing.

(d) Mary's supervising attorney is present at the closing.

(e) Mary's supervising attorney is present at the closing except for thirty minutes, during which time Mary continued to exchange documents and acknowledge the receipt of documents.

(f) During the closing, the attorney for the other party says to Mary, "I don't know why my client should have to pay that charge." Mary responds: "In this state that charge is always paid in this way."

■ ASSIGNMENT 4.20

John is a paralegal who works for the XYZ law firm, which is representing a client against the Today Insurance Company. The Company also employs paralegals who work under the Company's general counsel. One of these paralegals is Mary. In an effort to settle the case, Mary calls John and says, "We offer you $200.00." John says, "We'll let you know." Any ethical problems?

■ ASSIGNMENT 4.21

John Smith is a paralegal who works for Beard, Butler, and Clark. He sends out the following letter. Any ethical problems?

John Smith
Paralegal
310 High St.
Maincity, Ohio 45238
512-663-9410

June 1, 1991

State Unemployment Board
1216 Southern Ave.
Maincity, Ohio 45238

Dear Gentlepeople:

I work for Beard, Butler, and Clark, which represents Mary Anders, who has a claim before your agency. A hearing originally scheduled for June 8, 1991 has been postponed. We request that the hearing be held at the earliest time possible after the 8th.

Sincerely,

John Smith

JS:wps

■ ASSIGNMENT 4.22

In Section C of Chapter 2, there is a long list of tasks that paralegals have performed, and comments by paralegals working in the specialties covered. Identify any three tasks or paralegal comments that *might* pose ethical problems or problems of unauthorized practice. Explain why.

■ ASSIGNMENT 4.23

Compare the Affirmation of Professional Responsibility of NFPA with the Code of Ethics and Professional Responsibility of NALA, page 279. Make a list of the topics or themes covered in one of the documents but not in the other. Is there a difference in emphasis between the two documents?

■ ASSIGNMENT 4.24

Draft your own paralegal code as a class project. First, have a meeting in which you make a list of all the issues that you think should be covered in the code. Divide up the issues by the number of students in the class so that every student has roughly the same number of issues. Each student should draft a proposed rule on each of the issues to which he or she is assigned. Accompany each rule with a brief commentary on why you think the rule should be as stated. Draft alternative versions of the proposed rule if different versions are possible and you want to give the class the chance to examine all of them. The class then meets to vote on each of the proposed rules. Students will make presentations on the proposed rules they have drafted. If the class is not happy with the way in which a particular proposed rule was drafted by a student, the latter will redraft the rule for later consideration by the class. One member of the class should be designated the "code reporter," who records the rules accepted by the class by majority vote.

After you have completed the code, you should consider inviting attorneys from the local bar association to your class in order to discuss your proposed code. Do the same with officials of the closest paralegal association in your area.

☐ Chapter Summary

Attorneys are regulated by the highest court in the state, often with the extensive involvement of the state bar association. Since paralegals cannot practice law and cannot become full members of a bar association, they cannot be punished for a violation of the ethical rules governing attorneys. The American Bar Association is a voluntary association; no attorney must be a member. The ABA publishes ethical rules which the states are free to adopt, modify, or reject.

The current rules of the ABA are found in its *Model Rules of Professional Conduct.* These ethical rules require attorneys to be competent, to act with reasonable diligence and promptness, to charge fees that are reasonable, to avoid conduct that is criminal and fraudulent, to avoid asserting claims and defenses that are frivolous, to safeguard the property of clients, to avoid making false statements of law and fact to a tribunal, to withdraw from a case for appropriate reasons, to maintain the confidentiality of client information, to avoid conflicts of interest, to avoid improper communications with an opponent, to avoid improper solicitation of clients, to avoid improper advertising, to report serious professional misconduct of other attorneys, to avoid assisting nonattorneys engaged in the unauthorized practice of law, and to supervise paralegal employees appropriately.

Ethical opinions and guidelines exist in almost every state on the proper use of a paralegal by an attorney. All states agree that the title used for this employee must not mislead anyone about his or her nonattorney status, and that the employee must disclose his or her nonattorney status when necessary to avoid misunderstanding. Rules also exist on other aspects of the attorney-paralegal relationship, but not all states agree on what these rules should be. The following apply in most states:

Under attorney approval and supervision, paralegals in most states:

- can have their own business card
- can have their name printed on the law firm letterhead
- can sign law firm correspondence
- can give nonlegal advice
- can draft legal documents
- can attend a real estate closing
- can represent clients at agency hearings if authorized by the agency

With few exceptions, paralegals in most states:

- cannot give legal advice
- cannot conduct a deposition
- cannot sign formal court documents
- cannot supervise the execution of a will
- cannot make an appearance in court

Separate ethical rules and guidelines have been adopted by the National Association of Legal Assistants and by the National Federation of Paralegal Associations.

Key Terms

ethics	integrated bar association	Model Rules of Professional
sanctions	mandatory bar association	Conduct
national bar association	unified bar association	Model Code of Professional
state bar association	registration	Responsibility
local bar association	self-regulation	DR

EC
disbarment
suspension
interim suspension
reprimand
private reprimand
censure
public censure
admonition
probation
competence
malpractice
6th amendment
reasonable diligence
reasonable fee
retainer
minimum fee schedule
antitrust law
contingent fee
fee splitting
referral fee
forwarding fee
double billing
padding time sheets
insider trading
pirated software
frivolous positions
commingle funds
adversarial system

withdrawal
cured
impaired attorney
privileged
confidentiality
attorney-client privilege
work-product rule
discoverable
waiver
conflict of interest
divided loyalty
multiple representation
common representation
adverse interests
friendly divorce
switching sides
imputed disqualification
vicarious disqualification
Chinese wall
ethical wall
cone of silence
tainted/contaminated
    employee
quarantined paralegal
conflicts check
lateral hire
disinterested
in-person solicitation
barratry

ambulance chasing
attorney advertising
runner/capper
unauthorized practice of law
model·rule 5.3
tickler
associate/associated
business card
CLA
law-firm letterhead
law directory
legal advice
professional judgment
separate identity of document
real estate closing
deposition/deponent
supervision
delegatitis
second chair
freelance paralegal
Affirmation of Professional
    Responsibility (NFPA)
Code of Ethics and
    Professional
    Responsibility (NALA)
Model Standards and
    Guidelines for Utilization
    of Legal Assistants
    (NALA)

Introduction to the Legal System

■ Chapter Outline

Section A. Basic Terminology

Our legal system is really *three* systems consisting of independent but interconnected governments: federal government, state governments, and local (city or county) governments. The interrelationship among these levels of government is what is known as *federalism*. Each level of government has three *branches*: one that makes laws (legislative branch), one that carries out laws (executive branch), and one that interprets laws and resolves disputes that arise under them (judicial branch).

Federal Government.
Legislative branch: Congress
Executive branch: The President and the federal administrative agencies (see chart in Appendix B.)
Judicial branch: The U.S. Supreme Court, the U.S. Courts of Appeal, the U.S. District Courts, and other federal courts (see Figure 5.3).

State Government.
Legislative branch: The state legislature
Executive branch: The governor and the state administrative agencies
Judicial branch: The state courts (see Figure 5.2).

Local Government.
Legislative branch: City Council or County Commission
Executive branch: Mayor or County Commissioner and the local administrative agencies
Judicial branch: The local courts (see Figure 5.2).

Figure 5.1 provides an overview of the basic kinds of law that govern and that are produced by the above institutions.

Section B. Judicial Systems

1. Jurisdiction

There are fifty state court systems and a federal court system. Each court within a system is identified by its *jurisdiction*. The word jurisdiction has three meanings.

First, the word is often used to refer to the *geographic* area over which a particular court has authority. A state trial court, for example, has *geographic jurisdiction* to hear cases arising in a specific county or district of the state. A state supreme court, in contrast, may have geographic jurisdiction to hear appeals in cases arising anywhere in the state. Thus a state supreme court will often say "in this jurisdiction" when referring to its own state. The phrase has the same meaning as "in this state."

Secondly, the word *jurisdiction* refers to the *power* of a court over a defendant to adjudicate a dispute against that defendant. *Adjudication* is the process by which a court (or administrative agency) resolves a legal dispute through litigation. In order for the court to have the power to order the defendant to do anything (or to refrain from doing something), the court must have *personal jurisdiction* over the defendant. This is also called *in personam jurisdiction*. Personal jurisdiction is acquired through service of process on the defendant.

Thirdly, jurisdiction means the power that a court must have over the *subject matter* or over the particular kind of dispute that has been brought before it. Some of the more common classifications of *subject-matter jurisdiction* are:

(a) *Limited jurisdiction*
(b) *General jurisdiction*
(c) *Exclusive jurisdiction*
(d) *Concurrent jurisdiction*
(e) *Original jurisdiction*
(f) *Appellate jurisdiction*

(a) Limited Jurisdiction.   A court of *limited* (or *special*) *jurisdiction* can hear only certain kinds of cases. A criminal court is not allowed to take a noncriminal case, and a small claims court is authorized to hear only cases in which the plaintiff claims less than a certain amount of money as damages from the defendant.

Another way to look at a court of limited jurisdiction is to say it has a specified *subject-matter jurisdiction*. Its subject-matter jurisdiction is limited to cases that deal with designated subject matters only, such as criminal cases.

(b) General Jurisdiction.   A court of *general jurisdiction* can, with some exceptions, hear any kind of case as long as the case arises within the geographic

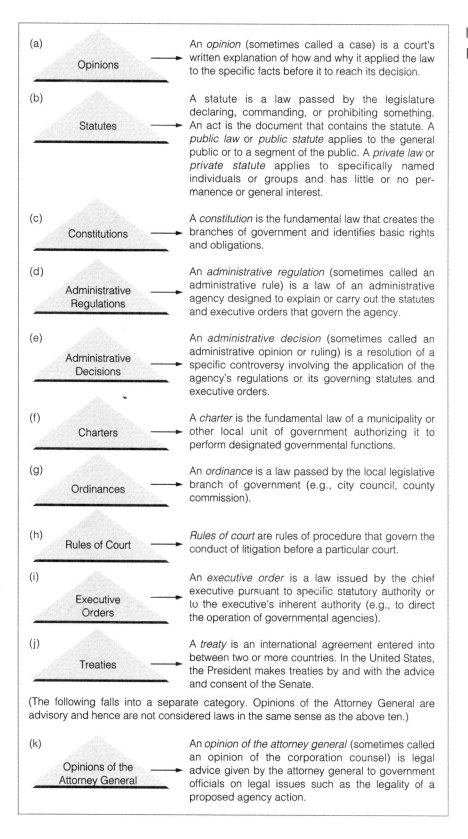

FIGURE 5.1
Kinds of Law

(a) Opinions — An *opinion* (sometimes called a case) is a court's written explanation of how and why it applied the law to the specific facts before it to reach its decision.

(b) Statutes — A *statute* is a law passed by the legislature declaring, commanding, or prohibiting something. An *act* is the document that contains the statute. A *public law* or *public statute* applies to the general public or to a segment of the public. A *private law* or *private statute* applies to specifically named individuals or groups and has little or no permanence or general interest.

(c) Constitutions — A *constitution* is the fundamental law that creates the branches of government and identifies basic rights and obligations.

(d) Administrative Regulations — An *administrative regulation* (sometimes called an administrative rule) is a law of an administrative agency designed to explain or carry out the statutes and executive orders that govern the agency.

(e) Administrative Decisions — An *administrative decision* (sometimes called an administrative opinion or ruling) is a resolution of a specific controversy involving the application of the agency's regulations or its governing statutes and executive orders.

(f) Charters — A *charter* is the fundamental law of a municipality or other local unit of government authorizing it to perform designated governmental functions.

(g) Ordinances — An *ordinance* is a law passed by the local legislative branch of government (e.g., city council, county commission).

(h) Rules of Court — *Rules of court* are rules of procedure that govern the conduct of litigation before a particular court.

(i) Executive Orders — An *executive order* is a law issued by the chief executive pursuant to specific statutory authority or to the executive's inherent authority (e.g., to direct the operation of governmental agencies).

(j) Treaties — A *treaty* is an international agreement entered into between two or more countries. In the United States, the President makes treaties by and with the advice and consent of the Senate.

(The following falls into a separate category. Opinions of the Attorney General are advisory and hence are not considered laws in the same sense as the above ten.)

(k) Opinions of the Attorney General — An *opinion of the attorney general* (sometimes called an opinion of the corporation counsel) is legal advice given by the attorney general to government officials on legal issues such as the legality of a proposed agency action.

Courtrooms in America

boundaries of that court. A *state* court of general jurisdiction can handle any
case that raises *state questions* (i.e., questions arising from the state constitution, state statutes, state regulations, or state common law); a *federal* court of
general jurisdiction can handle any case that raises *federal questions,* (i.e., questions arising from the federal constitution, federal statutes, federal regulations,
or other federal laws).

(c) Exclusive Jurisdiction.   A court of *exclusive jurisdiction* is the only court that can handle a certain kind of case. For example, it may be that the Juvenile Court has exclusive jurisdiction over all cases involving children under a certain age who are charged with acts of delinquency. If this kind of case is brought in another court, there could be a challenge on the ground that the court lacked jurisdiction over the case.

(d) Concurrent Jurisdiction.   Sometimes two courts have jurisdiction over a case; the case could be brought in either court. In such a situation, both courts are said to have *concurrent jurisdiction* over the case. For example, it could be that both the Family Court and a County Court have jurisdiction to enforce a child-custody order.

(e) Original Jurisdiction.   A court of *original jurisdiction* is the first court to hear and decide a case. It is also called a trial court or a court of first instance. In addition, it can be classified as a court of limited jurisdiction (if it can try only certain kinds of cases), or of general jurisdiction (if it can try cases involving any subject matter), or of exclusive jurisdiction (if the trial can take place only in that court), or of concurrent jurisdiction (if the trial can take place either in that court or in another kind of court).

(f) Appellate Jurisdiction.   A court with *appellate jurisdiction* can hear appeals from lower tribunals. An appeal is a review of what a lower court or agency has done to determine if there was any error. Sometimes a party who is dissatisfied with a lower court ruling can appeal as a matter of right to the appellate court (the court must hear the appeal); in other kinds of cases, the appellate court has discretion as to whether it will hear the appeal.

2. State Court Systems

(a) Courts of Original Jurisdiction.   Depending on the particular state, there may be one or more levels of trial courts (courts of original jurisdiction). These courts hear the dispute, determine the facts of the case, and make the initial determination or ruling. In addition, they may sometimes have the power to review cases that were initially decided by an administrative agency.

The most common arrangement is a two-tier system of trial courts. At the lower level are courts of limited or special jurisdiction, the so-called *inferior courts.* Local courts, such as city courts, county courts, or justice of the peace courts, often fall into this category. These courts may have original jurisdiction over relatively minor cases, such as violations of local ordinances and lawsuits involving small sums of money. Also included in this category are special courts that are limited to specific matters, such as surrogate courts or probate courts, which are limited to hearing matters involving the estates of deceased or mentally incompetent persons.

Immediately above the trial courts of limited jurisdiction are the trial courts of general jurisdiction, which usually handle more serious cases, such as violations of state laws or lawsuits involving large sums of money. The name given to the trial courts at this second level varies greatly from state to state. They are known as superior courts, courts of common pleas, district courts, or circuit courts. New York is especially confusing. There the trial court of general jurisdiction is called the *supreme court,* a label reserved in most states for the court of final appeals, the highest court in the system.

This two-tier system is not invariable. Some states may have only one court of original jurisdiction. Moreover, the individual levels may be segmented into divisions. A court of general, original jurisdiction, for example, may be broken up into specialized divisions such as landlord-tenant, family, juvenile, and criminal divisions.

(b) Courts of Appeal.   These courts rarely make the initial decision in a case. Their primary function is to *review* decisions made by lower courts in order to correct *errors of law.* That is, they will look to see if the lower court correctly interpreted and applied the law to the facts of the dispute. In this review process, appellate courts do not make their own findings of fact. No new evidence is taken, and no witnesses are called. The court limits itself to an analysis of the *trial court record* (transcripts of testimony and copies of the various documents that were filed, etc.) to determine if that lower court made any errors of law. Attorneys submit *appellate briefs* containing their arguments on the correctness or incorrectness of what the lower court did.

Depending on the state, there may be not one but two levels of appellate courts. The first level is the court of middle appeals, sometimes called an *intermediate appellate court.* The decisions of this court may in turn be reviewed by a second-level appellate court, the court of final appeals. This latter court, often known as the supreme court, is the highest court in the state, the court of final or last resort.

Figure 5.2 illustrates the lines of appeal in many state court systems.

3. Federal Court System

The federal court system, like those of the states, consists of two basic kinds of courts: courts of original jurisdiction (trial courts) and appellate courts.

(a) Courts of Original Jurisdiction.   The basic federal court at the trial level is the *United States District Court.* There are districts throughout the country, at least one for every state, the District of Columbia, Guam, the Virgin Islands, and Puerto Rico. The District Courts exercise original jurisdiction over most federal litigation and also serve as courts of review for many cases that were initially decided by federal administrative agencies.

In addition to the District Courts, there are several federal courts that exercise original jurisdiction over specialized cases. These include the United States Tax Court, the United States Claims Court, and the United States Court of International Trade. (See Figure 5.3.)

(b) Courts of Appeals.   The federal system, like almost half of the fifty state judicial systems, has two levels of appellate courts: middle appeals and final appeals. The primary courts at the middle level are the *United States Courts of Appeals.* These courts are divided into twelve geographic circuits, eleven of which are made up of groupings of various states and territories, with a twelfth for the District of Columbia. Their primary function is to review the decisions of the federal courts of original jurisdiction. In addition, the decisions of certain federal agencies, notably the National Labor Relations Board, are reviewed directly by the Court of Appeals without first going to the District Court. Finally, there is a specialized Court of Appeals called the Court of Appeals for the Federal Circuit. This court, created in 1982, reviews decisions of the United States Claims Court and the United States Court of International Trade, rulings of the Patent and Trademark Office, and some decisions of the federal District Courts where the United States government is a defendant.

FIGURE 5.2   Hierarchy of State Judicial System

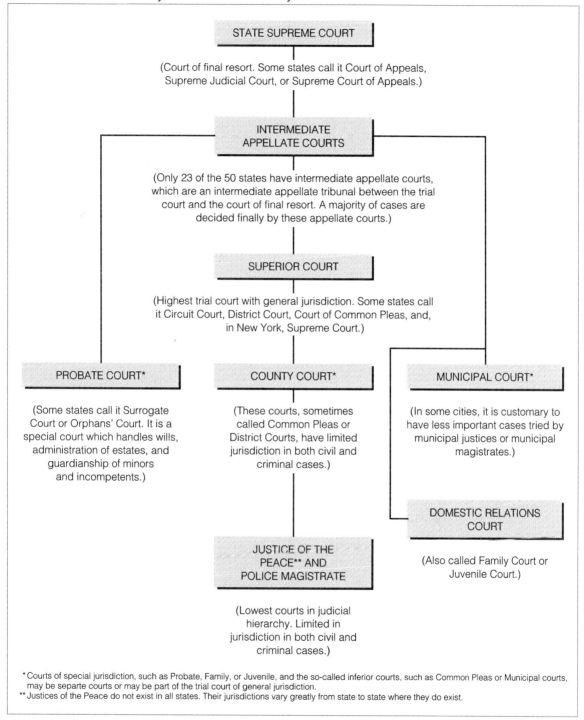

STATE SUPREME COURT

(Court of final resort. Some states call it Court of Appeals,
Supreme Judicial Court, or Supreme Court of Appeals.)

**INTERMEDIATE
APPELLATE COURTS**

(Only 23 of the 50 states have intermediate appellate courts,
which are an intermediate appellate tribunal between the trial
court and the court of final resort. A majority of cases are
decided finally by these appellate courts.)

SUPERIOR COURT

(Highest trial court with general jurisdiction. Some states call
it Circuit Court, District Court, Court of Common Pleas, and,
in New York, Supreme Court.)

PROBATE COURT*

(Some states call it Surrogate
Court or Orphans' Court. It is a
special court which handles wills,
administration of estates, and
guardianship of minors
and incompetents.)

COUNTY COURT*

(These courts, sometimes
called Common Pleas or
District Courts, have limited
jurisdiction in both civil and
criminal cases.)

MUNICIPAL COURT*

(In some cities, it is customary to
have less important cases tried by
municipal justices or municipal
magistrates.)

**DOMESTIC RELATIONS
COURT**

(Also called Family Court or
Juvenile Court.)

**JUSTICE OF THE
PEACE** AND
POLICE MAGISTRATE**

(Lowest courts in judicial
hierarchy. Limited in
jurisdiction in both civil and
criminal cases.)

* Courts of special jurisdiction, such as Probate, Family, or Juvenile, and the so-called inferior courts, such as Common Pleas or Municipal courts,
  may be separte courts or may be part of the trial court of general jurisdiction.
** Justices of the Peace do not exist in all states. Their jurisdictions vary greatly from state to state where they do exist.

Source: *Law and the Courts,* 20 (American Bar Association, 1974).

The federal court of final appeals is, of course, the *United States Supreme
Court,* which provides the final review of the decisions of all federal courts and
agencies. The Supreme Court may also review certain decisions of the state

FIGURE 5.3   Federal Judicial System and Flow of Cases to U.S. Supreme Court

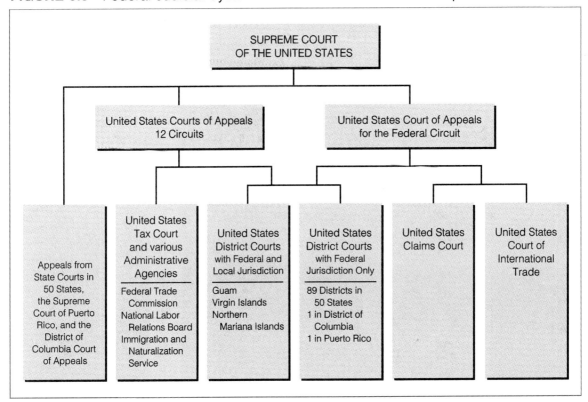

Source: United States Administrative Office of Courts.

courts when these decisions raise questions involving the United States Constitution or a federal statute. (See Figure 5.3.)

Figure 5.4 illustrates the division of the federal court system into twelve geographic circuits. Each circuit has its own United States Court of Appeals. The United States District Courts exist within these circuits.

 ## Section C. Administrative Agencies

An *administrative agency* is a unit of government whose primary mission is to carry out—or administer—the statutes of the legislature and the executive orders of the chief of the executive branch of government. At the federal level, the chief is the president; at the state level, it is the governor; and at most local levels, it is the mayor. As we will see in a moment, many agencies also have rule-making and dispute-resolution responsibilities.

Administrative agencies can have a wide variety of names. Here are some examples:

- Fire Department
- Board of Licenses and Occupations
- Civil Service Commission
- Agency for International Development

FIGURE 5.4   United States Courts of Appeals and United States District Courts

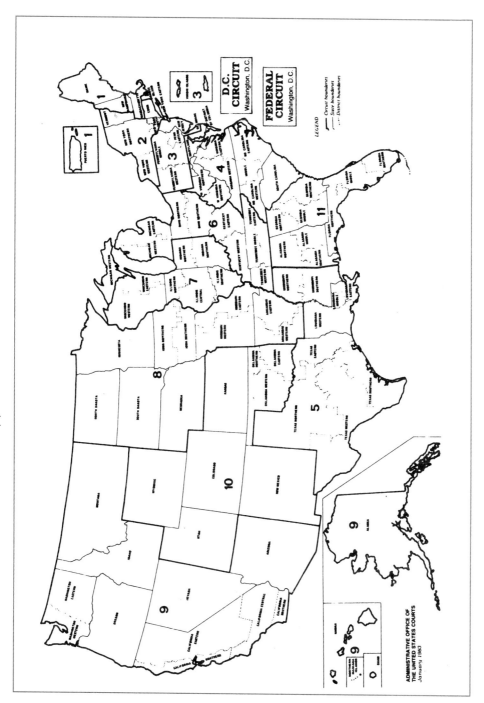

- Department of Defense
- Office of Management and Budget
- Legal Services Corporation
- Bureau of Taxation
- Internal Revenue Service
- Division of Child Support and Enforcement
- Social Security Administration

Certain types of agencies exist at all three levels of government. For example, there is a separate tax collection agency in each of the federal, state, and local governments. Other agencies, however, are unique to one of the levels. For example, only the federal government has a Department of Defense (DOD) and a Central Intelligence Agency (CIA). Nothing comparable exists at the state and local levels of government. The latter have police departments and the highway patrol, but their role is significantly different from the DOD and CIA.

For a list of some of the most important federal agencies, see Appendix B.

There are three main kinds of administrative agencies:

- *Executive department agencies*
- *Independent regulatory agencies*
- *Quasi-independent regulatory agencies*

Executive department agencies exist within the executive branch of the government, often at the cabinet level. Examples include the Department of Agriculture and the Department of Labor. These agencies are answerable to the chief executive, who usually has the power to dismiss those in charge of them.

Independent regulatory agencies exist outside the executive department and, therefore, outside the day-to-day control of the chief executive. Examples include the Interstate Commerce Commission, the Securities and Exchange Commission, and the Public Utilities Commission. Their function is usually to regulate an aspect of society—often a particular industry such as railroads, securities, and public utilities. In order to insulate these agencies from politics, those in charge usually cannot be removed at the whim of the chief executive.

A quasi-independent regulatory agency is a hybrid agency, often with characteristics of the two kinds just described. It often has more independence than an executive department agency, yet it might exist within the executive department.

In addition to carrying out laws, administrative agencies (particularly independent agencies) have *rule-making* functions and *dispute-resolution* functions. In this sense, the agency is acting like the legislature and like the courts:

- The agency often has the authority to write rules and regulations, which are laws. This is the agency's rule-making function. In this sense, the agency is "making law" like a legislature. Such laws are sometimes referred to as *quasi-legislation*.
- The agency has the authority to interpret the laws governing the agency and the laws created by the agency. Furthermore, it often has the authority to resolve disputes that arise over such laws. It will hold administrative hearings and issue administrative decisions. In this sense, the agency is acting like a court when the latter resolves, or adjudicates, disputes. The phrase *quasi-adjudication* means the process by which agencies act like courts in interpreting laws and resolving disputes.

- The agency's primary function, as we have seen, is to carry out or execute designated statutes and executive orders.

Here is an example of an agency using all three of these powers. The SEC (Securities and Exchange Commission):

- Makes laws, e.g., the SEC will write administrative regulations on insider stock trading.

- Resolves disputes, e.g., the SEC will hold a hearing to decide whether a company has violated a securities law. The end product of the hearing will be an administrative decision.

- Carries out laws, e.g., the SEC will accept filings of registration statements containing financial data on issuers of securities pursuant to statutes written by Congress and to securities regulations written by the SEC.

Section D. The Legislative Process

Figure 5.5 contains an outline of the steps that a bill goes through before it becomes a statute. The chart assumes that the legislature considering the bill is *bicameral,* i.e., consists of two houses. The two houses are referred to as the House and the Senate. (In some legislatures the houses may have different names, such as the Assembly and the Senate.) Legislatures with only one house are called *unicameral.* Very few state legislatures are unicameral. Local legislatures, however, such as city councils, are often unicameral.

The process of enactment can involve six major stages:

- Proposal
- Initial committee consideration
- Floor debate
- Conference committee consideration
- Floor debate
- Response of chief executive

The *legislative history* of a statute is what occurs at each of these stages.

(a) Proposal.   The idea for a statute can come from many sources. The chief executive of the government (for example, the president or governor) may initiate the process by sending the legislature a message in which the reasons for a proposed law are stated. Frequently an administrative agency has made a study of a problem, which is the impetus for the proposal. The agency will usually be the entity with responsibility for administrating the proposal if it is enacted into law.

The bar association may prepare a report to the legislature calling for the new legislation. The legislature or chief executive may have established a special commission to study the need for changes in the law and to propose changes where appropriate. The commission might consist of members of the legislature and outside experts. In some states there are ongoing law-revision commissions that frequently make proposals for legislation. In many areas there are councils of government made up of neighboring governments. Such councils often study problems and propose legislative changes. The National Conference of Com-

FIGURE 5.5 The Legislative History of a Statute—How a Bill Becomes a Law

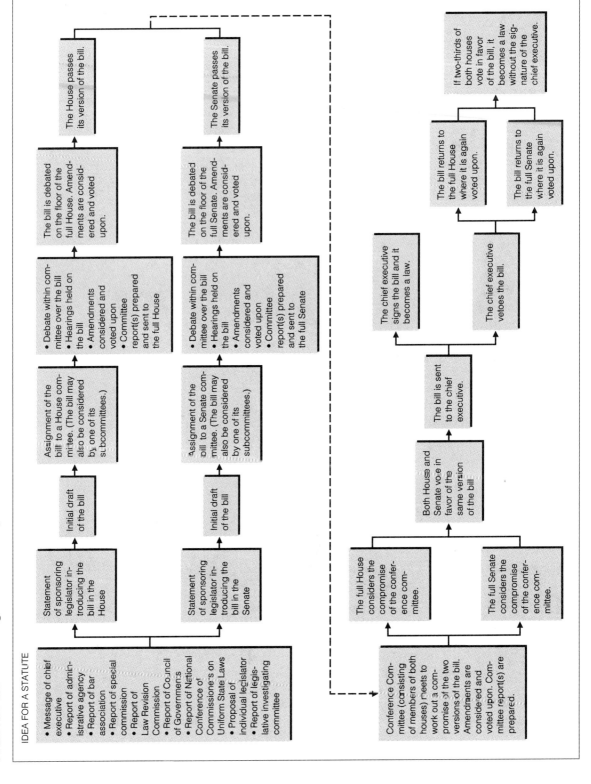

missioners on Uniform State Laws is an organization with members from each state. The conference makes proposals to the state legislatures for the enactment of laws where it deems uniformity to be desirable.

Finally, the idea for the legislation may be generated within the legislature itself. An individual legislator can always propose a *bill*. One or both houses of the legislature may have established an investigating committee to examine a problem and propose legislation where needed.

(b) Initial Committee Consideration.   The next step is for a member of the legislature to introduce the bill. This introduction is usually accompanied by a statement as to why the bill should be enacted. The bill may be introduced in only one of the houses or in both houses simultaneously by a member of each house. If the latter option is not used, the bill will often be introduced in the other house after it has been considered by the first house. As bills are introduced, they are assigned a consecutive number (S 250 is the 250th bill introduced in the Senate during the current session; HR 1753 is the 1753rd bill introduced in the House of Representatives during the current session).

Once the bill is introduced, it follows a similar procedure in each house. The bill is sent to the committee with responsibility over the subject matter of the bill—for example, a bill to change the criminal law might go the the Judiciary Committee. The initial draft of the bill might be considered by this committee and by one of its subcommittees. Hearings are held. Citizens and public officials give testimony for or against the bill. In some legislatures this testimony is transcribed so that a word-for-word record is made available. Legislators often propose amendments to the bill, which are voted on by the committee. The committee then issues a report summarizing why the bill is needed and what its major provisions are. If there is disagreement on the committee, a minority report is often prepared.

(c) Floor Debate.   The bill with its accompanying report(s) then goes to the floor of the house of which the committee is a part. The bill is debated by the full house. During the debate, which will usually be recorded or transcribed, questions are asked by members as to the meaning of certain provisions in the bill: what is covered and what is not. Amendments are often made from the floor and voted upon.

(d) Conference Committee Consideration.   Since both houses act independently of each other in considering the bill, it is rare that they will both produce exactly the same bill. Inevitably, the amendment process leads to different versions of the proposed law. To resolve these differences, a *conference committee* is established, consisting of key members of both houses, such as the chairpersons of the committees that initially considered the bill or the members who first introduced or sponsored the bill. A compromise is attempted in the conference committee. Amendments are considered and a final report of the conference committee is issued. Dissenting members of the committee might prepare a minority report. The majority report summarizes the major terms of the compromise and explains why it should be enacted by each house.

(e) Floor Debate.   The conference committee compromise then goes back to the floor of each house where more debate, explanations, and amendments are considered. Again, usually everything is recorded or transcribed. If both houses pass the same version of the bill, usually by a majority vote, it goes to the chief executive.

(f) Response of Chief Executive.   The bill becomes law if the chief executive signs it. When it is signed, the chief executive will sometimes make a statement as to why this action is being taken. If he or she *vetoes* the bill, or refuses to sign it, the bill goes back to the legislature, often with an explanation as to why it is being disapproved. If a designated number of legislators (usually two-thirds) in each house still vote in favor of the bill, it becomes law over the objection of the chief executive.

☐ Chapter Summary

There are ten main categories of laws: opinions, statutes, constitutions, administrative regulations, administrative decisions, charters, ordinances, rules of court, executive orders, and treaties. (In a special category are opinions of the attorney general.) These laws are written by one or more of the three branches of government (legislative, executive, and judicial) that exist within the three levels of government (federal, state, and local).

An understanding of jurisdiction is key to understanding our judicial system. Two of the main kinds of jurisdiction are: geographic jurisdiction, which specifies an area of the country over which a court can exercise its power, and subject-matter jurisdiction, which specifies the kinds of cases over which a court can exercise its power. There are six main kinds of subject-matter jurisdiction: limited, general, exclusive, concurrent, original, and appellate. Courts of original jurisdiction are the trial courts. There may be two levels of trial courts within a judicial system. There may also be two levels of courts with appellate jurisdiction.

There are three kinds of administrative agencies: executive department agencies, independent regulatory agencies, and quasi-independent regulatory agencies. Agencies serve three main functions: to carry out statutes and executive orders, to write rules and regulations, and to resolve disputes

that arise under laws over which the agency has responsibility.

The federal legislature (Congress) and most state legislatures are bicameral, that is, they consist of two houses. For a bill to become a statute, it must go through approximately six stages. First, the bill is proposed, and then introduced into one of the houses of the legislature. It may be introduced into the other house simultaneously or at a later date. Second, a committee of each house gives the bill initial consideration. If the committee votes in favor of the bill, it goes to the next stage. Third, all of the members of one of the houses debate and vote on the bill, and then all of the members of the other house debate and vote on the bill. Fourth, a conference committee made up of members of both houses considers the bill. The role of this committee is to try to reconcile any differences in the two versions of the bill passed by each house. Fifth, the bill goes back to the full membership of each house for a vote on what the conference committee produced. Sixth, the chief executive signs or vetoes the bill. If he or she vetoes or refuses to sign the bill, it can still become a statute if two-thirds of each house vote to override the chief executive. The legislative history of a statute consists of what happens during these six stages.

Key Terms

federalism
legislative branch
executive branch
judicial branch
opinion
case
statute
act
public law/public statute

private law/private statute
constitution
administrative regulation
administrative decision
ruling
charter
ordinance
rules of court
executive order

treaty
opinion of the attorney
   general
geographic jurisdiction
personal jurisdiction
in personam jurisdiction
adjudication
subject-matter jurisdiction
limited jurisdiction

special jurisdiction
general jurisdiction
state question
federal question
exclusive jurisdiction
concurrent jurisdiction
original jurisdiction
court of first instance
appellate jurisdiction
appeal as a matter of right
inferior court
surrogate court
review

trial court record
appellate brief
intermediate appellate court
supreme court
superior court
United States District Court
United States Court of
    Appeals
United States Supreme Court
administrative agency
executive department agency
independent regulatory
    agency

quasi-independent agency
rule-making function
quasi-legislation
quasi-adjudication
bicameral/unicameral
legislative history
uniform state laws
bill
floor debate
conference committee
veto

II

The Skills of a Paralegal

Contents

Introduction to Legal Analysis

■ Chapter Outline

Section A. The Structure of Legal
   Analysis
Section B. The Element-Identification
   Skill

Section C. The Issue-Statement Skill
Section D. The Definitions Skill
Section E. Briefing Court Opinions
Section F. Applying Court Opinions

 ## Section A. The Structure of Legal Analysis

Legal analysis is the process of connecting a rule of law to a set of facts in order to determine how that rule might apply to a particular situation. The goal of the process is to solve a legal dispute or to prevent one from arising. Here is a relatively simple example:

Rule +	Facts +	Issue +	Connection = (rule and facts)	Conclusion
§ 10. "Any business within the city must apply for and obtain a license to do business within the city limits."	Fran owns a grocery store in the city.	Is a grocery store in the city a "business" under § 10 requiring a license "to do business"?	A grocery store is a "business." Fran runs this business within the city.	§ 10 requires Fran to have a license.

Of course, not all legal analysis is this simple. *Yet the basic structure of a legal argument will always have this format.* Note the following characteristics of the process:

■ You start with a specific rule, such as a statute or regulation. You quote the relevant language exactly.

■ The major facts are stated.

■ The legal issue states the controversy in terms of specific language in the rule and specific facts that raise the controversy.

■ You draw the *connection* between specific language in the rule and specific facts. The analysis *is* this connection.

■ You reach a conclusion based on the above steps. The conclusion is phrased in terms of the rule.

More complicated example:

Rule +	Facts +	Issue +	Connection = (rule and facts)	Conclusion
§ 10. "Any business within the city must apply for and obtain a license to do business within the city limits."	Bill and his neighbors in the city have formed a food co-op through which members buy their food collectively from a wholesale company. All funds received by the co-op go for expenses and the purchase of food.	Is a non-profit co-op a "business" within the meaning of § 10 requiring a license "to do business"?	The city argues that the co-op is a business in the city. The co-op concedes that it is in the city but argues that it does not "do business," since the co-op does not earn a profit.	The co-op has the better argument. § 10 was not intended to cover non-profit ventures. Hence, the co-op does not have to have a license.

The following is a more detailed statement of the analysis, which is referred to as the "connection" in the above charts:

§ 10 provides as follows:

"Any business within the city must apply for and obtain a license to do business within the city limits."

There are two main *elements* to § 10:

1. Any business
2. Within the city

When the facts fit within these two elements, the entity in question must apply for and obtain a license to do business. The consequence of the rule is the need to be licensed. This consequence is mandated once both elements exist.

1. Any Business. The city claims that the co-op is a business. It does not matter to the city that profits in the traditional sense are not earned by the co-op. According to the city, the co-op members are "selling" goods to each other. A business is any entity that engages in any form of selling.

The co-op, on the other hand, argues that § 10 was not intended to cover co-ops. A business is an enterprise that makes a profit over and above expenses. Nothing of this kind occurs in the co-op. Everything taken in by the co-op goes out in the form of food purchases and expenses. Hence, the co-op is not a business and does not have to have a license.

2. Within the City. There is no dispute between the parties on this element. The city and the co-op agree that the co-op operates within the city limits. The only dispute in this case concerns whether the co-op is a business.

. . . .

If you had included legal research data on the meaning of § 10, the analysis would *also* have contained:

- A discussion of court opinions, if any, that interpret § 10
- A discussion of administrative regulations, if any, that implement § 10
- A discussion of the legislative history, if available, of § 10
- A discussion of secondary authority, if any, that interprets § 10, such as legal periodical literature and treatises

- A discussion of constitutional provisions, if any, that affect the applicability of § 10
- Etc.

The analysis, the facts, the issues, etc., are often presented in the format of a *memorandum of law,* which is simply a written explanation of what the law is and how it might apply to a fact situation.

We turn now to three skills that are important in legal analysis: the element-identification skill, the issue-statement skill, and the definitions skill.

 ## Section B. The Element-Identification Skill

All rules have consequences. There are rules that impose punishments, require payments, establish norms of behavior, institute procedures, etc. How do you determine when the consequence of a particular rule must be followed? The answer is: When *all* of the *elements* of that rule apply. In our example on § 10, note that the analysis proceeded through a discussion of the elements of § 10. An element is a component or portion of a rule. If you can show that all of the elements of a rule apply to a fact situation, then the rule itself—and its consequence—applies to the fact situation. The failure of any one of the elements to apply means that the entire rule cannot apply. In effect, each element is a precondition of the applicability of the entire rule.

The elements of § 10 were relatively short (business; within the city). This is not always so. How long should an element be? There is no absolute answer to this question. The two main criteria to keep in mind are these: (1) each element must be a precondition to the consequence of the entire rule, and (2) you should be able to discuss each element separately with relative ease.

Let us examine some additional examples:

> **§ 971.22. Change of place of trial.** The defendant may move for a change of the place of trial on the ground that an impartial trial cannot be had in the county. The motion shall be made at the time of arraignment.

Step one is to break the rule into its elements. The effect or consequence of the rule is to change the place of the trial. Ask yourself what must happen before this consequence will follow. Ask yourself what conditions or preconditions must exist before the result will occur. The answer will provide you with the elements of the rule:

1. Defendant
2. May move for a change of the place of trial
3. On the ground that an impartial trial cannot be had in the county
4. The motion must be made at the time of the arraignment

Hence, there are four elements to § 971.22. All four must exist before the place of the trial will be moved.

Suppose you are analyzing the following rule found in a statute:

> **§ 25–403.** A pharmacist must not sell prescription drugs to a minor.

As with almost all rules, this one is not already broken down into elements. You must identify the elements on your own. Ask yourself what conditions must exist before § 25–403 is violated, which would be the consequence of its applicability. Your answer will consist of its elements:

1. Pharmacist
2. Must not sell
3. Prescription drugs
4. To a minor

No violation exists unless all four elements of the statute are established. If, for example, a pharmacist sells simple aspirin (a nonprescription drug), he or she has not violated the statute. The third element cannot be established. Hence no violation, since one of the elements (preconditions) cannot be met.

For a number of reasons, rules such as statutes and regulations can be difficult to break into elements. For example, the rule may be long or may contain:

- Lists
- Alternatives
- Exceptions or provisos

Nevertheless, the same process is used. You must take the time to dissect the rule into its component elements. Examine the following rule as we try to identify its elements.

§ 5. While representing a client in connection with contemplated or pending litigation, a lawyer shall not advance or guarantee financial assistance to his client, except that a lawyer may advance or guarantee court costs, expenses of investigation, expenses of medical examination, and costs of obtaining and presenting evidence provided the client remains ultimately liable for such expenses.

Elements of § 5:

1. A lawyer
2. Representing a client in connection with contemplated litigation or in connection with pending litigation
3. Shall not advance financial assistance to his client or guarantee financial assistance to his client, except that the following is proper:
   a. lawyer advances or guarantees court costs, or
   b. lawyer advances or guarantees expenses of investigation, or
   c. lawyer advances or guarantees expenses of medical examination, or
   d. lawyer advances or guarantees costs of obtaining and presenting evidence

   as long as the client remains ultimately liable for all expenses (a–d).

When an element is stated in the alternative, list all the alternatives within the same element. Alternatives related to one element should be kept within the phrasing of that element. The same is true of exception or proviso clauses. State them within the relevant element, since they are intimately related to the applicability of that element.

In the above example, the most complicated element is the third—(3). Within it there are lists, alternatives, an exception, and a proviso. But they all relate to the same point—the propriety of financial assistance. None of the subdivisions of the third element should be stated as a separate element. Sometimes you must do some unraveling of a rule in order to identify its elements. This certainly had to be done with the third element of § 5. Do not be afraid to pick the rule apart in order to cluster its thoughts around unified themes that should stand alone as elements. Diagram the rule for yourself as you examine it.

If more than one rule is involved in a statute, regulation, constitutional provision, charter, ordinance, etc., treat one rule at a time. Each rule should have its own elements, and, when appropriate, each element should be subdivided into its separate components, as in the third element of § 5.

Once you have broken the rule down into its elements, you have the structure of the analysis in front of you. Each element becomes a separate section of your analysis. You discuss one element at a time, concentrating on those that pose the greatest difficulties.

Element identification has many benefits in the law, as demonstrated in Figure 6.1.

To a very large extent, as you can see in Figure 6.1, legal analysis proceeds by *element analysis.* A major characteristic of sloppy legal analysis is that it does not clearly take the reader (or listener) through the important elements of rules that must be analyzed.

FIGURE 6.1
The Benefits of Element Identification

- *Identifying Issues.* Once you identify the elements of a rule, the next step is to find the *elements* that are most likely to be in contention. These elements become the basis of legal issues (as we shall see in the next section).

- *Drafting a Complaint.* When drafting a legal complaint, you often organize your factual allegations around the *elements* of each important rule in the controversy. (The most important rule is called the *cause of action,* which is a legally acceptable reason for suing someone; negligence is an example.)

- *Drafting an Answer.* When drafting an answer to a complaint, you often state your defenses by alleging facts that support the *elements* of each defense. (Most defenses, such as the statute of limitation, are nothing more than rules designed to defeat the claims of another.)

- *Organizing an Interview of a Client.* One of the goals of interviewing a client is to obtain information on facts relevant to each of the *elements* of the potential causes of action and defenses in the case. Element analysis, therefore, helps you organize the interview and give it direction.

- *Organizing an Investigation.* One of the goals of investigation is to obtain information on facts relevant to each of the *elements* of the potential causes of action and defenses in the case. Element analysis, therefore, helps you organize the investigation and give it direction.

- *Conducting a Deposition.* During a deposition, many of the questions are designed to determine what facts the other side may be able to prove that support the *elements* of the potential causes of action and defenses in the case.

- *Organizing a Memorandum of Law.* One of the purposes of a memorandum of law is to tell the reader what rules might apply to the case, what *elements* of these rules might be in contention, and what strategy should be undertaken as a result of this analysis.

- *Organizing an Examination Answer.* Many essay examinations in school are organized around the key *elements* of the rules that should be analyzed.

- *Charging a Jury.* When a judge charges (that is, instructs) a jury, he or she will go over each of the *elements* of the causes of action and defenses in the case in order to tell the jury what standard to use to determine whether facts in support of those elements have been proven during the trial.

■ ASSIGNMENT 6.1

Break the following rules into their elements:

(a) § 75(b). A lawyer shall not enter into a business transaction with a client if they have differing interests therein and if the client expects the lawyer to exercise his professional judgment therein for the protection of the client.

(b) § 38. A person or agency suing or being sued in an official public capacity is not required to execute a bond as a condition for relief under this section unless required by the court in its discretion.

(c) § 1.2. A lawyer may not permit his legal assistant to represent a client in litigation or other adversary proceedings or to perform otherwise prohibited functions unless authorized by statute, court rule or decision, administrative rule or regulation or customary practice.

(d) § 179(a)(7). If at any time it is determined that application of best available control technology by 1988 will not assure protection of public water supplies, agricultural and industrial uses, and the protection and propagation of fish, shellfish and wildlife, and allow recreational activities in and on the water, additional effluent limitations must be established to assure attainment or maintenance of water quality. In setting such limitations, EPA must consider the relationship of the economic and social costs of their achievement, including any economic or social dislocation in the affected community or communities, the social and economic benefits to be obtained, and determine whether or not such effluent limitations can be implemented with available technology or other alternative control strategies.

Section C. The Issue-Statement Skill

After you have broken a rule into its elements, the next step is to identify the *element in contention*. That element then becomes the basis of a *legal issue*. An element is in contention when you can predict that the other side in the controversy will probably not agree with your interpretation of that element and/or with whether the facts support that element. If a rule has five elements and you anticipate disagreement over all of them, phrase five separate issues. If, however, only one of the five elements will probably be in contention, phrase only one issue. There is no need to waste time over elements that will most likely not be the basis of disagreement.

Legal issues are often phrased in *shorthand* such as "Does § 34 apply?" "Can a van be burglarized?" A more *comprehensive* phrasing of a legal issue would consist of:

■ A brief quote from the element in contention, and

■ Several of the important facts relevant to that contention

For example, suppose that you are analyzing the following rule and facts:

§ 92. The operator of any vehicle riding on a sidewalk shall be fined $100.

Facts: Fred rides his ten-speed bicycle on the sidewalk. He is charged with violating § 92.

The element breakdown and issue statement would be as follows:

Elements of § 92:

1. Operator
2. Any vehicle

3. Riding

4. On a sidewalk

Issue: Is a ten-speed bicycle a "vehicle" under § 92?

The parties will probably agree that Fred rode his bicycle on a sidewalk and that Fred was the operator of his bicycle. The first, third, and fourth elements, therefore, should not be be made into legal issues. The only disagreement will be over the second element. Hence it is the basis of an issue. Note the quote marks around the element in contention (vehicle) and the inclusion of an important fact that is relevant to this contention (it was a ten-speed bicycle).

■ ASSIGNMENT 6.2

Provide a comprehensive phrasing of the legal issue or issues in each of the following situations:

(a) *Facts:* Harry Franklin works for the XYZ Agency. In one of the Agency's personnel files there is a notation that Paul Drake, another Agency employee, was once arrested for fraud. Harry obtains this information from this file and tells his wife about it. (She also knows Paul.) Harry is unaware that Paul has told at least three other employees of his fraud arrest.

   Regulation: § 20(d). It shall be unlawful for any employee of the XYZ Agency to divulge confidential material in any file of the Agency.

(b) *Facts:* Jones has a swimming pool in his backyard. The pool is intended for use by the Jones family members and guests who are present when an adult is there to supervise. One hot summer night, a neighbor's child opens an unlocked door of a fence that surrounds the Jones' yard and goes into the pool. (There is no separate fence around the pool.) The child knows that he should not be there without an adult. No one else is at the pool. The child drowns.

   Statute: § 77. Property owners are liable for the foreseeable harm that occurs on their property.

Section D. The Definitions Skill

Language can frequently be defined broadly or narrowly. Assume that Jim meets a friend in a parking lot and says to him, "You can use my car." Jim is quite upset, however, when the friend returns five months later after driving the car through about twenty states. The friend asserts that he did nothing more than "use" the car. The question becomes: What is the definition of "use?"

Broad Definition: Use means to operate or employ something for any purpose and for any length of time.

Narrow Definition: Use means to operate or employ something for a reasonable purpose within a reasonable time.

The same dynamic is found when interpreting ambiguous language within elements in contention. Recall the bicycle example discussed in the preceding section:

§ 92. The operator of any vehicle riding on a sidewalk shall be fined $100.

Facts: Fred rides his ten-speed bicycle on the sidewalk. He is charged with violating § 92.

Issue: Is a ten-speed bicycle a "vehicle" under § 92?

This controversy may well turn on whether "vehicle" can be defined broadly or narrowly. Fred will argue that it should be interpreted narrowly, whereas the government will argue for a broad definition:

Broad Definition: **Vehicle means any method of transportation.**

Narrow Definition: **Vehicle means any motorized method of transportation.**

Whenever you have an element in contention that contains ambiguous language, you should put yourself in the shoes of each person in the controversy to try to identify what definition of the language each would propose. Think of a broad and a narrow definition, and state which side would argue which definition.

To help resolve a definition dispute, you would undertake some legal research—for example, you would try to find cases interpreting "vehicle" under § 92 and trace the legislative history of § 92. Often, however, you will *not* find the answer in the library. The precise question may never have arisen before. This is particularly true of recent statutes and regulations.

■ ASSIGNMENT 6.3

In each of the following problems, identify any ambiguous language in elements in contention. Give broad and narrow definitions of this language and state which side would argue which definition. Do not do any legal research.

(a) *Facts:* Alice Anderson is nine months pregnant. A police officer gives her a ticket for driving in a car-pool lane in violation of § 101. The officer said he gave her the ticket because she was alone in the car at the time.

   Regulation: § 101. Car-pool lanes can be used only by cars in which there is at least one passenger in the car with the driver.

(b) *Facts:* Mary is arrested for violating § 55. She is charged as a felon. She forced open the lock on the driver's side of a van at 5 P.M. Mary didn't know that the door on the passenger side was unlocked. She went into the back of the van and fell asleep on the floor. The police arrested her after waking her up at 9 P.M. The owner of the van claims that a $20 bill is missing. Mary had a $20 bill on her, but she said it was her own.

   Statute: § 55. A person who breaks and enters a dwelling at night for the purpose of stealing property therein shall be charged as a felon.

■ ASSIGNMENT 6.4

Analyze the problem in the following situations. Do not do any legal research. Simply use the facts and rules you are given. Be sure to include in your analysis what you have learned about elements, issues, and definitions.

(a) Susan is arrested for carrying a dangerous weapon. While in a hardware store, she got into an argument with another customer. She picked up a hammer from the counter and told the other customer to get out of her way. The customer did so and Susan put the hammer back. She was later arrested and charged with violating § 402(b), which provides: "It is unlawful for anyone to carry a dangerous weapon."

(b) It is against the law in your state "to practice law without a license" (§ 39). Fred is charged with violating this law. He told a neighbor that a certain parking ticket received by the neighbor could be ignored since the police officer was incorrect in issuing the ticket. In gratitude, the neighbor buys Fred a drink. (Assume that what Fred told the neighbor about the ticket was accurate and that Fred is *not* an attorney.)

(c) Ted and Ann are married. Ted is a carpenter and Ann is a lawyer. They buy an old building that Ted will repair for Ann's use as a law office. Ted asks Ann to handle the legal aspects of the purchase of the building. She does so. Soon after the purchase, they decide to obtain a divorce. Ted asks Ann if she will draw up the divorce papers. She does so. Ted completes the repair work on the building for which Ann pays him a set amount. Has Ann violated the rule stated in problem (a) in Assignment 6.1, page 316, above?

Section E. Briefing Court Opinions

The word *brief* has several meanings.

First, to *brief* a court opinion is to summarize its major components (e.g., key facts, issues, reasoning, disposition). Such a brief is your own summary of the opinion for later use. Second, a *trial brief* is an attorney's set of notes on how to conduct the trial. The notes (often placed in a *trial notebook*) will be on the opening statement, witnesses, exhibits, direct and cross-examination, closing argument, etc. This trial brief is sometimes called a trial manual or trial book. Third, the *appellate brief* is the formal written argument to a court of appeals on why a lower court's decision should be affirmed, modified, or reversed. It is submitted to the appellate court and to the other side.

Here our concern is the first meaning of the word brief—a summarization of the major components of a court opinion. Before we examine these components, we will study an opinion as it might appear in a library reporter volume.

The circled numbers are explained after the opinion.

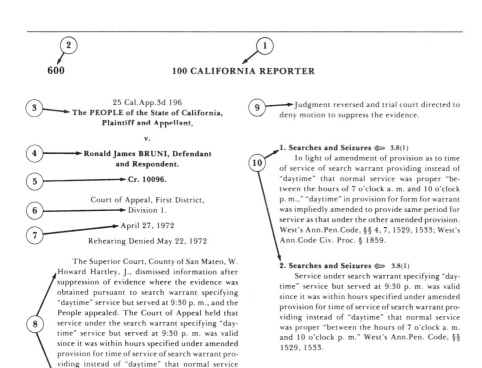

2

600   **100 CALIFORNIA REPORTER**   **1**

3
25 Cal.App.3d 196
**The PEOPLE of the State of California,
Plaintiff and Appellant,**

v.

4   **Ronald James BRUNI, Defendant
and Respondent.**

5   **Cr. 10096.**

6   Court of Appeal, First District,
Division 1.

7   April 27, 1972

Rehearing Denied May 22, 1972

8   The Superior Court, County of San Mateo, W. Howard Hartley, J., dismissed information after suppression of evidence where the evidence was obtained pursuant to search warrant specifying "daytime" service but served at 9:30 p. m., and the People appealed. The Court of Appeal held that service under the search warrant specifying "daytime" service but served at 9:30 p. m. was valid since it was within hours specified under amended provision for time of service of search warrant providing instead of "daytime" that normal service was proper "between the hours of 7 o'clock a. m. and 10 o'clock p. m."

9   Judgment reversed and trial court directed to deny motion to suppress the evidence.

1. Searches and Seizures ⟺ 3.8(1)

10   In light of amendment of provision as to time of service of search warrant providing instead of "daytime" that normal service was proper "between the hours of 7 o'clock a. m. and 10 o'clock p. m.," "daytime" in provision for form for warrant was impliedly amended to provide same period for service as that under the other amended provision. West's Ann.Pen.Code, §§ 4, 7, 1529, 1533; West's Ann.Code Civ. Proc. § 1859.

2. Searches and Seizures ⟺ 3.8(1)

Service under search warrant specifying "daytime" service but served at 9:30 p. m. was valid since it was within hours specified under amended provision for time of service of search warrant providing instead of "daytime" that normal service was proper "between the hours of 7 o'clock a. m. and 10 o'clock p. m." West's Ann.Pen. Code, §§ 1529, 1533.

Evelle J. Younger, Atty. Gen. of California, Edward P. O'Brien, Robert R. Granucci, Deputy Attys. Gen., San Francisco, for appellant.   (11)

William F. DeLucchi, Regalado & Lindquist, Redwood City, for respondent.

Smith, Judge.   (12)

The People appeal from a judgment dismissing an Information after suppression of evidence,   (13) where the evidence was obtained pursuant to a search warrant specifying "daytime" service, but   (14) which was served at 9:30 p. m. at night.

In 1970, section 1533 of the Penal Code was amended to eliminate the provision for "daytime" service for normal service of a search warrant. Instead of "daytime," the statute now specifies normal service as proper "between the hours of 7   (15) o'clock a. m. and 10 o'clock p. m." Apparently by oversight, the Legislature neglected to also amend the mandatory provisions under section 1529 of the Penal Code, which continues to require "daytime" service. An inconsistency exists as to the mandatory requirements of search warrants unless section 1529 of the Penal Code is read as having been amended by implication when section 1533 of the Penal Code was expressly amended. Otherwise, the only warrant an issuing magistrate could authorize, without possibly violating one or the other statute, would be one for unlimited service at any hour of day or night upon a showing of good cause. Nothing suggests that this was the legislative intent.

The provisions of the Penal Code "are to be construed according to the fair import of their terms, with a view to effect its objects and to promote justice." (Pen.Code. § 4.) "In the construction of a statute the intention of the Legislature . . . is to be pursued, if possible; and when a   (18) general and particular provision are inconsistent, the latter is paramount to the former." (Code Civ.Proc., § 1859.)   (16)

[1]   Under the definition in Section 7 of the   (10a) Penal Code, daytime is defined as "the period between sunrise and sunset." This general provision is clearly inconsistent with the particular provision relating to service of search warrants between the hours of 7 o'clock a. m. and 10 o'clock p. m. estab-   (18) lished under the amendment of section 1533 of the Penal Code. Under the general rules of statutory construction, we interpret "daytime" in the particular provisions of section 1529 of the Penal Code

(19)   as having been impliedly amended to provide the same period for service as that under amended section 1533 of the Penal Code.

(18)   " . . . 'where the language of a statute is reasonably susceptible of two constructions, one of which in application will render it reasonable, fair and harmonious with its manifest purpose, and another which would be productive of absurd consequences, the former construction will be adopted.' (citation); and 'if certain provisions are repugnant, effect should be given to those which best comport   (17) with the end to be accomplished and render the statute effective, rather than nugatory.'" (Dept. of Motor Vehicles of California v. Indus. Acc. Com. (1939) 14 Cal.2d 189, 195, 93 P.2d 131, 134.)

(10a)
(19)   [2]   We hold that the People are correct in their assertion that service was valid since it was within the hours specified under amended section 1533 of the Penal Code. See Tidwell v. Superior Court (1971) 17 Cal.App.3d 780, 786-787, 95 Cal.Rptr. 213.   (17)

This court has always been scrupulous in demanding a high standard for the admission of evidence pursuant to warrants. Our ruling today does not violate this standard. The integrity of our trial system in large measure depends upon the integrity of the evidence admitted at trial. The case before us deals with the timing of serving a warrant.   (21) If the case had involved other aspects of the warrant such as its specificity, our result would probably have been different.

The judgment is reversed, and the trial court is directed to deny the motion to suppress the   (20) evidence.

Jones, Judge (Concurring in result only).   (22)

Thomas, Judge (Dissenting).   (23)
If the California legislature intended to amend section 1529 of the Penal Code, it should have done so expressly. It is not the function of the judiciary to amend the statutes passed by the legislature. The public has a right to rely on the written language of statutes; in fact, we frequently admonish the citizenry if they ignore that language. For the courts to alter the language after the fact not only infringes upon the right of the legislature to be the sole entity under our system that can enact and amend legislation, but also is a signal to the public and to government officials that they can no longer trust the law as validly passed by the legislative branch. Both results are intolerable.

I would affirm the judgment below.

---

① The *California Reporter* is an unofficial reporter of state opinions in California. The "100" indicates the volume number of the reporter.

② The *Bruni* case begins on page 000. The citation of this case is *People v. Bruni*, 25 Cal. App. 3d 196, 100 Cal. Rptr. 600 (1972). The official cite is given at the top of the caption above the word PEOPLE.

③ When the *People* or the state brings an action, it is often a criminal case. This is an appellate court decision. Trial court decisions are appealed to the appellate court. The *appellant* is the party bringing the appeal because of dissatisfaction with the ruling or decision of the lower court. The state of California brought the case as the plaintiff and prosecutor in the lower court (Superior Court, County of San Mateo) and is now the appellant in the higher court (Court of Appeal, First District, Division 1).

④ Bruni was the defendant in the lower court since he was being sued or, in this case, charged with a crime. The appeal is taken against him by the People (appellant), because the lower court ruling was favorable to Bruni, to the dissatisfaction of the People. The party against whom a case is brought on appeal is called the *respondent.* Another word for respondent is *appellee.*

⑤ "Cr. 10096" refers to the *docket,* or calendar number of the case. "Cr." stands for *criminal.*

⑥ Make careful note of the name of the court writing the opinion. As soon as possible, you must learn the hierarchy of state courts in your state. In many states, there are three levels of courts: trial level, middle appeal level, and supreme level. (Most cases are appealed from the trial court to the middle appeal level, and then to the supreme level.) Here, we know from the title of the court (Court of Appeal) that it is an appellate court. It is not the supreme court, because in California the highest court is the California Supreme Court.

The name of the court is significant because of "legal authority." If the court is the highest or supreme court of the state, then the case would be applicable throughout the state. A middle appeals court case, on the other hand, applies only in the area of the state over which it has jurisdiction. When you see that the case was written by a trial or middle appeals court, you are immediately put on notice that you must check to determine whether the case was ever appealed subsequent to the date of the case. The main system for checking is called shepardizing.

⑦ When a case is being cited, only the year (here, 1972) is used, not the month or day (April 27). Sometimes, the date of the hearing or rehearing will be given as well as the date of the decision. The year of the decision is still the critical one for citation purposes.

⑧ Here the editors provide the reader with a summary of what the case says. The court did not write this summary; the editors did. It, therefore, is not an official statement of the law. It is merely an aid to the reader, who can quickly read this summary to determine whether the case covers relevant areas of law. This summary paragraph is often called the *syllabus.*

⑨ Here continues the unofficial summary, providing the reader with what procedurally must happen as a result of the April 27 case.

⑩ These are editor's *headnotes,* which are small-paragraph summaries of portions of the case. When the editors first read the case, they decide how many major topics or issues are covered in the case. Each of these topics is summarized in a headnote, all of which are then given consecutive numbers, here 1 and 2. These numbers correspond with the bracketed numbers [1] and [2] in the case itself. (See ⑩ₐ.) If, for example, you wanted to read the portion of the case that was summarized in the second headnote of the case, you would go to the text of the case that begins with the bracketed [2].

The headnotes also have *a topic and a key number,* here "Searches and Seizures ☞ 3.8(1)." Each headnote will also be printed in the *digests* of West Publishing Company. Digests are volumes that contain nothing but the headnotes of court opinions. You can find out what other courts have said about the same or similar points by going to the digest volumes, looking up the key topic and number of a headnote (e.g., Searches and Seizures ☞ 3.8(1)), and reading summary paragraphs from many court cases such as our case, *People v. Bruni.*

⑪ Here are the attorneys that represented the appellant and respondent on appeal. Note that the attorney general's office represented the People. The attorney general or the district attorney's office represents the state in criminal cases.

⑫ The opinion begins with the name of the judge who wrote the opinion, Judge Smith. In this spot you will sometimes find the words "The Court," *"Per curiam,"* or *"Memorandum Opinion,"* which simply means that the court decided not to mention the name of the individual judge who wrote the opinion for the court.

⑬ In reading or briefing a case, make note of the judicial history of the case to date. The lower court dismissed the information (similar to an indictment) against

Bruni after certain evidence was suppressed (declared inadmissible), and the People appealed this dismissal judgment.

If the words *information* or *suppression* are new to you, look them up in a legal dictionary before proceeding. Do this for every new word.

⑭ It is critical to state the facts of the case accurately. Here the facts are relatively simple: A search warrant that said "daytime" service was served at 9:30 P.M., and evidence was taken pursuant to this search warrant. Defendant objected to the admission of this evidence at trial. In most cases, the facts are not this simple. The facts may be given at the beginning of the case, or they may be scattered throughout the case. If you confront the latter situation, you must carefully read the entire case to piece the facts together. The facts are critical because you must assess how analogous or similar the facts of your own problem are to those of the case you are reading (assuming that the issues in the problem are covered in the case at all). If your facts are the same or substantially the same as the key facts of the case, then the law of the case will probably apply to your problem. If the facts of your problem are somewhat the same and somewhat different from those of the case, then it is much more debatable whether the case is analogous and therefore whether the law of the case applies.

⑮ The next critical stage of reading a case is to state the issue (or issues) that the court was deciding in the case. This can sometimes be a difficult task, since many cases are long and complicated. Judges often ramble. The issue in *People v. Bruni* is not difficult to state: Is evidence that was obtained pursuant to a daytime warrant but served at 9:30 P.M. admissible when there is an inconsistency in the statutes as to when service must take place?

According to the court, § 1533 is inconsistent with § 1529. Section 1529 requires a "daytime" service. The legal issue, stated another way, is whether § 1529 was amended by implication when § 1533 was amended to allow service up to 10:00 P.M. so that the evidence obtained at 9:30 P.M. would be admissible in court (if otherwise valid).

⑯ The court refers to other statutes to support the conclusion it will reach. Note the interrelationship of the statutory sections. One statute is interpreted by interpreting other statutes. Section 4 of the Penal Code ("Pen.Code") says that the sections of the Penal Code are to be interpreted ("construed") rationally in order to carry out their purpose or objective and to promote justice. Section 1859 of the Code of Civil Procedure ("Code Civ.Proc.") says that when there is a general and a particular section that are inconsistent, the latter is preferred.

The sequence of statutory interrelationship in this case is as follows:

- Section 1529 of the Penal Code says "daytime."
- Section 7 of the Penal Code defines daytime as sunrise to sunset.
- Section 1533 of the Penal Code, as amended, says between 7:00 A.M. and 10:00 P.M.
- Section 4 of the Penal Code and § 1859 of the Code of Civil Procedure provide principles of interpreting statutes that are inconsistent.

⑰ In the same manner, a court will refer to other cases to support its ruling. In this way, the court argues that the other cases are *precedents* for the case before the court. The court in *People v. Bruni* is saying that *Dept. of Motor Vehicles of California v. Indus. Acc. Com.* and *Tidwell v. Superior Court* are precedents for its own ruling.

⑱ Here is the reasoning of the court to support its ruling: If there is a general statute and a specific statute that are inconsistent, the court will adopt the interpretation that is consistent with the purpose of the statutory scheme. Specific provisions are preferred over general ones. This is what the legislature must have intended.

⑲ The result, or holding, of the court's deliberation of the issue must then be identified. The holding is that § 1529 was impliedly amended to authorize service up to 10:00 P.M. The holding is also called the court's ruling.

⑳ The procedural consequences of the court's resolution of the issue are then usually stated, as here, toward the very end of the case. The judgment of the lower court is reversed. The lower court cannot continue to suppress (i.e., declare inadmissible) the evidence seized at the 9:30 P.M. search.

An appeals court could take a number of positions with respect to a lower court's decision. It could affirm it; modify it (reverse it only in part); *remand* the case (send it back to the lower court) with instructions on how to proceed or how to retry the case, etc.

㉑ In theory, a judge must be very precise in defining the issue before the court—and in resolving only that issue. The judge should not say more than *must* be said to decide the case. This theory, however, is sometimes not observed. Judges will go off on tangents, giving long dissertations or speeches through their opinions. As indicated, this can make your job more difficult; you must wade through all the words to identify (1) the key facts, (2) the precise issues, (3) the precise reasoning, and (4) the precise holdings.

The worst tangent that a judge can stray into is called *dictum*. Dictum is a judge's or court's view of what the law is, or might be, on facts that are *not* before the court. Judge Smith indicated that the result of the case might be different if the warrant were not specific, that is, if it did not name the individual to be searched or what the investigator was looking for. This was not the situation in the *Bruni* case; therefore, Judge Smith's commentary or speculation is dictum.

㉒ On any court there may be several judges. They do not always agree on what should be done in a case. The majority controls. In *Bruni,* Judge Smith wrote the *majority opinion.* A *concurring opinion* is one that votes with the majority but adds its own views about the case. In *Bruni,* Judge Jones concurred but specified that he accepted only the result of Judge Smith's opinion. Normally, judges in such situations will write an opinion indicating their own point of view. Judge Jones did not choose to write an opinion. He simply let it be known that he did not necessarily agree with everything Judge Smith said; all he agreed with was the conclusion that the warrant was validly served. To reach this result, Judge Jones might have used different reasoning, relied on different cases as precedent, etc.

㉓ A *dissenting opinion* disagrees with part or with all of the opinion of the majority. Dissenting opinions are sometimes heated. Of course, the dissenter's opinion is not controlling. It is often valuable to read, however, in order to determine what the dissenter thinks the majority decided.

Having studied the *Bruni* case in this way, you should prepare a seven-part *brief:*

1. Facts: A search warrant that said "daytime" service was served at 9:30 P.M. Evidence was obtained during this search. The People (state) attempted to introduce this evidence at trial. Defendant Bruni objected.

2. Judicial History: The trial court dismissed the information against Bruni after refusing to consider the evidence seized pursuant to an improperly served warrant.

3. Issue: When § 1533 of the Penal Code was amended to allow service between 7:00 A.M. and 10:00 P.M., did the legislature impliedly also amend § 1529, which continued to require daytime service, so that evidence obtained pursuant to a warrant served at 9:30 P.M. can be admitted into evidence?

4. Result or Holding: Section 1529 was impliedly amended to conform to § 1533. The evidence seized pursuant to the search warrant can be admitted.

5. Reasoning: Courts will try to reconcile statutes that are inconsistent. If a general statute is inconsistent with a specific statute, the court will prefer the latter. The intent and purpose of the legislature is to be followed.

6. Procedural Consequences: The trial court's dismissal of the information is reversed. The trial must resume, and the evidence cannot be excluded on the basis of the time of service.

7. Subsequent Judicial History: As of the date of this brief, [here state whether there have been any subsequent decisions in this litigation; you obtain this information by shepardizing the case you are briefing].

■ **ASSIGNMENT 6.5**

Brief the Quinn opinion at the end of this chapter. Do first six parts of the seven-part brief.

Section F. Applying Court Opinions

As we have seen, a court opinion interprets one or more rules of law that are applied to the fact situation before the court. There are two main kinds of rules of law that are interpreted and applied in this way:

■ Enacted law
■ Common law

Enacted law consists of: *constitutional provisions* (created by a constitutional convention and by a combination of legislative and voter approval), *statutes* (created by the legislature), *administrative regulations* (created by agencies), *ordinances* (created by city councils and county boards), etc. **Common law** is judge-made law created by the courts when there is no controlling enacted law that governs the controversy before the court. For example, most of the law on negligence was initially created as common law by the courts because the legislature had not provided any statutes in this area. If, however, such statutes did exist, the courts would have to apply them. Since statutes are superior in authority to common law, new statutes can always change common law. Statutes that bring about such change are called *statutes in derogation of the common law.*

The starting point in your analysis is a set of facts presented to you by a client or by your instructor for a school assignment. The goal is to apply the court opinion to this set of facts. The opinion reached a certain result, called a holding, or ruling. The conclusion of your legal analysis of the opinion will be your assessment of whether this holding applies to the set of facts presented to you. How do you reach this assessment?

■ First, you *compare* the rule that was interpreted and applied in the opinion with the rule that you have uncovered through legal research as potentially applicable.

■ Second, you *compare* the facts given to you by the client or by your instructor with the key facts in the opinion.

Rule Comparison

Suppose your client is charged with a violation of § 23(b) of the state code on the payment of certain taxes. One of your first steps is to go to the law library and find § 23(b). You want to know whether § 23(b) applies to your client. You do an element analysis of the statute, you identify the issue(s), and you do a definitions analysis in the manner discussed earlier in this chapter. In the library you also look for court opinions. Your search is for court opinions that interpreted and applied § 23(b). You would not try to find opinions that interpreted housing or pollution statutes. You focus on opinions that cover the *same* rule involved in the case of the client—here, § 23(b). This is also true of the common law. If the client has a negligence case, for example, you search for opinions that interpret the law of negligence.

Rule comparison in the analysis of opinions is fairly simple. The general principle is: you compare the rule involved in your client's case (or school assignment) with the rule interpreted and applied in the opinion, and you proceed only if the rule is exactly the same. While there are some exceptions, this principle will be sufficient to guide you most of the time.

Fact Comparison

Here is the heart of the analysis. Before the holding of an opinion can apply, you must demonstrate that the key facts of the opinion are substantially the same as the facts in the client's case (or school assignment). If the facts are exactly the same or almost exactly the same, the opinion is said to be *on all fours* with your facts. If so, then you will have little difficulty convincing someone that the holding of the opinion applies to your facts. It is rare, however, that you will find an opinion on all fours. Consequently, careful analysis of factual similarities and differences must be made. In general, if the facts are substantially similar, the ruling applies; if they are substantially different, it does not.

You must make a determination of what the *key facts* are in the opinion, since it is these facts alone that are the basis of the comparison. A key fact is a very important fact—a fact that was crucial to the conclusion or holding of the court. In a divorce opinion, for example, it will probably not be key that a plaintiff was thirty-three years old. The court would have reached the same result if the plaintiff was thirty-two or thirty-four. Age may have been irrelevant or of very minor importance to the holding. What *may* have been key is that the plaintiff beat his wife, since without this fact the court may not have reached the ruling that the ground of cruelty existed. You carefully comb the opinion to read what the judge said about the various facts. Did the court emphasize certain facts? Repeat them? Label them as crucial or important? These are the kinds of questions you must ask yourself to determine which facts in the opinion were key.

Let us assume that you have been able to identify the key facts of opinion. Your next concern is comparing these facts and the facts of your own problem. For example:

Your Facts	The Case: *Smith v. Apex Co.*
Client sees an ad in the paper announcing a sale at a local store. He goes to the back of the store and falls into a pit. There was a little sign that said *danger* near the pit. The client wants to sue the store owner for negligence in failing to use reasonable care in preventing his injury. The law office assigns a paralegal to research the case. The paralegal finds the case of *Smith v. Apex Co.* and wants to argue that it applies.	This case involved a man (Smith) who is looking for an address. He is walking down the street. He decides to walk into an office building to ask someone for help. While coming down the corridor, he slips and falls on a wet floor. There was a small sign in the corridor that said *wet floor*, which Smith saw. Smith sued the owner of the building (Apex Co.) for negligence. The court held that the owner was negligent for failure to exercise reasonable care for the safety of users of the building.

First, identify all factual similarities:

- The client was in a public place (a store). Smith was also in a public place (an office building).

- Both situations involved some kind of warning (the *danger* sign and the *wet floor* sign).
- The warning in both situations was not conspicuous (the *danger* sign was "little"; the *wet floor* sign was "small").

Next, identify all factual differences:

- The client was in a store, whereas Smith was in an office building.
- Your case involved a hole or pit, whereas *Smith v. Apex Co.* involved a slippery surface.
- The client was there about a possible purchase whereas Smith was not trying to transact any business in the office building.

Next, identify any factual gaps:

- Smith saw the *wet floor* sign, but we do not know whether the client saw the *danger* sign.

Ninety percent of your legal analysis is complete if you have been able to make the above identifications. Most students do a sloppy job at this level. They do not carefully pick apart the facts in order to identify similarities, differences, and gaps.

Once you have done this properly, you make your final arguments about the opinion:

- If you want the holding in the opinion to apply, you emphasize the similarities between your facts and the key facts in the opinion. If any of your facts differs from a fact in the opinion, you try to point out that this is not significant since the latter was not a key fact in the opinion.
- If you do not want the holding in the opinion to apply, you emphasize the differences between your facts and the key facts in the opinion. If any of your facts is similar to a fact in the opinion, you try to point out that this is not significant since there is still a dissimilarity with at least one of the key facts in the opinion.

. . . .

Factual gaps sometimes pose a problem. If the factual gap is in the facts of your client's case, you simply go back to the client and ask him or her about the fact. In the above case, for example, the paralegal asks the client whether he saw the "danger" sign. Suppose, however, that the factual gap is in the opinion itself. Assume that your client was running when he fell into the pit, but that the opinion does not tell you whether Smith was running, walking, etc. You obviously cannot go to Smith or to the judge who wrote the opinion and ask. You must make a guess of what the judge would have done in the opinion if Smith was running at the time he slipped on the corridor floor. You may decide that it would have changed the result or that this additional fact would have made no difference to the ruling reached.

We turn now to an overview of how *Smith v. Apex Co.* would be applied to the client's case in a memorandum of law. The client's case and the opinion involve exactly the same rule—the law of negligence. Assume that the element in contention in this rule is the failure to use reasonable care.

Issue. Did the store use "reasonable care" for the safety of users of the store when the only warning of a pit in the store was a small *danger* sign near the pit?

Facts.   The client saw an ad in the newspaper announcing a sale. He went to the back of the store and fell into a pit. There was a small sign that said *danger* near the pit.

Analysis.   An opinion on point is *Smith v. Apex Co.*, 233 Mass. 578, 78 N.E.2d 422 (1980). In this opinion, the court found the owner of an office building liable for negligence when Smith slipped on a wet corridor floor in the building. There was a small *wet floor* sign in the corridor. This opinion is substantially similar to our own client's case. Both were in public buildings where owners can expect people to be present. In both situations, the warning was insufficient. The *wet floor* sign in the opinion was "small." The *danger* sign in our situation was "little." Because of all these important similarities, it can be argued that the holding in *Smith v. Apex Co.* applies.

It is true that in the opinion the judge pointed out that Smith saw the sign. Our facts do not state whether the client saw the *danger* sign in the store. This should not make any difference, however, since the judge in the opinion would probably have reached the same result if Smith had not seen the *wet floor* sign. In fact, the case would probably have been stronger for Smith if he did *not* see the sign. The building was dangerous in spite of the fact that users of the building such as Smith could see the sign. Obviously, the danger would be considered even greater if such users could not see the sign. We should find out from our client whether he saw the *danger* sign, but I do not think that it will make any difference in the applicability of the holding in *Smith v. Apex Co.*

The store owner will try to argue that the opinion does not apply. The argument might be that a pit is not as dangerous as a wet floor, since a pit is more conspicuous than a wet floor and hence not as hazardous. A user is more likely to notice a hole in the floor than to know whether a floor is slippery enough to fall on. Our client could respond by pointing out that the pit was in the back of the store where it may not have been very noticeable. Furthermore, the wet floor in the opinion was apparently conspicuous (Smith saw the *wet floor* sign), yet in the opinion the judge still found the defendant liable.

■ ASSIGNMENT 6.6

In the following situations, point out any factual similarities, differences, and gaps between the client facts and the facts of the opinion.

(a) *Client Facts:* Jim is driving his car 30 MPH on a dirt road at night. He suddenly sneezes and jerks the steering wheel slightly, causing the car to move to the right and run into Bill's fence. Bill sues Jim for negligence.

Opinion: A pedestrian brings a negligence action against Mary. Mary is driving her motorcycle on a clear day. A page of a newspaper unexpectedly flies into Mary's face. Since she cannot see where she is going, she runs into a pedestrian crossing the street. The court finds for Mary, ruling that she did not act unreasonably in causing the accident.

(b) *Client Facts:* Helen is the mother of David, age four. The state is trying to take David away from Helen on the ground that Helen has neglected David. Helen lives alone with David. She works part time and leaves David with a neighbor. Helen's job occasionally requires her to travel. At one time she was away for a month. During this period, David was sometimes left alone, since the neighbor had to spend several days at the hospital. When David was discovered alone, the state began proceedings to remove David on the ground of neglect.

Opinion: The state charged Bob Thompson with the neglect of his twins, aged ten. The state wishes to place the twins in a foster home. Bob is partially blind.

One day he accidentally tripped and fell on one of the twins, causing severe injuries to the child. Bob lives alone with the twins but refuses to hire anyone to help him run the home. The court ruled that Bob did not neglect his children.

■ ASSIGNMENT 6.7

Salem is a factory town of 500 inhabitants in Hawaii. The factory employs 95% of the workers in the town. The town has only two private attorneys: Ann Grote and Timothy Farrell. Forty of the employees have decided to sue the factory over a wage dispute. Ann Grote represents all these employees. She works alone except for her only employee, Bob Davis, a paralegal. In this litigation, the factory is represented by Timothy Farrell who has no employees—no secretaries and no paralegals. Grote and Farrell are young attorneys who have just begun their practices. Their only clients are the forty employees and the factory, respectively. The litigation has become quite complicated. Several months before the case is scheduled to go to trial, Farrell offers Davis a job as a paralegal at double the salary he is earning with Grote. He accepts the offer. Grote goes to court seeking a preliminary injunction against Davis and Farrell, which would bar them from entering this employment relationship.

Apply *Quinn v. Lum and Cronin, Fried, Sekiya & Kekina,* printed below, to the facts of the case of *Grote v. Davis and Farrell.* Do not do any legal research. Limit yourself to the application of this one opinion based on the guidelines of this chapter. (*Quinn* is an actual opinion from a state court in Hawaii.)

Quinn v. Lum and Cronin, Fried, Sekiya & Kekina
Civ. No. 81284
Hawaii Court of Appeals

On January 25, 1984, Richard K. Quinn, Attorney at Law, a Law Corporation, filed suit against Rogerlene Lum, a member of the Hawaii Association of Legal Assistants (HALA) and formerly legal secretary with the Quinn firm, for injunctive relief based on the allegation that Mrs. Lum possesses confidential client information from her work as Quinn's legal secretary, which information would be transmitted to the co-defendant, Mrs. Lum's new employer, Cronin, Fried, Sekiya & Kekina, Attorneys at Law, if she were to begin her employment with the Cronin firm as a legal assistant.

On or about January 3, 1984 Mrs. Lum notified Quinn that she had accepted a position as a paralegal with the Cronin firm. Quinn subsequently discussed and corresponded with Mr. Cronin regarding the hiring of Mrs. Lum, who was scheduled to begin work with the Cronin firm on January 30, 1984. Mr. Cronin repeatedly refused Quinn's request that she not be hired by the Cronin firm.

On January 26, a hearing on the application for a temporary restraining order was heard by Judge Philip T. Chun of the Circuit Court of the First Circuit, State of Hawaii. The application was denied.

Quinn alleges in the pleadings filed with the Court in Civil No. 81284 that Mrs. Lum's employment with the Quinn firm from December 1, 1982 to January 17, 1984, and as Mr. Quinn's secretary from April 25, 1983 to January 17, 1984, included attendance at the firm's case review committee meetings. Confidential discussions occurred concerning case evaluation, settlement evaluation, strategy, and tactics between Quinn, his associates, and their clients.

Cronin et al. are attorneys of record for the plaintiffs in *Firme v. Honolulu Medical Group and Ronald P. Peroff, M.D.* Quinn's firm represents the defendants. The case was set for trial on March 19, 1984. According to exhibits attached to the records filed in the instant case, Mr. Cronin recognized the *Firme* situation and agreed that Mrs. Lum would not be involved in the *Firme* case in her new employment, nor would his firm "[ever] seek to obtain any information from her concerning cases with which she was involved while in [Quinn's] office, nor would we have her work on any while here." Mr. Cronin goes on to say in his January 24 letter to Quinn that Quinn should consult with his clients in the *Firme* case as to whether Quinn's "attempt . . . to stop Mrs. Lum from working for [the Cronin firm] is with their approval."

Quinn also alleges that while his firm is known in the Honolulu legal community as one which represents hospitals, doctors, and other health care providers, the Cronin firm is known as a plaintiff medical malpractice firm. Quinn lists in several pleadings that on more than one occasion, these firms found themselves adversaries in the same cases.

[Quinn contends] that this action was brought not to "bar Lum from working as a legal secretary or even as a paralegal, since that would be ludicrous given the size of Hawaii's legal community." In fact, Quinn states he would have "no objection to Lum's working for any other law firm in Hawaii other than one which specializes in medical malpractice plaintiffs' work, like [Cronin's]."

A subsequent hearing on the original complaint for injunctive relief was then held in Judge Ronald Moon's court on February 6. Plaintiff's motion for a preliminary injunction that would bar such employment "for at least two years" was denied, with the judge noting *Quinn v. Lum* as a case of first impression.

The Court explained its decision in light of the standards to be met before a preliminary injunction could be issued, as dealt with in depth by Mrs. Lum's attorney, David L. Fairbanks, who is also the current President of the Hawaii State Bar Association.

The standards which must be met in order to obtain a preliminary injunction, as listed by Judge Moon, follow:

1. The Court did not feel there was a substantial likelihood that plaintiff would prevail on the merits. If an injunction were to be issued, it would:
   "[E]ssentially prevent a paralegal or legal secretary [or] attorney from joining any law firm that may have had some case in the past, . . . cases pending at the present time, or potential cases which may be worked on in the future" (Transcript of the Hearing, page 82).
2. The evidence is lacking regarding irreparable damage to Richard Quinn's clients.

3. The public interest would not be served by issuing such an injunction.

When an attorney enters practice in the State of Hawaii, he or she agrees to abide and be governed by the Hawaii Code of Professional Responsibility. This code does not attempt to govern the ethical actions of the non-attorneys. While Canon 37 of the American Bar Association's Code of Professional Responsibility, adopted pre-1971, states that a lawyer's employees have the same duty to preserve client confidences as the lawyer, this Canon is not included in the Hawaii code. Compliance, therefore, with the same rules of ethics guiding the Hawaii attorney is currently left to the discretion—and conscience—of the non-attorney.

If an attorney in Hawaii breaches the Code of Professional Responsibility, the office of Disciplinary Counsel may choose to investigate the matter and may pass the matter on to the Disciplinary Board and, possibly, to the Hawaii Supreme Court for adjudication.

If an employee of a law office becomes suspect of some breach of ethics or acts of omission, the employing attorney becomes responsible for the employee's deeds. For example, if a legal secretary fails to file the complaint the day the Statute of Limitations expires thinking the next day would suffice, it is the attorney who is responsible to the client. The attorney can fire the secretary "for cause" but the attorney, nevertheless, stands responsible. It appears the only way for an attorney to further censor the employee directly is via a civil suit for tortious damages.

Whether a permanent injunction can or will be granted has yet to be seen in this case. What is clear is that neither the office of Disciplinary Counsel nor the Hawaii Supreme Court would or could become involved; they have no jurisdiction over the non-attorney working in a law office,

Chapter Summary

Legal analysis is the process of connecting a rule of law to a set of facts in order to determine how that rule might apply to a particular situation. The goal of the process is to solve a legal dispute or to prevent one from arising. The structure of legal analysis is always the same: a rule and facts lead to a legal issue, which is generally phrased as a question. That question is answered by drawing a connection between the language of the rule and the facts, producing a conclusion.

An important skill in legal analysis is the ability to break a rule down into its elements. An element is simply a component or portion of a rule. If all the elements apply to a fact situation, then the rule applies to the fact situation. If one element does not apply, then the rule does not apply. Hence each element of a rule is one of the preconditions of the applicability of the entire rule. A legal issue is often phrased to ask whether one of the elements applies to the facts. (This element is sometimes re-

(Continued on next page)

☐ Chapter Summary (Continued)

ferred to as the element in contention or the element in controversy.) The answer may depend on whether the element is to be interpreted broadly or narrowly.

To brief an opinion means to identify its major components: facts, judicial history, issue, holding, reasoning, and the procedural consequences of the holding. In addition, it is often essential to determine the subsequent history of the opinion. There are two main steps in applying an opinion to a set of facts from a client's case. First, you compare the rule (which will either be an enacted law or a common law) that was interpreted in the opinion with the rule you are considering in the client's case. With limited exceptions, the opinion cannot apply unless these two rules are the same. Second, you compare the key facts in the opinion with the facts of the client's case. In general, the opinion will apply if these facts are the same or are substantially similar.

Key Terms

legal analysis
elements
cause of action
defense
memorandum of law
legal issue
element in contention
shorthand issue
comprehensive issue
broad/narrow definition
brief
trial brief
trial notebook
trial manual
trial book
appellate brief

People
appellant
respondent
appellee
docket number
shepardizing
syllabus
headnote
topic and key number
digests
attorney general
per curiam
memorandum opinion
precedent
holding
ruling

remand
dictum
majority opinion
concurring opinion
dissenting opinion
enacted law
common law
statute in derogation of the
    common law
rule comparison
fact comparison
on all fours
key fact
fact similarities
fact differences
fact gaps

7

Legal Interviewing

■ Chapter Outline

■ Section A. The Context of Interviewing in Litigation

There are at least three kinds of legal interviews:

1. The initial client interview
2. The follow-up client interview
3. The field interview involving someone other than the client

In the initial client interview, the interviewer introduces the client to the kind of legal services offered by the office, identifies legal problems, and explains the way in which the office will handle the case. Follow-up interviews occur after the initial interview. The client is asked about additional facts and is consulted on a variety of matters that require his or her attention, consent, and participation. Finally, there is the field interview conducted during investigation, in which the interviewer seeks out a great diversity of people for a wide range of purposes. Investigation will be examined in the next chapter. Here our focus will be the *initial client interview*.

Interviewing is among the most important skills used in a law office. Since it appears to be relatively easy to engage in interviewing (all you need is a person to interview and some time), it is commonly assumed that legal interviewing, like good conversation, requires little more than intelligence and a pleasing personality. This misconception often leads to incomplete and sloppy interviewing. Legal interviewing is much more than conversation. They are similar in that both frequently involve building a relationship and exchanging information. In legal interviewing, however, the goal is to help solve a client's problem. In order to do this, a relationship must be established between the interviewer and client that is warm, trusting, professional, and goal-oriented.

Paralegals in different settings have varied duties and authority. In a private law office, an attorney will usually conduct the initial interview and assign the paralegal the limited task of gathering detailed information from the client on a specific topic. For example, a paralegal may be asked to help a bankruptcy client detail debts and financial entanglements by listing them all on a worksheet. On the other hand, in a government agency or in a government-funded legal service office, the paralegal's interviewing responsibilities can be extensive. For example, a paralegal may conduct the initial interview with a client and remain the primary office contact for the client throughout the resolution of the case.

The initial client interview is critical because it sets the foundation for the entire litigation process. (See Figure 7.1.) The facts obtained from this interview are further pursued through field investigation; the laws governing these facts are researched in the law library; the facts and the governing law are informally argued between counsel for the parties in an effort to settle the case through negotiation; if there is no settlement, a trial is held in which the facts are formally established; finally, the process ends with an appeal. Everything begins with the facts obtained through the initial client interview.

■ Section B. The Format of an Intake Memo

Before analyzing the interviewing process, we should look briefly at one of the end products of the interview—the *intake memo*. This is the document the paralegal writes on the basis of notes taken at the interview. The intake memo

FIGURE 7.1
Interviewing in
Context

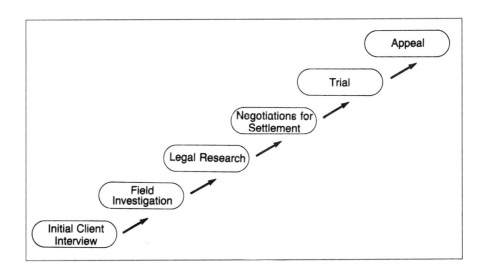

goes first to the supervisor and then into a newly opened case file on the client. The memo often has five parts:

1. Heading.   The heading provides the following information at the top of the first page:

- Who wrote the memo
- The supervisor in charge of the case
- The date the memo was written
- The date the interview was conducted
- The name of the case
- The office file number of the case
- The kind of case (general area of the law)
- The subject matter of the memo following the notation "RE"

2. Personal Data.

- Name of the client
- Home address
- Phone numbers where client can be reached
- Age of client
- Marital status
- Place of employment of client
- Etc.

3. Statement of the Assignment.   The first paragraph of the memo should state the precise objective the paralegal was given in conducting the interview.

4. Body of the Memo.   Here the facts are presented in a coherent, readable manner according to a number of possible organizational principles:

- A chronological listing of the facts so that the events are unfolded as a story with a beginning, middle, and end
- A categorizing of the facts according to the major topics or issues of the case, each with its own subject heading under which the relevant facts are placed
- Any other format called for by the supervisor

5. Conclusion.   Here a number of things could be included:

- A brief summary of the major facts listed in the body of the memo
- The impressions of the paralegal of the client, such as
  - how knowledgeable the client appeared to be
  - how believable the client appeared to be
- A list of the next steps, for example:
  - what further facts should be sought through investigation
  - what legal research should be undertaken
  - any other recommendations on what should be done on the case based on what was learned during the interview
- A list of anything the paralegal told the client to do, for example:
  - bring in specified documents relevant to the case

FIGURE 7.2
Intake Memo

Inter-Office Memo

To: Ann Fuller, Supervisor   **Case:** John Myers vs. Betsy Myers
From: Jim Smith, Paralegal   **File Number:** 91-102
Date of Memo: March 13, 1991   **Kind of Case:** Child Custody
Date of Interview: March 12, 1991   **Re:** Intake Interview of John Myers

Personal Data:

Name of Client: John Myers
Address: 34 Main Street, Salem, Massachusetts 01970
Phone: 966-3954 (H) 297-9700 (x 301) (W)
Age: 37
Marital Status: Married but separated from his wife, Betsy Myers
Employment: ABC Construction Co., 2064 South Street, Salem, Massachusetts 02127

You asked me to conduct a comprehensive intake interview of John Myers, our client, in order to obtain a listing of his assets and the facts surrounding his relationship with his children.

A. ASSETS
John Myers owns . . .

- check on further facts and call back
- return for another interview

In Figure 7.2 there is a sample of the introductory parts of an intake memo:

Section C. What Facts Do You Seek? Guides to the Formulation of Questions

Unless the paralegal knows what to accomplish in an interview, valuable time will be wasted. For example, suppose a client is being interviewed concerning the grounds (legally sufficient reasons) for a divorce. The paralegal does not simply write down *all* the facts about the marriage and the client's problems in it. The facts must be clustered or arranged in categories that are relevant to grounds for divorce. Unless paralegals have this objective in mind before and during the interview, they may end up with such a confusing collection of facts they'll have to conduct a second interview to go over matters that should have been covered initially. This does not mean that the paralegal cannot talk about anything other than what is directly related to the objective, but it does mean that each interview must have a definite *focus*.

There are six major ways a paralegal can achieve focus in the formulation of questions to be asked of a client:

- Instructions of the supervisor for the interview
- Checklists
- Legal analysis
- "Fact particularization"
- Common sense
- Flexibility

These methods are designed to help you avoid all the following examples of an *ineffective* interview:

- You fail to seek the information that the supervisor wanted you to obtain.

> "If you don't know where you're going, when you get there you'll be lost."
> Yogi Berra

- You miss major relevant facts.
- You fail to obtain sufficient detail on the major relevant facts.
- You fail to ask questions about (and record) the extent to which the client was sure or unsure about the facts given you.
- You fail to pursue leads the client provides about other relevant themes or topics that may not have been part of the supervisor's explicit instructions.

The Instructions of the Supervisor for the Interview

These instructions, of course, control what you do in the interview. As indicated above, you may be asked to do a limited interview or a comprehensive one. Be sure to write down what the supervisor wants from the interview. One concern that frequently arises is the amount of detail desired. Attorneys like facts. During three years of law school, they were constantly asked by their law professors, "What are the facts?" The likelihood is that the attorney for whom you work will want considerable detail from the interview. Even if you are told to limit yourself to obtaining the basic facts from the client, you may find that the supervisor wants a lot of detail about those basic facts. When in doubt, the safest course is to be detailed in your questioning. If possible, try to sit in on an interview conducted by your supervisor in order to observe his or her method of questioning and the amount of detail sought. Also, examine some closed case files that contain intake memos. Ask the supervisor if any of these memos are exemplary, and if so, why. Once you have a model, it can be very useful as a guide.

Checklists

The office where you work may have checklists that are used in conducting interviews. For some kinds of cases, such as probate or estate matters, the checklists may be extensive. If such checklists are not available, you should consider writing your own for the kinds of cases in which you do a good deal of interviewing.

Caution is needed, however, in using checklists:

- You should find out why individual questions were inserted in the checklist.
- You should be flexible enough to ask questions not on the checklist when your interview assignment calls for such adaptation.

A checklist must be viewed as a guide that should be adjusted to adapt to the case and client in front of you rather than as a rigid formula from which there can never be deviation.

Legal Analysis

Extensive legal analysis does not take place while the interview is being conducted. Yet *some* legal analysis may be needed to conduct an intelligent interview.

Most of the questions you ask in the interview must be *legally relevant*, which means that the answer is needed in order to determine whether a particular legal principle governs. It takes some understanding of legal analysis to apply the concept of legal relevance intelligently. It could be dangerous for the paralegal to be asking questions by rote, even if checklists are used. The question and answer process is a little like a tennis match—you go where the ball is hit or it passes you by.

Suppose that you are interviewing a client on an unemployment compensation claim. The state denied the claim because the client is allegedly not "available for work." You cannot conduct a competent interview unless you know the legal meaning of this phrase. From this understanding you can formulate questions that are legally relevant to the issue of whether the client has been and is "available for work." You will ask obvious questions such as:

What is your present health?

Where have you applied for work?

Were you turned down and, if so, why?

Did you turn down any work and, if so, why?

Suppose that during the interview, the client tells you the following:

There were some ads in the paper for jobs in the next town, but I didn't want to travel that far.

At this point you must decide whether to pursue this matter by inquiring about the distance to the town, whether public transportation is available, the cost of such transportation, whether the client owns a car, etc. Again, legal analysis can be helpful. Does "available for work" mean available in the same area? Is one *un*available for work because of a refusal to make unreasonable efforts to travel to an otherwise available job in another area? What does unreasonable mean? Definitional questions such as these must go through your mind as you decide whether to seek more details about the ads for work in the other town. These are questions of legal analysis. *You must be thinking while questioning.* Some instant mental analysis should be going on all the time. This does not mean you must know the answer to every legal question that comes to mind while interviewing the client. But you must know something about the law and must be flexible enough to think about legal questions that should be generated by unexpected facts provided by the client.

When in doubt about whether to pursue a line of questions, check with your supervisor. If he or she is not available, the safest course is to pursue it. As you acquire additional interviewing experience in particular areas of the law, you will be better equipped to know what to do. Yet you will never know everything. There will always be fact situations that you have never encountered before. Legal analysis will help you handle such situations.

Fact Particularization (FP)

"Fact particularization" is perhaps one of the most important concepts in this book. To *particularize a fact* means to ask an extensive series of questions

FIGURE 7.3

Fact Particularization

The investigator must *particularize* facts collected thus far:
1. By assuming that the facts are woefully incomplete, and
2. By assuming that there is more than one version of the facts, and
3. By identifying a large number of basic who, what, where, why, when, and how questions which, if answered, would provide as complete a picture of what happened as is possible to obtain at this time

about that fact in order to explore its uniqueness. Fact assessment is critical to practice of the law; fact particularization is critical to the identification of the facts that must be assessed. FP is a fact-collection technique. It is the process of viewing every person, thing, or event as unique—different from every other person, thing, or event. Every important fact a client tells you in an interview should be particularized. You do this by asking a large number of follow-up questions once you have targeted the fact you want to explore.

FP can be a guide to the formulation of questions in a number of situations:

- In a client interview
- In investigations
- In drafting interrogatories
- In preparing for a deposition
- In examining witnesses on the stand at trial

In legal interviewing, the starting point for the FP process is an important fact that the client has told you during the interview. Examples include: "I tried to find work"; "the car hit me from the rear"; "the pain was unbearable"; "the company was falling apart"; "he told me I would get the ranch when he died"; "he fired me because I am a woman"; etc. Then you ask the client eight categories of questions about the fact that is being particularized. (See Figure 7.4.)

The eight categories are not mutually exclusive, and all eight categories are not necessarily applicable to every fact that you will be particularizing. There is no definite order in which the questions must be asked as long as you are comprehensive in your search for factual detail. The point of FP is simply to get the wheels of your mind rolling so that you will think of a large number of questions and avoid conducting a superficial interview.

Time Details

When did the fact occur or happen? Find out the precise date and time. The interviewer should be scrupulous about all dates and times. If more than one event is involved, ask questions about the dates and times of each. If the client is not sure, ask questions to help jog the memory and ask the client to check his or her records or to contact other individuals who might know. Do not be satisfied with an answer such as, "It happened about two months ago." If this is what the client says, record it in your notes, but then probe further. Show the client a calendar and ask about other events going on at the same time in an effort to help him or her be more precise.

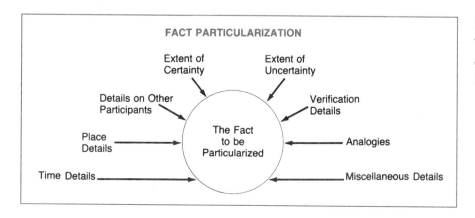

FIGURE 7.4

The Categories of Fact Particularization

Place and Environment Details

Be equally scrupulous about geography. Where did the event occur? Where was the thing or object in question? Where was the client at the time? Ask the client to describe the surroundings. Ask questions with such care that you obtain a verbal photograph of the scene. If relevant, ask the client to approximate distances between important objects or persons. You might want to have the client draw a diagram, or you can draw a diagram on the basis of what you are told and ask the client if the drawing is accurate. Ask questions about the weather or about lighting conditions. You want to know as much as you can about the environment or whatever the client could observe about the environment through the senses of touch, sight, hearing, and smell.

Details on Other Participants

Who else was involved? Ask questions about who they were, their roles, their age, appearance, etc., if relevant. Where were they at the time? When did they act? Why did they act? Why did they fail to act? Could you have anticipated what they did or failed to do? Why or why not? Have they ever acted or failed to act in this way before? Ask questions designed to obtain a detailed picture of who these other participants were and their precise relationship to the fact being particularized.

Extent of Certainty/Uncertainty

Everything the client tells you can be placed somewhere on the spectrum of certainty:

Absolutely Certain	Substantially Certain	Fairly Certain	Have A Vague Certainty	Unsure	Do Not Know

It would be a big mistake, for example, to record that the client said a letter was received two weeks ago when in fact the client said. "I think it came two weeks ago." Do not turn uncertainty into certainty by sloppy listening and sloppy recording in your intake memo of what the client said. Of course, it may be possible for a client to be uncertain about a fact initially but then become more certain of it with the help of your questioning. If so, record this transition by saying, "The client was first unsure of who else was present, but then said she was fairly certain that Fred was there."

Explain to the client right at the beginning how critical it is for you to obtain accurate information. Encourage the client to say "I'm not sure" when that's the case. It is important that the client be relaxed and unthreatened. It would not be wise for you to keep asking, "Are you sure?" following every fact the client tells you. Yet you must find out where on the spectrum of certainty a fact falls. Temper your probe with tact and sensitivity.

Verification Details

The fact that the client tells you something happened is *some* evidence that it happened. Verification data is evidence that supports what the client has said. Verification data is *additional* evidence to support the client. Always pursue such verification details. Ask yourself how you would establish the truth of what the client has said if the client suddenly disappeared and you had to rely exclusively on other sources. Inquire about documents (such as letters or check stubs) that support the client's statements. Inquire about other people who might be available to testify to the same subject. Ask the client questions that will lead you to such verification details. This approach does not mean that you do not trust the client, or that you think the client is lying. It is simply a good practice to view a fact from many perspectives. You are always seeking the strongest case possible. This calls for questioning about verification details.

Analogies

Some facts that you are particularizing (e.g., "the pain was unbearable"; "I was careful"; "it looked awful"; "I was scared") are difficult to pin down. In the interview, you should ask the client to explain such statements. Sometimes it is helpful to ask the client to use analogies to describe what is meant. An analogy is simply explaining something by comparing it to something else. For example, you ask the client:

What would you compare it to?

Was it similar to anything you have ever seen before?

Have you observed anyone else do the same thing?

Have you ever been in a similar situation?

Did it feel like a dentist's drill?

You ask the client to compare the fact to something else. Then you ask about the similarities and differences. Through a series of directed questions you are encouraging the client to analogize the fact he or she is describing to some other fact. This is done in a further attempt to obtain as comprehensive a picture as possible of what the client is saying.

Miscellaneous Details

Here you simply ask about any details that were not covered in the previous categories of questions. Include questions on anything else that might help in particularizing the fact under examination.

■ ASSIGNMENT 7.1

In this assignment, FP will be role-played in class. One student will be selected to play the role of the client and another, the role of the paralegal interviewer. The rest of the class will observe and fill out the FP Score Card on the interview.

Instructions to Interviewer. You will not be conducting a complete interview from beginning to end. You will be trying to particularize a certain fact that's given to you. Go through the eight categories of FP described above. Use any order of questioning that you want. Probe for comprehensiveness. Your instructor will select one of the following facts, which will be used as the basis of the interview:

(a) "I was hit in the jaw by Mary."

(b) "He neglects his children."

(c) "I have not been promoted because I am a woman."

Your opening question to the client will be, "What happened?" The client will make one of the three statements above. You then use the process of FP to particularize this statement.

Instructions to Client. The interviewer will ask you what happened. Simply make one of the three statements above as selected by the instructor. Then the interviewer will ask you a large number of questions about the statements. Make up the answers—ad lib your responses. Do not, however, volunteer any information. Answer only the questions asked.

Instructions to Class. Observe the interview. Use the following score card to assess how well you think the interviewer particularized the fact.

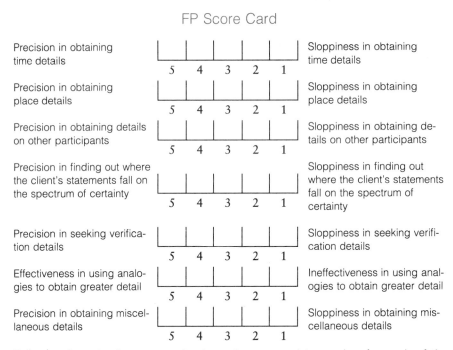

FP Score Card

	5	4	3	2	1	
Precision in obtaining time details						Sloppiness in obtaining time details
Precision in obtaining place details						Sloppiness in obtaining place details
Precision in obtaining details on other participants						Sloppiness in obtaining details on other participants
Precision in finding out where the client's statements fall on the spectrum of certainty						Sloppiness in finding out where the client's statements fall on the spectrum of certainty
Precision in seeking verification details						Sloppiness in seeking verification details
Effectiveness in using analogies to obtain greater detail						Ineffectiveness in using analogies to obtain greater detail
Precision in obtaining miscellaneous details						Sloppiness in obtaining miscellaneous details

Following the interview, put a check on the appropriate number for each of the above categories of assessment. A "5" score means you thought the interview was very precise or effective in fulfilling the goal of FP. A "1" score means the opposite. Also, make notes of questions that you think the interviewer should have asked. These questions, and your scores, will be discussed in class after the interview.

Common Sense

Common sense is another major guide to determining what questions to ask, achieving comprehensiveness, and giving the interview a focus. Though law is full of legalisms and technicalities, good judgment and common sense are still at the core of the practice of law. It is common sense, for example, to organize an interview by having the client tell the relevant events chronologically in the form of a story with a beginning, middle, and end. It is common sense to follow up on a topic the client mentions with further questioning even though you had not anticipated the topic. If the client says something you do not understand, common sense dictates that you ask what the client means before continuing with the interview. At times, it may be common sense to stop the interview for a moment to obtain further guidance from your supervisor.

Flexibility

In the previous discussion, the importance of flexibility was mentioned a number of times. You must be prepared to expect the unexpected and you must be relaxed. Although you lead the interview and give it direction, you must be ready to go where the interview takes you. It would be potentially disastrous for you to block out topics that arise simply because they were not part of your game plan in conducting the interview or are not on your checklist. As with so many areas of the law, you may not know what you are looking for until you find it. In interviewing a client about incorporating a business, for example, you may stumble across a lead from something the client says that could involve fraud or criminal prosecution on a matter unrelated to the incorporation. Don't block this out. Pursue what appears to be reasonably related to the law office's relationship with the client. Check with your supervisor. Again, let common sense be your guide. Flexibility is one of the foundations of common sense.

■ ASSIGNMENT 7.2

Interview a classmate for the purpose of writing his or her resume. Assume that this person wants to work for a law firm eventually. After you conduct the interview, write the resume. It should include the following categories of information:

- *Basic data* (name, address, phone, marital status, etc.)
- *Career objective* (what does the person hope to be doing—hope to be accomplishing—in the immediate future? five years from now?)
- *Education* (begin with current school and proceed back, including names of schools, dates of attendance, degrees or certificates awarded, etc.)
- *Prior employment* (begin with most recent work and proceed back, including names of employers, addresses, dates of employment, titles, responsibilities, etc.)
- *Community activities* (volunteer work, etc.)

The trouble with most resumes in that they focus only on events and rarely spend enough space listing specific skills and accomplishments. To identify them, you need to ask questions such as:

- Have you ever supervised other people? How many? To do what tasks?
- Have you had responsibility for handling someone else's money?
- Have you ever had to write a budget?
- Have you ever had the responsibility of evaluating someone else?
- Have you ever written a proposal?
- What kind of reports have you written?
- What work products have resulted from your previous employment and schooling? For instance, have you ever drafted a complaint? In what area of the law and under what circumstances? Have you done any legal research? On what specific issues and under what circumstances?
- Have you ever written a speech and delivered it?
- Have you ever run for any elective office in a club or other organization?
- Etc.

Ask questions such as these to try to identify items that should be considered for the resume. When someone reads the resume, what impression would they get of the individual? A self-starter? Someone who can act without constant supervision? An unstable person who moves from job to job to job? A doer? A person with enthusiasm? A live person or a collection of statistics? When you are conducting the interview, be sure to bring out facts that will enable you to place the person in a positive light in the resume.

There is no length limitation to the resume you prepare after the interview. Your goal is to particularize the person you are interviewing. (A resume that is actually used in a job search will have to be relatively brief. See Chapter 2.)

Type the resume and make at least one photocopy. Give the copy to the person you interviewed. Ask that person to read the resume and give it *as many* of the following ratings as he or she feels are applicable:

Rating I: The resume describes me to a "T."

Rating II: I would definitely hire me on the basis of this resume!

Rating III: The resume is substantially accurate, but there are some factual errors in it.

Rating IV: The facts in the resume are fairly accurate, but it's rather flat; it doesn't describe me as a live person.

Rating V: I hardly recognized myself.

Rating VI: The person described in this resume is impersonating me!

Rating VII: Nice try, but. . . .

Before you hand the resume in to the teacher, indicate on the top of the front page the rating(s) your interviewee gave the resume.

 ## Section D. What Does the Client Want?

There are a number of assumptions that can be made about many clients:

- They are not sure what they want.
- They are not aware of what legal and nonlegal options are available to help solve the problem that exists.
- The problem probably involves other legal problems about which the client is unaware and about which even you may be unaware at the outset.

Suppose that a client walks into the office and says, "I want a divorce." The following observations *might* be possible about the client:

- The client has an incorrect understanding of what a divorce is.
- The client says she wants a divorce because she thinks that this is the only legal remedy available to solve her problem.
- If the client knew that other remedies existed (e.g., annulment, judicial separation, a support order) she would consider these options.
- What the client is really troubled about is the fact that her husband beats the kids; a divorce is the only way she thinks she can stop it.
- The client does not want a divorce. She is being pressured by her husband to institute divorce proceedings. He threatened her with violence if she refuses.
- The client consciously or unconsciously wants and needs an opportunity to tell someone how badly the world is treating her and, if given this opportunity, she may not want to terminate the marriage.
- If the client knew that marriage counseling was available in the community, she would consider using it before taking the drastic step of going to a law office for a divorce.

If any of these observations is correct, think of how damaging it would be for someone in the law office to take out the standard divorce forms and quickly fill them out immediately after the client says, "I want a divorce." This response would not be appropriate without first probing beneath the statement to determine what in fact is on the client's mind. Some clients who speak only of divorces and separation agreements are receptive to and even anxious for reconciliation. The danger exists that the client might be steered in the direction of divorce because no other options are presented to her or because no one takes the time to help her express the ideas, intentions, and desires that are lurking beneath the otherwise clear statement, "I want a divorce."

This is not to say that you must psychoanalyze every client or that you must always distrust what the client tells you initially. It is rather a recognition of the fact that *most people are confused about the law and make requests based on misinformation about what courses of action are available to solve problems.* Common sense tells us to avoid taking all statements at face value. People under emotional distress need to be treated with sensitivity. In view of the emotions involved and the sometimes complicated nature of the law, we should not expect them to express their intentions with clarity all the time.

■ ASSIGNMENT 7.3

A client walks into the office where you work and makes the statements that follow. What areas do you think would be reasonable to probe to determine if the statement is an accurate reflection of what the client wants? What misunderstandings do you think the client might have? What further questions should you ask to be sure that you have identified what the client wants?

(a) "I want to commit my husband to a mental institution."

(b) "I can't control my teenage son anymore. I want him placed in a juvenile home."

(c) "I want to put my baby daughter up for adoption."

(d) "I want to dissolve my business."

(e) "I want to sell my house."

(f) "I'm fed up with that department store. I want to sue the store so that it goes out of business."

Section E. Human Relations and Communications Skills in Interviewing

---

■ ASSIGNMENT 7.4

Write down your answers to the following questions. When you have finished this chapter, come back to what you have written and ask yourself whether your perspective has changed.

(a) List some of the times you have interviewed someone. List some of the times you have been interviewed by someone.

(b) Describe what you feel are the central ingredients of a good interview in any setting.

(c) Describe a bad interview. From your experience, what are some of the worst mistakes an interviewer can make?

(d) Describe what you think are some of your strong and weak points as an interviewer.

Thus far our main emphasis has been on obtaining the facts. We now pursue this theme in the broader context of human relations and communications skills. This will raise some basic questions about who you are, how you view other people, how you are perceived by others, how you handle sensitive problems in the lives of others, etc.

Interviewing is a reflection of your personality. There are no absolute answers to interviewing problems; there is no such thing as the "perfect interview." There is such a thing, however, as an interview that works, that achieves its purpose. We need to find out what works in a legal interview.

In the following assignment, you will observe an interview role-played in class. After watching this interview, you will be asked to deduce some principles of communication involved in interviewing.

■ ASSIGNMENT 7.5

In this assignment, two students will role-play a legal interview in front of the class. The rest of the class will observe the interview and comment on it.

Instructions to Client. You will role-play the part of a client. A month ago you sprained your back while lifting a computer and carrying it from one room to another. You are an accountant. When you came into work that day you found the computer on your desk. It did not belong there and you did not know how it got there. You decided to move it to another desk. That was when you sprained your back.

You have come to the law office for legal advice. You have already seen an attorney in this office who has agreed to take your case. An interviewer has been assigned to conduct an interview with you to obtain a complete picture of what happened. This interview will now be role-played in front of the class.

The basic facts involve the computer, as indicated above. You can make up all other facts to answer the questions that will be put to you by the interviewer. Make up the name of the company for which you work, make up the details surrounding the accident, etc. You can create *any* set of facts as long as your answers are reasonably consistent with the basic facts given to you above.

Instructions to Interviewer. You will play the role of the interviewer in the case involving the sprained back. You are a paralegal in the office. All you know about the case thus far is that the office has agreed to represent the client and you have been assigned to interview the client for detailed information about the client and about the accident. Start off by introducing yourself and stating the purpose of the interview. Then proceed to the questions that you want to ask.

You do not need to know any law in order to conduct the interview. Let common sense be your guide. To compile a comprehensive picture of the facts as this client is able to convey them, what questions would you ask? Consult the material on fact particularization (FP) as you prepare and formulate questions.

The class will observe you in order to assess the manner and content of the interview. A good deal of constructive criticism may develop from the class discussion. As you listen to the criticism, try to be as objective as you can. It is difficult to conduct a comprehensive interview and probably impossible to conduct one flawlessly. For every question that you ask, there may be twenty observations on how you could have asked it differently. Hence, try not to take the comments personally.

Instructions to Class. You will be watching the interview involving the sprained back. You have two tasks:

1. Fill out a LICS (Legal Interview Communications Score) form. After the interview, take a moment to score the interview according to the LICS form that follows. The teacher will ask you to state the total score you gave the interview or to submit this score to someone who will calculate the average score from all students' scores.

2. Identify as many dos and don'ts of interviewing as you can. If you were writing a law office manual called *How to Interview,* what would you include? What guidance would you give an interviewer on taking notes during the interview, asking follow-up questions, maintaining eye contact with the client, etc.? After you observe the interview, discuss specific suggestions on what an interviewer should or should not do. Ideas will come to mind while you are filling out the LICS form. Following

Legal Interviewing Communications Score (LICS)

How to Score: You will be observing the role-playing of a legal interview and evaluating the interviewer on a 100-point scale. These 100 points will be earned in the four categories listed below. The score is not based on scientific data. It is a rough approximation of someone's oral communication skills in a legal interview. The interpretation of a score is as follows:

90–100 Points: Outstanding Interviewer
80–89 Points: Good Interviewer
60–79 Points: Fair Interviewer
0–59 Points: A Lot More Work Needs to Be Done

(Of course, the LICS does *not* assess the interviewer's ability to *write* an intake memorandum of law for the file. See Section B of this chapter.)

Category I: Factual Detail

On a scale of 0–80, how would you score the interviewer's performance in asking enough questions to obtain factual comprehensiveness? How well was FP performed?
(An 80 score means the interviewer was extremely sensitive to detail in his or her questions. A 0 score means that the interviewer stayed with the surface facts, with little or no probing for the who-what-where-why-when-how details. The more facts you think the interviewer did *not* obtain, the lower the score should be.)

Category I Score: [   ]

Category II: Control

On a scale of 0–10 how would you score the interviewer's performance in controlling the interview and in giving it direction?
(A 10 score means the interviewer demonstrated an excellent sense of control and direction in terms of knowing what his or her objectives were while asking the questions and in using the interview to meet those objectives. A 0 score means the interviewer rambled from question to question or let the client ramble from topic to topic.)

Category II Score: [   ]

Category III: Earning the Confidence of the Client

On a scale of 0–5 how would you score the interviewer's performance in gaining the trust of the client and in setting him or her at ease?
(A 5 score means the interviewer appeared to do an excellent job of gaining the trust and confidence of the client. A 0 score means the client seemed to be suspicious of the interviewer and probably doubted his or her professional competence. The more the interviewer made the client feel that he or she was genuinely concerned about the client, the higher the score. The more the client obtained the impression that the interviewer was "just doing a job," the lower the score.)

Category III Score: [   ]

Category IV: Role Identification

On a scale of 0–5 how well did the interviewer explain his or her role and the purpose of the interview?
(A 5 score means the interviewer took the time to explain clearly what his or her job was in the office and what he or she hoped to accomplish in the interview. A 0 score means either that the interviewer gave no explanation at all or mumbled through an explanation without being sensitive to whether the client understood.)

Category IV Score: [   ]

Total Score: [   ]

the class discussion on the dos and don'ts of interviewing, your teacher may ask you to make a written list of these dos and don'ts to hand in later. Also include thoughts that come to you after class.

After observing an interview, discussing it in class, and thinking about it, your class might collect all the written dos and don'ts and consolidate them into a manual of legal interviewing principles that reflects the best thinking of your class.

■ ASSIGNMENT 7.6

In your area there are probably many television programs in which some form of interviewing takes place—news programs, talk shows, etc. The instructor will select a program to be aired within the next few days. It should be a program that everyone in the class will be able to watch. Take notes on the communications skills of the interviewer for the program. Make comments on the following topics:

- *The setting of the interview.* How did it facilitate or detract from communication?
- *Focus.* What techniques or mannerisms of the interviewer facilitated or detracted from the interview's focus or direction?
- *Listening.* Was the interviewer a good listener? Explain.
- *Style of questioning.* How would you characterize the interviewer's style?
- *Self-image.* What image was the interviewer trying to project of himself or herself? Why? Did it work? Why or why not?
- *Achieving the purpose of the interview.* What purpose do you think the interviewer had in conducting the interview? Was it achieved? Why or why not?
- *Handling resistance.* Did the person being interviewed appear to resist any of the questions? If so, how was this handled by the interviewer? How should it have been handled?
- Make a list of dos and don'ts of interviewing that you deduced from watching the interview.

Make a copy of your comments and send it to the person who conducted the television program along with an explanation of this class assignment interview. If you receive a reply, share it with the class.

Communications Checklist
for Legal Interviewing

Purpose: There are no absolute rules on how to interview. There are, however, a number of considerations that you should have in mind while interviewing. The following questions are designed to increase your sensitivity about the manner in which an interview is conducted. *The more aware an interviewer is of the factors that might affect communication, the greater the likelihood that an effective interview will result.* These factors are posed below as questions or as a communications checklist. The checklist items are not mutually exclusive. Nor is there universal agreement on how some of these questions should be answered.

_____ Do I fully understand the purpose of this interview? Do I know what my supervisor wants me to accomplish?

_____ How do I prepare for this interview? From an office manual checklist? By talking with others who have conducted similar interviews in the past? Trial and error?

_____ Do I want to conduct this interview? Do I view this interview as my thousandth? Do I wish someone else would do this interview? Do I feel that I am doing the office a favor in conducting the interview? Do I feel that I am doing the client a favor? Has the day long passed when I view each interview as a potential learning experience?

_____ Where should the interview be conducted? In my office? At the client's home or place of work? Would it make any difference?

_____ How am I dressed? Do I dress to suit *my* personal taste? Have I thought about the impact my clothes and appearance may have on the client and on the effectiveness of the interview? Am I secure enough to ask the opinion of a colleague? How could I encourage a colleague to give me an honest opinion on how I come across to people?

_____ Do I have enough time to conduct this interview? If not, on whom will I take out my frustration?

_____ How should I introduce myself to the client? I understand my title and everyone else in the law office understands my title. Does this automatically mean that the client will understand my title? Should I assume that the client won't care? Does the client think I am an attorney? Does the client think that I am experienced and competent in this kind of case? After the interview, if the client were asked by a friend or relative who I was, what would the client say other than "someone who works in the office"? To what extent does the client need to know my job description and background?

_____ How is my office arranged? Professionally? Casually? How private is the interview? Can anyone overhear my conversation with the client?

_____ Do I know what client confidentiality means? Do I have a clear understanding of when confidentiality is violated? Do I appreciate the gray areas? Does the client understand his or her confidentiality rights? Should I make specific assurances to the client about confidentiality?

_____ Do I know what legal advice is? Do I know how to answer questions that directly or indirectly ask me for legal advice?

_____ Do I use a questionnaire in the interview? If so, do I know why each question is on the questionnaire? How closely do I follow the questionnaire? Do I know when I can deviate from it? Is it only a guide or is it something that I must follow rigorously?

_____ What should I say, if anything, to the client about the questionnaire?

_____ Do I take notes on what the client says? If so, what do I say to the client, if anything, about the fact that I am taking notes?

_____ How extensive are my notes? What am I doing to increase the speed of my note-taking?

_____ In answering questions, clients are certain about some facts, but uncertain about others. Do I know how to take notes about *both* kinds of answers? Do I fall into the trap of taking notes on only concrete answers of the client? Do I understand the importance of articulating on paper (in my client intake memo) when the client *thinks* something happened, or *probably* did something on a given date?

_____ How do I help the client recall factual details?

_____ How do I help the client unravel complicated facts so that the "story" of the case can be told coherently—for instance, chronologically?

_____ Do I know how to *particularize* a fact by asking all the appropriate who-what-where-why-when-how questions concerning the fact? Am I scrupulous about dates, places, verification details, etc.?

_____ Do I ask follow-up questions to help the client give more specific factual detail? Or do I let the interview wander from topic to topic, question to question, answer to answer?

_____ When the client answers a question by saying, "I'm not sure," or "Maybe," do I ask questions designed to help the client remember with greater specificity? (If no greater specificity is possible, see the standard above on the importance of stating when the client was ambiguous or unsure about a fact.)

_____ Do I make the distinction between facts that establish what happened and facts that help verify someone's version of what happened? Do I ask questions that elicit both kinds of facts?

_____ Is the client answering my questions? If not, is it due to the manner in which I am asking the questions?

_____ Am I condescending to the client? Do I know when I am condescending?

_____ Do I talk distinctly?

_____ Do I use words the client cannot understand, such as legal jargon or terms of art? Since most people do not want to admit that they don't understand a word or phrase, how do I know whether the client understands everything I am saying?

_____ Interviewers have a mental picture or at least a general idea of the topic of the interview, such as a car accident. What do I do when something comes up during the interview that does not fall into the pigeonhole of this mental picture or general idea? Do I block it out of my mind? How do I know that I *don't* block it out?

_____ Have I made the client feel welcome?

_____ Am I aware of the impact and importance of attentive listening? Am I one of the few attentive listeners around?

_____ Do I build the client's ego? Do I understand that ego building is not achieved merely by praising someone?

_____ Am I offended if the client does not build my ego? Am I aware of my ego needs in an interview?

_____ Am I willing to say to the client, "I don't know"?

_____ How do I handle the client's embarrassment over one of my questions?

_____ How do I handle my own embarrassment over one of my questions or over one of the client's answers? Am I aware of the embarrassment?

_____ How do I handle the client's irritation over one of my questions?

_____ How do I handle my own irritation over an answer to one of my questions? Am I aware of the irritation?

_____ How do I handle a client who is telling me something I do not believe?

_____ When I have personal knowledge of some aspect of what the client is saying, do I record the client's perspective or my own? Do I know the difference?

_____ When, if ever, should I role-play with the client? (For example, if I am trying to help the client recall a conversation, I might take the role of the other party in the conversation to see if it aids recollection.)

_____ Have I determined what the client wants? Do I know what his or her expectations are?

_____ At the conclusion of the interview, have I made it clear to the client what I will do, what the office will do, and what the client is to do as the next step?

_____ Am I a good interviewer? How do I know? Who has evaluated me? How can I obtain feedback on the quality of my interviewing skill? Who is around whom I respect enough to give me this feedback? How can I approach this person? For 99% of us, intensive criticism is unsettling and threatening to us—even if it is constructive. What makes me think that I fall into the 1% category?

Section F. Analysis of a Legal Interview

What follows is an analysis of a hypothetical interview involving Sam Donnelly, a senior citizen who walks into a law office seeking legal assistance. He will be interviewed by Jane Collins, a paralegal in the office. We will assume that her attorney–supervisor has instructed her to find out as much as possible about his problem. Since the office is government funded, the question of fees will not be involved. In analyzing this interview, our central concern will be the techniques or principles of communication that can be effective in interviewing.

[Setting: There is a knock at Jane Collins' door. She gets up from her chair, goes over to the door, opens it, and says to the man facing her (as she extends her hand for a handshake):]

Paralegal: *Hello, my name is Jane Collins. Won't you come in?*

Suppose that the paralegal did not go to the door to greet the client, and instead merely called from her chair, "Come in," in a loud voice. Do you think that it makes any difference whether the interviewer walks over to the client or not? When an individual walks with someone into a room, is the individual saying "come share my room with me"? If, on the other hand, the individual is seated at her desk and calls the visitor in, is the message to the visitor likely to be: "This is my room; I am in control of it; you may enter"? Consciously or unconsciously, the interviewer may want to project herself as a figure of authority to the client.

The interviewer cannot assume that the client will approve of and be receptive to everything the interviewer does simply because the interviewer is trying to help. It may be more appropriate to assume that the client is confused about who the interviewer is, and therefore will be somewhat suspicious of what the interviewer does until trust has been established.

Principle: The interviewer has the responsibility of building a relationship of trust with the client.

Studies have shown that clients rate "evidence of concern" as being even more significant than the results they obtain from a law office.[1] Furthermore, for the relationship between office personnel and the client to work, the client must feel that the office has a genuine interest in the client as a person.

Paralegal: *Let me take your coat for you. Won't you have a seat?* [*The paralegal points the client toward a chair that is at the opposite end of the desk where the paralegal sits. They face each other.*]

Note the seating arrangement the paralegal selects as illustrated in diagram A. "I" stands for interviewer and "C" stands for client.

Diagram A

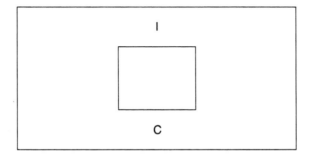

---

[1]H. Freeman & H. Weihofen, *Clinical Law Training, Interviewing and Counseling: Text and Cases,* 13 (1972).

A number of other seating arrangements could have been used:

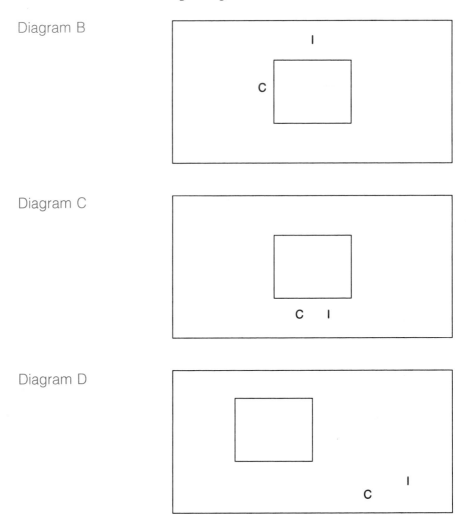

Diagram B

Diagram C

Diagram D

The chairs can be arranged so that the interviewer and the client sit at opposite ends of a desk (diagram A), diagonally across a desk (diagram B), at the same end of a desk (diagram C), or at another end of the room away from the desk altogether (diagram D). Seating arrangements are usually made at the convenience of the "owner" of the office. Rarely is enough thought given to how a particular arrangement may help or hurt the flow of communication. Sometimes the seating arrangement will create an austere and official atmosphere; other settings may be close and warm.

Principle: Select a seating arrangement that will maximize communication.

Of the four seating arrangements diagrammed above, which do you think would be most effective? Which would you feel most comfortable with? Which do you think the client would be most comfortable with? A number of factors can help you answer these questions. First, there is probably no single seating arrangement that will be perfect for all situations. The interviewer must be flexible enough to experiment with different arrangements. Will you be taking notes while interviewing? If so, do you want the client to be able to see what you are writing? Would this make him more at ease? If so, which arrangements would facilitate this? Do you want to project yourself as an authority figure? Do you, on the other hand, want the client to feel closer to you and not to have the impression that you are hiding behind a desk? Do you think it would ever be wise to change a seating arrangement in the middle of an interview? If a particular arrangement is used for the initial interview, do you think a different arrangement might ever be appropriate for follow-up interviews with the same client? When the client lifts his head, do you want him to be looking straight at you (diagram A) or do you think that it might be more comfortable for him to be able to face his head in other directions (diagram B) without appearing to scatter his attention?[2]

Of course, an office is much more than an arrangement of desks and chairs. Describe the potential benefits or disadvantages of the following:

1. Numerous posters on the wall contain political slogans
2. A half-dozen citations, certificates, and degrees are on the wall
3. The desk is cluttered with papers and books
4. The room is completely bare except for two chairs and a desk
5. The interviewer is dressed very casually
6. The interviewer is wearing a formal three-piece suit
7. The interviewer is smoking, eating lunch, or drinking coffee
8. The interviewer has no ashtray in the room
9. A "Please don't smoke" sign is on the wall
10. An open case file of another client is on the interviewer's desk
11. The secretary keeps knocking on the door or calling the paralegal on the phone for emergencies that require immediate attention
12. The paralegal does not have her own office and talks to the client with secretaries or other personnel around

Generally speaking, room settings that are extreme should always be avoided. Furthermore, the paralegal must be scrupulous in preserving the *confidentiality* of a client's case. Item 10 is therefore totally inappropriate. What about item 12?

Principle: Always be sensitive to the client's right to confidentiality.

Client: *It's a little hard getting around lately.*
Paralegal: *What do you mean?*
Client: *Oh, I just ache all over, you know, and on a hot day like this . . . my asthma gets up and, you know, I can hardly breathe sometimes. I'm sorry. I'm just a little out of breath coming up the stairs and all.*
Paralegal: *Well, just take your time and relax a bit.*
Client: *It's these bus drivers . . . I don't have a car; I lost it. It's not easy to get around . . . [Pause] Well, I feel a little better now.*
Paralegal: *Uh-huh.*
Client: *My wife is sick, and me, I'm not feeling too good. I've been sick going on three years. It goes back about eight or nine years. The last two or three years, I honestly haven't been able to do anything.*
Paralegal: *Sir, I didn't get your name.*
Client: *Donnelly, Sam Donnelly, the wife's name is Sarah.*

---

[2]See also White, *Architectural Suggestions for a Law Office Building,* 9 Practical Lawyer 66 (No. 8, 1956).

In this sequence, it's perhaps more significant to note what the paralegal did *not* say than what she did say. It may have been very tempting for the paralegal to have begun by asking the client, "What's the problem?" as soon as he sat down. Instead, the paralegal allowed the client to talk about what was on *his* mind. The interview did not begin by the paralegal directing the course of the interview through questions or comments. There are a number of benefits to this approach. First, the client is given an opportunity to relax; he is not immediately pressured by questions. Second, the message that comes across is that the paralegal is interested in the client as a person. The client obviously wants someone to listen to his story of how the world is mistreating him. He's sick; he can't get around, etc. Avoid dismissing such talk as either irrelevant to the interview or as typically senile. Much more sensitivity is required. Apparently this client is old and without substantial means. Perhaps to him the most significant information about his life is that he is old and sick. It is an extremely important event to him to be able to share this with someone else and to have his story listened to with concern. Third, by letting the client talk, indeed, by letting him ramble on a bit, the paralegal may be able to collect information not as easily obtained by pointed questioning at the outset.

There are, of course, limitations in this approach. The paralegal does not have all day to interview this client. Other tasks may be waiting to be done. In the interview under analysis, however, the exchange was relatively short; it took a matter of seconds before the paralegal began to direct the attention of the client to such basic data as his name. It is not always easy to break off the conversation in this way. The interruption must be handled with tact.

> **Principle: The interviewer should consider the advantages of permitting the client to say what is on his mind at the outset instead of beginning with a series of questions.**

If the client has nothing to say at the outset, then of course the paralegal will have to take the initiative with questions such as, "How are you today?" "Is there anything I can help you with?" or "I understand you've come to this office about a legal matter."

Soon after the interview begins, the paralegal should be taking notes on what the client is saying. The notes should be extensive. The paralegal should say something about the notes to the client such as, "I hope you don't mind if I make a few notes on what you say so that I don't forget anything." This should set the client's mind at ease about her writing. The client will probably respect the paralegal for this thoroughness and consideration in explaining the writing to him. In addition to aiding the paralegal's memory, the notes serve another important function: recordkeeping. In a law office, every case must be adequately documented. Personnel other than the paralegal will probably be working on the case at many stages. A well-kept case record can save a great deal of time and ensure accuracy. After the interview, the paralegal should take the time to compose a coherent report (intake memo) on the interview from her notes.

> **Principle: The interviewer should take notes and explain to the client why she is doing so.**

The paralegal is always looking for clues (or flags) of potential legal problems. From the brief exchange between the paralegal and Mr. Donnelly, a number of such problems may have surfaced. At some point in the interview, the paralegal must ask questions about them if the client does not volunteer further information. Note that the client may not know which of his problems are legal and which are not. He may have come in with one problem on his mind but reveal a number of others as he speaks. Here again we see the value of letting the client talk. This approach is much more beneficial than saying to the client, "Tell me all your legal problems." It is the job of the interviewer to assist the client in identifying such problems. What are some of his potential legal problems that require further inquiry?

- He lost his car. Was it stolen or repossessed?
- He is sick. Is he getting proper medical attention? Is he receiving all the public medical services to which he is entitled?
- His wife is sick; same questions as to her.
- Is there an emergency that requires immediate attention?

The last question is essential. Very early in the interview, the paralegal must determine whether a crisis exists with respect to such matters as health or housing. If so, then the office must act immediately either through legal proceedings or by helping the client obtain government emergency social services.

> **Principle: The interviewer is always alert to the flags indicating potential legal problems.**
>
> Paralegal: *Mr. Donnelly, I am a paralegal . . .*
> Client: *A what?*
> Paralegal: *A paralegal. I am not an attorney. My job is to get some preliminary information so that when you do see a lawyer, he'll be able to help you a lot more quickly.*

Do you think that the client understands who Jane Collins is? If he were asked what a paralegal is, what do you think he would answer? What obligation does the interviewer have, if any, to be sure that the client knows whom he is talking to before asking him for personal information?

> **Principle: It should be made absolutely clear to the client that the paralegal is not an attorney.**
>
> Client: *I don't have any money, and I went to these welfare people and they won't put me on the program. They say I'm not sick enough. And I haven't been able to do a solid day's work in, oh, two and a half years now. Every once in a while I do a little bit and I have to lay down for hours. Go to the doctor a couple times a month. I've been to the hospital two or three times. So, you know, I don't really know how or what you can do about this. I really don't. I don't know what to do. My wife has been sick too.*
> Paralegal: *Everything's been hitting you at once, it seems.*

Note again how the client's story is beginning to unfold. The paralegal learns for the first time that Mr. Donnelly has been to a welfare department and has been told that he does not qualify for a program because he is not sick enough. Most assuredly, this information should go into the paralegal's notes for further questioning. Clients sometimes tell their stories piecemeal rather than in a coherent fashion. The job of the interviewer is to put these pieces together.

How would you characterize the paralegal's statement that, "Everything's been hitting you at once, it seems"? Patronizing? Sympathetic? Unprofessional? What effect do you think it had on the client? Do you think that, with this statement, the paralegal is taking sides? Suppose the paralegal said, "It sounds like the government is really trying to do you in," or "Well, of course, you know, Mr. Donnelly, the government is made up of a large group of people and it's almost impossible for them to please everyone." Would these be appropriate opinions for the paralegal to express, if she believes either of them? Shouldn't she be honest about her feelings?

Generally, it is more appropriate for the paralegal to be *neutral* in the expression of personal opinions. It is not the paralegal's job to comment on the evils of government or to be apologetic about government. This does not mean, however, that she should always refrain from expressing personal feelings about subjects. If the client is telling a horror story about his life, it would be only natural for the paralegal to react with surprise or dismay. This is fine as long as the paralegal does not lose perspective and objectivity in trying to gather all the facts.

> **Principle: The interviewer should exercise self-restraint in the expression of personal opinions or feelings. Remain neutral unless it would be awkward and unnatural not to express oneself in the context of the interview.**

It is all too tempting for a paralegal to become overly involved in the emotional aspects of assisting people with legal problems. The paralegal must retain composure in a milieu where tempers can run high and where facts can change rapidly. The best legal service can be provided by someone with a cool head. Again, this does not necessarily mean that the paralegal cannot identify with the very real frustrations and problems of the client. Objectivity is not inconsistent with empathy.

Paralegal: *Mr. Donnelly, before we get down to the specifics of your case, I need to ask you a few questions. As you may know, this office does not charge clients for its services as long as the client lives within the area served by this office and does not have income above a certain level. We provide free service to low-income clients.*

Client: *Well, I'll tell you, I think I could pass the test, yes ma'am! I have a little nest egg, but I haven't been able to work over the years . . .*

Paralegal: *How much do you have left?*

Client: *I have about $500, $600 in the bank.*

Paralegal: *Uh-huh.*

Client: *But I'll tell you, that's about to be eaten up. I don't have a car. It's really hard to get around on the bus. Other than that, the wife's got a little bit of jewelry, a wedding ring, stuff like that. And that's about it.*

Paralegal: *Do you rent an apartment?*

Client: *Yes, we do.*

Paralegal: *What about Social Security. Do you receive any income there?*

Client: *Well, we get a little bit of Social Security.*

Paralegal: *How much is that?*

Client: *$305 a month. I can't live on that. My wife is taking work into the house like . . . She's been sick lately. We don't have the money coming in.*

Paralegal: *Do you have any children?*

Client: *No.*

Paralegal: *Okay, Let me ask you a couple of other questions. I want to make sure that I have the street right. You want to give that to me?*

Client: *Delores, 1429 Delores Street, Apartment 7B.*

Paralegal: *What about a phone? Still have it?*

Client: *Yes. The number is 824-8027.*

Paralegal: *824-8027. Fine. Well, it's pretty clear that you're eligible for our services.*

Client: *Very good, I sure do need it.*

Paralegal: *Okay, I've got some other questions that I want to ask you, and if there are things that you want to say, just stop me. If you have any questions, just stop me and ask.*

Client: *Okay.*

The paralegal was correct in stating that government-funded legal service offices do not charge clients for their services as long as they live within a designated geographical area and meet an income test. Regulations exist on how much income and assets a family can have in order to be eligible. The paralegal (or sometimes the receptionist) has the job of determining eligibility based on office charts.

Matters of income and wealth are intensely personal and must be approached with great delicacy. A rapid-fire series of questions such as, "Do you work?" "How much do you make?" "How much do you have in the bank?" "Do your relatives give you money?" can be very demoralizing. The common complaint against bureaucracy is the distance and impersonality with which it deals with the public. There is absolutely no reason why a law office must act in the same manner, no matter how busy it is.

Note that the client was somewhat hesitant about answering some of the questions and took every opportunity to demonstrate how poor he was. This is understandable. Perhaps he was not aware of the fact that the office was *not* actively looking for ways to disqualify people and that he will normally be taken at his word on eligibility. The dignity of the client requires that the interviewer not assume that everything said is a lie until proven otherwise.

Principle: Whenever an interviewer is asking a client for personal information, the client should clearly know why the information is needed. It should be taken with great sensitivity.

Paralegal: *Mr. Donnelly, do you have any papers with you . . . anything that was sent to you concerning the problem that you want some help with?*

Client: *Yes, I brought it along here. I'm not sure I understand it all.*

Paralegal: *Okay, let's take a look at it.*

Now the paralegal has gotten through the preliminaries, and the central core of the interview is about to begin. There are a number of options available. Here the paralegal began concretely by asking a directed or close-ended question, one that required the client to focus on a very specific area—the legal papers. This is usually a good way to begin. The event that convinces clients that they should receive legal help is often the receipt of papers, either through the mail or delivered (served) to them in person. The papers may be confusing and upsetting.

Principle: As soon as possible, the interviewer should try to focus on concrete matters that are bothering the client.

There are other ways that the paralegal could have proceeded. The paralegal could have asked, "What's the problem?" or "What's on your mind?" These are *open-ended questions.* They invite the client to respond in a wide variety of ways within the general confines of the question. Unlike the directed or *close-ended question,* the client is given control of the situation when asked an open-ended question. The danger of such a question is that the client will ramble on at great length, providing irrelevant as well as relevant data. It may be difficult for the paralegal to follow the answer. On the other hand, the client may have a need to vent his frustrations in this way. It is often important to "get it off his chest" and have someone listen to the complete story. Once the client has been allowed to experience this catharsis, he may be better able to relate to the more directed questions of the interviewer.

> **Principle: Interviewers must be sensitive to when clients are ready to answer directed questions.**

Another approach would be to refer back to something the client said earlier in the interview. For example, the paralegal could have said, "Mr. Donnelly, you said earlier that you applied for a program. Could you tell me a little bit more about that?" It can be reassuring for the client to know that the interviewer has been listening to what he has been saying and wants to know more.

One of the most effective ways to assist a client is to help him give the facts in sequence. "When did you become ill?" "How was the illness treated?" "When did you apply at the welfare department?" "What happened next?" The client has one large story to tell and perhaps a series of substories. Each story can be conceived of as a unit with a beginning, middle, and end. Helping the client reconstruct the stories chronologically will aid him in recalling details and will assist the paralegal in later organizing notes for the office file.

> Paralegal: *This is a letter from the welfare department denying your application for disability payments. When did you get this, Mr. Donnelly?*
> Client: *Oh, just a couple of weeks ago. They don't know what they are talking about! I can't understand why they are lying. They are not giving me the respect I am entitled to.*

Clients are very much inclined to think in terms of opinions, conclusions, and characterizations, as opposed to facts. A primary objective of the interviewer is to identify the *facts*. The client's interpretations of the facts may be important. However, the discussion must go beyond or behind the interpretations to cover the basic factual questions: who, when, where, how, etc.? When a client gives an opinion or a characterization of a fact or series of facts, the interviewer must ask the client to talk about what led to the interpretation. When and if a client becomes involved in an agency proceeding or a court hearing, the referee or judge will focus primarily on the facts that are alleged. Hence it is the job of the interviewer, as early as possible, to uncover as many underlying relevant facts as she can.

> **Principle: An interviewer should always encourage a client to spell out all the facts that led him to a particular conclusion or interpretation of what happened or is happening.**

The paralegal asked the client when he had received the letter. From the paralegal's study of welfare law, she knows that there are certain requirements that must be met whenever the welfare department makes decisions. One such requirement relates to the time span between the date of the decision and the date the client is notified of the decision. Another problem is the length of time the client has to appeal after receiving written notice of a decision.

> Paralegal: *Why did you wait two weeks to come in?*
> Client: [Mr. Donnelly slumps a little in his chair and looks around the room.]
> Paralegal: *Well, it's not that important.*

Here the paralegal has asked a "why question," potentially calling into question either the client's motives or his competence. Luckily, the paralegal picked up on the inappropriateness of the question right away from the client's nonverbal cues (change in seating posture and apparent loss of attention). If the "why information" is important, it may be better to wait until later to try to obtain it. The paralegal must always be alert to *nonverbal communication:* mannerisms, gestures, silence, etc.

> **Principle: The interviewer must be able to interpret nonverbal forms of communication.**

> Paralegal: *Well, Mr. Donnelly, what I'd like to do is find out a little bit more about what happened. When did you first apply?*
> Client: [A long silence.]
> Paralegal: *Mr. Donnelly, when did . . .*
> Client: *I'm not sure.*

This particular client is very opinionated and may have taken offense at the interviewer's sudden shift from his (the client's) opinions ("they are lying") to the "why inquiry" and the cold facts ("When did you first apply?"). A client who is silent or who uses comments such as "I'm not sure" or "I don't know" may be on a different wavelength from the interviewer. The client often has his own agenda and expectations from the interview. Of course, the statement "I don't know" may mean nothing more than the absence of knowledge, just as silence may simply mean that the client needs more time or guidance to remember the facts. On the other hand, they could be a signal to the interviewer that communication is breaking down. There are a number of ways to deal with this. The interviewer could change the topic for the moment. She could ask the client if anything is troubling him. Or, she could simply proceed and try to play it by ear. In Mr. Donnelly's case, all that may be required is giving him the opportunity to express his opinions as often as possible. This is fine as long as they do not interfere with the fact-gathering function of the interview.

> **Principle: Interviewers must be able to recognize client discomfort or non-cooperation and to deal with it flexibly.**

> Paralegal: *Could I ask you what you mean when you say that they are not treating you with respect?*
> Client: *I am disabled and they tell me I'm not. It's plain for anyone to see.*
> Paralegal: *What we would have to do then, Mr. Donnelly, is to try to show that they are wrong.*
> Client: *Yes, very wrong.*
> Paralegal: *And to do it, what we need to do is get a complete picture of all the facts so that when we challenge them, we will be able to do it correctly. So, I'd like to start by your giving me an estimate (in days, weeks, or even months) of how long ago you first applied.*
> Client: *I think it was a month ago. I have it written down at home.*

How would you analyze this exchange? What do you think the paralegal did that was or was not effective? Note the sensitivity with which the paralegal is questioning the client. The first time the paralegal asked him when he initially applied, she got no response. When she asked the same question less directly (in terms of estimates), she had greater success.

> **Principle: The style or manner of questioning should flexibly fit the unfolding and often shifting context of the interview.**

> Paralegal: *Looking at your letter here, I see that it was signed by Ralph Smith of the welfare department. After you leave, I will call him and ask him*

about things such as the date you applied. In addition, I'd appreciate it if you would call me when you get home and have had time to look at your own notes of when you applied. Could you do that?

Client: *Yes, I will.*

Whenever practical, it is wise to have the client take some steps on his own behalf. This tends to ensure a sense of involvement and cooperation between office staff and client. It also is a step in the direction of accuracy, since the client is often in the best position to collect certain facts or perform certain tasks.

Principle: Whenever practical, the interviewer should ask the client to perform tasks on his own to aid the office in handling the case.

Exactly how much you can ask a client to do depends on the circumstances. Some clients may be willing and able to do a good deal, such as help locate a lost relative or make a written list of all known debts. Again, however, this aspect of legal services must be handled with care. The client cannot be asked to do the job of the paralegal or the attorney.

The paralegal told the client that she was going to call the welfare department. The client should be told what steps the office proposes on his behalf. A client needs to know what action will be taken.

Principle: As often as possible, the office should explain the concrete steps it proposes to take on behalf of the client.

Paralegal: *Time and again, here in the office, we have clients who are unsure about such basic things as dates, amounts, what was signed, and so on. Of course, you can't be expected to have a record of everything. We have to be practical. All I'm saying is that it's a good idea for a person to keep a record of as many basic things as possible.*

Here we have the paralegal stepping out of her role as interviewer and becoming a teacher. This can be upsetting to some clients; others will appreciate it very much. Here, the lecture on keeping records is fundamental, since documentation is fundamental in the law.

Paralegal: *Okay, fine. Just as soon as you can call me, please do it. Now I want to ask you some questions about your medical history. First, let's get back to this letter. It says that your application for Aid for the Totally Disabled was denied because they say you are not disabled. It also says that they examined the medical records you brought with you. Is that right?*

Client: *Yes, I brought my papers there.*

Paralegal: *Do you have these papers with you now?*

Client: *No, they are at home. Do you want me to bring them to you?*

Paralegal: *Yes, would you? Why don't you take this piece of paper and make a note of the things you should do. First, you are going to call me to let me know the date you first applied. Then you are going to bring me the medical records that the welfare department looked at when they were deciding on your application. Do you have all that?*

Client: *Yes, I think so.*

Paralegal: *Could you give me the name and address of the doctor who most recently examined you?*

Client: *Dr. Edward Zuder of 7th Avenue; I don't know the exact address.*

Paralegal: *What other doctors have examined you?*

Client: *Well, I'm not sure. There was one that I saw a few months ago in Mason County.*

Paralegal: *Do you remember the doctor's name?*

Client: *Johnson, or Thompson, I don't recall fully. I think my wife would know. I'll ask her. She's better at names than me.*

Paralegal: *That would be fine. Have her do that. In fact, Mr. Donnelly, what I am going to need is a list of every doctor that you have seen within the last five years. When you bring me your medical records, a lot of the names and addresses will be there. Some may not be. Just try to remember—you and your wife—as many as you can. Why don't you add that to the list of things you are going to do? With your permission, I will call some of them for some basic information.*

Client: *For five years? Why do you need all that?*

Paralegal: *I know it's a lot of information, but from experience we know that old medical records are often very important. We should be prepared.*

Client: *Well, I'll get what I can.*

The paralegal is probing for information. Probing is important but sometimes difficult to do. The client should never feel that he is being interrogated or cross-examined. It is obvious that Mr. Donnelly cannot be pushed much further. He cannot be expected to recall all the information the paralegal is seeking. When he was surprised at being asked for information dating back five years, he may have been reacting not simply to the difficulty of obtaining such data but also to the possible implication that the paralegal doubted his claim. Do you think that the client felt that he had to prove something *to the paralegal?*

Principle: Probing is a valid technique of data-gathering, but it must be used with care to avoid making the client uncomfortable.

The paralegal did not simply rely on probing the client to obtain information. Jane Collins has a talent for trying different approaches to data-gathering. She asked the client to check his records and call her, and she also asked him to bring records to her. Finally, *she* will take the initiative in making some calls herself. These are a series of comprehensive steps calculated to obtain facts and to cross-check the validity of facts.

The steps used by the paralegal demonstrate the intimate relationship between interviewing and investigation. The interviewer lays the groundwork for the investigative function (which in this office may or may not be performed by the same paralegal). Both the interviewer and the investigator seek relevant facts that can be verified or documented. If names, dates, and witnesses must be tracked down in the field by the investigator, the process is begun by a thorough interview.

The same is true of the informal and formal advocacy function. At some later point, the office may try to negotiate the case with the welfare department through informal advocacy in order to obtain what the client wants without resorting to a formal agency hearing or a court proceeding. If informal advocacy does not work, formal advocacy at agency hearings or in court may be tried. All these steps begin with and are dependent on a competent initial client interview. The groundwork is established at this level with fact and problem identification on the one hand and a trustful, cooperative client on the other.

Principle: Interviewing is intimately connected with and is the foundation for investigation, negotiation, and formal advocacy.

Client: *Do you think I have a chance of winning?*

Paralegal: *Well, we're going to study your case carefully. I can tell you definitely that you do have a right to fight the department for denying your application. This could mean forcing them into a fair hearing. Before any final decision on strategy is made, however, I and one of the attorneys here in the office will be checking with you.*

Client: *I see.*

Has the paralegal given the client legal advice? The paralegal is interpreting administrative regulations on challenging welfare decisions in reference to a particular client's case.

Generally, if an administrative agency authorizes a lay person to represent clients before it, this authorization includes the right to give legal advice in preparation for such representation. The welfare department provides such authorization. Hence, the paralegal can give legal advice to Mr. Donnelly in this case. If there is no specific authorization for lay representation at agency hearings, then the paralegal cannot give legal advice. Normally, no such authorization exists when the case involves traditional divorce, landlord-tenant, consumer fraud, or other court cases. In such cases, the role of the paralegal is limited to fact-gathering in interviewing and investigation, preliminary drafting of legal documents for attorneys, legal research, etc. Of course, in every case, a paralegal can give clients legal advice when the advice is specifically dictated by an attorney. In such situations, the paralegal is merely relaying a message from the attorney to the client.

Principle: The paralegal must know what legal advice is and when she can and cannot give it to clients.

The paralegal properly instructed the client on how the office functions in handling cases: paralegals work closely with attorneys, and both are in regular communication with the client.

The paralegal used the phrase "fair hearing" without explaining that this is the technical procedure used by the welfare department to permit clients to challenge its actions. The client, on the surface, appeared to understand when he said, "I see." It is more probable, however, that the client was simply covering up his confusion by being polite.

Principle: Technical terms (i.e., jargon) should either be rejected in favor of understandable English or explained clearly to clients.

Paralegal: *Well, I think that we have gone about as far as we can today. Is there anything else that you want to tell me, anything that I should know? Are you sure you've told me everything?*

Client: *What do you mean?*

Here again it is possible that the client could take offense to this last question. The client might be thinking, "Doesn't she trust me? I've tried to tell her everything." On the other hand, experienced interviewers know that clients have a natural inclination to overstate their case, to highlight what they feel are the good points of their case, and to minimize anything negative about their case. They may fear that the office will not take their case if it knew the whole story. Furthermore it may take more than one interview for the client to place his full trust in the paralegal or in the office as a whole. Nevertheless, the interviewer must pursue every aspect of the case, even that which may be damaging. Better to learn everything now so that the office can be prepared for potentially negative factors than to be surprised at a hearing with information that is damaging.

While it is true that the paralegal must try to uncover everything, there are effective and ineffective ways of going about it. The approach taken by the paralegal here does *not* appear to be effective. The blanket question she asked is not likely to communicate the message that she needs to know everything. She was indirect, vague, and potentially condescending. If the paralegal suspected that there were aspects of the case that the client was concealing, she should have asked specific questions designed to determine whether her suspicions were valid. Furthermore, she should have explained to the client why it is important to provide all the facts. Perhaps this would necessitate some explanation to the client of how our *adversarial system* of justice works. When advocates for clients go before referees, judges, or juries, it is their duty to present the best case possible for the client. It is the job of the advocate for the other side to point up the negative aspects of the case. The advocate for the client, however, must be ready in advance to respond to what the other side will say. Hence the necessity of knowing everything as soon as possible. The key point that must be made to the client is that the office will not refuse to serve a client simply because he doesn't have a perfect case.

> **Principle: Interviewers must uncover both the positive and damaging aspects of a case.**

Paralegal: *I have a few forms here that I would like you to sign. They simply give this office your authority to represent you and to look at your welfare and medical records. You'll sign these here, won't you?*
Client: *You want me to sign this here?*
Paralegal: *Yes, would you?*
Client: *Okay, should my wife sign?*
Paralegal: *No, that won't be necessary.* [Client signs.] *Fine.*

Asking the client to sign papers is always a delicate matter. Very often, the client does not know what he is signing. The interviewer should assume that the client is confused about the signing. The client should be given the chance to read over what he is being asked to sign and encouraged to ask questions about what he doesn't understand. Not only is this good practice as a matter of courtesy, but it is also good training for the client to read carefully and ask questions about *any* papers *before* signing.

> **Principle: Before a client is asked to sign anything, the interviewer should be sure that the client knows what he is signing, why he is being asked to sign, and that it is up to the client to decide whether he wants to sign.**

Whenever a question is asked and the answer is strongly stated or implied in the question, we have a *leading question*. Leading questions are potentially dangerous because of the manipulative way in which words are put into the mouth of the person being asked the question. Here are some examples: "Mr. Jones, you knew that it was past midnight when you called, isn't that right?" "Wasn't it past midnight when you called?" Leading questions attempt to pressure the individual to answer in a certain way. This is not to say that a person asking leading questions is always devious. People can ask leading questions without even realizing it. They may feel that they are helping out by asking the question in this manner.

Now, look again at the statement "You'll sign these here, won't you?" Is this a leading question? Should the question have been asked in this way?

Principle: Interviewers must be able to recognize their own leading questions and to understand the dangers of such questions.

Paralegal: *Just a couple of points before we conclude, Mr. Donnelly. You said something earlier about having lost your car. What did you mean?*

Client: *Well, I had to give it to my nephew. It wasn't safe for me to drive, you know. I've been very ill lately.*

Paralegal: *I see. What about your wife? You said that she was sick. Has she applied to the welfare department for the same benefits that you applied for?*

Client: *Why, no. I never thought of her going ahead. Do you think I should?*

Paralegal: *You certainly can't lose anything. It's up to you if you want to give it a try.*

Here the paralegal is going back to her notes to ask about matters that she noted earlier. This is the sign of a thorough interview. The office is interested in all legal aspects of the client's needs. The paralegal may have suspected creditor or car repair problems. It was totally appropriate to check this out. The law is critical, however, of attorneys who try to stir up legal problems and who go on so-called fishing expeditions to discover legal problems of citizens in order to generate business for themselves. Such stirring up of litigation is frowned on. This was not the case here, however. The paralegal properly inquired about issues suggested by what the client told her.

The suggestion to the client that his wife apply for benefits raises another question about the role of the paralegal and the office. Clients should not be pressured, persuaded, or urged to take courses of action. The task of the office is to lay out *options* for the client, explain the merits and demerits of each option, and leave it for the client to decide what he wants to do. If the client asks for a recommendation on what option to choose, an answer should be given, but it should always be made clear to the client that he has the final responsibility to decide what he wants to do. The paralegal in this case acted properly. She did not urge Mr. Donnelly to do anything. She made the client aware of the option concerning his wife and responded to the client's specific request for her opinion about whether he should take the option.

Principle: The interviewer should not pressure the client to take any course of action.

Paralegal: *Okay, Mr. Donnelly, let's leave it at that. If you don't have any more questions, we can conclude now. I will be talking to an attorney about your case shortly. You will call me concerning the date we spoke about, bring me your medical records, and put together a list of the doctors who treated you in the last five years. I will call Mr. Smith at the welfare department to find out what I can from him. If your wife wants to talk to me about applying, have her come by or call me. We'll be glad to help her in any way we can.*

Client: *Okay, and I thank you.*

Paralegal: *Thank you for coming by. I hope we can help you. Good-bye.*

Client: *Good-bye.*

The paralegal's final comment is very significant. It is important not to leave the client with the impression that the office is definitely going to win the case. It would be easy to raise this expectation in the mind of the client, since undoubtedly this is what he wants to believe. More realistically, all the office can say is that it will do the best it can for the client and that no guarantees of success can be given. The comment "I hope we can help you" is appropriate to convey this message.

> **Principle: The interviewer must not raise false expectations in the mind of the client about what the office will be able to do.**

■ ASSIGNMENT 7.7

Form a circle of chairs centered around a single chair in the middle. The student sitting in the middle will play the role of the client. The students in the circle (numbering about ten) will be the interviewers, in rotation. The instructor will ask one of the students to begin the interview. As this student runs into difficulty during the interview, the student to his or her right picks up the interview, tries to resolve the difficulty in his or her own way, and then proceeds with the interview. If *this* student cannot resolve the difficulty, the student to his or her right tries, and so on. The objective is to identify as many diverse ways of handling difficulties as possible in a relatively short period. No interviewer should have the floor for more than a minute or two at any one time. The student playing the role of the client is given specific instructions about how to play the role—that is, sometimes he or she is asked to be shy; other times, demanding. The client should not overdo the role, however. He or she should respond naturally within the role assigned. Here are four sets of instructions to attempt this "interview in rotation."

(a) The interviewer greets the client and says, "I am a paralegal." The client is confused about what a paralegal is. The interviewer explains. The client is insistent upon a comprehensive definition that he or she can understand.

(b) The client comes to the law office because he or she is being sued for negligent driving. The interviewer asks the client if he or she must wear eyeglasses to drive. The answer is *yes*. The interviewer then asks if he or she was wearing eyeglasses during the accident. The client is very reluctant to answer. (In fact, the client was not wearing glasses at the time.) The client does not appear to want to talk about this subject. The interviewer persists.

(c) The client is being sued by a local store for $750.00 in grocery bills. The client has a poor memory and the interviewer must think of ways to help him or her remember. The client wants to cooperate but is having trouble remembering.

(d) The client wants to sue an auto mechanic. The client gives many opinions, conclusions, and judgments (such as: "The mechanic is a crook," "I was their best customer," "The work done was awful.") The interviewer is having difficulty encouraging the client to state the facts underlying the opinions. The client insists on stating conclusions.

After each exercise, the class should discuss principles, guidelines, and techniques of interviewing.

■ ASSIGNMENT 7.8

Below are two additional role-playing exercises to be conducted in class.

(a) The instructor asks the class if anyone was involved, in any way, in a recent automobile accident. If someone says *yes*, this student is interviewed by another class member whose job is to obtain as complete a picture as possible of what happened. At the outset the interviewer knows nothing other than that some kind of an automobile accident occurred.

(b) The instructor asks the class if anyone has recently had trouble with any government agency (like the post office or sanitation department). If someone says *yes*, this student is interviewed by another class member whose job is to obtain as complete a picture as possible of what happened. The interviewer at the outset knows nothing other than the fact that the person being interviewed has had some difficulty with a government agency.

■ ASSIGNMENT 7.9

When an office represents a debtor, one of the paralegal's major responsibilities may be to interview the client in order to write a comprehensive report on the client's assets and liabilities. Assume that your supervising attorney has instructed you to conduct a comprehensive interview of the client in order to write such a report. Assets are everything the client *owns* or has an interest in. Liabilities are everything *owed;* they are debts. These are the only definitions you need; you do not need any technical knowledge of law to conduct this interview. All you need is common sense in the formulation of questions.

Your instructor will role-play the client in front of the room. It will be a collective interview. Everyone will ask questions, but you will each write individual reports on the interview based on your own notes. Raise your hand to be recognized. Be sure to ask follow-up questions when needed for factual clarity and comprehensiveness. You can repeat the questions of other students if you think you might elicit a more detailed response. Any question is fair game as long as it is directly or indirectly calculated to uncover assets or liabilities. There may be information the client does not have at this time, such as bank account numbers. Help the client determine how such information can be obtained later. In your notes, state that you asked for information that the client didn't have and state what the client said he or she would do to obtain the information. To achieve comprehensiveness, you must obtain factual detail. This means that you go after names, addresses, phone numbers, dates, relevant surrounding circumstances, verification data, etc. In short, we want Fact Particularization. Take detailed notes on the questions asked by every student (not just your own questions) and the answers provided in response. You will have to write your report based on your own notes.

The heading of your report will be as follows:

Inter-Office Memorandum

To: [name of your instructor]

From: [your name]

Date: [date you prepared the report]

RE: Comprehensive Interview of

_____

Case File Number: _____

(Make up the case file number.) The first paragraph of your report should state what your supervisor has asked you to do in the report. Simply state what the assignment is. Organization of the data from your notes is up to you. Use whatever format you think will most clearly communicate what you learned from the client in the interview.

Chapter Summary

Interviewing is conversation for the purpose of obtaining information. In a law office, legal interviewing is designed to obtain facts that are relevant to the identification and eventual resolution of a legal problem. These facts are often reported in a document called an intake memo. Six major guides exist to the kinds of questions that should be asked during a legal interview. The most important is the instructions of the supervisor on the goals of the interview. Other guides include preprinted checklists for certain kinds of interviews, legal analysis to help you focus on issues such as relevance, "fact particularization" as a device to achieve comprehensiveness, and, finally, common sense and flexibility to help you remain alert and responsive as the interview unfolds.

A good deal of sensitivity is needed when interviewing clients. They are sometimes confused about the law and about what they want from the law.

There are a large number of factors that inhibit or facilitate communication. For example, the professional appearance of the office and of the interviewer, the seating arrangement in the office, the preservation of confidentiality, the explanation of the paralegal's role and status, the readiness of the client to answer open-ended and directed questions, the use of leading questions, the timing of probing questions, the exploration of damaging and favorable aspects of the case, the sequencing of questions designed to elicit a chronological recitation of the facts, sensitivity when covering personal matters, and the use of jargon. Finally, the paralegal must be alert to the danger of giving legal advice during the interview.

Key Terms

initial client interview	legal analysis	open-ended question
follow-up interview	legally relevant	nonverbal communication
field interview	fact particularization	probing
intake memo	analogies	legal advice
RE	confidentiality	jargon
grounds	directed question	adversarial system
checklists	close-ended question	leading question

8

Investigation in a Law Office

■ Chapter Outline

 Section A. The Nature and Context of Investigation

Investigation is the process of gathering additional facts and verifying presently known facts in order to advise a client about solving a legal problem or about preventing a legal problem from occurring. In Chapter 7 on legal interviewing, we examined six major guides to fact gathering:

■ Instructions of the supervisor

■ Checklists

■ Legal analysis

■ Fact Particularization (FP)

■ Common sense

■ Flexibility

You should review these guides now since they are equally applicable to investigation. Fact Particularization (FP) is especially important.

· · · · · · · · · · · · · · · ·

1. Investigative techniques are often very individualistic. Styles, mannerisms, and approaches to investigation are often highly personal. Through a sometimes arduous process of trial and error, the investigator develops effective techniques. While some of these techniques come from the suggestions of fellow investigators, most are acquired from on-the-job experience.

2. It is impossible to overemphasize the importance of hustle, imagination, and flexibility. If there is one characteristic that singles out the effective investigator, it is a willingness to dig. While many investigation assignments may be relatively easy (e.g., photograph the ceiling of a bathroom that a tenant claims is falling down), most assignments are open-ended in that the range of options and possible conclusions to a problem are extensive. The answer is not always there for the asking. For such assignments, investigators must be prepared to identify and pursue leads, be unorthodox, and let their feelings, hunches, and intuition lead where they will. In short, the formal principles of investigation must give way to hustle, imagination, and flexibility.

Good investigators are always in pursuit. They are on the offensive and don't wait for the facts to come to them. They know that legwork is required. They know that 50% of their leads will become dead ends. They are not frightened by roadblocks and therefore do not freeze at the first hurdle. They know that there are no perfect ways of obtaining information. They know that they must take a stab at possibilities and that it takes persistent thinking and imagination to come up with leads. At the same time, good investigators are not fools. They do not pursue blind alleys. After being on the job for a while, they have developed a feel for what is or is not a reasonable possibility or lead. They have been able to develop this feel because, when they first started investigating, they had an open mind and were not afraid to try things out.

3. Investigators may not know what they are looking for until they find it.   As with legal interviewing and legal research, good investigation may sometimes live a life of its own in terms of what it uncovers. There are two kinds of investigation assignments: the closed-ended assignment (where the end product is carefully defined in advance, such as the photograph assignment mentioned in the tenant case), and the open-ended assignment (where the investigator begins with only the general contours of a problem and is asked to fill in the facts). An example of an open-ended assignment is to find out as much as possible about the case of a client charged with burglary. In the open-ended assignment (and in some closed-ended ones), investigators are walking into the unknown. They may have no idea what they will uncover. Suppose in the burglary assignment the investigator sets out to focus on whatever is relevant to the burglary charge and in the process discovers that a homicide was involved, as yet unknown to the police. The investigator had no idea that she would find this until she found it. Suppose that the law firm has a client who is charging his employer with racial discrimination and, in the process of working on the case, the investigator discovers that this employee had a managerial job at the company and that several of the workers under him have complained that *he* practiced sex discrimination against them. The investigator had no idea that she would uncover this until it was uncovered. In short, an open mind is key when undertaking an assignment.

4. Investigation and interviewing are closely related.   The interviewer conducting the initial client interview has two responsibilities: to help identify legal problems and to obtain from the client as many relevant facts on those problems as possible. The starting point for the investigator is the report or intake memo (see Chapter 7) prepared by the interviewer on what the client said. It is either clear from this report what the investigation needs are, or they become clear only after the investigator and his or her supervisor have defined them more precisely.

The investigator should approach the interview report with a healthy skepticism. Thus far, all the office may know is what the client has said. The perspective of the office is therefore narrow. Without necessarily distrusting the client's word, the investigator's job is to verify the facts given during the interview and to determine whether new facts exist that were unknown or improperly identified during the interview. The interview report should not be taken at face value. New facts may be revealed or old facts may for the first time be seen in a context that gives them an unexpected meaning. The investigator must approach a case almost as if the office knows nothing about it or as if what the office knows is invalid. By adopting this attitude, the investigator will be able to give the case an entirely different direction when the product of the investigation warrants it.

5. *The investigator must be guided by goals and priorities.*   It is one thing to say that the investigator must be open-minded enough to be receptive to the unexpected. It is quite another to say that the investigator should start in a void. The starting point is a set of instructions from the supervisor. How clear a supervisor is about an investigation assignment may vary with each assignment. For example:

■ Supervisors may have a very definite idea of what they want.

■ Supervisors think they know what they want but are not sure.

■ Whatever conception supervisors have about what they want, they are not effective in explaining it to the investigator.

■ Supervisors have no idea what they want other than a desire to obtain as many facts about the case as possible.

The first responsibility of the investigator is to establish communication with the supervisor. With as much clarity as possible, determine what the supervisor wants accomplished through the investigation.

6. *There is a close relationship among investigation, negotiation, and trial.* There are two ultimate questions that should guide the investigator's inquiry into every fact being investigated:

■ How will this fact assist or hurt the office in attempting to settle or negotiate the case without a trial?

■ How will this fact assist or hurt the office in presenting the client's case at trial?

A large percentage of legal claims never go to full trial; they are negotiated in advance. Opposing counsel have a number of bargaining sessions in which attempts are made to hammer out a settlement acceptable to their clients. Very often they discuss the law that they think will be applicable if the case goes to trial. Even more often they present each other with the facts that they think they will be able to establish at trial. Here the investigator's report becomes invaluable. As a result of this report, the attorney should be able to suggest a wide range of facts that could be used at trial ("we have reason to believe . . ." or "we are now pursuing leads that would tend to establish that . . ." etc.). The attorney's bargaining leverage is immeasurably increased by a thorough investigation report.

If negotiations do not produce a settlement, the investigator's report can help the attorney in a number of ways:

■ Determining whether to go to trial

■ Deciding what witnesses to call

■ Choosing questions to ask of witnesses

■ Deciding how to impeach (i.e., contradict or attack the credibility of) opposing witnesses

■ Determining what tangible or physical evidence to introduce

■ Deciding how to attack the tangible or physical evidence the other side will introduce

The investigator should be familiar with the standard, pretrial *discovery devices:* depositions, interrogatories, requests for admissions, medical examination reports, etc. A *deposition* is a pretrial question-and-answer session conducted outside of court, usually in the office of one of the attorneys. The attorney asks questions of the other party (or of a witness of the other party) in order to obtain facts that will assist in preparing for trial. Depositions are often transcribed so that typed copies of the session are available. The same objective exists with the use of *interrogatories,* except that the questions and answers are usually submitted in writing rather than in person. An interrogatory is simply a question. A *request for admission* is a statement of fact submitted by one party to another. The latter is asked to admit or deny the statement. Those that are admitted do not have to be proven at trial. A request for a medical examination will be granted by the judge when medical issues are relevant to the trial.

Investigators can be of assistance during this discovery stage by helping the attorney decide what questions to ask in a deposition or in an interrogatory, what admissions to request, whether to ask for a medical examination, etc.

After the discovery devices have been used, the investigator should carefully study all the facts these devices disclosed in order to:

■ Cross-check or verify these facts, and

■ Look for new leads (names, addresses, incidents) that should be the subject of future investigation.

7. It is important to distinguish between absolute proof of a fact and some evidence of a fact. Investigators must not confuse their role with that of a judge or jury in deciding truth or falsity. The function of investigators is to identify reasonable options or fact possibilities. To be sure, they can speculate on whether a judge or jury would ever believe a fact to be true. But the presence or absence of absolute proof is not the test that should guide them in their investigations. The tests that an investigator should apply in determining whether to pursue a fact possibility are:

■ Am I reasonable in assuming that a particular fact will help establish the case of the client? Am I reasonable in assuming that if I gather enough evidence on such a fact, a judge, jury, or hearing officer *might* accept it as true?

■ Am I reasonable in assuming that a particular fact will help to challenge or discredit the case of the opposing party? Am I reasonable in assuming that if I gather enough evidence on such a fact (evidence that will challenge or discredit the case of the other side) a judge, jury, or hearing officer *might* accept it as true?

You should also approach the case from the perspective of the opponent, even to the point of assuming that you work for the other side! What facts will the opponent go after to establish its case? What is the likelihood that such facts will be accepted? Again, do not confuse proof with evidence.

8. The investigator must know some law. Investigators do not have to be experts in every area of the law or in any particular area of the law in order to perform their job. For their field work to have a focus, however, they must have at least a general understanding of evidence, civil procedure, and the areas of the law governing the facts of the client's case. They must know, for example, what *hearsay* and *relevance* mean. They must understand basic procedural steps in litigation in order to see where fact gathering can be used and how it is often used in different ways at different steps in the litigation process. Some substantive law is also needed. In a divorce case, for example, the investigator must know what the grounds for divorce are in the state. The same kind of basic information is needed for every area of the law involved or potentially involved in the client's case. Such knowledge can be obtained:

- In paralegal courses or seminars
- Through brief explanations from the supervisor
- By talking to experienced attorneys and paralegals whenever they have time to provide their perspective on the law.
- By reading a chapter in a legal treatise or a section in a legal encyclopedia that provides an overview of the relevant area of the law.

9. *The investigator must know the territory.*   When you are on the job as an investigator, it is important to begin acquiring a detailed knowledge of the makeup of the city, town, or state where you will be working. Such knowledge should include:

- The political structure of the area: Who is in power? Who is the opposition? In what direction is the political structure headed?
- The social and cultural structure of the area: Are there racial problems? Are there ethnic groupings that are diffused or unified? Are there different value systems at play?
- The contacts that are productive: If you want something done at city hall, whom do you see? Does the director of a particular agency have any control over the staff? What agencies have "real services" available? What court clerk is most helpful?

It is usually very difficult for the investigator to acquire this knowledge in any way other than going out into the field and obtaining it through experience. Others can provide guidance, and often will. In the final analysis, however, you will probably discover that what others say is biased or incomplete. You must establish your own network of contacts and sources of information. First and foremost, you must establish your credibility in the community. People must get to know and trust you. Simply by announcing yourself as an investigator (or by presenting a printed card indicating title and affiliation), you will not find instant cooperation from the community. You must *earn* this cooperation. If you gain a reputation as arrogant, dishonest, opportunistic, or insensitive, you will quickly find that few people want to deal with you. An investigator could be in no worse predicament.

Often the best way to learn about an area and to begin establishing contacts is by being casual and unassuming. Have you ever noticed that insurance agents often spend three-fourths of their time talking about the weather, sports, politics, the high cost of housing, etc., *before* coming to their sales pitch? Their approach is to relax you, to find out what interests you, to show you that they are human. Then they hit you with the benefits of buying their insurance. The investigator can learn from this approach not only in establishing contacts at agencies and in the community generally, but also in dealing with prospective witnesses on specific cases.

Section B. Fact Analysis: Organizing the Options

The process of structuring or organizing fact options may initially appear to be complex and cumbersome. But the process can become second nature to you once you understand it, try it out, evaluate it, modify it, and find it helpful. It is, of course, perfectly proper to adopt any process that you find effective. Whatever method you use, you need to develop the *discipline* of fact analysis as soon as possible.

There are a number of fundamental characteristics of facts that should be kept in mind:

■ Events take place.

■ Events mean different things to different people.

■ Different people, therefore, have different versions of events.

■ Inconsistent versions of the same event do not necessarily indicate fraud or lying.

■ Although someone's version may claim to be the total picture, it probably will contain only a piece of the picture.

■ In giving a version of an event, people usually mix statements of *why* the event occurred with statements of *what* occurred.

■ Whenever it is claimed that an event occurred in a certain way, one can logically expect that certain signs, indications, or traces (evidence) of the event can be found.

Given these truisms, the investigator should analyze the facts along the lines indicated in Figure 8.1. It is possible for a single client's case to have numerous individual facts that are in dispute. Furthermore, facts can change, or people's versions of facts can change in the middle of a case. Each new or modified fact demands the same comprehensive process of fact analysis that is outlined in Figure 8.1.

Obtaining different versions of a fact may be difficult because the differences may not be clear on the surface. Of course, every fact will not necessarily have multiple versions. It is recommended, however, that you assume there will be more than one version until you have demonstrated otherwise to yourself. Undoubtedly, you must do some probing in order to uncover the versions that exist. Better to do so now than to be confronted with a surprise at trial or at an agency hearing.

People will not always be willing to share their accounts or versions of facts with you. If you are not successful in convincing them to tell their story, you may have to make some assumptions of what their story is *likely* to be and to check out these assumptions.

 Section C. Distortions in Investigation

Investigators are not mere newspaper reporters or photographers who simply report what they see, hear, or otherwise experience. You have a much more dynamic role. In a very significant sense, you sometimes have the power of controlling what someone else says about the facts. This can have positive and negative consequences.

Starting Point:
All the facts you presently have on the case
Procedure:
■ Arrange the facts chronologically. ■ Place a number before each fact that must be established in a legal proceeding.
State the Following Versions of Each Fact:
Version I: The client's Version II: The opponent's (as revealed to you or as assumed) Version III: A witness's Version IV: Another witness's Version V: Any other reasonable version (e.g., from your own deductions)
As to Each Version:
■ State precisely (with quotes if possible) what the version is. ■ State the evidence or indications that tend to support the version according to persons presenting the version. ■ State the evidence or indications that tend to contradict this version. ■ Determine how you will verify whether the evidence or indications exist.

FIGURE 8.1

Fact Analysis in Investigation

At its worst, this can mean that you are not listening to the person or that you are asking questions in such a manner that you are putting words into the person's mouth. The primary technique that can bring about this result is the *leading question.* A leading question is a pressure question, one that contains (or suggests) the answer in the statement of the question. For example, "You were in Baltimore at the time, isn't that correct?" "You earn over $200 a week?" "Would it be correct to say that when you drove up to the curb, you didn't see the light?"

Questions can intentionally or unintentionally manipulate someone's answer by including a premise that has yet to be established. It takes an astute person to say to such questions, "I can't answer your question (or it is invalid) because it assumes another fact that I haven't agreed to." In the following examples of questions and answers, the person responding to the question refuses to be trapped by the form of the question:

Q: How much did it cost you to have your car repaired after the accident?
A: It's not my car and it wasn't an accident; your client deliberately ran into the car that I borrowed.

. . . .

Q: Have you stopped beating your wife?
A: I never beat my wife!

. . . .

Q: Can you tell me what you saw?
A: I didn't see anything; my brother was there and he told me what happened.

The last leading question containing the unestablished premise can be highly detrimental. Suppose the question and answer went as follows:

Q: Can you tell me what you saw?
A: The car was going about 70 MPH.

In fact, the person answering the question did not see this himself; his brother told him that a car was traveling at this speed. There are a number of reasons why this person may have failed to tell the investigator that he didn't see anything first-hand:

- Perhaps he did not hear the word *saw* in the investigator's question.

- He may have wanted the investigator to think that he saw something himself; he may want to feel important by conveying the impression that he is special because he has special information.

- He may have felt that it was not significant enough to correct the investigator's false assumption; he may have thought that the investigator was more interested in *what* happened than in *who* saw what happened.

Whatever the reason, the investigator has carelessly put himself or herself in the position of missing a potentially critical fact, namely that the person is only talking from hearsay.

Another way to blur communication is by completely avoiding some topics and concentrating only on selected ones. If you do not ask questions about certain matters, intentionally or otherwise, you are likely to end up with a distorted picture of a person's version of the facts. For example, assume that Smith and Jones have an automobile collision. The investigator, working for the attorney that represents Jones, finds a witness who says that she saw the accident. The investigator asks her to describe what she saw, but fails, however, to ask her where she was at the time she saw the collision. In fact, she was sitting in a park over two blocks away and could see the collision only through some shrubbery. The investigator didn't ask questions to uncover this; it wasn't volunteered. The investigator, therefore, walks away with a potentially distorted idea of how much light this individual can shed on what took place. This is similar to the distortion that can result from the use of questions that contain an unestablished premise.

Yet there may be instances in which these techniques have beneficial results. First of all, a leading question can help jar someone's memory so that they are better able to recall the facts. If, however, this individual is constantly in need of leading questions in order to remember, you have strong reason to suspect that, rather than being merely shy, inarticulate, or in need of a push now and then, the person knows little or nothing.

Suppose that the witness being questioned is uncooperative or has a version of the facts that is damaging to the client of the investigator's office. It may be that the techniques described in this section as normally improper can be used to challenge a version of the facts. A leading question with an unestablished premise, for example, may catch an individual off guard and give the investigator reasonable cause to believe that the person is not telling the truth.

Suppose that the person being questioned is not hostile but is neutral, or seemingly so. The way in which such individuals are questioned may help them emphasize certain facts as opposed to others. Once witnesses have committed themselves to a version of the facts, either completely on their own or with some subtle help from the questioner, there is a good chance that they will stick by this version because they do not want to appear to be vague, uncertain, or inconsistent later. An investigator who takes such a course of action, however, must be extremely careful. You are taking certain risks, not because your conduct is illegal or unethical, but because a witness who needs subtle pressuring in order to state a version of the facts in a certain way is probably going to be a weak witness at trial or at an agency hearing. On cross-examination, the witness may fall apart.

 ## Section D. Sources of Evidence/Sources of Leads

Evidence is that which is used to prove or disprove a fact. Testimonial evidence is what someone says. Physical or tangible evidence is what can be seen or touched. A *lead* is simply a path to potentially admissible evidence. Of course, evidence is often its own lead to other evidence.

In Figure 8.2, there is a partial checklist containing some of the standard sources of evidence and leads at the investigator's disposal. (The list is not presented in order of priority.)

FIGURE 8.2

Checklist on the Standard Sources of Evidence and Leads

- Statements of the client
- Documents the client brings or can obtain
- Information from attorneys involved with the case in the past
- Interrogatories, depositions, other discovery devices; letters requesting information
- Pleadings (such as complaints) filed thus far in the case
- Newspaper accounts; notices in the media requesting information
- General records of municipal, state, and federal administrative agencies
- Business records (such as cancelled receipts)
- Employment records, including job applications
- Photographs
- Hospital records
- Informers or the "town gossip"
- Surveillance of the scene
- Reports from the police and other law enforcement agencies (see Figure 8.3)
- Fingerprints
- School records
- Military records
- Information that may be voluntarily or involuntarily provided by the attorney for the other side
- Use of alias
- Bureau of vital statistics and missing persons

- Court records
- Worker's Compensation records
- Office of politicians
- Records of Better Business Bureaus and consumer groups
- Telephone book
- Boat register
- *Polk Directory*
- *Reverse Directory*
- Accounts of eyewitnesses
- Hearsay accounts
- Automobile register (DMV)
- County assessor (for real property)
- Tax assessor's offices
- County election records
- Post office (record of forwarding addresses)
- Object to be traced (such as an auto)
- Credit bureaus
- Reports of investigative agencies written in the past
- Resources of public library
- Associations (trade, professional, etc.)
- *Who's Who* directories
- Insurance Company Clearing House
- Standards and Poor's *Register of Directors and Executives*
- Telling your problem to a more experienced investigator and asking for other leads
- Shots in the dark

Section E. Gaining Access to Records

It is easy to say that the investigator should check records for evidence and leads; but sometimes it is quite difficult to gain access to these records. There are four categories of records:

1. Those already in the possession of the client or of an individual willing to turn them over to you on request

2. Those in the possession of a governmental agency or of a private organization and available to anyone in the public

FIGURE 8.3
Request for Copy
of Peace Officer's
Accident Report

REQUEST FOR COPY OF PEACE OFFICER'S ACCIDENT REPORT
(PLEASE SUBMIT IN DUPLICATE)

Statistical Services   Date of Request _____
Texas Department of Public Safety
P.O. Box 15999   Claim or Policy No. _____
Austin, Texas 78761–5999

Enclosed is a (check)(money order) payable to the Texas Department of Public Safety in the amount of

$_____ for (check service desired):

☐ Copy of Peace Officer's Accident Report - $4.00 each

☐ Certified Copy of Peace Officer's Accident Report - $8.00 each

for the accident listed below:

Please provide as accurate and complete information as possible.

ACCIDENT DATE _____
                   MONTH   DAY   YEAR

ACCIDENT LOCATION _____
                            COUNTY   CITY   STREET OR HIGHWAY
WAS ANYONE
KILLED IN THE ACCIDENT? _____ If So, Name of one Deceased _____

INVESTIGATING AGENCY AND/OR OFFICER'S NAME (IF KNOWN) _____

| DRIVER'S FULL NAME | DRIVER INFORMATION (If Available) | | ADDRESS |
	DATE OF BIRTH	TEXAS DRIVER LICENSE NO.	
1. _____			
2. _____			
3. _____			

Texas Statutes allow the investigating officer 10 days in which to submit his report.
Requests should not be submitted until at least 10 days after the accident date to allow time for receipt of the report.

The Law also provides that if an officer's report is not on file when a request for a copy of such report is received, a certification to that effect will be provided in lieu of the copy and the fee shall be retained for the certification.

Mail To _____

Mail Address _____

City _____ State _____ Zip _____

Requested By _____ Phone # _____

3. Those in the possession of a governmental agency or of a private organization and available only to the client or to the individual who is the subject of the records

4. Those in the possession of a governmental agency or of a private organization and claimed to be confidential except for in-house staff

There should obviously be no difficulty in gaining access to the first category of records unless they have been misplaced or lost, in which event the person who once had possession would ask the source of the records to provide another copy. As to records in the latter three categories, the checklist in Figure 8.4 should provide some guidelines on gaining access.

Section F. Evaluating Testimonial and Physical Evidence

At all times, you must make value judgments on the usefulness of the evidence that you come across. There are a number of specific criteria that can be used to assist you in assessing the worth of what you have. The checklists in Figures 8.6 and 8.7 may be helpful in determining this worth.

Section G. Interviewing Witnesses

1. Know what image you are projecting of yourself.   In the minds of many people, an investigator is often involved in serious and dangerous undertakings.

---

1. Write, phone, or visit the organization and ask for the record.

2. Have the client write, phone, or visit and ask for it.

3. Draft a letter for the client to sign that asks for it.

4. Have the client sign a form that states that he or she gives you authority to see any records that pertain to him or her and that the client specifically waives any right to confidentiality with respect to such records.

5. Find out if one of the opposing parties has the record and, if so, ask them to send you a copy.

6. Find out if others have it (such as a relative of the client or a co-defendant in this or in a prior court case) and ask them if they will provide you with a copy.

7. For records available generally to the public, find out where these records are and go use them.

8. If you meet resistance (fourth category of records), make a basic fairness pitch to the organization as to why you need the records.

9. Find out (by legal research) if there are any statutes, regulations, or cases that arguably provide the client with the right of access to the records—for example, through the *Freedom of Information Act* (FOIA). (See Figure 8.5.)

10. Let the organization know that your office is in the process of establishing a legal basis to gain access to the records and that the office is contemplating initiating litigation to finalize the right.

11. Solicit the intervention of a politician or of some other respectable and independent person in trying to gain access.

12. If the person who initially turns down the request for access is a line officer, appeal the decision formally or informally to his or her supervisor, and up the chain of command to the person with final authority.

FIGURE 8.4
Guidelines to Gaining Access to Records

FIGURE 8.5
Sample FOIA
Letter

Agency Head or FOIA Officer
Title
Name of Agency
Address of Agency
City, State, Zip

                                    Re: Freedom of Information Act (FOIA) Request.

Dear _____:
    Under the provisions of the Freedom of Information Act, 5 U.S.C. 552, I am requesting access to (identify the records as clearly and specifically as possible).
    If there are any fees for searching for, or copying, the records I have requested, please inform me before you fill the request. (Or: . . . please supply the records without informing me if the fees do not exceed $_____.)
[Optional] As you know, the FOIA permits you to reduce or waive fees when the release of the information is considered as "primarily benefiting the public." I believe that this request fits that category and I therefore ask that you waive any fees.
[Optional] I am requesting this information (state the reason for your request if you think it will assist you in obtaining the information).
    If all or any part of this request is denied, please cite the specific exemption(s) that you think justifies your refusal to release the information, and inform me of the appeal procedures available to me under the law.
    I would appreciate your handling this request as quickly as possible, and I look forward to hearing from you within [ten] days, as the law stipulates.

                                    Sincerely,

                                    Signature
                                    Name
                                    Address
                                    City, State, Zip

Source: U.S. Congress. House. Committee on Government Operations. *A Citizen's Guide on How to Use the Freedom of Information Act and the Privacy Act Requesting Government Documents,* 95th Congress, 1st sess. (1977).

What reaction would you have if a stranger introduced himself or herself to you as an investigator? Would you be guarded and suspicious? You may not want to call yourself an investigator at all. You may want to say "My name is _____, I work for (name of law office) and we are trying to get information on _____." On the other hand, you may find that you are most effective when you are direct and straightforward.

Can you think of different people who would respond more readily to certain images of investigators? The following is a partial list of some of the images that an investigator could be projecting by dress, mannerisms, approach, and language:

- A professional
- Someone who is just doing a job
- Someone who is emotionally involved in what he or she is doing
- A neutral bystander
- A friend
- A manipulator or opportunist
- A salesperson
- A wise person
- An innocent and shy person

Checklist to Use If the Witness Is Speaking from First-Hand (Eyewitness) Information	Checklist to Use If the Witness Is Speaking from Second-Hand (Hearsay) Information
■ How long ago did it happen? ■ How good is the memory of this witness? ■ How far from the event was the witness at the time? ■ How good is the sight of the witness? ■ What time of day was it and would this affect vision? ■ What was the weather at the time and would this affect vision? ■ Was there a lot of commotion at the time and would this affect vision or ability to remember? ■ What was the witness doing immediately before the incident? ■ How old is the witness? ■ What was the last grade of school completed? ■ Employment background? ■ What is the reputation of the witness in the community for truthfulness? ■ Was the witness ever convicted of a crime? Are any criminal charges now pending against him or her? ■ Is the witness an expert on anything? ■ What are the qualifications of the witness? ■ Is the witness related to, an employee of, or friendly with the other side in the litigation? Would it be to this person's benefit, in any way, to see the other side win? ■ Does any direct evidence exist to corroborate what this witness is saying? ■ Does any hearsay evidence exist to corroborate it? ■ Is the witness willing to sign a statement covering what he or she tells the investigator? Is he or she willing to say it in court? ■ Is the witness defensive when asked about what he or she knows?	■ How well does the witness remember what was told to him or her by the other person (the declarant) or what the witness heard him or her say to someone else? ■ How is the witness sure that it is exact? ■ Is the declarant now available to confirm or deny this hearsay account of the witness? If not, why not? ■ Under what conditions did the declarant allegedly make the statement (for example, was declarant ill)? ■ Is there other hearsay testimony that will help corroborate this hearsay? ■ Does any direct evidence exist to corroborate this hearsay? ■ How old is the witness? How old is the declarant? ■ What are the educational and employment backgrounds of both? ■ Is either of them related to, an employee of, or friendly with the other side in the litigation? Would it be to the benefit of either of them to see the other side win? ■ Is the witness willing to sign a statement covering what he or she tells the investigator? Is he or she willing to say it in court? ■ Is the witness defensive when asked about what he or she was told by the declarant or what he or she heard the declarant say to someone else? ■ Are there any inconsistencies in what the witness is saying? ■ How does the witness react when confronted with the inconsistencies? Defensively? ■ Are there any gaps in what the witness is saying? ■ Does the witness appear to exaggerate?

FIGURE 8.6

Checklist on the Validity of Testimonial Evidence

Continued

FIGURE 8.6

Checklist on the
Validity of
Testimonial
Evidence
—Continued

Checklist to Use If the Witness Is Speaking from First-Hand (Eyewitness) Information	Checklist to Use If the Witness Is Speaking from Second-Hand (Hearsay) Information
■ Are there any inconsistencies in what the witness is saying? ■ How does the witness react when confronted with the inconsistencies? Defensively? ■ Are there any gaps in what the witness is saying? ■ Does the witness appear to exaggerate? ■ Does the witness appear to be hiding or holding anything back?	■ Does the witness appear to be hiding or holding anything back? ■ What is the reputation of the witness in the community for truthfulness?

You must be aware of (a) your own need to project yourself in a certain way, (b) the way in which you think you *are* projecting yourself, (c) the way in which the person to whom you are talking perceives you, and (d) the effect that all this is having on what you are trying to accomplish.

2. *There are five kinds of witnesses: hostile, skeptical, friendly, disinterested or neutral, and a combination of the above.* Hostile witnesses want your client to lose; they will try to set up roadblocks in your way. Skeptical witnesses are not sure who you are or what you want in spite of your explanation of your role. They are guarded and unsure of whether they want to become involved. Friendly witnesses want your client to win and will cooperate fully. *Disinterested* or neutral witnesses don't care who wins. They have information that they will tell anyone who asks.

If the hostile witness is the opposing party who has retained counsel, it is unethical for the investigator to talk directly with this person without going through his or her counsel (see Chapter 4). If the hostile witness is not a party but is closely associated with a party, you should check with your supervisor on how, if at all, to approach such a witness.

To complicate matters, it must be acknowledged that witnesses are seldom totally hostile, skeptical, friendly, or neutral. At different times during the investigation interview, and at different times throughout the various stages of the case, they may shift from one attitude to another. While it may be helpful to determine what general category witnesses fit into, it would be more realistic to view any witness as an individual in a state of flux in terms of what he or she wants to say and what he or she is capable of saying.

3. *The investigator must have the trust of the witness.* You have the sometimes difficult threshold problem of sizing up the witness from whom you are trying to obtain information. What are some of the states of mind that such witnesses could have?

■ They may want to feel important.

■ They may want to be "congratulated" for knowing anything, however insignificant, about the case.

■ They may want absolute assurance from you that they won't get into trouble by talking to you. They shy away from talk of courts, lawyers, and law.

Checklist for Written Material	Checklist for Nonwritten Material
■ Who wrote it? ■ Under what circumstances was it written? ■ Is the original available? If not, why not? ■ Is a copy available? ■ Who is available to testify that the copy is in fact an accurate copy of the original? ■ Is the author available to testify on what he or she wrote? If not, why not? ■ Is there any hearsay testimony available to corroborate the authenticity of the writing? ■ Is there any other physical evidence available to corroborate the authenticity of the writing? ■ What hearsay, direct evidence, or physical evidence is available to corroborate or contradict what is said in the writing? ■ Can you obtain sample handwriting specimens of the alleged author?	■ Who found it and under what circumstances? ■ Where was it found? ■ Why would it be where it was found? Was it unusual to find it there? ■ Who is available to identify it? ■ What identifying characteristics does it have? ■ Who owns it? Who used it? ■ Who owned it in the past? Who used it in the past? ■ Who made it? ■ What is its purpose? ■ Does it require laboratory analysis? ■ Can you take it with you? ■ Can you photograph it? ■ Is it stolen? ■ Is there any public record available to trace its history? ■ What facts does it tend to establish? ■ Was it planted where it was found as a decoy?

FIGURE 8.7

Checklist on the Validity of Physical (Tangible) Evidence

■ They may be willing to talk only after you have given full assurance that you will never reveal the source of the information they will give you.

■ They may be willing to talk to you only in the presence of their friends.

■ If they know your client, they may want to be told that you are trying to keep the client out of trouble.

■ They may want the chance to meet you first and then have you go away in order to decide whether they want to talk to you again.

■ They may not be willing to talk to you until you fulfill some of their needs— for example, listen to their troubles; act in a fatherly or motherly manner; play subtle, seductive games; etc.

In short, the investigator must gain the trust of individuals by assessing their needs and by knowing when they are ready to tell you what they know. If you take out your notebook immediately upon introducing yourself, you are probably too insensitive to establish the communication that's needed.

4. The investigator must assess how well the witness would do under direct and cross-examination. As witnesses talk, ask yourself a number of questions:

■ Would they be willing to testify in court? Whatever the answer to this question is now, are they likely to change their minds later?

■ Would they be effective on the witness stand?

■ Do they know what they are talking about?

- Do they have a reputation for integrity, credibility, or truthfulness in the community?
- Are they defensive?
- Would they know how to say "I'm not sure" or "I don't understand the question," as opposed to giving an answer for the sake of giving an answer (e.g., to avoid being embarrassed)?
- When they talk, are they internally consistent?
- Do they know how to listen as well as talk?
- Do they understand the distinction between right and wrong, truth and lying?

Section H. Special Investigative Problems: Some Starting Points

Judgment Collection

The person who wins a money judgment in court is called the *judgment creditor*. Unfortunately, collecting that judgment can be a difficult undertaking. An investigator may be asked to assist the law firm in ascertaining the financial assets of a particular individual or corporation against whom the judgment was obtained, called the *judgment debtor*.

One of the best starting points for such an investigation is government records. The following is a partial list of records available from the county clerk's or court office:

- Real property tax assessments
- Personal property tax assessments
- Filings made under the Uniform Commercial Code
- Federal tax liens
- Court dockets—to determine whether the judgment debtor has been a plaintiff or defendant in prior litigation
- Inheritance records—to determine whether the judgment debtor has inherited money or other property (determined by checking records of surrogate's court or probate court that handles inheritance and trust cases)

Such records could reveal a good deal of information on the financial status of the party under investigation.

For corporations that are judgment debtors, check the records of state and federal government agencies (such as the Secretary of State and the Securities and Exchange Commission) with whom the corporation must file periodic reports or disclosures on its activities and finances. You should also check with people who have done business with the corporation (customers or other creditors) as well as with its competitors in the field. These records and contacts could provide good leads.

Missing Persons

An investigator may be asked to locate a missing heir, a relative of a client, a person who needs to be served with process in connection with current litigation, etc. A missing person generally is not difficult to locate—unless this person does not want to be found. The first step is to send a registered letter to the person's last-known address, "return receipt requested," which asks the post office to send you back a notice of who accepted the letter. Other possible leads:

- Relatives or friends
- Former landlord, neighbors, mail carrier, and local merchants in the area of the last-known address
- Local credit bureau
- Police department, hospitals
- References listed on employment applications
- Naturalization certificate, marriage record, drivers license, car registration
- Ad in the newspaper

Background Investigations

Figure 8.8 presents a form used by a large investigative firm for its general background investigations on individuals. The first part of the form seeks information regarding identification of the subject. The antecedent data covers prior history.

■ ASSIGNMENT 8.1

Which of the following statements do you agree or disagree with? Why? For those statements that you are unsatisfied with, how would you modify them to reflect your own view?

(a) Investigation is a separate profession.

(b) There is a great difference between investigation conducted by the police and that conducted by a paralegal working for a law office.

(c) An investigator is an advocate.

(d) It is impossible for the investigator to keep from showing his or her own personal biases while in the field investigating.

(e) There is often a need for a separate investigation to verify the work of another investigation.

(f) A good investigator will probably be unable to describe why he or she is effective. There are too many intangibles involved.

(g) It is a good idea for an investigator to specialize in one area of the law, such as automobile negligence cases.

(h) If someone is willing to talk to and cooperate with an investigator, there is reason to suspect that this person is trying to manipulate the investigator.

■ ASSIGNMENT 8.2

If you were Tom in each of the following situations, what specific things would you do to deal with the situation?

(a) On September 1st, Tom decides that he wants to enter a community college. School opens in five days. There are only two colleges that still allow time for registration. Both are about the same distance from his home and he can afford both. Tom's problem is that he doesn't know enough about either college to make a decision. He works full-time from 9 to 6 and *must* continue to work right up to the first day of school in order to be able to finance his education.

Continued

FIGURE 8.8

Background
Investigations

Identification of Subject

1. Complete Name _____ Age _____ SS# _____ Marital Status _____

Spouse's Name; Pertinent Info _____

Children's Names and Ages _____

2. Current Residence Address and Type of Neighborhood _____

How Long at Present Address—Prior Residence Info _____

3. Business Affiliation and Address, Position, Type of Bus. _____

Antecedent History

1. Place & Date of Birth _____

Parents' Names & Occupations _____

Where Did They Spend Their Youth? _____

2. Education—Where, Which Schools, Dates of Attendance _____

Degree? What Kind? _____Any Other Info Pertaining to Scholastic Achievement, Extracurric. Activities _____

3. First Employer, to Present—F/T or P/T, Position or Title, Job Description, Exact Dates of Employment, Type of Company _____

4. Relationship with Peers, Supervisors, Subordinates—Where Do His or Her Abilities Lie? Any Outside Activities? Reputation for Honesty, Trustworthiness, Integrity? Does He or She Work Well Under Pressure? Anything Derogatory? If So, What Are Details? Reasons for Leaving? Would They Rehire? Salaries? Health? Reliability? Job Understanding? Willingness to Accept Responsibility? _____

Continued

_____
_____
_____
_____
_____
_____

If Self-Employed—What Was the Nature of the Business? With Whom Did He or She Deal? Corp. Name? _____

Date & Place of Incorporation _____

Who Were Partners, If Any? _____

What % of Stock Did Subj. Own? _____Was Business Successful? _____What Happened to It? _____

If Sold, to Whom? _____Any Subsid. or Affiliates? _____
_____
_____

5. What Is His or Her Character or Personality Like? Did Informer Know Him or Her Personally? _____

Hobbies? _____

Family Life? _____

Even-Tempered? _____ Loner or Joiner? _____

Introverted, Extroverted? _____ Written or Oral Abilities? _____

Does Informer Know Anyone Else Who Knows Subj.? _____
_____

6. Credit Information _____
_____
_____

7. Litigation _____Civil _____Criminal _____Bankruptcy _____

State _____Federal _____Local _____
_____
_____

8. Banking—Financial: Bank _____

Types of Accounts—Average Bal. _____

How Long Did Subj. Have Accounts? _____Any Company Accounts?
_____

Is He or She Personally Known to Officers of the Bank? _____Any Borrowing?_____

Secured or Unsecured? _____If Secured, by What? Do They Have Financial Statement on the Subj.? _____

What Is His or Her Net Worth? _____Other Assets? Real Estate _____

Stocks _____

Equity in His or Her Co., etc. _____
_____

FIGURE 8.8

Background Investigations
—*Continued*

■ **ASSIGNMENT 8.2—*Continued***

(b) Tom teaches a second-grade class. It is the end of the school day on Friday and the bus is in front of the school ready to take his class home. If the students are not out in time for the bus, it will leave without them. It is 2:50 P.M. and the bus is scheduled to leave at 3:05 P.M. Tom discovers that his briefcase is missing from the top of his desk.

(c) Tom is the father of two teenagers, Ed and Bill. He comes home one day and finds a small package of marijuana in the front hall. He immediately suspects that Ed or Bill left it there. He turns around and goes out to look for them.

(d) Tom's son, Bill, has been accused of using abusive language in front of his teacher. Tom calls the teacher, who refuses to talk about it. The teacher refers Tom to the principal. The principal refuses to talk about it and refers Tom to the assistant superintendant at the central office.

(e) Tom's sister is ill. She received a letter from a local merchant where she often buys goods on credit. The letter informs her that she owes $122 and that unless she pays within a week "legal proceedings will be instituted" against her. She calls Tom and tells him that she paid the bill by sending $122 in cash last week. She asks Tom to help her.

(f) Tom works for a local legal service office. The office has a client who wants to sue her landlord because the kitchen roof is falling down. Tom is assigned to the case.

(g) A welfare department has told a client that it is going to terminate public assistance because the client's boyfriend is supporting her and her family. The client denies this. Tom is assigned to the case.

(h) A client has been to the office seeking help in obtaining a divorce. She claims that her husband beat her. Tom is assigned to the case.

(i) Sam owes Tom $1,000. When Tom asks for his money, Sam tells him that he is broke. Tom suspects differently.

(j) Tom's uncle once lived in Boston. After spending two years in the Army, he started traveling across the country; he has not been heard from for five years. Tom wants to locate his uncle.

■ **ASSIGNMENT 8.3**

How would you find the following information:

(a) The average life span of a lobster.

(b) The maiden name of the wife of the first governor in your state's history.

(c) The assessed property tax value of the tallest commercial building in your city in 1980.

(d) The number of vehicles using diesel fuel that drove in or through the state last month.

(e) The salary of the air traffic controller with the most seniority on duty on the day last year when the nearest airport experienced the largest rainfall of the year.

Note on the Need for a License

In some states, investigators must be licensed. What about paralegals who are assigned investigation tasks by their supervising attorneys? A literal reading of the licensing statute might lead to the conclusion that such paralegals must be licensed along with traditional, self-employed private investigators. Often, however, the legislature will make an exception to the licensing requirement for employees of attorneys who engage in investigation under the attorney's supervision. Paralegal associations have been active in seeking these exemptions for paralegals. The main opposition to such exemptions has come from organizations of private investigators, who allegedly seek to impose roadblocks to paralegal investigation in order to secure more business for themselves.

Section I. Evidence and Investigation

There is a close relationship between investigation and the law of evidence. One of the aims of investigation is to uncover and verify facts that will eventually be *admissible* in court. Admissibility is determined by the law of evidence. When attorneys are negotiating a case to try to reach a settlement in order to avoid a trial, they frequently talk (and argue) about the admissibility of the facts in the event that a trial does occur.

Evidence in General

Evidence is that which is used to prove or disprove a fact, as indicated earlier.

Admissible evidence is evidence that the judge will permit the jury to consider. Admissible evidence does not mean that the evidence is true. It simply means that there are no valid objections to keep the evidence out. The jury is free to conclude that it does not believe the evidence that the judge ruled admissible.

Direct evidence is evidence (usually from personal observation or knowledge) that tends to establish a fact (or to disprove a fact) without the need for an inference.

Circumstantial evidence is evidence of one fact from which another fact can be inferred.

Example: The police officer says, "I saw skid marks at the scene of the accident." This statement is:

Direct evidence	■ that the police officer spoke these words. ■ that skid marks were at the scene of the accident.
Circumstantial evidence	■ that the driver of the car was speeding (this is the inference that can be drawn from the officer's statement).

Examples of *direct* evidence that someone was speeding would be: an admission by the driver that he or she was speeding, radar results, testimony of people who saw the car being driven, etc.

Investigation Guideline:
Direct evidence is preferred over circumstantial, although both kinds of evidence may be admissible. It is important that you are able to identify the inference in the circumstantial evidence. Then try to find direct evidence of whatever was inferred.

Relevance

Relevant evidence is evidence that reasonably tends to make the existence of a fact more probable or less probable than it would be without that evidence. Relevancy is a very broad concept. It simply means that the evidence may be helpful in determining the truth or falsity of a fact involved in a trial. The test of relevancy is common sense and logic. If, for example, you want to know whether a walkway is dangerous, it is relevant that people have slipped on this walkway in the immediate past. Prior accidents under the same conditions make it more reasonable for someone to conclude that there is danger.

All relevant evidence is not necessarily admissible evidence. It would be highly relevant, for example, to know that the defendant told his attorney he was driving 80 MPH at the time of the accident, yet the attorney-client privilege would make such a statement inadmissible. Also, relevant evidence is not necessarily conclusive evidence. The jury will usually be free to reject certain relevant evidence and to accept other relevant evidence that is more believable. Relevancy is a *tendency* of evidence to establish or disestablish a fact. It may be a very weak tendency. Prior accidents may be relevant to show danger, but the jury may still conclude, in light of all the evidence, that there was no danger.

> **Investigation Guideline:**
> Let common sense be your main guide in pursuing relevant evidence. So long as there is some logical connection between the fact you are pursuing and a fact that must be established at trial, you are on the right track.

■ ASSIGNMENT 8.4

Examine the following four situations. Discuss the relevance of each item of evidence being introduced.

(a) Mrs. Phillips is being sued by a department store for the cost of a gas refrigerator. Mrs. Phillips claims that she never ordered and never received a refrigerator from the store. The attorney for Mrs. Phillips wants to introduce two letters: (1) a letter from Mrs. Phillips' landlord stating that her kitchen is not equipped to handle gas appliances and (2) a letter from another merchant stating that Mrs. Phillips bought an electric refrigerator from him a year ago.

(b) Phil Smith has been charged with burglary in Detroit on December 16, 1986. His attorney tries to introduce testimony into evidence that on December 7, 8, 11, 15, and 22, 1986, the defendant was in Florida.

(c) Al Neuman is suing Sam Snow for negligence in operating his motor vehicle. Al's attorney tries to introduce into evidence the fact that Snow currently has pending against him four other automobile negligence cases in other courts.

(d) Jim is on trial for the rape of Sandra. Jim's attorney wants to introduce into evidence (1) the fact that Sandra subscribes to *Cosmopolitan* magazine, (2) the fact that Sandra is a member of AA, and (3) the fact that Sandra is the mother of Jim's child, who was born three years ago when they were dating. They separated in bitterness five months after the birth and never married.

Competence of Witnesses

A witness is competent to testify if the witness:

- understands the obligation to tell the truth
- has the ability to communicate
- has knowledge of the topic of his or her testimony

Children or mentally ill persons are not automatically disqualified. They are competent to testify if the judge is satisfied that the above criteria are met.

The competence of a witness must be carefully distinguished from the credibility of the witness. *Competency* is simply a ticket into the trial. *Credibility* goes to the *weight* of the evidence. This weight is assessed by the trier of fact—usually the jury. Competence goes to whether that witness will be allowed to testify at all. The jury may decide that everything said by a competent witness has little weight or is unworthy of belief.

Lay Opinion Evidence

An opinion is an inference from a fact. For example, after you watch George stagger down the street and smell alcohol on his breath, you come to the conclusion that he is drunk. The conclusion is the inference. The facts are the observation of staggering and the smell of alcohol on his breath. Technically, a lay witness should not give opinion evidence. He or she must state the facts and let the trier of fact form the opinions. (Under certain circumstances, expert witnesses *are* allowed to give opinions on technical subjects not within the understanding of the average layperson.) The problem with the opinion rule, however, is that it is sometimes difficult to express oneself without using opinions, as when a witness says it was a sunny day or the noise was loud. Courts are therefore lenient in permitting opinion testimony by lay witnesses when the witness is talking from his or her own observations and it would be awkward for the witness not to express the opinion. If people regularly use opinions when discussing the topic in question, it will be permitted.

> **Investigation Guideline:**
> Know when a person is stating an opinion. Even though an opinion may be admissible, you should assume that it will *not* be admissible. Pursue all of the underlying facts that support the inference in the opinion. In the event that the person is not allowed to testify by using the opinion, be prepared with a list of the underlying facts the person relied on for the opinion.

■ ASSIGNMENT 8.5

Make a list of the questions that you would ask in order to uncover the underlying facts that formed the basis of the following opinions:

(a) He was insane.

(b) She couldn't see.

(c) It was cold out.

(d) He was traveling very fast.

Hearsay

If evidence is *hearsay*, it is inadmissible unless one of the exceptions to the hearsay rule applies. Hearsay is testimony in court, or written evidence, of a statement made out of court when the statement is offered to show the truth of matters asserted therein and thus resting for its value on the credibility of the out-of-court asserter.[1]

> **Example:**
> Sam, a witness on the stand, says, "Fred told me on the street that he was speeding."

Note the conditions for the presence of hearsay:

---

[1] E. Cleary, ed., McCormick's *Handbook of the Law of Evidence*, 584 (1972).

Testimony in court	The witness, Sam, is on the stand.
Statement made out of court	The statement by Fred was made on the street and not in court.
Offered to assert the truth of the matter in the statement	Assume that the purpose of the attorney questioning Sam is to show that Fred was speeding—that is, that the statement is true.
The value of the statement depends on the credibility of the out-of-court asserter	Fred is the out-of-court asserter. The value of the statement depends on how believable or credible *Fred* is.

If the statement is not offered to prove the truth of the matters asserted in the statement, it is not hearsay. Suppose, for example, that the attorney wants to prove that Fred was alive immediately after the accident—that death was not instantaneous. The above statement would be admitted to prove that Fred actually said something, in other words, that Fred was alive enough to make a statement. If the testimony of the witness is offered to prove simply that the words were spoken by Fred rather than to prove that Fred was speeding, then the statement is not hearsay. The testimony that "Fred told me on the street that he was speeding" would therefore be admissible. The jury would have to be cautioned to examine the testimony for the limited purpose for which it is offered and not to consider it evidence that Fred was speeding.

Conduct intended as a substitute for words can also be hearsay. For example, the witness is asked, "What did Fred say when you asked him if he was speeding?" The witness answers, "He nodded his head yes." This testimony is hearsay if it is offered to prove that Fred was speeding. Conduct—nodding the head—was intended as a substitute for words.

Investigation Guideline:
Know when hearsay exists so that you can try to find alternative, nonhearsay evidence to prove the truth of the assertions made in the hearsay.

■ ASSIGNMENT 8.6

Is hearsay evidence involved in the following situations? Examine the four conditions of hearsay in each.

(a) Tom is suing Jim for negligence. On the witness stand, Tom says, "Jim was speeding at the time he hit me."

(b) Tom is suing Jim for negligence. While Tom is on the stand, his attorney introduces into evidence a mechanic's bill showing that the repair of the car cost $178.

(c) Mary and George were passengers in Tom's car at the time of the collision with Jim. George testifies that just before the collision, Mary shouted, "Look out for that car going through the red light!"

(d) He told me he was God.

■ ASSIGNMENT 8.7

Smith is being sued for assaulting Jones, who later died. Smith is on the stand when the following exchange occurs. How would you rule on the objection?

Counsel for Smith: "Did you strike the decedent, Jones?"
Smith: "Yes."
Counsel for Smith: "Did Jones say anything to you before you struck him?"

Smith: "Yes, he told me that he was going to kill me."
Counsel for Jones's estate: "Objection, your honor, on the grounds of hearsay. Smith cannot give testimony on what the decedent said since the decedent is obviously not subject to cross-examination."

There are a limited number of exceptions to the hearsay rule that have the effect of making evidence admissible even if it fulfills all the conditions of hearsay.

1. Admissions.   An *admission* is an out-of-court statement made by a party to the litigation that is inconsistent with a position the party is taking in the litigation. Example: Tom is being sued for negligence in driving a car that resulted in a collision at night. After the accident, Tom told the victim that he was driving. (Before the trial, Tom died of unrelated causes.) At the trial, the attorney for Tom's estate is claiming that Tom was only a passenger in the car. The victim's testimony that Tom said he was driving is admissible hearsay since it is an admission by a party—Tom.

2. Declarations against Interest.   A *declaration against interest* is an out-of-court statement made by a nonparty (who is now unavailable) when the statement is against the interest of the nonparty. Example: Fred sues Bob for stealing Fred's car. Bob introduces a statement of Kevin, who is now dead, that he (Kevin) stole the car. The testimony is admissible hearsay, since it is a declaration by Kevin, who is unavailable, that is against the interest of Kevin.

3. Dying Declaration.   A *dying declaration* is an out-of-court statement concerning the causes or circumstances of death when made by a person whose death is imminent. Example: Tom dies two minutes after he was hit over the head. Seconds before he dies, he says, "Linda did it." Tom's statement is admissible hearsay since it is a dying declaration. Some courts limit this exception to the hearsay rule to criminal cases. Other states would also allow it to be used in a civil case, such as in a civil battery or wrongful death case against Linda.

4. Business Entry.   A *business entry* is an out-of-court statement found in business records made in the regular course of business by someone whose duty is to make such entries. (This also applies to records of non-businesses such as universities, government agencies, or associations.) Example: A party seeks to introduce into evidence a hospital record containing a description of the plaintiff's condition when admitted to the emergency room. The record was made by the supervising nurse who is not in court. The record containing the description of the plaintiff's condition is admissible hearsay as a business entry made in the regular course of business by someone whose duty is to make such a report (assuming that the supervising nurse has this duty).

5. Spontaneous Declaration.   A *spontaneous declaration* is an out-of-court statement or utterance made spontaneously during or immediately after an exciting event by an observer of the event. Example: On the witness stand, Fred says, "I heard John say 'Oh my God, the truck just hit the child.' " This testimony is admissible hearsay as a spontaneous declaration.

6. Declaration of Bodily Feelings, Symptoms, and Conditions.   A *declaration of bodily feelings, symptoms, and conditions* is an out-of-court statement or utterance made spontaneously about the person's present bodily condition. Example: On the witness stand, Carol says, "My husband told me he had a sharp pain in his stomach." This testimony is admissible hearsay as a declaration of present bodily condition.

7. Declaration of Mental State of Mind. A *declaration of mental state of mind* is an out-of-court statement made about the person's present state of mind. Example: On the witness stand, Len says, "The manager said she knew about the broken railing and would try to fix it." This testimony is admissible hearsay as a declaration of mental state of mind.

8. Declaration of Present Sense Impression. A *declaration of present sense impression* is an out-of-court statement that describes an event while it is being observed by the person making the statement. Example: On the witness stand, Bill says, "As the car turned the corner, a bystander turned to me and said, 'She'll never make it.' " This testimony is admissible hearsay as a declaration of present sense impression.

NOTE: Exceptions 5–8 are referred to as the *res gestae* exceptions; the statements or utterances are all closely connected or concurrent with an occurrence.

Privilege

A *privilege* in the law of evidence is the right to refuse to testify or the right to prevent someone else from testifying on a matter.

1. Privilege against Self-Incrimination. An accused person cannot be compelled to testify in a criminal proceeding or answer incriminating questions that directly or indirectly connect the accused to the commission of a crime.

2. Attorney-Client Privilege. A client and an attorney can refuse to disclose any communications between them whose purpose was to facilitate the provision of legal services for that client. The attorney cannot disclose the communication without the permission of the client.

3. Doctor Patient Privilege. A patient and doctor can refuse to disclose any confidential (private) communications between them that relate to medical care. The doctor cannot disclose the communication without the permission of the patient.

4. Clergy-Penitent Privilege. A penitent and a member of the clergy can refuse to disclose any confidential (private) communications between them that relate to spiritual counseling or consultation. The minister, priest, or rabbi cannot disclose the communication without the permission of the penitent.

5. Marital Communications. A husband and wife can refuse to disclose confidential (private) communications between them during the marriage. One spouse can also prevent the other from making such disclosures. Both spouses must agree to the disclosure. This privilege does not apply to litigation between spouses, such as divorce litigation.

6. Government Information. Some information collected by the government about citizens is confidential and privileged. Examples include adoption records and tax records. The privilege would not prevent use of the information to prosecute the citizen in connection with the citizen's duty to provide accurate information. It would, however, prevent third parties from gaining access to the confidential information.

Investigation Guideline:

When a privilege applies, look for alternative, nonprivileged sources of obtaining the information protected by the privilege.

Best Evidence Rule

To prove the contents of a private (nonofficial) writing, you should produce the original writing unless it is unavailable through no fault of the person now seeking to introduce a copy of the original e.g., it was destroyed in a storm.

Authentication

Authentication is evidence that a writing (or other physical item) is genuine and that it is what it purports to be—for example, the testimony of witnesses who saw the document being prepared.

Parol Evidence Rule

Oral evidence cannot be introduced to alter or contradict the contents of a written document if the parties intended the written document to be a complete statement of the agreement.

Section J. Taking a Witness Statement

There are four major kinds of *witness statements:*

1. Handwritten statement
2. Recorded statement in question-and-answer format (on audio or video tape)
3. Responses to a questionnaire that is mailed to the witness to answer
4. A statement taken in question-and-answer format with court reporters

The most common kind of statement is the first, which we shall consider here.

In a handwritten statement, the investigator writes down what the witness says, or the witness writes out the statement himself or herself. There is no formal structure to which the written statement must conform. The major requirements for the statement are clarity and accuracy.

The statement should begin by identifying (1) the witness (name, address, place of work, names of relatives, and other identifying data that may be helpful in locating the witness later); (2) the date and place of the taking of the statement; and (3) the name of the person to whom the statement is being made. See the example of a witness statement in Figure 8.9.

Then comes the body of the statement, in which the witness provides information about the event or circumstance in question (an accident that was observed, what the witness did and saw just before a fire, where the witness was on a certain date, etc.) It is often useful to have the witness present the facts in a chronological order, particularly when many facts are involved in the statement. It is important that the witness give detailed facts, such as facts demonstrating that the witness was in a good position to observe the event, to lend credibility to the statement.

At the end of the statement, the witness should say that he or she is making the statement of his or her own free will, without any pressure or coercion from anyone. The witness then signs the statement. The signature goes on the last page. Each of the other pages is also signed or initialed. If others have watched the witness make and sign the statement, they should also sign an *attestation clause,* which simply states that they observed the witness sign the statement.

FIGURE 8.9

Witness Statement

Statement of John Wood

I am John Wood. I am 42 years old and live at 3416 34th Street, N.W., Nashua, New Hampshire 03060. I work at the Deming Chemical Plant at region circle, Nashua. My home phone is 966-3954. My work phone is 297-9700 ×301. I am married to Patricia Wood. We have two children, Jessica (fourteen years old) and Gabriel (eleven years old). I am making this statement to Rose Thompson, a paralegal at Fields, Smith and Farrell. This statement is being given on March 13, 1986 at my home, 3416 34th Street, NW.

On February 15, 1986, I was standing on the corner of. . . .

Before the witness signs, he or she should read the entire statement and make any corrections that need to be made. Each correction should be initialed by the witness. Each page should be numbered with the total number of pages indicated each time. For example, if there are four pages, the page numbers would be "1 of 4," "2 of 4," "3 of 4," and "4 of 4." The investigator should not try to correct any spelling or grammatical mistakes made by the witness. The statement should exist exactly as the witness spoke or wrote it. Just before the signature of the witness at the end of the statement, the witness should say (in writing), "I have read all _____ pages of this statement, and the facts within it are accurate to the best of my knowledge."

Investigators sometimes use various tricks of the trade to achieve a desired effect. For example, if the investigator is writing out the statement as the witness speaks, the investigator may *intentionally* make an error of fact. When the witness reads over the statement, the investigator makes sure that the witness catches the error and initials the correction. This becomes added evidence that the witness carefully read the statement. The witness might later try to claim that he or she did not read the statement. The initialed correction helps rebut this position.

Not all witness statements are eventually admitted into evidence at the trial. They may be admitted to help the attorney demonstrate that the pretrial statement of the witness is inconsistent with the testimony of this witness during the trial itself. The main value of witness statements is thoroughness and accuracy in case preparation. Trials can occur years after the events that led to litigation. Witnesses may disappear or forget. Witness statements taken soon after the event can sometimes be helpful in tracking down witnesses and in helping them recall the details of the event.

■ **ASSIGNMENT 8.8**

Select any member of the class and take a witness statement from this person. The statement should concern some accident in which the witness was a participant or an observer. The witness, however, should not be a party to any litigation growing out of the accident. You write out the statement from what the witness says in response to your questions. Do not submit a statement handwritten by the witness except for his or her signature, initials, etc. Assume that you (the investigator-paralegal) work for the law firm of Davis and Davis, which represents someone else involved in the accident.

 Section K. The Settlement Work-Up

One of the end products of investigation is the *settlement work-up,* which is a summary of the major facts obtained through investigation, client interviewing, answers to interrogatories, deposition testimony, etc. The work-up, in one form or another, is used in negotiation with the other side or with the other side's liability insurance company in an effort to obtain a favorable settlement in lieu of trial.

In Figure 8.10, there is a memo containing data for a proposed settlement work-up.[2] Note its precision and attention to detail. Excellent FP (Fact Particularization, see Chapter 7) had to be used as the basis of this report.

<table>
<tr><td>

Interoffice Memorandum

To: Mary Jones, Esq.
From: Katherine Webb, Paralegal
Date: October 12, 1975
Re: Joseph Smith vs. Dan Lamb et al.
   Case Summary—Settlement Work-Up

I. Facts of Accident:

   The accident occurred on September 6, 1973, in Orange, California. Joseph Smith was driving westbound on Chapman Avenue, stopped to make a left turn into a parking lot, and was rear-ended by the one-half-ton panel truck driven by Dan Lamb.
   The defendant driver, Mr. Lamb, was cited for violation of Vehicle Code Sections 21703 and 22350, following too close, and at an unsafe speed for conditions.

II. Injuries:

   Severe cervical and lumbar sprain, superimposed over pre-existing, albeit asymptomatic, spondylolisthesis of pars interarticulus at L5-S1, with possible herniated nucleus pulposus either at or about the level of the spondylolisthesis; and contusion of right knee.
   Please see attached medical reports for further details.

III. Medical Treatment:

   Mr. Smith felt an almost immediate onset of pain in his head, neck, back, and right knee after the accident and believes that he may have lost consciousness momentarily. He was assisted from his car and taken by ambulance to the St. Joseph Hospital emergency room, where he was initially seen by his regular internist, Raymond Ross, M.D.
   Dr. Ross obtained orthopedic consultation with Brian A. Ewald, M.D., who reviewed the multiple X-rays taken in the emergency room and found them negative for fracture. Lumbar spine X-rays did reveal evidence of a spondylolisthesis defect at the pars interarticulus of L5, but this was not felt to represent acute injury. Dr. Ewald had Mr. Smith admitted to St. Joseph Hospital on the same day for further evaluation and observation.
   On admission to the hospital, Mr. Smith was placed on complete bed rest, with a cervical collar and medication for pain. On September 10, neurological consultation was obtained with Michael H. Sukoff, M.D., who, although he did not find any significant objective neurological abnormality, felt that there might be a herniated disc at L4-L5, with possible contusion of the nerve roots.
   Drs. Ewald and Sukoff followed Mr. Smith's progress throughout the remainder of his hospitalization. He was continued on bed rest, physiotherapy, and medication, and fitted with a lumbosacral support. He was ultimately ambulated with crutches and was discharged from the hospital on September 25, 1973, with instructions to continue to rest and wear his cervical collar and back brace.
   On discharge from the hospital, Mr. Smith was taken by ambulance to the Sky Palm Motel in Orange, where his wife and children had been staying during his hospitalization. Arrangements were made for home physiotherapy and rental of a hospital bed, and Mr. Smith was taken by ambulance on the following day to his residence at the Riviera Country Club in Pacific Palisades.
   After returning home, Mr. Smith continued to suffer from headaches, neck pain, and severe pain in his lower back, with some radiation into both legs, especially the right. He

</td></tr>
</table>

FIGURE 8.10
Settlement
Work-Up

Continued

---

[2]Prepared by Katherine Webb, Legal Assistant at Cartwright, Sucherman, Slobodin & Fowler, Inc., San Francisco, California.

FIGURE 8.10
Settlement
Work-Up—
Continued

was totally confined to bed for at least two months following the accident, where he was cared for by his wife. Daily physical therapy was administered by Beatrice Tasker, R.P.T.

Mr. Smith continued to receive periodic outpatient care with Dr. Ewald. By the end of December, 1973, Mr. Smith was able to discontinue the use of his cervical collar and was able to walk, with difficulty, without crutches. At the time of his office visit with Dr. Ewald on December 21, he was noted to be having moderate neck discomfort, with increasingly severe low back pain. At the time, Dr. Ewald placed Mr. Smith on a gradually increasing set of Williams exercises and advised him to begin swimming as much as possible.

Mr. Smith continued to be followed periodically by Dr. Ewald through March 1974, with gradual improvement noted. However, Mr. Smith continued to spend the majority of his time confined to his home and often to bed, using a cane whenever he went out. In addition, he suffered periodic severe flareups of low back pain, which would render him totally disabled and would necessitate total bed rest for several days at a time.

During this period of time, Mr. Smith also experienced headaches and blurred vision, for which Dr. Ewald referred him to Robert N. Dunphy, M.D. Dr. Dunphy advised that the symptoms were probably secondary to his other injuries and would most likely subside with time.

On April 1, 1974, Mr. Smith consulted Dr. Ewald with complaints of increased back pain following an automobile ride to San Diego. Dr. Ewald's examination at that time revealed bilateral lumbar muscle spasm, with markedly decreased range of motion. Due to his concern about the extremely prolonged lumbar symptoms, and suspecting a possible central herniated nucleus pulposus, Dr. Ewald recommended that Mr. Smith undergo lumbar myelography. This was performed on an inpatient basis at St. Joseph Hospital on April 4, 1974 and reported to be within normal limits.

Mr. Smith continued conservative treatment with Dr. Ewald through February 1974, following the prescribed program of rest, medication, exercise, and daily physiotherapy administered by his wife. He was able to graduate out of his lumbosacral support by approximately October 1974, resuming use of the garment when he experienced severe flareups of low back pain.

In his medical report dated January 2, 1975, Dr. Ewald stated that he expected a gradual resolution of lumbar symptomatology with time. However, in his subsequent report, dated January 10, 1975, Dr. Ewald noted that since his original report, Mr. Smith had suffered multiple repetitive episodes of low back pain, secondary to almost any increase of activity. At an office visit on February 25, Mr. Smith was reported to have localized his discomfort extremely well to the L5-S1 level, and range of motion was found to have decreased to approximately 75%. Since his examination in February, Dr. Ewald has discussed at length with both Mr. Smith and his wife the possibility of surgical intervention, consisting of lumbar stabilization (fusion) at the L5-S1 level, secondary to the spondylolisthesis present at that level. Dr. Ewald has advised them of the risks, complications, and alternatives with regard to consideration of surgical stabilization, noting that surgery would be followed by a six- to nine-month period of rehabilitation, and further warning that even if the surgical procedure is carried out, there is no guarantee that Mr. Smith will be alleviated of all of his symptomatology.

As stated in Dr. Ewald's medical report dated March 10, 1975, Mr. Smith is himself beginning to lean toward definite consideration with regard to surgery, although he is presently continuing with conservative management.

Dr. Ewald recommends that in the event Mr. Smith does choose to undergo surgery, a repeat myelogram should be performed in order to rule out, as much as possible, the presence of a herniated nucleus pulposus either above or at the level of the spondylolisthesis.

IV. Residual Complaints

Mr. Smith states that his neck injury has now largely resolved, although he does experience occasional neck pain and headaches. However, he continues to suffer from constant, severe pain in his low back, with some radiation of pain and numbness in the right leg.

Mr. Smith notes that his low back pain is worse with cold weather and aggravated by prolonged sitting, walking, driving, or nearly any form of activity. He finds that he must rest frequently and continues to follow a daily regimen of swimming, Williams exercises,

Continued on next page

pain medication, and physiotherapy administered by his wife. He also has resumed the use of his lumbosacral brace.

Mr. Smith was an extremely active person prior to the accident, accustomed to working twelve to sixteen hours per day and engaging in active sports such as tennis. Since the accident, he has had to sell his business and restrict all activities to a minimum, because he has found that any increase in activity will trigger a flareup of low back pain so severe that he is totally incapacitated for several days at a time.

As stated by Dr. Ewald, Mr. Smith is now seriously considering the possibility of surgical stabilization, despite the risks and complications involved. He has always viewed surgery as a last resort but is now beginning to realize that it may be his only alternative in view of his prolonged pain and disability. However, he currently intends to delay any definite decision until after the summer, during which time he intends to increase his swimming activity and see if he can gain any relief from his symptomatology.

V. Specials

(Copies of supporting documentation attached hereto.)

A. Medical:

1. Southland Ambulance Service (9/6/73)	$ 37.00
2. St. Joseph Hospital (9/6–9/25/73)	2,046.29
3. Raymond R. Ross, M.D. (Emergency Room, 9/6/73)	25.00
4. Brian A. Ewald, M.D. (9/6/73–4/28/75)	604.00
5. Michael H. Sukoff, M.D. (9/10–9/22/75)	140.00
6. Wind Ambulance Service (9/25/73)	39.50
7. Wind Ambulance Service (9/26/73)	89.00
8. Beatrice Tasker, R.P.T. (9/21–10/22/73)	825.00
9. Abbey Rents (Rental of hospital bed and trapeze bar, 9/25–11/25/73)	222.00
10. Allied Medical & Surgical Co. (Purchase of cane, 1/10/73)	10.45
11. Rice Clinical Laboratories (2/1/74)	4.00
12. Robert N. Dunphy, M.D. (2/1–4/15/74)	95.00
13. St. Joseph Hospital (X-rays and lab tests, 2/9/74)	156.00
14. St. Joseph Hospital (Inpatient myelography, 4/23–4/24/74)	251.60
15. Medication	357.70
Total Medical Expenses	$4,902.54

B. Miscellaneous Family Expenses

(During plaintiff's hospitalization, 9/6–9/25/75.)

1. Sky Palm Motel (Lodging for wife and children)	$1,050.50
2. Taxicab (9/6/73)	2.45
Total Miscellaneous Expenses	$1,052.95

C. Wage Loss

At the time of the accident, Mr. Smith was employed as president and co-owner, with Mr. George Frost, of the Inter Science Institute, Inc., a medical laboratory in Los Angeles.

Continued on next page

FIGURE 8.10

Settlement Work-Up— *Continued*

FIGURE 8.10

Settlement
Work-Up—
Continued

As stated in the attached verification from Mr. Mamikunian, Mr. Smith was earning an annual salary of $48,000.00, plus automobile, expenses, and fringe benefits.

In a telephone conversation with Mr. Frost on May 6, 1975, he advised me that the Inter Science Institute had grossed $512,000.00 in 1973 and $700,000.00 in 1974. He further confirmed that prior to the accident of September 6, 1973, both he and Mr. Frost had been approached on at least two to three different occasions by companies, including Revlon and a Canadian firm, offering substantial sums of money for purchase of the business. On the basis of the foregoing, both Mr. Smith and Mr. Frost place a conservative estimate of the value of the business at $2,000,000.00.

Due to injuries sustained in the subject accident, Mr. Smith was unable to return to work or perform the necessary executive and managerial functions required in his position as president and part owner of the business. As a result, on or about October 26, 1973, while still totally incapacitated by his injuries, Mr. Smith was forced to sell his 50% stock interest in the Inter Science Institute for a total sum of $300,000.00.

On the basis of the prior estimated value of the business at $2,000,000.00, *Mr. Smith sustained a loss of $700,000.00 in the sale of his one-half interest in Inter Science Institute, Inc., in addition to the loss of an annual salary of $48,000.00, plus automobile, expenses, and fringe benefits.*

Even if one were to assume that the sale of his interest in the business was reasonable value, Mr. Smith has sustained a loss in salary only in the sum of *$84,000.00* to date, based on an annual salary of $48,000.00 for one year and nine months up to June 12, 1975.

Chapter Summary

The goal of investigation is to obtain new facts and to verify facts already known by the office. It is a highly individualistic skill where determination, imagination, resourcefulness, and openness are critical. A good investigator has a healthy suspicion of preconceived notions of what the facts are when this might interfere with uncovering the unexpected. In the search for the facts, the investigator is concerned with truth in the context of the evidence that will be needed to establish that truth in court. But the standard that guides the search is not absolute truth or proof; the guideline of the investigator is to pursue whatever degree of evidence (large or small) that is reasonably available.

People often have different perspectives on what did or did not happen, particularly in regard to emotionally charged events. When different versions of facts exist, the investigator must seek them out.

Competent investigation requires a knowledge of the standard sources of information; an ability to use the techniques of gaining access to records, and an ability to evaluate the trustworthiness of testimonial and physical evidence.

Investigators must be aware of the image they project of themselves, be prepared for witnesses with differing levels of factual knowledge, be ready for witnesses who are unwilling to cooperate, and be able to gain the trust of witnesses.

The law of evidence is an important part of the investigator's arsenal. This should include an understanding of: admissible evidence, the distinction between direct evidence and circumstantial evidence, the nature of relevance, when a witness is competent to give testimony and to state an opinion, the nature of hearsay and the eight exceptions that allow hearsay to be admitted. Investigators need to understand the effect of the privilege against self-incrimination, the attorney-client privilege, the doctor-patient privilege, and the confidentiality of some government information. They must also understand the best evidence rule, the authentication of evidence, and the parol evidence rule.

Two important documents that are the products of competent investigation are: a witness statement, which is taken to preserve the testimony of an important witness, and a settlement work-up, which is an advocacy document that compiles and organizes facts in an effort to encourage a favorable settlement.

Key Terms

impeach
discovery devices
deposition
interrogatories
request for admissions
evidence
testimonial evidence
physical evidence
tangible evidence
Freedom of Information Act
disinterested witness
admissible evidence
direct evidence
circumstantial evidence
relevant evidence

competency
credibility
lay opinion evidence
hearsay
admissions
declaration against interest
dying declaration
business entry
spontaneous declaration
declaration of bodily feelings
declaration of mental state of
   mind
declaration of present sense
   impression
res gestae exceptions

privilege
privilege against self-
   incrimination
attorney-client privilege
doctor-patient privilege
clergy-penitent privilege
marital communications
best evidence rule
authentication
parol evidence rule
witness statement
attestation clause
settlement work-up

Computer Literacy for Paralegals: An Introduction to the Use of Computers in a Law Office

with Dale Hobart*

■ Chapter Outline

■ Section A. Law Offices, Computers, and Paralegals

It is very doubtful that you will work in an office without computers. For many medium and large law offices, computers dominate the practice of law and the management of the law office. If you flipped through the pages of a bar association magazine or legal newspaper, you would probably find that two-thirds of the advertising is from computer manufacturers, vendors, and consultants. Paralegals are an integral part of this computer environment, as demonstrated by the surveys presented in Figures 9.1 and 9.2 and by the comments of paralegals that begin on page 402.

How do paralegals feel computers have affected their professional lives? The following comments, while not representative of all paralegals, help provide an answer.

---

*Director of Legal Assistant Program and Assistant Director of Academic Computing, Ferris State College

FIGURE 9.1   Survey on Computer Use

Employment and Salary Survey 1990 (Rocky Mountain Legal Assistants Association, 1990) Question: Do you personally use a computer for any of the following? (Answer based on 470 responses from paralegals.)	Task	Yes	Percent Responding
	■ Word Processing	331	77
	■ Docketing	94	22
	■ Conflicts Check	24	6
	■ Litigation Support	181	42
	■ Timekeeping/Billing	87	20
	■ Other	95	22

PARALEGAL COMMENTS:

General

"These amazing little machines are filled with micro-chips, circuit boards, disks, and many other magical parts about which I know nothing! What I do know is how much more efficient I am with my PC."[1]

"In the last few years, the computer has become a desirable, if not indispensable, tool of the legal profession, and, in fact, it is somewhat ironic that this new tool has caused typing skills to enjoy a comeback in popularity. Efficient use of the computer keyboard not only facilitates drafting of legal pleadings but also the use of a variety of software programs. While word processing programs are the programs most widely used by legal assistants, [other software used includes:] programs for file organization, document retrieval, calculation, spreadsheet formulation, and research. . . ."[2]

Corporate Law

Some paralegals have become adept at tailoring general business programs, such as spreadsheet and database management programs, to different areas of legal practice. "When I worked . . . for a major corporation, I was responsible for the shareholder relations program. This required monthly analysis of the company's shareholder base. Rather than have a transfer agent compile the information for a handsome fee, I prepared the report on an IBM PC using Lotus 1-2-3."[3]

Criminal Law

"We were confronted with more than 300 boxes of documents stored in a depository in Houston" that contained evidence that had to be classified so that it would be available for the trial attorney. To do that, the attorney "started building a database, using teams of paralegals to code and input the information." The judge allowed the attorney to connect his computer and fax machine

■ Not so many years ago, computers were fancy tools only big firms could afford. Even firms with computers were inclined to keep them out of sight, off the polished oak desks of their lawyers, many of whom made it a point of pride not to be able to type. Those days are gone forever.
Paul Reidinger, American Bar Association Journal (1991).
■

---

[1]Eastwick, *JLA's Seminar/Workshop on Personal Computers in the Law Office,* JLA News 4, Issue 12 (Jacksonville Legal Assistants, January 1988).
[2]Schueneman, *Software Brings Typing Back to the Future,* 3 TALAFAX 3, No. 3 (Tucson Ass'n of Legal Assistants, 1991).
[3]B. Bernardo, *Paralegal* (Peterson's Guides, 1990).

FIGURE 9.2

Computers in the Law Office

**Results of 1989 Wage,
Benefit & Utilization Survey**

(Legal Assistants of New Mexico, 1989)

Question: What types of tasks do you use your computer for? (Answer based on 103 responses. Paralegals could check more than one task.)

71 Word Processing
49 Document Control
41 Case Evaluation and Management
39 Document Assembly/Forms Fill-in
39 Preparing Charts and Exhibits
36 Database Research (WESTLAW & LEXIS)
33 Full-text Data Storage and Retrieval
29 Database Research (nonlegal)
22 Calendaring/Date Reminder (tickler) System
13 Networking/E-Mail (Electronic Mail)
13 Accounting/Billing
 9 Calculating/"Number Crunching"
 5 Desktop Publishing
 4 Conflicts Checking
 5 Other

Question: Which computer do you use? (Answer based on 96 responses from paralegals.)

Number	Computer Used
62	IBM or Compatible PC
4	Apple PC
1	IBM Displaywriter
9	Portable and/or laptop
20	Other

Question: Does your firm provide you with your own PC or terminal, or do you share it with other users? (Answer based on 101 responses.)

60 Use own PC or terminal
17 Share a PC or terminal
24 N/A

Question: Which word processing software program does your office use? (Answer based on 80 responses.)

Number	Software Used
47	WordPerfect
14	Wang
4	Microsoft Word
3	Displaywrite
18	Other (e.g., DEC, Lanier)

Question: Does your firm use a computerized litigation support system? (Answer based on 103 responses.)

71 YES
29 NO
 3 N/A

Question: When your firm orders the transcript of a hearing or a deposition, it is provided on disk so that it can be used with your in-house database system? (Answer based on 95 responses.)

50 YES
40 NO
 5 N/A

Question: Has your firm used an outside computer consultant when acquiring computer hardware and/or software? (Answer based on 95 responses.)

66 YES
27 NO
 2 N/A

---

in the courtroom with the computer and fax machine in the law office. In effect, the attorney was "wired into the network back at the office, which is staffed with paralegals who have access to all kinds of information which can be faxed or sent by computer back into the courtroom immediately." [4]

---

[4]Keeva, *Document Analysis in Criminal Litigation,* 76 American Bar Ass'n Journal 80 (May 1990).

Estates and Trusts

Ann Cook, legal assistant at Pepper, Hamilton & Scheetz of Philadelphia, saw a demonstration of a software package for fiduciary accounting and immediately began urging her firm to move in that direction. "After seeing it, I was no longer satisfied writing the same information several times for each different purpose when all I had to do was input it once and then push buttons. . . . We've now expanded our system to do estate planning calculations which manually were cumbersome and expensive to produce. Eventually, we would like to connect our system into a data bank like Standard & Poors, so that we can get instant evaluations of stock and bond values."[5]

Insurance

In the case management area, Norman Strizek works with insurance firms. He's "created databases so they can track separately every litigation case they're involved in, and [identify] which law firm is handling each part; what they're billed each quarter; the status of the litigation; responsible attorneys and paralegals, with phone numbers; due dates of different filings and who is handling each. It helps the insurer manage all their litigation."[6]

Litigation

"When the portable PC is not used for data retrieval, the legal assistant can use it to take notes." Julie Hoff, a litigation legal assistant for ten years, "cites an example of a legal assistant who put her portable to work in an efficient manner during a recent trial in Minneapolis. While the witness was testifying, the legal assistant summarized the proceedings on her portable computer. At the end of each day, she printed her notes and they were used in the preparation of [cross] examination for the next day and for future witnesses."[7]

"I never leave home without my laptop!" says Laurie Roselle, the Litigation Paralegal Manager at Rogers & Wells in New York. She "types in taxis, commutes with her desktop portable, pulls cases and does actual memos." She says, "You have to use every minute—and you can bill the time."[8]

Professional Responsibility

Jane Palmer is the conflict-of-interest specialist at Hogan and Hartson in Washington D.C. Working under the supervision of an attorney, Jane spends "more than half her time at the computer on requests for information." She "does all the research on every prospective client" for the firm's offices in Washington D.C., Maryland, Virginia, London, and Brussels "to find out who are the related parties in the matter they are bringing." She "uses her database to see if Hogan and Hartson has ever represented any party on any side of the matter, or been adverse to them. The databases are a client list, accounting and

[5]Troop, *Paralegals Are Taking the Lead Through Computers,* 2 Legal Assistant Today 21 (Winter 1985).
[6]Milano, *Novel Way Paralegals Are Using Computers,* 8 Legal Assistant Today 22, 110 (March/April 1991).
[7]*Law Office Trends: Portable PCs in the Courtroom,* Merrill Advantage, 6 (Spring 1989).
[8]Milano, see footnote 6 at p. 23.

billing information, and addresses." "I draw on that for searches, and add to it every day, updating the information." Building on the accounting department's database, Palmer uses Informatics, software designed for conflicts, which connects to accounting and is used for both functions.[9]

Torts

"Moving on to a tetracycline case involving five pharmaceutical firms, he computerized 40,000 documents. . . ." His "team did the coding." [10]

McCarthy, Palmer, Volkema & Becker is a plaintiff's tort litigation firm in Columbus Ohio. "Computers are an important part of the legal assistants' daily work environment. In place of the message slips and paper memos, the desks of the attorneys and paralegals are adorned with personal computers. Since the firm's beginning, all of the attorneys, legal assistants, secretaries and receptionists have been networked. All telephone messages are transferred from the receptionist via E-mail (Electronic Mail). The main function of the computer, however, is as a warehouse for client file information. The attorney and legal assistant can access the computer from the name and phone number of the judge, opposing counsel, adjuster, treating physician or expert, without pulling a large file from the filing cabinet. An electronic calendar is also available on the system. Firm members now have a means for scheduling meetings with more than one attorney and/or legal assistant without leaving their desks. The computer will notify the person . . . of any conflicts. No more telephone tag or running from one calendar to another." [11]

 ## Section B. Survival Strategies

When you walk into your first paralegal job, be prepared to encounter some sophisticated equipment. Our goal in this chapter is not to make you an expert in any particular product or system, rather the goal is to provide you with some of the fundamentals so that you will be in a better position to benefit from the inevitable on-the-job training in the computer products and systems used by a particular law office. We will assume in this chapter that you are a beginner. Even if you are well-versed in computers generally, you'll be a beginner with respect to computer programs that have been (and will be) designed for law offices. Our starting point is a series of survival strategies presented in Figure 9.3. As we begin our exploration of computer use in the practice of law, keep these strategies in mind.

 ## Section C. Terminology

The world of the computer, like the world of law, has its own language. Initially, this language can be very confusing. Persistence and time, however, will help rectify this problem.

---

[9]Milano, see footnote 6 at p. 24.
[10]Milano, see footnote 6 at p. 24.
[11]Overly, *Innovations in Law Office Automation*, 6 LACO Letter 12 (Legal Assistants of Central Ohio, December 1990).

FIGURE 9.3

Computer Survival Strategies: A Paralegal Tackles a New Program in the Law Office

Stage I: Identify Your "Help" Resources

■ Find out whether there is anyone in the office who already knows how to use the program who would be willing to answer your questions about it. If possible, this should be someone other than—or in addition to—your supervisor.

■ Ask if the program you will be using has an 800 number that you can call for assistance.

■ Ask if the program has an *online tutorial* which explains the basics. If so, ask someone to start the tutorial for you.

■ Ask if the program has a *"HELP" key* that can be used while you are running the program. If so, ask how to use it.

■ Find the manual for the program (called the *documentation*). Turn to the index, if one exists. Select some familiar terms in the index, such as *capitalization.* Turn to the pages for such items and try to follow the instructions provided for them.

■ Start a computer notebook in which you write definitions of new terms, steps to follow for certain tasks, steps you took just before you seemed to make a mistake, questions that you want to ask someone later, etc.

■ Expect to learn a new vocabulary. (*Boot*, for example, has nothing to do with what goes on your foot.)

Stage II: Learn the Big Seven Tasks

Learn the seven essential tasks that apply to most programs:

■ How to turn on the computer, *load* the program, and start using it

■ How to create a new document or file with the program

■ How to save a document or file

■ How to call up (or retrieve) a document or file that was created and saved earlier

■ How to make a copy of the document or file

■ How to turn on the printer and print a document or file

■ How to exit from the program and turn the computer off

Stage III: Take the Initiative

■ Find out if your local paralegal association is offering a seminar on computer use. Attend it. If none is planned, call the president of the association and suggest that one be offered.

■ Read the local bar association journals to find out what computer seminars are offered by the bar or by CLE (Continuing Legal Education). Attend some that are relevant to your job.

■ Photocopy a chapter from the computer manual at the office. Take the chapter home and read it over the weekend.

■ Ask librarians in your area how you can find magazine reviews of the program that you use. Read those reviews.

■ Find out if there is a *users group* in your area that meets every month to discuss the program, such as a WordPerfect Users Group. Attend the meetings of this group.

■ Organize a "specialty section" of your paralegal association that consists of paralegals who use the program. Members of this section would meet periodically to learn from each other and to discuss common problems with the program.

First we begin with some basic definitions:

Hardware.   The computer and its physical parts. Hardware is what you take out of the box and plug together when you purchase a computer system. It is any part of the system that can be physically touched.

Backup.   To copy information that a computer uses. Copies should be made regularly just in case the original is destroyed.

Command.   A word or character typed into the computer to tell the computer what to do next.

Data.   Information of any type that can be used by computers. The data may consist of numbers, words, or pictures.

Typical desktop computer system

Disk Drive (also called a disk).   In this chapter, we will use the term *disk drive* (rather than disk) to describe the part of your hardware that is used to store and retrieve programs and information to and from diskettes (see next definition). The disk drive has the capability of placing program information on a diskette. This is often referred to as *writing information to the diskette.* The disk drive also has the capability of "reading" the information from the diskette into the computer. If the information is a program, the program can then be "run" (see definition below) by the computer. Disk drives can be hard or floppy. A *floppy disk* drive is one that can use diskettes. The diskettes can be easily inserted and removed from the disk drive. *Hard disks,* on the other hand, cannot be removed without taking the hardware apart. Furthermore, they have a much greater memory capacity than diskettes. A 40 megabyte hard disk, for example, will be

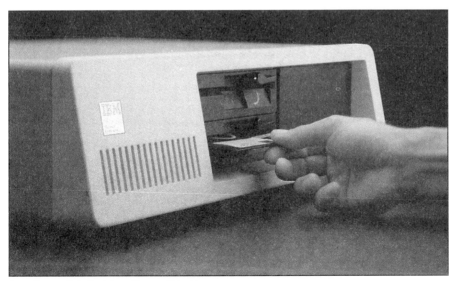

Inserting a diskette into a floppy disk drive

able to hold approximately 40 million *bytes* of information—about 20,000 pages of text. (One byte is the storage equivalent of one letter of the alphabet, or one punctuation mark, or one blank space.) It would take over one hundred regular-sized diskettes to store the same amount of data.

Diskette.   Sometimes these are also called disks, floppy disks, or just floppies. In this chapter, the term *diskette* will be used. A diskette is a flat piece of plastic, 3½ inch or 5¼ inch in size, that is covered with the same magnetic substance used on a magnetic tape. Information is placed on the diskette in a manner similar to the way music is stored on a cassette. The information can be a program or data to be used by a program. This information can then be read into the computer for the computer to use.

Boxes containing 3½-inch and 5¼-inch diskettes

File.   A file refers to any information that a computer can use and that is stored or kept together as a group. A file can consist of data or a program. (For the meaning of *file* in a database program, see Figure 9.5.)

k.   A measure of capacity. Each k equals one kilobyte, which is 1,024 bytes (see definition of byte above). The letter k often refers to the amount of information that can be kept on your diskette. It can also refer to the work area in the computer. The work area is the amount of space available to the computer for keeping programs and information that will be used. When microcomputers were new, 64k was considered a great deal of memory (see definitions below). Today, however, many of the programs require 640k or more to function properly.

Language.   A program that allows a computer to understand commands and carry them out. BASIC, COBAL, and PASCAL are among the most common computer languages.

Laptop.   A portable computer that can be powered by rechargeable batteries.

Typical laptop computer system

Load.   To move or transfer a program or information from a disk drive into the computer.

Memory.   The area inside a computer that contains programs, and data that programs help generate.

Microcomputer.   A computer that is small enough to fit on a desk. The term is not clearly defined because the power of small computers has increased dramatically in the past few years.

Monitor.   A TV-like device that is part of the hardware of the computer. On the screen the monitor displays whatever commands you type at the keyboard—and displays information in response to those commands.

Operating System.   A program that is in charge of what is displayed on the screen, what is sent to the printer, and all other facets of the operation of a computer. In effect, the operating system serves the function of traffic cop or central manager. There are a variety of operating systems available, such as DOS or MS-DOS, OS/2, UNIX, GEOS, HFS (Macintosh), and NextStep. In some of the systems, you type certain commands on the keyboard. In others, you use a small pointer device called a *mouse* to point to pictures (graphics or icons) on the screen that stand for the same kind of commands that you would otherwise "type in." To execute the command, you push (or *click*) a button on the mouse. An important development in this area is *Windows* from Microsoft. This is a mouse-pointer program that allows a user to run several large programs (such as word processing, database management, spreadsheet) simultaneously. To take advantage of this *multitasking* capacity, a number of the older operating systems are issuing what they call their *windows-based* operating system. Furthermore, many software manufacturers are rushing to release versions

A monitor displaying text on screen

of their products for the *windows environment*, e.g., WordPerfect for Windows.

Run.   To cause a program to be loaded into the computer from a disk drive and to begin performing its task.

Save.   To cause a program or data that is in the computer memory to be moved or stored on a diskette or hard drive.

Computer with mouse

Software.   The programs that allow you to perform tasks such as word processing, database management, and spreadsheet calculations. To use a program, you must get it into the computer. This is usually done by transferring the program from a diskette or from the hard drive.

 ## Section D. Hardware

Many people make the mistake of buying a computer first and then trying to figure out what to do with it. This is not the best approach. If you know what you want to do, you should *first find the software* that can do the job and *then buy the computer* that will run that software.

When investigating available programs, you will probably discover that we live in an IBM world. At the present time, most business application programs are designed first for an IBM or *compatible* computer and then are developed for others. There are many computers that are IBM compatible.

The word *compatible,* or compatible computer, is used in several senses. At a minimum, the word simply means that the information or data files created on an IBM computer can also be used by another computer. At the other end of the spectrum of compatibility, some non-IBM computers not only will use information or data from an IBM computer but will also run most software designed for an IBM computer.

Once software has been selected, the next step is to choose a computer. One of the first considerations is how much memory should be purchased for the computer. Most come with a minimum of 640k. For multipurpose software, it is advisable to obtain considerably more.

The next item of hardware to consider is the disk drive. Disk drives are used to load programs into the computer and to store letters, documents, and other information. There are several combinations of disk drives for a microcomputer, but only two that make sense for business applications.

One choice is two floppy drives (a disk drive that uses diskettes to store data). These are disk drives that use removable diskettes that are usually 3½ or 5¼ inches in diameter. The disk drives should be *dual sided,* meaning that the disk drive is capable of writing on both sides of the diskette. It should also be able to store information on a diskette in *condensed* mode. This mode is referred to as *double-density.* Therefore, a two-floppy-drive machine should have dual sided, double-density disk drives. This will often be abbreviated DS DD. Two disk drives are needed to make the use of a computer faster and easier. If only one disk drive is available, the user is often required to change the diskette in the drive while using the computer. This is time-consuming and frustrating.

The more common choice for business purposes is a computer with one floppy disk drive and one hard disk drive. A hard disk normally used in a microcomputer can hold much more information than a diskette. This means that most of the programs and data that are used from day to day can be kept on the hard disk, making use of the computer more convenient. There is no need to locate and insert a new diskette to change programs on a hard disk system. All the programs that you normally need can be stored on the hard disk and accessed directly. Unlike a diskette, a hard disk cannot be easily removed from the machine. If finances allow, a hard disk is preferable either in the computer itself or externally as part of a network. (A *network,* as we will see below, is created when several computers are connected together.) You will find that it is nearly impossible to have too much disk storage capacity.

You'll need a monitor as part of your system. Monitors usually come in one of two formats: monochrome or color. The monochrome may be either black and white, green, or amber. Most users prefer the green or amber screen monitors. Color is tempting, but unless the computer is going to be used for color graphics or presentations, monochrome is better. Color can be hard on the eyes, though this is beginning to change. As computers become more sophisticated, color quality will improve.

To obtain a printed copy of what has been entered into the computer, you need a printer. There are many different kinds of printers available:[12]

- *Dot Matrix Printer.* This printer uses tiny pins that press against or punch a ribbon to create a pattern of dots.

Daisy wheel

- *Daisy Wheel Printer.* This printer uses a "daisy wheel," a device (resembling a flower) that contains the alphabet and other characters on spokes. The printer spins the wheel to find the character, which then strikes the ribbon.

- *Ink Jet Printer.* This printer uses a stream of ink sprayed on paper to produce the print. The ink comes from a cartridge rather than a ribbon.

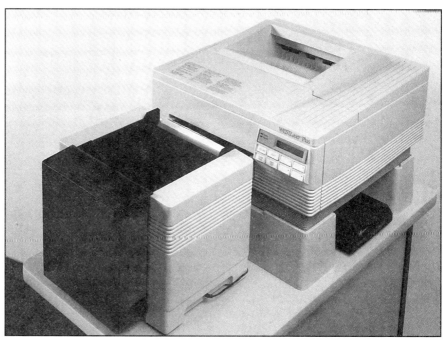

Laser printer: HP LaserJet III Printer

---

[12]Electronic Industries Association, *How to Buy a Personal Computer,* 14 (1990).

■ *Laser Printer.* This printer uses a laser beam of light to reproduce images. Special cartridges are needed to print text or graphics. It operates very much like a copy machine. Because of their versatility, speed, and high quality, laser printers have become standard in law offices.

A *network* is another important hardware item used by law offices. It will allow you to connect many computers together, enabling them to share (a) information, (b) a hard disk, or (c) printers. For example, a network can make it possible for everyone in a law office to have access to wills, pleadings, or other frequently used documents without each person needing separate copies on individual diskettes. A network can be cost-efficient since it can provide the means for many computers to share some of the more expensive parts of a system.

A *modem* is needed for any law office wishing to use its computer for communications. The modem makes it possible for a computer to send and receive information using regular telephone lines.

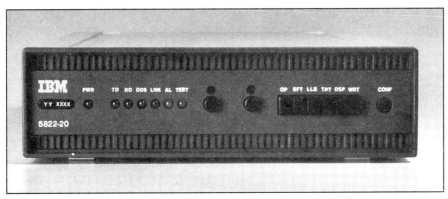

An external modem

Many other hardware options are available. The list just given covers the basics and is sufficient to satisfy the needs of most users.

 Section E. Software

There are four basic types of software available:

■ Word processing
■ Database management
■ Spreadsheets
■ Communications
■ The fifth and latest kind of software consists of a combination of all four

There are two ways of making a rational choice when selecting software. One is to try out the programs *before* purchasing them. This will work best for someone with experience who knows what to look for. Testing software yourself can be very time consuming. If you have neither the background nor the time to develop the needed expertise (months are needed), consult an expert. Generally the expert should *not* be someone connected with the local computer store who has an interest in selling you the software that is in stock. A person within your own office is often the best expert. There are a surprising number of people who develop such expertise on their own.

1. Word Processing Software

Use a *word processor* instead of a typewriter for writing. It makes little sense to use a typewriter for anything other than addressing one envelope or filling in a simple printed form. Any letter, memo, pleading, brief, or other typed material is easier to prepare with word processing. Once you have used a good word processor, you will be very reluctant to sit at a traditional typewriter again. Since a large volume of writing is done in the law office, a word processor can be a great productivity tool.

Many law offices have used *dedicated word processing* for a long time. A dedicated word processor is one that can do only word processing and none of the other functions that a computer can perform. It is not a computer. The capabilities of the dedicated word processor, however, are now available on computers that can do word processing and other jobs for less cost than the single-purpose or dedicated word processors of old.

The most elemental difference between a word processor and the familiar manual or electric typewriter becomes apparent when you prepare a document for the first time. For example, unlike a traditional typist, the computer user does not listen for a bell in order to know whether he or she is at the end of a line. The computer will automatically move a word down to the next line when the end of a line is reached. This feature is called *word wrap*. There is no need to pause or slow down. The only time you strike the carriage return key is at the end of a paragraph. When a typing error is made at the computer keyboard, there is no need to reach for the bottle of correction fluid. Nor is there ever a need to worry about a messy final draft caused by insertions or corrections. With the computer you simply go back and correct the error(s). If you left out a letter or sentence, you can easily insert it. The line, in effect, opens up to allow this insertion. If you typed the wrong letter, you can quickly type the correct one directly over the wrong one. If there are too many letters, just press the delete key over the excess letters. Furthermore, there is no need to worry about what such changes will do to paragraph alignment. The computer will take care of it. The task of typing becomes infinitely easier. Someone with limited typing skills soon becomes a confident and competent typist. (See Figure 9.4 for a list of common word-processing terms.)

Easy text entry is just the beginning. Once a document has been put into the computer, it can be used over and over again. Standard paragraphs can be saved, modified, and inserted whenever needed. Documents can be designed so that names are entered once and then automatically included in the final output at fifty different locations. Standard documents can be rearranged by moving paragraphs and sentences within the document. Large or small parts of a document may be moved, deleted, or duplicated to create the final document.

A helpful feature on many word processors is the spelling checker. After a document has been typed, you can activate a spelling program. Different types of spelling programs exist, all of which are based on a large number of words in the program's dictionary. The simpler programs place a mark on any word *not* contained in the program's dictionary. You have probably misspelled such words. You can then review and correct the marked words as needed. More sophisticated spelling programs not only mark a word that is not in the program's dictionary, but also present several possible correct spellings. Spelling

TERM	DEFINITION
Automatic pagination	A feature that enables a word processor to number the pages of the printed copy automatically.
Block	A group of characters, such as a sentence or paragraph.
Block movement	A feature that allows the user to define a block of text and then perform a specific operation on the entire block. Common block operations include block move, block copy, block save, and block delete..
Boldface	Heavy type; for example, **this is boldface**.
Character	A letter, number, or symbol.
Character enhancement	Underlining, boldfacing, subscripting, and superscripting.
Control character	A coded character that does not print but is part of the command sequence in a word processor.
Cursor	The marker on the display screen indicating where the next character can be displayed.
Default setting	A value used by the word processor when it is not instructed to use any other value.
Deletion	A feature by which a character, word, sentence, or larger block of text can be removed from the existing text.
Editing	The act of changing or amending text.
Format	The layout of a page; for example, the number of lines and the margin settings.
Global	An instruction that will be carried out throughout an entire document. For example, change the word *avenue* to *street* everywhere in the document.
Header	A piece of text that is stored separately from the text and printed at the top of each page.
Incremental spacing	A method by which the printer inserts spaces between words and letters to produce justified margins; also called microspacing.
Insertion	A feature in which a character, word, sentence, or larger block of text is added to the existing text.
Justification	A feature that makes lines of text even at the margins.
Menu	A list of commands or prompts on the display screen.
Print formatting	The function of a word processor that communicates with the printer to tell it how to print the text on paper.
Print preview	A feature that enables the user to view a general representation on the screen of how the document will look when printed.
Screen formatting	A function of a word processor that controls how the text will appear on the screen.
Scrolling	Moving a line of text onto or off the screen.
Search and find	A routine that searches for, and places the cursor at, a specified series or string of characters.
Search and replace	A routine that searches for a specified character string and replaces it with the specified replacement string. See global.
Status line	A message line above or below the text area on a display screen that gives format and system information.

FIGURE 9.4

Frequently Encountered Word Processing Terms

Continued

FIGURE 9.4
Frequently
Encountered Word
Processing Terms
—*Continued*

TERM	DEFINITION
Subscript	A character that prints below the usual text baseline.
Superscript	A character that prints above the usual text baseline.
Text buffer	An area set aside in memory to hold text temporarily.
Text editing	The function of a word processor that enables the user to enter and edit text.
Text file	A file that contains text, as opposed to a program.
Virtual representation	An approach to screen formatting that enables the user to see on the screen exactly how the printed output will look.
Word wrap	The feature in which a word is moved automatically to the beginning of the next line if it goes past the right margin.
WYSIWYG	What you see (on the screen) is what you get (when the screen is printed).

Source: S. Mandell, *Introduction to Computers Using the IBM and MS-DOS PCs with Basic,* 3d ed., 216 (West, 1991).

checkers are great for catching transposed letters, easily overlooked by a proofreader. (You will be told, for example, that you need to change the spelling of th*ie*r to th*ei*r.) Be aware that a spelling checker will not tell you that you used "to" when you should have used "two" or "too." Since all these words are correctly spelled, they will not be marked by the program.

Word processors can print out a document in many formats. You can change formats if you discover that you are not satisfied with the format of your document. A variety of formats or formatting styles can be selected. The type can be *right justified* (meaning that the right hand margin of the text is even) or have a ragged right edge. Left margins can be set at many different places throughout the document. Pages can be numbered or unnumbered, and the numbering can start with any digit you choose. Most word processors can include footnotes and keep the textual material that has been footnoted on the same page with the footnote even if you later insert a lot of material on this page. Many word processors can place the same heading at the top of each page without your having to retype the heading for all the pages in the document. A few word processors come with the capability of creating indexes for the document. You simply mark the word or phrase that is to be included in the index and run the index part of the program. An index is then created with all the page numbers for each location of the word or phrase in the document.

Probably the most powerful capability of a word processor is called *merge printing*. It allows you to combine several whole files and to place data from one file into specific locations in another.

Merge printing whole files is very useful in creating documents with standard paragraphs. Each paragraph is usually saved in a computer file with its own name. When you wish to include the paragraph in a document, you simply enter the proper code and the name of the file. When you print out the document, the paragraph will be included at the location indicated without the necessity of retyping it.

Merging data from one file into another allows the creation of letters or other documents with appropriate names and addresses included in the finished document at all the proper places. This can be particularly useful in mailing the same document to many people. Code words are used for the placement of each bit of information such as the street address, the city, and the state. Once the code words are created, the street address, city, or whatever is represented by the code word, will be included in the final document wherever the code word is found.

When selecting a word processing program, the first step is to determine what current tasks could be done better and more efficiently with a word processing program. If the law office uses standard forms or standard language in documents or mass mailings (such as billings), a word processor with good merge capabilities is very helpful.

If you already have word processing capabilities, you may be considering a change in your system. It is critical to determine whether the current system performs all the tasks you need. If it does, you probably shouldn't change your system. The current system is known by the current users, and retraining can be very disruptive. Do not buy new software just to have the latest program. When new programs are first sold, they frequently have defects *(bugs)*. Some of the defects can be serious. If the new features are not critical to your operation, wait six months. After that time, most of the bugs will be found and fixed by the manufacturer (and the price may go down). Let someone else be the guinea pig.

Many magazines review word processors and other software programs. Go to the library and find at least three reviews on a software program that you are thinking of purchasing. Read them carefully. Usually you will find a consensus within the reviews.

Examples of available computer magazines

2. Databases

Database software is used to store and organize information. The information is entered into the database in an organized manner so that the computer can extract it, reorganize it, consolidate it, summarize it, and create reports from it. As a business management tool in a law office, a database is used for timekeeping, calendars, ticklers, billing, and client records. (See Figure 9.5.) As a case management tool, it can be used for document control in cases that have a large number of documents that must be indexed and cross-referenced. Also, as we shall see, WESTLAW and LEXIS are services that consist of hundreds of databases used for legal research.

Entering information into the database usually requires someone to sit at a terminal and manually type in the information. (Machines called *scanners* are able to enter text without typing, but they are generally more effective in taking in graphics than text.) If the database is to contain documents, each document entered will need an ID code, a brief description of the document, and index words for it. One of the major features of a database is that it can serve as a large index, thereby allowing rapid retrieval of information.

Once all the data has been entered, the database can be used to retrieve, compare, or compile information. To perform any of these functions, you need to search the database. There are two ways to search a database: *key word* searches and *full text* searches.

A *key word* search is like looking through the index of a book. The data base program will build an index using information that it is told to use for the index. The computer searches through this index and displays all information associated with the key word. For example, assume that you create a database to keep the membership list for your paralegal association, and you instruct the database program that you want an index created using the state in the address of members of the association. You could then ask the computer to list all members from Ohio or any other state. This type of search can be completed very quickly. The quality of the results of such a search depends on how well indexed the database is. If the person who made the list of index words for each document did not do a very good job, the search will not be very productive. Poor

FIGURE 9.5

Frequently Encountered Database Management Terms

TERM	DEFINITION
Database	A grouping of independent files into one integrated whole that can be accessed through one central point; a database is designed to meet the information needs of a wide variety of users within an organization.
Data Manager	A data management software package that consolidates data files into an integrated whole, allowing access to more than one data file at a time.
Data Redundancy	The repetition of the same data in several different files.
Field	A subdivision of a record that holds a meaningful item of data, such as an employee number.
Record	A collection of related data fields that constitutes a single unit, such as an employee record.
File	A group of related data records, such as employee records.

Source: S. Mandell, *Introduction to Computers Using the IBM and MS-DOS PCs with Basic*, 3d ed., 514–15 (West, 1991).

indexing causes either too little or too much information to be reported from the search.

The second way to search a database is called a *full-text* search. With this type of search, the computer will examine *all* the information stored by the database program, not just the contents of an index. You might, for example, create a document-control database that contains a summary of the document, including important dates, names, and events. A full-text search would be a search of all the words in the summaries of the documents that were entered in the database. The computer will look through the summaries and display a list of documents that meet the search criteria. If, for example, the documents that were entered into the database concerned an automobile accident and you wished to find all the documents that referred to Helen Johnson (who is the chief witness for the opposition), you could make a full-text search of the document summaries and receive a list of all the documents that mention Helen Johnson.

To make a search, the computer must be told what to search for and where to search for it. This is called the *search criteria*. Many large databases allow search criteria that use the words AND, OR, and NOT. A search criteria using such words might be:

GUN AND ROBBERY AND NOT BANK

This would cause a search of the database to return a list of documents in which the summary had the words *gun* and *robbery* but exclude any summary that also contained the word *bank*. The problem with this type of search is that if the word *holdup* were used instead of *robbery* in the summary of one document, that document would not be found by the search. To find that document, the following search criteria must be used

GUN AND (ROBBERY OR HOLDUP) AND NOT BANK

The parentheses show that the OR applies only to *robbery* and *holdup*. If you did not think of the word *holdup* at the time you phrase your search request, an important document would be missed because you did not use the same words as the person who wrote the summary for the database. In a moment, we will examine how search requests are made on the major legal research services, WESTLAW and LEXIS.

Most database programs can perform several simple tasks. Calendar control is one of them. A database is very efficient in keeping trial and appointment calendars for a law office. Each attorney can receive a printed calendar of appointments for the day. All office calendars can be kept on one computer so that scheduling can be done without creating time conflicts among the attorneys.

A database could also be designed to print out a list of all the cases for the office where the statute of limitations is due to expire during the coming month.

Name, address, family status, phone numbers, case type, and other pertinent information for all the clients of a law firm can be kept in a database. This information could be used for mass mailings of informational letters about certain types of cases to those clients. The database can also be used to identify the types of cases handled by different attorneys in the office and the completion time for each type. This information is very helpful in making management and marketing decisions for the law firm.

For more complex tasks, the usefulness of the computer increases. Timekeeping and billing can be made more efficient with a good database program. There are many database programs designed specifically to perform timekeeping and billing tasks. For different clients, these programs can handle multiple rates for attorneys and paralegals. We will examine this in more detail in Chapter 10 on law office administration.

The database also makes it possible to analyze which types of cases are more profitable to the law firm and which people are more productive in terms of billed hours. Of course there are other factors that must still be evaluated subjectively. The attorney who brings in new clients for the law firm could very well show up poorly on a billable-hours evaluation. Like all other tools, the numbers produced by a computer must be evaluated in perspective.

Databases can be very useful for document control. For example, they can keep track of the content and location of thousands of documents in an antitrust case. Document-control programs were once available only for large computers and were very expensive. Consequently, document control with computers was used only in very large cases. Today, programs have been developed that enable small computers to perform many document control functions.

WESTLAW and LEXIS

WESTLAW and LEXIS are commercial services that are available to anyone who wishes to perform (and pay for) CALR—Computer-Assisted Legal Research. These services can give you access to a vast amount of material, such as the full text of federal and state court opinions, federal and state statutes, federal and state administrative regulations, loose-leaf services, treatises, law review articles, directories of attorneys, and financial data. West Publishing Company, which offers WESTLAW,[13] and Mead Data Company, which offers LEXIS, have user agreements which must be signed before you will be allowed to use their services. The agreement establishes the fees to be paid for the different services available. You gain access to these services by using your PC, personal computer (or a custom terminal), which is connected by telephone lines to computers with vast storage capacities. Data is thereby searched *online*.

Assume that you are working on a case in which a client developed cancer after smoking for many years. You want to know if the client can bring a product-liability claim against the tobacco industry. You would need to formulate a question—called a *search query*—for the computer. The query would ask the computer to find cases involving product liability and cigarettes. Here is an example of such a query used in WESTLAW:

cigar! tobacco smok! /p product strict! /5 liab!

Later, we will examine the meaning of such queries and how to write them. For now, we simply want to give you an overview of what is available.

The screen in Figure 9.6 shows a recent case *(Forster v. R. J. Reynolds Tobacco Co.)* that would be retrieved by WESTLAW, using the above query. After looking at a large number of such cases, you might want to ask the computer to give you a list of citations of every case that fits your query. The screen in Figure 9.7 presents such a list. (It includes the *Forster* case as well as others that fit the query.) If you have a printer connected to your computer, you can ask for a printout of any of these screens.

Every citation to a case that you obtain through CALR can be taken to a traditional law library where you can read the case in a reporter volume. Of

---

[13]The assistance of Laura C. Mickelson is gratefully acknowledged for the material on WESTLAW.

FIGURE 9.6

PAGE 1

Citation	Rank(R)	Rank(P)	Database	Mode
437 N.W.2d 655	R 2 OF 8	P 1 OF 37	MN–CS	T

57 U.S.L.W. 2604, 8 UCC Rep. Serv.2d 370
(Cite as: 437 N.W.2d 655)

John FORSTER, et al., Respondents,

v.

R.J. REYNOLDS TOBACCO COMPANY, Erickson Petroleum Corporation, d/b/a Holiday
Station Stores, Inc., Petitioners, Appellants.
No. C1-87-2170.
Supreme Court of Minnesota.
April 14, 1989

Smoker who developed lung cancer brought **products liability** action against manufacturer and retailer of **cigarettes**. The District Court, Hennepin County, Jonathan Lebedoff, J.,
granted motion of manufacturer and retailer for summary judgment on ground that claims
were preempted, and appeal was taken. The Court of Appeals, 423 N.W.2d 691, reversed.
On further review, the Supreme Court, Simonett, J., held that: (1) state tort claims based
on state-imposed duty to warn are impliedly preempted by Federal **Cigarette** Labeling and
Advertising Act, while other state tort claims are not preempted, and (2) federal Act does
not preempt state tort claims based on failure to warn which predate its effective date.
Affirmed in part, reversed in part, and remanded for further proceedings.

COPR. (C) WEST 1991 NO CLAIM TO ORIG. U.S. GOVT. WORKS

Case retrieved in WESTLAW, with search words in bold print

course, you can also read the case on the computer screen or you can read a
printout of the case, but it is usually cheaper to read material in a library volume
than to read it online. The computer is excellent for searching, not necessarily
for extensive reading.

The *Forster* case was decided in 1989. Suppose that you wanted to know
what has happened to the case since 1989. Has it been overruled? Has it been
cited by other courts? There are three different updating or validation services
on WESTLAW that can give you further information about cases like *Forster*.
They are Insta-Cite (see Figure 9.8), Shepard's Preview (see Figure 9.9), and
Shepard's Citations (see Figure 9.10).

In litigation, there is often a need to find experts who may be able to provide consultation and, if needed, deposition or trial testimony.[14] One of the
specialized searches that can be performed by computer is a search for such
experts. Figure 9.11 presents an example of the results of this kind of search
from the Forensic Services Directory (FSD) database in WESTLAW.

LEXIS works in a similar way, with many of the same features. Suppose,
for example, that you wanted cases in which a juror concealed his or her bias.

---

[14]See Runde, *Computer Assisted Legal Research*, 10 Facts and Findings 13 (NALA, July/August
1983).

FIGURE 9.7

CITATIONS LIST   Total Documents: 8
Database: MN-CS

    1. Minn.App., 1991.
Andren v. White-Rodgers Co., a Div. of Emerson Elec. Co.
(To be reported at: 465 N.W.2d 102)

    2. Minn. 1989. Forster v. R.J. Reynolds Tobacco Co.
437 N.W.2d 655, 57 U.S.L.W. 2604, 8 UCC Rep.Serv.2d 370

    3. Minn.App. 1988. Forster v. R.J. Reynolds Tobacco Co.
423 N.W.2d 691, 56 U.S.L.W. 2664

    4. Minn.App. 1988. Holstad v. Southwestern Porcelain, Inc.
421 N.W.2d 371, 5 UCC Rep.Serv.2d 912

    5. Minn. 1985. Bixler by Bixler v. J.C. Penney Co., Inc.
376 N.W.2d 209

    6. Minn.App. 1984. Dalager v. Montgomery Ward & Co., Inc.
350 N.W.2d 391

    7. Minn. 1979. Armstrong v. Mailand 284 N.W.2d 343, 11 A.L.R.4th 583
188 N.W.2d 426, 290 Minn. 321

    8. Minn. 1971. LEE v. CROOKSTON COCA-COLA BOTTLING COMPANY
188 N.W.2d 426, 290 Minn. 321

END OF CITATIONS LIST
             COPR. (C) WEST 1991 NO CLAIM TO ORIG. U.S. GOVT. WORKS

List of cases retrieved in WESTLAW

You would instruct LEXIS to find cases in which the word *bias* appears in proximity to the words *juror* and *conceal* or *concealing*. See Figure 9.12.

Once you have examined a number of these cases, you can ask the service to display a list of citations of all the cases discovered when LEXIS fulfilled your search request. See Figure 9.13. (Compare Figure 9.7 with Figure 9.13.)

Formulating a Query

We turn now to one of the critical skills in using WESTLAW and LEXIS: formulating a research question or *query*. Our examination of this skill will explore the following topics:

(a) Universal Character (*) and Root Expander (!) for WESTLAW and LEXIS

(b) WESTLAW Queries:

- The OR connector
- The AND connector (&)
- The sentence connector (/s)
- The paragraph connector (/p)
- The BUT NOT connector (%)

FIGURE 9.8

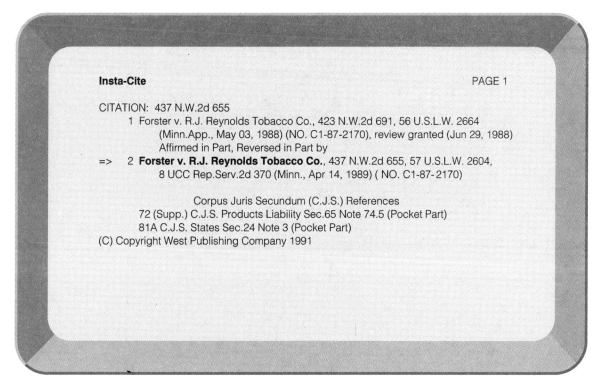

Insta-Cite   PAGE 1

CITATION: 437 N.W.2d 655
       1 Forster v. R.J. Reynolds Tobacco Co., 423 N.W.2d 691, 56 U.S.L.W. 2664
         (Minn.App., May 03, 1988) (NO. C1-87-2170), review granted (Jun 29, 1988)
         Affirmed in Part, Reversed in Part by
=>   2 **Forster v. R.J. Reynolds Tobacco Co.**, 437 N.W.2d 655, 57 U.S.L.W. 2604,
        8 UCC Rep.Serv.2d 370 (Minn., Apr 14, 1989) (NO. C1-87-2170)

            Corpus Juris Secundum (C.J.S.) References
        72 (Supp.) C.J.S. Products Liability Sec.65 Note 74.5 (Pocket Part)
        81A C.J.S. States Sec.24 Note 3 (Pocket Part)
(C) Copyright West Publishing Company 1991

Insta-Cite, an updating or validation service in WESTLAW

- The numerical connector (/n)
- Phrase searching (" ")

(c) LEXIS Queries:

- The OR connector
- The AND connector
- The numerical connector (w/n)
- The AND NOT connector
- Phrase searching

(d) Field Searches:

- Title search
- Synopsis search
- Topic search
- Digest search
- Judge search

(e) Find and Read

(a) Universal Character (*) and Root Expander (!) for WESTLAW and LEXIS

An important technique in the formulation of queries in either WESTLAW or LEXIS is the proper use of the asterisk (*) as a universal character, and the exclamation mark (!) as a root expander. The discussion below of these and

FIGURE 9.9

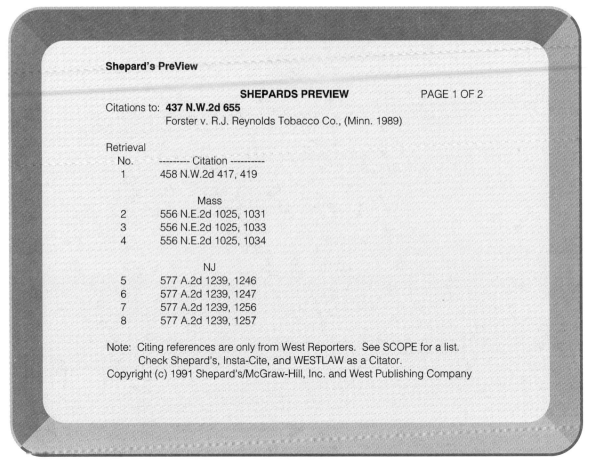

Shepard's PreView

SHEPARDS PREVIEW   PAGE 1 OF 2

Citations to: **437 N.W.2d 655**
              Forster v. R.J. Reynolds Tobacco Co., (Minn. 1989)

Retrieval
  No.   -------- Citation ----------
   1   458 N.W.2d 417, 419

                    Mass
   2   556 N.E.2d 1025, 1031
   3   556 N.E.2d 1025, 1033
   4   556 N.E.2d 1025, 1034

                     NJ
   5   577 A.2d 1239, 1246
   6   577 A.2d 1239, 1247
   7   577 A.2d 1239, 1256
   8   577 A.2d 1239, 1257

Note: Citing references are only from West Reporters. See SCOPE for a list.
       Check Shepard's, Insta-Cite, and WESTLAW as a Citator.
Copyright (c) 1991 Shepard's/McGraw-Hill, Inc. and West Publishing Company

Shepard's PreView in WESTLAW

other query-formulation techniques will cover searches for cases, although the techniques are generally applicable when searching any kind of document available in the databases and files of WESTLAW and LEXIS.

The Universal Character (*)   Suppose that you asked the computer to find cases that contained the following word anywhere in the case:

                    marijuana

This search will not find a case that spelled the word *marihuana*. If, however, you changed your query to:

                    mari*uana

you would pick up cases under both spellings. The asterisk stands for any character or letter. Hence the above search will also pick up cases that contained the words *maribuana, marituana,* or *marizuana*—if such words existed in any of the cases in the database or file you are searching. Since the asterisk stands for any character, it is called the universal character. It is most commonly used when searching for cases that contain a proper name you are having trouble

FIGURE 9.10

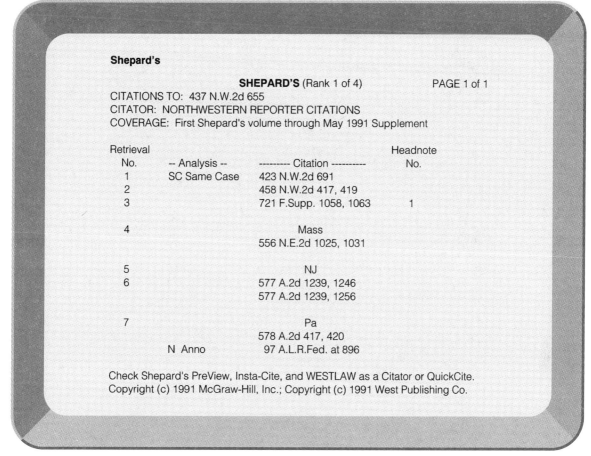

Shepard's in WESTLAW

spelling. If, for example, you were looking for cases decided by a judge whose name is spelled *Falen* or *Falon*, you can enter the query as:

fal*n

You are not limited to one universal character per word. For example, the following search:

int**state

will give you cases containing the word *interstate* and cases containing the word *intrastate*. Similarly, the query:

s****holder

will give you cases containing the word *stockholder,* cases containing the word *stakeholder,* and cases containing the word *shareholder*.

Root Expander (!)   Next we consider the exclamation mark (!) as a root expander. When this mark is added to the root of a word, it acts as a substitute for one or more characters or letters. If your query is:

litig!

FIGURE 9.1

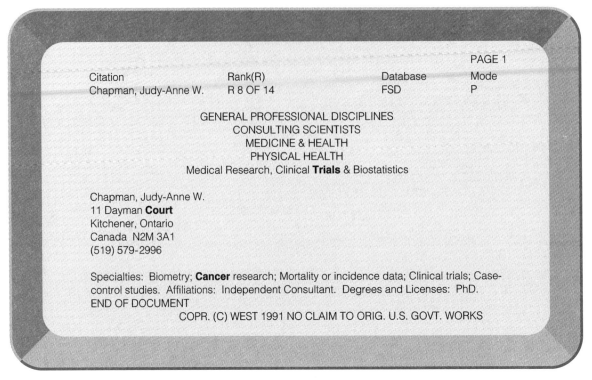

```
                                                                        PAGE 1
Citation                  Rank(R)                 Database      Mode
Chapman, Judy-Anne W.     R 8 OF 14               FSD           P

                    GENERAL PROFESSIONAL DISCIPLINES
                        CONSULTING SCIENTISTS
                         MEDICINE & HEALTH
                          PHYSICAL HEALTH
              Medical Research, Clinical Trials & Biostatistics

Chapman, Judy-Anne W.
11 Dayman Court
Kitchener, Ontario
Canada  N2M 3A1
(519) 579-2996

Specialties:  Biometry; Cancer research; Mortality or incidence data; Clinical trials; Case-
control studies. Affiliations:  Independent Consultant. Degrees and Licenses:  PhD.
END OF DOCUMENT
            COPR. (C) WEST 1991 NO CLAIM TO ORIG. U.S. GOVT. WORKS
```

Search for expert witnesses in WESTLAW

you will find cases containing one or more of the following words: litig, litigable, litigate, litigated, litigating, litigation, litigator, litigious, litigiousness. The root expander is quite powerful and can be overused. The query:

tax!

will lead you to cases containing any one or more of the following words: tax, taxability, taxable, taxation, taxational, taxes, taxi, taxicab, taxidermy, taxidermist, taxied, taximeter, taxing, taxis, taxiway, taxon, taxonomist, taxonomy, taxpayer. This will undoubtedly lead to cases that are beyond the scope of your research problem.

Plurals.   Finally, it is not necessary to use universal characters or the root extender to obtain the regular plural of a word. The query:

guest

will give you cases containing the word *guest* and cases containing the word *guests*. Entering the singular form of a word will automatically search the plural form of that word.

Next we will focus on special guidelines for formulating WESTLAW queries and LEXIS queries.

(b) WESTLAW Queries

When formulating a query in WESTLAW, *connectors* can be used to show the relationship between the words in the query. Connectors link query words

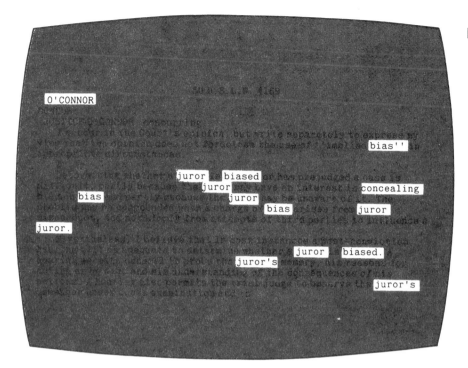

FIGURE 9.12

Case retrieved in LEXIS, with search words highlighted

FIGURE 9.13

List of cases retrieved in LEXIS

together to give the query more direction. The main connectors in WESTLAW are:

- The OR connector
- The AND connector (&)

- The sentence connector (/s)
- The paragraph connector (/p)
- The BUT NOT connector (%)
- The numerical connector (/n)

After explaining how to use each of these connectors, we will examine how to search for phrases on WESTLAW through the use of quotation marks (" ") in queries.

The OR Connector   The simplest connector in WESTLAW is OR, which can be expressed by typing the word *or* between two words, or by leaving a blank space between the words. This connector instructs WESTLAW to treat the two words as alternatives and to find cases that contain either or both words. Hence, the query:

doctor or physician

or the query:

doctor physician

will find the following cases:

- A case that contains the word *doctor,* but not the word *physician*
- A case that contains the word *physician,* but not the word *doctor*
- A case that contains both the word *doctor* and the word *physician*[15]

Similarly, the query:

attorney or lawyer or counsel

or the query:

attorney lawyer counsel

will find the following cases:

- A case that contains the word *attorney* but not the words *lawyer* or *counsel*
- A case that contains the words *attorney* and *lawyer* but not the word *counsel*
- A case that contains the words *attorney* and *counsel* but not the word *lawyer*
- A case that contains the word *lawyer* but not the words *attorney* or *counsel*
- A case that contains the words *lawyer* and *attorney* but not the word *counsel*
- A case that contains the words *lawyer* and *counsel* but not the word *attorney*
- A case that contains the word *counsel* but not the words *attorney* or *lawyer*
- A case that contains the words *counsel* and *lawyer* but not the word *attorney*
- A case that contains the words *counsel* and *attorney* but not the word *lawyer*
- A case that contains all three words: *attorney* and *lawyer* and *counsel.*

The AND Connector (&)   When you use the & connector in your WESTLAW query, you are asking WESTLAW to find cases that contain every word joined by &. The query:

paralegal & fee

---

[15]In all of these examples, remember that the service will retrieve cases containing these words and their plurals, such as physician, physicians; doctor, doctors.

will find cases in which the word *paralegal* and the word *fee* are found. The query will not find cases containing only one of these words.[16]

The Sentence Connector (/s)   The sentence connector (/s) requires the search words to appear in the same sentence in the case.[17] The query:

paralegal /s termin!

will find cases in which the word *paralegal* is found in the same sentence as the word *terminable* or *terminal* or *terminate* or *terminating* or *termination* or *terminator* or *terminology* or *terminus*. Here are examples of two sentences from two different cases that this query would retrieve:

Case #1:
> "The **paralegal** did not receive notice of the allegation until the letter of **termination** arrived the next day."

Case #2:
> "The patient's **terminal** condition was negligently diagnosed in a report obtained by the **paralegals** of the opposing counsel." [18]

The Paragraph Connector (/p)   The paragraph connector (/p) requires the search words to appear in the same paragraph in the case. The query:

paralegal /p certif!

will find cases in which the word *paralegal* is found in the same paragraph as the word *certifiable* or *certificate* or *certified* or *certification* or *certifier* or *certify* or *certifying*.

The BUT NOT Connector (%)   The BUT NOT connector (%) excludes everything that follows the percentage mark, %. The query:

paralegal % fee

or

paralegal but not fee

will find every case in which the word *paralegal* appears, except for those cases in which the word *fee* plus the word *paralegal* appear in the case. Perhaps you are looking for every case that mentions the word *paralegal* other than those involving paralegal fees.

The Numerical Connector (/n)[19]   The numerical connector (/n) requires search words to appear within a specified number[20] of words of each other in the case. The query:

paralegal /5 license*

---

[16]It is also possible to write this query as *paralegal and fee* (rather than use the ampersand, &), but this is not recommended.

[17]The sentence connector (/s) and the paragraph connector (/p) are referred to as the *grammatical connectors.*

[18]Note that in case #2, the order in which the search terms appear in the sentence is not the order of the words in the query itself. If you want to limit the search to cases that contain the search words in the sentence in the order presented in the query, you would phrase the query as follows: paralegal + s termin!

[19]The numerical connector can also be expressed as w/n. For example: paralegal w/5 fee. As we will see, LEXIS also uses w/n in its numerical connector. Only on WESTLAW can you use /n.

[20]Up to 255.

will retrieve any case in which the word *paralegal* appears within five words of the word *license,* or within five words of the word *licensed.* Here is an example of a line from a case that this query would retrieve:

"... the **paralegal** had no **license** from the state."[21]

A case with the following line, however, would *not* be retrieved by this query because there are more than five words between the search words of the query:

"... **paralegals**, as well as notaries and process servers, are not **licensed.**"

Phrase Searching (" ") Thus far, our examples of queries have involved searches for individual words in cases. Suppose, however, that you wanted to search for phrases such as *drug addict, habeas corpus,* or *legal assistant.* If your query was:

legal assistant

WESTLAW would interpret the space between these two words to mean OR. hence, it will retrieve

- Any case in which the word *legal* appears but the word *assistant* does not appear
- Any case in which the word *assistant* appears but the word *legal* does not appear
- Any case in which both the word *legal* and the word *assistant* appears

This could lead to thousands of cases, the vast majority of which would have nothing to do with legal assistants.[22] To avoid this problem, we need a way to tell WESTLAW not to interpret the space between the search words to mean OR. This is done by placing quotation marks around any phrase (or group of words) that you want WESTLAW to search as a unit. Hence our query should read:

"legal assistant"

In a moment, we will see that LEXIS does not require quotation marks when conducting a phrase search since LEXIS does not interpret every space as an OR.

(c) LEXIS Queries

When using LEXIS, connectors are also used in formulating a query. While there are some similarities between the connectors in WESTLAW and in LEXIS, the differences are significant. The main connectors in LEXIS are:

- The OR connector
- The AND connector
- The numerical connector (w/n)
- The AND NOT connector

---

[21]In this example, the words in the sentence are presented in the order of the words in the query—paralegal before license. The query, however, would not require this order unless you use a + sign before the number: paralegal + 5 license*. Another way to ensure this order would be to phrase the query: paralegal pre/5 license*.

[22]WESTLAW will probably flash a message on the screen warning you that your search query may retrieve a large number of cases and suggesting that you rephrase your query to make it narrower.

After examining these connectors, we need to compare how to search for phrases in LEXIS and in WESTLAW.

The OR Connector The OR connector tells LEXIS to treat the two words joined by OR as alternatives. The query:

merger or acquisition

will find the following cases:

- A case that contains the word *merger* but not the word *acquisition*
- A case that contains the word *acquisition* but not the word *merger*
- A case that contains both the word *merger* and the word *acquisition*

Hence the OR connector in LEXIS is similar to the OR connector in WEST-LAW, except that LEXIS does not interpret a space between two words as an OR.

The AND Connector When you use the AND connector in your LEXIS query, you are asking LEXIS to find cases that contain every word joined by AND. The query:

paralegal and fee

will find cases in which the word *paralegal* and the word *fee* are found. The query will not find cases containing only one of these words. (In WESTLAW, the preferred way to achieve this result is by using the & connector.)

The Numerical Connector (w/n) The numerical connector (w/n) of LEXIS requires search words to appear within a designated number of words of each other in the case. The query:

paralegal w/5 license

will retrieve any case in which the word *paralegal* appears within five words of the word *license*.[23]

The AND NOT Connector The AND NOT connector in a LEXIS query excludes everything that follows AND NOT. The query:

paralegal and not fee

will find every case in which the word *paralegal* appears, except for those cases in which the word *fee* plus the word *paralegal* appear in the case.[24]

Phrase Searching Recall that phrase searching in WESTLAW required the use of quotation marks around any phrase, since WESTLAW interprets spaces between words in a phrase to mean OR. This is not so in LEXIS, since LEXIS does not equate spaces with ORs. Hence to search for a phrase in LEXIS, you do not

---

[23]The number (n) of words that can be used as the numerical connector in LEXIS is any number up to 255. But LEXIS does not count words such as *the, be,* and *to.* LEXIS considers them "noise words." The numerical connector in WESTLAW also goes up to 255. See footnote 20. But WEST-LAW counts every word. In the LEXIS numerical query, if you wanted the words in the case to exist in the order in which the words are listed in the query, use the pre/n connector. For example: paralegal pre/5 license. See also footnote 21.

[24]Another way to phrase this query is: paralegal but not fee. The latter phrasing would make this LEXIS connector the same as the connector in WESTLAW that serves this function.

need to use quotation marks around the phrase. Simply state the phrase. In LEXIS, the query:

$$legal\ assistant$$

will lead to cases in which the phrase *legal assistant* is found. It will not lead you to cases in which the word *legal* appeared but not the word *assistant*, and vice versa.

■ ASSIGNMENT 9.1

Below you will find five separate queries. If they were used in either WESTLAW or LEXIS, what words in the documents would they find?

(a) para!

(b) assign!

(c) crim!

(d) legis!

(e) e****e

■ ASSIGNMENT 9.2

On page 420, the following query was given as an example of a WESTLAW query:

$$cigar!\ tobacco\ smok!\ /p\ product\ strict!\ /5\ liab!$$

Explain this query. State what the symbols mean. What is the query designed to find? Assume that you are using the query to find cases in one of the databases of WESTLAW.

■ ASSIGNMENT 9.3

You are looking for cases in which a paralegal is charged with the unauthorized practice of law.

(a) Write the query for WESTLAW.

(b) Write the query for LEXIS.

■ ASSIGNMENT 9.4

You are looking for cases in which a law firm illegally failed to pay overtime compensation to its paralegals.

(a) Write the query for WESTLAW.

(b) Write the query for LEXIS.

■ ASSIGNMENT 9.5

You would like to know what judges in your state have said about paralegals.

(a) Write several queries for WESTLAW.

(b) Write several queries for LEXIS.

(d) Field Searches

In addition to full-text searches, both WESTLAW and LEXIS allow you to conduct searches that are limited to information found in certain parts of cases or other documents. On LEXIS, these parts are called *segments*. The segments of cases are: name, court, writtenby, dissentby, counsel, number, etc. On WESTLAW, these p1rts are called *fields*. The fields of cases are: title, synopsis, topic, digest, judge, :tc. Here is a fuller explanation and some examples of field searches on WESTLAW:

Field Searches on WESTLAW

Title (abbreviated *ti*). The title field contains only the names of the parties to a case. Use this field to retrieve a case if you know the case name. The computer quickly will retrieve your case and display it so you can either read it online or print it to read at a later time. Suppose, for example, that the title of the case you wanted to read was *Pennzoil v. Texaco.* Once you select the database you want, a title field search for this case would be as follows:

ti (pennzoil & texaco)

Synopsis (abbreviated *sy*). The synopsis field contains a summary of the case prepared by the editorial staff of WESTLAW. This summary includes the facts presented by the case, the holding of the lower court, the issues on appeal, and the resolution of those issues. The names of majority, concurring, and dissenting judges are also included in the synopsis field. Since general legal concepts are used to describe the issues before the court, this is a good field in which to run a conceptual search. A conceptual search is helpful for finding cases that fall into a legal category or classification, such as domicile, adverse possession, or product liability. The digest field (to be considered below) also allows you to conduct a search via concepts. Hence it is often worthwhile to combine the synopsis and digest fields in a single search. For example:

sy, di ("product liability")

Topic (abbreviated *to*). Each small-paragraph summary in the West digests is assigned a topic classification, such as criminal law, bankruptcy, and divorce. West has tens of thousands of cases summarized under these topics. If you already know a topic classi-

fication, you can conduct a WESTLAW search that is limited to this topic field. For example:

to (criminal)
to (bankruptcy)
to (divorce)
to ("product liability")

Digest (abbreviated *di*). In addition to a topic classification, every small-paragraph case summary in a West digest contains the name or title of the case, the name of the court that decided it, the citation of the case, and the rest of the summary itself, known as a headnote. All of this information (topic, title, court, citation, headnote) is contained within what is called the digest field of WESTLAW. Here is an example of a search in this field:

di (paralegal)

This search will find every case that has the word paralegal anywhere in a small-paragraph case summary of a West digest. To make sure that your search finds cases mentioning legal assistants as well as those mentioning paralegals, the search would be:

di (paralegal "legal assistant")

As indicated above, it is often wise to combine searches in the digest and synopsis fields.

Judge (abbreviated *ju*). If you wanted to find cases written by a particular judge, e.g., Justice William Brennan, you could conduct a search in the judge field:

ju (brennan)

When run in the database containing opinions of the United States Supreme Court (sct), this search will give you every majority opinion written by Justice Brennan.

(e) Find and Read

Suppose that you already have the citation of a case or other document, and you simply want to read it. But you are not in a traditional law library that has the bound volumes you need. If you have access to WESTLAW or LEXIS, there is a relatively easy way to retrieve what you want. On WESTLAW, use the *find* command (abbreviated *fi*). On LEXIS, use the *lexstat* command (abbreviated *lxt*) when you are looking for a statute and the *lexsee* command (abbreviated *lxe*) when you are looking for cases or any other documents available through this route.

Using the *find* command of WESTLAW, here are four examples that retrieve documents in the Supreme Court Reporter (sct), the United States Code Annotated (usca), the Code of Federal Regulations (cfr), and the Federal Register (fr). All of these examples assume that you already know the volume numbers, page numbers, section numbers, etc. indicated. You simply want to find these documents and read them on your computer screen.

```
fi 97 sct 451
fi 18 usca 1968
fi 9 cfr 11.24
fi 52 fr 22391
```

Using the *lexstat* command of LEXIS, here is an example that locates a statute in United States Code Service (uscs); and using the *lexsee* command, here are three examples that locate material in Columbia Law Review (colum l rev), American Law Reports, Federal (alrfed), and an IRS Revenue Ruling (rev rul). Again, all of these examples assume that you already know the volume numbers, pages numbers, section numbers, etc. indicated.

```
lxt 11 uscs 101
lxe 07 colum l rev 1137
lxe 44 alrfed 148
lxe rev rul 88-2
```

3. Spreadsheet Programs

Most law offices can clearly see the usefulness of word processing and database programs. The usefulness of a spreadsheet, however, is a little more difficult to appreciate. A spreadsheet can be helpful for almost any project that requires the use or manipulation of numbers. It is a good management tool for creating budgets and tracking expenses of a law firm. Most spreadsheet programs have built-in functions that will make intricate calculations, such as determining present net value, loan repayment schedules, averages, and many other statistical functions.

A spreadsheet allows you to create large groups of interrelated numbers. Once this is done, changing one of the numbers allows you to see what happens to all the others. A spreadsheet can quickly recalculate the values of all the numbers that are dependent on the one that was changed. (See Figure 9.14.) For example, with a spreadsheet you can create a program that will calculate the size of payments on a loan based on the amount, length, and interest rate that apply to the loan. If you change the numbers displayed on the screen for the amount, for the length, or for the interest rate of the loan, the spreadsheet will recalculate the payment size.

A spreadsheet consists of a series of boxes called cells. Numbers and other information can be placed directly into the boxes from the keyboard. Once the

TERM	DEFINITION
Cell	A storage location within a spreadsheet used to store a single piece of information relevant to the spreadsheet.
Coordinates	The column letter and row number that define the location of a specific cell.
Formula	A mathematical expression used in a spreadsheet.
Label	Information used for describing some aspect of a spreadsheet. A label can be made up of alphabetic or numeric information, but no arithmetic can be performed on a label.
Value	A single piece of numeric information used in the calculations of a spreadsheet.
Window	The portion of a worksheet that can be seen on the computer display screen.

Source: S. Mandell, *Introduction to Computers Using the IBM and MS-DOS PCs with Basic,* 3d ed., 409 (West 1991).

FIGURE 9.14

Terms Associated with Electronic Spreadsheets

information is stored in a box, it can be a source for formulas in other boxes. When a box containing a formula is displayed on the screen, the result of the formula is seen, not the formula itself. If any of the numbers in the boxes used by a formula are changed, the display for the box with the formula will reflect this change. For example, let us assume that we have a small spreadsheet program with three boxes. (Large, sophisticated spreadsheets can have thousands of boxes.) Each of our three boxes has a name that refers to the information in them. We will name our boxes A, B, and C.

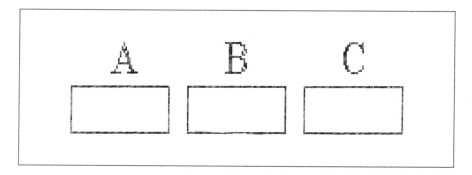

If we placed the number 5 in box A and the number 2 in box B, we could then combine this information in box C by entering the formula A + B into box C.

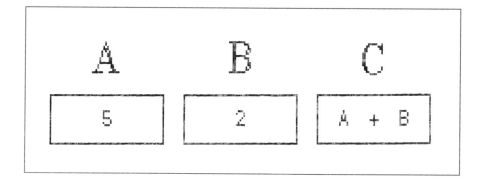

Box C would then display the number 7.

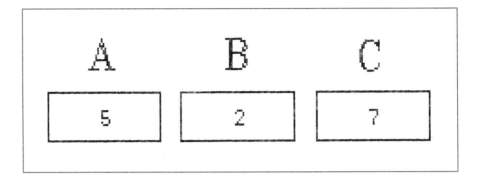

We could change the formula in box C to read (A + B) * 2 (here, the * means *times* on most computers).

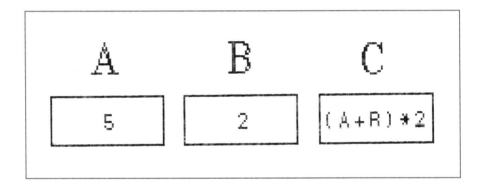

C would now read 14.

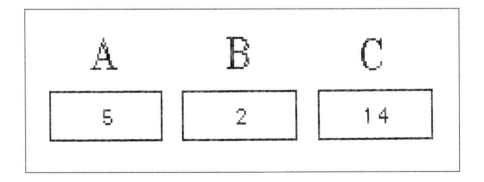

Now if we change the number in box A from 5 to 4, box C would read 12; (4 + 2) * 2 = 12.

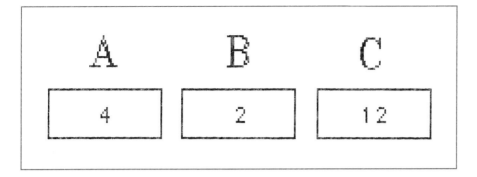

Our small spreadsheet example can be made more complicated. Let us start over. Place the number 2 in box A. Then place the formula A + 2 in box B. Box B will now contain the number 4; 2 + 2 = 4. We could now place the formula A * B in box C. Box C would now display the number 8; 2 * 4 = 8.

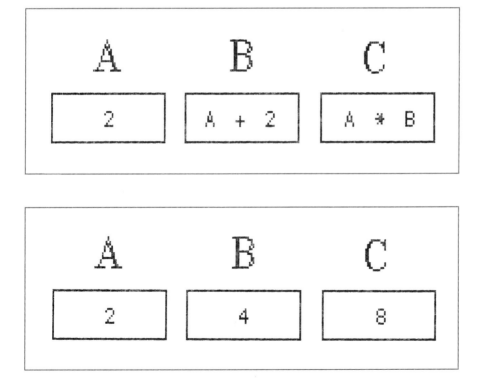

Any time we change the number that is in box A, the numbers displayed in both box B and C will change. If the number 4 is placed in box A, box B will show the number 6; 4 + 2 = 6, and box C will display the number 24; 6 * 4 = 24.

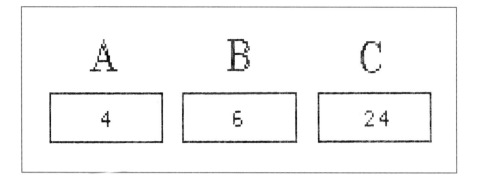

On a large spreadsheet, many cells (boxes) can depend on information from formulas in other cells. Sophisticated models and project formulas, therefore, can be created using a spreadsheet program.

When creating large models you must guard against making circular references. For example, place the formula (A * C) in box B and the formula (A * B) in box C.

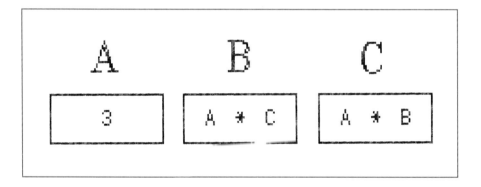

No matter what number is entered in box A, box B looks to box C for information and box C looks to box B for information. Some spreadsheet programs will get stuck on these two formulas and stop dead. Other spreadsheets will run through the calculations for the two boxes ten or twenty times and then stop.

The capability of a spreadsheet to perform a whole series of calculations based on formulas and numbers makes it possible for you to do in minutes or seconds what once took accountants hours or days. The spreadsheet is perfect for doing what users call "what ifs." Suppose you were considering the purchase of a house and wanted to figure out what the monthly payments would be. Three factors determine the size of the payments: the interest rate, the length of the mortgage, and the amount of the loan. Using the proper financial formulas, you could create a spreadsheet that would let you enter an interest rate, the number of years, and the amount that you wished to borrow. In seconds the spreadsheet would display the monthly mortgage payment based on those numbers. You can then play "what if" and change one or more of the numbers to see what happens to the payment level as the interest rate went down, the length of the mortgage increased, the amount of the loan was greater, etc. (See Figure 9.15.)

A spreadsheet used as a "what if" device can be very helpful in a law office for working out damage projections and settlement offers, particularly struc-

FIGURE 9.15

Spreadsheet
Mortgage
Cost Display

```
                 Real Estate Financial Analysis

                          Assumptions

        House Price:                $35,900.00
        Downpayment:                  1,795.00
                                    ------------------
        Amount Financed:             34,105.00
        Interest Rate %:                  9.75
        Number of Yrs Financed:          20.00
        Calculated Payment:           $323.49
```

tured settlements where the payments are spread over a period of time and take account of the value of money in the future according to an agreed-on formula. Once the relationship of the various elements of damages is determined, different interest and inflation assumptions can be tested. You can determine how these assumptions will influence the amount of damages that would be necessary in a particular case. For example, assume you are trying to project lost wages of an injured plaintiff. Interrelated formulas can be created to determine this damage calculation. One of the formulas would project potential salary over the working life of the person, starting with the current salary and adding increases over time. The increase would be a percent of salary. The formula created can allow for changing the percent increase so that different increase assumptions may be tested quickly. Another formula can take the results from the salary calculations and determine how many dollars would be needed today to create an amount equal to the future income. Various rates of return can be tested with this formula. Used in a similar manner, a spreadsheet can be productive for estate planning and real estate projections.

Most of the current spreadsheet programs have the capability of creating graphs from the numbers they produce. They can create line, bar, and pie charts in many different formats. Bar charts can be made to appear three dimensional or can be stacked one above the other. If the computer has a color monitor, the bars representing different items can be displayed in various colors.[25]

There are many applications for spreadsheets that can be obtained by purchasing a *template* to perform the needed task. A template is a set of formulas sold with instructions on its use. A federal income tax template, for example, will contain all the lines and forms of a tax return. The template covers each part of the tax form on which information must be entered, and calculates the taxes based on the information entered. The template then prints the form as a completed tax return. Templates are available for almost any type of business calculation. There are small bookkeeping programs, purchase-lease comparison programs, linear regression programs, and many others.

Some publishers of spreadsheets claim that bookkeeping and other *database* applications can be performed using their programs. This is true to a limited extent. These bookkeeping and database systems are limited and awkward, however, and hence of little practical use in most law offices. Bookkeeping and

---

[25]When you need a hard copy of the chart, laser printers are often very effective. If high-quality charts are needed in color, a *plotter* can be used. A plotter is a device that will hold a pen to a piece of paper and draw lines as instructed by commands you enter into the computer.

database manipulation should be performed on programs designed for that purpose rather than with spreadsheet programs.

■ ASSIGNMENT 9.6

Barklay is a freelance paralegal. He shares an office with three others: Adams, Cordier, and Davis. The expenses of the office are rent, phone, electricity, gas, postage meter, and secretarial service. They agree to the following allocation of expenses: rent will be $185 per person; the cost of electricity and gas will be split evenly among the four of them; everything else will be apportioned according to actual use and cost.

The four will have the following bill-paying responsibilities: Barklay will pay the phone and secretarial bills; Adams will pay the rent; Cordier will pay the electricity and gas bills; and Davis will pay the postage bill. At the end of every month, each will make an accounting of what was paid. They will then calculate who owes what to whom based on their agreement of how expenses are to be allocated.

Here are the figures for last month. Adams ran up $122 in phone calls, Barklay $85, Cordier $77, and Davis $19. Postage use was $22.50 for Adams, $14.20 for Barklay, $66.85 for Cordier, and $10.31 for Davis. The bill for secretarial services showed that Adams owes $118.00, Barklay $100.33, Cordier $84, and Davis $44. The electric bill was $29.03. The gas bill was $11.16.

The bills were paid on time. In Parts I and II of this assignment, you will be setting up a spreadsheet to calculate each person's share of the expenses, using the following basic structure as a guide:

	A Adams	B Barklay	C Cordier	D Davis
ROW				
1 Rent				
2 Amt. Paid				
3 Bal. Due				
4 Phone				
5 Amt. Paid				
6 Bal. Due				
7 Electricity				
8 Amt. Paid				
9 Bal. Due				
10 Gas				
11 Amt. Paid				
12 Bal. Due				
13 Postage				
14 Amt. Paid				
15 Bal. Due				
16 Secretarial				
17 Amt. Paid				
18 Bal. Due				
19 Grand Totals Due from Each				

Part I

For each category of expense, fill in the figures you are given for last month. Do not do any math at this time, but state the formulas that you would use to arrive at all of the mathematical calculations. For example, if you must divide $11.16 by 4, phrase the formula as follows: (11.16/4). Or, if you must add Row 13 for all four individuals, phrase the formula as follows: (A13 + B13 + C13 + D13).

Next, do all the calculations based on your formulas.

Part II

Assume that there is a three percent tax on the phone calls over and above the amounts stated. Change your spreadsheet setup accordingly.

4. Communications

Finally we come to one of the most recent microcomputer developments. Communications software makes it possible to call up WESTLAW or LEXIS to do legal research over telephone lines. Such programs also make it possible to contact people or businesses and communicate with their computers. You can send or receive letters, statistical information, programs, or insults! Anything that can be put on paper or into a computer can be sent from one computer to another over telephone lines.

For successful computer communications, there are two necessary components: a modem and communications software. A *modem* is a piece of hardware that is plugged into your computer on one end and into your telephone line on the other. The modem controls the transmission of information over telephone lines. The communications software controls the information sent to the modem that is to be transmitted over telephone lines. When two computers are transmitting information to one another over telephone lines, each one must have a modem and a communications program. The two modems transmit the information that they are told to send by the communications software.

For the modems to be able to do this, they must be "speaking" with the same code and "talking" at the same speed. Most modems sold today use the same code, but they do not all communicate at the same speed. Some can communicate at more than one speed. The speed of transmission is stated in terms of *baud* or the *baud rate*. Three hundred baud is the minimum used today; many modems can transmit and receive information at this speed. If large amounts of information are being sent, however, 300 baud is very slow. The higher the baud rate, the less time it takes to send the same information. Twelve hundred baud is today's high-speed standard. As modem technology improves, 2400 baud modems are becoming available. The only drawback with higher (faster) baud rates is that the error rate goes up with the speed. When more information is squeezed into the same space, the equipment used must be more sensitive. Unfortunately sensitive equipment may be less able to distinguish static from the information being sent on the telephone line. Therefore, at higher transmission rates, the information is more likely to become garbled. This problem must be controlled by the communications software.

When selecting communications hardware, keep in mind the amount of information that you wish to send or receive. The greater the amount of bulk transmission used, the greater the need for high-speed modems. If you will be using the communications system mostly for reading or examining materials immediately on screen, 1200 is a sufficient communications speed.

When purchasing software for communications, higher cost does not necessarily mean better software. There are commercial software packages available that are expensive yet difficult to use. You may need a thick instruction manual and a degree in computer science to use them. Other communications packages are available in the *public domain,* meaning that the programs are available to the public without charge. Some are easy to use and will satisfy ninety percent of users requiring communications software.

Developing the skills necessary for communications can be difficult. Once you have started, however, stopping can be just as hard or harder! It is a fascinating and challenging area of the computer world. A great deal of information about sources of software, user special-interest groups, "adult" bulletin boards, etc. is available through electronic *bulletin boards.* A bulletin board is an inexpensive version of large commercial database information services, such as WESTLAW and Dialog. The bulletin board contains information centered around a common interest. Users can obtain this information, exchange messages to each other, find buyers or sellers for certain products, etc. Your phone bill could become very large if you are addicted to calling bulletin boards around the country.

5. Combinations

We have examined four types of programs: word processing, database management, spreadsheets, and communications. You can now obtain software packages that contain all four types in one program. These are often called *integrated* packages. They are programs that require computers with large amounts of memory. The reason for creating an integrated package is to simplify the process of moving information from one application to another. If, for example, you have information in your database that you wish to manipulate with a spreadsheet program, the task of moving the information from a format that a database understands to one that a spreadsheet understands can be monumental or impossible. An integrated package makes it possible.

The big question is, "Do you really need an integrated package?" If you are not sure, the answer is probably *no.* If you frequently find yourself wishing that you could put a graph from your spreadsheet into a letter or wishing that you could easily get your database information into a spreadsheet, then you do need integrated software.

Section F. The Real Investment: Time

Thus far we have examined the relative expense of some of the hardware and software options. The greatest cost by far, however, is *time.* For the system to be implemented successfully, time must be invested both before and after acquisition of the system. Considerable time must be spent before the purchase of a system to determine what the law office needs. If this is not carefully done, the system probably will not fulfill the office's needs. After the system is acquired, time must be spent implementing the system and training all members of the staff to use its capabilities properly. If the time invested before or after installation is insufficient, the microcomputer system will be a failure.

Another costly but necessary element for the successful implementation of a computer system is a guru. The guru is the one who has a knack for figuring out and solving most of the system's problems. The guru will be a person in the office who has a system at home, or who, when introduced to the training, learns quickly and wants to take the system manuals home to see how the thing "really" works. Encourage this person. Meanwhile, other staff members need to take over some of this person's duties. Having someone present in the office who can respond to a crisis saves time and minimizes frustration.

Other cost factors that must be considered involve "down time" and lost data. *Down time* occurs when the computer breaks. No matter how good, expensive, or reliable your equipment may be, sooner or later it will fail. Many firms have discovered that microcomputers are so inexpensive, they purchase one or more to keep in the closet just to replace the unit that breaks down. This is often less expensive than having to wait a day, week, month, or six months for the defective computer to be repaired.

The loss of data can be even more expensive. Some data, of course, is irreplaceable. Other data can be replaced or reconstructed only at great cost. Nothing can compare to the horror of realizing that the diskette you just erased contained the only copy of the brief you have been working on for months. Every system should have regular backup procedures. There should be at least one backup copy of all data, and for particularly valuable or difficult-to-reconstruct data, two backup copies are recommended. If possible, a backup copy of important diskettes should be kept at a place other than where the day-to-day or working copies are located. This backup is an added expense, but it's not nearly as costly as the destruction of data by fire, magnet, or other calamity.

■ ASSIGNMENT 9.7

Each student will make a presentation in front of the class on a computer product—a hardware or software product. You can select your own product, but it must be approved in advance by your teacher.

The setting will be a mock meeting of members of a law firm (attorneys, paralegals, and secretaries) who have assembled to listen to you. You have come to the meeting to make a sales presentation on the product.

You have several objectives:

(a) *To introduce yourself.* You are the representative of the company that makes the product. Use your own name. Make up some brief facts about yourself as representative, such as how long you have been with the company.

(b) *To provide something visual about the product.* You do not have to bring the product with you. Try to obtain a brochure on it. If not available, try to obtain a photo of the product. For example, you might be able to photocopy an ad that has a picture of the product. At the very least, you should prepare a diagram or drawing of the product or of some important aspect of it. Circulate the brochure, photo, ad, diagram, or drawing to the group while you are talking.

(c) *To describe the product.* State what the product does. What is its purpose? How is it used in a law office? What are its benefits? Who is supposed to use it in the office? How will the product improve efficiency or increase profit? How does the product compare with competing products on the market? How much does it cost? Try to cover as many of these areas as possible.

The product you select must meet the following characteristics:

■ It is a brand product that is currently on the market.

■ It is a product that is either designed exclusively for law offices or is widely used in law offices.

■ It is not a product that you work with every day (if you already work in a law office). The goal of this assignment is to force yourself to learn about a *new* product and to communicate what you have learned to others.

■ It is a product that no one else in the class has covered in a presentation. (The teacher will enforce this guideline by approving the products in advance.)

The best starting point in locating a product is to go to any law library and look through ads in bar association journals (state or national) and ads in legal newspapers (state or national). Many of these ads have 800-numbers you can call for more information. Once you have identified a product, ask a librarian how you can find out if any reviews of that product have been published. (Manufacturers of the product are often very willing to send you copies of favorable reviews.) You might also obtain a lead to products by talking to someone who works in a law office.

No one is expected to have intimate familiarity with the product (although you may want to give a contrary impression as part of your sales presentation).

Your goal is give information about the product that you learn by:

- Reading ads
- Reading brochures
- Talking with company representatives (locally, if available, or via an 800-number)
- Reading reviews
- Talking with someone in a law office in your area that already uses the product

---

■ ASSIGNMENT 9.8

Smith, Smith & Smith is a forty-attorney law firm that was established thirty years ago. It employs eight paralegals, ten secretaries, a librarian, a receptionist, a file clerk, and a part-time maintenance worker. The firm handles a great variety of cases: personal injury litigation, worker's compensation, government contracts, antitrust, domestic relations, estates and trusts, taxation, bankruptcy, commercial law, etc.

The founder and leader of the firm is John Smith, who practiced law with his father in the 1920s before he set up the present firm with his two children, Mary and David Smith. They are full partners in the firm.

For years, John Smith practiced law "the old fashioned way." "If it was good enough for my father," he is fond of saying, "it's good enough for me." The consequence of this attitude is that Smith, Smith & Smith is managed today in almost the same manner that it was run thirty years ago. Almost everything is done by hand. All the secretaries have typewriters. John agreed to purchase electric typewriters only five years ago. These machines do nothing but type. There are a few dictaphones, but they are seldom used.

Payroll, billing, document control, etc. are all done by hand. The law firm consists of a suite of fifty rooms, almost half of which contain nothing but records and files.

Six months ago John Smith died. Mary and David are now in full control of the firm. At a recent bar association meeting, Mary and David listened to a presentation on the use of computers in the practice of law. Mary was fascinated by the presentation and is ready to restructure the law firm with the introduction of computers throughout the office. David (who believed that his father and grandfather were incapable of making a mistake) is skeptical. David does not see any reason to change the way the firm practices law. Yet he agrees that the idea of computer use is worth exploring.

Mary and David agree to hire you as a computer consultant. You specialize in giving advice to attorneys in the use of computers in the management of a law firm and in the practice of law.

(a) Name some areas where you think Smith, Smith & Smith might be able to use computers in the office. Explain why.

(b) What do you think some of David's objections might be to the introduction of computers in these areas? How would you respond to these objections?

Chapter Summary

Like almost every other aspect of our society, the law office has been substantially altered by the computer. Since there is a tremendous diversity in computer products available, it is unlikely that any paralegal will walk into a new office, particularly a large one, and be totally familiar with all of the hardware and software programs in use. Hence, you must expect to go through a large and ongoing dose of on-the-job computer training. Standard survival techniques can help, such as finding out if any of the products have an 800-number helpline that you can call, taking advantage of online tutorials, and using help keys.

Fairly soon you should learn a relatively small list of computer terms. The list includes *hardware, software, backup, data, hard-disk drive, operating system, modem, laser printer,* etc. The four major kinds of software programs are word processing, database management, spreadsheets, and communications. A fifth kind combines the other four.

Word processing software is a substitute for the traditional typewriter, bottle of correction fluid, and scissors that were once used to cut-and-paste a report together. Now you can use the word processor to type the text of a report, to insert additional text, to move text around, and to make other corrections on a computer screen (monitor) so that you can see the finished product before the report is printed. This feature, plus many others, makes word processing the most widely used software in offices and homes throughout the country.

Database software allows you to store, organize, and retrieve a large body of information. The office can design its own database, and it can purchase access to commercial databases such as WESTLAW and LEXIS. One of the critical skills in this area is the ability to formulate a question, or query, for the computer to answer. Most queries ask the computer to find data within a designated database. In formulating a query, you need to know how to use the universal character (*) and the root expander (!). You also need to know when to use connectors (such as the OR connector, the AND connector, and the numerical connector) to specify the relationship among the search words in the query in order to give the search more direction. You also need to know how to search for phrases, how to conduct field and segment searches, and how to perform simple "find" searches when you already have the citation to something you want to read.

Spreadsheet software allows you to make financial calculations and solve mathematically oriented problems with much greater ease than with traditional calculators. Endless "what if" questions can be answered based on variables entered into the program.

Communications software makes it possible for computers to "talk" with each other, through a modem, over telephone lines. Finally, software exists that allows the user to combine or integrate word processing, database management, spreadsheets, and communications capabilities.

Key Terms

online tutorial
help key
documentation
CLE
users group
hardware
backup
command
data
disk drive
floppy disk
hard disk
byte
diskette
floppy

file
k
language
laptop
memory
microcomputer
monitor
operating system
mouse
windows
multitasking
run
save
software
hardware

compatible
dual sided
double-density
network
dot matrix printer
daisy wheel printer
ink jet printer
laser printer
modem
word processor
dedicated word processing
word wrap
spelling checker
automatic pagination
block

block movement
boldface
character
character enhancement
control character
cursor
default setting
deletion
editing
format
global
header
incremental spacing
insertion
justification
right justified
menu
print formatting
print preview
screen formatting
scrolling
search and find
search and replace
status line
subscript
superscript
text buffer
text editing
text file

virtual representation
WYSIWYG
merge printing
bugs
database
data manager
data redundancy
field
record
file
scanner
key-word search
full-text search
search criteria
WESTLAW
LEXIS
online search
search query
universal character (*)
root expander (!)
connectors
OR connector
AND connector
sentence connector
paragraph connector
grammatical connector
BUT NOT connector
numeral connector
phrase searching

noise words
AND NOT connector
segment search
field search
title search
synopsis search
topic search
digest search
headnote
judge search
fi
lexstat (lxt)
lexsee (lxe)
spreadsheets
cell
coordinates
formula
label
value
window
plotter
template
communications
baud rate
public domain
bulletin board
integrated packages
down time

Introduction to Law Office Administration*

■ Chapter Outline

 Section A. The Practice of Law in the Private Sector

There are over 700,000 attorneys in the United States—one for every 360 citizens. (This is double the number that existed in 1970.) By the year 2000 the number is expected to grow to 1,000,000.[1]

About 70% of attorneys practice in private law offices. Another 10% work for corporations in corporate practice. The remainder practice in the public sector for government, for legal aid and legal service offices, for organizations such as unions, trade associations, and public interest groups, or do not practice law at all. In this chapter, our primary focus will be on attorneys who practice law in relatively large private offices, although other practice settings will also be covered.

In the private sector, law is practiced in a variety of settings:

■ Sole practice

■ Office-sharing arrangement

■ Partnership

---

*Portions of this chapter were originally written with Robert G. Baylor, Business Manager at Manatt, Phelps, Rothenberg, and Tunney, Los Angeles. Others who have reviewed this chapter and provided valuable commentary include Dorothy B. Moore, Kathleen M. Reed, Michele A. Coyne, Patsy R. Pressley, Deborah L. Thompson, and Shawn A. Jones.

[1]Stanton, *Stepping Up to the Bar,* 35 Occupational Outlook Quarterly 3 (Spring 1991).

- Professional corporation
- Corporate legal department

Sole Practice

A *sole* (or solo) *practice* often refers to an attorney who practices alone. More accurately, it means a sole proprietorship in which one attorney owns and manages the firm. Anyone who works for this attorney, including another attorney, is an employee who receives a salary. They are not entitled to a share of the profits of the office in addition to a salary.

Sole practitioners are generalists or specialists. A generalist is the equivalent of a doctor in general practice. An attorney who is a *general practitioner* often tries to handle all kinds of cases. If, however, the case is unusually complex or if the attorney is very busy with other cases, he or she might consult with an attorney in another office or refer the case to another attorney. Other sole practitioners specialize. Their practice might be limited, for example, to tax, criminal, or patent and trademark cases, or—more commonly—to personal injury cases.

Most sole practitioners have very few employees. There is a secretary, who often performs many paralegal functions along with the traditional clerical responsibilities of typing, filing, and reception work. He or she may also perform bookkeeping chores. The most common job title of this individual is "legal secretary," although occasionally he or she will be known as a "paralegal/secretary." You will sometimes find job ads for small offices seeking paralegals with clerical skills. These skills are often phrased more positively as administrative or word processing skills, but they are, in essence, clerical. In recent years, however, many sole practitioners have begun to hire one or more paralegals who have minimal or no clerical duties.

The office may employ a part-time *law clerk* who is a student currently in law school. It may also employ one or more other attorneys. Again, in a sole practice these attorneys do not share in the profits of the office.

Office-Sharing Arrangement

Occasionally, a sole practitioner will allow a newly admitted attorney to use the facilities of the office in exchange for some nonpaid help on the practitioner's cases. A more formal arrangement would be two or more attorneys with independent practices who share the use and cost of administration such as rent, copy machine, other equipment, library, secretarial help, etc. They do not practice law together as a partnership or corporation, although they may assist each other during periods of vacation, illness, or other emergencies. To avoid the conflict-of-interest and confidentiality problems discussed in Chapter 4, they must be careful in the selection of clients and in discussions about their cases with each other.

Partnership

A law partnership is a group of individuals who practice law jointly and who share in the profits and losses of the venture. Its revenues come from client fees. If the partnership is relatively large, it will probably be organized into a series of departments based on client needs (such as an antitrust department, a litigation department, etc.) and will be managed through a series of committees (such as a recruitment committee, a library and records committee, etc.) based on the variety of support services available to the attorneys. See Figure 10.1 for an example of the organization structure of a large law firm.

There are many different categories of attorneys in a large partnership, the most common of which are:

- Partners
- Associates
- Staff attorneys
- Of counsel
- Contract attorneys

1. *Partners*

Partners contribute the capital that is needed to create the firm and to expand it as needed. They decide whether to merge with other firms, and, indeed,

FIGURE 10.1   Large Law Firm Organization Chart: An Example

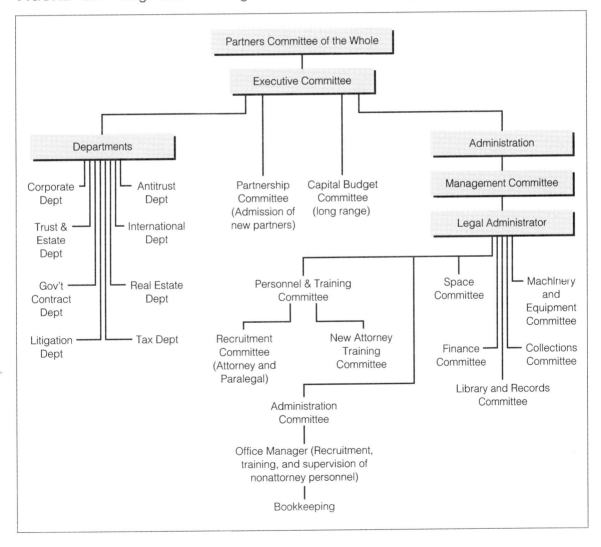

whether to go out of business altogether. Partners share the profits and losses of the firm pursuant to an elaborate partnership agreement. They decide how the firm should be managed, when to take on new partners, what attorneys, paralegals, and other employees to hire, etc. Most of this is done through a variety of administrative staff. In short, the partners own the firm. There may be different categories of partners in a firm (for example, senior partner and junior partner) depending on factors such as the amount of capital the attorney contributed to the firm and how involved he or she is in the firm's management. As we will see, a distinction is also sometimes made between equity and nonequity partners.

Generally, partners are not on salary in the traditional sense, although they do receive a periodic *draw*, which is an advance against profits in some firms and an overhead expense in others.

2. Associates

Associates are attorney employees of the firm. Often, they are hired right out of law school while studying for the bar examination. As students, they may have worked for the firm as a law clerk. Other associates, however, are hired from other law firms. They are known as *lateral hires*. (When partners and paralegals switch law firms, they also are referred to as lateral hires.) After a certain number of years at the firm, e.g. seven, associates are usually considered for partnership. If they are *passed over* for partner, they often leave the firm to practice elsewhere, although a few may be invited to stay as a *permanent associate* or a *senior associate*.

In some firms, there is a movement away from the "up-or-out" system that adds great tension to the ranks of associates. To encourage good people to stay, the firms have created different tiers of partners. For example, a firm might create the category of *nonequity partner* or *income partner*, to be distinguished from the *equity partner* or *capital partner*. The latter is a full partner in the sense of owning the firm and sharing in its profits and losses. A nonequity or income partner, on the other hand, is an individual who has not made, or who does not aspire to become, a full partner. In effect, he or she is often little more than a permanent associate with a more inviting title.

(Hence paralegals are not the only workers who are frustrated by a lack of career ladders in the legal profession. As we saw in Chapter 1, the paralegal field has been slowly developing career ladders, e.g., from case clerk to paralegal to senior paralegal and paralegal supervisor. Attorneys also want career ladders beyond the traditional associate-partner regime. Equally slowly, the profession has been responding to this need.)

3. Staff Attorneys

Staff attorneys (sometimes called *second-tiered attorneys*) are hired with the understanding that they will never be considered for partnership. This is what distinguishes them from associates.

4. Of Counsel

There is no fixed definition of an attorney who is *of counsel* to a firm. He or she may be a semiretired partner, a part-time attorney, or a full-time attorney who is considering a long-term relationship with the firm. Not all firms use the title "of counsel." Some prefer "special counsel" or simply "counsel."

5. Contract Attorneys

Contract attorneys (sometimes called *project attorneys*) are hired when the firm has a temporary shortage of attorneys, or needs expertise in a certain area for a limited period. Often paid on an hourly basis, the contract attorney is not a full-time employee.

Professional Corporation

In most states, it is possible for attorneys to incorporate their practice of law as a *Professional Corporation* (P.C.), e.g., "Jamison & Jamison, P.C." This is done primarily for tax purposes. From a tax and estate-planning perspective, it is often more advantageous to organize as a corporation than as a partnership. Like any corporation, a professional corporation has stockholders (the owners), directors, and officers—all of whom are attorneys. The operation of a professional corporation is practically identical to the operation of a traditional partnership. A client would hardly notice the difference.

Corporate Legal Department

Many large corporations have a *law department* headed by a *general counsel* who may also be a vice-president of the company. Other attorneys in this office can include deputy or associate general counsel, senior attorneys, staff attorneys, etc. They are the in-house attorneys who handle the day-to-day tasks of advising the company on legal matters. They have one client—the corporation that hires them and that pays them a salary. Frequently, paralegals work with these attorneys. In 1983, the ratio of paralegals to attorneys was 0.15-to-1. In 1990, the ratio increased to 0.21-to-1.[2] Other support personnel may include legal administrators, legal secretaries, word processing and data processing operators, clerks, librarians, and records managers.

There are, of course, no client fees. Funds to operate the department come directly from the corporate treasury. If expertise is needed that is not available in the department, such as trial experience in a certain specialty, the general counsel will hire outside attorneys from law firms.

■ Section B. The Legal Administrator and the Legal Assistant Manager: Overview of Administration in a Large Law Firm

The practice of law is a profession, but it is also a business. The larger the practice, the more likely its business component will be managed by individuals whose main or sole responsibility is administration. While the owners of a law firm have ultimate responsibility for administration, they often delegate this responsibility to others. For example, there may be a managing partner, often an attorney with a small case load or none at all. More and more firms are hiring new categories of management personnel who are not attorneys. We will focus on two such individuals: the *legal administrator* and the *legal assistant manager*. One way to obtain an overview of management is to examine the job descriptions of such individuals.

---

[2]Wilber, *Support Staffing Ratios*, National Law Journal S6, col. 2 (May 20, 1991).

The legal administrator works under the supervision of the managing partner or of a management committee of the firm. The range of this person's responsibility, and of the business component of the practice of law, can be seen in the job description in Figure 10.2.

Again, this job description fits an individual who works for a law office that is fairly large. The support staff for such an office can also be quite extensive. Here are some examples:[3]

Administrative Support Staff in a Large Law Office

Legal Administrator	Secretaries
Legal Assistant Manager	Data Processing Operators
Personnel Manager	Word Processing Supervisor
Records/File Manager	Word Processors
Employee Benefits Manager	Proofreaders
Recruiter	Docket Clerks
Director of Marketing	Computer Specialists
Facilities Manager	Equipment Managers
Risk Manager	File Room Clerks
Office Manager	Librarian
Financial Manager	Library Aides
Credit/Collections Manager	Messengers/Pages
Chief Financial Officer/Comptroller	Copy Room Clerks
Bookkeepers	Mail Clerks
Analysts	Purchasing Clerks
Payroll Specialists	Receptionists
Accounts Payable Clerk	Telephone Operators
Accounts Receivable Clerk	Reservation Clerks
Time and Billing Assistants	

Prominent on this list is the legal assistant manager, whose job description is presented in Figure 10.3.

Section C. Expenses

How does a large law firm spend the fee income that it receives? There are a number of organizations that conduct surveys to answer this question. One of the largest is the Altman Weil Pensa Survey of Law Firm Management. Some of the highlights of its 1990 survey are presented in Figure 10.4. The data was collected from 647 law firms with more than 16,000 attorneys.

Section D. Timekeeping

Abraham Lincoln's famous statement that a "lawyer's time is his stock in trade" is still true today. Effective timekeeping is therefore critical to the success of a law firm. In some firms, it is an obsession, as typified by the following story. A senior partner in a very prestigious Wall Street law firm walked down the corridor to visit the office of another senior partner. Upon entering the room, he was startled to find his colleague on the floor writhing in pain, apparently

---

[3]R. Green, ed., *The Quality Pursuit* 69 (American Bar Association, 1989).

Summary of Responsibilities

The legal administrator manages the planning, marketing, and business functions, as well as the overall operations of a law office. He or she reports to the managing partner or the executive committee and participates in management meetings. In addition to general responsibility for financial planning and controls, personnel administration (including compensation), systems, and physical facilities, the legal administrator also identifies and plans for the changing needs of the organization, shares responsibility with the appropriate partners for strategic planning, practice management, and marketing, and contributes to cost-effective management throughout the organization.

WHETHER DIRECTLY OR THROUGH A MANAGEMENT TEAM, THE LEGAL ADMINISTRATOR IS RESPONSIBLE FOR MOST OR ALL OF THE FOLLOWING:

Financial Management:

- ☐ Planning
- ☐ Forecasting
- ☐ Budgeting
- ☐ Variance analysis
- ☐ Profitability analysis
- ☐ Financial reporting
- ☐ Operations analysis
- ☐ General ledger accounting
- ☐ Rate analysis
- ☐ Billing and collections
- ☐ Cash flow control
- ☐ Banking relationships
- ☐ Investment
- ☐ Tax planning and reporting
- ☐ Trust accounting
- ☐ Payroll and pension plans
- ☐ Other related functions

Systems Management:

- ☐ Systems analysis
- ☐ Operational audits
- ☐ Procedures manual
- ☐ Cost-benefit analysis
- ☐ Computer systems design
- ☐ Programming and systems development
- ☐ Information services
- ☐ Records and library management
- ☐ Office automation
- ☐ Document construction systems
- ☐ Information storage and retrieval
- ☐ Telecommunications
- ☐ Litigation support
- ☐ Conflict-of-interest docket systems
- ☐ Legal practice systems
- ☐ Other related services

Facilities Management:

- ☐ Lease negotiations
- ☐ Space planning and design
- ☐ Office renovation
- ☐ Purchasing and inventory control
- ☐ Reprographics
- ☐ Reception/switchboard services
- ☐ Telecommunications
- ☐ Mail messenger services
- ☐ Other related functions

Human Resource Management:

- ☐ Recruitment, selection, and placement
- ☐ Orientation, training, and development
- ☐ Performance evaluation
- ☐ Salary and benefits administration
- ☐ Employee relations
- ☐ Motivation and counseling
- ☐ Discipline
- ☐ Termination
- ☐ Worker's compensation
- ☐ Personnel data systems
- ☐ Organization analysis
- ☐ Job design, development of job descriptions
- ☐ Resource allocation
- ☐ Other human resource management functions for the legal and support staff

AS A MEMBER OF THE LEGAL ORGANIZATION'S MANAGEMENT TEAM, THE LEGAL ADMINISTRATOR MANAGES AND/OR CONTRIBUTES SIGNIFICANTLY TO THE FOLLOWING:

General Management:

- ☐ Policymaking
- ☐ Strategic and tactical planning
- ☐ Business development
- ☐ Risk management
- ☐ Quality control
- ☐ Organizational development
- ☐ Other general management functions

FIGURE 10.2
Legal Administrator: Job Description (Association of Legal Administrators)

Continued

FIGURE 10.2

Legal
Administrator:
Job Description
(Association of
Legal
Administrators)
—*Continued*

Practice Management:	Marketing:
☐ Attorney recruiting	☐ Management of client-profitability analysis
☐ Attorney training and development	
☐ Legal assistant supervision	☐ Forecasting of business opportunities
☐ Work-product quality control	☐ Planning client development
☐ Professional standards	☐ Marketing legal services: enhancement of the firm's visibility and image in the desired markets
☐ Substantive practice systems	
☐ Other related functions	

Job Requirements

Knowledge: Has familiarity with legal or other professional service organizations, and experience managing business operations, including planning, marketing, financial and personnel administration, and management of professionals.

Skills and Abilities: Able to identify and analyze complex issues and problems in management, finance, and human relations, and to recommend and implement solutions. Able to manage office functions economically and efficiently, and to organize work, establish priorities, and maintain good interpersonal relations and communications with attorneys and support staff. Excellent supervisory and leadership skills, as well as skills in written and oral communication. Demonstrated willingness and ability to delegate.

Education: Graduation from a recognized college or university with major coursework in business administration, finance, data processing, or personnel management, or comparable work experience.

due to a heart attack. Standing there, he could think of only one thing to say to him: "Howard, are your time sheets in?" [4]

In some firms, the pressures of the clock on attorneys and paralegals can be enormous:

[Y]oung lawyers often are shocked to discover their new employer's time expectations. Many firms in major cities require as many as 2,400 billable hours

FIGURE 10.3   Legal Assistant Manager

Legal Assistant Manager: Job Description
Attorneys' Guide to
Practicing with Legal Assistants
(State Bar of Texas, 1986)[5]

General Responsibilities:

The legal assistant manager has overall responsibility for administration of the program. Formal training programs responsive to the needs of the various sections and to the professional development of legal assistants are identified and established by this individual. He or she works with the supervising attorneys, providing assistance in staff-ing and in resolving legal assistant-related conflicts between sections and between individuals.

Specific Duties:

A. Development and utilization of legal assistant skills

   1. Work with the supervising attorneys. Become and remain familiar with the nature and amount of work done by each lawyer in the firm.

   2. Work with the supervising attorney. Develop and submit to the Practice Management Committee a written analysis of each

---

[4]Margolis, *At the Bar*, New York Times B13 (September 7, 1990).
[5]The job title used in the Guide is Legal Assistant Coordinator. Legal Assistant Manager or Paralegal Manager, however, is more common.

FIGURE 10.3   Legal Assistant Manager—*Continued*

lawyer's work, identify the portions which should be performed by a legal assistant, and update this information on an annual basis.

3. Develop a training program for the supervising attorneys.
4. Develop a short introductory presentation for lawyers in each section to demonstrate the types of tasks for which legal assistants should be used.
5. Meet with each new attorney in the firm to explain the legal assistant program, thus ensuring the utilization of legal assistants by new attorneys.
6. Develop an orientation program for new legal assistants and conduct orientation sessions with each new legal assistant.
7. Develop an in-house training program for all new legal assistants and conduct or supervise the training provided by others.
8. Receive notice of each lawsuit docketed in the Litigation Section and assign a legal assistant to each lawsuit.
9. Assign legal assistants to all files which require the assistance of a legal assistant.
10. Receive notice of the assignment of all or major parts of Special Projects to attorneys, and assign a legal assistant to each Special Project.
11. Monitor the progress of legal assistant use in each section and develop changes in the legal assistant support program as needed.
12. Consult with each legal assistant and each supervising attorney individually at appropriate intervals, perhaps quarterly, to identify problems and possible solutions.
13. Conduct monthly meetings of the legal assistants to keep them informed.
14. Work with the supervising attorney in the development of written procedures for inclusion in the firm's manual concerning the use of legal assistants.
15. Evaluate the need for support staff for legal assistants and work with firm administrator to ensure that legal assistants have adequate support.

B. Legal assistant supervision

1. Supervise the development of procedure manuals for legal assistants in each section for review by the supervising attorneys.

2. Review legal assistant time records to ensure proper preparation and to monitor workloads.
3. Coordinate evaluations of legal assistants.
4. With the respective supervising attorneys, conduct a performance interview with each legal assistant.
5. Ensure that all section staff meetings and similar meetings are open to legal assistants.
6. Monitor both quality and quantity of work assignments to legal assistants.

C. Reporting

Prepare and submit to the Practice Management Committee a quarterly report showing:

1. Approximate hours spent by each legal assistant on work from each lawyer.
2. The number of assignments carried out by each assigned legal assistant for each lawyer.
3. The same information for backup work done by the legal assistants in each section.

D. Professional development for legal assistants

1. Set objectives for and help plan in-house professional instruction for legal assistants.
2. Review all notices received in the firm regarding seminars.
3. Develop and implement schedules of continuing in-house and outside training for each legal assistant to ensure timely completion of required formal and enhancement instruction.

E. Personnel

1. Recruit, interview, and hire legal assistants.
2. Maintain a personnel file for each legal assistant.
3. Anticipate and correct unsatisfactory assignments and inadequate or inappropriate staffing.
4. Assign backup responsibility after consultation with legal assistants and supervising attorneys.
5. Provide assistance in resolving legal assistant conflicts between individuals.
6. Evaluate office space requirements for legal assistants and work with firm administration in providing office space for legal assistants.

FIGURE 10.4

1990 Survey of
Law Firm
Economics

During the past five years, the average overhead costs per attorney was $93,648, an increase of 51%. The average law firm spent:

- $34,121 per attorney for support staff (excluding paralegals). This constituted 16.5% of the gross revenue of the firm. This is the same percentage that existed in 1984. (Apparently, the large investment in law office automation between 1984 and 1990 did *not* result in significant net staff cost savings.)

- $28,718 per attorney for general expenses, such as insurance of all kinds, printing, meetings, postage, and office supplies not charged to clients. This constituted 13.9% of the gross revenue of the firm, an increase of 69% between 1985 and 1990.

- $8,323 per attorney for paralegals. This constituted 4.0% of gross revenue, an increase of 67% between 1984 and 1990.

- $15,462 per attorney for occupancy expenses. This constituted 7.5% of gross revenue, an increase of 49% between 1985 and 1990.

- $4,672 per attorney for equipment. This constituted 2.3% of gross revenue, an increase of 10% between 1985 and 1990.

- $2,352 per attorney for library and reference expenses. This constituted 1.1% of gross revenue, an increase of 33% between 1984 and 1990.

The median number of billable hours were:

- 1,706 for partners/shareholders (up from, 1,571 in 1984)
- 1,820 for associates (up from 1,738 in 1985)
- 1,400 for paralegals in 1989

The median billing rates were:

- $150 per hour for partners/shareholders
- $100 per hour for associates
- $55 per hour for paralegals

per year. When one considers that many full-time employees outside of the law only *work* 2,000 hours per year, the time commitment required by these firms is staggering.[6]

The cry for billable hours is thought by many to be at the heart of much of the problem. Many legal assistants as well as attorneys have quotas of billable hours. Zlaket [the President of the State Bar of Arizona] stated that some firms require 2,200 hours a year and he deems this to be outrageous. He suggested that this only leads to padding of bills and time sheets, and it leads to unnecessary work that will be paid by somebody.[7]

The ethical dimensions of this problem are considered in Chapter 4. Here our concern is the administration of the timekeeping and billing system.

. . . .

After the initial client interview, the accounting starting point can be a *New File Worksheet* (see Figure 10.5). It is also sometimes referred to as a *New Matter Sheet* or a *New Business Sheet*. The New File Worksheet becomes the source document for the creation of all the necessary accounting records involved in working on the case or matter of a client.

Attorneys and paralegals must keep an accurate account of the time they spend on behalf of a client. An example of a form they can use is the *Daily Time*

---

[6]Walljasper, *I Quit!*, Wisconsin Lawyer 16 (March 1990).
[7]Morris, *Join the Effort to Restore Respect to the Legal Profession*, The Digest 3 (Arizona Paralegal Ass'n, April 1989).

FIGURE 10.5
New File Worksheet

Billing No. _____
Date _____Opened _____Closed

Client (Check one)

___ INDIVIDUAL

_____
      Last   First   Middle Initial

___ ENTITY

_____
   (Use complete name & common abbreviations; place articles [e.g., The] at end.)

___ CLASS ACTION

_____
          (File Name, ex.: Popcorn Antitrust Litigation)

Matter (Check One)

___ NON-LITIGATION   _____

___ LITIGATION   _____

         _____ Approved for litigation by—MUST BE INITIALED by submitting attorney!!

Nature of the Case

   Area of law code _____   Summary of work or dispute: _____

   _____

Client Contact (N/A for Class Actions)

   Name: _____
   Company: _____
   Street: _____
   City, State, Zip: _____
   Telephone: _____

Billing Address (N/A for Class Actions)

   Name: _____
   Company: _____
   Street: _____
   City, State, Zip: _____
   Telephone: _____

Team Information (Use initials)

   ____ ____ ____   Managing Attorney(s) (for non-litigation cases only)
   ____ ____ ____   Bill Review Attorney(s)
   ____ ____ ____   Originating Attorney(s)
   _____ Calendar Attorney (for litigation cases only)
   _____ Legal Assistant (for litigation cases only)
   _____ Secretary to Calendar Attorney (for litigation cases only)

Referral Source (Check one)

___ Existing Client   _____
                              (Name)

___ Non-Firm Attorney   _____
                              (Name)

___ Firm Attorney or Employee _____

___ Martindale-Hubbell

___ Other   _____

Continued

FIGURE 10.5 New File Worksheet—*Continued*

Fee Agreement (Check those that apply)

___ Hourly

___ Contingent _____%

___ Fee Petition

___ Fixed Fee $_____ or Fixed Range from $_____ to $_____

___ Retainer $_____

___ Letter of Retainer sent by _____ on _____
       (Initials) (Date)

Statement Format (Check those that apply)

Do you want identical disbursements grouped?   _____ Yes _____ No

Do you want attorney hours reflected on *each* time entry?   _____ Yes _____ No

Do you want fees extended on *each* time entry?   _____ Yes _____ No

---

Conflict Check

Conflict Check Completed By: _____   **Date:**_____
          (Initials)

Conflict Check Not Needed: _____
      (Initials of Submitting Person)

Check One:

_____ No conflicts

_____ Potential conflict with the following existing parties (from computer system):

     _____

     _____

     (Or attach computer printout from Conflict Check System.)

***New Adverse Parties:**

_____

_____

_____

***New Related Parties** (for Class Actions, Named Plaintiffs Only):

_____

_____

_____

*Will be entered into computer system by Bus. Dept. *AFTER* approval by Managing Partner.

Closed File

Date Closed: _____   **Atty. or Sec. Initials:** _____

_____ Attach Pleadings and/or File Indexes. If indexes are not available, attach brief description of what is contained in the file(s). SEND FILES, THIS FORM, AND INDEX TO FILE ROOM.

Routing Lists

(Initial)

	New File:	Date:	Closed File:	Date:
Submitted by	_____	_____	_____	_____
Sec. of Submitting Person	_____	_____	_____	_____

Continued

FIGURE 10.5 New File Worksheet—*Continued*

Managing Partner	______	______	______	______
Business Department	______	______	______	______
File Department	______	______	______	______
Firm Newsletter	______	______	______	______
Docket for Litigation	______	______	______	______
EnviroLaw (Computer Center) Add?	______			
IdeaLaw (Computer Center) Add?	______			
JobLaw (Computer Center) Add?	______			
Pulse—See Fred Farrell				

Sheet (see Figure 10.6). This sheet becomes the journal from which all time entries are posted to individual client ledger pages.

Law firms normally use tenths of an hour (increments of six minutes) as the base unit for the measurement of time, although a few firms still use one-fourth of an hour as their base for recording time. *Hourly Time and Rate Charts* (see Figure 10.7) can later be used to translate these time fractions into dollars and cents for billing purposes; or this can be quickly accomplished by computer. Attorneys and paralegals note their activities on the Daily Time Sheet each time during the day that they work on a particular matter. The information from these Daily Time Sheets can then be typed on *time tickets* (see Figure 10.8) or into a computer database.

These time tickets are usually perforated or shingled. For offices still using a manual system, this facilitates easy separation so that they can be subsequently sorted into alphabetical order for quick posting to client ledger cards. The tickets can be processed in several different ways. One is to retain the individual tickets in an open tray in alphabetical order for eventual retrieval and tabulation for billing; another would be to use gummed backs for pasting directly onto a client ledger card; or the ticket may be used as a source document for transcribing onto a *Master Ledger Card* (see Figure 10.9); or the ticket could

FIGURE 10.6
Daily Time Sheet

DAILY SERVICE REPORT OF: DATE:

ANS -Answer	DEPO -Deposition	K -Contract	O -Order	RES -Research
APP -Appearance or Attending	DIC -Dictation	L -Legal	OP -Opinion	REV -Revision
ARG -Argue or Argument	DOC -Document	LT -Letter to	P -Preparation	S -Settlement
BR -Brief	DR -Drafting	LF -Letter from	PL -Plaintiff	TF -Telephone from
COMP -Complaint	F -Facts	MT -Memorandum to	PR -Praecipe	TT -Telephone to
CW -Conference-Office	FL -File	MF -Memorandum from	PRT -Pretrial	TR -Trial
CWO -Conference-Outside Office	H -Hearing	MOT -Motion	R -Reading and Review	TRV -Travel
DEF -Defendant	INV -Investigation	NEG -Negotiation	REL -Release	W -Witness
DEM -Demurrer	INT -Interview			

CLIENT (State billing division or department)	MATTER	DESCRIPTION OF WORK (Use abbreviations above)	TIME	
			Hours	10ths

FIGURE 10.7

Hourly Time ×
$ Hourly Rate

RATE: TIME:	$20	$25	$30	$35	$40	$45	$50	$55	$60	$65	$70	$75
0.10 hour	2 00	2 50	3 00	3 50	4 00	4 50	5 00	5 50	6 00	6 50	7 00	7 50
0.20	4 00	5 00	6 00	7 00	8 00	9 00	10 00	11 00	12 00	13 00	14 00	15 00
0.30	6 00	7 50	9 00	10 50	12 00	13 50	15 00	16 50	18 00	19 50	21 00	22 50
0.40	8 00	10 00	12 00	14 00	16 00	18 00	20 00	22 00	24 00	26 00	28 00	30 00
0.50	10 00	12 50	15 00	17 50	20 00	22 50	25 00	27 50	30 00	32 50	35 00	37 50
0.60	12 00	15 00	18 00	21 00	24 00	27 00	30 00	33 00	36 00	39 00	42 00	45 00
0.70	14 00	17 50	21 00	24 50	28 00	31 50	35 00	38 50	42 00	45 50	49 00	52 50
0.80	16 00	20 00	24 00	28 00	32 00	36 00	40 00	44 00	48 00	52 00	56 00	60 00
0.90	18 00	22 50	27 00	31 50	36 00	40 50	45 00	49 50	54 00	58 50	63 00	67 50
1.00 hour	20 00	25 00	30 00	35 00	40 00	45 00	50 00	55 00	60 00	65 00	70 00	75 00
2.00	40 00	50 00	60 00	70 00	80 00	90 00	100 00	110 00	120 00	130 00	140 00	150 00
3.00	60 00	75 00	90 00	105 00	120 00	135 00	150 00	165 00	180 00	195 00	210 00	225 00
4.00	80 00	100 00	120 00	140 00	160 00	180 00	200 00	220 00	240 00	260 00	280 00	300 00
5.00	100 00	125 00	150 00	175 00	200 00	225 00	250 00	275 00	300 00	325 00	350 00	375 00
6.00	120 00	150 00	180 00	210 00	240 00	270 00	300 00	330 00	360 00	390 00	420 00	450 00
7.00	140 00	175 00	210 00	245 00	280 00	315 00	350 00	385 00	420 00	455 00	490 00	525 00
8.00	160 00	200 00	240 00	280 00	320 00	360 00	400 00	440 00	480 00	520 00	560 00	600 00
9.00	180 00	225 00	270 00	315 00	360 00	405 00	450 00	495 00	540 00	585 00	630 00	675 00
10.00 hours	200 00	250 00	300 00	350 00	400 00	450 00	500 00	550 00	600 00	650 00	700 00	750 00

FIGURE 10.8

Time Ticket

DATE	NAME	CLIENT	MATTER	CLIENT REFERENCE NUMBER	TIME

DESCRIPTION:

Posted:

FIGURE 10.9

Master
Ledger Card

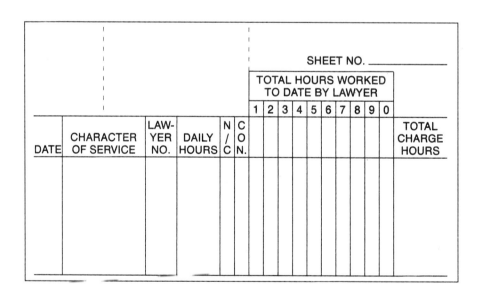

be keyed directly from the Daily Time Sheet of the attorney or paralegal and used as an input document for the firm's computerized system.

If you have never kept close track of your time, you will find that the task requires a great deal of effort and discipline; it does not come naturally to most of us. The key to performing the task effectively is to do it consistently and comprehensively until it becomes second nature. Even nonbillable activities should be accounted for, such as performing administrative chores, helping to develop standard forms, or taking a lunch break. A senior attorney or other supervisor will then be in a better position to determine the best allocation of an employee's efforts, now and in the future.

Tory Barcott, a Certified Legal Assistant in Anchorage, makes a number of important points about timekeeping:[8]

> It "sometimes scares me a little to contemplate clients paying" $10.00 or more "for every six minutes of our time." To survive in this world, the legal assistant must possess the accuracy and efficiency of a Swiss watch. "I keep one of those small, cheap, adhesive digital clocks where it can't be missed or covered with paperwork. Sticking it to my phone, in the middle of my desk, works best for me. The first step in performing any task is to record the time on my time sheet. I do this before retrieving the file, making a phone call," or going to meet a supervising attorney. The clock is also helpful in recording the time when a task is interrupted by anything unrelated to the current client matter. "I take notes on the start and stop times exactly as displayed on my digital clock." Some Saturdays, while absently attending to household chores, "I'll glance at the clock and catch myself thinking, 'that floor took only 0.4 to clean.' " This is a sure sign that the discipline of timekeeping has been internalized!

For other recommendations on effective timekeeping, see Figure 10.10.

Computer programs have been developed to provide assistance in keeping track of time. In one program, for example, there is a menu on the screen that you use to tell the computer the following information (with relatively few keystrokes): what project you are working on, whether the time is billable, what client the project is for, the nature of the work you are doing, the time you begin the project, the times you are interrupted, and the completion time. An internal computer clock keeps track of the time until you tell it to stop and resume. You can also "input" costs connected with the case, such as postage and photocopying charges. The data you enter into the computer can be sent to the accounting department and to the supervising attorney for eventual billing. The computer can use the data in other ways as well, as the following discussion demonstrates.

> Computers . . . can take an initial item of data such as a specific transaction:
>
> Attorney RLR Met with client ACME to discuss research needs, 2 hours, July 2
>
> and use the data over and over again in various ways. For example, the data may be sorted by attorney to give a listing of all the hours worked by the attorney on that day or in that month for all clients. It may be sorted by client to give a listing of all the hours worked for a particular client. It may be used to produce a preliminary or final bill. The data may be merged with other data to price the hours spent and to provide additional billing information. The same data may be matched with other data to list the total hours billed for the client that year or even total hours still unbilled. The Meeting With Client might be encoded as MWC and the firm, for whatever reason, might build statistics on how much meeting with clients occurred for all clients. . . .
>
> Computerization not only allows one entry to provide a great deal of output but it speeds the entry. Special codes can be used for such items as the name of the lawyer (RLR), the name of the client (ACME) and the type of work done (e.g., MWC, above). The user may not even need to enter a billing rate ($100 per hour) since some systems can automatically search the lawyer or client information to find a rate. Or the system may look at the transaction code (Processed Application for State Trademark abbreviated as AST) and disregard all hourly rates, using the $175 fixed fee automatically associated with that type of work. Some computer systems can keep track of the hours spent on all trade-

---

[8]Barcott, *Time Is Money*, AALA News (Alaska Ass'n of Legal Assistants, April 1990).

FIGURE 10.10

Effective
Timekeeping
Techniques[9]

- Always have your time sheet and pen at your side, ready for entries.
- If available, use a dictating machine for time only. Regularly tell the machine what you are doing—for example, as soon as you hang up the phone.
- When you begin a project, make a list of each task involved. Note the time you begin each task. Note the time of interruptions and the completion time. If additional tasks are needed for the project, add them to the list.
- In addition to a project list of tasks to be completed over a period of days, weeks, or longer, compile a **daily to-do list.** This will help you organize your day and focus on the time dimensions of what you do.
- Whenever possible, complete a project before moving on to another one. This facilitates timekeeping.
- Conduct your own study of your nonbillable hours, such as interruptions, pro bono work, interoffice conferences on administrative matters, breaks, clerical work, lunch. At the end of a pre-determined period, e.g., two weeks, identify the largest categories of your nonbillable time. Determine whether you can do anything to cut this time down. You may want to show your study to a supervisor to encourage him or her to delegate some of your nonbillable tasks to others who do not bill by the hour, or who bill at a lower rate than you do.

mark cases, multiply by the lawyer's basic rate and determine at the end of the year if the $175 fee is profitable for this type of work.

Entry by computer is also faster and easier. Computers prompt the operator for information and require it before allowing the operator to move on. The details are often immediately verified to see if they are consistent with other data in the computer. Correction speed is also improved. If a lawyer sees a printout of the work done for a client and realizes that there was an error, it can be easily corrected without much retyping. For example if an entry were made for a meeting with a client, when the meeting was actually with the client's witness, the error can usually be changed with a single entry. And all other places where the data are used are automatically changed as well.[10]

Section E. Billing

There are least nine different methods of billing, according to the Law Practice Management Section of the American Bar Association. See Figure 10.11.

In addition to fees for services, a law firm usually recovers out-of-pocket expenses (called *disbursements* or costs) that the firm incurs while working on the case, e.g., court filing costs, witness fees, copying charges, long-distance phone calls, out-of-town transportation, and lodging for attorneys and paralegals.

The fees and costs to be paid by the client should be spelled out in the *retainer.* Unfortunately, not everyone uses this word in the same way. Its meaning should be made clear in the agreement between attorney and client. In a general sense, a retainer is the contract of employment between the attorney and client. More specifically, it sometimes refers to an amount of money paid to assure that an attorney will be available to work for a particular client, and

---

[9]Rucker, *Effective Timekeeping: A Legal Assistant's Point of View,* Newsletter (Houston Legal Assistants Ass'n, August 1987); Serrano, *The Member Connection,* Facts & Findiongs 7 (NALA, December 1986).

[10]P. Maggs & J. Sprowl, *Computer Applications in the Law,* 172–74 (1987).

- *Hourly Rate.* A designated amount per hour. An hourly rate is "bundled" if overhead is included in this rate. It is "unbundled" if the various charges are broken out separately.

- *Fixed Fee.* A flat fee for services.

- *Full Contingent Fee.* The amount of the fee is based on a percentage of the recovery, if any. This arrangement is often used in personal-injury cases.

- *Hourly Plus Fixed Fee.* A specified hourly rate is used until the nature and scope of the problem are defined, and a fixed fee is used thereafter.

- *Hourly Reduced or with Contingent.* A discounted hourly rate, sometimes combined with a contingent fee.

- *Blended Hourly Rate.* One rate is set depending on the mix of partners and associates working on the case.

- *Lodestar.* A lodestar is a mathematical formula used by federal courts and some state courts. It is based on a multiplier and relies on hourly rates and various other factors.

- *Value Billing.* The bill is not based solely on the time required to do the work. Instead, the amount to be paid is based on the complexity of a legal problem, the expertise it demands of an attorney, and on the sheer number of hours devoted to the matter. An estimate is often given to the client at the outset. This amount may eventually go higher or lower based on the factors used to determine value.

- *Percentage Fee.* The fee is a percentage of the amount involved in the transaction, such as the assets to be probated in an estate, the cost of real estate to be transferred, or the amount received as damages in a personal-injury case.

FIGURE 10.11

Methods of Billing[11]

hence unavailable to work for the client's competitor. When the attorney does work for the client, the latter pays fees in addition to the retainer, plus the out-of-pocket costs of the attorney. Another meaning of retainer is the amount of money or other assets paid by the client as a form of deposit or advance payment against future fees and costs. Additional money is paid only when the deposit or advance runs out. The agreement should specify whether money or other assets from the client are refundable if the client terminates the relationship because he or she decides not to pursue the matter.

The actual billing process differs from firm to firm, and occasionally differs from case to case within the same firm. Client billing sometimes occurs only after the matter is completed. More commonly, a client is billed monthly, quarterly, or semiannually. An administrator in the firm usually works with the billing attorney to prepare the bill. When a matter is called for billing, the administrator may prepare a billing memorandum (the *draft bill*) which specifies the disbursements of the firm in connection with the matter, plus the amount of time each attorney and paralegal has spent on the matter (along with the billing rate of each). For example:[12]

- *Attorney Jones: $1,000.* This attorney, who has a billing rate of $200 an hour, spent five hours on the matter. (5 × $200 = $1,000).

- *Attorney Smith: $800.* This attorney, who has a billing rate of $100 an hour, spent eight hours on the matter. (8 × $100 = $800).

- *Paralegal Kelly: $500.* This paralegal, who has a billing rate of $50 an hour, spent ten hours on the matter. (10 × $50 = $500).

---

[11]See Marcotte, *Billing Choices*, 75 American Bar Ass'n Journal 38 (November 1989); and *Value Billing Gaining Popularity*, Tennessee Bar Journal 9 (January/February 1990).
[12]Darby, *Of Firms and Fees: The Administrator's Role*, 8 Legal Management 34, 39 (March/April 1989).

The billing attorney has three choices: (1) Bill the total of the actual amounts. In our example, this would produce a bill of $2,300 ($1,000 + $800 + $500). (2) *Write-down* the matter by subtracting a certain amount, such as $300. This would produce a bill of $2,000. (3) *Write-up* the matter by adding an amount, such as $600. This would produce a bill of $2,900. This adjustment downwards or upwards is known as *valuing the bill.* An increase is sometimes called a premium adjustment; a decrease, a discount adjustment. The decision to adjust is based on factors such as the potential liability exposure of the firm (leading to a write-up) and the relative inexperience of an attorney or paralegal working on the matter (leading to a write-down). If, for example, recently hired attorneys or paralegals take an unusually long time to complete a task they never performed before, a write-down may be appropriate so that the client does not have to bear the full cost of their on-the-job training. See Figure 10.12 for an example of a bill sent to a client covering work of attorneys and paralegals on a matter.

 ## Section F. Administrative Reports

There are different types of administrative reports that naturally "fall out" of the timekeeping and billing process. The more common reports used by law firms are:

1. Billable hours delinquent time reports
2. Billable hours analysis
3. Nonbillable time analysis
4. Accounts receivable reports
   a. Accounts receivable ledger
   b. Cash receipts journal
   c. Open invoice report
   d. Accounts receivable *aging report*[13]
      - billing by client (cumulative for a year)
      - billing by attorney (cumulative for a year)
   e. Departmental profitability analysis

These reports could be available on a regular schedule such as weekly, monthly, annually, or on request as needed. In any event, the raw data will be available and should be developed and stored in such a fashion as to accommodate easy retrieval, tabulation, and display for the legal administrator and managing partner, with summary totals being available for presentation to the entire firm. All this historical data can be compared to the results of the preceding year for the same period to measure quickly "how we are doing this year;" can be compared to the budget or any other acceptable benchmark; can be used as danger signals to prompt remedial action where appropriate; can be used as

---

[13]An *aging report* is one of the most common reports developed by accountants to provide management with the time outstanding of accounts receivables. For example, an *aged accounts receivable* will set forth how many of the total receivables are less than thirty days old, how many are thirty to fifty-nine days old, how many are sixty to ninety days old, and how many are more than ninety days old. It is a truism that the older an account receivable is, the less collectable it is. Therefore, management needs to know how old the account is in order to put the emphasis on collecting it before it becomes so old that it is worthless.

Rubin, Rinke, Pyeumac & Craigmoyle
1615 Broadway, Suite 1400
Oakland, California 94612-2115
(415) 444-5316
Tax ID 94-2169491

April 10, 1991

IBM Corporation
Norm Savage
3133 Northside Parkway
Atlanta GA   33033

Statement for Professional Services Rendered

Re: Chapter 11   (IBM-1)
     Reorganization

Description of services

04/17/91   Receipt and review of contracts regarding Ar-
           monk home office liquidation.

04/18/91   Meeting with opposing attorney regarding
           court appearance in Atlanta in late October
           of 1991.

04/21/91   Receipt and review of depositions from seven
           hundred forty three (743) claimants to Austin
           plant parking facilities.

04/22/91   Meeting with officers of the corporation to dis-
           cuss liquidation of office furniture in all
           branch offices. Scheduling of 2000 simultane-
           ous garage sales in marketing managers'
           driveways to be advertised during next year's
           Super Bowl.

Total for legal services rendered $797.50

	Hours	Rate	
Partners	4.00	125	500.00
Paralegals	3.50	85	297.50

Reimbursable expenses

04/17/91	Lunch meeting with opposing attorney.	185.17
04/27/91	Atlanta Bankruptcy Court filing fee due September 1, 1990.	55.00
04/29/91	Photocopies	5.69
04/29/91	Long distance telephone charges	36.90

Total expenses $282.76

Total current charges $1080.26

Source: Computer Software for Professionals, Inc., LEGALMASTER

FIGURE 10.12
Bill Sent to Client
Involving Attorney
and Paralegal
Services

the basis for compensation schedules; can provide the firm with all necessary data for complying with government regulations (such as tax laws governing the firm's income); and can be used as a general audit and control device.

A well-thought-out system should give the managers of the law firm effective control and provide additional meaningful data for:

1. Firm Management Reports
   a. Firm activity and work status
   b. Summary aging of work in progress
   c. Summary aging of uncollected bills
   d. Summary of billings and realizations
   e. Uncollected bills written off
   f. Nonlegal staff charges to work in progress
2. Practice Analysis Reports[14]
   a. Staff utilization
   b. Attorney practice experience
3. Partner Responsibility Reports
   a. Partners' work in progress summary
   b. Partners' work in progress aging
   c. Partners' uncollected bills
   d. Partners' billing and realizations
4. Work in Progress and Billing Reports
   a. Work in progress ledger—detail
   b. Work in progress disbursements—detail
   c. Billing memorandum
   d. Delinquent diaries
   e. Client billing history
5. Special Purpose Reports
   a. Billings by introducing attorney
   b. Billings by assigned attorney
   c. Allocations to prior partnerships
6. Special Management Reports as Required

One of the reports that could be generated from the basic timekeeping records is an analysis of how much time paralegals are investing in client matters. This analysis is the same kind of analysis that the firm would want regarding time invested by attorneys. Sometimes large firms also keep track of time invested by secretaries and other nonattorneys, but generally this is not done. More commonly, firms keep track of attorney time and paralegal time spent on client matters. Firms need time expenditures in order to evaluate profit centers, costs, allocation of work among attorneys and paralegals, etc.

. . . .

---

[14]A "practice analysis report" can be very helpful to a firm. It analyzes where the firm is investing its time, how much money it is earning from specific areas of the practice, where its costs lie, and hence how much profit is being earned from the various areas of practice. Specifically, a practice analysis could develop such information for probate practice, litigation practice, general corporate practice, banking practice, antitrust practice—any of the "specialties" that are identifiable within a firm. Beyond the economic impact, the firm can use these "practice analysis reports" to be sure that all are carrying their fair share of work.

We will now examine representative formats for some reports that are often used in law office administration.

Work Summary

Each attorney in the firm should routinely complete a form such as that illustrated in Figure 10.13, "Work Summary," so that the managing partner of the firm can evaluate the workload of the firm each week. The managing partner should then be able to assign new work or reallocate work to attorneys on the basis of this Work Summary in conjunction with a review of time utilization reports developed from the timekeeping system. Paralegals also fill out Work Summary sheets, depending on the nature of the work they're doing. If they are working for many attorneys in one department, the department head and the paralegal supervisor, if any, often require copies of the Work Summary report in order to keep track of the work being done.

Cash Flow Projection

Many firms have cash flow problems, but only a few use mathematical methods to determine projected needs. One approach, as suggested by the form in Figure 10.14, is to determine anticipated cash receipts for the period under consideration by adding to the ending cash balance a certain percentage of new billings (the firm can anticipate payment within thirty days from approximately 50% of new billings, with the remaining bills being paid over a sixty-day to one-year period, depending on the firm's attentiveness to receivable collections), plus the anticipated collection from the more than sixty-day-old account receivables, to arrive at "total estimated cash resources," from which the firm can subtract out-of-pocket costs anticipated for the time period, and arrive at a "projected cash balance." The firm can then quickly determine whether it needs

FIGURE 10.13
Work Summary

FIGURE 10.14

Cash Flow
Projection

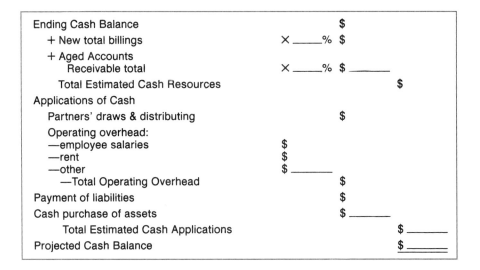

to borrow supplemental cash from the bank, or cut overhead, or take whatever remedial action may be necessary.

Chargeable Hour Schedule

The Chargeable Hour Schedule summarizes the actual hours invested by the attorneys and paralegals on a month-by-month basis (see Figure 10.15). To refine this schedule further and make it more informative, multiply hours by billing rates to arrive at a total dollar value of an attorney's or a paralegal's investment in the practice each month.

Aged Accounts Receivable

A list of clients, showing the amount due from each client as of a specified date, is known as a Schedule of Accounts Receivable. This schedule can be refined to indicate the number of days outstanding since the original billing date, normally into the following categories: 0–29 days old, 30–59 days old, 60–90 days old, and older than 90 days. This now becomes known as the Aged Accounts Receivable report.

The schedule in Figure 10.16 is common throughout most businesses. Law firms generally do not develop such a schedule, yet this can be a critical tool in the collection process. It should be prepared each month so that the managing partner and legal administrator can quickly determine where a special effort may be needed in the collection process, evaluate the status of receivables, and adjust cash-flow predictions in accordance with the status of the receivables.

Budget Reports

The annual budget should be one of the very first items management develops. It can be combined with income statements to give the firm current information on the firm's financial health. See Figure 10.17. Traditionally, law firms have had little understanding or control over their financial destiny and, as a consequence, they generally tend to react to problems on a crisis basis. The use of an annual budget and other such planning tools would virtually eliminate or greatly minimize crises throughout the year. The trend is for law firms to be

FIGURE 10.15
Chargeable Hour Schedule

	Jan.	Feb.	Mar.	April	May	June	July	Aug.	Sept.	Oct.	Nov.	Dec.	Total
Partners:													
A													
B													
C													
D													
Total Partners													
Associates:													
A													
B													
C													
D													
E													
F													
G													
Total Associates													
Paralegals:													
A													
B													
C													
Total Paralegals													
TOTAL FIRM													

more and more businesslike in their management style, and many firms will probably be implementing more sophisticated budgetary procedures.

Section G. The Procedures Manual in a Small Office: Mail, Copying, and Filing

Law offices often have a procedures manual to cover different aspects of law office administration. The following excerpts are from a manual in a relatively small firm.[15]

Incoming Mail

Before touching sophisticated areas, the manual should start with some fairly straightforward routines. A prime candidate is incoming mail. A suggested statement for the manual begins at the top of page 471.

---

[15]Adapted from Light, *The Procedure Manual: Mail, Copying and Filing Rules*, 26 The Practical Lawyer 71 (January 1980). Copyright 1980 by the American Law Institute. Reprinted with permission of The Practical Lawyer.

FIGURE 10.16

Aged Accounts
Receivable
Billed—Not Yet
Collected

Billing Attorney	Client Name	Legal Services	Disburse-ments	Total Due		Current To 30 Days	31–60 Days	61–90 Days	91–180 Days	More Than 6 Mos. Old
	(Alphabetic listing by client)	$	$	$		$	$	$	$	$
	.									
	.									
	.									
	.									
	.									
	TOTAL, ALL CLIENTS	$	$	$		$	$	$	$	$
	% Distribution	%	%	100%		%	%	%	%	%
	TOTAL RECAP BY BILLING ATTORNEY				% to total					
	(Total by billing lawyer)	$	$	$	%	$	$	$	$	$
	.				%					
	.				%					
	.				%					
	TOTAL ALL LAWYERS				100%					

FIGURE 10.17

Income Statement with Budget

```
11/16/86                      CLARK, LOWREY & SMITH
PERIOD 9                      ATTORNEYS AT LAW                                      PAGE 1

                         INCOME STATEMENT WITH BUDGET
```

ACCT NO	DESCRIPTION	CURRENT PERIOD				YEAR TO DATE			
		THIS YEAR	%	BUDGET	%	THIS YEAR	%	BUDGET	%
	INCOME								
	INCOME ACCRUAL								
400	FEES: INCOME FROM CLIENTS	42356.00		19000.00		229247.57		228000.00	
100	OTHER INCOME/RECEIPTS	1836.23		700.00		9232.88		8400.00	
480	INCOME PRODUCING PROPERTY	.00		350.00		3790.00		4200.00	
	TOTAL INCOME ACCRUAL	44192.23		20050.00		242270.37		240600.00	
	EXPENSES								
	PAYROLL								
500	SALARY: SECRETARIAL	2975.30	6.7	1500.00	7.5	17851.00	7.4	18000.00	7.5
501	SALARY: WORD/DATA PROC.	1100.00	2.5	650.00	3.2	7556.45	3.1	7800.00	3.2
502	SALARY: PARALG & CLERKS	1875.18	4.2	2000.00	10.0	20632.15	8.5	24000.00	10.0
503	SALARY: ATTORNEYS	11400.00	25.8	6000.00	29.9	68400.00	28.2	72000.00	29.9
504	SALARY: OTH NON-OWN EMPL	1050.00	2.4	700.00	3.5	7804.00	3.2	8400.00	3.5
	TOTAL PAYROLL	18400.48	41.6	10850.00	54.1	122244.40	50.5	130200.00	54.1
	NON-PAYROLL EMPLOYEE COSTS								
510	FICA & UNEMPLOY TAXES	838.77	1.9	420.00	2.1	5038.77	2.1	5020.00	2.1
514	RETIREMENT BENEFITS	746.00	1.7	370.00	1.8	4446.00	1.8	4440.00	1.8
518	TRAINING & EDUCATION	250.00	.6	300.00	1.5	3660.00	1.5	3600.00	1.5
519	OTHER EMPLOYEE COSTS	.00	.0	150.00	.7	1674.00	.7	1800.00	.7
	TOTAL NON-PAYROLL EMPL COST	1834.77	4.2	1240.00	6.2	14818.77	6.1	14860.00	6.2
	OCCUPANCY EXPENSES								
520	OFFICE RENT	2940.00	6.7	750.00	3.7	10290.00	4.2	9000.00	3.7
521	PARKING	240.00	.5	80.00	.4	1003.85	.4	960.00	.4
523	REAL EST TAXES & INS	382.00	.9	185.00	.9	2245.78	.9	2200.00	.9

Source: Computer Legal Systems, Inc.

Mail: Incoming

In addition to sorting mail by addressee, the individual responsible for the morning mail should:

1. Date-stamp *everything* with the "Received" stamp. Exceptions are books received on approval or original documents such as deeds that have been mailed to the office for recording or filing elsewhere. Whenever possible, stamp the date in the same location on every document. This will make it easier for someone to read the dates when perusing through a large file.

2. When an incoming document requires reference to previous papers, place the appropriate file with it.

3. If you can draft a response to the incoming document, prepare a draft and place it with the document.

4. Return receipts for certified mail should be stapled to the copies of the documents to which they correspond.

5. File the following documents immediately without circulation:

   ■ Pocket parts or supplements to treatises in the library.

   ■ All loose-leaf page supplements.

   ■ The paperback supplements to the state statutes and the United States Code Annotated or United States Code Service.

6. For informational purposes, prepare a "Daily Checks and Bills Received" sheet using the format in Figure 10.18.

Incoming mail may have to be photocopied and distributed to others—for example, to paralegals for specific assignments or to clients for their information. In some firms, special stamps are used such as the following:

FOR INFORMATION ONLY—NO ACTION REQUIRED

Copying Charges

Failure to record legitimate copying charges for later billing to the client constitutes a drain on the firm's financial resources.

1. Register on the alphabetical list that is kept on or near the copying machine the client's name, if not already there, and the number of copies.

2. Copies that are not to be charged to any client should be noted as "office" copies or "N/C" copies.

Received on January 6, 1991		
CHECKS		
Hammerlee	(title search)	$380.00
Mid-Penn	136.55 C.A.	3961.43
PNB	164.80 C.A.	724.80
Kalp, Arn	2.25 C.A.	62.25
BILLS		
Wagners	(clips and rubber stamps)	12.72
Rec'd vol. 97 of *Supreme Court Reporter*		

FIGURE 10.18

Daily Checks and Bills Received

3. On at least a monthly basis, the member of the staff who is responsible for copy charges should post them to the respective client accounts.

Filing System

Rules and Comments

The importance of a good filing system cannot be overestimated. Lost and misplaced papers are the obvious result of a poor system. But the damage can run even deeper. Deadlines can be missed, leading to one of the most common causes of malpractice claims against attorneys. Hours may be lost in ferreting through files for crucial documents that cannot be found. Appellate briefs might be poorly prepared because files are not in a readily usable form that would allow drafters to gather information and prepare the briefs in an orderly fashion. Particular tasks might be overlooked because attorneys, often subconsciously, dread having to search for needed information or simply do not know how to tell a member of the staff to compile what is needed.

Some firms use an exclusively *alphabetical filing system*. For example, all the documents for the Allen Construction Corporation case would be filed just before all the documents for the Allenson estate case. Such a system is not as effective as a *numerical filing system* accompanied by an alphabetical card index. Here is an example of the categories of cases (or client matters) that could be used in a numerical filing system:

001–099	Large clients
100–199	Wills and estate planning
200–349	Real estate: purchase and sale
350–399	Estate administration and trusts
400–499	Domestic relations, excluding divorce and custody masterships
500–549	Personal injury, including worker's compensation
600–649	Litigation, excluding personal injury
700–749	Corporations and partnerships
750–799	Financing, bonds, industrial developments, and similar matters
800–849	Tax, excluding estate planning
900–999	Miscellaneous files not appropriate for any other category
1000–1499	Printed forms, applications, and other miscellaneous documents
1500–1999	Bar Association and non-client-related matters
2000–2049	Bankruptcy
2100–2149	Divorce and custody masterships and arbitration panels
2200–2299	Criminal matters

These numerical categories vary widely from office to office according to size and type of practice. Large firms spread the brackets and use higher numbers. A two digit number representing the year would precede each of the number categories. Hence, 92.287 would be a real estate matter opened in 1992. Anytime a significant block of cases does not fit within a particular category, it is relatively easy to create a new category.

A numerical filing system with an alphabetical card index is preferable since it:

■ Reduces the misplacement of files. For some reason, individuals are more likely to place files in correct numerical order than in correct alphabetical order. For example, a purely alphabetical system would have difficulty handling the industrial development project for a client named Jones who owns North Marine Industries involving a local development agency bearing the acronym SIFT. While someone may think of the project as "Jones: SIFT-North Marine Industries," others may look for the file under "North Marine Industries: SIFT." Cross-referencing within a card index (see below) almost eliminates this problem when a numerical filing system is used.

■ Permits the grouping of files by subject matter, such as litigation or real estate. Such a system can be useful if, for example, the firm wants to contact all clients for whom wills were prepared within the past five years.

■ Allows easier reference on memoranda, correspondence, and client lists. It is certainly simpler to jot "86.267" on a title abstract sheet than "Stankiewicz: Purchase of Real Estate (1986)."

■ Allows cross-referencing within the card index. The index cards *can* be alphabetical. You can create cards under any variety of headings that you think a user might try to use. Each card would refer to the files under their numerical entry.

■ Automatically brings old files to the front of the filing system, acting almost as a tickler system.

■ Allows the immediate identification of the year of a particular file by the first two digits of the file index, such as, "86.589" for a 1986 file.

■ Facilitates the differentiation of files that may have confusingly similar designations. "Jones: Personal Injury (1981)" and "Jones: Property Settlement Agreement (1983)" would probably be stored next to one another in an *alphabetical* system and would have the tendency not only to be filed in the wrong alphabetical order but to attract each other's papers. But in a *numerical* system, although the index cards would probably be neighbors, the physical separation of the folders in the file cabinet would be more likely to prevent the misplacing of documents among the files.[16]

■ Adapts to computerization, when that time comes (see next section).

■ Eases the handling of closed files. Under an alphabetical system, when the firm is ready to "retire" a particular file, two choices are available—continue to file alphabetically, or switch to a sequential closed-file numbering system, with files placed one after the other as they are closed, regardless of their alphabetical designations. The first choice leads to the situation in which all the files from I through Z have to be moved if H grows rapidly (for example, nobody anticipated that the Half-Penny National Bank would become the firm's most active client). The second alternative requires an alphabetical card index to allow for the retrieval of particular closed files. It would already exist under the numerical system.

Depending on the size of the office, a library-like system may be needed in which files are checked out of the file room in much the same manner that books are checked out of a library. While administratively burdensome, this system at

---

[16]One possible difficulty with a numerical filing system is the confusion of file 91.325 with file 92.325. The multicolored file folders that are available from stationery suppliers offer a ready solution to this potential problem. If blue folders were used for 1991, red for 1992, and green for 1993, a file is not likely to be misplaced, and if it is in the wrong spot, it will stand out. In order to have the benefit of a fully integrated system, color-matching index cards should be used for the alphabetical index.

least ensures an ability to trace missing files. Overly strict measures, however, might backfire. For example, an attempt to prevent attorneys from ever holding files in their office might discourage them from initially storing any of their files in the filing room.

Closed Files

The filing cabinets in the main office contain only files on which work is being done, on which work is likely to be done in the near future, or that are likely to be used for reference in a current matter. Closed file procedures are designed to save active file space as well as allow for easy retrieval of retired information. Theoretically, if the firm's practice is stable, its main filing cabinets should maintain a constant size, while the real accumulation of paper occurs in the closed file storage area.

Generally, only the billing attorney may declare a file closed. Such a decision is not crucial or irreversible because the file can be retrieved easily. It is better to close a file than to keep it around. The fewer the active files, the more manageable the filing system.

When a file is to be closed, one way to do it is to "Pendaflex" it to the individual responsible for file closings, who then:

1. Assigns a CF (closed file) number to the file. This will be the next number for the year, with the first file closed during the calendar year 1992 receiving the number CF 92.001.

2. Places the CF number on the file's alphabetical index cards.

3. Writes the CF number on the file label.

4. Places the file in the "upstairs" CF filing drawer. The upstairs CF filing drawer contains recently closed files that may be needed. These files are sent upstairs for a time, before being relegated to the basement or other permanent storage area.

The closed files are permanently stored in boxes clearly labeled with the first and last CF file number. To retrieve a closed file, simply check the alphabetical index card, obtain the CF number, and find the file in storage. In some firms, closed files are placed on microfilm after a designated time. Most of the original file is then destroyed. Future access and copying of such files are achieved through microfilm readers and printers.

■ Section H. Computer-Based Records Management System in a Large Office

How One Law Firm Automated Its Records Management

Patricia Patterson, Director of Legal Information Services,
Schiff Hardin & Waite, Chicago, Illinois
21 American Association of Law Libraries Newsletter 291 (April 1991)

By the end of the next decade, it is likely that all records managers will have considered, tested, or installed some sort of computer-based records management system. From the smallest to the most complex central file system, computer automation offers the possibility of a cost-effective method for increasing management efficiency. But for many records information managers, jumping into a computerized system may not be conceptually or economically feasible at this time. Their problems probably fall into one or more of the following categories:

1. Insufficient financial resources to purchase a completely computerized system.

2. A non-standard records system that may require a specially customized computer program.

3. Management reluctant to commit to a new way of doing business.

4. Records personnel must be retrained, at great time and expense, to become computer literate and understand a computer system.

If your situation falls into one of these categories, you can take it upon yourself to solve some of these problems.

First of all, and let me emphasize [that] a successfully Automated Records Management System is:

- User Designed and Implemented
- Easy to Use and Accessible
- Online in Real Time
- Multi-User (Multiple/Simultaneous Users)
- Application Based and Controlled
- Management Supported

Using my own experience as a working example, I would like to discuss each of these criteria.

When I assumed the responsibilities of the Schiff Hardin and Waite Records Department, I inherited a large problem. Data entry operators had been employed three years prior to my arrival to capture our 350,000 3 × 5 card file information onto magnetic tape. The Records Department was behind in its duties of opening new files, tracking file locations, and checking for conflicts of interest. In addition, the Records Department still had two people keying all of the file card and cross reference card information into batches of data onto magnetic type. Management directed me to guide the department into the twenty-first century by installing a computer system capable of using the data that the firm had spent significant time and money on over the previous four years. My background was in library management, and I was responsible for the Schiff library, so I was accustomed to working with large volumes of information.

My first task was to select a computer company to convert the data stored on nine reels of magnetic tape. We needed this data reformatted into a structure that could be loaded to an online database. Over 350,000 records of data had been keyed with very little control over checking the validity of client numbers, dates, attorney numbers, etc. Previous computer consultants employed by Schiff had not thoroughly planned for the next step. That being the case and with the keying of data nearly complete, an implementation decision was needed.

At that time, we contacted the firm of Micom Systems, Inc., of North Muskegon, Michigan. Micom had been doing custom programming and computer services work for law firms since 1969. Their proposal to convert our data to a database format and clean up the duplicate entries and as much of the erroneous

editing as possible was accepted by the firm in the fall of 1987. Micom, using its IBM 4341 computer and IBM assembler language, converted the data by January, 1988.

My next task was to select an online database on which to use our newly converted data. After researching all of the records management software packages on the market, we concluded that they were inappropriate for our application. Because of Micom's knowledge of our data and experience with online law firm systems, we selected them to develop our records management system. With our data now ready for use, and after years of keying in the data, we were naturally anxious for the system to be operational. However, Schiff's two IBM System 36s were filled to capacity with litigation support and accounting functions. There was no room for a 250 million-character records management system on either of our two computer systems. Therefore, we chose to install communications equipment and a dedicated 9600 baud line to Micom's IBM mainframe 200 miles from our Chicago office.

Micom personnel studied our information storage and reporting needs. They then designed our system to meet current, as well as future needs. Operational requirements and key functions of the system included:

1. All data from the conversion loaded and accessible.

2. User-friendly system with a short learning curve.

3. An adaptable system that could be changed quickly and easily.

4. Online interactive with additions, changes, and deletions immediately available.

5. Online conflict of interest searching with results printed on demand.

6. File cards and labels printed online using local printers.

7. Accommodation of the complex structured file identification system Schiff already had in place.

As I will list later on, the records management system has many features that address our information needs. The key ones, previously stated, were the driving force behind Micom selecting IBM CSP (Cross System Product) as its development language. Because of CSP's ability to run across IBM platforms, Micom could develop and initially run the system on their IBM mainframe. Then when Schiff installs an IBM AS/400 or networked IBM PS/2s, Micom can port the system to run on either of these computer systems. This software portability across platforms was a positive factor in our decision to use Micom to develop our system.

The Schiff requirements for an automated records management system originated from attorney needs and expectations. Accurate and thorough conflict checking is a necessity and rates the highest priority. Our system provides timely and complete new client screening based on all of the data stored in the records management system. Our attorneys need rapid opening of new files and swift retrieval of stored files. We have the ability to track folders and identify files easily and quickly with very few keystrokes or screen changes. Quick locating of a client's file folders is important whether the file is located in someone's office or in a box at an off-site storage facility. Attorney and secretary requests for file locations and identifications are handled by our staff of 11 using this system. Most requests of this type are handled by phone. New, revised, or additional file labels are printed on demand by the Records Center staff.

Our system has performed as we had hoped it would, allowing us to proceed with add-on enhancements. For example, we are now in the installation phase of a bar coding subsystem. This will enable us to print a bar code label with a unique client/matter number for each file created in the Records Center. Using a fixed scanner in our Records Department, we will scan the bar codes of all folders that leave the Records Center. Both the location and file folder identification will be scanned online directly into the computer system. All file folders leaving the Records Center at night will be batch-scanned into an IBM PS/2 and transferred to the IBM mainframe the next morning. Periodically we will scan all folders in attorneys'

offices using portable, hand-held scanners. This procedure will give us the ability to track folder movements between attorney offices.

One feature of our system which saves additional time is the box storage system. This system tracks all box storage; both on, and off-site. Folder movement into and out of boxes is monitored, as are all pick-ups and deliveries. This system provides us with reports of all pick-ups and deliveries by date to enable us to verify our warehouse service bill more easily.

The Conflict of Interest System deserves more comment. This system is fully integrated into our Records Management System. Our personnel can hot key to the full text search process at any time. Then, using . . . commands, they can completely search our file records data. The data is displayed in our record structure format with the "hits" highlighted. We also have the ability to print any or all of the occurrences immediately. This efficient system has saved us countless hours of work.

While you may not be ready to adopt the automated records system that I have described, I hope the process we went through at Schiff Hardin & Waite will alert you to the advantages offered by computerized records management systems. Just be certain that the system you select addresses your specific information needs. The future is upon us, and we must knowledgeably embrace the technology on which it is based.

Scanning coded files in records department

■ **ASSIGNMENT 10.1**

In the practice of law, time is money. Hence you must develop the discipline of recording your time. Supervisors will later decide what portions of your time are billable—and to what clients. Step one is to compile a record of your time.

To practice this discipline, fill out a Daily Time Sheet for a day that you select. On *one* sheet of paper, record (in a chart form that you design) everything (approximately) that you do *in six minute* intervals over a continuous eight-hour period. Once you design your chart, *it should take you no more than about fifteen minutes to fill it out* during the eight-hour period. You do not, however, fill it out at one time; you fill it out at appropriate times throughout the eight hours.

Select an eight-hour period in which you are engaged in a fairly wide variety of activities. If possible, avoid an eight-hour period that contains any single activity lasting over two hours. Draw a chart covering the eight-hour period. At the top of the chart, place your name, the date of the eight-hour period that you used, and the starting/ending times of the eight-hour period. The period can be within a school day, a workday, a day of leisure, etc.

Using abbreviations, make specific entries on your activities within the eight hours—in six-minute intervals. For example, "Reading a chapter in a real estate school text" might be abbreviated as RE-R. "Driving to school" might be abbreviated as D-Sch. "Purely personal matters" (such as taking a shower) might be abbreviated as PPM. You decide what the abbreviations are. On the back of the sheet of paper containing the chart, explain what the abbreviations mean. When an activity is repeated in more than one six-minute interval, simply repeat the abbreviation.

One format for the chart might be a series of vertical and horizontal lines on the sheet of paper. This will give you a small amount of space on which to insert your abbreviations for each six-minute interval. Design the chart any way that you want, keeping in mind the goal of the exercise: to enable someone else to know what you did within the eight-hour period.

On page 459, there is an example of a Daily Time Sheet (Figure 10.6) used in a law office. Note that the last column says "hours" and "10ths." A 10th of an hour is six minutes. Do *not* follow the format in Figure 10.6. Use the guidelines listed above, e.g., place your abbreviations on the other side of the sheet of paper that you submit.

■ **ASSIGNMENT 10.2**

Mary Davis is a paralegal who has been working at the law firm of Smith & Smith for five years. The firm consists of two attorneys, Sam and Karen Smith, a husband and wife attorney team. There is one other employee, Jane Jones, who has just been hired as a paralegal trainee. This person, a high school graduate, was a homemaker for fifteen years. She has had no outside employment or training. The firm has one secretary who spends most of his time typing bills to be sent to clients and acting as the receptionist.

Smith & Smith has a family-law practice, handling mostly divorces. It takes two main kinds of cases: (1) contested divorces, where the husband and wife cannot agree on one or more critical issues (such as custody, property division, or amount of alimony); and (2) uncontested divorces, where everything is agreed on. While most of the firm's clients are plaintiffs who have filed for divorce, the firm also represents defendants on occasion.

Uncontested cases involve a fair amount of paperwork plus at least one court appearance, where the attorney obtains the approval of the court on what the parties have agreed to do. Contested cases involve extensive paperwork and many court appearances in which the disputed issues are resolved by the court—unless a settlement is eventually reached by the parties.

Almost every case requires the preparation of the following documents:

- Retainer (in which the client hires the firm)
- Intake Memorandum (reporting on a long interview with the client, during which extensive information is obtained about spouses, children, addresses, employment, facts of marriage, length of time in the county, bank accounts, residences, cars, other property owned, family health conditions, kinds of insurance, stocks, bonds, pension plans, debts already incurred, budget data, etc.)
- Complaint (stating the grounds for divorce)
- Answer (responding to the complaint)
- Letters to opposing counsel requesting information
- Motions to the court requesting temporary alimony or maintenance, child custody and support, and attorney fees
- Motion for a Restraining Order (to prevent either side from transferring assets and to prevent harassment)
- Motion to Produce (a formal request that the other side turn over designated items, such as pay stubs, copies of tax returns, bank statements, and insurance policies)
- Agreement on Property Division, Custody, and Support (uncontested cases only, unless a settlement is eventually reached in contested cases)
- Interrogatories (in which one party sends written questions to the other)
- A Notice of Deposition (informing the other to appear at a designated place, such as at the office of one of the attorneys, to answer questions)
- Proposed Final Decree of Dissolution of the Marriage

In the office, Mary prepares the Intake Memorandum based on an interview that she conducts with the client. This occurs after the retainer is signed and one of the attorneys goes over the case with the client. Mary prepares the first draft of all the other documents listed above.

Mary conducts the intake interview with the client alone. Since she has done so many of these interviews, she knows from memory what questions to ask. When she was first hired, she watched the attorneys interview and so learned what to ask and how to conduct an interview on her own. Whenever anything unusual came up during the interview, she left the room to find one of the attorneys for guidance. She took extensive notes on what the client said and later typed her notes for the Intake Memorandum.

Whenever Mary needed to draft one of the documents, she went to the firm's closed-case files to try to find a model that she could adapt. Since she had legal research skills, she also sought help from texts (such as practice books) found in the law library. The more experienced Mary became, however, the less she had to resort to the old files and the law library. The attorneys were amazed at her ability to find and retain whatever she needed to prepare so many different kinds of documents. They developed tremendous trust in Mary. For many cases, the documents never seemed to vary except for the names of the parties and particular financial figures. A fair number of times, however, different situations arose—for example, the parties had prior marriages or a child was retarded and therefore required special care following the divorce. Starting from scratch, Mary used her experience and skills to draft the proper documents to accommodate these situations.

Mary was also responsible for opening case files for all new clients. Each time the firm accepted a client, she took an accordion folder and typed the name of the client on it. Scattered throughout the folder were handwritten notes (from Mary or the attorney in charge of the case) describing some event that was relevant to the case. The documents were not placed in the folder in any particular order. This, however, did not create much difficulty since Mary was so familiar with all of the files. Only occasionally were things lost or misfiled.

The reason that the firm has decided to hire another paralegal is that Mary has announced that in six months she is going to leave the firm for another position. The receptionist also gave notice that he is leaving. Neither is dissatisfied with the firm; it is simply time to move on. The firm tried to find an experienced paralegal to replace Mary, but could not. Hence it just hired Jane Jones who, as indicated, has had no experience or training. The firm will replace the receptionist with a full-time typist and a full-time receptionist who will also be available for messenger assignments.

The firm is in a panic. The caseload is increasing at a rapid pace. There is some talk of hiring an additional attorney who has just graduated from law school and passed the bar, but no definite decision has yet been made. The big worry is the effect of Mary's departure in six months.

Sam Smith's solution is to have Jane Jones, the paralegal trainee, follow Mary around, observing everything Mary does during her last six months in the hope of absorbing as much as possible.

Karen Smith has a different approach. "Why don't we create some management systems and then train everyone on them?" Sam is very skeptical, but willing to listen.

Assume that you work for a law office management consulting firm. Karen and Sam Smith have asked you to prepare a report on how the office can systematize and manage its divorce practice so that Jane Jones—and *anyone* else—can come in, learn the system on their own (or almost on their own) and become functioning members of the team.

State how you would go about handling this task. If you think more than one system is needed, describe what they are. What facts do you want to obtain on how the firm now operates? How would you go about getting these facts? State any problems that you anticipate in obtaining these facts and how these problems might be resolved. Then describe what you would do with what you learn. State how the system or systems would operate. Give examples. Detail any problems you anticipate in implementing the system or systems and how these problems might be handled. If you feel that the firm needs different kinds of equipment, describe what is needed and how it would be used within the system or systems that you propose. State the benefits that the system(s) might provide. Also describe any difficulties that might exist in the system(s). In short, provide a comprehensive but realistic report. Don't try to oversell what you propose. Assume that the main audience of your report will be attorneys who are uninformed about the management dimensions of a law office.

☐ Chapter Summary

Our examination of law office administration began with an overview of the different settings in which attorneys practice law in the private sector in the United States and of the different kinds of attorneys found in each setting.

A sole practice consists of one attorney who owns the practice even if he or she employs other attorneys. The others do not share in the profits and losses of the firm. To save on expenses, several sole practitioners may enter into an office-

sharing arrangement under which the attorneys share expenses for office space, secretarial help, library materials, etc.

In a partnership, the equity or capital partners share in the profits and losses of the firm and control its management, often through a committee or department structure. Associates are attorneys in the firm who hope one day to be invited to become partners. There are, however, special categories of associates created for those who do not become

(Continued on next page)

☐ Chapter Summary *(Continued)*

partners, such as senior associate and permanent associate.

Other categories of attorneys who might be hired by a law firm include staff attorneys, of counsel attorneys, and contract attorneys. For tax and estate-planning purposes, many states allow attorneys to practice law as a professional corporation. There is little practical difference, however, between the administration of a partnership and a professional corporation.

Finally, there are attorneys who practice law in the legal departments of corporations. They are employees of the corporation, which is their sole client.

Large law offices may have many nonattorney employees to help manage the office. These employees have become increasingly influential because of the sharp rise in overhead costs in recent years. Among the most prominent is the Legal Administrator. Also, if there are more than a few paralegals in the office, a Legal Assistant Manager is often hired to help administer the office's system for recruiting, hiring, training, and monitoring the progress of paralegals.

There is considerable pressure on attorneys and paralegals to keep track of their time with precision. The accounting records and financial health of the law firm depend on it. At least nine different methods of billing exist: hourly rate, fixed fee, full contingent fee, hourly plus fixed fee, hourly reduced or with contingent, blended hourly rate, lodestar, value billing, and percentage fee. The method of paying this bill (including disbursements) should be spelled out in the retainer. The amount actually paid by a client is not determined until there has been a valuing of the bill, which might result in a write-up, a write-down, or no change.

An efficient law firm uses administrative reports to help it keep track of and manage the practice. Among the most important are the practice analysis report, work summary, cash flow projection, chargeable hour schedule, aged accounts receivable, and budget reports.

A busy law firm receives a great deal of mail, does a great amount of copying, and files a great many documents. It is important for the paralegal to learn what method the firm uses for these tasks. While some offices file alphabetically, many firms have found that numerical filing is more effective. Offices with large caseloads, and hence many documents to file and store, often use a computerized system of record management.

Key Terms

sole practice
general practitioner
law clerk
office sharing
partnership
partner
draw
associate
lateral hire
passed over
permanent associate
senior associate
nonequity partner
income partner
equity partner
capital partner
staff attorney
second-tiered attorney
of counsel
contract attorney
project attorney
professional corporation

corporate legal department
general counsel
in-house attorney
legal administrator
legal assistant manager
timekeeping
new file worksheet
new matter sheet
daily time sheet
hourly time and rate chart
time ticket
master ledger card
hourly rate
bundled/unbundled
fixed fee
full contingent fee
hourly plus fixed fee
hourly reduced or with
    contingent
blended hourly rate
lodestar
value billing

percentage fee
disbursements
retainer
billing memorandum
draft bill
write down
write up
valuing the bill
premium adjustment
discount adjustment
aging report
practice analysis report
work summary
cash flow projection
chargeable hour schedule
aged accounts receivable
annual budget
alphabetical filing system
numerical filing system
bar coding

Paralegal Associations and Related Organizations

PARALEGAL ASSOCIATIONS (NATIONAL)

(Membership statistics, where known, are presented in brackets.)

National Association of Legal
   Assistants [15,000]
1601 S. Main St., Suite 300
Tulsa, OK 74119
918-587-6828

National Federation of Paralegal
   Associations [17,500]
P.O. Box 33108

Kansas City, MO 64114
816-941-4000

(NALA and NFPA have numerous affiliated local paralegal associations. NALA affiliates are indicated by one asterisk (*) below; NFPA affiliates are indicated by two asterisks below (**). The addresses of these local associations change frequently. If the address given below turns out to be incorrect, contact the national office of NALA or NFPA for a more current address. Local associations without an asterisk are unaffiliated at the time of publication.)

PARALEGAL ASSOCIATIONS (STATE)

ALABAMA

Alabama Association of Legal
   Assistants (*) [215]
P.O. Box 55921
Birmingham, AL 35255

Huntsville Association of
   Paralegals
P.O. Box 244
Huntsville, AL 35804-0244

Mobile Association of Legal
   Assistants [75]
P.O. Box 1988
Mobile, AL 36633

ALASKA

Alaska Association of Legal
   Assistants (**) [130]
P.O. Box 101956
Anchorage, AK 99510-1956

Fairbanks Association of Legal
   Assistants (*)
P.O. Box 73503
Fairbanks, AK 99707

Juneau Legal Assistants Association
   (**) [20]
P.O. Box 22336
Juneau, AK 99802

ARIZONA

Arizona Association of Professional
   Paralegals (**) [50]
P.O. Box 25111
Phoenix, AZ 85002

Arizona Paralegal Association (*)
P.O. Box 392
Phoenix, AZ 85001
602-258-0121

Legal Assistants of Metropolitan
   Phoenix (*)

P.O. Box 13005
Phoenix, AZ 85002

Southeast Valley Association of
   Legal Assistants (*)
% Sandy Slater
1707 N. Temple
Mesa, AZ 85203

Tucson Association of Legal
   Assistants (*)
P.O. Box 257
Tucson, AZ 85702-0257

ARKANSAS

Arkansas Association of Legal
   Assistants (*)
P.O. Box 2162
Little Rock, AR 72203-2162

CALIFORNIA

California Alliance of Paralegal
   Associations [4000]

P.O. Box 2234
San Francisco, CA 94126
415-576-3000

California Association of Freelance
  Paralegals [94]
P.O. Box 3267
Berkeley, CA 94703-0267
213-251-3826

Central Coast Legal Assistant
  Association (**) [70]
P.O. Box 93
San Luis Obispo, CA 93406

Central Valley Paralegal
  Association
P.O. Box 4086
Modesto, CA 95352

East Bay Association of Paralegals
  [200]
P.O. Box 29082
Oakland, CA 94604

Inland Counties Paralegal
  Association
P.O. Box 292
Riverside, CA 92502-0292

Kern County Paralegal Association
  [63]
P.O. Box 2673
Bakersfield, CA 93303

Legal Assistants Association of
  Santa Barbara (*)
P.O. Box 2695
Santa Barbara, CA 93120
805-965-7319

Los Angeles Paralegal Association
  (**) [1150]
P.O. Box 241928
Los Angeles, CA 90024
213-251-3755

Marin Association of Legal
  Assistants
P.O. Box 13051
San Rafael, CA 94913-3051
415-456-6020

Orange County Paralegal
  Association (**) [490]
P.O. Box 8512
Newport Beach, CA 92658-8512
714-744-7747

Paralegal Association of Santa
  Clara County (*)

P.O. Box 26736
San Jose, CA 95159

Redwood Empire Association of
  Legal Assistants
1275 4th St. Box 226
Santa Rosa, CA 95404

Sacramento Association of Legal
  Assistants (**) [271]
P.O. Box 453
Sacramento, CA 95812-0453

San Diego Association of Legal
  Assistants (**) [450]
P.O. Box 87449
San Diego, CA 92138-7449
619-491-1994

San Francisco Association of Legal
  Assistants (**) [975]
P.O. Box 26668
San Francisco, CA 94126-6668
415-777-2390

San Joaquin Association of Legal
  Assistants
P.O. Box 1306
Fresno, CA 93715

Sequoia Paralegal Association
P.O. Box 3884
Visalia, CA 93278-3884

Ventura County Association of
  Legal Assistants (*)
P.O. Box 24229
Ventura, CA 93002

COLORADO

Association of Legal Assistants of
  Colorado (*) [106]
% Alma Rodrigues
4150 Novia Dr.
Colorado Springs, CO 80911

Rocky Mountain Legal Assistants
  Association (**) [440]
P.O. Box 304
Denver, CO 80201
303-369-1606

CONNECTICUT

Central Connecticut Association of
  Legal Assistants (**) [290]
P.O. Box 230594
Hartford, CT 06123-0594

Connecticut Association of
  Paralegals, Fairfield County (**)
  [135]
P.O. Box 134
Bridgeport, CT 06601

Connecticut Association of
  Paralegals, New Haven (**)
  [100]
P.O. Box 862
New Haven, CT 06504-0862

Legal Assistants of Southeastern
  Connecticut (**) [55]
P.O. Box 409
New London, CT 06320

DELAWARE

Delaware Paralegal Association
  (**) [295]
P.O. Box 1362
Wilmington, DE 19899

DISTRICT OF COLUMBIA

National Capital Area Paralegal
  Association (**) [620]
1155 Connecticut Ave. N.W.
Wash. D.C. 20036-4306
202-659-0243

FLORIDA

Broward County Paralegal
  Association
% Leigh Williams
Ruden, Barnett, McClosky
P.O. Box 1900
Ft. Lauderdale, FL 33302

Dade Association of Legal
  Assistants (*)
% Maxine Stone
14027 S.W. 84th St.
Miami, FL 33183

Florida Legal Assistants (*)
% Nancy Martin
P.O. Box 503
Bradenton, FL 34206

Jacksonville Legal Assistants (*)
P.O. Box 52264
Jacksonville, FL 32201

Orlando Legal Assistants (*)
% Roxane MacGillivray
Akerman, Senterfitt & Eidson

P.O. Box 231
Orlando, FL 32802

Pensacola Legal Assistants (*)
% Deborah Johnson
Levin, Middlebrooks & Mabie
226 S. Palafox St.
Pensacola, FL 32581

Volusia Association of Legal
  Assistants (*)
P.O. Box 15075
Daytona Beach, FL 32115-5075

GEORGIA

Georgia Association of Legal
  Assistants (**) [820]
P.O. Box 1802
Atlanta, GA 30301

Southeastern Association of Legal
  Assistants of Georgia (*)
% Debra Sutlive
2215 Bacon Park Drive
Savannah, GA 31406

South Georgia Association of Legal
  Assistants (*)
% Martha Tanner
L. Andrew Smith, P.C.
P.O. Box 1026
Valdosta, GA 31603-1026

HAWAII

Hawaii Association of Legal
  Assistants (**) [150]
P.O. Box 674
Honolulu, HI 96809

IDAHO

Idaho Association of Legal
  Assistants (*) [54]
P.O. Box 1254
Boise, ID 83701

ILLINOIS

Central Illinois Paralegal
  Association (*)
% Debra Monke
GTE North Inc.
1312 E. Empire St.
Bloomington, IL 61701

Illinois Paralegal Association (**)
  [1059]

P.O. Box 857
Chicago, IL 60690
312-939-2553

Independent Contractors
  Association of Illinois
6400 Woodward Ave.
Downers Grove, IL 60516

Peoria Paralegal Association
% Sharon Moke
1308 Autumn Lane
Peoria, IL 60604

INDIANA

Indiana Legal Assistants (*)
% Dorothy French
14669 Old State Rd.
Evansville, IN 47711

Indiana Paralegal Association (**)
  [300]
P.O. Box 44518, Federal Station
Indianapolis, IN 46204

Michiana Paralegal Association
  (**) [40]
P.O. Box 11458
South Bend, IN 46634

IOWA

Iowa Association of Legal
  Assistants [400]
P.O. Box 335
Des Moines, IA 50302-0337

Paralegals of Iowa, Ltd.
P.O. Box 1943
Cedar Rapids, IA 52406

KANSAS

Kansas Association of Legal
  Assistants (*) [138]
% Jimmie Sue Marsh
Foulston & Siefkin
700 Fourth Financial Center
Wichita, KS 67202

Kansas City Association of Legal
  Assistants (**)
P.O. Box 13223
Kansas City, MO 64199
913-381-4458

Kansas Legal Assistants Society
  (**) [190]
P.O. Box 1657
Topeka, KS 66601

KENTUCKY

Kentucky Paralegal Association
  [232]
P.O. Box 2675
Louisville, KY 40201-2657

Lexington Paralegal Association
  (**) [80]
P.O. Box 574
Lexington, KY 40586

Louisville Association of Paralegals
  (**) [182]
P.O. Box 962
Louisville, KY 40201

LOUISIANA

Baton Rouge Paralegal Association
P.O. Box 306
Baton Rouge, LA 70821

Lafayette Paralegal Association
P.O. Box 2775
Lafayette, LA 70502

Louisiana State Paralegal
  Association [200]
P.O. Box 56
Baton Rouge, LA 70821-0056

New Orleans Paralegal Association
  (**) [190]
P.O. Box 30604
New Orleans, LA 70190

Northwest Louisiana Paralegal
  Association (*)
P.O. Box 1913
Shreveport, LA 71166-1913

Southwest Louisiana Association of
  Paralegals
P.O. Box 1143
Lake Charles, LA 70602-1143

MAINE

Maine Association of Paralegals (*)
P.O. Box 7554
Portland, ME 04112

MARYLAND

Baltimore Association of Legal
  Assistants (**) [140]
P.O. Box 13244
Baltimore, MD 21203
301-576-BALA

MASSACHUSETTS

Berkshire Association for
Paralegals and Legal Secretaries
% Nancy Schaffer
Stein, Donahue & Zuckerman
54 Wendell Ave.
Pittsfield, MA 01201

Central Massachusetts Paralegal
Association (**) [80]
P.O. Box 444
Worcester, MA 01614

Massachusetts Paralegal
Association (**) [440]
P.O. Box 423
Boston, MA 02102
617-642-8338

Western Massachusetts Paralegal
Association (**) [50]
P.O. Box 30005
Springfield, MA 01102-0005

MICHIGAN

Legal Assistants Association of
Michigan (*)
% Cora Webb
Woll, Crowley, Berman
315 S. Woodward
Royal Oak, MI 48067

Legal Assistant Section [400]
State Bar of Michigan
440 E. Congress, 4th Fl.
Detroit, MI 48226

Legal Assistants Section
State Bar of Michigan
306 Townsend St.
Lansing, MI 48933-2083
517-372-9030

MINNESOTA

Minnesota Association of Legal
Assistants (**) [972]
P.O. Box 15165
Minneapolis, MN 55415

Minnesota Paralegal Association
(*)
% Tracy Blanshan
Kennedy Law Office
724 SW First Ave.
Rochester, MN 55902

MISSISSIPPI

Gulf Coast Paralegal Association
942 Beach Drive
Gulfport, MS 39507

Mississippi Association of Legal
Assistants (*)
P.O. Box 996
600 Heritage Bldg.
Jackson, MS 39205

Paralegal Association of Mississippi
P.O. Box 22887
Jackson, MS 39205

MISSOURI

Gateway Paralegal Association
P.O. Box 50233
St. Louis, MO 63105

Kansas City Association of Legal
Assistants (**) [470]
P.O. Box 13223
Kansas City, MO 64199
913-381-4458

Southwest Missouri Paralegal
Association [80]
2148 South Oak Grove
Springfield, MO 65804-2708

St. Louis Association of Legal
Assistants (*) [434]
P.O. Box 9690
St. Louis, MO 63122

MONTANA

Big Sky Paralegal Association
P.O. Box 2753
Great Falls, MT 59403

Montana Paralegal Association
P.O. Box 693
Billings, MT 59101

NEBRASKA

Nebraska Association of Legal
Assistants (*)
P.O. Box 24943
Omaha, NE 68124

NEVADA

Clark County Organization of
Legal Assistants (*)
% Angel A. Price

3800 S. Nellis #235
Las Vegas, NV 89121

Sierra Nevada Association of
Paralegals (*)
P.O. Box 40638
Reno, NV 89504

NEW HAMPSHIRE

Paralegal Association of New
Hampshire (*)
% Frances Dupre
Wiggin & Nourie
P.O. Box 808
Manchester, NH 03105

NEW JERSEY

Central Jersey Paralegal
Association
P.O. Box 1115
Freehold, NJ 07728

Legal Assistants Association of
New Jersey (*) [260]
P.O. Box 142
Caldwell, NJ 07006

South Jersey Paralegal Association
(**) [160]
P.O. Box 355
Haddonfield, NJ 08033

NEW MEXICO

Legal Assistants of New Mexico
(**) [200]
P.O. Box 1113
Albuquerque, NM 87103-1113
505-260-7104

NEW YORK

Adirondack Paralegal Association
% Maureen Provost
Bartlett, Pontiff, Stewart
One Washington Street
Box 2168
Glen Falls, NY 12801

Legal Professionals of Dutchess
County
51 Maloney Rd.
Wappingers Falls, NY 12590

Long Island Paralegal Association
(**) [130]

P.O. Box 31
Deer Park, NY 11729

Manhattan Paralegal Association
[515]
200 Park Ave., Suite 303 East
New York, NY 10166
212-986-2304

Paralegal Association of Rochester
(**) [170]
P.O. Box 40567
Rochester, NY 14604

Southern Tier Association of
Paralegals (**) [45]
P.O. Box 2555
Binghamton, NY 13902

Western New York Paralegal
Association (**) [275]
P.O. Box 207
Buffalo, NY 14202
716-862-6132

West/Roc Paralegal Association
(**) [130]
Box 101
95 Mamaroneck Ave.
White Plains, NY 10601

NORTH CAROLINA

Cumberland County Paralegal
Association
P.O. Box 1358
Fayetteville, NC 28302

Metrolina Paralegal Association
P.O. Box 36260
Charlotte, NC 28236

North Carolina Paralegal
Association (*)
% T. William Tewes
Fuller & Corbett
P.O. Box 1121
Goldsboro, NC 27533-1121

Professional Legal Assistants
P.O. Box 31951
Raleigh, NC 27622
919-821-7762

Raleigh Wake Paralegal
Association
P.O. Box 1427
Raleigh, NC 27602

Triad Paralegal Association
Drawer U
Greensboro, NC 27402

NORTH DAKOTA

Red River Valley Legal Assistants
(*)
P.O. Box 1954
Fargo, ND 58106

Western Dakota Association of
Legal Assistants (*)
P.O. Box 7304
Bismarck, ND 58502

OHIO

Cincinnati Paralegal Association
(**) [380]
P.O. Box 1515
Cincinnati, OH 45201
513-244-1266

Cleveland Association of Paralegals
(**) [480]
P.O. Box 14247
Cleveland, OH 44114

Greater Dayton Paralegal
Association (**) [160]
P.O. Box 515, Mid City Station
Dayton, OH 45402

Legal Assistants of Central Ohio
(**) [270]
P.O. Box 15182
Columbus, OH 43215-0812
614-224-9700

Northeastern Ohio Paralegal
Association
P.O. Box 9236
Akron, OH 44305

Toledo Association of Legal
Assistants (*) [176]
P.O. Box 1322
Toledo, OH 43603

OKLAHOMA

Oklahoma Paralegal Association
(*)
P.O. Box 18476
Oklahoma City, OK 73154

Tulsa Association of Legal
Assistants (*)
P.O. Box 1484
Tulsa, OK 74101

OREGON

Oregon Legal Assistants
Association (**) [340]

P.O. Box 8523
Portland, OR 97207

Pacific Northwest Legal Assistants
(*)
P.O. Box 1835
Eugene, OR 97440

PENNSYLVANIA

Berks County Paralegal Association
544 Court St.
Reading, PA 19601
215-375-4591

Central Pennsylvania Paralegal
Association (**) [70]
P.O. Box 11814
Harrisburg, PA 17108

Keystone Legal Assistant
Association (*)
% Catrine Nuss
3021 Guineveer Drive, Apt. B4
Harrisburg, PA 17110

Lancaster Area Paralegal
Association
% Rosemary Merwin
Gibble, Kraybill & Hess
41 East Orange St.
Lancaster, PA 17602

Paralegal Association of
Northwestern Pennsylvania (**)
[40]
P.O. Box 1504
Erie, PA 16507

Philadelphia Association of
Paralegals (**) [775]
1411 Walnut St., Suite 200
Philadelphia, PA 19102
215-564-0525

Pittsburgh Paralegal Association
(**) [400]
P.O. Box 2845
Pittsburgh, PA 15230

Wilkes-Barre Area Group
% Tom Albrechta
6 East Green St.
West Hazelton, PA 18201

RHODE ISLAND

Rhode Island Paralegal Association
(**) [200]
P.O. Box 1003
Providence, RI 02901

SOUTH CAROLINA

Charleston Association of Legal
  Assistants
P.O. Box 1511
Charleston, SC 29402

Columbia Association of Legal
  Assistants (**)
P.O. Box 11634
Columbia, SC 29211-1634

Greenville Association of Legal
  Assistants (*)
P.O. Box 10491 F.S.
Greenville, SC 29603

Paralegal Association of the Pee
  Dee [31]
P.O. Box 5592
Florence, SC 29502-5592

SOUTH DAKOTA

South Dakota Legal Assistants
  Association (*) [61]
% Louise Peterson
May, Johnson, Doyle
P.O. Box 1443
Sioux Falls, SD 57101-1443

TENNESSEE

Memphis Paralegal Association
  (**) [105]
P.O. Box 3646
Memphis, TN 38173-0646

Middle Tennessee Paralegal
  Association (**) [145]
P.O. Box 198006
Nashville, TN 37219

Southeast Tennessee Paralegal
  Association
% Calecta Veagles
P.O. Box 1252
Chattanooga, TN 37401

Tennessee Paralegal Association (*)
P.O. Box 11172
Chattanooga, TN 37401

TEXAS

Alamo Area Professional Legal
  Assistants [245]
P.O. Box 524
San Antonio, TX 78292

Capital Area Paralegal Association
  (*) [252]
% Chris Hemingson
Pope, Hopper, Roberts & Warren
111 Congress, Suite 1700
Austin, TX 78701

Dallas Association of Legal
  Assistants (**) [799]
P.O. Box 117885
Carrollton, TX 75011-7885

El Paso Association of Legal
  Assistants (*) [106]
P.O. Box 121
El Paso, TX 79941-0121

Fort Worth Paralegal Association
  [226]
P.O. Box 17021
Fort Worth, TX 76102

Houston Legal Assistants
  Association
P.O. Box 52266
Houston, TX 77052

Legal Assistant Division [2046]
State Bar of Texas
P.O. Box 12487
Austin, TX 78711
512-463-1383

Legal Assistants Association/
  Permian Basin (*)
P.O. Box 10683
Midland, TX 79702

Legal Assistants Professional
  Association (Brazos Valley)
P.O. Box 925
Madisonville, TX 79702

Northeast Texas Association of
  Legal Assistants (*) [29]
P.O. Box 2284
Longview, TX 75606

Nueces County Association of
  Legal Assistants (*)
% Joyce Hoffman
Edwards & Terry
P.O. Box 480
Corpus Christi, TX 78403

Southeast Texas Association of
  Legal Assistants (*) [130]
% Janie Boswell
8335 Homer
Beaumont, TX 77708

Texarkana Association of Legal
  Assistants (*) [40]
P.O. Box 6671
Texarkana, TX 75505

Texas Panhandle Association of
  Legal Assistants (*) [63]
% Lisa Clemens
Morgan, Culton
P.O. Box 189
Amarillo, TX 79105

Tyler Area Association of Legal
  Assistants [94]
P.O. Box 1178
Tyler, TX 75711-1178

West Texas Association of Legal
  Assistants (*) [44]
P.O. Box 1499
Lubbock, TX 79408

UTAH

Legal Assistants Association of
  Utah (*)
P.O. Box 112001
Salt Lake City, UT 84147-2001
801-531-0331

VERMONT

Vermont Paralegal Association [80]
% Trudy Seeley
Langrock, Sperry & Wool
P.O. Drawer 351
Middlebury, VT 05753

VIRGINIA

American Academy of Legal
  Assistants
1022 Paul Avenue N.E.
Norton, VA 24273

Peninsula Legal Assistants (*)
% Diane Morrison
Jones, Blechman, Woltz & Kelly
P.O. Box 12888
Newport News, VA 23612

Richmond Association of Legal
  Assistants (*) [318]
% Vicki Roberts
McGuire, Woods, Battle & Boothe
One James Center
Richmond, VA 23219

Roanoke Valley Paralegal
  Association (**) [70]

P.O. Box 1505
Roanoke, VA 24001
703-224-8000

Tidewater Association of Legal
   Assistants (*)
% Claire Isley
Wilcox & Savage
1800 Sovran Center
Norfolk, VA 23510

VIRGIN ISLANDS

Virgin Islands Paralegals (*)
% Eloise Mack
P.O. Box 6276
St. Thomas, VI 00804

WASHINGTON

Washington Legal Assistants
   Association (**) [453]
2033 6th Ave., Suite 804
Seattle, WA 98121
206-441-6020

WEST VIRGINIA

Legal Assistants of West Virginia
   (*)
% Mary Hanson
Hunt & Wilson
P.O. Box 2506
Charleston, WV 25329-2506

WISCONSIN

Paralegal Association of Wisconsin
   (**) [380]
P.O. Box 92882
Milwaukee, WI 53202
414-272-7168

WYOMING

Legal Assistants of Wyoming (*)
% Nancy Hole
Brown & Drew
123 West First St.
Casper, WY 82601

OTHER ORGANIZATIONS

Alberta Association of Legal
   Assistants
% Mackimme Mathews
700, 401 9th Ave. SW
P.O. Box 2010
Calgary, AB Canada T2P 2M2

American Association for Paralegal
   Education
10100 Santa Fe Dr., Suite 105
P.O. Box 40244
Overland Park, KS 66204
913-381-4458

American Association of Law
   Libraries
53 W. Jackson Blvd., Suite 940
Chicago, IL 60604
312-939-4764

American Association of Petroleum
   Landsmen
4100 Fossil Creek Blvd.
Fort Worth, TX 76137
817-847-7700

American Bar Association
750 N. Lake Shore Dr.
Chicago, IL 60611
312-988-5000
312-988-5618 (Standing
   Committee on Legal Assistants)
202-331-2200 (Wash. D.C. office)

American Paralegal Association
P.O. Box 35233
Los Angeles, CA 90035

American Society of Notaries
918 16th St., NW
Wash. D.C. 20006
202-955-6162

American Society of Questioned
   Document Examiners
1432 Esperson Bldg.
Houston, TX 77002
713-227-4451

Association of American Law
   Schools
1201 Connecticut Ave., NW
Wash. D.C. 20036
202-296-8851

Association of Federal Investigators
1612 K. ST., NW, Suite 506
Wash. D.C. 20006
202-466-7288

Association of Legal
   Administrators
175 E. Hawthorn Parkway
Vernon Hills, IL 60061-1428
312-816-1212

Association of Transportation
   Practitioners
1211 Connecticut Ave., NW
Wash. D.C. 20036
202-466-2080

Canadian Association of Legal
   Assistants
P.O. Box 967
Station "B"

Montreal, Quebec, Canada H3B
   3K5

Coalition for Paralegal and
   Consumer Rights
1714 Stockton St., Suite 400
San Francisco, CA 94133

Federal Criminal Investigators
   Association
P.O. Box 1256
Detroit, MI 48231
512-229-5610

HALT (Help Abolish Legal
   Tyranny)
1319 F. St. NW, Suite 300
Wash. D.C. 20004
202-347-9600

Independent Association of
   Questioned Document
   Examiners
403 W. Washington
Red Oak, IA 51566
712-623-9130

Institute of Law Clerks of Ontario
Suite 502, 425 University Avenue
Toronto, ON Canada M5G 1T6

Institute of Legal Executives
Kempston Manor
Kempston, Bedford England

International Association of Arson
   Investigators
5428 Del Maria Way

Louisville, KY 40291
502-491-7482

International Association of Auto
  Theft Investigators
255 S. Vernon
Dearborn, MI 48124
313-561-8583

Legal Assistant Management
  Association
638 Prospect Ave.
Hartford, CT 06105-4298
203-232-4825

National Association for Law
  Placement
166 Conn. Avenue, Suite 450
Wash. D.C. 20009
202-667-1666

National Association of Document
  Examiners
20 Nassau St.
Princeton, NJ 08542
609-924-8193

National Association of Enrolled
  Agents
6000 Executive Blvd., Suite 205
Rockville, MD 20852
800-424-4339

National Association for
  Independent Paralegals

635 5th St. West
Sonoma, CA 95476
800-542-0034
800-332-4557

National Association of Law Firm
  Marketing Administrators
60 Revere Drive, #500
Northbrook, IL 60062
708-480-9641

National Association of Law
  Placement
1666 Connecticut Ave. NW
Wash. D.C. 20009
202-667-1666

National Association of Legal
  Secretaries
2250 East 73d St., Suite 550
Tulsa, OK 74136-6864
918-493-3540

National Association of
  Professional Process Servers
306 H. St. NE
Wash. D.C. 20002
202-547-5710

National Indian Paralegal
  Association
7524 Major Ave.
Brooklyn Park, MN 55443

National Legal Assistant
  Conference Center
2444 Wilshire Blvd., Suite 301
Santa Monica, CA 90403

National Notary Association
8236 Remmet Ave.
Canoga Park, CA 91304-7184
818-713-4000

National Organization of Social
  Security Claimants
  Representatives
19 E. Central Ave., 2nd Fl.
Pearl River, NY 10965
800-431-2804

National Paralegal Association
P.O. Box 406
Solebury, PA 18963
215-297-8333

National Resource Center for
  Consumers of Legal Services
1444 Eye St. NW
Wash. D.C. 20005
202-842-3503

National Shorthand Reporters
  Association
118 Park St., SE
Vienna, VA 22180
703-281-4677

Federal Government Organization Chart

The Government of the United States

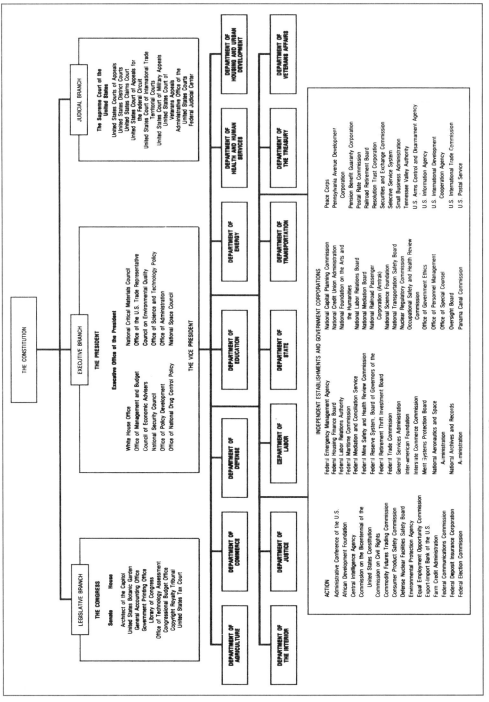

Source: United States Government Manual 1989-90.

Federal Job Information

Office of Personnel Management Federal Job Information Centers

Contact the Federal Job Information Center, which is nearest the location where you would like to work, for information on the job opportunities in that area and the forms needed to apply.

ALABAMA
Huntsville:
Building 600, Suite 341
3322 Memorial Pkwy., South
35801-5311
(205) 544-5802

ALASKA
Anchorage:
222 W. 7th Ave., #22,
99513-7572
(907) 271-5821

ARIZONA
Phoenix:
Century Plaza Bldg., Rm. 1415
3225 N. Central Ave., 85012
(602) 640-5800

ARKANSAS
(See Oklahoma Listing)

CALIFORNIA
Los Angeles:
9650 Flair Drive
Ste. 100A
El Monte, 91731
(818) 575-6510

Sacramento:
4695 Watt Ave., North Entrance
95660-5592
(916) 551-1464

San Diego:
Federal Bldg., Room 4-S-9
880 Front St., 92188
(619) 557-6165

San Francisco:
P.O. Box 7405, 94120
(Located at 211 Main St.,
2nd Floor, Room 235)
(415) 974-5627

COLORADO
Denver:
P.O. Box 25167, 80225
(303) 969-7050
(Located at 12345 W. Alameda
Pkwy., Lakewood)

*For Job Information (24 hours a
day) in the following States, dial:*
Montana: (303) 969-7052
Utah: (303) 969-7053
Wyoming: (303) 969-7054
*For forms and local supplements,
dial:* (303) 969-7055

CONNECTICUT
Hartford:
Federal Bldg., Room 613
450 Main St., 06103
(203) 240-3096 or 3263

DELAWARE
(See Philadelphia Listing)

DISTRICT OF COLUMBIA
Metro Area:
1900 E St., N.W., Room 1416,
20415
(202) 606-2700

FLORIDA
Orlando:
Commodore Bldg., Suite 150
3444 McCrory Pl., 32803-3701
(407) 648-6148

GEORGIA
Atlanta:
Richard B. Russell Federal Bldg.,
Room 940A, 75 Spring St., S.W.,
30303
(404) 331-4315

HAWAII
Honolulu (and other Hawaiian
Islands and Overseas):
Federal Bldg., Room 5316
300 Ala Moana Blvd., 96850
(808) 541-2791
Overseas Jobs—(808) 541-2784

IDAHO
(See Washington Listing)

ILLINOIS
Chicago:
175 W. Jackson Blvd., Room 530
60604
(312) 353-6192
(For Madison & St. Clair Counties,
see St. Louis, MO listing)

INDIANA
Indianapolis:
Minton-Capehart Federal Bldg.,
575 N. Pennsylvania St., 46204
(317) 226-7161

(For Clark, Dearborn, & Floyd Counties, see Ohio listing)

IOWA
(816) 426-7757
(For Scott County see Illinois listing; for Pottawattamie County, See Kansas listing)

KANSAS
Wichita:
One-Twenty Bldg., Room 101
120 S. Market St., 67202
(316) 269-6794
(For Johnson, Leavenworth, and Wyandotte Counties, dial
(816) 426-5702)

KENTUCKY
(See Ohio listing: for Henderson County, see Indiana listing)

LOUISIANA
New Orleans:
1515 Poydras St., Suite 680, 70112
(504) 589-2764

MAINE
(See New Hampshire Listing)

MARYLAND
Baltimore:
Garmatz Federal Building
101 W. Lombard Street, 21201
(301) 962-3822

MASSACHUSETTS
Boston:
Thos. P. O'Neill, Jr. Federal Bldg.
10 Causeway St., 02222-1031
(617) 565-5900

MICHIGAN
Detroit:
477 Michigan Ave., Rm. 565,
48225
(313) 226-6950

MINNESOTA
Twin Cities:
Federal Building, Room 501
Ft. Snelling, Twin Cities, 55111
(612) 725-3430

MISSISSIPPI
(See Alabama Listing)

MISSOURI
Kansas City:
Federal Building, Rm. 134
601 E. 12th Street, 64106
(816) 426-5702

(For Counties west of and including Mercer, Grundy, Livingston, Carroll, Saline, Pettis, Benton, Hickory, Dallas, Webster, Douglas, and Ozark)

St. Louis:
400 Old Post Office Bldg.
815 Olive St., 63101
(314) 539-2285
(For all other Missouri counties not listed under Kansas City above)

MONTANA
(See Colorado Listing)

NEBRASKA
(See Kansas Listing)

NEVADA
(See Sacramento, CA Listing)

NEW HAMPSHIRE
Portsmouth:
Thomas J. McIntyre Federal Bldg.
Room 104
80 Daniel Street, 03801-3879
(603) 431-7115

NEW JERSEY
Newark:
Peter W. Rodino, Jr., Federal Bldg.
970 Broad Street, 07102
(201) 645-3673
In Camden, dial (215) 597-7440

NEW MEXICO
Albuquerque:
Federal Building
421 Gold Avenue, S.W., 87102
(505) 766-5583

NEW YORK
New York City:
Jacob K. Javits Federal Bldg.
26 Federal Plaza, 10278
(212) 264-0440, 0441, or 0442

Syracuse:
James M. Hanley Federal Building
100 S. Clinton Street, 13260
(315) 423-5660

NORTH CAROLINA
Raleigh:
P.O. Box 25069
4505 Falls of the Neuse Rd.
Suite 450, 27611-5069
(919) 856-4361

NORTH DAKOTA
(See Minnesota Listing)

OHIO
Dayton:
Federal Building, Rm. 506
200 W. 2nd Street, 45402
(513) 225-2720
(For Van Wort, Auglaize, Hardin, Marion, Crawford, Richland, Ashland, Wayne, Stark, Carroll, Columbiana counties and all counties north of these see Michigan listing)

OKLAHOMA
Oklahoma City:
(Mail or phone only)
200 N.W. Fifth St., 2nd Floor, 73102
(405) 231-4948
TDD-(405) 231-4614
For Forms, dial (405) 231-5208

OREGON
Portland:
Federal Bldg., Room 376
1220 S.W. Third Ave., 97204
(503) 326-3141

PENNSYLVANIA
Harrisburg:
Federal Bldg., Room 168
P.O. Box 761, 17108
(717) 782-4494

Philadelphia:
Wm. J. Green, Jr., Federal Bldg.
600 Arch Street, 19106
(215) 597-7440

Pittsburgh:
Federal Building
1000 Liberty Ave., Rm. 119, 15222
(412) 644-2755

PUERTO RICO
San Juan:
Federico Degetau Federal Building
Carlos E. Chardon Street
Hato Rey, P. R. 00918
(809) 766-5242

RHODE ISLAND
Providence:
Pastore Federal Bldg.
Room 310, Kennedy Plaza, 02903
(401) 528-5251

SOUTH CAROLINA
(See Raleigh, NC Listing)

SOUTH DAKOTA
(See Minnesota Listing)

TENNESSEE
Memphis:
200 Jefferson Avenue
Suite 1312, 38103-2335
(901) 521-3958

TEXAS
Dallas:
(Mail or phone only)
1100 Commerce St., Rm. 6B12,
75242
(214) 767-8035

San Antonio:
8610 Broadway, Rm. 305, 78217
(512) 229-6611 or 6600

UTAH
(See Colorado Listing)

VERMONT
(See New Hampshire Listing)

VIRGINIA
Norfolk:
Federal Building, Room 500
200 Granby St., 23510-1886
(804) 441-3355

WASHINGTON
Seattle:
Federal Building
915 Second Ave., 98174
(206) 442-4365

WEST VIRGINIA
Phone only:
(513) 225-2866

WISCONSIN
For Dane, Grant, Green, Iowa,
Lafayette, Rock, Jefferson,
Walworth, Milwaukee, Waukesha,
Racine, and Kenosha counties call
(312) 353-6189

(For all other Wisconsin counties
not listed above see Minnesota
listing)

WYOMING
(See Colorado Listing)

How to Start a Freelance Paralegal Business

by Linda Harrington

The best way to get into business is to do it, not talk forever about it. In fact, you may be doing it before you know that you are actually running a business.

The conservative approach to getting into freelance business it to take work on the side while you maintain a salaried position. When your side business interferes with your job, then you must decide whether or not the business is enticing enough to promote. If it is not, give up the business, keep the salaried job, and be thankful to have learned a lesson in an undramatic way about running a business.

If the business is satisfying and if you enjoy it, the time has come to devote more time and energy to it. Therefore, you will be resigning your salaried job to tackle a business.

Perhaps you have impressed your current employer enough so that he, she, or it will be your client after you resign.

Preliminary Considerations in Getting Started

What is your area of expertise? Is it likely to generate some cash for you if you go freelance? One of the areas to avoid is claimants' personal injury work where it's contingent, that is, the attorney will get a fee contingent upon success in court. It's been my experience that attorneys will pay you when they get paid on a case. So if you're working for an attorney who will pay you when that attorney gets paid and that attorney loses the case, then it's likely you won't get paid.

I work in probate. Everyone knows that death and taxes are inevitable. That being the case, I find it a very lucrative and interesting area.

An extremely important aspect of being a freelance paralegal is having a network. A network can be one of two kinds: first, a network of prior employers who respect your skills a lot and will use you when you go freelance; second, the network of your peers that's developed through paralegal associations and contacts. Both are equally important; one does not substitute for the other. I found that my activities in the local association have been extremely rewarding. They have given me leadership opportunities, the ability to learn current law from the people who work in large law firms, and a chance to meet friends who have the same kind of responsibilities I do. For the most part, my job leads have come from people I worked for before I became a freelancer.

The other part of the network to explore is the school system. The local paralegal programs can assist you a great deal in establishing a freelance business. For one thing you can teach there, and that provides some of the income you need when you're first starting a business. (The income does come slowly in a new business.) Second, if you're teaching, you're meeting people who will one day be your peers—and that's expanding your professional network. Third, many paralegal programs have work-study experiences available for the students. The students are placed in offices where they get on-the-job training. I have lots of them come to my office. That keeps my overhead down. I give the student on-the-job training in all aspects of probate and death taxes, and in return, I have people to staff my office. It benefits the school, my office, and the students as well. So there are resources, lots of resources, available from the local schools.

A high level of expertise is something that I would like to stress. I have seen a lot of people come out of paralegal training programs and not get their dream job. They then decide that they're going to open freelance business operations, knowing not too much about the practical reality of dealing with attorneys, not to mention the practical reality of working as a paralegal. *I would think that you'd need about four or five years' experience in your field before attempting to go freelance.* The first reason, of course, is that you want to have strength in your practice area and be able to handle some of the problems that you will later encounter as a freelance paralegal.

The second reason is that you have to know about attorneys. You have to know about their personalities, you have to be able to manage the problems that they often present. I tell all my students that attorneys now have to pass "arrogance" before they are allowed to take the Bar exam, and you have to learn how to deal with this attitude in as cheerful a manner as you possibly can. Dealing with attorneys is just as important an area of expertise to develop as any other aspect of expertise in a practice field. If you're going to go freelance, you have to handle the situation of hundreds of attorneys calling you up, each one considering himself or herself the most important person in the world. You have to deal with that reality.

The most important things I had to learn were to keep a sense of humor and to remember to be compulsive. Some people say that I'm a workaholic; I prefer to state that I work hard. I work very, very hard. The things that most people think are available in freelance work are independence and free time. The reality is that they don't always exist. If your office does not get the work done, the buck stops with you. You can't blame your staff. The final responsibility rests on your shoulders. If everybody else leaves and the computer breaks down, you must still perform. If you don't get it done, you face the possibility of jeopardizing your entire business operation.

Other Practical Suggestions

Step 1.   Have business cards printed. The cards should state your name, area of specialty, and telephone number.

Have an answering service. A business answering service provides a real, live voice to a caller, not a recording. It is reassuring to a potential customer to hear "a live one" on the line. Limit the service to the hours 9–5 to keep the cost of the service down.

Have "call waiting" installed by the phone company. This feature enables one line to handle several calls at once by a mere flick of a button.

Have "call forwarding" installed by the phone company. This feature enables you to have incoming calls automatically forwarded to the telephone number of your choice. If you are waiting for an important call but have a visit to make, you can have your call forwarded to your destination automatically.

Step 2. Systematize your operation immediately. The systems you will need are:

1. Calendar system
2. Timekeeping system
3. Billing system
4. Filing system for both open and closed matters
5. Procedural manual for your area of specialty

A *calendar system* should include: a master calendar that is easily spotted among clutter; a pocket calendar, which you must carry at all times; and some sort of statute-of-limitations reminder system. Many companies offer calendar systems at relatively low cost. Two are: Safeguard Business Systems and Lawfax System.

A *timekeeping system* should include: a master time record repository (separate from the case file), time slips, and decision-making on your part concerning standard charges for services and costs. It is easiest to assign a set charge for a particular service, subject to increases for complications or quirks. For example, typical time charges will be incurred for telephone calls. Assign a minimum charge for each call. Each duty should have a minimum charge assigned to it. In this way, your billing will reflect all applicable charges for the particular service involved in the transaction as well as your research, investigation, and other "write up" expenses. Costs such as photocopies should also reflect the time involved to perform the service. Therefore, standard mark-up for costs is advisable. Naturally, these are matters that are internal to the business. Therefore, establish your standards and then keep your mouth shut.

A *billing system* should include a retainer, which is received when the case work comes in, and a statement for services submitted at an advantageous time and in a personal manner which makes it clear that a bill is an important document to the sender. Set up a system for billing that is realistic. If your clients are most likely to pay on the 30th of the month, send your bills on the 25th. If your clients will not pay the bill until the receipts from the case are received, bill at the end of the work. Billing is as much psychology as anything else. Figure out when the client will want to pay and bill at that time.

A *filing system* for open cases will include: a repository for case documents, an identification system for file labels, a spot for the files to be stored; and a case matter sheet that generally describes the client, the case, and the work to be done, as well as the billing arrangements between you and the client. Casework can be stored in file folders, in binders, in boxes, and a number of other places. Make sure that all cases are stored in the same fashion and that the case files are easily located.

Closed cases should be stored and retained. A closed file system should be a numerical system. For this type of system, you need: file folders, a card file to store the case name and closed file number (retained in alphabetical order by case), and a central register to show the numbers used for previously closed files, so that the number chosen for a closed file will not have been used previously.

A procedural manual will contain: standard correspondence sent for the particular areas of law you specialize in, standard (completed) court forms used in your field, instructions to others concerning processing the documents. A procedural manual can also contain information concerning special and standard requirements of area courts, if your work involves preparing and filing court papers. The latter will help you avoid procedural errors and will save time, if it is updated regularly.

Step 3. Fix your goals, make a budget, and prepare to stick to them.

Fixing a goal involves knowing why you want to run a business. There are many reasons to want to be in business for yourself. Some are: ego gratification—now you are going to get recognition for how great you've always known you are; free time—now you can set your own hours and go to the beach whenever you want; money—now you are going to get a piece of the action and get rich.

Caution: be prepared for reality. None of your original goals will be unchanged if you are still in business one year later. Most of the people you work for will never be impressed by your brilliance—you said you could do the work, you did do the work, so what's the big deal? If you are successful, the last thing you will have is free time. Even in the beginning, your clients will want to see you or talk to you when *they* want to do so, not when you want them to. Most attorneys feel that if you only knew that they wanted to talk to you, you would jump to attention at four in the morning and be grateful for the phone call. All the money you earn will be hard earned. When you finally do earn money, some of it will go to your staff, some to your landlord, some to the IRS, and some to you.

To keep your wits about you, you must budget and you must set limits. How much of what you want do you have to receive in order to stick with it? If you want ego gratification, how many clients have to tell you you are great to make the business worthwhile? If you want free time, how much free time do you have to have to make the business worthwhile? If you want money, how much profit must you make to make the business worthwhile? The "how much" is your minimum. Obviously, the sky is the limit.

If you do not get your minimum, are you willing to quit? If not, do not go into business.

You can generally figure out how you are doing by using the following calculation: Monthly gross $\times$ 12 = Year's gross. Do not count on new business to get you by. Count on the status quo as far as income is concerned to figure out how much money you will make by December 31 and budget accordingly. If you need income from the business to pay your personal bills, how much do you need monthly? Does this leave any money to run the business? Of the money that is left, how much will be required for telephone, answering service, supplies, and other fixed expenses? Now how much is left? Use the rest for expansion of your business (equipment purchases, rent, personnel, etc.).

Step 4. Develop realistic employee relationships.

If you have done everything you can do to avoid hiring your first employee and that is not enough to keep pace with your work or to allow you the time off you desire, then it is time to hire help.

Accept what you are. You are the owner of a very small business and cannot offer big-firm benefits, bonuses, or vacations to your prospective employee.

Also, you are a person who wishes to protect your business position, so you do not want to hand your business over to a potential competitor. Last, you are a person who has certain expectations concerning job performance, productivity, and attendance. You have developed your own ideas about what constitutes a good job in your field.

Do not hire a friend. Being someone's boss does not improve a friendship when you also own the business.

Hire someone trainable. A trainable person is likely to be a recent graduate from a paralegal school. The fact that an applicant has sought education in the field and completed some or all of it is a strong indication that the person has an interest in the field and a desire for practical experience.

Do not hire someone just like you. You are the person who decided to start up the business, who worked (slaved?) to get it going, who knows everything, and who does not want to work so hard now. If you hire someone just like you, you will have two people not wanting to work so hard (you and your employee) *or* one who wants to start a business and has access to all your clients.

Establish a trial employment first. Whether you're hiring a work-study student at minimum wage from a local paralegal program or hiring an experienced person from some other source, set a review period or termination period for the relationship. Tell your employee what that period is and stick to it.

Be realistic about your employee. Because you are a small business, you cannot compete with larger firms that will offer your employee a better deal after the employee has experience and training. Therefore, accept the fact that the employee will probably move on. Tell the employee that you accept this fact and will help the person find a better position after the training has been completed (one to two years, usually). This will motivate the employee to learn as much as possible and to do a good job. This will also avoid you taking the job move personally, which any sensible employee will consider after becoming competent on the job.

Be sure you understand the tax and insurance requirements for your employee. You must have an employer I.D. number, you must withhold taxes and social security and state disability insurance, you must file quarterly reports with the taxing authorities and provide your employee with a W-2 at year end, you must have Worker's Compensation Insurance, and you must contribute as the employer into the unemployment fund and to Social Security. Each employee's salary is hardly your total cost in keeping that employee.

Have your employee work on your premises. This is mandatory during the training period, at bare minimum, so that you can become familiar with the employee's work habits and control work production.

Review the employee's time slips. The time slip review will educate you concerning how long a particular job takes the employee to perform, how many hours during the day the employee devotes to office matters, and how the cases are progressing.

Fire the hopeless. When you know that an employee is not going to work out, do not wait for the realization to come to the employee. It never will. Call the person into your office, look the person in the eyes, and tell the person how wonderful he or she is and how many fantastic qualities he or she has and how unfortunate it is that the job is so miserable for such a terrific individual and that the job just isn't good enough for such a talented person. *Or* call the person in and tell him or her that the employment is not working out and that you wish to ask for his or her resignation, to avoid the stigma to the employee of being fired. *Or* call the person in and tell him or her that you can no longer tolerate his or her presence and that he or she is fired. In whatever way you can do it, be sure that it gets done as soon as you have given up hope for improvement. That's your money that your employee is taking home every two weeks. Nothing rankles so much as feeling that you are paying for a mistake again and again.

Reward the hearty. Go out to lunch for a chat and pay the bill. Send the employee home early or give him or her a surprise day off after a hard week. Leave town yourself and let him or her have the office to himself or herself. Give bonuses when a difficult case is completed. Give a raise of one-day off a week. Compliment the employee for work well done.

Accept criticism. Your employee will probably be compelled to express criticism of the systems in your office or, perhaps, your own style. So what? This is how good ideas get born. Think about the recommendations and, if they are good ones, change your office systems.

 Conclusion

The worst way to get into business is to assume that there is no way you can fail (90% of all new businesses do fail, the Small Business Administration says), to buy the most expensive equipment, rent the most costly office space, get the most sophisticated telephone system, and generally count on the birds in the bushes before they land in your hand. Hope that you are able to start building your business slowly so that you will have time to learn about building and problem solving. Give it a good try. If it works out and if you like it, keep going. If it works out and you do not like it, or if it does not work out, then give it up and congratulate yourself on having given it a good try-out.

Murphy's Law for Paralegals

1. The day you wear comfortable, ugly old shoes is the day you are called into the managing partner's office or have to meet with an important client.

2. The day you wear attractive, stylish pumps that pinch your toes, bite your instep and chafe your heels is the day that you have to serve papers at Nick Tahou's and the Eastern School of Music—before 11 A.M. or after 2 P.M.

3. The night when you have a date, theatre tickets, or fifteen dinner guests due at 7:30 is the night you have to stay late.

4. The day your car is in the garage and you carpooled is the day that you receive a 15-hour project that has to be done before you go home.

5. Your mother, your husband, your boyfriend or your bookie always calls when the boss is standing in your office.

6. Clients that work near you never have to sign anything. The number of documents that need to be signed by a client increases in proportion to the number of miles between their home or office and your office.

7. Whatever you lost is what everyone must have immediately.

8. Whatever can't be found was last in the possession of a paralegal.

9. Whatever needs to be hand delivered or picked up is always beyond the messenger's responsibility.

10. The day you have liverwurst and onion for lunch is the day that you have to attend an unscheduled meeting with an important client or another attorney.

11. The volume of Carmody-Wait 2nd that you require to prepare a motion is always missing from the library.

12. Nobody ever asks you about subjects with which you are familiar. If you are an expert on the mating habits of mosquitoes, you will be asked to digest a deposition or prepare research about the malfunction of the farabus and ullie pin connection in Yugoslavian lawnmowers.

Ciaccia, *Murphy's Laws for Paralegals*, 9 Newsletter 12 (Dallas Ass'n of Legal Assistants, Sept. 1985).

# Glossary

AAfPE American Association for Paralegal Education.

ABA American Bar Association.

Accounts Receivable A list of who owes money to the office, how much, how long the debt has been due, etc.

Accreditation The process by which an organization evaluates and recognizes a program of study (or an institution) as meeting specified qualifications or standards.

Acquit To find not guilty.

Act *See* Statute.

Ad Damnum The amount of damages claimed in the complaint.

Adjudication The process by which a court resolves a legal dispute through litigation. The verb is *adjudicate*.

Administrative Agency A unit of government whose primary mission is to carry out or administer the statutes of the legislature and the executive orders of the chief of the executive branch.

Administrative Code A collection of administrative regulations organized by subject matter.

Administrative Decision A resolution of a controversy involving application of the regulations of an administrative agency or its governing statutes and executive orders. Also called a *ruling*.

Administrative Hearing A proceeding at an administrative agency presided over by a hearing officer (e.g., an Administrative Law Judge) to resolve a controversy.

Administrative Law Judge A hearing officer who presides over a hearing at an administrative agency.

Administrative Procedure Act The statute that governs aspects of procedure before administrative agencies.

Administrative Regulation A law of an administrative agency designed to explain or carry out the statutes and executive orders that govern the agency. Also called a *rule*.

Admiralty Law An area of the law that covers accidents and injuries on navigable waters. Also called *maritime law*.

Admissible Evidence Evidence that a judge will allow a jury to consider.

Admission An out-of-court statement made by a party to the litigation that is inconsistent with a position the party is taking in the litigation. (An exception to the hearsay rule.)

Admonition A nonpublic declaration that the attorney's conduct was improper. This does not affect his or her right to practice. Also called a private reprimand.

ADR Alternative dispute resolution.

Adversarial Hearing A proceeding in which both parties to a controversy appear before a judge.

Adversarial Memorandum *See* Memorandum of Law.

Adversarial System Justice and truth have a greater chance of emerging when parties to a controversy appear before a neutral judge and jury to argue their conflicting positions.

Adverse Interests Opposing purposes or claims.

Adverse Judgment A judgment or decision against you.

Advice *See* Professional Judgment.

Advocacy An attempt to influence actions of others.

Affiant *See* Affidavit.

Affidavit A written statement of fact in which a person (called the affiant) swears that the statement is true.

Affiliate Member *See* Associate Member.

Affirmation of Professional Responsibility A statement of the ethical guidelines of the National Federation of Paralegal Associations.

Affirmative Defense A defense that is based on new factual allegations by the defendant not contained in the plaintiff's allegations.

Agency Practitioner An individual authorized to practice before an administrative agency. This individual often does not have to be an attorney.

Aging Report A listing of accounts receivable indicating the time outstanding on each account.

ALA Association of Legal Administrators.

Allegation A claimed fact.

Ambulance Chasing Aggressively going to individuals with potentially good claims as plaintiffs (e.g., personal-injury victims) to encourage them to hire a particular attorney. If the attorney uses someone else to do the soliciting, the latter is called a *runner*. If this other person uses deception or fraud in the solicitation, he or she is sometimes called a *capper*.

Amicus Curiae Brief A friend-of-the-court brief. An appellate brief submitted by someone who is not a party to the litigation.

Analogous Sufficiently similar in the facts and law being applied. Also referred to as *on point*.

Annotated Code/Annotated Statutes A collection of statutes organized by subject matter, along with notes and commentary.

Annotation The notes and commentary that follow opinions printed in A.L.R., A.L.R.2d, etc.

Answer The pleading that responds to or answers the allegations of the complaint.

Antitrust Law The law governing unlawful restraints of trade, price fixing, and monopolies.

APA *See* Administrative Procedure Act.

Appeal as a Matter of Right The appeal of a case that an appellate court must hear; it has no discretion on whether to take the appeal.

Appearance Going to court to act on behalf of a party to the litigation. The first time this is done, the attorney files a *notice of appearance*.

Appellant The party bringing an appeal because of dissatisfaction with something the lower tribunal did.

Appellate Brief A document submitted to an appellate court containing arguments on whether a lower court made errors of law.

Appellate Jurisdiction The power of a court to hear an appeal of a case from a lower tribunal to determine whether it made any errors of law.

Appellee The party against whom an appeal is brought. Also called the *respondent*.

Appendixes Additions to a volume or document printed after the body of the text.

Apprentice A person in training for an occupation under the supervision of a full member of that occupation.

Approval The recognition that comes from accreditation, certification, licensure, or registration. The ABA uses *approval* as a substitute for the word *accreditation*.

Approval Commission A group of individuals who investigate whether a paralegal school meets the criteria for approval established by the ABA.

Arbitration In lieu of litigation, both sides agree to allow a neutral third party to resolve their dispute.

Arraignment A court proceeding in which the defendant is formally charged with a crime and enters a plea.

Arrest To take someone into custody in order to bring him or her before the proper authorities.

Assigned Counsel An attorney appointed by the court and paid with government funds to represent an individual who cannot afford to hire an attorney.

Associate An attorney employee of a law firm who hopes eventually to become a partner.

Associated Pertaining to an attorney who is an associate in a law firm.

Associate Member A nonattorney who is allowed to become part of—but not a full member of—a bar association. Sometimes called *affiliate member*.

Attestation Clause A clause stating that a person saw a witness sign a document.

Attorney Attestation A signed statement by an attorney that a paralegal applying for membership in a paralegal association meets designated criteria of the association, e.g., is employed as a paralegal.

Attorney–Client Privilege A client and an attorney can refuse to disclose communications between them whose purpose was to facilitate the provision of legal services for the client.

Attorney General The chief attorney for the government. *See also* Opinion of the Attorney General.

Attorney of Record The attorney who has filed a notice of appearance. *See also* Appearance.

Attorney Work Product *See* Work-Product Rule.

Authentication Evidence that a writing or other physical item is genuine and is what it purports to be.

Authority Anything that a court could rely on in reaching its decision.

Authorized Practice of Law Services that constitute the practice of law which a nonattorney has authorization to provide. *See also* Practice of Law, Professional Judgment.

Automatic Pagination A feature that enables a word processor to number the pages of the printed page automatically.

Background Research Checking secondary sources to give you a general understanding of an area of law that is new to you.

Backup To copy information.

Bail Property or a sum of money deposited with the court to ensure that the defendant will reappear in court at designated times.

Bailiff A court employee who keeps order in the courtroom and renders general administrative assistance to the judge.

Bar Prevent or stop.

Bar Coding A series of lines of different widths that can be read by a scanner.

Barratry Stirring up quarrels or litigation; illegal solicitation of clients.

Barrister   A lawyer in England who represents clients in the higher courts.

Bar Treaties   Agreements between attorneys and other occupations on what law-related activities of these other occupations do and do not constitute the unauthorized practice of law.

Baud Rate   A unit of measurement used to indicate the speed of transmission over a modem.

Below   (1) The lower tribunal that heard the case before it was appealed. (2) Later in the document.

Best Evidence Rule   To prove the contents of a private writing, the original writing should be produced unless it is unavailable.

Beyond a Reasonable Doubt   There is no reasonable doubt that every one of the elements of the crime has been established.

Bias   Unfairly leaning in favor of or against someone; the potential for unfairness because of prior knowledge or involvement, leading to possible preconceptions and a lack of open-mindedness.

Bicameral   Having two houses in the legislature. If there is only one house, it is *unicameral.*

Bill   A proposed statute.

Billable Tasks   Those tasks requiring time that can be charged to a client.

Billing Memorandum   A draft client bill which states disbursements, time expended, and billing rates of those working on the matter.

Blended Hourly Rate   A rate is set depending on the mix of partners and associates working on the case.

Blind Ad   A want ad that does not print the name and address of the prospective employer. The contact is made through a third party, e.g., the newspaper.

Block   A group of characters, e.g., a word, a sentence, a paragraph. Block movement is a feature of a word processor that allows the user to define a block of text and then do something with that block, e.g., move it, delete it.

Board of Appeals   The unit within an administrative agency to which a party can appeal a decision of the agency.

Boilerplate   Standard language that is commonly used in a certain kind of document.

Boldface   Heavier or darker than normal type.

Bond   A sum of money deposited in court to ensure compliance with a requirement.

Brief   *See* Appellate Brief, Brief of a Case, Trial Brief.

Brief of a Case   A set of notes on the essential parts of a court opinion, e.g., facts, issues, holding, reasoning.

"Bugs"   Manufacturing or design errors that exist in products such as computer hardware or software.

Bulletin Board   An inexpensive, relatively small, user-run version of a commercial information service.

Bundled/Unbundled   An hourly rate is *bundled* if overhead is included in this rate. It is *unbundled* if the various charges are broken out separately.

Burden of Proof   The responsibility of proving a fact at trial.

Business Entry   An out-of-court statement found in business records made in the regular course of business by someone whose duty is to make such entries. (An exception to the hearsay rule.)

Byte   The storage equivalent of one letter, one punctuation mark, or one blank space typed into the computer.

CALR   Computer-Assisted Legal Research.

Capital Partner   *See* Income Partner.

Capper   *See* Ambulance Chasing.

Career Ladder   A formal promotion structure within a company or office.

Case   (1) A legal matter in dispute or potential dispute. (2) The written decision of a court. *See also* Opinion.

Casebook   A law-school textbook containing numerous edited court opinions.

Case Clerk   An assistant to a paralegal; an entry-level paralegal.

Case Manager   An experienced legal assistant who can coordinate or direct legal assistant activities on a major case or transaction.

Cause of Action   A legally acceptable reason for suing.

Cell   A storage location within a spreadsheet, used to store a single piece of information that is relevant to the spreadsheet.

Censure   A formal disapproval or declaration of blame. *See also* Reprimand.

Certificated   Having met the qualifications for certification from a school or training program.

Certification   The process by which a nongovernmental organization grants recognition to an individual who has met qualifications specified by that organization. *See also* Specialty Certification.

Certified   Having complied with or met the qualifications for certification.

Certified Legal Assistant (CLA)   The title bestowed by the National Association of Legal Assistants on a paralegal who has passed the CLA exam and has met other criteria of NALA. *See also* Specialty Certification.

Certified PLS A Certified Professional Legal Secretary. This status is achieved after passing an examination and meeting other requirements of NALS, the National Association of Legal Secretaries.

CFLA Certified Florida Legal Assistant. To earn this title, a paralegal must first pass the CLA (Certified Legal Assistant) exam of NALA, and then pass a special exam on Florida law.

Character A letter, number, or symbol. Character enhancement includes underlining, boldfacing, subscripting, and superscripting.

Chargeable Hour Schedule A report that summarizes hours invested by attorneys and paralegals, usually on a monthly basis.

Charge to Jury Instructions to the jury on how to go about determining the facts and reaching its verdict.

Charter The fundamental law of a municipality or other local unit of government authorizing it to perform designated governmental functions.

Chinese Wall Steps taken to prevent a tainted employee (attorney, paralegal, or secretary) from having any contact with the case of a particular client in the office. The employee is tainted because he or she has a conflict of interest with that client. A Chinese wall is also called an *ethical wall*. A tainted employee is also called a *contaminated employee*. Once the Chinese wall is set up around the tainted employee, the latter is referred to as a *quarantined employee*.

Circumstantial Evidence Evidence of one fact from which another fact can be inferred.

Citation A reference to any written material. It is the "address" where the material can be found in the library. Also called a *cite*.

Cite (1) A citation. (2) To give the volume and page number, name of the book, etc. where written material can be found in a library.

Cite Checking Reading every cite in a document to determine whether the format of the cite conforms to the citation rules being used (e.g., the Bluebook rules), whether the quotations in the cite are accurate, etc.

Civil Dispute One private party suing another, or a private party suing the government, or the government suing a private party for a matter other than the commission of a crime.

CLA *See* Certified Legal Assistant.

Claims-Made Policy Insurance that covers only claims actually filed (i.e., made) during the period in which the policy is in effect.

CLAS Certified Legal Assistant Specialist (an advanced certification status of NALA).

CLE Continuing Legal Education. Undertaken after an individual has received his or her primary education or training in a law-related occupation.

Clergy-Penitent Privilege A member of the clergy and a penitent can refuse to disclose communications between them that relate to spiritual counseling or consultation.

Closed-Ended Question A relatively narrow question (e.g., how old are you?) that discourages the interviewee from rambling. Also called a *directed question*.

Closing The event during which steps are taken to finalize the transfer of an interest in property.

Code A set of rules, organized by subject matter.

Codefendant More than one defendant being sued in a civil case (or prosecuted in a criminal case) in the same litigation.

Code of Ethics and Professional Responsibility A statement of the ethical guidelines of the National Association of Legal Assistants.

Codify To arrange material by subject matter.

Command An instruction typed into a computer.

Commingling Mixing general law firms funds with client funds in a single account.

Common Law Judge-made law in the absence of controlling statutory law or other higher law. *See also* Enacted Law.

Common Representation *See* Multiple Representation.

Communications A program that allows computers to communicate with each other, usually through telephone lines. *See also* Modem.

Compatible (1) Information generated on an IBM computer that can also be used by another computer. (2) A program designed for an IBM computer that can also be run by other computers.

Competence, Attorney Having the knowledge and skill that is reasonably necessary to represent a particular client.

Competent (evidence) Capable of giving testimony because the person understands the obligation to tell the truth, has the ability to communicate, and has knowledge of the topic of his or her testimony.

Complaint The pleading filed by the plaintiff that tries to state a claim or cause of action against the defendant.

Concurrent Jurisdiction The power of a court to hear a particular kind of case, along with other courts that could also hear it.

Concurring Opinion An opinion written by less than a majority of the judges on the court that agrees with the *result* reached by the majority but not with all of its reasoning.

Conference Committee A committee made up of members of both houses of the legislature which meets to try to resolve differences in the versions of a bill that each house passed.

Confidential That which should not be revealed; pertaining to information that others do not have a right to receive.

Conflict of Interest Divided loyalty that actually or potentially places one of the participants to whom undivided loyalty is owed at a disadvantage. *See also* Divided Loyalty.

Conflicts Check A check of the client files of a law firm to help determine whether a conflict of interest might exist between a prospective client and current or past clients. The person performing this check is often called a *conflicts specialist.*

Conflicts of Law An area of the law that determines what law applies when a choice must be made between the laws of different, coequal legal systems, e.g., two states.

Confrontation The right to face your accuser.

Connectors Characters, words, or symbols used to show the relationship between the words and phrases in a query.

Constitution The fundamental law that creates the branches of government and that identifies basic rights and obligations.

Contaminated Paralegal *See* Chinese Wall.

Contest To challenge.

Contingent Fee A fee that is dependent on the outcome of the case.

Contract Attorney *See* Project Attorney.

Contract Paralegal A self-employed paralegal who often works for several different attorneys on a freelance basis. *See also* Freelance Paralegal.

Control Character A coded character that does not print but is part of the command sequence in a word processor.

Coordinates In a spreadsheet program, the column letter and row number that define the location of a specific cell.

Corporate Counsel The chief attorney of a corporation. Also called the *general counsel.*

Corporate Legal Department The law office within a corporation containing salaried attorneys (in-house attorneys) who advise and represent the corporation.

Counterclaim A claim or cause of action against the plaintiff stated in the defendant's answer.

Court of First Instance A trial court; a court with original jurisdiction.

Credentialization A form of official recognition based on one's training or employment status.

Credible Believable.

Criminal Dispute A suit brought by the government for the alleged commission of a crime.

Cross-examination Questioning the witness called by the other side after direct examination.

Cured Corrected.

Cursor The marker on the display screen indicating where the next character can be displayed.

Daisy Wheel Printer A printer which uses a device resembling a flower that contains the alphabet and other characters on spokes.

Damages An award of money paid by the wrongdoer to compensate the person who has been harmed.

Data Information that can be used by a computer.

Database A program used to store and organize information; a grouping of independent files into one integrated whole that can be accessed through one central point.

Data Manager A data management software package that consolidates data files into an integrated whole, allowing access to more than one data file at a time.

Data Redundancy The repetition of the same data in several different files.

Decision *See* Administrative Decision, Opinion.

Declaration against Interest An out-of-court statement made by a nonparty to the litigation that is against the interest of that nonparty. (An exception to the hearsay rule.)

Declaration of Bodily Feelings An out-of-court statement or utterance made spontaneously about the person's present bodily condition. (An exception to the hearsay rule.)

Declaration of Mental State of Mind An out-of-court statement made about the person's present state of mind. (An exception to the hearsay rule.)

Declaration of Present Sense Impression An out-of-court statement that describes an event while it is being observed by the person making the statement. (An exception to the hearsay rule.)

Dedicated Word Processor A system that can perform only word processing tasks.

Deep Pocket Slang for the person or organization with enough money or other assets to be able to pay a judgment.

Default Judgment A judgment for the plaintiff because the defendant failed to appear or to file an answer before the deadline.

Default Setting A value used by the word processor when it is not instructed to use any other value.

Defense An allegation of fact or the presentation of a legal theory that is offered to offset or defeat a claim or demand.

"Delegatitis" An inordinate fear of delegating tasks to others.

Deletion A feature of a word processor that allows you to remove a character, word, sentence, or larger block of text from the existing text.

Demurrer Even if the plaintiff proved all the facts stated in the complaint, a cause of action would not be established.

Denturist A nondentist who produces and dispenses removable dentures directly to the public.

Deponent *See* Deposition.

Deposition A pretrial discovery device consisting of a question-and-answer session involving a party or witness designed to assist the other party prepare for trial. The person who is questioned is called the *deponent*.

Depo Summarizer An employee whose main job is digesting discovery documents.

Dictum A statement made by a court that was not necessary to resolve the specific legal issues before the court. The plural of dictum is dicta.

Digesting Summarizing discovery documents. *See also* Depo Summarizer.

Digests (1) Volumes that contain summaries of court opinions. These summaries are sometimes called *abstracts* or *squibs*. (2) Volumes that contain summaries of annotations in A.L.R., A.L.R.2d, etc.

Directed Question *See* Closed-Ended Question.

Direct Evidence Evidence that tends to establish a fact (or to disprove a fact) without the need for an inference.

Direct Examination The first questioning of a witness you have called.

Disbarment The temporary or permanent termination of the right to practice law.

Disbursements Out-of-pocket expenses.

Disciplinary Rule (DR) *See* Model Code of Professional Responsibility.

Discount Adjustment A write down (decrease) in the bill.

Discoverable Obtainable through one of the devices of pretrial discovery, e.g., interrogatories.

Discovery Pretrial devices designed to assist a party prepare for trial. *See* Deposition, Interrogatories.

Disinterested Not working for one side or the other in a controversy or other legal matter; not deriving benefit if one of the sides prevails.

Disk Drive Hardware used to store and retrieve programs and information to and from diskettes.

Diskette A flat piece of plastic on which information can be placed or removed by the computer.

Disqualification *See* Vicarious Disqualification.

Dissenting Opinion An opinion that disagrees with the result and the reasoning used by the majority.

District Court *See* United States District Court.

Diversity of Citizenship The parties to the litigation are from different states, and the amount in controversy exceeds the amount specified by federal statute.

Divided Loyalty The responsibility of protecting the interest of parties who are competitors or are otherwise at odds with each other. *See also* Conflict of Interest.

Docket Number The number assigned to a case by the court.

Doctor-Patient Privilege A doctor and a patient can refuse to disclose any confidential (private) communications between them that relate to medical care.

Document Clerk An individual whose main responsibility is to organize, file, code, or digest litigation or other client documents.

Documentation The manual on operating a computer; the accompanying documents.

Dot Matrix Printer A printer which uses tiny pins that press against or punch a ribbon to create a pattern of dots.

Double Density The disk drive can store information on the diskette in condensed mode.

Downtime The period during which the computer is unavailable because of technical difficulties.

DR Disciplinary Rule. *See* Model Code of Professional Responsibility.

Draft Write.

Draft Bill *See* Billing Memorandum.

Draw A partner's advance against profits.

Dual Sided The disk drive is capable of writing on both sides of the diskette.

Dying Declaration An out-of-court statement concerning the causes or circumstances of death made by a person whose death is imminent. (An exception to the hearsay rule.)

EC Ethical Consideration. *See* Model Code of Professional Responsibility.

Editing In word processing, the act of changing or amending text.

EEOC Equal Employment Opportunity Commission, a federal agency that investigates job discrimination.

Element A portion of a rule which is a precondition of the applicability of the entire rule. The *element in contention* is the element of the rule about which the parties cannot agree. The disagreement may be over the meaning of the element or how it applies to a given set of facts.

Enacted Law Law written by the legislature (statutes), by the people (constitutions), and by an administrative agency (regulations). Law that is not the product of adjudication. *See* Adjudication.

En Banc By the entire court.

Enrolled Agent An individual authorized to represent taxpayers at all administrative proceedings within the Internal Revenue Service—this person does not have to be an attorney.

Enrollment *See* Registration.

Entry-Level Certification Certification of individuals who have just begun their careers.

Equity Partner A full owner of a law firm. *See also* Income Partner.

Estate All the property left by a decedent from which his or her debts can be paid.

Et al. And others.

Ethical Wall *See* Chinese Wall.

Ethical Consideration (EC) *See* Model Code of Professional Responsibility.

Ethics Rules embodying standards of behavior to which members of an organization are expected to conform.

Et Seq. And following.

Evidence That which is offered to help establish or disprove a factual position. A separate determination must be made on whether a particular item of evidence is relevant or irrelevant, admissible or inadmissible, etc.

Exclusive Jurisdiction The power of a court to hear a particular kind of case, to the exclusion of other courts.

Execution Carrying out or enforcing a judgment.

Executive Branch The branch of government that carries out, executes, or administers the law.

Executive Department Agency An administrative agency that exists within the executive branch of government, often at the cabinet level.

Executive Order A law passed by the chief executive pursuant to a specific statutory authority or to the executive's inherent authority.

Exempt Employee An employee who is not entitled to overtime compensation under the Fair Labor Standards Act because the employee is a professional, administrative, or executive employee. Paralegals are nonexempt, except for paralegal managers.

Ex Parte Hearing A hearing at which only one party is present. A court order issued at such a hearing is an *ex parte order.*

Fact Particularization A technique designed to help you list numerous factual questions in order to obtain a comprehensive picture of all the facts that are relevant to a legal matter.

Facts & Findings A periodical of the National Association of Legal Assistants.

Fair Labor Standards Act The federal statute that regulates conditions of employment such as when overtime compensation must be paid. *See also* Exempt Employee.

Federalism The coexistence of, and the interrelationships among, the state governments and the federal government, particularly with respect to the powers of each of these levels of government.

Federal Question A legal question that arises from the application of the United States Constitution, a statute of Congress, or a federal administrative regulation.

Fee-Generating Case The case of a client who can pay a fee out of the damages awarded or from his or her independent resources.

Fee Splitting A single client bill covering the fee of two or more attorneys who are not in the same firm.

Felony A crime punishable by a sentence of one year or more.

Field A subdivision of a record that holds a meaningful item of data, e.g., an employee number.

Field Search In WESTLAW, a search that is limited to a certain part of cases in its databases.

File A group of related data records, e.g., employee records.

Filed Formally presented to a court.

First Instance, Court of A trial court; a court with original jurisdiction.

Fixed Fee A flat fee for services. A set amount paid regardless of the outcome of the case or the amount of time needed to complete it.

Floppy Disk A disk drive that can use diskettes.

Format In word processing, the layout of the page, e.g., the number of lines and margin settings.

Formbook   A manual that contains forms, checklists, practice techniques, etc. Also called a *practice manual* or *handbook.*

Formula   A mathematical expression that is used in a spreadsheet.

Forum   The court where the case is to be tried.

Forwarding Fee   *See* Referral Fee.

FRCP   Federal Rules of Civil Procedure.

Freedom of Information Act   A statute that gives citizens access to certain information in the possession of the government.

Freelance Paralegal   A self-employed paralegal who works for several different attorneys, or a self-employed paralegal who works directly for the public. Also referred to as an *independent paralegal.*

Friendly Divorce   A divorce proceeding in which the parties have no significant disputes between them.

Full-Text Search   A search through all of the information in a database.

Functional Resume   A resume that clusters skills and talents together regardless of when they were developed.

General Counsel   The chief attorney in a corporate law department.

General Jurisdiction   The power of the court (within its geographic boundaries) to hear any kind of case, with certain exceptions.

General Practitioner   An attorney who handles any kind of case.

General Schedule (GS)   The pay-scale system used in the federal government.

Geographic Jurisdiction   The area of the state or country over which a court has power to render decisions.

Global   In word processing, an instruction that will be carried out throughout the document.

Go Bare   To engage in an occupation or profession without malpractice insurance.

GOD   The "Great Overtime Debate." *See* Exempt Employee.

Grand Jury   A special jury whose duty is to hear evidence of felonies presented by the prosecutor to determine whether there is sufficient evidence to return an indictment against the defendant and cause him or her to stand trial on the charges.

Grounds   Reasons.

Group Legal Services   A form of legal insurance in which members of a group pay a set amount on a regular basis, for which they receive designated legal services. Also called *prepaid legal services.*

GS   *See* General Schedule.

Guideline   Suggested conduct that will help an applicant obtain accreditation, certification, licensure, registration, or approval.

HALT   Help Abolish Legal Tyranny, an organization that seeks to reform the legal profession, primarily by eliminating the monopoly of attorneys over the practice of law.

Handbook   *See* Formbook.

Harassment   *See* Hostile Environment, Quid Pro Quo Harassment.

Hard Disk   A disk drive that cannot be removed without taking the hardware apart.

Hardware   The computer and its physical parts.

Header   In word processing, a piece of text that is stored separately from the text and printed at the top of each page.

Heading   The beginning of a memorandum that lists who the memo is for, who wrote it, what it is about, etc.

Headnote   A small-paragraph summary of a portion of a court opinion, written by a private publisher.

Hearing Examiner   One who presides over an administrative hearing.

Hearsay   Testimony in court, or written evidence, of a statement made out of court when the statement is offered to show the truth of matters asserted therein, and thus resting for its value on the credibility of the out-of-court asserter.

Holding   A court's answer to one of the legal issues in the case. Also called a *ruling.*

Hornbook   A treatise that summarizes an area of the law.

Hostile Environment Harassment   Pervasive unwelcome sexual conduct or sex-based ridicule which unreasonably interferes with an individual's job performance or creates an intimidating, hostile, or offensive working environment.

Hourly Plus Fixed Fee   A specified hourly rate is used until the nature and scope of the problem are defined; a fixed fee is used thereafter.

Id.   Same citation as immediately above.

Impaired Attorney   An attorney with a drug or alcohol problem.

Impaneled   Selected, sworn in, and seated.

Impeach   To challenge; to attack the credibility of.

Imputed Disqualification   *See* Vicarious Disqualification.

Income Partner A special category of partner who does not own the firm in the sense of a full equity or capital partner. Also called a *permanent associate* and a *non-equity partner.*

Incremental Spacing In word processing, a method by which the printer inserts spaces between words and letters to produce margins that are justified. Also called *microspacing.*

Independent Contractor One who operates his or her own business and contracts to do work for others who do not control the details of how that work is performed.

Independent Paralegal *See* Freelance Paralegal.

Independent Regulatory Agency An administrative agency (often existing outside of the executive department) created to regulate an aspect of society.

Indictment A formal document issued by a grand jury accusing the defendant of a crime. *See also* Grand Jury.

Indigent Poor, unable to pay for needed services.

Inferior Court A lower court.

Information A document accusing the defendant of a crime (used in states without a grand jury system).

Informational Interview An interview in which you find out about a particular kind of employment. It is *not* a job interview.

Infra Below, mentioned or referred to later in the document.

In-house Attorney An attorney who is an employee of a business corporation. *See* Corporate Legal Department.

In Issue In dispute or question.

Ink Jct Printer A printer that uses a stream of ink sprayed on paper to produce the print.

In Personam Jurisdiction *See* Personal Jurisdiction.

In Re In the matter of.

Insertion In word processing, a feature by which a character, word, sentence, or larger block of text is added to the existing text.

Instrument A formal document that gives expression to a legal act or agreement, e.g., a mortgage.

Intake Memo A memorandum that summarizes the facts given by a client upon becoming a client of the office.

Integrated Bar Association A state bar association to which an attorney must belong in order to practice law in the state. Also called a *mandatory* or *unified bar association.*

Integrated Package A software program that enables the user to use more than one kind of program simulta-

neously, e.g., word processing, database management, spreadsheet.

Intellectual Property Law The law governing patents, copyrights, trademarks, and trade names.

Interim Suspension A temporary suspension, pending the imposition of final discipline.

Interlocutory Appeal An appeal of a trial court ruling before the trial court reaches its final judgment.

Intermediate Appellate Court A court with appellate jurisdiction to which parties can appeal before they appeal to the highest court in the judicial system.

Interrogatories A pretrial discovery device consisting of written questions sent by one party to another to assist the sender of the questions to prepare for trial.

Intra-agency Appeal An appeal within an administrative agency, before the case is appealed to a court.

Jailhouse Lawyer A paralegal in prison, usually self-taught, who has a limited right to practice law and to give legal advice to fellow inmates if the prison does not provide adequate alternatives for legal services. Also known as a *writ writer.*

Jargon Technical language; language that does not have an everyday meaning.

Job Bank A service that lists available jobs, usually available only to members of an organization.

Judgment The decision of the court on the controversy before it.

Judgment Creditor The party to whom damages must be paid.

Judgment Debtor The party who must pay damages.

Judicare A system of paying private attorneys to provide legal services to the poor on a case-by-case basis.

Judicial Branch The branch of government with primary responsibility for interpreting laws and resolving disputes that arise under them.

Jurisdiction The power of a court. *See also* Geographic Jurisdiction, Subject-Matter Jurisdiction.

Justification In word processing, a feature for making lines of text even at the margins.

K A measure of capacity in a computer system.

Key Fact A critical fact; a fact that was very important or essential to the holding of the court.

Key-Word Search A search through a list of specified words that function like an index to a database.

Label Information used for describing some aspect of a spreadsheet.

LAMA Legal Assistants Management Association.

Landmen Paralegals who work in the area of oil and gas law. Also called *land technicians.*

Language A program that allows a computer to understand commands and to carry them out.

Laptop A portable computer, often powered by a rechargeable battery.

Laser Printer A printer that uses a laser beam of light to reproduce images.

Lateral Hire An attorney, paralegal, or secretary who has been hired from another law office.

Law Clerk An employee of an attorney who is in law school studying to become an attorney or who has graduated from law school and is waiting to pass the bar examination. In Ontario, Canada, a law clerk is a trained professional doing independent legal work, which may include managerial duties, under the direction and guidance of a lawyer, and whose function is to relieve a lawyer of routine and administrative matters and to assist a lawyer in the more complex ones.

Law Directory A list of attorneys.

Law Review A legal periodical published by a law school. Sometimes called a *law journal.*

Lay Opinion Evidence The opinion of someone who is not an expert.

Leading Question A question that suggests an answer within the question.

Legal Administrator An individual, usually a nonattorney, with broad management responsibility for a law office.

Legal Advice *See* Professional Judgment.

Legal Analysis The process of connecting a rule of law to a set of facts in order to determine how that rule might apply to a particular situation. The goal of the process is to solve a legal dispute or to prevent one from arising.

Legal Assistant *See* Paralegal.

Legal Assistant Clerk A person who assists a legal assistant in clerical tasks such as document numbering, alphabetizing, filing, and any other project that does not require substantive knowledge of litigation or of a particular transaction. *See also* Document Clerk.

Legal Assistant Division A few state bar associations, e.g., Texas, have established special divisions which paralegals can join as associate members.

Legal Assistant Manager A person responsible for recruiting, interviewing, and hiring legal assistants who spends little or no time working on client cases as a legal assistant. He or she may also be substantially involved in other matters pertaining to legal assistants, e.g., training, monitoring work assignments, designing budgets, and overseeing the billing of paralegal time. Also known as a *paralegal manager.*

Legal Bias *See* Bias.

Legal Executive A trained and certified employee of a solicitor in England; the equivalent of an American paralegal but with more training and credentials.

Legal Insurance *See* Group Legal Services.

Legal Issue A question of law; a question of what the law is, or what the law means, or how the law applies to a set of facts. If the dispute is over the truth or falsity of the facts, it is referred to as a *question of fact* or a *factual dispute.*

Legalman A nonattorney in the Navy who assists attorneys in the practice of law.

Legal Technician A self-employed paralegal who works for several different attorneys, or a self-employed paralegal who works directly for the public. Sometimes called an *independent paralegal* or a *freelance paralegal.*

Legislation (1) The process of making statutory law. (2) A statute.

Legislative Branch The branch of government with primary responsibility for making or enacting the law.

Legislative History All of the events that occur in the legislature before a bill is enacted into a statute.

Letterhead The top part of stationery which identifies the name and address of the office (often with the names of selected employees).

Leverage The ability to make a profit from the income-generating work of others.

LEXIS The legal research computer service of Mead Data Co.

Liable Legally responsible.

Licensed Independent Paralegal A paralegal who holds a limited license. *See* Limited Licensure.

Licensure The process by which an agency of government grants permission to persons meeting specified qualifications to engage in an occupation and to use a particular title.

Limited Jurisdiction The power of a court to hear only certain kinds of cases. Also called *special jurisdiction.*

Limited Licensure The process by which an agency of government grants permission to persons meeting specified qualifications to engage in designated activities that are now customarily (although not always exclusively) performed by another license holder, i.e., that are part of someone else's monopoly.

Limited Practice Officer A nonattorney in Washington state who has the authority to select and prepare designated legal documents pertaining to real estate closings.

Litigation The formal process of resolving legal controversies through special tribunals established for this purpose. The major tribunal is a court.

Load To move a program or information from a disk drive into the computer.

Lodestar A mathematical formula based on a multiplier which relies on hourly rates and other factors.

Magistrate A judicial officer having some but not all the powers of a judge.

Majority Opinion The opinion whose result and reasoning is supported by at least half plus one of the judges on the court.

Malpractice Serious wrongful conduct committed by an individual, usually a member of a profession.

Mandatory Bar Association *See* Integrated Bar Association.

Marital Communications A husband and a wife can refuse to disclose communications between them during the marriage.

Maritime Law *See* Admiralty Law.

Market Rate The prevailing rate in the area.

Martindale–Hubbell A national directory of attorneys.

Mediation In lieu of litigation, a neutral third party (the mediator) tries to encourage the parties to a dispute to reach a compromise.

Memorandum of Law A memorandum is simply a note, a comment, or a report. A legal memorandum is a written explanation of what the law is and how it might apply to a fact situation.

Memory The area inside the computer that contains programs, and data which the programs help generate.

Menu In word processing and other programs, a list of commands or prompts on the display screen.

Merge Printing In word processing and other programs, a feature that allows a user to combine whole files and to place data from one file into specified locations in another.

Microcomputer A computer small enough to fit on a desk.

Minimum-Fee Schedule A published list of fees recommended by a bar association.

Misdemeanor A crime punishable by a sentence of less than a year.

Model Code of Professional Responsibility An earlier edition of the ethical rules governing attorneys recommended by the American Bar Association. The Model Code consisted of Ethical Considerations (ECs), which represented the objectives toward which each attorney

should strive, and Disciplinary Rules (DRs), which were mandatory statements of the minimum conduct below which no attorney could fall without being subject to discipline.

Model Rules of Professional Conduct The current set of ethical rules governing attorneys recommended by the American Bar Association. These rules revised the ABA's earlier rules found in the Model Code of Professional Responsibility.

Model Standards and Guidelines for Utilization of Legal Assistants A statement of ethical and related guidelines of the National Association of Legal Assistants.

Modem A device that allows one computer to send and receive information using regular telephone lines.

Monitor A display screen; a TV-like device used to display what is typed at the keyboard and the response of the computer.

Mouse A clicking device used as a partial substitute for typing commands into a computer.

Multiple Representation Representing more than one side in a legal matter or controversy. Also called *common representation*.

Multitasking Having the capacity to run several large programs simultaneously.

NALA National Association of Legal Assistants.

NALS National Association of Legal Secretaries. *See also* Certified PLS.

National Paralegal Reporter A periodical of the National Federation of Paralegal Associations.

Neighborhood Legal Service Office A law office that serves the legal needs of the poor, often publicly funded.

Network Several computers connected together to share printers or hard disk drives.

Networking Establishing contacts with a relatively large number of people who might be helpful to you later. Similarly, you become such a contact for others.

NFPA National Federation of Paralegal Associations.

Nonadversarial Proceeding Only one party appears in the proceeding, or both parties appear but they have no real controversy between them.

Nonbillable task A task for which an office cannot bill a client.

Nonequity Partner *See* Income Partner.

Nonexempt Employee *See* Exempt Employee.

Nonrebuttable Presumption *See* Presumption.

Notary Public A person who witnesses (i.e., attests to the authenticity of) signatures, administers oaths, and performs related tasks. In Europe, a notary often has more extensive authority.

Occurrence Policy   Malpractice insurance that covers all occurrences (e.g., a negligent error or omission) during the period the policy is in effect, even if the claim is not actually filed until after the policy expires.

Of Counsel   An attorney with a special status in the firm, e.g., a semiretired partner.

Office Sharing   Attorneys with their own independent practices who share the use and cost of administration such as rent, copy machine, etc.

OJT   On-the-job training.

On All Fours   The facts are exactly the same, or almost the same.

Online   Within the control of, or coming from, a central computer; in communication with a computer; through equipment under the control of a central processing unit.

Open-Ended Question   A relatively broad question or request (e.g., "tell me about yourself") that forces the interviewee to organize his or her thoughts and to exert a relatively large measure of control over the kind and quantity of information provided.

Operating System   A program that controls the overall operation of the computer, allowing it to do anything.

Opinion   A court's written explanation of how and why it applied the law to the specific facts before it to reach its decision. Also called a *case*. Opinions are printed in volumes called *reporters*.

Opinion of the Attorney General   Formal legal advice given by the attorney general to government officials.

Ordinance   A law passed by the local legislative branch of government (e.g., city council).

Original Jurisdiction   The power of a court to hear a particular kind of case initially. A trial court has original jurisdiction.

Outstanding   Still unresolved; still unpaid.

Overhead   The operating expenses of a business, e.g., cost of office space, furniture, equipment, insurance, clerical staff.

Padding   Adding something without justification.

Paralegal   A person with legal skills who works under the supervision of an attorney or who is otherwise authorized to use those skills; this person performs tasks that do not require all the skills of an attorney and that most secretaries are not trained to perform. Synonymous with *legal assistant*.

Paralegal Manager   *See* Legal Assistant Manager.

Paralegal Specialist   A job classification in the federal government.

Paraphrase   To rephrase something in your own words.

Parol Evidence Rule   Oral evidence cannot be introduced to alter or contradict the contents of a written document if the parties intended the written document to be a complete statement of the agreement.

Partner, Full   An attorney who contributes the capital to create the firm and to expand it, who shares the profits and losses of the firm, who controls the management of the firm, and who decides whether the firm will go out of existence.

Partnership   A group of individuals who practice law jointly and who share in the profits and losses of the venture.

People   The state or government.

Percentage Fee   The fee is a percentage of the amount involved in the transaction or award.

Per Curiam   By the court. A court opinion that does not name the particular judge who wrote the opinion.

Personal Jurisdiction   The court's power over a particular person. Also called *in personam jurisdiction*.

Personal Liability   Being responsible because of what you wrongfully did or wrongfully failed to do. *See also* Vicarious Liability.

Petition   (1) A formal request or motion. (2) A complaint.

Physical Evidence   That which can be seen or touched. Also called *tangible evidence*.

Physician Assistant   An individual who is qualified by academic and clinical training to provide patient care services under the supervision and responsibility of a doctor of medicine or osteopathy.

PI Cases   Personal injury (tort) cases.

Plaintiff   The party initiating the lawsuit.

Plead   To deliver a formal statement or response.

Pleading   A paper or document filed in court stating the position of one of the parties on the cause(s) of action or on the defense(s).

Plotter   A device that will hold a pen to a piece of paper and draw lines as instructed by commands you enter into the computer.

PLS   Professional Legal Secretary. *See also* Certified PLS.

Practice Analysis Report   A report that analyzes where the firm is investing its time, where its income and profit are coming from, the amount of disbursements, etc.

Practice of Law Engaging in any of the following activities on behalf of another: representation in court, representation in an agency proceeding, preparation of legal documents, or providing legal advice.

Pre-evaluation Memo A memorandum sent to a supervisor before a formal evaluation in which the employee lists the following information (since the last formal evaluation): major projects, functions on those projects, names of co-workers on the projects, evidence of initiative, quotations on the quality of work, etc.

Premium Adjustment A write up (increase) of a bill.

Prepaid Legal Services *See* Group Legal Services.

Presumption An assumption that a certain fact is true. It is rebuttable if the court will consider evidence that it is false, and nonrebuttable if no such contrary evidence will be considered.

Print Formatting The function of a word processor that communicates with the printer to tell it how to print the text on paper.

Print Review In word processing, a feature that enables you to view a general representation on the screen of how the document will look when printed.

Private Law Firm A law firm that generates its income from the fees of individual clients.

Private Reprimand *See* Admonition.

Private Sector An office where the funds come from client fees or the corporate treasury.

Privilege A special benefit, right, or protection. In the law of evidence, a privilege is the right to refuse to testify or to prevent someone else from testifying.

Privilege against Self-Incrimination Persons cannot be compelled to testify in a criminal proceeding or to answer incriminating questions that directly or indirectly connect themselves to the commission of a crime.

Probation Supervised punishment in the community in lieu of incarceration. In the field of ethics, probation means: to allow an attorney to continue to practice, but under specified conditions, e.g., submit to periodic audits, make restitution to a client.

Pro Bono Work Services that one volunteers to provide another at no charge.

Procedural Law The rules that govern the mechanics of resolving a dispute in court or in an administrative agency, e.g., a rule on the time a party has to respond to a complaint.

Professional Corporation The organization of a law practice as a corporation.

Professional Judgment Relating or applying the general body and philosophy of law to a specific legal problem. When communicated to a client, the result is known as *legal advice*.

Project Attorney An attorney who works either part-time or full time over a relatively short period. Also referred to as a *contract attorney*.

Prosecution (1) Bringing a criminal case. (2) The attorney representing the government in a criminal case. (3) Going through the steps to litigate a civil case.

Prosecutor The attorney representing the government in a criminal case.

Public Benefits Government benefits.

Public Censure. *See* Reprimand.

Public Defender An attorney who is paid by the government to represent low-income people charged with crimes.

Public Domain Available for use without permission or cost; not protected by copyright.

Public Sector An office where the funds come from charity or the government.

Quarantined Paralegal *See* Chinese Wall.

Quasi-adjudication An administrative decision of an administrative agency which has characteristics of a court opinion.

Quasi-independent Agency An administrative agency that has characteristics of an executive department agency and of an independent regulatory agency.

Quasi-judicial Like or similar to a court.

Quasi-legislation A regulation of an administrative agency that has characteristics of the legislation (statutes) of a legislature.

Query A question that asks a computer to find something in its database.

Question of Law/Question of Fact *See* Legal Issue.

Quid Pro Quo Harassment Using submission to or rejection of unwelcome sexual conduct as the basis for making employment decisions affecting an individual.

Rainmaker A person who brings fee-generating cases into the office.

RE Concerning

Reasonable Fee A fee that is not excessive in light of the amount of time and labor involved, the complexity of the case, the experience and reputation of the attorney, the customary fee charged in the locality for the same kind of case, etc.

Rebuttable Presumption *See* Presumption.

Record (1) The official collection of all the trial pleadings, exhibits, orders, and word-for-word testimony that took place during the trial. (2) A collection of data fields that constitute a single unit, e.g., employee record.

Referral Fee A fee received by an attorney from another attorney to whom the first attorney referred a client. Also called a *forwarding fee*.

Registered Agent An individual authorized to practice before the United States Patent Office. He or she does not have to be an attorney.

Registration The process by which individuals or institutions list their names on a roster kept by an agency of government or by a nongovernmental organization. The agency or organization will often establish qualifications for the right to register, and determine whether applicants meet these qualifications. Also called *enrollment*.

Regulation Any governmental or nongovernmental method of controlling conduct. *See also* Administrative Regulation.

Relevance That which reasonably has a bearing on something; that which tends to help establish a fact as true or as false, as present or as missing. Evidence is relevant when it reasonably tends to make the existence of a fact more probable or less probable than it would be without that evidence.

Remand Send the case back to a lower tribunal with instructions from the appellate court.

Reporters Volumes containing the full text of court opinions.

Reprimand A public declaration that an attorney's conduct was improper. This does not affect his or her right to practice. Also called a *censure* and a *public censure*.

Request for Admissions A pretrial discovery device consisting of a series of written factual statements that a party is asked to affirm or deny.

Res Gestae Exceptions Exceptions to the hearsay rule that consist of statements or utterances closely connected to or concurrent with an occurrence.

Res Judicata A judgment on the merits will prevent the same parties from relitigating the same cause of action on the same facts.

Respondeat Superior Let the superior answer. An employer is responsible for the wrongs committed by an employee within the scope of employment.

Respondent *See* Appellee.

Retainer (1) The contract of employment between attorney and client. (2) An amount of money paid by a client to make certain that an attorney will be available to work for him or her. (3) The amount of money or other assets paid by the client as a form of deposit or advance payment against future fees and costs.

Review To examine in order to determine whether any errors of law were made. *See also* Appellate Jurisdiction.

Right Justified In word processing, an even right side margin.

Root Expander (!) The exclamation mark stands for one or more characters or letters added to the root of a word.

Rule *See* Administrative Regulation, Rules of Court.

Rule-Making Function Writing administrative regulations.

Rule of Three Gross revenue generated through paralegal billing should equal three times a paralegal's salary.

Rules of Court Rules of procedure that govern the conduct of litigation before a particular court.

Ruling *See* Administrative Decision, Holding.

Run To cause a program to (1) be loaded into the computer from a disk drive and (2) begin to perform its task.

Runner *See* Ambulance Chasing.

Sanction (1) A penalty or punishment imposed for unacceptable conduct. (2) To authorize or give approval.

Satisfy To comply with a legal obligation.

Save To cause a program or data that is in the computer memory to be moved or stored on a diskette or hard drive.

Scanner A machine that allows a user to enter text and graphics without traditional typing.

Screen Formatting In word processing and other programs, a feature that controls how the text will appear on the screen.

Scrolling In word processing and other programs, moving a line of text onto or off the screen.

Search and Find In word processing and other programs, a routine that searches for and places the cursor at a specified string of characters.

Search and Replace In word processing and other programs, a routine that searches for a specified string of characters and replaces it with another string.

Search Criteria/Query A computer research question; what you ask the computer in order to find something in a database.

Second Chair A seat at the counsel's table in the courtroom used by an assistant to the trial attorney during the trial.

Second-Tiered Attorney *See* Staff Attorney.

Section (§) A portion of a statute, regulation, or book.

Segment Search In LEXIS, a search that is limited to a certain part of cases in its databases.

Self-Regulation   A process by which members of an occupation or profession establish and administer the rules on who can become a member and when members should be disciplined.

Senior Legal Assistant   An experienced legal assistant with the ability to supervise or train other legal assistants. He or she may have developed a specialty in a practice area.

Service Company   A business that sells particular services, usually to other businesses.

Service of Process   The delivery of a formal notice to a defendant ordering him or her to appear in court to answer the allegations of the plaintiff.

Settlement Work-up   A summary of the major facts in the case presented in a manner designed to encourage the other side (or its insurance company) to settle the case.

Sexual Harassment   *See* Hostile Environment, Quid Pro Quo Harassment.

Shepardizing   Using the volumes of *Shepards' Citations* in order to obtain the data available in these volumes, e.g., whether a case has been appealed, whether a statute has been repealed.

Slip Law   A single act passed by the legislature and printed separately, often in a small pamphlet. It is the first official publication of the act.

Slip Opinion   A single court opinion, which for many courts is the first printing of the case.

Software   Computer programs for performing tasks such as word processing and database management.

Sole Practice   A single attorney owns and manages the law firm.

Solicitor   (1) A lawyer in England who handles day-to-day legal problems of clients with only limited rights to represent clients in certain lower courts. *See also* Barrister. (2) In the United States, some high government attorneys are called solicitors, e.g., the Solicitor-General of the United States who argues cases before the United States Supreme Court for the federal government.

Special Interest Group   An organization that serves a particular group of people, e.g., a union.

Special Jurisdiction   *See* Limited Jurisdiction.

Specialty Certification   Official recognition of competency in a particular area of law. The National Association of Legal Assistants, for example, has a specialty certification program to recognize a person as a Certified Legal Assistant Specialist (CLAS). A paralegal must first become a Certified Legal Assistant (CLA), and then pass one of NALA's specialty exams. *See also* Certified Legal Assistant.

Spelling Checker   A computer software program that checks the spelling of words entered through a word processing program.

Spontaneous Declaration   An out-of-court statement or utterance made spontaneously during or immediately after an exciting event by an observer. (An exception to the hearsay rule.)

Spreadsheet   A ledger or table used for financial calculations and for the recording of transactions.

Staff Attorney   A full-time attorney who has no expectation of becoming a full partner. Sometimes called a *second-tiered* attorney.

Staffing Agency   An employment agency providing part-time employees for businesses. Often the business pays the agency, which in turn pays the employee.

Standard Form   A preprinted form used frequently for various kinds of transactions or proceedings.

State Question   A legal question that arises from the application of the state constitution, a state statute, or a state administrative regulation.

Status Line   In word processing and other programs, a message line above or below the text area on a display screen that gives format and system information.

Statute   A law passed by the legislature declaring, commanding, or prohibiting something. The statute is contained in a document called an *act*. If the statute applies to the general public or to a segment of the public, it is called a *public law* or *public statute*. If the statute applies to specifically named individuals or to groups—and has little or no permanence or general interest—it is called a *private law* or *private statute*.

Statute in Derogation of the Common Law   A statute that changes the common law. *See* Common Law.

Statute of Limitations   The period within which the lawsuit must be commenced or it can never be brought.

Statutory Code   A collection of statutes organized by subject matter.

Stay   To delay the enforcement or the execution of a judgment.

Stipulated   Agreed to.

Subject-Matter Jurisdiction   The power of the court to resolve a particular category of dispute.

Subscript   In word processing and other programs, a character that prints below the usual text baseline.

Subscription   The signature of the attorney who prepared the complaint.

Substantive Law   The nonprocedural rules that govern rights and duties.

Summons   A formal notice from the court ordering the defendant to appear.

Superior Court   Usually a trial court.

Superscript   In word processing and other programs, a character that prints above the usual text baseline.

Superseded   Outdated and replaced.

Supervising Legal Assistant   Someone who spends about fifty percent of his or her time supervising other legal assistants and about fifty percent on client cases as a legal assistant.

Supra   Above, mentioned or referred to earlier in the document.

Supremacy Clause   The clause in the United States Constitution that gives the federal government supremacy over state and local governments in regulating designated areas.

Supreme Court   The highest court in a judicial system. (In New York, however, the supreme court is a trial court.)

Surrogate Courts   A special court with subject-matter jurisdiction over wills, probate, guardianships, etc.

Suspension   The removal of an attorney from the practice of law for a specified minimum period, after which the attorney can apply for reinstatement.

Sustain   To affirm the validity of.

Syllabus   (1) A one-paragraph summary of an entire court opinion, usually written by a private publisher rather than by the court. (2) In *Shepard's Citations*, the syllabus refers to the headnotes of an opinion that summarize a portion of the opinion.

System   An organized method of performing a recurring task.

Tainted Paralegal   *See* Chinese Wall.

Tangible Evidence   *See* Physical Evidence.

Template   A set of formulas created to perform a designated task.

Testimonial Evidence   That which someone says.

Text Buffer   In word processing and other programs, an area set aside in memory to hold text temporarily.

Text Editing   In word processing and other programs, the function that enables the user to enter and edit text.

Text File   In word processing and other programs, a file that contains text, as opposed to a program.

Tickler   A reminder system that helps office staff remember important deadlines.

Topic and Key Number   The system used by West Publishing Company to organize the millions of small-paragraph summaries of court opinions in its digests.

Tort   A private wrong or injury other than a breach of contract or the commission of a crime, although some breaches of contract and crimes can also constitute torts.

Transcribed   Copied or written out word for word.

Transcript   A word-for-word account.

Treatise, Legal   A book written by a private individual (or by a public official writing as a private citizen) that provides an overview, summary, or commentary of a legal topic.

Treaty   An international agreement between two or more countries.

Trial Book   *See* Trial Brief.

Trial Brief   An attorney's set of notes on how to conduct a trial, often placed in a *trial notebook*. Sometimes called a *trial manual* or *trial book*.

Trial Notebook   A collection of documents, arguments, and strategies that an attorney plans to use during a trial. Sometimes referred to as the *trial brief*. (It can mean the notebook in which the trial brief is placed.)

Unauthorized Practice of Law   Services that constitute the practice of law, which a nonattorney has no authorization to provide. *See also* Practice of Law, Professional Judgment.

Unbundled   *See* Bundled.

Unicameral   *See* Bicameral.

Unified Bar Association   *See* Integrated Bar Association.

Uniform State Law   A proposed statute presented to all the state legislatures by the National Conference of Commissioners on Uniform State Laws.

United States Court of Appeals   The main federal appellate court just below the United States Supreme Court.

United States District Court   The main federal trial court.

United States Supreme Court   The highest court in the federal judicial system.

Universal Character   (*) The asterisk stands for any character or letter in a query.

User Group   Individuals using the same computer product who meet to discuss their experiences with it.

Value   A single piece of numeric information used in the calculations of a spreadsheet.

Value Billing   The amount to be paid is based on the complexity of the legal problem, the expertise required of the attorney, and the number of hours devoted to the matter.

Valuing the Bill   Determining whether there should be a write up or a write down of the bill.

Veto   A rejection by the chief executive of a bill passed by the legislature.

Vicarious Disqualification   A law firm cannot continue to represent a client or cannot accept a new client because it has hired someone (attorney, paralegal, or secretary) who has a conflict of interest with that client.

Vicarious Liability   Being responsible because of what someone else has wrongfully done or wrongfully failed to do. *See also* Personal Liability.

Virtual Representation   In word processing and other programs, an approach to screen formatting that enables the user to see on the screen exactly how the printed output will look.

Voir Dire   The oral examination of prospective jurors for purposes of selecting a jury.

Wage and Hour Division   The unit within the U.S. Department of Labor that administers the Fair Labor Standards Act, which governs overtime compensation and related matters. *See also* Exempt Employee, Fair Labor Standards Act.

Waiver   The loss of a right or privilege because of an explicit rejection of it or because of a failure to claim it at the appropriate time.

WESTLAW   The legal research computer service of West Publishing Co.

Window   In a spreadsheet program, the portion of a worksheet that can be seen on the computer display screen.

Word Processor   A computerized system of entering, editing, storing, retrieving, etc. data.

Word Wrap   A word is automatically moved to the next line if it goes past the right margin.

Work-Product Rule   Notes, working papers, memoranda, or similar documents and tangible things prepared by the attorney in anticipation of litigation are not discoverable. *See also* Discoverable.

Write Down   Deduct an amount from the bill.

Write Up   Add an amount to the bill.

Writ Writer   *See* Jailhouse Lawyer.

WYSIWYG   What You See (on the screen) Is What You Get (when the screen is printed).

■ Index

■ C

Paralegal Associations: Local

1. Determine how many paralegal associations exist in your state (or in any state where you hope to work). See Appendix A.

2. Photocopy the following form, fill out one form for each association you identify in step one, and mail the form to each association.

Date: _____

Dear Paralegal Association:

    I am a student at the following paralegal school:

_____

Would you be kind enough to answer the following questions:

    1. Can paralegal students be members of your association? If so, what are the dues for students?

    2. Does your association have a mentor program where an experienced paralegal member provides guidance or advice to new members?

    3. Do you have a student rate for subscriptions to your newsletter?

    4. Does your association have a job bank service? If so, can student members take advantage of this service?

    5. Would your association consider conducting a "Career Day" in which experienced paralegal members of your association describe work in different employment settings in the state?

Any other information you can send me about the association would be greatly appreciated.

    I hope to hear from you.

Sincerely,

_____

My Address: _____

                _____

                _____

Source: Statsky, *Essentials of Paralegalism* (West)

Paralegal Associations: National

Please send me information about the Federation.

My Name and Address: Clip this form and mail to:

_____   Nat'l Federation of Paralegal
                                                         Associations
_____   P.O. Box 33108
                                                         Kansas City, MO 64114
_____

Statsky, *Essentials of Paralegalism* (West)

Please send me information about NALA.

My Name and Address: Clip this form and mail to:

_____   Nat'l Association of
                                                         Legal Assistants
_____   1601 South Main St., Suite 300
                                                         Tulsa, OK 74119
_____

Statsky, *Essentials of Paralegalism* (West)

Please send me information about PLA

My Name and Address: Clip this form and mail to:

_____   Professional Legal
                                                         Assistants, Inc.
_____   P.O. Box 31951
                                                         Raleigh, NC 27622
_____

Statsky, *Essentials of Paralegalism* (West)